MOST SECRET WAR

MOST SECRET
WAR

❖

R. V. JONES

WORDSWORTH EDITIONS

First published in Great Britain 1978
By Hamish Hamilton Ltd
90 Great Russell Street, London WC1B 3PT

Copyright © 1978 by R. V. Jones

This edition published 1998
by Wordsworth Editions Limited
Cumberland House, Crib Street, Ware,
Hertfordshire SG12 9ET

ISBN 1 85326 699 X

© Wordsworth Editions Limited 1998

Wordsworth® is a registered trade mark of
Wordsworth Editions Limited

Printed and bound in Great Britain
by Mackays of Chatham plc, Chatham, Kent.

DEDICATION

To all those in Nazi-occupied Europe who in lone obscurity and of their own will risked torture and death for scientific intelligence, like 'Amniarix' (Jeannie Rousseau, Vicomtesse de Clarens), Leif Tronstad, Thomas Sneum, Hasagar Christiansen, A. A. Michels, Jean Closquet, Henri Roth, Yves Rocard, Jerzy Chmielewski, and the author of the Oslo Report: to reconnaissance pilots like Tony Hill: to radio observers like Eric Ackermann and Harold Jordan: and to the men of the Bruneval Raid. For 'courage is the quality that guarantees all others'.

CONTENTS

FOREWORD

by the Vicomtesse de Clarens

*who, then known by the name 'Amniarix', gave ten months'
warning of the V-bombardment of London (see pages 350–375)*

A MAN such as Churchill should have written the foreword to this
fascinating work, which reveals extraordinary intuition, based on
encyclopaedic knowledge; but once again, its author has done the
unexpected, and asked the little man at the other end of the string to
introduce his work. The honour is great; the gratitude being no smaller,
I felt I could not dodge.

Seeing side by side the drawings of German radars he made 'sight
unseen', and the actual drawings that the Germans themselves made, for
instance, is flabbergasting. But reading is still more enlightening: each
episode tells the story of a major breakthrough in pure knowledge and
into the enemy's weaponry and strategy. It also tells the story of many
men and women who painstakingly collected the information that either
led to discovery or confirmed intuition. Professor Jones speaks of them
with such understanding that it is only fitting to tell him how important
it is to know for certain—and not only to surmise—that the mountain of
apparently unrelated data was sorted, checked, reassembled, turned into
useful information and then used for directing action.

Those who worked underground in constant fear—fear of the
unspeakable—were prompted by the inner obligation to participate in
the struggle; almost powerless, they sensed they could listen and observe.
During the war, they could but hope that what they did would be of
some service, but seldom knew for sure. Now, those who survive and
those who keep the memory of the dead will have the proof that indeed
no information, however irrelevant at first sight, was left unsearched.
All was used in the gigantic puzzle Professor Jones and his team fitted
together.

How rewarding!

Some of us were told to collect pedestrian facts; others were given specific instructions; others still were asked to keep ears and eyes open for the unusual, the improbable; all were working in small, compartmented fields in almost complete isolation—the price to pay for lessening danger—and yet saw friend after friend, comrade after comrade fall into the ever gaping trap.

It is not easy to depict the lonesomeness, the chilling fear, the unending waiting, the frustration of not knowing whether the dangerously obtained information would be passed on—or passed on in time—or recognized as vital in the maze of the 'couriers'.

This book, in addition to being invaluable for the historian, will give the poor soldier in the field an unexpected bird's-eye view of those years.

I for one, having made it a rule not to stir old memories, did not meet Professor Jones until 33 years after the events. The encounter was a great personal experience but also shed a clear light on the past; from what he tells us, our efforts were worth it.

Thank you dear, unique, Reg.

Amniarix.

Acknowledgements

Much of this book is based on my World War II reports; these are Official documents, and I must therefore thank the Controller of Her Majesty's Stationery Office for permission to quote and to use sketches and photographs from them. Other material has come from my wartime colleagues Sir Geoffrey Tuttle, Colonel James Langley, Mr. Leslie Mitchell, Mr. Thomas Sneum, Professor Yves Rocard and Commodore Paul Møtch. I am grateful to some old and respected opponents— General Josef Kammhuber, Dr. Hans Plendl, and Colonel Viktor von Lossberg for their photographs, and to Herr Fritz Trenkle and the Deutsches Museum, Munich for photographs of Knickebein and Wotan installations and of V-2 rockets respectively. I am similarly grateful for photographs from the Ministry of Defence and the Imperial War Museum, and from the Editor of *After The Battle* Magazine. I also acknowledge help from Mr. Brian Johnson of the British Broadcasting Corporation, Mr. Simon Welfare of Yorkshire Television, Dr. Rupert Cecil, Professor A. T. Hatto, Dr. Colin Knight, Professor Nicholas Kurti, Mr. James Sharp and the Wiener Library.

Besides referring to the relevant Official Histories, I have drawn freely on books by other authors who had consulted me while they themselves were writing. They include Ronald Clark (*The Rise of the Boffins*, Phoenix House, 1962 and *Tizard*, Methuen, 1965), David Irving (*The Mare's Nest*, Kimber, 1964, *The Virus House*, Kimber, 1967, and *The Rise and Fall of the Luftwaffe*, Weidenfeld & Nicolson, 1973), James Leasor (*Green Beach*, Heinemann, 1975), George Millar (*The Bruneval Raid*, The Bodley Head, 1974) and Alfred Price (*Instruments of Darkness*, Kimber, 1967 and Macdonald & Jane's, 1977). I have also drawn on Marie-Madeleine Fourcade's *Noah's Ark*, the story of her 'Alliance' network (Allen & Unwin, 1973), George Martelli's *Agent Extraordinary*, the story of Michel Hollard (Collins, 1960), and Jozef Garlinski's *Poland, S.O.E. and the Allies* (Allen & Unwin, 1969).

Sir Charles Frank, Colonel John Day, Mr. Robin Denniston, Mr. Robert Newton, and Group Captain E. B. Haslam (of the Air Historical Branch of the Ministry of Defence) all read the first draft, and I have been most grateful for their comments and help. In this same direction I have also had the benefit of advice from Mr. James Heard, Mr. George Greenfield, Mr. Roger Machell and Mr. Joseph Kanon. Photographs and diagrams, often from difficult wartime originals, have been prepared by Messrs. G. Coull, G. Shepherd and T. Wratten; and both drafts of the text have been admirably typed by my secretary, Mrs. Maida Pirie. The index was made by Mrs. D. L. Mackay, of Duns.

INTRODUCTION

THIS BOOK tells of the rise of Scientific Intelligence in warfare as I saw it in World War II. It is thus a personal memoir in which I hope that general readers may find some entertainment, intelligence officers some working examples of their trade, historians some matters of interest, and scientists some instruction in the value of sticking to basic principles.

The work took me into several fields of warfare, and it has not been easy to summarize these fields in a single title. I had long decided that if ever I were to write a book on Intelligence its title should be *Merchants of Light*, in allusion to the first scheme for a scientifically enlightened state, the *New Atlantis* of Francis Bacon. As a recognized and important section of his scientific society he had twelve fellows 'that sail into foreign countries under the names of other nations (for our own we seek to hide) who bring us the books and abstracts and patterns of experiments of all other parts. These we call merchants of light.' I am advised, however, that this is not a 'selling' title and, although I believe that it is no less relevant to this book than *The Seven Pillars of Wisdom* and *The Road to Endor* were to their respective contexts, and although *Merchants of Light* would admit the happy subtitle *Never a Dull Moment*, I have searched widely for an alternative.

One that I would certainly have considered, had it not already been most appropriately used by Alfred Price, is *Instruments of Darkness*, which comes from *Macbeth*: 'the instruments of darkness tell us truths, win us honest trifles, to betray's in deepest consequence.' It is peculiarly fitting for the great night battles fought in the air first over Britain and then over Germany. And mention of truth invites the adaptive plagiarism of another recent title to *Bodyguard of Truth* or of the motto of the Central Intelligence Agency 'And ye shall know the truth and the truth shall make you free' to, perhaps, *Shall the truth make free?* or again, some derivative of Robert Peel's comment to Lyon Playfair 'I am indeed sorry that you are compelled to make so unfavourable a report, but the knowledge of the whole truth is one element of security'.

Since this is a book about a war in which I was involved, another Shakespearean title *With Advantages* might have served to remind me of the dangers of personal recollection: 'old men forget; yet all shall be forgot but he'll remember with advantages what feats he did that day'. And since it is also a book about Intelligence its title might be found somewhere in King John's pained stricture: 'Oh, where hath our intelligence been drunk, where hath it slept?' But since the Intelligence with which I was concerned was in the main both sober and continent, a more apposite title might be the inscription on the Pillars of Hercules which was *Ne Plus Ultra*, because one function of this book may be to relate the contribution of what has been called *The Ultra Secret* to those of other forms of intelligence.

The simple title *Watchdog* had some appeal, because this is how I regarded myself; but it would run the gauntlet of any critic who knows his Shakespeare well enough to strike home with 'the watch-dogs bark, Bow wow. Hark hark! I hear the strain of strutting Chanticleer cry Cock-a-diddle-dow!' And that in turn suggests yet another possibility: the call of the German air controllers to their nightfighters at the end of a night's operations—'ENGÜLTIG KRÄHE'—*Final Crow* but this gets ominously near *Last Trump*.

The writings of Winston Churchill are a resplendent source of inspiration, for they scintillate with such phrases as 'the gleaming wings of science'. And indeed he wrote his own account of some of the episodes that I am going to describe, introducing them under the title *The Wizard War* with the comment 'no such warfare had ever been waged by mortal men'. Referring to me he quoted that part of *The Ingoldsby Legends* which might suggest *Jones Depones* as a boisterous title for my own book; but the mention of the surname might invoke memories of the man who addressed the Duke of Wellington with 'Mr. Jones, I believe?' and met with the riposte 'If you believe that you will believe anything'.

Inevitably, *The Secret War* suggests itself; it has been the title of a recent television series dealing with some of the episodes in this book. But apart from the fact that two other but unrelated books have already used the title, the definite article sounds somewhat vainglorious. Churchill himself wrote of our work that 'this was a secret war' and so *A Secret War* would have the highest credentials. Finally, hesitating between the vainglory of the definite and the timidity of the indefinite articles I realized that neither was necessary and that confusion with other books could be avoided by going to the superlative—blatant though it sounds, it fairly reflects the fact that the affairs that I shall describe were mainly in the 'most secret' (=American top secret) category when they happened.

Even so, the title goes somewhat against the grain, for although the events of which I tell occurred on the average 35 years ago, and although they have now become available to the public through the 30-year rule, I would still have an ingrained reluctance to write of them; but the 70 or more reports that I wrote during World War II are now available for inspection in the Public Records Office, and the major secrets such as Ultra and Double Cross have been released. Moreover more than 30 other books have described one facet or other of my own activities; and a permanent record of events as I saw them will, I hope, give some sense of perspective.

As for sources, I kept no diary during the war partly because I would not have had time, partly because I could not have foreseen its historical value, and also because the keeping of diaries was expressly forbidden. But it happened that whenever I felt that one of my intelligence investigations had reached the stage where it was worth presenting to the operational staffs, I wrote a report about it; and the resultant series of reports has been my major source, along with the diagrams and lantern slides that I retained for my post-war lectures at the Air Staff College. In addition, the many books that have been written in the intervening years have added to my knowledge and I have drawn on them freely.

A point that I must emphasize is that I am describing events as I saw them; although I have been as objective as possible, I may well have not been able always to give credit where it was deserved. I can imagine, for example, that some brilliant work was done by Resistance Organizations in the Occupied Territories on the V-weapons which failed to get through to me, or which for one reason or another I failed to appreciate, and that any survivors will be justly disappointed not to find their services acknowledged. To them I apologize. Again, I have described scientific and technical developments in Germany as I saw them at the time; and although I have sometimes compared the state of our knowledge with what was actually happening in Germany, this book is not a definitive history of German military technology or more than a sketchy account of some of the major new German weapons.

The passage of time, while permitting greater detachment in viewing events, has unhappily borne away some of those to whom I owe much. These include among my immediate colleagues Harold Blyth, Denys Felkin, 'Bimbo' Norman, Rowley Scott-Farnie, Hugh Smith, Peter Stewart, and Claude Wavell. I hope that this book will give their relatives some idea of the value of what they did.

Although I can only write of what became known to me and which therefore affected the course of the war, I much hope that the episodes that I witnessed will show the debt that we in Britain—and in America—owe to the men and women of many nations who worked for Intelligence in one form or another. And in a Britain that has been drifting downstream ever since 1945, I hope that this story will show one facet of what we could achieve no more than 40 years ago, and what therefore—since a people cannot change its basic make-up so quickly—we could do again if we could only replace the present mood of self-seeking easement by a sense of purpose and service.

In recording some of the heights of bravery and self-sacrifice to which men and women rose in our work, I hope that the book will prove more than just a good story. Although it has been pruned of undue anecdote, I have from time to time described my personal circumstances and feelings; I have inevitably mentioned some of the difficulties that I encountered, and I have had to record how things went wrong at the end of the war. In this I have tried to avoid rancour; my object has been to show future Intelligence Officers, and others, the kind of difficulties that they may have to face, in the faith that whether they meet with personal triumph or disaster their work will have been worthwhile.

PART ONE

CHAPTER ONE

The Men Who Went First

IN 1939 I was a Scientific Officer on the staff of the Air Ministry in London, and for the past four years I had been involved in problems of defending Britain from air attack. For reasons that will later become evident I had been exiled since July 1938 to the Admiralty Research Laboratory at Teddington; and it was there in May 1939 that I received a telephone call that changed the course of my life, and perhaps that of many another. It came from the Secretary of Sir Henry Tizard's Committee for the Scientific Survey of Air Defence, A. E. Woodward-Nutt: he said that he would like to see my work, and we agreed on a visit a few days later.

As I showed him the work, I sensed that there might be some deeper reason for his visit, and I told him so. He replied that there was indeed another reason: Tizard and his colleagues did not know what the Germans were doing in applying science to air warfare, and our Intelligence Services were unable to tell them. So it had been agreed that a scientist should be attached to these Services for a period to discover why they were producing so little information, and to recommend what should be done to improve matters. 'I thought of you,' said Woodward-Nutt, 'and I wondered whether you would be interested.' My reply was immediate: 'A man in that position could lose the war—I'll take it!' We agreed that we ought to give the Admiralty Research Laboratory time to replace me and so the date for my move over to Intelligence should be 1st September 1939.

It turned out that we had hit the very day on which the Second World War started. This book is primarily an account of my part in that war, which was to attempt to anticipate the German applications of science to warfare, so that we could counter their new weapons before they were used. Much of my work had to do with radio navigation, as in the Battle of the Beams, and with radar, as in the Allied Bomber Offensive and in the preparations for D-Day and in the war at sea. There were also our efforts against the V-1 (flying bomb) and V-2 (rocket) Retaliation

Weapons and—although fortunately the Germans were some distance from success—against their nuclear developments. In all these fields I had the ultimate responsibility for providing Intelligence, and my main object now is to describe how we built up our pictures of what the Germans were doing. But Intelligence is of little use unless it leads to action, and so I must in some vital instances also describe what went on in Whitehall before action was finally taken. These episodes brought me into contact with many of those responsible for the conduct of the war from Winston Churchill downwards. Also coming naturally into my narrative will be examples of the heroism of some of our Serving personnel and of those many helpers who joined the cause of Allied Intelligence in the Nazi-occupied territories.

As with many others who played a part in 1940, my own preparation for the Second World War started years earlier; without the experience that we had gained then, we could have done little until too late in the war. I must therefore recall some of the incidents from my earlier days that sensitized me to the work that I was about to do.

I was born on 29th September 1911; and in a sense, my earliest background was that of the Grenadier Guards. My father had served from Guardsman to Sergeant in the South African and First World Wars, and had been in the King's Company in the last stages of the Retreat from Mons. Offered a Commission, he refused to leave his friends; he survived Neuve Chapelle, where the battalion lost sixteen out of its twenty-one officers and 325 of its men, and where he himself was to have been recommended for the Victoria Cross; two months later he was very badly wounded at Festubert in May 1915. In hospital and convalescent home for a year, he became a guard at M.I.5 headquarters and later a Drill Sergeant at Aldershot. My childhood was steeped in the Regimental tradition of discipline, precision, service, endurance, and good temper. It was steeped, too, in the experiences of the air raids on London, all of which I went through with my mother and sister. The shattered houses that I saw then, and the suspense of waiting for the next bomb, remained in my memory as the Second World War approached.

In 1916 I went to my first school, St. Jude's, Herne Hill in South London. It was a Church school, and religion was of course a prominent feature: the war had plenty of examples of self-sacrifice to which our teachers could point, and I particularly remember being told of an officer who had saved his men by throwing himself onto a grenade that was about to explode. From St. Jude's I went in 1919 to the one elementary school in the neighbourhood to which my mother prayed I should not be sent, Sussex Road, Brixton, because it was so rough. It certainly was tough, the future of my contemporaries encompassing everything from barrow boy to millionaire scrapmerchant and trade union peer. But I found genuine friendship and decency, and I can still talk on equal terms with some of the stallholders in London street markets. And we had devoted teachers like E. C. Samuel, a great Welshman who had taught one of my uncles before me; and despite the fact that his class numbered 55 he found time to give me personal tuition in algebra, so that I was solving simple simultaneous equations before I was ten. He told me that he himself had been to college, but that all his swans had turned out to be geese, and that he would like to see me go far. Thanks to his help, I won a London Junior County Scholarship in 1922, and went to Alleyn's School, Dulwich.

But before I left Sussex Road a trivial incident occurred that helped to shape the course of my life. It was the first Boat Race after the war. However partisan the undergraduates of Oxford and Cambridge might have felt about the outcome, they were almost as conscientious objectors compared with the belligerent boys of the typical London school of the period, which temporarily split into violently opposed factions. My first acquaintance with the strife, having previously never heard of either Oxford or Cambridge, was when an older boy asked me 'Which are you, Oxford or Cambridge?' Perhaps because he had put Oxford first, I replied 'Oxford'. It turned out that he was Cambridge, so he promptly punched me on the nose and knocked me down. From that moment I swore undying enmity to Cambridge, and the incident may have been at least as significant as any other in the course of my subsequent career.

For me, the move to Alleyn's meant a new era of discipline. We were forbidden to run anywhere in the school except on the playing fields. Many of our masters had been in the Army, and the Officers' Training Corps was one of the strongest activities in the school. I was in it, or its predecessor, the Cadet Corps, for the next seven years. Even now, we still drink at the annual dinner to the memory of the Old Boys who fell in the Wars.

As for my own career in the O.T.C., my father expected me to be turned out as smartly as a Guardsman, with such details as puttees finishing not more than one half inch beyond the top of the fibula. The incident that probably gave him most satisfaction and most annoyance was when I was in summer camp and the parade was inspected without warning by a colonel in the Coldstream Guards. It happened that I had not had time to clean my brass that day, and I expected to be in trouble. To my surprise, the colonel complimented me on the smartness of my turnout and my father was as pleased with the fact that even with a day's unpolished brass I had impressed a Coldstream colonel as he was annoyed by the fact that I had not cleaned it.

When it came to qualifying for a Commission by taking Certificate A in 1928, I decided to put the power of prayer to the test. Previously I had been taught to pray for anything that I hoped would come about, and this of course included passing examinations. By now my doubts were being aroused and since it did not particularly matter whether I passed Certificate A or not, I decided to experiment by not praying. I thought that I had made a mess of the papers, so it was 'one up' for God. When the results came out I did not even trouble to look at the noticeboard, and was surprised when one of my contemporaries grasped my hand and told me that I had broken the school record. It was about the only school record that I ever held and, although I readily acknowledge my debt to a most Christian upbringing, I have never prayed since.

Our headmaster, R. B. Henderson, was a strong influence. After morning prayers he would address the whole school on any topic of his choice, but it generally lay either in the direction of service to the school, community, or country, or in the importance of being good at cricket. In fact, his instructions ruined my cricket, because he taught us that by far the most important thing when batting was to have your bat in the twelve o'clock high position as the ball left the bowler's arm, and that you should then bring the bat down in a vertical swing. The result, as far as I was concerned, was that I could hardly ever get the bat down before the ball was past my crease and I had been clean bowled. It was only after I went to Oxford and gave up the twelve o'clock fetish that I managed to make many runs.

Others of his admonitions were more effective. On 21st March he would remind us that this was the anniversary of the Germans' last great offensive in 1918 which had occasioned Haig's 'backs to the wall' order. He stressed how much we owed to our fathers who had stood fast at that time, and how the time could come again when we should have to follow their example. In a sixth form lesson on the theory of forgiveness he elaborated this theme, arguing that forgiveness could only take place when a sinner had repented. We could therefore not forgive the Germans because they had never expressed regret for the war and, he added, 'Mark my words, as soon as they're strong enough they'll be at us again!'

He exerted considerable pressure on the brightest boys to get them to study classics. It turned out that I was rather better at Latin than I was in science, but I had already decided that science was what I wanted to do. Fortunately, he did not regard his budding scientists as completely lost, and he provoked us with a weekly lesson on anything ranging from Greek tragedy to Gothic architecture, with Aristotelian philosophy thrown in. The effect that he had on us by opening cultural windows—because some of us looked through them with the hope of proving him wrong—was out of all proportion to the amount of time that his lessons occupied.

One incident in my first year of physics at the age of 12 will show how well taught we were, and indicate one of the factors that sensitized me, years later, to what was going to happen at Coventry. We had a new and enthusiastic physics master who set us more homework than I could manage; and at the end of more than two hours when the supposed allocation was 45 minutes, I had to solve a problem in specific heats. I worked the answer out to thirteen places of decimals, knowing perfectly well that this was quite unjustified, and in fact getting the answer wrong. The master promptly sent for me, saying that surely I knew better than to work out an answer to that degree of meaningless precision. I replied that I did, but that I thought he would like an answer matching the length of the homework that he had set us. The result was that he moderated his demands, but the point of the story in this context is that as fourth form schoolboys we already well knew how many places of decimals were justified in particular measurements: its significance was to be evident at Coventry in 1940.

Life was not easy. I sometimes felt like giving up, when I contrasted my situation with that of some of my classmates who could turn to their parents for help. All that my mother could say, now that I was beyond her academic attainment, was 'Stick it!', and somehow I stuck. In retrospect, such encouragement was far more valuable than any detailed help. Too many parents are superficially solicitous over their children, and I have come to appreciate Edward III's restraint over the Black Prince at Crecy: 'Let the boy win his spurs!'

My main hobby in my schooldays was, as with many other boys of my generation, the making of radio receiving sets. There has never been anything comparable in any other period of history to the impact of radio on the ordinary individual in the 1920's. It was the product of some of the most imaginative developments that have ever occurred in physics, and it was as near magic as anyone could conceive, in that with a few mainly home-made components simply connected together one could conjure speech and music out of the air. The construction of radio receivers was just within the competence of the average man, who could thus write himself a passport to countries he could never hope to visit. And he could always make modifications that might improve his aerial or his receiver and give him something to boast about to his friends. I acquired much of my manipulative skill through building and handling receivers: when at last I could afford a thermionic valve in 1928, I built a receiver that picked up transmissions from Melbourne, which that station acknowledged by sending me a postcard carrying the signatures of the English Test Team.

My interest in radio, coupled with an instinct that physics was the most basic of the sciences, permanently biased me in that direction. I had originally intended to be a chemist, but by the time I went to Oxford, my choice had finally settled on physics. Actually, the school had wanted me to try for a scholarship at Cambridge in mathematics, but to the astonishment of my masters I refused to enter, remembering my experience at the first Boat Race and saying that I had been Oxford ever since (although we had been defeated nearly every year) and I was not going to change now. Had someone pointed out to me that if I got to Cambridge I might have a chance of working with Rutherford, my blind loyalty to Oxford might have been sorely tried—if I had believed him, for to work with Rutherford seemed beyond dreams. As it was, I was happy to be tutored by a new Oxford graduate in physics who had just joined the school and who was to do much for it over the next forty years, 'Inky' Incledon, and I was awarded an Open Exhibition at Wadham College in 1929.

I immediately came to appreciate the atmosphere of Wadham. Built of soft Cotswold stone, its frontage on Parks Road was trim, its hall and quadrangle beautifully proportioned, and its garden delightful. If incense were needed for Matthew Arnold's 'Last Enchantments of the Middle Ages' it could well be the autumn smell of burning twigs in Wadham garden.

T. C. Keeley was my tutor; and in addition to physics he offered wisdom. He warned us that if another war broke out there would be a disastrous period for six months while those who had reached high positions on inadequate abilities in peacetime would have to be replaced. He also introduced us to some of the comic achievements of administrators. He had been at the Royal Aircraft Establishment at Farnborough during the First War, and apart from their unhappily naming their first airship 'The Mayfly', which didn't, they had at one stage changed the method of packing bombs into crates, with the result that a crate arrived at Farnborough bearing the legend 'Caution! The bombs in this crate are packed in a different manner from that formerly used. Compared with the old methods the bombs are now packed upside down, and the crate must therefore be opened at the bottom. To prevent confusion, the bottom has been labelled "Top".'

Keeley had been brought from Farnborough to Oxford by the Professor of Experimental Philosophy, Frederick Alexander Lindemann, who had succeeded to that Chair and to the Headship of the Clarendon Laboratory in 1919. A natural physicist, he was also a champion tennis player, and a man of great courage. At Farnborough during the war he had worked out the method of recovering an aircraft from a spin, which had hitherto been a nearly fatal condition, and despite defective vision in one eye he had learned to fly to put his theory to the test. It developed into a manoeuvre that has been standard ever since.

I first came to Lindemann's notice at the end of my first term of physics in 1931, somewhat accidentally. At the Terminal Examination I found that the paper was divided into two parts, the questions in the first part being different and much more challenging than those in the rest of the paper. The rubric advised candidates to spend at least an hour on the first part, and I became so interested in them that I failed to notice that my watch had stopped. Only in the last quarter of an hour of the three hours allocated did I realize that time had passed, and I could only scribble brief answers for the second part. It turned out that the questions that had so interested me had been set by Lindemann himself, and that he was looking much more for physical insight than for the retailing of existing knowledge. A few days later he told me that he had never had his questions answered so effectively; and even though I told him this was partly because I had spent nearly three times as long on them as I ought to have done, he talked of a possible Fellowship after I had taken Finals.

I was duly awarded a First in 1932, and was granted a Research Studentship to work for a doctorate. Again, the subject of my research was somewhat accidental. There was a spectrometer for examining infra-red radiation in the laboratory. It was an extremely tricky instrument, and the man who had been using it previously was now so tired of it that he persuaded Lindemann that someone else ought to take it over. As it seemed to offer a prospect for both theory and experimental work, I agreed to take it on, and found within the first week that its infra-red detector was broken. Lindemann suggested that I should therefore make a new one, and I became involved in designing and making new infra-red detectors—an activity which on and off I was to pursue over the next thirty years. This quickly brought me into conflict with Lindemann, who had novel ideas on how infra-red detectors should be made, but after some time I found that he had been leading me up a garden path because he had made some erroneous assumptions he had not troubled to check. When I told him so, he accused me of a defeatist attitude, and, stung by his comments, I began to follow my own ideas.

At the same time, he continued to talk to me about more general matters, perhaps because he realized that in several directions we had similar interests. I can recall walking back to Wadham one evening in 1933 from the Clarendon, just after Hitler came to power. He pointed out to me that the world was heading towards dictatorships, with Stalin in Russia, Mussolini in Italy, Hitler in Germany; and Roosevelt had just won the Presidential Election in America. He wondered whether we should be able to survive without becoming a dictatorship ourselves.

Within a few weeks the Oxford Union Society passed its notorious resolution which had been either proposed or supported by C. E. M. Joad, that 'Under no circumstances will this house fight for King and Country'. I was not a member of the Union, but I was disgusted. The news of the motion reverberated round the world. A. J. P. Taylor in his *English History 1914–1945* says that there is no documentary evidence that it had any effect on the dictators; but Churchill in *The Gathering Storm* said that Lord Lloyd, who was on friendly terms with Mussolini noted how the latter had been struck by the resolution and 'In Germany, in Russia, in Italy, in Japan, the idea of a decadent, degenerate Britain took deep root and swayed many calculations'. And in the *Daily Telegraph* of 4th May 1965, Erich von Richthofen wrote, 'I am an ex-officer of the old *Wehrmacht* and served on what you would call the German General Staff at the time of the Oxford resolution. I can assure you, from personal knowledge, that no other factor influenced Hitler more and decided him on his course than that "refusal to fight for King and Country", coming from what was assumed to be the intellectual elite of your country.'

I wrote my next letter home in the light of a comment that I once heard my mother make to someone else during the First War that much as she would hate me to go, I would not be a son of hers if I were not fighting. I told her not to judge Oxford by the aspiring politicians in the Union, and although most of my colleagues were at that time pacifists, I thought that many of us would fight. I certainly would, although it might not be quite in the front-line way that she and my father would be expecting, because it was quite possible that there would be essential jobs that only physicists could do.

I must have felt more strongly than most of my contemporaries, none of whom can I recall being particularly worried about the rise of Hitler, or about the need to develop our defences. Lindemann was the only man I can recall talking to me about it, and in that respect we were clearly fellow spirits. Many of my contemporaries thought that a pacifist approach could be effective in resisting dictatorships, and there was much enthusiasm for a silly play that was broadcast more than once which pictured a small buffer state between two much larger states preventing a war by massing unarmed on their frontiers to resist the passage of tanks from the opposing sides. The tank commanders were supposed to have refrained from driving their tanks over the bodies of the unarmed pickets. These were the days of the well-intentioned but unrealistic League of Nations Union.

I took my doctorate in 1934 at the age of 22. My differences with Lindemann over research work had reached the point where it seemed that I could no longer continue in the Clarendon, and I was awarded a Senior Studentship in Astronomy in Balliol, with the objective of henceforward working in the University Observatory with H. H. Plaskett on the infra-red spectrum of the Sun. To my surprise Lindemann then told me that he regretted that our differences had been so great, and even though I was now formally on the Observatory staff, he would be glad for me to continue working in his laboratory as long as I pleased. My prospects looked good: my doctorate was out of the way, and by the time the Balliol Studentship terminated there was the likelihood of a Commonwealth Fellowship to Mt. Wilson for two years, after which there was to be a Travelling Fellowship with half my time being spent in Oxford and the other in South Africa, to which the Radcliffe Observatory was moving. The money had been provided by Lord Nuffield's purchase of the Observatory site in Oxford for the new medical school, and the Fellowship had been specially instituted with me in mind.

At this same time, July 1934, I had one of my greatest strokes of fortune. For a month that summer I became tutor to a Christchurch undergraduate, Mark Meynell, who came from Hoar Cross, a stately home in Staffordshire. His parents were Colonel and Lady Dorothy Meynell. The family very quickly accepted me, starting with the younger daughter, Rachel, followed by her elder sister Dorothy and brother Hugo. These were the last days of the traditional English country house, with weekend parties full of gracious living and good company. Over the years I have been much indebted to the Meynells for this experience of their way of life, and for very warm friendship. I had now, as it were, seen everything of English life from the street market to the stately home, and it left me with none of the class bitterness that has since so bedevilled English politics. My England was that of Rupert Brooke and Robert Falcon Scott who wrote in the last pages of his diary as he was dying in the tent in Antarctica: 'I do not regret this journey which shows that Englishmen can endure hardships, help one another and meet death with as great fortitude as ever in the past.' If the time came, this England would be worth fighting for.

So the stage was now set for the events of 1935. But this chapter may properly end with an incident from 1919 which will serve as both paradigm and parable. It was the 22nd of March and the Victory Parade of the Brigade of Guards. My mother and I were standing somewhere in the great crowd near Hyde Park Corner, and I had my first experience of an individual perceiving a truth that was staring the crowd in the face, and yet all the rest failing to see it until it was spelled out for them. As Company after Company came by, the crowd burst into cheer after cheer. And then there came a company that was different—all its men were in civilian clothes. The cheering died away, the crowd was subdued. What were civilians doing in a parade like this? Were they recruits who had joined in time to miss the war? I shared the disappointment that these drab men should interlope among the splendid Guardsmen. And then the hush was broken by the indignant voice of a woman crying 'Cheer the men in civvies—*they were the men who went first*'. It was absolutely true, for these were the survivors of the 'Old Contemptibles', already demobilized on the rule of 'first in, first out'.

The shamed crowd apologized with thundering cheers. Although I have not spoken of it in the fifty years since, I remember because the voice had been my own mother's. And one of the men in civvies, marching unmistakably as a Guardsman even though, thanks to Festubert, his left arm was three inches short, was my father.

CHAPTER TWO

Friends and Rivals

THE WEEK that I went to Hoar Cross, *The Times* published on 8th August a letter from Lindemann headed 'Science and Air Bombing'. This read:

Sir, In the debate in the House of Commons on Monday on the proposed expansion of our Air Forces, it seemed to be taken for granted on all sides that there is, and can be, no defence against bombing aeroplanes and that we must rely entirely upon counter-attack and reprisals. That there is at present no means of preventing hostile bombers from depositing their loads of explosives, incendiary materials, gases, or bacteria upon their objectives I believe to be true; that no method can be devised to safeguard great centres of population from such a fate appears to me to be profoundly improbable.

If no protective contrivance can be found and we are reduced to a policy of reprisals, the temptation to be 'quickest on the draw' will be tremendous. It seems not too much to say that bombing aeroplanes in the hands of gangster Governments might jeopardize the whole future of our Western civilization.

To adopt a defeatist attitude in the face of such a threat is inexcusable until it has definitely been shown that all the resources of science and invention have been exhausted. The problem is far too important and too urgent to be left to the casual endeavours of individuals or departments. The whole weight and influence of the Government should be thrown into the scale to endeavour to find a solution. All decent men and all honourable Governments are equally concerned to obtain security against attacks from the air and to achieve it no effort and no sacrifice is too great.

Once again, he was using his favourite 'defeatist attitude' but there was great force to what he said. Baldwin had stated in Parliament on 10th November 1932 that 'the bomber will always get through' and the summer air exercises of 1934 had seemed to provide ample confirmation.

Lindemann was very strongly supported by his friend Winston Churchill, who was some twelve years his senior. They had first met in 1921 when Lindemann had partnered Mrs. Churchill in an exhibition tennis tournament for charity at Eaton Hall, the home of the Duke of Westminster. At first sight so different, the two men quickly saw each other's qualities. Churchill, who counted eating, drinking, and smoking among his pleasures, valued Lindemann's keenness of mind and his bravery as a test pilot. Lindemann, the non-smoking and abstaining vegetarian, valued Churchill's supreme quality of action inspired by warm humanity and lively imagination. The anchor points of their friendship were courage, patriotism and humour; in these each matched the other. Love of good language and prowess in sport, Lindemann in tennis and Churchill in polo, were also matters of common ground.

Over the ten years following their first meeting, Churchill came to depend on Lindemann for advice ranging from the future of science in warfare to the design of the fountains in his gardens at Chartwell. From 1932 onwards, when Lindemann lost his other political friend, Lord Birkenhead, he and Churchill were drawn much closer together in the alarm they both felt about the rise of Nazi Germany. They did their utmost to awaken the country in general and the politicians in particular. They had even gone to visit Stanley Baldwin during his holiday at Aix les Bains in 1934 and had mooted the idea of forming a special sub-committee of the Committee of Imperial Defence.

As often happens, someone else had a rather similar idea. He was a scientific civil servant, A. P. Rowe, the Personal Assistant to H. E. Wimperis, the Director of Scientific Research in the Air Ministry. In June 1934 Rowe had warned the Ministry that 'unless science evolved some new method of aiding our defence, we were likely to lose the next war if it started within ten years'. In the resulting discussions Wimperis in November 1934 proposed the formation of a Committee for the Scientific Survey of Air Defence, and Henry Tizard was selected as Chairman.

Henceforward both Lindemann and Tizard were to be major factors in my life; and since much has been made of their differences, it is interesting to compare their careers up to this point in the story. Lindemann had been born in 1886 at Baden-Baden, his father being a wealthy engineer of Alsatian origin but who left Alsace after it was ceded to Germany in 1871 and became a British citizen. Tizard had been born in 1885, his father being Captain T. H. Tizard of the Royal Navy and of

Huguenot descent; in fact, on hearing the Tizards described as 'more English than the English' Henry had remarked, 'With a name like mine, you have to be!' Lindemann had been at preparatory school in Scotland, and then went to Darmstadt and thence to university in Berlin, where he became a research student under Walther Nernst and took his Ph.D. in 1910. There he met Tizard as a fellow research student, Tizard having been at Westminster School and at Magdalen College Oxford, where he read Chemistry. While Tizard returned to Oxford, Lindemann stayed in Berlin for further research with Nernst, and produced some very distinguished work. At the outbreak of war in 1914 both men were abroad—Lindemann still in Germany, Tizard with the British Association in Australia. Both hurried home, Lindemann finding his niche in the Royal Aircraft Establishment at Farnborough and Tizard in the Royal Flying Corps. Both became test pilots, although each had defective vision in one eye. At the end of the war Tizard returned to Oxford, and successfully canvassed for Lindemann to be elected to the vacant Chair of Experimental Philosophy. So far they had been the best of friends.

It is difficult to be sure regarding the first rift in their relations. They could always argue vehemently on simple questions of science, such as the most efficient way of packing oranges into a box—whether the oranges in adjacent layers should lie with each orange directly over the one below, or should instead nestle as closely as possible into the spaces between the oranges in the layer below. Retrospectively, Tizard thought that Lindemann may have resented not being put onto government committees because Tizard had not given him sufficient support after Tizard himself had become Secretary of the Department of Scientific and Industrial Research. But whatever real or imaginary grievance Lindemann may have harboured, he now—in 1935—felt that he had plenty. He and Churchill had made all the political running for something drastic to be done about Air Defence; they did not think that the Air Ministry was to be entrusted with it, for the Ministry had given Baldwin the advice that 'the bomber will always get through'. Lindemann and Churchill therefore wanted the problem to be considered at the higher level of the Committee of Imperial Defence which should form a special Sub-Committee for Air Defence. As recently as 27th November 1934 Lindemann had met Tizard at the Royal Society and solicited his aid in pressing for this Sub-Committee to be formed.

Whether or not Tizard had already been informally approached by Wimperis is not clear, but on 12th December he was formally asked to Chair the Air Ministry's own Committee. On 10th January 1935 the

Prime Minister, Ramsay MacDonald, agreed with Lindemann and Churchill that a C.I.D. Sub-Committee for Air Defence should be formed, only to find afterwards that the Air Ministry had just set up its own Committee which it was claimed would be sufficient. When Lindemann and Churchill were informed of this fait accompli, it seemed to them that the Ministry had prevaricated so as to gain time to form its own Committee and so forestall any move at a higher level. Lindemann found himself left out and his old friend Tizard preferred, along with A. V. Hill and P. M. S. Blackett. He would have had to be almost superhuman not to feel resentful. So an erstwhile friendship was succeeded by an acrimonious rivalry—I can recall Lindemann parodying Omar Khayyam with something along the lines of 'The Blackett and the Tizard keep the courts where Trenchard once did sleep'.

At the outset, Tizard and his Committee—and Britain—had a tremendous stroke of luck, for on 18th January 1935 Wimperis saw R. A. Watson-Watt of the Radio Research Station at Slough, and asked him to advise 'on the practicability of proposals of the type colloquially called "death ray"', the idea being the creation of a sufficiently strong beam of electromagnetic waves which would heat up anything in their path to the point where living tissue would be destroyed or bombs automatically exploded. Watson-Watt had given the problem of calculating the amount of power employed to his assistant A. F. ('Skip') Wilkins, and the latter quickly calculated that the power involved would be far beyond current technology. When he handed the calculation to Watson-Watt the latter said, 'Well, then, if the death ray is not possible, how can we help them?' Wilkins replied that he knew that Post Office engineers had noticed disturbances to radio reception when aircraft flew in the vicinity of their receivers, and that this phenomenon might be useful for detecting enemy aircraft.

The Post Office observations had been made in 1931, and indeed rather similar observations had been made at H.M. Signal School in 1923. Moreover, Marconi had proposed in 1922 to detect ships by means of reflected radio waves and in 1931 W. A. S. Butement and P. E. Pollard of the Signals Experimental Establishment at Woolwich had devised and made a pulsed radio system on a wavelength of about 50 centimetres for detecting ships, and a rather similar system was in course of being installed on the French liner *Normandie* for detecting icebergs. As regards air defence in Britain, though, it was Wilkins' remark to Watson-Watt that started the serious development of radar.

A brief note from Watson-Watt was available to the Tizard Committee at its first meeting on 28th January 1935 and by 14th February Tizard had received a more detailed memorandum. On 26th February the first test was held near Daventry, using radio waves from one of the transmitters there in the 49 metre band, and with a Heyford bomber as a target flying at a height of ten thousand feet and piloted by Squadron Leader R. S. Blucke. The test was immediately successful, and the British development of radar could now start in earnest. So from the very first, the Tizard Committee had been presented with the basic solution to the greatest of the problems that it had to face.

On the same day, 14th February, that Tizard had discussed with Watson-Watt and others over lunch at the Athenaeum the paper Watson-Watt had produced, Lindemann and Churchill were joined by Austen Chamberlain in meeting Ramsay MacDonald, who finally agreed that an air defence sub-committee of the Committee of Imperial Defence should be formed, notwithstanding the existence of the Tizard Committee. It appears from Lindemann's notes that the Prime Minister even agreed to get the Tizard Committee wound up. The C.I.D. Sub-Committee met for the first time on 11th April under the Chairmanship of Lord Swinton, who suggested that Churchill should be made a member. Churchill agreed, provided that Lindemann would be made a member of the 'Technical Sub-Committee', which was how Churchill regarded the Tizard Committee.

I knew very little of all this, and was brought into the field in a manner which involved neither Lindemann nor Tizard. It started with a ring on the bell of my lodgings at 10 St. Michael's Street on the morning of Saturday 16th February 1935. My landlady informed me that I had visitors, and these turned out to be Commander Paul H. Macneil, a retired officer of the U.S. Navy, and his wife, Ruth. They had come to England in the hope of selling to the Air Ministry a detection system for aircraft based on the infra-red or heat radiation emitted by aircraft engines. They were due to give a demonstration at the Royal Aircraft Establishment on the following Thursday, and at the last moment the vital detecting element in their apparatus had broken down. Resourcefully, Macneil had contacted the Institute of Physics in London and asked whether there was anyone in England who could make him a replacement detector in a hurry.

It happened that a few months before I had published a paper on the design of infra-red detectors, and the Institute of Physics suggested that Macneil should get in touch with me. I was fascinated with Macneil's ideas, and told him that I would try. I thought that at worst I could only waste four days of my life, because he said that it would be no good unless the detector could be made by Wednesday evening. I therefore evolved a new design on Sunday, and spent the next three days and nights with very little sleep, only to fail. At about 2 a.m. on the day fixed for the trial I telephoned Macneil to tell him that I had failed, but he replied that this did not matter because the trial had been postponed for a fortnight, so perhaps I would try again. Over the next few months I saw a good deal of the Macneils in their flat above Prunier's, from which we viewed the 1935 Jubilee Procession. I was with Macneil at Croydon aerodrome at about this time when he undoubtedly detected the Imperial Airways aircraft as they taxied for take-off.

So at just about the same time that radar was at the nascent stage, I became involved with infra-red at a similar stage. Lindemann did not come into my room for a week or two; but when he did, and asked me what I was doing, I told him that this very interesting job had come up, and that I was seeing what I could do to detect aircraft by infra-red. His immediate comment was 'You ought not to be doing that for an American inventor, you ought to be doing it for the Government!' He went on to say that he had proposed the idea himself in 1916 but that no one had done anything about it. Unwittingly, I had presented him with an argument that he could use against the Tizard Committee, for he could now say that while Tizard and his friends were sitting around a table talking, he, Lindemann, had a man in his laboratory actually doing something about air defence. Towards the end of April I had a long talk with him, and as a result he may well have begun to press for something to be done officially about infra-red, for the minutes of the Tizard Committee for 16th May contained the following entry: 'The Committee considers that the detection of heat radiation from an aircraft engine or of energy radiated by an aircraft engine magneto offer no prospect of success; each of these methods has been the subject of experiments'. Indeed, A. B. Wood, a distinguished physicist on the Admiralty staff, had made trials with infra-red at Farnborough in 1927 which indicated that infra-red was unpromising, and his findings could be supported by the argument that the infra-red radiation coming out of an aircraft engine could easily be screened by an extra cowling, and that even if it did get out, it would not penetrate cloud. Finally, whereas radar gave an indication of the range as well as the direction of the target, infra-red could at best give direction only.

As usual when faced by opposition, Lindemann produced a plausible counter-argument. Although engines could be screened, there was far more heat energy coming out in the exhaust gases than that which would be radiated by the engine, and these gases, too, would radiate and so they should be detectable. To satisfy Lindemann the Committee then agreed that some trials should be made at Farnborough. The trials were to be undertaken by an impartial body, the National Physical Laboratory, but even then Lindemann said that he would only accept them if I were present as an expert observer on his behalf. I was therefore surprised when Dr. J. S. Anderson of the N.P.L. telephoned me and asked if he could borrow my infra-red aircraft detector. He explained that the N.P.L. had no suitable equipment but that Mr. Wimperis had told him that Lindemann had said I had an infra-red detector which flashed lights whenever an aircraft flew in front of it. I explained that I had no such thing and Anderson seemed so crestfallen, saying he now had no hope of doing the trials, that I offered to help him out by at least making a detector that should be capable of settling the point about exhaust gases.

I realized that Lindemann had made what I subsequently came to recognize as a characteristic overstatement. I had sometime before told him that, from what I had seen of Macneil's experiments, it should be possible to make a much better system by oscillating the detector mirror so that any hot source in the field of view was alternatively focused on and off the detector element, giving rise to a rhythmic signal which could easily be recognized against its background. For this a fast detector would be required, and if one could be made its rhythmic fluctuations could be used to generate an alternating current which could be amplified electronically, rather than detected by a galvanometer. Once we had the possibility of electronic amplification, we could begin to give visual warning of the presence of an infra-red source, and could even make a pattern of lights which would indicate the direction of the source. These were all ideas that I considered feasible but which no one had pursued, and which Lindemann must in his mind have converted into a fictitious reality before he told the other members of the Tizard Committee about them.

There would be no time to build such an apparatus before the Farnborough trials. So I spent most of October 1935 making something much simpler that should resolve the question Lindemann had raised. On 4th November I set the equipment up on the roof of the Instrument Building at Farnborough to examine aircraft suitably staked on the ground as their engines were raised to full revolutions. Whereas Anderson was to have done the trials and I was to have been the observer, our roles were reversed. It quickly became evident that although there was ample infra-red radiation being emitted by a hot engine, this could be easily screened, and by interposing a movable aircraft spare wing in front of the engine I showed that there was little infra-red getting out from the hot gases in the exhaust. After a few days I returned to Oxford and wrote the report, sending it to Anderson for his agreement before I showed it to Lindemann. The latter was understandably annoyed that he had had no chance to question our findings before they had received the authority of the National Physical Laboratory, but I thought that this would be the end of the matter. His argument had been so plausible that there must be a factor he had overlooked: this turned out to be the fact that the gases had indeed radiated infra-red as he expected, but they radiated it in the very bands of wavelength that are strongly absorbed by the carbon dioxide and water vapour in the Earth's atmosphere, and so become almost undetectable at more than very short ranges. With current technology, as opposed to that of forty years ago, the small amounts of energy that do get through can now be detected, and in any event engines are much more powerful and therefore emit much more, but the exploitation of the technique lay far in the future.

My report to the Tizard Committee had the opposite effect to that which I expected. Instead of the Committee deciding that nothing further should be done about infra-red, they asked me to see whether I could develop an airborne infra-red detector so that it could be mounted on a nightfighter and thus detect bombers. Quite possibly their engines would not be screened, and quite often they would be flying in clear conditions without cloud; and although airborne radar was possible, it might not work at short ranges owing to the fact that the pulse coming back from the bomber would be swamped by the pulse still emitted by the fighter. There could thus be an awkward gap in the interception technique over the last thousand yards or so, which infra-red detection might fill. It seemed that the Tizard Committee had been so surprised by the objectivity of the report coming out of Lindemann's laboratory that they were ready to support further work there.

CHAPTER THREE

The Clarendon Laboratory
1936–1938

MY WORK on the airborne infra-red project was to start on 1st January 1936, and I was to receive an honorarium of £100 for four months' work and an extra £50 for equipment. If the latter seems a paltry sum now, it was large compared with what many of us in laboratories in the '30's were accustomed to. And since these laboratories were the cradles for most of the scientists who were later to contribute so substantially to World War II, it may be worth giving some impression of the Clarendon as a typical laboratory.

When Lindemann took it over in 1919 it had long been moribund. Perhaps because he had found his activities in World War I so absorbing, he never again settled down to serious research, although with F. W. Aston he proposed a method of separating isotopes, and with G. M. B. Dobson diagnosed the existence of a high temperature layer in the upper atmosphere, and with T. C. Keeley devised a new form of electrometer. These were the most successful examples of the diversity of his mind, and he started off his relatively few research students over a wide range of projects where they had no expert help, so it was very much a matter of 'sink or swim' for them. Two or three graduates would start research each year, and roughly the same number leave after two years; since there were no more than six Fellowships in physics in the whole university, there was little chance of one of these becoming vacant for a new worker to fill. The Cavendish under Rutherford at Cambridge obviously had much greater attractions for serious physicists, and so for Lindemann's first fifteen years he had rather an odd assortment to choose from. Even so, his was a lively laboratory where not only was good physics done but also its fifteen to twenty members had a number of other achievements to their credit. Derek Jackson, later to be Chief Airborne Radar Officer in Fighter Command, for example rode in the Grand National. James Griffiths, subsequently President of Magdalen, was a member of Leander. Two others, 'Snooks' Gratias and Jack Babbitt, were ice hockey blues, and Hylas Holbourn was Laird of Foula in the Shetland Islands. And for some years T. C. Keeley and E. Bolton King made the best photoelectric cells in the world.

It is not clear how long it would have taken the Clarendon to establish its reputation unaided, for in 1933 there occurred the exodus of Jewish and other scientists from Germany, and Lindemann was among the first to offer them refuge. We thus had an invigorating influx of physicists including Erwin Schrödinger, the London brothers, Leo Szilard, Franz Simon, Nicholas Kurti and Kurt Mendelssohn; especially in low temperature research they rapidly advanced the Clarendon to a world reputation.

By way of technical help, we had just two mechanics in the workshop, A. H. Bodle and W. Stonard. I owed much to both of them. Bodle lived with his wife and daughter in a lodge just outside the laboratory, and I was often invited in for a late night cup of tea. Frequently in the evenings would come the sounds of trios being played with Mrs. Bodle at the piano, Marion with the violin and Bodle with the viola. Physically a little man with Napoleon as his hero, Bodle had largely taken refuge in books as an escape from the buffeting of the world. He urged me not to remain as uneducated as he believed the typical physicist to be, and he recounted with awe once hearing Lindemann quote Herodotus. I promptly read Herodotus, and was impressed by his penchant for good stories, and with his honesty as an historian when he told that, while he himself found it hard to believe, the Phoenicians who claimed to have sailed round the south of Africa said that the sun then rose on the other side. This observation simultaneously established Herodotus as honest and added to the credibility that the Phoenicians had really gone as far south as they claimed—a point of narrative technique that I was later to use in trying to get the Germans to accept some of our deceptions as genuine. Encouraged by Bodle I went on to read Plutarch and Thucydides, and even the Icelandic Sagas, all of which were to be sources of inspiration during the coming war.

Besides the Jewish refugees, we now had a German physicist of much my own age, Carl Bosch, working in the laboratory. His father was also Carl Bosch, a very fine man who had shared the Nobel Prize in 1931 for high-pressure chemistry. He was President of I.G. Farben Industrie, and his prestige was so great that he was elected by his fellow scientists as President of the Kaiser Wilhelm Gesellschaft, as one of the few men big enough to stand up to the Nazis.

I first heard about Bosch from some of the others in the Clarendon, who told me that he was a great practical joker. There was something challenging about their tone, and I wondered whether they had said similar things about me to Bosch, with the object of getting us to play practical jokes on one another. Fortunately for me, and perhaps unfortunately for the rest of the Clarendon, he happened to be in the Laboratory a few evenings later. Since 'the Prof' himself tended to set the pattern by not arriving before 11 a.m., not a great deal of work was done during our mornings, and it was customary for a few of us to come back after dinner and work well past midnight, and sometimes all night. On this particular evening when Bosch and I first met, we started to chat and the subject worked round to the tricks that one could do with a telephone. Bosch told me that he had worked on an upper floor of a laboratory from which he could see into the windows of a block of flats, and he had found that the occupant of one of them was a newspaper reporter. The telephone in the flat was visible through the window, and Bosch telephoned the reporter pretending to be his own professor. He said that he had just invented a marvellous instrument that could be attached to any ordinary telephone, and which would enable the user to see what was going on at the other end. This was around 1933, when the possibilities of television were just being mooted. The reporter was, of course, incredulous, and the supposed professor offered to give him a demonstration. He told the reporter to point the telephone towards the middle of the room and to stand in front of it and assume any attitude he liked, such as holding one arm up, and when he returned to the telephone he would be told exactly what he had done. Bosch, of course, could see perfectly well what he had done simply by looking through the window. The reporter was appropriately astonished, with the result that the following morning there appeared a most enthusiastic article about Bosch's professor and his marvellous invention, together with a detailed description of the demonstration.

Bosch and I then happily discussed variations on the telephone theme and ultimately I said that it ought to be possible to kid somebody to put a telephone into a bucket of water. I outlined to Bosch the various moves, and we were laughing about the prospect of their success and wondering whom we should select as a victim when one of my colleagues, Gerald Touch, came into the Laboratory and asked why we were so amused. He shared our amusement at the prospect of the bucket of water, and he offered to return to his digs, where several research students resided, and to watch while one or other of them answered the telephone, so as to report whether my plan had been successful.

We therefore waited about twenty minutes and then I telephoned Gerald Touch's digs. Before anyone could answer I rang off again, and repeated this procedure several times, in order to create the impression that someone was trying to ring the number but that something must be wrong. After this spell of induction, I dialled the number again, and heard a voice which I recognized as belonging to a very able research student in chemistry—in fact he had won the Senior Scholarship in Chemistry in the whole University that year. Reverting to the tongue that was my second language, the Cockney that came from my early schooling, I explained that I was the telephone engineer and had just received a complaint from a subscriber who was trying to dial the number and who had failed to get through. From the symptoms that he described I would say that either his dial was running a bit too fast or there was a leak to earth somewhere at the receiving end. I added that we would send a man round in the morning to check the insulation, but it was just possible that the fault could be cleared from the telephone exchange if only we could be quite sure what it was. A few simple tests would check whether this were so, and if the victim would be good enough to help us with these tests, whoever it was who wanted to get through might be able to do so the same evening. Would the victim therefore help with the tests? Immediately, of course, he expressed a readiness to do so, and I explained that I would have to keep him waiting while I got out the appropriate manual so that we could go through the correct test sequence.

I realized that he was so firmly 'hooked' that I could even afford to clown, and I persuaded him to sing loudly into the telephone on the pretext that its carbon granules had seized up. By this time, of course, all the residents of the household had now been alerted, and watched with some amazement the rest of his performance. I told him that his last effort had cleared the microphone and that we were now in a position to trace the leak to earth.

I explained that I would put on a testing signal, and that every time he heard the signal that particular test had proved okay. The appropriate signal was very simply generated by applying my own receiver to its mouthpiece, which resulted in a tremendous squawk. As I had also asked him to listen very carefully for it, he was nearly deafened the first time I did it. I then asked him to place the receiver on the table beside him and touch it. I could, of course, hear the noise of his finger making contact, and immediately I repeated the squawk. When he picked up the receiver I told him that that test had been satisfactory and that we must now try some others, and I led him through a series of antics which involved him holding the receiver by the flex, and as far away from his body as possible, at the same time standing first on one leg and then on the other. When I had given him time to reach each position I duly transmitted the squawk, and thus got him engrossed in listening for it. After this series of tests I told him that we were now getting fairly near the source of the trouble, and that all we now needed was a good 'earth'.

When he asked what that would be I said, 'Well, sir, have you got such a thing as a bucket of water?' He said that he would try to find one, and within a minute or two he came back with the bucket. When he said, 'Well, what do we do now?' I told him to place the bucket on the table beside the telephone and to put his hand into the water to make sure that he was well earthed and then to touch the telephone again. When he did this, he duly heard the appropriate squawk; and when he picked up the receiver again I told him that there was now only one final test and we would have it clinched. When he asked what this was I asked him to pick up the receiver gently by the flex, and hold it over the bucket and then gently lower it into the water. He was quite ready to do so when Gerald Touch, who had been rolling on the floor with agonized laughter, thought the joke had gone far enough, and struggled to his feet. While not wishing to give the game away, he thought that he ought to stop our victim from doing any further damage, and he started to remonstrate, saying that putting the telephone into the water would irretrievably damage it. Our victim then said to me, 'I'm very sorry about this but I'm having some difficulty. There is a chap here who is a physicist who says that if I put the telephone into the water it will ruin it!' I could not resist saying, 'Oh, a physicist is he, sir. We know his kind—they think they know everything about electricity. They're always trying to put telephones right by themselves and wrecking them. Don't you worry about him, sir, it's all in my book here.' There was a great guffaw at the other end of the telephone while the victim said to Gerald Touch, 'Ha, ha, you hear that—the engineer said you physicists are always ruining telephones because you think you know all about them.' 'I'm going to do what he tells me.' As he tried to put the telephone into the water Gerald Touch seized his two wrists so as to try to stop him. They stood, swaying in a trial of strength over the bucket and the victim being the stronger man was on the point of succeeding. I heard

Touch's voice saying 'It's Jones, you fool!', and our victim, a manifest sportsman, collapsed in laughter.

Bosch and I collaborated on several further occasions. On one we had Leo Szilard go to call on the *Daily Express* in Fleet Street because I had faked a telephone call from the editor asking Szilard to confirm that he had recently invented a radioactive death ray. We were astonished at the strength of Szilard's reaction—it was not until long after World War II that I found that he had just taken out a secret patent on the possibility of a uranium chain reaction and had assigned the patent to the British Admiralty. Telephone hoaxes were easy to play because one had only to produce a convincing impression in the single communications channel of the telephone: a hoax which had to appear genuine to the victim's eye as well as his ear was much more difficult. Telephone hoaxes were so easy, in fact, that I ultimately graduated from the practical joke to the theoretical, being content to work out the various moves without trying them on the prospective victim, in the near-certainty that he would have fallen for them. Moreover, it was not very sporting to play jokes which had no chance of rebounding; and I sometimes aimed at creating a comic situation from which I could only extricate myself by thinking more quickly than the victim. Trobridge Horton, my lodgings mate, once remarked that he could not understand why I took such risks: my reply was that an academic life gave us no exercise in quick thinking, and that I had a hunch that the practice that jokes gave in quick thinking would one day come in useful.

Arising from my friendship with Carl Bosch, an opportunity for quick thinking soon arose. He was as much interested in military matters as I was myself, and he told me that the Maginot Line was not as impregnable as it was supposed to be because corrupt contractors had put in considerably less concrete than they had been paid for. On Friday 1st November 1935 he told me that he was off to London for the weekend. I was staying in Oxford until Monday, when I would have to go to Farnborough for the vital infra-red trials about the exhaust gases, but of course I did not tell him about this. My Saturday was normal up to teatime, which I spent with others from the Clarendon, as usual, in Elliston and Cavell's. On our return we found a tall stranger, a German, in the Laboratory and he explained that he was looking for Carl Bosch; he himself was Dr. Hans W. Thost, the correspondent of the *Völkische Beobachter* (the *People's Observer*). I said that I was pretty sure that Bosch had gone to London, but that I would telephone his digs. Returning from the telephone I found that one of my colleagues had taken Thost into my room, where my infra-red detecting equipment was assembled ready for packing. Now a newspaper correspondent might easily be a cover-occupation for a spy, and here he was in the room along with equipment which was about to be used in a secret trial. If he spotted it, and started to ask questions, it could be awkward. I therefore thought that it would be a good idea to give him something to think about, and generally distract his attention. So on the spur of the moment I invented a preposterous story which seemed harmless enough at the time, but could have had unforeseen and unhappy consequences if we had lost the coming war.

I told Thost that I had a certain amount of sympathy with Hitler, and could see why he had pushed out the Jews. Thost almost clicked his heels together with an 'Ach, so!' and said that if it were not for the Nazis he would not have his present job. But I went on to wonder whether Hitler had done such a good thing for Germany after all. 'What do you mean?' asked Thost. 'Well', I replied, 'they are very clever and if they started to plot against Germany there could be trouble. For example', I added, 'I know that there is a great anti-Nazi organization run by the Jewish refugees in Britain.' With a highly sibilant 'Sso!' Thost pulled out a pencil, stretched his arm to expose a stiff white cuff and started to write notes upon it. 'Oh yes', I went on, 'I thought everyone knew about it. Why, the headquarters are here in Oxford!' 'So, here in Oxford!' repeated Thost at the same time inscribing it on his cuff. 'Not only that', I added, 'but here in this Laboratory. The headquarters is in that room over there, and Franz Simon is the head of it.' 'Franz Simon' wrote down Thost. I then said that any friend of Bosch's was a friend of mine, and since Bosch was away I would be delighted to offer him dinner. 'No, no', said Thost, 'I must get back to London at once!' And off he went.

Three weeks later I read on the placards as I went to dinner 'R.A.F. SPY SCARE'. Being interested in both spies and the R.A.F., I bought a paper but the story conveyed nothing to me—it concerned a Dr. Goertz who had been arrested for making a sketch of the aerodrome at Manston in Kent. Two days later I had a letter from my mother, who had the same interest in spies, saying how glad she was that they had got Dr. Goertz and how sorry she was that Dr. Thost had got away. I was puzzled because there was no mention of Thost in my paper, and I could not remember having told her that he had visited me in Oxford. So I wrote home asking her how she knew about Thost.

She replied that if only I would read a decent paper like the *Daily*

Sketch instead of *The Times*, I should be better informed. She sent me the article from *The Sketch* and there undoubtedly was Thost's photograph alongside that of Goertz. It turned out that Thost was one of Goertz's acquaintances, at the least, and that he had been made *persona non grata* by the Home Office, because the security authorities were convinced that he was a spy without having enough evidence to convict him. So this was round No. 2 of the escapade—I really had had a German spy in the room, and had distracted him from the infra-red apparatus with this cock-and-bull story about the anti-Nazi organization.

We thought no more of it for the next two years; but in August 1937 there was a bout of expulsion of newspaper correspondents between Britain and Germany. We had expelled three correspondents, the Germans retaliated, and this had raised the question of whether newspaper correspondents were really spies or not. As I later heard the story Simon and Nicholas Kurti were over in Paris doing some low temperature experiments with the big electro-magnet at Bellevue, when they were astonished by an article in a paper published by the Jewish emigrés (probably the *Pariser Tageszeitung*), which said that the British had been thoroughly justified in their action. One of their own reporters had somehow obtained a copy of Thost's report back to his masters on how he had come to be so unsuccessful as to be expelled from Britain. In it he said that while he was in London he had obtained evidence of a great anti-Nazi organization run by the Jewish refugees in Britain, with its headquarters in Oxford and headed by the Jew Simon. Thost had gone up to Oxford to investigate the matter and had succeeded in penetrating the headquarters where he had spoken to two Englishmen. One had immediately gone to the telephone to warn the Jew Simon of Thost's presence, and Simon had clearly used his influence with the English police to get Thost thrown out of the country.

Simon and Kurti came back to Oxford with this astonishing story, having no idea of the true explanation. At least, this is how I heard the story at the time, although it must be mentioned that Nicholas Kurti has no recollection of reading the newspaper in Paris. But Thost certainly published in 1939 a book *A National Socialist in England 1930–1935* in which he stated that he had reported on the activities of Jewish emigrés in England. Fortunately, all ended very well; but when, at the end of the war I was shown a list of all the men to be rounded up by the Nazis if their invasion was successful, there was Simon's name.

Carl Bosch left Oxford on 31st July 1936; as we said goodbye at Oxford station, I remarked that we might next meet again in our respective front lines. We were not in fact to see one another again for forty years, but in a way we were to meet long before that, for Bosch was to design the radio beam system that guided some of the V-2 rockets, and he was frequently to be called in by the German Air Force to help unravel the latest radio devices that we had fitted to our bombers.

The next member of the Clarendon who was subsequently to affect my own career in World War II was James Tuck, who joined the Laboratory from Manchester in October 1937, and who at that time was a remarkable combination of social naïveté and technical astuteness. In the later stages of the war he was to work at Los Alamos, and one of his American colleagues told me that without Tuck's contribution to the fusing mechanism it is doubtful whether the atomic bombs of 1945 could have been exploded. But in 1937, he seemed to be an innocent who had unwittingly strayed into a den of practical jokers. At first, with his attempts to be 'more Oxford than Oxford' with coloured shirts and corduroy trousers, we did not know whether he was genuinely sophisticated or not. And then he almost took our breath away by asking us at tea time whether any of us had ever made any money at horse racing. We were so taken aback that we said 'No' and he proceeded to tell us why he had asked. It turned out that he had recently married, and was trying to keep himself and his wife on a normal research student-ship. This was obviously going to be difficult, but he had been following a tipster in the *Daily Express* with some such name as 'Jubilee' or 'Captain Juniper' and the newspaper from time to time published details of his score for the season, from which it appeared to Tuck that all he had to do was to distribute his grant on 'Jubilee's' various tips and he would make a very useful profit by the end of the year. Unfortunately, Tuck said, as soon as he had started to do this, the tipster's rate of success had fallen off, and he was rapidly getting out of pocket.

By now, we realized that he was dead serious, and I told him that we had said 'No' because we knew that this was likely to happen to any of us who started betting without a deep study of the subject. However, with the Prof it was different. He, too, faced Tuck's problem on a larger scale in that the University gave him much too small a grant on which to run the Clarendon. As a result, the Prof had taken to betting, and the reason that he was never in the Laboratory before 11 a.m. was that he was in his rooms in Christ Church studying the form for the day, and the reason that he was closeted with Keeley for half an hour or so before noon was that they were on the telephone to various book-makers laying out their bets. To our delight, Tuck swallowed this completely and over the next two or three days we gradually enlarged the story, each succeeding detail becoming more outrageous.

Finally, the story spread to the workshop, who overdid it. They told Tuck that the Prof had made so much money out of the Turf that he had had a fit of conscience, and had decided that he ought to plough some of the money back, with the result that he had founded the Lindemann Stakes of fifty guineas with two thousand added. At that point, Tuck saw that he was having his leg pulled, and he came into tea this time saying, 'Ha, ha, you chaps. Jolly funny! It was a good story while it lasted, but now I have seen through you, and you'll never catch me again!' I now agreed that he had had his initiation and was therefore one of us from now on, and that it would be quite useless of us to try and pull his leg again. However, within a few minutes I had worked the subject round to what an unusual lot we were. Douglas Roaf was Eastern Counties Ballroom Champion (which was untrue) and the Prof had been Tennis Champion of Sweden. Tuck said, 'Now you are at it again, but you don't catch me this time—I am going to call your bluff!' Now Lindemann used to come in to tea, in which he never partook, but usually stood somewhat aloofly away from the main party. I had the impression he felt he ought to be there but somehow could not quite join in. On this occasion, though, he was dragged in by Tuck who went up to him and said, 'I say, Professor, these silly asses are trying to tell me that *you* were Tennis Champion of Sweden!' The Prof was taken aback by Tuck's familiarity, and more or less froze him with a restrained, 'As a matter of fact, I was.' Tuck thereupon recoiled, and decided that perhaps some of our tall stories were true.

So we could now put him through the same cycle until he had reached a suitable stage of disbelief again, and I then told him that Derek Jackson owned nearly half of *The News of the World* and rode in the Grand National every year. Tuck promptly tackled Jackson. It was hardly fair, in that it was indeed highly improbable that a distinguished spectroscopist should also be a Grand National rider, but it was quite true. I once asked Derek why, with all his money, he took spectroscopy so seriously. 'Why, man,' he replied, 'you must have something to do in the summer when you can't hunt!' With his affluence he was accustomed to privileged treatment, one of the privileges being a first class corner seat with its back to the engine. Whenever he failed to find one he simply pulled the communication cord. The first time he did this, at Paddington, he got away with it by writing a straightforward apology. The second time, he pulled the cord so violently that it broke. He was then sent up to Oxford in a specially cleared compartment with a frightened little guard, who thought he was mad, all to himself. That time he got away with it by threatening to bring an action on behalf of the public, pointing out that the train had been sent out of Paddington in a defective condition, because it had no communication cord, and there might be some unfortunate woman about to be ravished who would in her distress tug at the communication cord, to no avail. The third time, his defence was that the train had been sent out of Paddington one minute early and, knowing the reputation of the Great Western Railway for punctuality, he had thought of all those regular travellers who would have been expecting to catch the train in the last minute and who would now find it gone; but this time he was fined. His response to Tuck's incredulity that he rode in the Grand National is better imagined than described.

The atmosphere in the Laboratory was gradually changing, as to some extent I was myself. The Laboratory boy, Basil, even asked me what was happening—I seemed so much more serious than I had been two years before. The reason was simple enough—I was engrossed in the air defence problem. And despite the fact that Lindemann himself clearly felt the same way, I had to endure ragging from my contemporaries as a militarist for switching from pure research to air defence. They, along with most of our countrymen, seemed blind to what was happening in Germany; and yet the sight of a cinema newsreel of a Nazi rally should have been enough to open their eyes. These were the days when the Socialist-controlled London County Council suppressed the Cadet Corps in the London schools. While retrospectively we may sympathize with the anti-war feelings of those who knew the horrors of trench warfare in World War I, with all the doubts that these threw on the higher leadership, it should have been obvious that their actions were encouraging the very danger that they hoped to avoid.

In 1936 and 1937 the predominant feeling in Oxford was still pacifist, as far as the University was concerned. But it was different among working men; I knew a number of them through the City of Oxford Rifle Club, which I had joined, and they warmly supported my suggestion that we should try to form an anti-aircraft battalion. I therefore wrote on 1st November 1937 to the First Anti-Aircraft Division at Hillingdon:

I can offer to form a committee of representatives of municipal bodies and local firms, to consider the problem of raising, say, 1,000 men in

Oxford, provided that the War Office would provide equipment and instruction. Presumably the way would be to establish a Territorial battalion here. Before we can start a recruiting campaign, we must be able to tell people what obligations they entail by joining, and we must also have some indication that the War Office will take the matter seriously. I believe that we can get the men—perhaps not a thousand (although Oxford has a population of 80,000), but at any rate enough to make it worth while. Despite the pacifist reputation of the university, the spirit in the town is good. . . .'

The war broke out before anything was done. Another of my efforts may have been more fruitful. Shortly before I left Oxford in March 1938 the Germans annexed Austria, and the scales at last fell from the eyes of my contemporaries. They were now almost anxious to do something for defence, but there was no organization ready if their enthusiasm ever materialized to the point of action. I therefore wrote to D. R. Pye, the new Director of Scientific Research, at the Air Ministry on 18th March. After discussing some minor details of my work, I went on:

The main purpose of this letter is to raise a far more important question: it seems very obvious, but since I have not heard it considered perhaps you will forgive me for mentioning it.

The events of the past week have made the research people here realize that the position is more serious than they had thought. Yesterday one of them asked me what he should do in the event of war: he wanted to do something active, and pointed out there was nobody to tell him what to do. In the past, most scientists have tended to be conscientious objectors; following this spontaneous move, I investigated the feelings of other members of the laboratory, and found that out of eighteen people questioned, only two were now conscientious objectors. Most of the remainder wanted to do scientific military research, while one or two of the more pugnacious would prefer to take more vigorous measures. . . .

The point is this: if war were to break out tomorrow the scientific directorates of the services would find themselves overwhelmed by volunteers, and much valuable time would be wasted in finding out what posts they were best suited for, and the necessary—and as far as I know unforeseen—expansion would have to be effected.

I am suggesting therefore that the research workers in the universities should be asked what they want to do, and to state their lines of specialization, should they elect to join the scientific staffs during war-time. You would then know your prospective personnel, and could arrange your necessarily expanded programme accordingly. The men could then be informed where they were to be stationed, and laboratory accommodation arranged. They could start practically at the outbreak of war, and no time would be wasted.

I received an interim reply from Pye saying that he would later reply more fully, but he never did. Fortunately, Tizard took the matter up; and by the outbreak of war many university physicists had been told where their services could best be applied.

CHAPTER FOUR

Inferior Red
1936–1938

THE SEQUENCE of events that led to my leaving Oxford in March 1938 had started in January 1936 with my work on infra-red detection of aircraft for the Tizard Committee. Within two months I had made some new detecting elements and had designed and built an electronic amplifier that caused a spot of light to broaden into a band whenever a faint source of heat came into the field of view of the detector, the breadth of the band increasing as the source grew stronger. Besides serious measurements, the equipment could do two 'party tricks': one was to scan a rack of tools, from which I had asked a visitor to withdraw one and then replace it, and I could then tell him which one it had been, because the few seconds' contact with his hand had warmed it slightly. The other demonstration was to shine a torch at a black screen and then switch it off. The detector could then be made to scan the screen and discover where the spot of light from the torch had previously fallen, even up to a minute afterwards, because the light had been converted into heat, in an amount imperceptible to the senses, and this heat was now being re-radiated.

The first visitor to see the demonstration was Watson-Watt, who came to talk to Lindemann on 24th February 1936. He was looking for recruits for the Air Ministry Research Establishment that he was setting up at Bawdsey Manor on the Deben Estuary just north of Felixstowe. Lindemann had recommended Gerald Touch, who was just finishing his doctorate, and who had been our reporter for the telephone-in-the-bucket-of-water incident. He was to be a significant influence in my career over the next few years, and a lifelong friend. Although he was not exactly like the research student of whom Edward Appleton said, 'He was the kind of man for whom no experimental difficulty was too great to be thought of', Gerald could usually see trouble ahead. Even when things were going well he would say, 'That's all very well, Reginald, but, you see, the trouble is . . .' But he was an able experimenter of complete honesty, and Watson-Watt wisely accepted Lindemann's recommendation.

Watson-Watt may well have discussed other matters with Lindemann on this visit; they had known one another since the Farnborough days of World War I, and it would be natural for them to discuss the whole air defence problem. Lindemann seemed to conclude that Watson-Watt needed more support than the Tizard Committee was giving him, for on 12th June 1936, he arranged to take Watson-Watt to meet Churchill. As could be expected, Lindemann had not been an easy member of the Tizard Committee, and had been pressing some of his own schemes, such as aerial mines supported on parachutes. His association with politicians was resented by other members of the Committee, and his introduction of Watson-Watt to Churchill behind the backs of the Committee was almost the last straw. Following what Watson-Watt told him, Churchill was critical of the Tizard Committee at the C.I.D. Sub-Committee meeting on 15th June. The Tizard Committee was due to write a progress report within a few weeks, and Lindemann insisted on writing a minority report, which went into the Official Records dated 20th July.

Among the conclusions from which Lindemann dissented was one not to give aerial mines a highest priority. In the event he appears to have been wrong, for the mines were a failure when tried in 1940, but they were hardly less realistic than several of the schemes backed by the Committee, including one to floodlight the whole of southern England. As for the mines, they were not just a debating point as far as Lindemann was concerned, for when the work on mines had been held up because a 'Queen Bee' pilotless aircraft could not be made available by the Air Ministry, Lindemann offered to pilot the plane himself to see what happened when planes ran into wires from which mines could be suspended, just as he had also done during World War I. As for radar, he agreed with the Committee that it should have the highest priority, but he made the sensible point that this would only be effective if a similar priority were given to develop the communications system by which the radar data would be transmitted to fighter controllers and by which instructions could be sent to our fighters. Such points might have been listened to in a less charged atmosphere, but by now the other members of the Tizard Committee were exasperated, partly because of Lindemann's communicating his ideas to Churchill when their defects had already been pointed out at the Tizard Committee, and partly because he was now standing for Parliament, on the air defence issue. After the

Tizard Committee meeting of 15th July, Blackett and Hill offered their resignations. Swinton, the Air Minister, refused to accept them, and instead dissolved the Committee in order to reform it again without Lindemann.

Much has been made of the differences between Lindemann and the Committee. In retrospect, there was some right on both sides: far from holding up radar in favour of infra-red, as has sometimes been suggested, Lindemann earned Watson-Watt's gratitude, and the latter afterwards wrote, 'He gave to the radar team support, at the highest level, which was indispensable both psychologically and organizationally.' Personally, if I had had to discuss with anyone on the Tizard Committee a problem requiring physical insight, I would have valued Lindemann's judgement most. I can recall an incident from those days when an inventor had put up a proposal to the Committee of what is now called inertial navigation. It was dismissed by the Committee because the members said that it was well known that you could not establish the speed of an aircraft other than by measuring relative to the air in which the aircraft was moving and the wind would therefore always cause errors. This is true enough of a pitot tube but, as Lindemann pointed out to me, the proposal was perfectly sound if one used, as the inventor suggested, accelerometers. One could then integrate all the accelerations to which the aircraft had been subjected since it left the ground; this would give velocity, and a further integration would give position relative to the point of take-off.

Tizard had more common sense than Lindemann, but to some extent he also had luck. Not only was radar presented to him, as it were, on a plate, but also he was dealing with a body of serving officers in Fighter Command who realized they would be in grave difficulty if the Germans attacked. They were therefore prepared in their predicament to look at any ideas coming from the scientists. True, Tizard had done as much as anybody, and perhaps more, to persuade the Royal Air Force to be receptive, but even he could not succeed if the officers concerned were complacent. Following the success of his original committee for surveying air defence, it was proposed that he should head a similar committee to look into problems of air offence. This second committee was set up towards the end of 1936, and some members were common to both committees. And yet, despite the brilliant example in defence, the work for offence was, as Tizard himself said, a failure. The basic explanation was that the officers concerned with bombing operations were complacent and convinced that they could hit their targets without scientific aids, and so they were not prepared to listen even to Tizard.

Most of the Tizard Committee arguments were of course far above my head. While it was in turmoil in June 1936 I had been at Farnborough trying out my infra-red equipment on the ground. It satisfactorily detected aircraft in flight—the speeds make odd reading now, a Westland Wapiti flying past at 70 m.p.h. With its small size the detector seemed worth taking a step further, at least to the stage of designing an airborne version. I was now in my second four months of work for the Tizard Committee. Churchill had commented at the C.I.D. Sub-Committee that he had understood that a man in Oxford had been paid £100 for four months work, and was shortly to receive another £100 for another four months, and he asked whether something more ought not to be done.

My own position was that the Balliol post ran out at the end of September, and had my astronomical career been continuing I should have gone to Mount Wilson for the next two years. I applied for a Commonwealth Fellowship with Mount Wilson in mind, but I was worried that war might break out within the following two years, and if this happened I wanted to be in England rather than America. I told the Commonwealth Committee that there was a chance that even if I were offered a Fellowship I would feel that I had to give air defence the first priority, if the Air Ministry decided that it wanted me to continue the work after September 1936. This in fact happened, and I was appointed as a Scientific Officer and a full-time member of the Air Ministry staff from 5th October 1936, and accredited to the Royal Aircraft Establishment at Farnborough even though I was still to work in Oxford. My salary was £500 per annum which, low though it may seem now, was higher than that of any other scientist of my age in Government service.

In the meantime three of my friends had left Oxford. The first was Carl Bosch; the second was Gerald Touch, who left to join Watson-Watt at Bawdsey on 8th August. The third was F. C. Frank, my exact contemporary, in the Chemistry School. I had first seen Charles Frank when we tried for Scholarships in December 1928, his cherubic and intellectual countenance prominent among those at the top of the Balliol Hall steps, anxious to get at the examination papers as quickly as possible. In our first year I had seen him coming away from Blackwell's clutching a great textbook of chemistry with an air of anticipatory delight, and also on the river as cox of one of the Lincoln torpids. We hardly met until we were postgraduates, when he shared lodgings with one of my friends, and we discovered that we had much in common.

Although he was a theorist, he clearly appreciated experimental dexterity, and although I was an experimenter I found that he could expound theory in terms that I could understand. We grew closer together with each year and so, when on 13th July 1936 he left to work with Peter Debye in Berlin for two years, I could tell him my thoughts about the prospects of war, and ask him to watch for anything that might affect our ideas about defence.

The next stage of the infra-red work was to make a detector capable of operating in an aircraft. On 16th October I attended a meeting of the Tizard Committee for the first time, and outlined what I saw of the possibilities, including a device for converting infra-red into visible radiation so that one could form in effect a thermal picture of a scene in which the warmer regions would show up as brighter. The Committee appeared reconciled to the fact that despite their differences with Lindemann I should continue to work in his Laboratory. He was in the middle of his Election campaign for Parliament, and on 30th October Winston Churchill came to Oxford to speak in his support. On the following morning Lindemann brought him to the Clarendon, and showed him my work. This was the first sight that I had of Churchill, and I remember well the impression that he created on all of us. He looked so tired and florid that our general verdict was 'Poor old Winston—he can't last much longer!'

During the winter I constructed a new infra-red detector for mounting in an aircraft, the main difficulty being to render it sufficiently immune from the vibration to which all aircraft of that period were susceptible; besides simple detection, it was capable of giving an indication of whether the target was to the right or left, and up or down. I was at this time joined by George Pickard, who had just completed his doctorate in low temperature physics and who, like me, now became a member of the Air Ministry staff. We took the detector to Farnborough in April 1937, and on 27th April I flew with the equipment, and managed to detect another aircraft in flight. As far as I know, this was the first occasion on which one aircraft was detected from another in flight by infra-red means.

Over the next few months we made good progress. I showed that even if the engines of an aircraft were screened it could still be detected because of the heating of its wings and fuselage caused by the compression of the air in front of it (aerodynamic heating) and I also started to grow large crystals of materials that would transmit infra-red radiation. When it seemed that, if we developed the detector to the operational stage, it would have to be mounted in single seater fighters (for these were what the Air Staff intended to use at night) there would obviously be a difficult stage where the pilot of the trial aircraft would need to know a good deal about infra-red. I thought that the simplest method of dealing with this stage would be for me to learn to fly fighters, and I therefore suggested to D. R. Pye that I join the Oxford University Air Squadron with this in mind. It came to nothing because the Commanding Officer found that he was up against a regulation that allowed him to take only undergraduates as cadets; and although I was still only 24 I was a doctor with two years' seniority. The Air Staff were not worried—I was told that they had plenty of men who could fly aeroplanes.

In June 1937 I paid my first visit to Bawdsey at Gerald Touch's invitation and with Watson-Watt's approval. I had already guessed what they were doing, since the radar equipment on the liner *Normandie* had been described in the press. The technique of detecting aircraft by echoes arising from reflected radio waves was obviously much more powerful than the infra-red method that I had been asked to pursue, although there might be a possible gap at short range which infra-red would serve to cover. At the same time, radar had some disadvantages. One was that with its relatively long wavelength of 1·5 metres it would be difficult to obtain accurate indications of the direction of the target, and these would certainly be needed for a satisfactory interception. Another weakness occurred to me when Gerald Touch said that the method was so sensitive that it could detect a wire hanging from a balloon at forty miles. All one might therefore need to do to render the system useless would be to attach wires to balloons or parachutes at intervals of half a mile or a mile, and the whole radar screen would be so full of echoes that it would be impossible to see the extra echo arising from an aircraft.

The Air Defence Research Sub-Committee had recorded in its minutes of 2nd July, regarding infra-red: 'Considerable progress has been made. Work should continue in view of the possible application of the results to other problems.' I was not informed of this comment and its cryptic significance, but a month or two later Lindemann told me that Churchill had said that he understood from the Sub-Committee that they were going to shut down my infra-red work. I replied that infra-red certainly had its limitations of not being useful through cloud and of not giving an indication of range, but that radar, too, was vulnerable, especially to a 'smoke screen' of spurious radar reflections which only need be lengths of wire half a wavelength long. Lindemann told me that he would get Churchill to raise this point at the Sub-Committee. When I subsequently asked him what had happened he said that Tizard and Watson-Watt had rather 'looked down their noses' at the suggestion. My conversation with Lindemann about 'smoke screen' reflections was effectively the beginning of what came to be known in Britain as 'Window' and in America as 'Chaff' but for many years I had no evidence other than my own memory, which I could not expect others to accept. However, when Alfred Price was writing *Instruments of Darkness* he found a memorandum in Lindemann's files, dated 8th March 1938, which ran:

Lest too much reliance be placed upon the R.D.F. methods, it is perhaps worth pointing out that certain difficulties may easily be encountered in actual use.

Though undoubtedly excellent for detecting single aircraft or squadrons thereof, flying together, it seems likely that great difficulties may be encountered when large numbers of aeroplanes attacking and defending are simultaneously in the air, each sending back its signals.

This difficulty may be very materially increased if the enemy chooses to blind the R.D.F. operator by strewing numbers of oscillators in the appropriate region. Such oscillators need consist merely of thin wires fifty to a hundred feet long which could easily be suspended in suitable positions from toy balloons or even, if only required for half-an-hour or so, from small parachutes. As far as the R.D.F. detector is concerned, each one would return an echo just like an aeroplane.

The first formal indication that I had that our work might close was when I was summoned to a meeting of the Tizard Committee on 21st October 1937, when the Committee at least seemed anxious that the work should be removed from Oxford. Tizard invited me to lunch on 8th November, to discuss the future in more detail, and I received dire warnings from Lindemann as to the artfulness to which I might be subjected. To my surprise, Tizard started in the most friendly manner by saying to me, 'I don't suppose that you can remember the last war!' I replied that not only could I remember the war, and its air raids, but that I could remember my father leaving for France on 11th November 1914, and that I could recall incidents from 1913 when I could not have been more than eighteen months old. 'In that case', said Tizard, 'you have the longest memory of any man I know—except myself. Do you know, I can distinctly remember having had a bottle!'

There could hardly be much guile in a man starting an acquaintance in such an informal manner, and we had a very cordial discussion. He referred to 'this ridiculous quarrel between me and Lindemann' and went on to tell me that Lindemann had been godfather to his sons. At the same time, he thought that it would be better if I would break with Lindemann, and come to Imperial College, of which he was Rector, and continue the infra-red work there. I was not anxious to leave Oxford for London, and so in that respect the discussion was fruitless.

On 3rd December I again visited Bawdsey, and this time was put under pressure by Watson-Watt regarding the relative merits of infrared and airborne radar. Gerald Touch actually worked in the Airborne Radar Group whose head was E. G. Bowen and which included an outstanding young electrical engineer, Robert Hanbury Brown. They had achieved a tremendous feat in getting airborne radar to work, and there was no question that it was going to be superior to infra-red. I had the impression, however, that Watson-Watt was not a good enough physicist to realize how slender a threat infra-red had always been to him, and something about his tactics aroused my resentment. Our discussion, which he had assured me was 'off the record', was reported back to the Air Ministry, and it seemed that somehow he wished to get me under his direct control. He seemed unwilling to face the fact that radar, too, had its weak points. This suspicion, which could be attributed to my highly personal viewpoint, was many years afterwards confirmed by A. P. Rowe, who succeeded Watson-Watt as Superintendent at Bawdsey. Writing to me in 1962 of the 'Window' episode, Rowe said, 'When I took over from W-W at Bawdsey, I found that it was "not done" to suggest that the whole idea would not work. . . . What I want to emphasize is that from no one at no time did I hear a breath of anything like window.'

In the meantime, I continued to work at infra-red, and proposed a pulsed searchlight in which the range of an aircraft could be directly measured by optical pulses, and the glare of the light scattered back by the lower atmosphere could be eliminated. This subsequently was developed as 'Lidar' the optical analogue of radar. But on 28th January 1938 I received a letter from D. R. Pye saying, 'I have decided that in view of the urgency of some of our other defence problems, the Air Ministry programme as a whole will best be served by employing yourself and Pickard elsewhere. I have suggested 31st March as a suitable date for the termination of the Air Ministry research work at the Clarendon.'

I was very annoyed, not so much at the justice of the decision, but of the way it had come about. The Tizard Committee had encouraged me to work on infra-red at the expense of my own career, and only two months before Tizard himself had been inviting me to continue the infra-red work at Imperial College. I had burnt my academic boats, for while my contemporaries had been continuing with their normal researches, I had been working to my utmost on developments which could not be published, on security grounds, even though we ourselves did not intend to use them. I had lost my chances of an academic appointment and was now a civil servant. At the same time, convinced that war was almost inevitable, I did not wish to leave the defence field, although I certainly wanted to get well away from Watson-Watt, Tizard and the rest, where I felt that I had been a pawn in a distinctly unpleasant game. I had almost made up my mind to join my father's old regiment, the Grenadiers.

At that very time, my father lost the sight of one eye, and there was a danger that the other would go too, and I had to face the problem of his being unable to work and therefore of my helping him and my mother. I could not do this on a guardsman's pay, and the most sensible thing would be to continue on some work that would maintain my relatively high salary, even if it meant working with Watson-Watt. I therefore saw Watson-Watt on 4th February, and told him frankly my personal position and also my dislike of his method of approach. On his side I must admit that I must have seemed an even more problematic 'handful' than will have so far appeared from this account. For, having decided that I was selling myself, I was determined to get the best price I could, not so much for myself as for the men who were already working at Bawdsey.

I had, of course, seen Bawdsey mainly through the eyes of Gerald Touch, who was not given to taking a rosy view of anything. Undoubtedly, they had had to start in the old manor house at Bawdsey in very uncomfortable circumstances, and the Air Ministry had done very little to provide reasonable amenities. I thought that by drawing attention to all my prospective discomforts, I might help to get the amenities improved; but it must have made me appear a very awkward personality to Watson-Watt and Rowe.

However, it was agreed that I should go to Bawdsey, and I received a formal letter from the Superintendent of Farnborough instructing me to report for duty at Bawdsey on 1st April. Pickard was not to go with me, but instead to Farnborough; and I saw our mechanic, W. S. Driver, into another job. As for my own preparations, I knew that Bawdsey had a lawn some three hundred yards long and so I thought that I would take up archery. I would, perhaps, acquire a rather exotic dog such as a Saluki; and since there would be plenty of secluded time I would buy many of the books that I knew I ought to have read. Of all the books that I acquired, the one which I have valued most was Bartlett's *Quotations*. Years afterwards I found that Churchill at Bangalore had done exactly the same thing: 'It is a good thing for an uneducated man to read books of quotations. Bartlett's *Familiar Quotations* is an admirable work, and I studied it intently. The quotations when engraved upon the memory give you good thoughts. They also make you anxious to read the authors and look for more.'

Just as I was leaving for Bawdsey I received a telegram instructing me not to report to Bawdsey but instead to Air Ministry Headquarters in London. Watson-Watt had now been promoted from being Super-intendent at Bawdsey to take charge of a new Directorate of Com-munications Development in the Air Ministry, and as such he would have control of infra-red work as well as of radar and communications generally. There was therefore no need for me to be posted to Bawdsey to be under his control, and in any event both he and Rowe were apprehensive about the disruptive influence I would represent. He had therefore arranged a meeting with the other two Services, and had persuaded them that infra-red should be continued, after all, on an inter-Service basis. The Admiralty Research Laboratory at Teddington was suggested as a suitable establishment, and I was to be posted there as the Air Ministry representative and placed directly under a Principal Scientific Officer in the Admiralty Service. I was thus to be removed as far as possible from any place where I could cause trouble and to be disciplined in the tradition of the Senior Service. Actually, the complete *volte face* by Watson-Watt took the Admiralty so much by surprise that they could not be ready for some months, and I was therefore attached to the new Directorate in Air Ministry to cool my heels.

In preparation for the move to Bawdsey my car was already loaded with my books and other possessions and so I drove instead to my parents' home in Herne Hill and reported for duty at the Air Ministry the following morning. I can remember my feelings on leaving the Clarendon and Oxford for the last time. It would be easy to be sorry for myself. My prospects, which had appeared so bright in 1934, with Mount Wilson and South Africa in view, were now, less than four years later, completely shattered. Instead of a pleasant academic life I now faced a relatively dull one in a Government establishment, where I would be subservient to men who knew far less about infra-red than I did, and only my father's situation had stopped me from breaking out of it. This was a rotten reward for three years of desperate work, from which I could not even recover the kudos of papers in scientific journals. I wanted never again to become involved with Lindemann, Tizard, or Watson-Watt.

CHAPTER FIVE

Exile

MY EXILE from active research in air defence did not start exactly as planned, for instead of being at the Admiralty Research Laboratory I was attached to Group Captain H. Leedham, the Assistant Director of Instrument Research and Development in Air Ministry Headquarters. A Regular officer of high principles, he was also a lay preacher; and I had already appreciated his friendly support in my arguments with Watson-Watt. Although office work was not really to my taste, the experience could be useful—and so it was to prove.

I found myself being given a widening range of jobs. Occasionally, I had something practical to do such as the acceptance trials of the first airborne television equipment for the R.A.F. Sometimes I would put up ideas myself. One that was to have later importance was a method by which a bomber could locate itself by receiving radio pulses sent out simultaneously by three ground stations. From the time interval between the pulses from any two of the stations being received by the bomber, it could tell that it was on a particular hyperbolic curve about the two stations as foci, and from the intersection of this hyperbola with another similarly determined from the interval between the pulses from one of the first two stations and the third one, the bomber could determine precisely where it was. The idea was turned down because the radio engineers said that the radio waves used would have to be short ones, and that these would not curve sufficiently round the earth to give a useful range. I found this surprising, but was not in a position to contradict them.

I was, incidentally, astonished by the complacency that existed regarding our ability to navigate at long range by night. The whole of our bombing policy depended on this assumption, but I was assured that by general instrument flying, coupled with navigation by the stars, Bomber Command was confident that it could find pinpoint targets in Germany at night, and that there was therefore no need for any such aids as I had proposed. I was not popular for asking why, if this were true, so many of our bombers on practice flights in Britain flew into hills.

The job that afforded me most interest was to examine the reports that occasionally came in from the Air Intelligence branches. These were usually very slight, but I tried to extract every possible item of information out of them, and I started to interact with Air Intelligence. Finally, a report came in that the Germans were undertaking some very high frequency radio developments on the Brocken, a well-known mountain in the Harz. Now I already knew something about the Brocken, because of the optical phenomenon known as the 'Brocken Spectre' or 'Brocken Ghost' which arises if you stand on the summit and the sun throws your shadow on a cloud below. If the conditions are right, you see your shadow with a saintly rainbow-coloured halo around its head. I decided that I would see if I could beat the official Intelligence Service in discovering more about whatever was happening on the Brocken, and so I wrote to Charles Frank explaining my interest in meteorological phenomena of the optical variety, and that I would be grateful for a first-hand account of the Brocken ghost. Before I heard from him, my time at the Air Ministry came to an end. I had in the meantime found so many jobs to do that five new Sections were set up to take them over; the Sections thus set up were to continue throughout the War.

On 2nd July I went to Teddington, and parked my car in the grounds of the National Physical Laboratory. I knew that the Admiralty Research Laboratory adjoined it, but was not certain of the way. A mild-looking man passed me and I enquired if he could tell me the way. He said that he was going there himself, and so we walked chatting pleasantly on a fine summer morning. He told me where I would find Dr. E. G. Hill, who was to be head of the Infra-Red Group, and so I made my way to Hill's office. Hill said that he had instructions to take me to the Superintendent, who wanted to see me before I started work. So we went together to the Superintendent's office, and he turned out to be the very man of whom I had asked the way. He then surprised me by more or less reading the riot act to me, and saying that he understood that I had hitherto worked in a university laboratory, and that I would find things different in a Government establishment, and that in particular I would be under direct orders from my superior officer, Dr. Hill. It struck me that he was overdoing things a bit, and I could very easily have exploded. However, his attitude did not altogether accord with what I would have expected of the very pleasant man who had guided me to the Laboratory, and I guessed that something must have happened. If indeed I lost my temper, this would confirm the suspicions that he obviously had. I therefore took the dressing-down as meekly as I possibly could, and he finally ran out of steam. Hill and I then departed, and as we were walking back, Hill said, 'I'm sorry about that. Someone has been talking about you—do you know a man called Watson-Watt?'

I intended to lie as low as possible, but within the hour an opportunity occurred that I could not resist. The next step in the disciplinary process was to overawe me with the Official Secrets Act. I was shown the Laboratory copy of the Act and asked to sign a certificate to the effect that I had read the Official Secrets Act (1911) and understood it. I could not resist adding a postscript to my signature: 'The 1920 Act is also worth reading.' Actually, having been interested in official secrets I had some time before purchased from the Stationery Office copies of both Acts to see how they applied to my work and to anyone who might try to reveal it. It was almost incredible that the security authorities in the Admiralty had not been aware of the later Act, and I awaited results. The certificate was duly taken back to the Laboratory office and a little later a despatch rider was sent up to the Admiralty to check whether there really was an Act in 1920. The upshot of the affair occurred on the following afternoon when the Superintendent, whose name I now knew to be Chaffer, sent for me and said that now that I had been with them for two days they had seen quite enough to realize that what they had heard about me was entirely unjustified, and that he wished to apologize for what he had said at our first interview, and that he hoped I would have a happy time at A.R.L. Chaffer was a gentleman, and this was true generally of his staff. They made me very welcome, and I much enjoyed my time with them.

Curiously, before he became a civil servant Chaffer had been a mathematics schoolteacher, and among his pupils had been E. A. Milne, one of our professors at Oxford. An interesting brush thereby occurred between Milne and an officer at A. R. L., Colonel Kerrison, who had been seconded to the Laboratory for the development of predictors for A.A. gunfire. Kerrison was a very able mathematician, but Chaffer thought that some of his mathematics ought to be checked, and had sent the calculations to Milne. The latter replied saying that Kerrison was wrong, and that this was only to be expected from someone who knew no more mathematics than a colonel in the army. The story was that Kerrison had thereupon written to Milne saying, 'Dear Milne, With reference to what you were saying about colonels, you may recall that in 1941 you gained the second scholarship at Trinity, Cambridge. The first scholar did not take up his scholarship but went to fight for his country. He was, Yours sincerely, A. V. Kerrison.' I once asked Kerrison whether the story was true: he told me that he had not sent the letter but the facts were correct.

Another impressive character at A.R.L. was Stephen Butterworth. He was one of a small class of applied mathematicians with a strong practical outlook that this country produced in his generation, the most notable instances being, of course, G. I. Taylor and A. A. Griffith. Butterworth modestly held that his one claim to fame was that as an Examiner he had once failed Captain P. P. Eckersley, the Chief Engineer of the B.B.C. Despite his retiring nature he opened up warmly to me, and I was sorry to observe that more than one careerist in the Admiralty had climbed on Butterworth's back by exploiting his work. Happily, his true merit and their defects were to show up in 1939.

The head of Group E, as the Infra-Red Group was known, was E. G. Hill, who too was a gentleman. He was then aged about forty-five, and had graduated at Bristol. Having been in the R.A.M.C. in the First War, he had a pronounced interest in physiological phenomena, and had spent a long time at H.M. Signal School at Portsmouth on various problems of signalling, especially with infra-red. I learned a great deal of wisdom and naval lore from him, including a comment by Admiral Burmister that, 'There is not, there never has been, and there never will be a completely satisfactory system of recognition. For you have to take grave positive action on a negative result,' i.e. you have to shoot your opponent out of the ocean, the grave positive action, if he does not make the right recognition signal, which is a negative result that may also have been caused by a breakdown in whatever device that he has been provided with to identify himself. As it was not unknown for sailors painting ship to also paint over the infra-red recognition lights, the force of the Admiral's dictum was easy to appreciate.

And then there was the Head Porter, generally known as Deputy Superintendent, whose name happened to be Reginald Jones. He was accorded his second title because this accurately reflected his function— he was an indispensable factotum who looked after the affairs of the Laboratory far more effectively than any of the rest of us. In 1938, when the Laboratory was given a fairly palatial new building, the design was left to one of the Principal Scientific Officers and a Ministry of Works architect. The building was almost ready for occupation when the Deputy Superintendent, performing one of his other functions, took in the Superintendent's usual tray of afternoon tea, with the comment, 'I suppose that you will be wanting tea when we move over to the new building, sir?' 'Of course', replied the Superintendent. 'Well, then, sir, you are not going to get it!' 'Why not. Are you going on strike?' 'Certainly not, sir—but there's no electric point to boil my electric kettle!' And then as the extent of this peculiarly civil service disaster sank in, he added, 'And what's more, sir, there is no electric point in the whole building.' 'How do you know this?' asked the Superintendent. 'I've looked at the plans, sir, and what's more there's no gas and no running water except in the lavatories.' And he was absolutely right. The scientist and the architect between them had omitted all services except electric light, and water for the lavatories. The concrete floors were already set, and their lordships asked us to do with an absolute minimum of facilities for the first six months, after which the necessary alterations could be counted as dilapidation. Even so, the conduits had to be chipped into the concrete floors so that electric cables could be laid. My namesake was one of the towers of strength on which the rest of humanity depends. He had been a Chief Yeoman of Signals in the Battleship *Malaya* at Jutland, and I vowed that if ever I had a laboratory of my own I would try to find another Chief Yeoman as Head Porter; and when the time came, twenty-five years later, I did.

But even with all the gentlemanliness of A.R.L., I could not help feeling the difference in tempo from that which I had been accustomed to in Air Defence. I felt rather like Winston Churchill did when he was removed from his post as First Lord in 1915: 'Like a sea-beast fished up from the depths, or a diver too suddenly hoisted, my face threatened to burst from the fall in pressure. I had great anxiety and no powers of relieving it; I had vehement convictions and small power to give effect to them.' Where he took to painting, I took to glass-blowing, at which I was already fairly good. I spent much energy in constructing an elaborate vacuum system, but I had still plenty left, and some of it almost inevitably went into practical jokes of one form or another.

In fact, when the Superintendent heard of some of my efforts he let it be known to me unofficially that he would be grateful if a new member of staff, who was being unduly inquisitive, could be kept away from the true scent of what Group E was doing. He was an enthusiastic optician, and there really was no harm in his enquiries—it was just that he took a lively interest in everything around him. But it could be an opportunity for entertainment, and a few days after I had been apprised of the Superintendent's desire, I happened to meet the optician in another laboratory, and he clearly treated me as an authority. In the middle of one conversation about technological possibilities, the question had come up of how useful it would be if one had a material that was both transparent to light and a conductor of electricity. Turning to me he said, 'But we haven't got transparent metal, have we doctor?' 'No,' I replied and then after a thoughtful pause, 'Well, no, not officially.' He jumped with enthusiasm and said, 'So that's what Group E is doing.' It was not difficult then to lead him on to discovering that what we were trying to do was to build a transparent and invisible battleship. We had produced enough metal to make an invisible torpedo boat, but were having difficulty because the crew were still visible, as was the wake.

The summer of 1938 wore on to Munich time. I had arranged a visit to Bawdsey, and had now received a letter from Charles Frank to say that he did not believe in ghosts but would be glad to discuss their nature with me at any time. Since he was home in Ipswich, it was possible to see him on my way back from Bawdsey, where I had found A. P. Rowe in a state of some alarm in case the Germans raided his establishment as soon as the War started. When I met Charles Frank he told me that he had immediately grasped the significance of my letter about the Brocken, and had burned it at once. He had taken a trip to see what was going on, and had brought back a picture postcard of the new television-tower that had been erected on its summit. German Air Force personnel were generally around the area, and one thing that he observed neither of us has been able to explain. It was an array of posts rather like Belisha beacons with wooden pear-shaped objects at the top.

There was also, incidentally, the story that whatever was in the tower at the summit was able to paralyse internal combustion engines. As usually reported, the phenomenon consisted of a tourist driving his car on one of the roads in the vicinity, and the engine suddenly ceasing to operate. A German Air Force sentry would then appear from the side of the road and tell him that it was no use his trying to get the car going again for the time being. The sentry would, however, return and tell him when he would be able to do so. The sentry appeared in due course, and the engine started. Incidentally, we did not believe the story, the explanation of which I was to find later, but we thought that it might be a good idea to start the same tale going in England to see whether it would puzzle the Germans. The story spread rapidly, and we heard of it from time to time, with ever increasing detail. The last I heard of it was a family of Quakers, who of course never lie, driving across Salisbury Plain when the engine of their car stopped. In due course a soldier appeared and told them that it would now start again, and so they were able to continue on their way.

I returned to London on the evening of Monday 26th September, and felt the tense calm of the London streets as people braced themselves for the seemingly inevitable war. There was something of the feeling that reached its culmination after Dunkirk. I was unhappy in not having more to do at Teddington, and spent my evenings distributing gas masks—more than two thousand in three days.

Then came Chamberlain's return with his pathetic scrap of paper and his 'Peace in our time' speech. I was as angry as a cat which has just been robbed of its mouse. Those who felt like that were a minority among the almost hysterical majority who thought that Chamberlain had done a great thing, but when I went into the Air Ministry with Charles Frank's information about the Brocken the following morning I found that the Air Staff were convinced that Chamberlain had only postponed the reckoning. As it happened, the official Intelligence Service, which I had also briefed about the Brocken while I had been stationed at Headquarters, came up with some further information, but Charles and I between us had beaten them by a day, and his description of activities on the Brocken was much more detailed. This, as it turned out, did not go unnoticed.

On my return to A.R.L., I found some general laughter over what had happened at the height of the crisis. Someone had thought that in case of air raids some shelter trenches ought to be dug, and there had been a general call for volunteers. A large squad of physicists had therefore been assembled and they had sallied forth on to the playing fields armed with spades and sandbags. A little while later they were observed trudging sadly back, driven by an irate little woman. She was Vera Cain, the captain of the Women's Hockey team, and they had chosen to try to dig their trenches in the middle of her pitch. She had heard of their intentions, and had gone to the Director, Sir Charles Darwin, and had convinced him that there were many more sensible places to dig trenches. But even if she had not had his authority I doubt whether anyone could have stood up to her. I know, for we were married in 1940.

We became engaged on St. Patrick's Day 1939, and began to pay various social visits, particularly to Oxford. One Saturday evening in the summer we had met Jim and Elsie Tuck, and I can remember standing at a bus stop in the High while Jim told me about the discovery of nuclear fission, and the possibility that an atomic bomb might one day be made. He said that it looked as though the idea had already been

conceived in Germany and that, indeed, from one paper it appeared that
one of the German physicists was trying to warn the rest of the world.

I would have been interested in the matter anyway, but what now
made my interest acute was the visit I had had a few weeks before
from A. E. Woodward-Nutt, which I have described in the opening
chapter. Tizard had found there was little information coming through
from Germany, and so it had been proposed that a scientist of some
standing (Tizard may have had in mind Thomas Merton, who had
worked with M.I.6 in World War I and who was an eminent spectroscopist) should be appointed to conduct an enquiry into our Intelligence
Services, and recommend what should be done to improve them. The
Treasury, however, had refused financial support, saying that science was
international and that British scientists should be able to tell how their
opposite numbers were thinking by talking to them at conferences, and
that this should cost nothing. Faced with this frustrating reply, Woodward-Nutt had remembered my interest in Intelligence matters with the
Thost and Brocken stories, and so he suggested that I could be transferred
to Intelligence, and that this would cost the Air Ministry nothing. This
was the main reason that I found myself in my war post.

CHAPTER SIX

The Day Before War Broke Out

MY LAST few months at the Admiralty Research Laboratory went quickly, and I began to think about my new work. On 15th March Hitler had invaded Czechoslovakia and on 7th April Mussolini had taken over Albania. The treachery of the Munich Agreement was at last obvious, even to Chamberlain; he now gave a guarantee to Poland, and so all would depend on whether the Germans would be satisfied with their present gains. By early August this seemed increasingly unlikely, and then on 23rd August came the astonishing news of the non-aggression pact between Germany and Russia. The invasion of Poland appeared to be only a matter of time, and for me it seemed now or never for a short holiday. Ever since 1934 I had spent early September at Hoar Cross, and this year my visit could be conveniently sandwiched between leaving Teddington and starting in Air Intelligence. Moreover, the Meynells had invited Vera as well, so with some misgivings we left Teddington shortly after the news of the German pact with Russia came through.

If the next few pages seem to hold up my narrative of the war, they may serve to provide a moment of comedy before a cataclysm of high tragedy, for they give a glimpse of a carefree and gracious life that the war was to sweep away for ever.

Life at Hoar Cross was as pleasant as it had always been. I took my pistols with me; these were something of a joke with the Meynells because I would disappear for hours and they never knew what I was going to bring back. My bag was mainly rabbits but over the years I had also shot hares, stoats, pigeons, crows, and jays. On the first Sunday of this particular holiday, which happened to be the last Sunday in August, I was reconnoitring a copse to assess the prospects for the week. I saw a great deal of wild life in this way, since it was necessary to stand completely still for perhaps half-an-hour at a stretch before an animal or bird would timidly come into view, and in the meantime I often saw things that I would have missed on an ordinary walk.

That particular morning a rabbit loped across a footpath not more than fifteen yards from where I was standing, and its leisurely pace completely misled me as to what was to happen next: a full-grown fox came trotting, equally leisurely, after the rabbit. My thoughts during the two or three seconds that the fox was visible were very mixed. First, I had never shot a fox, a difficult target for a pistol; indeed, this was the first time I had ever seen a fox within range. Secondly, it was Sunday morning, and thirdly, this was the ancestral home of Hugo Meynell, known the world over as the father of English foxhunting. I had the pistol in my hand and the fox in my sights, just to see whether I could hit it, but I finally controlled myself enough not to pull the trigger. When I returned to lunch I told Vera, but she refused to believe that I had deliberately not fired. She said that it was much more likely that I had been so surprised by the fox that I had been paralysed.

The following day I was out with the pistol when, about eighty yards away, I saw something peering at me from behind a bush. This was a fox's head in silhouette, and all I could think of was showing Vera that I could shoot foxes if I wanted to. Foxhunting or not, I took careful aim and fired: the fox slumped over dead. Then, of course, came the reckoning. I was quite pleased with myself to have shot such a wary animal, and at this range, but it would require some explaining. When I went back to tea I quietly confessed to Colonel Meynell who—instead of being annoyed—was much amused. He told me, regretfully, that perhaps I ought to bury the body quietly, since the Hunt had been over that very ground during the morning and had failed to draw any foxes or cubs at all. So that was the end of my fox.

On the following Thursday, 31st August, Lady Dorothy asked Vera and me if we would mind going with her to another country house in the afternoon, since a neighbouring Earl was holding an 'at home', and she felt obliged to take a party across. Moreover, there was to be some tennis; she knew that Vera was good at the game and it would help if our party was strengthened in this respect. I myself was unable to play since I had been badly stung on the ankle while out shooting the previous day, but if Vera went I obviously had to go too. No sooner had Lady Dorothy told us about the party than her elder son, Hugo, started to warn us against going. 'I'll tell you exactly what will happen. People will be standing about and then someone will say, "What about tennis?" and (mentioning the Earl's Viscount son, by now in his forties) will say, "Ah yes, tennis!"; then he will go and get his racquet, which is an old triangular one with a great knob on the handle, and he will bring out two odd-job men who will start to put the net up. But the net rope won't be long enough and they'll have to go and get a bit of string. When he starts to play, he'll hit a ball hard into the net and the string will break and things will have to start all over again. And at some stage in the game he will trip over a manhole in the middle of the court.'

We laughed at this obvious caricature of a country tennis party, but he insisted it was a truthful picture. Indeed, Colonel Meynell seemed to give it some support for he told us that the Viscount had been an officer in his battery during the 1914–18 War. He was so untidy that Colonel Meynell in an effort to shame him into smartening himself up had said, 'Look here, if you will get yourself a new pair of breeches I'll pay half the cost!' The Viscount duly appeared in a new pair of breeches and a few months later the Colonel received a bill from a firm of west-end tailors 'To one half the Viscount Blank's breeches'.

We left with Lady Dorothy in high curiosity. I was enjoying the prospect much more than Vera, because she was attired in a way not altogether suitable for tennis, despite the fact that she had often preached to me that if you were playing a sport you ought to be properly dressed for it. She had indeed brought tennis dress to Hoar Cross, but it included shorts rather than a skirt. At lunch she had mentioned the fact, fearing that shorts were perhaps a little too modern for the kind of party that we appeared to be in for, and Colonel Meynell agreed. In that case, there was nothing for it but to wear a party dress, actually an attractive dark blue American dress with rather a long skirt. Her ensemble was completed by gloves and a large floppy hat.

When we arrived we found that Hugo was not quite right, in that tennis had already started and two formidable girls were thumping the ball about the court more in the spirit of a County match. Moreover they were attired in very brief shorts. When their game was over, the Viscount suggested that a four should be made up, and Lady Dorothy said that Vera would like to play. Vera was very apologetic, saying that she had not come dressed for tennis because she thought that shorts might be out of place. 'You are quite right, my dear,' said the very positively voiced daughter of the house. 'We *never* wear shorts here!' Perhaps the general embarrassment caused by this remark, for it was surely within earshot of the two Amazons, may have contributed to the subsequent course of affairs.

I watched Vera miserably go on to the tennis court to partner the Viscount against the two girls who had obviously assessed the amount of tennis that she had played by her blue dress. She seemed to be about half their size. I have rarely enjoyed myself so much. I knew how annoyed Vera was having to play in this habit, and I also suspected that the Amazons were in for a surprise. Moreover, there was enough already right about Hugo's predictions to make me hope that the rest might well come true. The Viscount's racquet was, for example, triangular and it did have a ball-end to its handle. There *was* a piece of string connecting the too-short net rope to one of the posts. While there was not exactly a *manhole* in the middle of the court, there was for some curious reason a drainage hole like a miniature hydrant.

As play got under way, I watched the growing bewilderment of the Amazons as the little thing in the party dress began to hit the ball even harder than they could. The Quixotic figure of the Viscount grew as appreciative of his partner as the Don would have been if his 'Dulcinea del Toboso' had suddenly appeared on the court. His enthusiasm waxed full: 'Well done, partner! Splendid shot, partner!' And then in ecstasy at one of Vera's further efforts, 'Oh, I *have* got a good partner!' Emulating the Don in the Sierra Morena, he cut a series of wild capers one of which caused him to trip over the manhole, crash into the net, get himself tangled up with it, and break the string. Laughter overwhelmed me and I fell off my chair. The odd-job men were duly summoned to repair the net with a new piece of string, and Vera carried the Viscount to a triumphant victory.

After tea his father, the Earl, suggested that I might walk round the garden with him. It was a magnificent garden, landscaped by Capability Brown. As we walked, we chatted about the international situation and of the prospect of war. The Earl summed up, 'I don't believe in it—I tell you, my boy, Hitler's bluffing. Yes, the man's bluffing. There will be no war!' Twelve hours later the Germans were marching into Poland.

CHAPTER SEVEN

The Secret Weapon

As the German tanks and dive bombers attacked Poland, Britain became tensely calm. Trains full of evacuated children left our large cities, and those of us at Hoar Cross spent Saturday 2nd September collecting evacuees from the local railway station and taking them to their pre-arranged billets. The pathos of these bewildered children, torn from their parents by unpredictable danger, indelibly impressed me with sympathy for the innocents in war.

The British Ultimatum to Germany expired on 3rd September 1939. It was a Sunday, and Vera had accompanied the Meynells to morning service at church. Jean, Hugo Meynell's wife, and Rachel Meynell had stayed in the house, and the three of us listened to Neville Chamberlain's speech at a quarter past eleven. The Prime Minister sounded like a decent, if ineffectual, man who had been badly let down; and as he said 'It is evil things that we shall be fighting against', we at least felt that Britain had done everything possible, in fact too much, to accommodate German demands.

So we were, for the second time in our lives, at war. My immediate reaction was one of discomfiture, in that the most likely target in the event of a blitzkrieg would be London, and that I ought not to be comfortably away in Staffordshire. At the same time there was a sneaking relief at being out of London entirely legitimately, and therefore being able to weigh up the odds. The next few days were typical of those in a family decently prepared to do what it could. Hugo moved to join his Territorial Regiment, the Staffordshire Yeomanry—he was to be badly wounded at El Alamein. Rachel put on her Red Cross uniform—her mother had long been President of the Red Cross for Staffordshire—and Vera and I returned to London.

There had been no air attack, although there had been a false alarm immediately after Chamberlain's speech. I reported for duty to the Directorate of Scientific Research, which I found packing up its files in Berkeley Square House, in preparation for evacuating to Harrogate. I read what I could of the files that yet had to be packed and which might be useful as briefing regarding the development of new military weapons and techniques in this country.

Woodward-Nutt introduced me to Wing Commander F. W. Winterbotham, the Head of the Air Intelligence branch designated as A.I.1(c) which was, although I did not know it, the Air component of M.I.6, the Secret Intelligence Service. It was agreed that I should be attached to Winterbotham's Section after I had read the rest of the files in Harrogate. A few days later I drove north, the only incident of interest being a Montagu's Harrier flying across the Great North Road, the only time in my life that I have seen one.

I thought about the job that I now had to do. In some ways it suited me perfectly. I could see it as one of the very outposts of our national defences—it could not win the war but a failure to detect the development of a new German weapon could easily lead to disaster. This was what I had meant in my immediate comment on being offered the job by Woodward-Nutt. So, as with my father in 1914, I would hope to be among the first or the last. And had I been old enough to think about it—which I was not—I might have consciously wondered at the experience that, with two weeks still to go to my twenty-eighth birthday, I had already accumulated which was all going to be useful in the new job. My main weakness was in not being able to speak German—a legacy of the bias in school in favour of French—but against that I had gained much from school, and from home and Oxford. I had five years' post-doctoral experience, especially in problems of observation, detection and navigation. I had worked in the Admiralty Research Laboratory and had been at sea with the Navy; I had the background of the Grenadiers coupled with seven years in the O.T.C. and more recently with the Air Defence Experimental Establishment at Biggin Hill and the Chemical Defence Establishment at Porton; I had been on the staff at Farnborough and had flown with the Royal Air Force. I knew both Lindemann and Tizard—and I also knew how different operational conditions in battle, or at least in trials, were from the calm of the laboratory. I had worked in Air Ministry Headquarters. Finally I had hoaxed the German Intelligence Service.

The first trial was soon to come, for I had hardly been in Harrogate a week when Hitler made a speech at Danzig on 19th September 1939, in which, according to the Foreign Office translation, he said that he had a secret weapon against which no defence would avail. This caused Mr. Chamberlain as Prime Minister to ask the Intelligence Services if they knew what the secret weapon was. They were only too glad to be able to reply that they had just appointed a man for the very purpose, and would ask him to report. So I received an urgent call from Winterbotham to return to London, so that I could look through the files of the Secret Intelligence Service, and decide what the weapon must be.

As it turned out, this was a great stroke of luck. Instead of having to spend some months on the periphery of Intelligence, while those in charge summed me up and decided whether I would be sufficiently reliable, there was such an alarm that I was taken to the very heart of Intelligence, and all its secrets were laid bare to me. After a day or two at the Headquarters of M.I.6 at No. 54, Broadway, I was told to go to Bletchley Park, or 'Station X' as it was known, which was to be the evacuation headquarters of M.I.6, and where all its pre-war files now rested.

At Bletchley I shared a room with a most gentlemanly Squadron Leader, Courtleigh Nasmith Shaw, who had the traditional Air Force moustache and equally traditional drawl, and who had once been a cavalry officer. The relative informality of even military flying in those days enabled him to claim the endurance record for a Wapiti aircraft. What happened was that he had taken it from his own station to another for a lunch which was preceded, and doubtless followed, by a surfeit of what he termed 'lightning snifters'. Flying back across Salisbury Plain he realized that his personal endurance was about to be reached, and that he would have to land in order to relieve himself. Spotting a large field he put down the aircraft without any trouble, and taxied to a convenient corner. After he had done what he had to do, it struck him that it was a beautiful summer afternoon and that a nap in the shade would be much in order. He therefore went to sleep, to be awakened some time later by the noise of an aircraft engine. It turned out to be his own, which he had not switched off. Jumping into the aircraft in some alarm he promptly took off, only to curse himself for being so foolish because it was clear that an hour or two had gone by and that his fuel might be near exhaustion. However, the fuel situation was not too bad, since the engine had not used much while ticking over, and he got home safely, some two hours beyond the official endurance of a Wapiti, to find that a search alarm had been instituted for him.

The Wapiti was not the only episode in Courtleigh Shaw's varied life in which micturition played a part. Courtleigh, or 'Jane' as he was universally nicknamed in honour of a well-known rugger song, had actually been a spy. During a tour of Germany by car to locate new air-fields, he was accompanied by a suitable girlfriend, and the two of them were caught well within a forbidden area. They were taken by German Air Force guards to the airfield headquarters and interrogated. By making appropriate signs, Jane convinced the interrogator that nature was making undue demands on him, which he was too shy to mention in front of the girl, and was finally told the way to the lavatory while his girlfriend remained behind. In the best manner of the silly-ass Englishman he blundered into one door after another in an apparent search for the lavatory, excusing himself every time but in fact taking a look at what was going on in every room. He and the girl were finally released because the Germans could find nothing incriminating; but Jane told me that he was glad that he had made no marks on his maps. The worst thing that you can do, he said, was to use a pin instead of a pencil—although a pinprick cannot easily be seen from the right side of the map it is immediately obvious to any Intelligence Officer who knows the job and therefore holds the map up to the light.

Jane looked after me for the first few days at Bletchley, and introduced me to some outstandingly interesting colleagues. At our first lunch he whispered to me, 'See that chap opposite you—he's A. J. Alan.' This was the marvellous raconteur who used to fascinate B.B.C. listeners with his broadcast stories, and I found that most of the clues that I had spotted about him from his talks were correct. He was officially a civil servant, and had been at Oxford and, I think, Rugby. He was a cryptographer, which accounted for the reticence which surrounded him whenever anyone tried to discover his identity: his real name was Lambert. The most surprising thing about him was that, in contrast to the outrageously unconventional stories that he told, he himself was a model of regularity. At 11.30 precisely he would leave for a drink, usually with Oliver Strachey, another cryptographer, and return to work with the same punctuality. All his days were run on a mono-tonously regular timetable.

The following day I found myself sitting opposite a distinctly excitable professor of German, who turned out to be Frederick Norman of King's College London. He seemed to have no technical knowledge whatso-ever, and he was waxing furious about the recent loss of the aircraft carrier H.M.S. *Courageous*. 'Shocking show, shocking show!' he kept on saying, shaking his head from side to side at the same time. I asked him why he was so moved, and he told me that it was bad enough to lose an aircraft carrier but to lose all the aircraft as well was beyond the limit.

He said that she had taken some time to sink and so why couldn't they have flown off all the aircraft in the meantime? I pointed out to him that it is difficult enough to take off from an aircraft carrier in the ordinary way, but to try to do so from a deck that was listing would be almost impossible. 'I hadn't thought of that!' he said, and his technological ineptitude gave no clue to the enormous help he was to provide for me right through the war. A pleasant surprise at lunch was to encounter Joan Stenning, the daughter of the Warden of Wadham when I was an undergraduate. Again, we had no idea how the events of war were to throw us together.

One of the most remarkable men at Bletchley was universally known as 'Josh'. An outstanding cryptographer, he had built up a reputation for absentmindedness that even by the standard of his academic colleagues was unique. While I was at Bletchley he took part in the first interrogation of a prisoner of war from the German Air Force. This was a Lieutenant who had been shot down during the attack on our warships in the Firth of Forth on 16th October 1939. The party that was assembled to conduct the interrogation numbered four. The chief interrogator was S. D. Felkin, then a Squadron Leader who had served in World War I, and who had come back to the Air Force after being manager of Ideal Boilers in Paris. He was a good German speaker and, as it turned out, a brilliant interrogator. This first time, however, his technique had not yet developed, and it was agreed that he should be backed up by three experts. One was from the German Section of Air Intelligence; another was Flight Lieutenant Maggs, from the Y Service, or Signals Intelligence, who had a magnificent knowledge of the radio call signs used by German aircraft. I found that at any stage throughout the war I could telephone him asking him where an aircraft with a particular call sign had been heard before, and he could immediately give me its history. The third expert was Josh.

They had a preliminary meeting together, and decided that the first thing that they had to do was to establish a moral superiority over the prisoner. They were to sit on one side of a long table, and the prisoner was to be marched in and stood to attention between two guards as members of the interrogation panel fired questions at him. When they had settled themselves down, the door was thrown open and the prisoner marched in. He was a typical product of Nazi success. His uniform was smart, his jackboots were gleaming, and his movements executed with German precision. As he came to the centre of the room he was halted and turned to face the panel. No sooner had he executed his turn than he clicked his heels together and gave a very smart Nazi salute. For this the panel were unprepared, and none more so than Josh, who stood up as smartly, gave the Nazi salute and repeated the prisoner's 'Heil Hitler!' Then, realizing that he had done the wrong thing, he looked in embarrassment at his colleagues and sat down with such speed that he missed his chair and, to the prisoner's astonishment, disappeared completely under the table.

My final stroke of luck at Bletchley was that I was billeted with Sir Kenneth and Lady Macdonald at Winslow, along with Commander Edward Travis, who happened to be Deputy Head of the Government Code and Cipher School, the cryptographic headquarters that was officially part of M.I.6. The Head of the School was Commander Alexander Denniston, whom Travis was to succeed in 1942, but who had laid the foundations of our brilliant cryptographic successes. In our long evenings together Travis discussed with me his problems in cryptography, and in particular the problem of trying to 'break' the German Enigma machine. This was a very ingenious arrangement of three wheels, each one of which had a sequence of studs on each side, with each stud on one side being connected by a wire to a pin on the other side—the exact arrangement of the connections being one of the secrets of the machine—and the pin making contact with one of the studs on the next wheel. The machine had a typewriter keyboard, and it was worked rather like a cyclometer: every time the machine was operated to encode a letter, one wheel would be turned by one space; after this wheel had moved by enough spaces to turn it through one revolution, it would click its neighbouring wheel by one space. The wheels were thus never in the same position twice. The basic encoding was effected by the passage of an electric current through the studs so that when a letter was to be encoded, the appropriate key would be pressed on the keyboard, and the resultant coded letter would be determined by the appropriate conducting path through the studs, the studs on one wheel making suitable contact with the pins on the neighbouring wheel. A further touch of ingenuity was to add a reversing arrangement at the edge of the third wheel, again with studs cross-connected so as to send the current backwards through the wheels by yet another path. The returning current lit a small electric bulb which illuminated a particular letter on a second keyboard, and thus indicated the enciphered equivalent of the letter whose key had originally been pressed.

Travis told me that although the World War I generation of cryptographers, which included Oliver Strachey and Nigel de Grey (who had helped break the famous Zimmermann telegram) believed that machine codes would be unbreakable, some of his new generation of young cryptographers believed that Enigma could be broken, and that they had already got as far as working out what some of the cross wiring inside the wheels must be. A great step forward had recently been achieved through the Poles, who had stolen the wheels of an actual machine, and it was now therefore a question of building yet another machine which could rapidly try out all the possible combinations to see which one produced a plain text in German language. Even when you had the wheels, you needed to know the relative order in which they were placed, and the positions in which they were set at the beginning of a message, if you were to use the Enigma machine, and this was, of course, the knowledge that was still denied us and which had somehow to be recovered every time.

Travis introduced me to Alan Turing, the brilliant mathematician who later contributed so much to the development of computers and machine intelligence, and together we worked out ways in which the process might be done mechanically, with a machine that would recognize when genuine German was coming out by the frequencies with which various letters and diphthongs appeared. Actually, the way in which the problem was finally and brilliantly solved was not quite along that line of attack, but it had introduced me to the cryptographers and given me an understanding of their problems. And it had alerted them to mine.

While my evenings were spent discussing cryptography, my days went in perusing the S.I.S. files. These were not inspiring, for they were very weak on matters concerning science and technology, since (in common with most Ministers of the Crown and their Permanent Secretaries) the average S.I.S. agent was a scientific analphabet. The most entertaining file was undoubtedly one labelled 'Death Ray' which was a saga in itself. Over the years the S.I.S. had become tired of reporting death rays only to be slapped down by the Service Ministries, and one S.I.S. agent had been so convinced by a Dutch inventor that the S.I.S. finally decided to show the Service Ministries how wrong they were. It therefore actually provided the inventor with money to pursue his development so that they could present the Service Ministries with the genuine article. The latter part of the file consisted of reports of visits to the inventor to inspect his progress. Invariably he had an excuse for the apparatus not working, right up to the outbreak of war. At last, when it was clear that even the S.I.S. was not being fooled any longer and would therefore give him no more money, his final report stated that although the apparatus had been a failure as a death ray, he had discovered that it had remarkable properties as a fruit preserver, and he therefore offered this invention for exploitation by the S.I.S. in any venture that it might think appropriate.

The more I looked through the S.I.S. files, the more I was impressed by the paucity of useful information. At the same time, I could not help wondering, if there really were a secret weapon, why we had neither heard of it nor thought of it for ourselves. I began to suspect the Foreign Office translation, and to wonder what Hitler had actually said. Fortunately, a fellow guest during one of my visits to Hoar Cross had been Sir Roy Maconachie, who was Director of Talks at the B.B.C. I therefore telephoned him to see whether the B.B.C. had a record of Hitler's speech and, if so, they would allow one of my colleagues to listen to it again. Sir Roy arranged for this to be done and I asked 'Bimbo' Norman, whom I was now getting to know well, whether he would go. He duly went, and returned full of indignation at Hitler's grammar. But he was certain that Hitler had not said that he had a secret weapon, merely that he had a weapon with which Germany could not be attacked, just as England could not be attacked at sea because it had the Royal Navy. Norman's translation ran:

... And it is England who has already again begun the war on women and children with lies and deceit.

They have a weapon, which they believe to be unassailable, that is to say their Navy, and they say: 'Well, because we ourselves cannot be attacked with this weapon, we are justified in waging war with this weapon against women and children, not only those of our enemies but also if necessary those of the neutrals.'

But one should not deceive oneself on this point. The moment could arrive very quickly, when *we* would employ a weapon with which *we* cannot be attacked.

I hope that they will then not suddenly remember Humanity and the impossibility of waging war against women and children. We Germans don't hold with that at all. That is not our nature.

Also in this campaign I have issued orders to spare towns wherever possible. But naturally, if a column marches across the market square and is attacked by aeroplanes, it can happen that someone else is unfortunately sacrificed. . . .

The emphasis on 'we' in the fourth sentence reflects the emphasis which Hitler himself made in his speech. I ought to explain that the German for 'weapon' is 'waffe' which can either mean a particular weapon such as a rifle or a whole armed service (as Hitler himself had used to describe the Royal Navy)—and indeed the word for 'Air Force' in German is 'Luftwaffe'. And from the example that he quoted in the last sentence it was clear that he was in fact thinking of the Luftwaffe.

This was very much an anticlimax, and not popular with our own Admiralty, who had been encouraging me to say that the secret weapon was the magnetic mine, partly because a German prisoner of war had said so. But I had weighed up all the evidence as impartially as I could and, although I had the opportunity to alter my report before it was circulated on 11th November, I decided to let my conclusion stand.

The whole scare had arisen because the Foreign Office translators had put the vital clause differently. Instead of saying, 'We would employ a weapon with which we cannot be attacked,' they said, 'we would employ a weapon against which no defence would avail.' They added to the confusion a few days later when they helpfully reported that Hitler had disclosed something of the nature of the weapon, telling me that I had to look for a weapon which would blind and deafen its victims. On this occasion Hitler had said that if the allies attacked he would reply with a force that would deprive them of sight and hearing—but this merely happened to be an idiom for 'render them thunderstruck'. So the Foreign Office did not have much luck.

Although I had demolished the secret weapon, I did at the same time report my conclusions from a search of the S.I.S. files and summarized the results as follows:

Apart from the more fantastic rumours such as those concerned with machines for generating earthquakes and gases which cause everyone within two miles to burst, there are a number of weapons to which several references occur, and of which some must be considered seriously. They include:—

(1) Bacterial Warfare.
(2) New gases.
(3) Flame weapons.
(4) Gliding bombs, Aerial torpedoes and Pilotless aircraft.
(5) Long range guns and rockets.

(6) New Torpedoes, mines and submarines.
(7) Death rays, engine-stopping rays and magnetic guns.

The war would see how many of these forecasts would come to pass. In the meantime Hitler had done me a great service by securing my base in the very heart of Intelligence.

CHAPTER EIGHT

The Oslo Report

To COMPLETE my report on the secret weapon, I had returned to London at the beginning of November and been given an office in No. 54 Broadway alongside Fred Winterbotham, who had instructed his secretary, Daisy Mowat, to 'mother' me. Daisy, now Lady Currie, typed all my early reports; and very well she did them. Her sense of mischief would occasionally lead her to incorporate a deliberate mistake, which had to be watched for; and there was one occasion later in the war when the Prime Minister's Secretary telephoned and she told him that I was not available. By the time that I had retrieved the call from her extension I heard a grieved voice saying, 'This is Peck, the Prime Minister's Secretary—is that really Dr. Jones? I have just been talking to a most extraordinary lady who asserted that you had just jumped out of the window!' With some presence of mind I replied, 'Please don't worry, it's the only exercise that we can get.' It was this light-hearted background that gave Churchill cause to write in *Their Finest Hour* that I thought that my first summons to his Cabinet Room might be a practical joke.

The Old Chief of M.I.6, Admiral 'Quex' Sinclair, had just died. He was succeeded by Stewart Menzies, who had previously been Head of Section V of M.I.6, but I was not to meet him for another year. The highest ranking officer that I did meet in the early days was the Vice-Chief, Claude Dansey. Various things, mainly uncomplimentary, have been written about Dansey, but once again I had a stroke of fortune at the begining of my dealings with him. Evidently he had heard that there was now a scientist in the office, and he quickly came to see me. He delighted in intrigue, and what he wanted me to do was, in this instance anyway, altruistic on his part. It involved finding employment for a deserving physicist in a Government establishment. Fortunately I was able to do so, and this initial success put me into Dansey's good books—a fact for which I was later to be very thankful.

Whilst on the subject of scientific recruitment, I might mention that at Bletchley I met one of the keepers in the botany department of the Natural History Museum who had volunteered for the Navy. Because there was a shortage of cryptographers, the three Services were asked whether there were any among their recruits who had a cryptographic background, and the museum keeper was one of those discovered in this way because he had described his occupation as that of a 'cryptogamic botanist'. When he told me this my comment had been, 'The silly idiots, they ought to have known that it meant that you had a secret wife!' He gave me a most curious look—it was some time afterwards that I discovered that although he was indeed married, he also maintained a clandestine ménage.

Just as I was finishing the secret weapon report one evening, Fred Winterbotham came into my room and dumped a small parcel on my desk and said, 'Here's a present for you!' I asked him what its background was and he said that it had come from our Naval Attaché in Oslo. This was after the Attaché had received a letter, dropped privately through his letterbox, saying that if the British would like to know about various German scientific and technical developments, would we alter the preamble to our news broadcasts in German so as to say, 'Hullo, hier ist London . . .' instead of the normal preamble, and then our would-be helper would know that it was worth while to give us the information. The change had been duly made, and a package had then been put through the letterbox. It contained some seven pages of typewritten text and a sealed box. I can remember gingerly opening the box because it might easily have been a bomb, especially because of the extraordinary way in which it had appeared. But it turned out to be harmless, and inside there was a sealed glass tube, rather like an electronic valve which, in one sense, it was. It proved to be an electronic triggering device which, our correspondent said, had been developed so as to operate a proximity fuse in anti-aircraft shells. The principle of operation was that the shells were to be made in two electrically insulated halves, with suitable electronics to record the change in electrical capacitance between the halves whenever the shell was in the vicinity of a third body.

Besides the fuse and a description of its intended operation, there was a wide range of information, including the fact that the Junkers 88 was to be used as a dive-bomber. The German Navy was said to have developed remote-controlled rocket-driven gliders of about three metres span and three metres long, with radio control for launching by aircraft against enemy ships. The experimental establishment where this work was being carried out was Peenemünde—the first mention we had ever heard of this establishment.

The German Army was developing rocket projectiles of 80 centimetres calibre and stabilized by gyroscopes. The projectiles were not flying straight but in uncontrollable curves, and were therefore to be equipped with radio remote control. The report mentioned Rechlin, the German equivalent of Farnborough, about which we already knew. It also told us that in the raid by Bomber Command on Wilhelmshafen in September, our aircraft had been detected at a range of 120 kilometres by radar stations with an output of 20 kilowatts. It did not state the wavelength, but suggested that we should find this for ourselves and jam the transmissions. There was another radar system using paraboloid aerials and operating on wavelengths of around 50 centimetres.

There was also a system for finding the range of a friendly bomber by transmitting a signal on a wavelength of 6 metres, which was modulated at a low frequency. This signal was received by the aircraft and returned to the observing station on a somewhat different radio frequency so that, from the phase lag in the returned modulation, the distance of the aircraft could be determined. The observing station could then transmit this information to the bomber, so that he could position himself relative to some pre-determined target.

Finally, the Oslo report told us about two new kinds of torpedo developed by the German Navy. One was controlled by radio for the first part of its journey and then switched to acoustic homing with microphones on the head of the torpedo so that it could steer itself towards the ship by listening to the noise of its engines. The second type of torpedo had a magnetic fuse, and the writer of the report speculated that it was these torpedoes that had sunk the *Royal Oak* in Scapa Flow.

The report was obviously written by someone with a good scientific and technical background, and quite different from anything that I had so far seen in Intelligence. My first step was to take the electronic trigger tube down to my former colleagues at the Admiralty Research Laboratory, to get them to evaluate its performance. The report itself was circulated to the three Service Ministries, but nobody would take it seriously. The leading doubter was John Buckingham, the Deputy Director of Scientific Research at the Admiralty. When I tried to convince him he implied that I was an innocent in Intelligence work, and that the whole thing was a 'plant'. His argument was that the German hoaxers had overdone it, because it was very unlikely that any one man in Germany could have had such a comprehensive knowledge of developments in so many different fields. When I pointed out that at least some of the information was genuine, he said this was an old trick (as indeed it was) in which you give your victim something genuine that you know that he already knows, in the hope of convincing him that the rest of the report, which contains the hoax, is genuine. I pointed out that this was quite a remarkable hoax, since by now A.R.L. had found that the electronic tube was much better than anything that we had made in the same line, but I could not convince him. The report was thereafter disregarded in the Ministries, which did not even keep their copies, and all I could do was to keep my own copy and use it as a basis for much of my thought.

The value of the Oslo report was to become evident as the war proceeded, as it will in this book. I gave it publicity in my post-war lecture to the Royal United Services Institution on 19th February 1947, partly in the hope that whoever had written it would come forward if he had survived the war. But despite worldwide publicity, the only response I had was from the former Naval Attaché in Oslo, Hector Boyes, who was now a Rear Admiral. His letter said:

I was very much interested to read in *The Times* a résumé of your lecture at the United Services Institution.

Whilst serving as Naval Attaché Oslo I remember receiving the German letters.

At that period one was inundated with various anonymous correspondence which it was necessary to sift.

On translating the German correspondence there appeared to be matters of interest though one had a certain mistrust, the letters having been posted in Norway.

On arrival home after the evacuation I asked about the correspondence without much result. I forgot about it, having been appointed to Japan. Your lecture shows that the writer was genuine— Is there any chance of his being Norwegian? At one period I was in touch with a Norwegian engineer who had been working in Germany on U and E boats.

One thing against it being him is that the letters were written in excellent German.

It confirms the lack of interest that had been shown in the Ministries— unfortunately my position in 1940 after the Norwegian evacuation was too obscure for Captain Boyes and me to have met.

Inevitably, the question will be asked regarding my own ideas about the identity of the Oslo author. I believe that I know, but the way in which his identity was revealed to me was so extraordinary that it may well not be credited. In any event, it belongs to a later period, and the denouement must wait till then.

CHAPTER NINE

A Plan For Intelligence

A S INTEREST in the secret weapon died down, I was able to get on with the task for which I had gone to Intelligence. This was not to act as an Intelligence Officer myself, but to conduct a one-man enquiry into why so little scientific and technical information was being obtained by our Intelligence Services, and to recommend ways in which the arrangements could be improved. It was originally intended that the task should take me six months from 1st September: but the war had broken out, and something therefore needed to be done quickly. And so, after ten weeks which included the secret weapon and Oslo stories, I embodied my findings in a report entitled 'A Scientific Intelligence Service' which was completed on 7th December. The first page of this report ran:

A serious disparity in Scientific Intelligence between England and Germany almost certainly exists at the present time. This is due in part to the extra secrecy precautions observed in Germany, and in part to the lack of coordinated effort in our acquisition of information.

Parallels have frequently been drawn between the Peloponnesian War and that between England and Germany, but rarely more accurately than in the present connection. A similar disregard for Scientific Intelligence exists now in England to that which existed in Athens: Pericles, in a classic exposition of Athenian policy, stated:

'Our city is thrown open to the world, and we never expel a foreigner or prevent him from seeing or learning anything of which the secret if revealed to an enemy might profit him. We rely not upon management or trickery, but upon our own hearts and hands.' (Thucydides. II, 39.)

While it may be claimed that we do not completely emulate this abandon, yet the relative ease of obtaining, for example, air intelligence in this country, compared with the difficulty of even locating German aerodromes, renders the parallel sensibly true: Athens lost the war.

I went on to look at the aims of Scientific Intelligence:

The primary problem of a Scientific Intelligence Service is to obtain early warning of the adoption of new weapons and methods by potential or actual enemies. To tackle this problem, it is advisable first to consider its nature. The adoption of a fundamentally new weapon proceeds through several stages:

(1) General scientific research of an academic or commercial nature occurs which causes

(2) Someone in close touch with a Fighting Service, and who is aware of Service requirements, to think of an application of the results of academic research. If this application be considered promising

(3) Ad hoc research and small scale trials are performed in a Service laboratory. If these are successful

(4) Large scale Service trials are undertaken, which may lead to

(5) Adoption in Service.

The first stage is generally public, and is probably common knowledge to all progressive countries. Frequently, therefore, the idea is born almost simultaneously everywhere; its subsequent history depends on the attitude of the Services concerned. . . .

The third and fourth stages are more difficult to observe, and the only method of dealing with the former is direct espionage, or the observation of indiscretions by research personnel concerned. Sometimes the recruiting of new staff, who have already attained some eminence in research, will give a clue to the type of research. The supply of apparatus by commercial firms may also furnish clues. In many ways those are the most important stages at which a good Intelligence Service should be able to give timely warning to its Government, and every effort should be made to extract the utmost from any item of information. . . .

Information leaks out in five ways:

(1) Accidental indiscretions (including deciphered messages) of which there are always a large number and if these are pieced together a valuable impression may be gained.

(2) Indiscretions encouraged by alcohol and/or mistresses. The results obtained by these methods are all that can be expected.

(3) Information that cannot be kept secret and yet can give useful information to an enemy. R.D.F. transmissions are one example and, in time of war, loss of apparatus by contact with the enemy is another.

(4) Direct acquisition of information by placing agents in Military Research Departments. Such a method is difficult and hazardous, and comparatively little is obtained; its value is large.

(5) Information from disaffected nationals. Frequently this is unreliable and must always be checked.

A Scientific Intelligence Service starting at the present time would have to concentrate on (1) and (3), but the other ways should be exploited to best advantage.

After surveying what I had so far done to encourage the collection of more scientific and technical information I drew attention to an important weakness in our Intelligence cover in that there was no organization to listen to German transmissions that might be connected with radar or radio navigation:

Enquiries have shown that there has been no systematic observation of evidence indicating German R.D.F. transmissions. . . .

I outlined an organization in which there would be a central section with the following terms of reference:

Objects
(1) To ascertain the development of new weapons and improvement of existing ones by other countries.
(2) To mislead potential or actual enemies about our own weapons.
(3) To mislead the enemy about the success of his own weapons.
(4) To assist technically in espionage and its counter (including codes and ciphers, where technicians are becoming important at the expense of classical scholars).
(5) To coordinate Scientific and Technical Intelligence between the Services.

In addition to the Central Section there should be Scientific Intelligence branches attached to the Director of Naval Intelligence, the Director of Military Intelligence, and the Director of Air Intelligence. As regards the size of the staffs that would be needed I wrote that they should be kept as numerically small as possible, and that quality was much the most important factor.

When the report was completed it was circulated to the Directors of Intelligence and the Directors of Scientific Research in the Service Ministries and to Sir Henry Tizard, who promptly wrote congratulating me on the report and hoping that it would be accepted. The Director of Scientific Research at the Air Ministry, D. R. Pye, who was still nominally my Chief, wrote in the same vein. And for a time it looked likely that the report would be accepted, and that we should soon have a healthy organization. All three Directors of Intelligence agreed, as did two of the Directors of Scientific Research. D.S.R. Admiralty, advised by his Deputy Director J. Buckingham, was the only one to disagree: and on this one disagreement the whole scheme foundered.

Buckingham's argument appeared to have something to it. It was that, while he would like to see the collection of scientific information about the enemy encouraged, it should be assessed and interpreted not by an Intelligence organization but by scientific experts in the Scientific Directorates. He argued that these were the men best qualified because they were working on our own weapons, and that they would be in a better position to assess the incoming information if they had it undigested by someone who was less expert.

The fallacy in the argument was to be shown up by future episodes in the war. Plausible as it seems, the scientific experts in one country are not necessarily as good at assessing evidence as independent intelligence officers. It may happen for some reason that they have not developed a particular weapon either because they have not thought of it or, more likely, they have thought of it but have done some careless work which has led them to a wrong conclusion and have therefore decided that the development is not feasible. What sometimes happens is that a man thinks of an idea and tries it before the time is really ripe, and so he fails. He then invents a reason for his failure which overlooks his own deficiencies and blames instead the operation of some fundamental law. Thus, there was a doctrine that radio wavelengths of the order of 10 centimetres could not be generated by electronic valves because the time taken by the electrons to pass through the valve was much too great. This argument was fallacious, but was accepted by many scientists and engineers because we had become almost congenitally inclined to accept such 'postulates of impotence' in basic science. For example, the idea that you cannot send a signal with a greater speed than that of light led to the theory of relativity, with its amazingly fruitful results. The scientist is rather like Robert of Sicily in Longfellow's poem about the battle between Robert and the Angel. Once Robert was prepared to submit, the Angel gave him all he wanted. And if the scientist is humble enough to admit that there are some things that nature will not allow him to do, whole fields of science then become intelligible. Encouraged by the success of humility, he is therefore conditioned to look for basic reasons why something cannot be done.

This chapter may be leavened by telling how I came myself to see the fallacy in the argument about the impossibility of generating centimetre waves. It arose from a demonstration at Farnborough of a very powerful loudspeaker system and amplifier system that had been developed for installation in aircraft policing the North-West frontier of India. This policing was sometimes done by punishing marauding tribesmen by bombing their villages, after due warning. Someone thought that the warning would be all the more effective if it came as from the voice of God, bellowing out from an aircraft. When the apparatus had been perfected, it was demonstrated to the Air Staff at Farnborough by mounting a microphone on one side of the aerodrome, some two thousand feet away. If you spoke into the microphone you could hear your voice coming two seconds later across from the other side. All went well with the demonstration until one of the inspecting officers struck by the curiosity of hearing his delayed voice, started to laugh. Two seconds later there came back a laugh from the loudspeaker at which everybody laughed. Two seconds later the shower of laughter returned, and I like to think that by now the volume was so great that the returned laugh was picked up by the microphone and duly relayed once again, making a system that laughed by itself.

Apart from the comedy of the situation, there was an important lesson to be learnt. This was that the time of oscillations generated by the human voice is typically of the order of one thousandth of a second, and yet these were being faithfully generated by a system in which the transit time of sound across the aerodrome was some two seconds. This showed the fallacy in the argument about centimetric waves. What really mattered was not the transit time itself, but the regularity in the time of transit. So if electrons could be persuaded to travel at uniform speeds across the valve they could be made to generate oscillations of considerably shorter period and wavelength than the limit which the previous careless theory had predicted. What had gone wrong up to that time was that we had failed to make sufficiently regular streams of electrons; and when this difficulty was overcome new devices such as the klystron worked very successfully. It was an example of the wisdom of the Canadian biochemist de Vignaud that 'Nothing holds up the progress of science so much as the right idea at the wrong time'—a comment which is paralleled by 'Crow's Law' formulated by my late friend Mr. John Crow, Reader in English at King's College London: 'Do not think what you want to think until you know what you ought to know.'

After this digression, let us return to the events of 1939. Buckingham's argument had temporarily won the day, but I was later to show its its weakness. Experts on one's own side are indeed valuable in the assessment of Intelligence, but their real function is not to make the final assessment—they are in effect your spies on the laws of nature which are relevant to the particular weapon under development. Usually they will be correct in their observations, and indeed more correct than most of your other sources. But from time to time they will be wrong for the reasons that I have just described and such occasions usually turn out to be very important. Their evidence must therefore be weighed impartially together with that from all other sources, and if there is a substantial consensus from these other sources in conflict with what your own experts say, then their evidence must be questioned very carefully. Fortunately for us, the Germans operated throughout the war on Buckingham's system, and so were badly caught from time to time.

Such was Buckingham's opposition, however, that D. R. Pye wanted to recall me from Intelligence, just as he had recalled after a month or so the liaison officers he had sent out to the various Air Force Commands. I pleaded with him not to recall me, pointing out that I had been told that I would be appointed to Intelligence for six months in the first place, anyway, and I had another three months to run. I told him that I was convinced that sooner or later something useful would come from my presence in Intelligence, and that if there was to be no organization set up I would like to see what I could do, if necessary by myself. I had already suggested to him that reinforcements were needed, and that undoubtedly the first recruit that I wanted was my friend Charles Frank, both because of his outstanding ability as a scientist and his knowledge of Germany and the German language. When the prospects for the future organization had looked good, Pye had authorized me to approach Frank, who expressed willingness to join me in London. Pye now told me, however, that he could not authorize my recruiting any-body, and so I had to continue by myself, while Frank went to Porton.

CHAPTER TEN

The Phoney War

THE WINTER of the Phoney War gave me time to build up contacts with the various sources of intelligence and to brief them. There was relatively little air activity. In fact, Neville Chamberlain had stated in Parliament on 14th September that 'whatever be the lengths to which others may go, His Majesty's Government will never resort to the deliberate attack on women, children and other civilians for purposes of mere terrorism', a statement which he repeated on 15th February 1940. This makes curious reading in view of our bomber offensive in the later stages of the war, which showed how far high intentions can be gradually eroded. There was another Government statement at about the same time, reporting atrocities in the German concentration camps, but many of us thought that this statement must be partly propaganda and it was not therefore given its due weight.

Air activity in the early days of the war had shown that British aircraft were much more vulnerable than their German counterparts. Single bullets through fuel tanks proved enough to stop our bombers getting home from Kiel and Wilhelmshafen, whereas the German bombers in the Forth raid had taken many bullets with seemingly little inconvenience. The single bomber that we had shot down was found to have self-sealing tanks, and enquiry revealed that similar designs had been available in pre-war years for our aircraft, but had been rejected. In fact, a nearly satisfactory bullet-proof tank was developed before the end of World War I but, with peace, the specification had been altered to include crash-proof as well as bullet-proof characteristics, since crashes were then the major danger. As a result, every design submitted to the Air Ministry was taken to Farnborough, filled with liquid, and dropped over the side of one of the buildings onto concrete, where it inevitably broke up, and was therefore rejected. Some of the designs would in fact have been bullet-proof (this being achieved by a spongy rubber envelope which closed up again after a bullet had passed through it), but none could stand the fall of 60 ft. onto concrete. It proved a

1a H. V. Jones (No. 9223 Grenadier Guards), 1899

1b R. V. Jones, 1937

1c F. A. Lindemann (Photograph by A. H. Bodle)

1d H. T. Tizard (Photograph by Walter Stoneman, courtesy of R. W. Clark)

2a The Clarendon Laboratory. The top floor was where infra-red detectors were developed
(Photograph by A. H. Bodle, whose cottage is at left)

2b Hoar Cross, Staffordshire

3a T. C. Keeley, who ran the Laboratory during World War II

3b D. A. Jackson, later Chief Airborne Radar Officer, Fighter Command

Members of the Clarendon Laboratory, 1934–1936

A. G. Touch, who later developed anti-submarine radar

3d Carl Bosch, who developed the radio beam guidance for the V–2 rocket

4a Churchill in the Cabinet Room, 10 Downing Street, the scene of the Knickebein and Window meetings (*Cecil Beaton*)

4b The Cabinet underground meeting room, scene of the V-2 meetings. The wooden chair was Churchill's

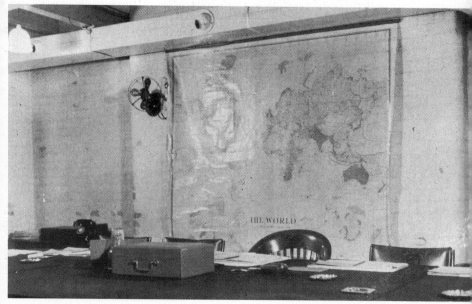

5a Vertical air photograph showing first Knickebein beam station to be found (near Cherbourg), September 1940 (R.A.F. photograph)

KNICKEBEIN

5b Small Knickebein (F. Trenkle)

Entrance to the operational dug-out of a Knickebein (X on Figure 8) erected south of Cherbourg in 1941

ERBAUT UNTER ADOLF HITLER

5d Large Knickebein, near Bredstedt, Schleswig Holstein 100 metres wide x 30 metres high (Photograph supplied by Herr F. Trenkle, who has tentatively drawn in the aerial arrays)

6a F. C. Frank

6b A. H. Smith (courtesy of Mrs. Helen Smith)

6c F. Norman (courtesy of Mrs. Jean Loudon)

6d S. D. Felkin (courtesy of Mrs. Charlotte Felkin)

7 A Wotan I or X-Beam transmitter. Inset: A Heinkel 111 with receiving antennae for X-Beams
(Photographs courtesy of F. Trenkle)

8a Wotan II or Y (or Benito) beam transmitter near Stavanger,
photographed by a Norwegian patriot

8b A Heinkel 111 of IIIKG26 fitted with a
Y-Beam antenna with its pilot Viktor von
Lossberg (see Plate 17d)

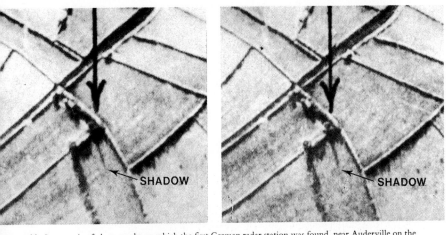

9a and b Stereo pair of photographs on which the first German radar station was found, near Auderville on the Hague Peninsula W.N.W. of Cherbourg. The scale of the original photographs on which the difference in the shadows was recognized by F. C. Frank was one quarter of this reproduction – the circular blast walls then appeared as only half a millimetre in diameter. On such clues pilots' lives had sometimes to be risked, and Intelligence had to depend (R.A.F. photographs)

9c Low oblique photograph of the Auderville Freyas taken by Flying Officer W. K. Manifould, 22 February, 1941 (R.A.F. photograph)

10a Bruneval. The dot on the arrowhead in front of the house was suspected to be a Würzburg radar (R.A.F. photograph)

10b Barbed wire at la Panne, Belgium, erected after the Bruneval Raid, thereby confirming suspicions that the object at the centre of the lower right enclosure was a Würzburg (R.A.F. photograph)

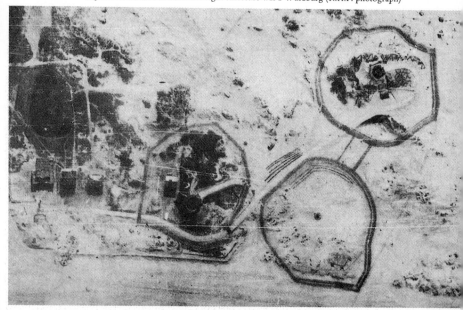

11a and b Tony Hill's photographs of the Würzburg at Bruneval, 5 December, 1941
(R.A.F. photographs)

C COMPANY (2nd PARA)

VILLA

WÜRZBURG

LA PRESBYTÈRE (100 GERMANS)

NAUMOFF

FROST

ASSEMBLY AND REARGUARD TIMOTHY (30 MEN)

DROP ZONE

ASSEMBLY

CHARTERIS (20 MEN) (PLAN)

ROSS

YOUNG (30 MEN) VERNON, COX

CSM STRACHAN HIT

VERNON COX HELD UP

TASKER (10 MEN)

SHARP (10 MEN)

WIRE

CHARTERIS DROPPED 1½ MILES

BRUNEVAL (20-40 GERMANS)

CHARTERIS

GUARD ROOM AND STRONG POINT

LANDING CRAFT

12 The terrain of the Bruneval Raid (Original photograph courtesy of *After The Battle Magazine*)

13a Photograph taken by the American Embassy in Berlin, 1941, of a Giant Würzburg on the Flak Tower in the Tiergarten

and c Tony Hill's photographs of Giant Würzburgs at Domburg, lay 1942 (R.A.F. photographs)

13d Giant Würzburg at a nightfighter control station in the Kammhuber Line, photographed by a Belgian patriot, 1943

14a Squadron Leader A. E. Hill, D.S.O., D.F.C.
(courtesy of Air Marshal Sir Geoffrey Tuttle)

14b Wing Commander G. W. Tuttle, O.B.E., D.F.
(courtesy of Air Marshal Sir Geoffrey Tuttle)

14c Photographic Reconnaissance Spitfire, Mark PR 19 (the PRU Memorial at R.A.F. Benson). Note the camera window between the pilot's seat and the R.A.F. Roundel used for low oblique photography. The Memorial Plaque reads:

THIS SPITFIRE PR19 STANDS AT BENSON IN COMMEMORATION OF THE OFFICERS AND AIRMEN WHO SERVED WITH THE PHOTOGRAPHIC RECONNAISSANCE UNIT AND SQUADRONS OF THE ROYAL AIR FORCE 1939–1945 REMEMBERING PARTICULARLY THOSE WHO FAILED TO RETURN.

NO. 1, 2, 3, 4 PRU'S

140, 540, 541, 542, 543, 544, 680, 681, 682 & 684 SQUADRONS

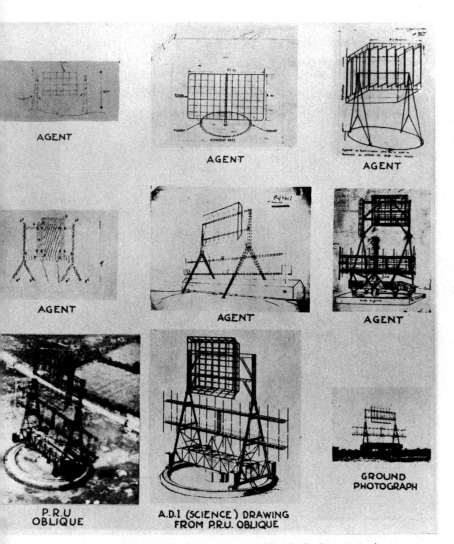

AGENT

AGENT

AGENT

AGENT

AGENT

AGENT

P.R.U
OBLIQUE

A.D.I (SCIENCE) DRAWING
FROM P.R.U. OBLIQUE

GROUND
PHOTOGRAPH

15 *Upper two rows:* Sketches made by different observers of 'Bernhard' radio navigational
stations, showing varying degrees of perception
Bottom row: l. to r. Air Reconnaissance low oblique: drawing made by Hugh Smith from
the air photograph: ground photograph

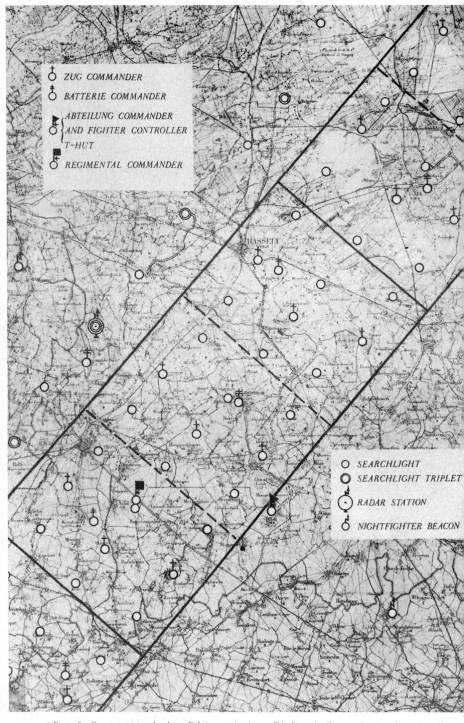

ZUG COMMANDER

BATTERIE COMMANDER

ABTEILUNG COMMANDER
AND FIGHTER CONTROLLER
T-HUT

REGIMENTAL COMMANDER

SEARCHLIGHT

SEARCHLIGHT TRIPLET

RADAR STATION

NIGHTFIGHTER BEACON

16 Part of a German map stolen by a Belgian patriot (agent Tégal) 20 April 1942, showing the entire radar and searchlight dispositions in one box (No. 6B) of the Kammhuber Line. The box of 27 searchlights occupies a front of 30 kilometres

lesson in the importance of making sure that the paper specification defined the essential requirement—I know of at least one other example, when one of my colleagues showed that, according to the War Office specification, the ideal material for making crash helmets for its motor-cycle despatch riders would have been plate glass.

In pursuance of the policy of not bombing civilians, the R.A.F. was ordered to fly over Germany dropping nothing more harmful than propaganda leaflets, and I began to look at the reports of the air crew, who frequently stated that they encountered coloured searchlights. Since I myself had put up the scheme for pulsing searchlights to make a form of optical radar, I wondered whether the colours might be due to the use of discharge tubes instead of carbon arcs in German searchlights for this same purpose. It ought to be possible to tell simply by looking at the searchlights with a small direct-vision spectroscope which would show a continuous spectrum of colour if the searchlights were ordinary ones, and relatively narrow bands of colour if they used discharge tubes. I therefore bought six such spectroscopes for distribution to the special observers from our own Anti-Aircraft Command who were flying with the leaflet raids.

I was astonished to receive a telephone call from Major Alfred Wintle, who said that he would like to talk to me about the problem. He was the Army officer who had been posted to Air Intelligence in 1938 to co-ordinate information about the German anti-aircraft (Flak) defences. In Germany these defences were part of the Luftwaffe, but in Britain A.A. guns and searchlights were operated by the Army. Since the German defences were of acute interest to the Royal Air Force, the Flak Intelligence Section was in the Air Ministry, inter-Service honour being salved by posting an Army officer to head it. One would have expected, therefore, the officer to be an anti-aircraft gun expert but instead Wintle was from The First The Royal Dragoons. He was indeed almost a cari-cature of the popular idea of a cavalryman—somewhat cadaverous, with a large reddish nose and a monocle. The last, however, was no affectation, for one of his eyes was almost useless. His moustache was neatly trimmed, and his uniform immaculate.

When I went to see him, I found him sharing a room with his assistant, who turned out to be Gilbert Frankau, the novelist. Finding that I was a doctor, Frankau seemed far more anxious to get my advice on how he could restore his virility than on what we should do about the German defences. Wintle suggested that our conference, to which by now he had summoned some others, would go better with sherry all round, and so he sent an Air Ministry messenger across to a pub on the other side of Whitehall. This made the conference unique among the many hundreds that I have attended in Government offices.

I was astonished when Wintle said, 'This is a damned good idea of yours, old boy, issuing direct-vision spectroscopes to the observers. But I have a better idea. Let's send out spectrographs, so that they can bring back photographs, which you and I can examine for ourselves.' A cavalryman who knew the difference between a spectroscope and a spectrograph was clearly someone to be reckoned with. He was remarkably unpopular for his cutting criticisms of most Intelligence reports. When one came in from an agent describing the German balloon barrage cable as being twenty millimetres in diameter and consisting of twenty strands each one millimetre thick, he simply wrote across it 'This is a mathematical impossibility' which indeed it was. On his desk rested a photograph of himself surrounded by various Air Staff officers across which he had written 'The brains of the Air Force'. He was to have an eventful war.

At about the same time, I was on the fringes of the magnetic mine alarm. During September the Germans began to lay magnetic mines around our ports and estuaries, and they caused a great deal of trouble. In fact, had they been used in sufficient numbers and with sufficient ingenuity they could have brought our economy to a standstill. Various countermeasures were devised, including degaussing. The highlight of the episode was the outstandingly gallant dismantling of a mine that had been laid on the foreshore at Shoeburyness on 22nd November by Lieutenant Commander Ouvry and Chief Petty Officer Baldwin. By rights it should have involved them in certain death, because we had expected that the Germans would have incorporated a fuse to explode the mine if anyone attempted to dismantle it. But, strangely, there was no such fuse, and great courage met its reward.

One of the participants in the magnetic mine discussions was my old friend James Tuck. Surprisingly, Lindemann had brought Tuck with him when he had come to the Admiralty from Oxford. Up to the outbreak of war Lindemann had tended to choose to talk more to 'yes men' than to those who would honestly differ from him, and I had expected that he would select one of the former. Instead Lindemann chose Tuck, who was certainly no 'yes man', and whose rough corners from Manchester had not been entirely rounded off by three years at Oxford. It was a very hopeful sign, for Tuck was both clever and honest, and just the man for straight action in a tight corner.

Tuck and his wife Elsie took a flat in Vandon Court in Petty France, and I often used to lunch with them. At the same time, I avoided making contact with Lindemann because I had had more than enough of the battle between him and Tizard. And now that I was in a position on the Air Staff, with Tizard also on the Air Staff, whereas Lindemann was at the Admiralty, I thought it best to make no move. Tuck told me that Lindemann frequently regretted the fact that he was not in touch with me; but having had a rough deal once, I certainly wanted to avoid any more trouble.

Tuck gave me valuable help because as assistant to Lindemann he came to know a great deal about our own developments. He had already warned me about the prospects for a nuclear bomb, and he continued to brief me in this field. I was thus able to learn that the prospects for the bomb had at first dimmed because of an apparent snag in the physics, but that Rudolf Peierls had seen the way round this snag. Tuck also told me about the development of the jet engine. I was therefore well briefed about what to look for in Germany.

Tuck himself had an interesting and eventful time. On Lindemann's behalf he had to attend various trials; one of these concerned new Army weapons, and he told me how in the lunch interval between demonstrations he had been shown into what he described as 'a stockade full of Generals'. There were tall thin Generals, short fat Generals, Generals with flowing moustaches, Generals with clipped moustaches, and Generals with no moustaches at all. Most of them nucleated around one General who was shorter, fatter and younger than any of the rest, and he was clearly regarded as the bright boy of the General Staff. What Tuck heard him say, to general approbation was, 'Of course, what we really need, chaps, is a gas that will go through gas masks.' This was hailed as a brilliant idea.

Another episode from this period concerned 'Job 74', a project designed to settle the controversy over whether bombers could sink battleships, which still went on despite the fact that Billy Mitchell had demonstrated years before that it could be done. It would obviously be expensive to allow bombers to try to sink our own battleships, so before the war a mock-up section of a battleship had been erected on a bombing range. It was called 'Job 74' and by the outbreak of war, it was still unscathed despite the various bombs that the Air Force had aimed against it.

In the meantime, there had been an important development in explosive charges, using what is known as the 'Munro Effect'. Munro had been an explosives tester in a U.S. Naval arsenal around 1900, and had noticed that when he exploded a test piece of cordite on a steel plate he found 'U.S. Navy' etched on the plate in mirror writing. Each piece of cordite had been stamped underneath with 'U.S. Navy' and it had been the hollows thus created that somehow focused the explosive effect. The effect was merely a curiosity for many years, but ultimately its potential was realized, and the 'hollow charge' resulted. In its simplest form this consisted of a block of explosive with a hollow cone on one face, the surface of the cone being thinly lined with a metal. If the charge were exploded in contact with armour plate, the metal liner was converted into an extremely hot tongue emerging from the axis of the cone, which proceeded to drill a deep hole in the plate.

Lindemann thought that such charges could be used in bombs against battleships, where they would easily penetrate the deck armour. He therefore proposed to explode a trial charge on the deck of Job 74. But by now the Admirals were almost as attached to Job 74 as they were to their real battleships. They argued that it was not sporting to place the charge in contact with the target, and insisted that an alternative rig of steel plates should be set up, each plate being tethered to the ground on suitable posts. Tuck was a witness of the test, which went wrong because one of the plates, weighing 50 tons, had not been properly fixed, and the force of the explosion caused it to bowl, cartwheel fashion, for one-and-a-half miles.

Tuck had his times with Lindemann. He came home one day extremely agitated. He told Elsie and me that he had just had a row with the Prof. It had started because Lindemann had badly exaggerated something Tuck had told him. Tuck had the idea of building a rocket with automatic controls so that it would run up a searchlight and therefore hit anything on which the searchlight was aimed. Many of us had previously had the same idea, and had soon found that it was at that stage impracticable, but Tuck had come in with a fresh mind and had put a scheme to Lindemann which involved building the electronic controls into a rocket of the type that was then being developed for anti-aircraft defence. The control section, Tuck estimated, would occupy about eighteen inches of the length of the rocket.

Lindemann became enthusiastic, and said that he would see whether he could get support from the War Office to make a few trial weapons. He came back telling Tuck that he had convinced them and that now all Tuck had to do was to make the weapon. It turned out that Lindemann had succeeded in convincing the War Office by telling them that

Tuck could make the electronics so small that they would occupy a length of only six inches. When Tuck realized how he had been committed to something that he could not do he flared up and, according to his words to me immediately afterwards, told the Prof that he had had 'enough of his bloody double-dealing'. A fierce row had ensued, and Tuck had retired to steady himself in the Admiralty bar before returning home. He thought that Lindemann would surely have finished with him; but to Lindemann's credit and good sense, he backed down and Tuck stayed.

My own association with Tuck ultimately led to my being trapped by Lindemann. The incident was trivial in itself, but without it Lindemann and I might not have come together until very much later and some aspects of the war might then have gone differently. It happened that I had telephoned Tuck one day to suggest that we lunch together, but he was out of his office and a colleague left a message on his desk saying that I would telephone again at a particular time. When I did so, the telephone was answered not by Tuck but by the Prof, who had seen the note on Tuck's desk and had sat by the telephone waiting for it to ring. He asked me why I had not been to see him, and I told him that my position was not easy because of my being on the Air Staff with Tizard but that if he would like me to come, I would do so. We arranged a meeting, and I at once went to Tizard to tell him that although I had stayed as low as possible, and well out of Lindemann's way, I was now compromised into meeting him, and I thought that Tizard ought to know. To my surprise Tizard replied, 'I'm glad. You could do some good. Tell him from me that I should be glad if we could stop this ridiculous quarrel at least for the period of the war and concentrate on fighting the Germans.' I went off delighted, seeing myself as the bearer of an olive branch, and about to effect the great reconciliation. It did not turn out that way— when I told Lindemann what Tizard had said, his only response was to give a mild snort and say, 'Now that I am in a position of power, a lot of my old friends have come sniffing around!' So that was that.

One of my diversions during the Phoney War period was to join a Committee which Tizard had proposed with the aim of tapping the knowledge of Jewish emigrés about developments in Germany. Its chairman was C. H. Lander, a professor of engineering at the City and Guilds Institute, with British and German Jews as its main members. I was the one Anglo-Saxon apart from the chairman, and the only member in a Government position. Simon Marks, the head of Marks and Spencer, was one of the members, and we met in his headquarters. The most outstanding member of the Committee was Chaim Weizmann, who had an immense oriental presence—in fact the only other man I have ever known with such a presence was the Mahdi. I was embarrassed to find myself treated by Weizmann as the official representative of His Majesty's Government, and he and the others seemed to imagine that they had only to suggest to me that something should be done, and H.M.G. would immediately do it. It turned out that they could not help much with information about technical processes in Germany, and so they turned to suggesting bright ideas by which Britain could win the war. Later some of the Jewish refugees helped Intelligence most courageously by going back under cover to Germany.

It was from my contact with one refugee that I found at last the explanation for the stories about engine-stopping rays. This particular refugee had been an announcer at the Frankfurt radio station, and I therefore wondered whether he might know anything about the work on the nearby Feldberg television tower that was said to be one of the engine-stopping transmitters. When I told him the story he said that he had not heard it, but he could see how it might have happened. When the site for the transmitter was being surveyed, trials were done by placing a transmitter at a promising spot, and then measuring the field strength that it would provide for radio signals in the areas around it. Since the signals concerned were of very high frequency, the receivers could easily be jammed by the unscreened ignition system of the average motor car. Any car travelling through the area at the time of the trial would cause so much interference as to ruin the test. In Germany, with its authoritarian regime, it was a simple matter to decide that no cars should run in the area at the relevant time, and so sentries were posted on all the roads to stop the cars. After the twenty minutes or so of a test the sentries would then tell the cars that they could proceed. In retailing the incident it only required the driver to transpose the first appearance of the sentry and the stopping of his engine for the story to give rise to the engine-stopping ray.

Radar and radio aids to navigation were of course very much in my mind the whole time, and I was much excited by a recorded fragment of conversation between two prisoners of war that was given a very limited circulation by Denys Felkin from his headquarters at Cockfosters. One prisoner was telling the other about something which he called the the 'X-Gerät' or X-Apparatus. The beginning of a thriller could hardly have had a more intriguing title. From what little he had said it appeared that the X-Apparatus was something to be used in a bomber and, if we had overheard correctly, it seemed to involve pulses, which were presumably radio pulses. I telephoned Felkin, telling him of my interest, and we arranged to meet at his club, The Bath.

After a cautious exchange of identity cards he listened to my ideas about what the device might be, so that he could prompt the prisoners by questions that they might afterwards discuss among themselves. We in fact obtained very little more, but I thought that I ought to draw attention to the problem, and on 4th March I reported that the X-Gerät was a bombing apparatus involving an application of pulse radio technique and that there appeared to be confusion in the minds of the prisoners between two separate systems:

(a) The setting up of a system of intersecting radio beams from German transmitters so that a small area of intersection occurs in which the characteristic signals of two stations combine and give a signal which might even be made to operate the bomb release gear automatically. The significance of the X as a cross supported this.

(b) The use of an elaborated form of radio altimeter perhaps scanning the ground below and giving the position of reflecting obstacles with sufficient accuracy for bombing.

I heard nothing more about the X-Apparatus, but there was an interesting fragmentary entry on a paper salvaged during March from a shot-down Heinkel aircraft with the call sign 1H+AC, which showed that it belonged to a bomber formation designated as Kampf Geschwader 26. Felkin drew my attention to the entry, of which the translation ran:

Navigational Aid: Radio Beacons working on Beacon Plan A. Additionally from 0600 hours Beacon Dühnen. Light Beacon after dark. Radio Beacon Knickebein from 0600 hours on 315°.

Much could be inferred from this entry. Ordinary radio beacons were standard navigational aids, and the navigator in a bomber could take bearings on them—knowing their positions, he could work out where he was. Typically if he were attacking England from Germany these bearings would lie somewhere to the east, say between 45° and 135° round from north. But 'Knickebein' seemed to be something different: 315° points due north-west, and in any event it seemed to be pre-set at the beacon itself. It therefore looked to me as though Knickebein might be some kind of beamed beacon which that day had been set to transmit in a north-westerly direction. By interrogation, Felkin obtained the further clue from one of the prisoners that it was something like the

4*

X-Apparatus, and that a short wave beam was sent that would not be more than a kilometre wide over London.

Meanwhile, Vera and I were married on 21st March and had found a very pleasant flat in Richmond Hill Court, a large-ish block situated near the brow of Richmond Hill. It was on the top floor, and commanded a view ranging from Kew Gardens round to Windsor Castle some ten miles away. With the wartime exodus from London, it had not been too difficult to find, because landlords were only too anxious to let their properties. A few weeks after we had settled in Richmond Hill Court, Gerald and Phyllis Touch came to spend the weekend with us; and as Gerald and I walked in Richmond Park on the Sunday morning I tried out my ideas on him. He was clearly in a good position to comment on the possibility of the X-Apparatus being something in the bomber which would emit pulses and from the reflected echoes show up towns, as in a map. Although he was largely responsible for this very device for use against ships, he did not think that it would work against towns because such a use would involve two contradictory requirements. In order to get sufficient sharpness of the radar beam to give useful information, a wavelength of a few centimetres would be necessary; but to give echoes that would show up towns, a much longer wavelength would be required, because with a short wavelength even the roughness of ploughed fields would give strong echoes which could be confused with those from towns. As it later turned out, this argument was incorrect, but it served its purpose in convincing me that the second of my two hypotheses about the X-Gerät was wrong, and this left only the possibility of intersecting beams.

A further encouragement to thinking about beams came from a lunch I had with Woodward-Nutt. At the beginning of the war he had suggested that he and I should lunch periodically to brief one another, with him providing a background about what was going on in our own developments and me supplying what I could about what was happening on the German side. At this particular lunch he mentioned to me that there had been a rumour from the French that the Germans had been setting up some kind of radio beam station on their frontier; and he added that he had consulted our own radio experts at Farnborough and had been surprised by the narrowness of a beam that they thought could be made.

It almost went without saying, though, that a narrow beam would require a short wavelength, and so I should be up against the old objection that I had encountered two years before in proposing the hyperbolic navigation system: short waves would not bend sufficiently around the curve of the earth to permit bombing at long range. I was therefore sensitive to any light that might be thrown on the point. One day I was talking to a relative newcomer to Signals Intelligence, Flight Lieutenant Rowley Scott-Farnie, a generous-natured rugby player who had badly injured a leg and who before the war had been in a bank. An enthusiastic radio amateur, he had joined the R.A.F. Signals Intelligence Service at the outbreak of war. Incidentally, our community of radio amateurs in Britain was to prove an invaluable reserve, both in Signals Intelligence and in Signals proper, as well as furnishing many of the staff for our rapidly increasing number of radar stations.

Scott-Farnie and I were discussing the possibility that the Germans might already be working on centimetric wavelengths, and wondering what our chances of interception were if they were doing so. Scott-Farnie showed me a short report by Mr. T. L. Eckersley of the Marconi Company, who was the country's leading expert in radio propagation. On a purely theoretical basis, Eckersley had computed the range at which a transmitter sited at the top of the Brocken (the earlier object of Charles Frank's and my attention) and working on a wavelength of 20 centimetres, could be heard. If Eckersley's calculations were correct, the waves would bend round the earth to a surprising extent, and might well be received by a bomber flying at twenty thousand feet over our east coast. I asked Scott-Farnie for a copy of Eckersley's map, which I placed in my files.

War had now started in earnest. On 9th April the Germans invaded Norway. There was an Intelligence lesson for us to learn, because a day or so before one of our reconnaissance aircraft had taken photographs of Bremen harbour, which was full of shipping for the intended invasion; but because this was our first photograph there was nothing with which to compare it, and so the photographic interpreters did not realize that the state in the port was anything other than normal. This taught us the value of routine cover.

A minor aspect of the Norwegian Campaign was afterwards related to me by Colonel Archie Crabbe of the Scots Guards. The Guards had instructions to land near Narvik and make contact with the local Norwegian Forces. Determined to do everything properly, despite the danger of the situation, they marched from the beach and set up head-quarters with neat precision, as though they might still have been at Pirbright. This *sang froid* defeated them in their main purpose, because the few cautious Norwegians who observed them decided that a Force behaving with such cool confidence in the prevailing military situation could only be German, and it took two days before they were able to make any contact with the Norwegians at all.

On 10th May the Germans invaded the Low Countries, and with astonishing ease captured the very strong and key fortress of Eben Emael, near Liège. No more than 85 glider-borne troops had mastered a garrison of 750: how had they done it? Hitler gave orders that the method was to be kept secret, and so I spent some time finding out. It transpired that, like ourselves, the Germans had at last decided to exploit the possibilities of the hollow charge: their troops had placed such charges on the cupolas of the fort, blowing holes in them and immobilizing the guns. It was an instance where both sides in secrecy had undertaken exactly the same development, in contrast to others like centimetric radar or the V-2 rocket, where one side built up an overwhelming lead.

Within a few days it was clear that our Army was in dire trouble. Once again, there was the kind of alarm that we had experienced at the beginning of the war, and S.I.S. wanted to ensure that the new Prime Minister, who had taken over on the same day as the invasion of Holland and Belgium, could not hold it against them for failing to warn him about any weapon that might appear, and so I was asked to up-date my secret weapon report. I did not like the way things were going, not only because of our military situation but because of the way people were 'flapping' about it. I therefore used the occasion to inject a sense of proportion and one of my opening paragraphs, which admittedly drew on the wisdom of my old colleague E. G. Hill at Teddington, ran:

> The particular object of this paper is to indicate the weapons to be used against England. The mine campaign has failed: the failure has been due in part to our effective reaction, and in part, perhaps, to a shortage of mines. The Norwegian campaign certainly risked the sacrifice of the entire German surface Navy. In the alleged timetable of Nazi expansion, there was to have been an interval of several years between the subjugation of Northern France and the conquest of England; perhaps in the interval a fleet was to have been built. If Germany is expecting a swift conclusion to the war with England, it therefore follows that her campaign now depends entirely on heavy attack by air. It is beyond the scope of this paper to comment upon either the feasibility or the wisdom of attempted invasion, but there is perhaps something in the view that actual invasion is not imminent,

but after a swift and heavy attack from the air, using all the weapons at his command, Hitler will then offer seductively moderate terms. This line of attack is largely dependent on the subjection of France, and probably represents the worst contingency we have to face. We might then find a force of four or five thousand aircraft of mixed types ready to attack us.

Following the same theme the report concluded:

In conclusion, some relief may be derived from the fact that despite rumours to the contrary, there are some responsible quarters in Germany which are preparing for a long war. It is a fact that the German War Department has advertised (10th April 1940) for an ersatz electrical accumulator, to be constructed almost entirely from materials found within the Reich. A prize of RM. 10.000 is offered, and the competition closes on 1st January 1941: clearly the German War Department expects still to be at war on that date.

What I said was not altogether popular at the time (23rd May 1940), because 1941 seemed an age away, and it was not easy to see how we were going to survive. But, as it turned out, the only point where I was wrong was that I thought that the bombing might come first and the peace offer later, whereas Hitler played things the other way round. At the same time, I did crystallize my warning about the beams:

It is possible that they have developed a system of intersecting radio beams so that they can locate a target such as London sufficiently accurately for indiscriminate bombing. No information is available regarding the wavelength to be employed, but the accuracy of location expected by the Germans is something like $\frac{1}{2}$ mile over London from the western frontier of Germany. Efforts are still being made to determine the probable wavelengths so that counter measures can be employed.

No doubt owing to the illegibility of my writing, Daisy Mowat had actually typed 'metre' instead of 'mile' in the second sentence, but even this did not create undue interest, and I still found myself with hardly enough to do. On 10th May Anthony Eden announced the formation of the Local Defence Volunteers, and before he had finished the broadcast I had telephoned Richmond police station to join. I attended the first few parades, with an enormous personal superiority, for no one else had any weapons, and I had six pistols and a rifle. But the records of the

L.D.V. show that on 13th August 1940, long before it became the Home Guard, I was given a discharge, ostensibly on the grounds that my services 'were no Longer Required', this being a curious euphemism for the fact that they were by then more urgently required elsewhere.

Winston began to make his speeches, and started to rally the country. We had heard L. S. Amery's ringing repetition of Cromwell's words a few days before in Parliament, 'You have sat too long here for any good you have been doing. Depart, I say, and let us have done with you. In the name of God, go!' And a new spirit was beginning to inspire the country. Winston made his 'Blood, tears, toil, and sweat' speech on 13th May, and we grimly prepared for the worst.

Around 20th May I well remember Fred Winterbotham's Deputy, John Perkins, coming into my office and going up to the map on my wall and saying, 'This is the situation. The Germans are here and here and here and our Army is cut off and retreating to the sea at Dunkirk. The Chiefs of Staff think that we shall be lucky if we get twenty thousand out.' The position seemed hopeless and yet by the end of the month we had recovered three hundred thousand.

The country was fired by the epic of the small boats that had sailed, some as many as seven times, into the teeth of the Luftwaffe to bring back our Army; and among those who took their boats to Dunkirk was my cousin Reg Mytton. I heard of the Commander-in-Chief, Lord Gort, standing on the beach with two Guardsmen as loaders while he tried to shoot down German dive bombers with a rifle. He also told one of his staff officers, Captain George Gordon Lennox, that however few of the Army could be evacuated, priority was to be given to the R.A.F. pilots who had parachuted from aircraft shot down over the beach head, for they would be vital to the final fight for Britain. And whereas most other regiments had straggled back, the Grenadiers had sent an R.S.M. to Dover to pick up any Grenadiers and drill them, exhausted as they were, to march off the quay in formation as though it were Horseguards. The Navy were so indignant at witnessing this Spartan treatment that the R.S.M. was the object of many Able-Bodied cat-calls, but tradition had been preserved.

The trains from the Channel ports passed through Herne Hill, and my parents' home was in sight of the station. Vera and I spent the afternoon of Saturday 25th May with them, watching the trains packed with dishevelled troops on their way to Victoria, where my colleague Freddie Wintle recounted the scene:

Times may change in other respects, but the Guards never do. I was at Victoria Station when the army remnants started arriving back from Dunkirk. There were a good many trainloads of them. I was deeply shocked with the appearance of the first lot.

About the third trainload turned out to be a couple of companies of Foot Guards. What a contrast! They were glorious to see. They fell in on the platform, dressed, and marched out at attention, not even looking at the girls in the crowd of onlookers. Every Guardsman had his full equipment and his rifle. Everything was polished and properly adjusted. Thank God, I thought, that ass Hore-Belisha can never undermine the Guards. The sight of them was like a tonic—with a very large gin in it—which I promptly had in their honour.

CHAPTER ELEVEN

The Crooked Leg

AFTER THE drama of Dunkirk the next few days were surprisingly quiet. Early in June the Tizard Committee met in Oxford, and I was asked to attend. The Committee had to face the prospect that Lindemann, whom it had earlier rejected, was now Scientific Adviser to the Prime Minister. But the one memory that I have of the meeting is of Sholto Douglas, then the Deputy Chief of Air Staff, asking, 'Can anyone tell me what the Germans are up to? For the past few days Manston [the R.A.F. aerodrome near Dover] has been packed full of our aircraft flown back from France and presenting an ideal target—and yet no German aircraft has attacked!' It all confirmed my impression that the Germans had been surprised by their own success, and now had no coherent plan for the immediate future.

We experienced some sporadic night raids in the first few days of June and, in view of our later failures, our nightfighters shot down a misleadingly large proportion of the attackers. I still had not enough to do, and so decided to spend the day of 11th June at the Admiralty Research Laboratory, to see what my former colleagues were doing. During the day I received two telephone calls, one from Group Captain Blandy, the Head of the R.A.F. 'Y' Service (which intercepted German radio signals), and the other from Lindemann. Each asked when I would be back in London; and when I said that I expected to spend all day at Teddington but would return if they wished, the answer in each case was that tomorrow would do.

On the morning of 12th June, therefore, I went to see Blandy; and as I sat down he slowly pulled open a drawer of his desk and produced a scrap of paper and handed it to me saying, 'Does this mean anything to you? It doesn't seem to mean much to anybody here.' On the paper I read:

'KNICKEBEIN, KLEVE, IST AUF PUNKT 53 GRAD 24 MINUTEN NORD UND EIN GRAD WEST EINGERICHTET'.

There, once again, was 'Knickebein'; and 'Kleve' could be the west German town that we knew as Cleves, where Anne came from. If so the translation would run: 'Cleves Knickebein is confirmed (or established) at position 53° 24' north and 1° west.' The geographical position referred to was a point in England, roughly on the Great North Road a mile or so south of Retford. I immediately told Blandy that it meant everything to me, and that it suggested that the Germans had a radio beam transmitter called Knickebein set up at Cleves, on the nearest German soil to England, and that the existence of the beam had been confirmed one way or another at this position over England. I quickly recognized that it was a decoded message, because I knew that during the preceding two months Bletchley had begun to be successful in decoding some of the Enigma messages. This particular one had been sent by the Chief Signals Officer of Flieger Korps IV at 1455 hours on 5th June, and had been decoded four days later. By this time a stream of decodes was coming from Bletchley into Winterbotham's office; somehow this one had been missed but had then been spotted by an air-minded cryptographer, very probably Josh of the Interrogation Panel, and sent up to Blandy. I told the latter how the message had confirmed my previous thoughts and how I proposed to follow it up.

I then went across to the Cabinet Offices to see Lindemann for only the second time in the whole war; and had I gone to see him first instead of Blandy the course of the next few days, and perhaps the winter of 1940, might have gone quite differently. He told me that he had sent for me because he would like to hear what I knew about German radar. I told him that I was convinced that it existed, and mentioned details from the Oslo Report and also the fact that L. H. Bainbridge-Bell, whom the Admiralty had sent out to survey the wreck of the *Graf Spee*, had reported that she had radar-type aerials. The later information, which should have been quite conclusive, seemed somehow to be ignored in Whitehall, which for many months more continued to debate whether the Germans had radar. As a final point I told Lindemann that I had just received the Knickebein message, and that I was convinced that the Germans had an intersecting beam system for bombing England; and if they could make narrow beams for navigation they could also make narrow beams for radar. Lindemann immediately said that the beams would not work for radionavigation, because they would have to use short waves which would not bend round the curvature of the earth. Armed with Eckersley's computations, I told him that, contrary to what he supposed, they would. I then returned to my office to take stock of the situation.

While I had been at Teddington, a party from the Air Staff headed by Group Captain D. L. Blackford, an enthusiastic and friendly officer then in the Plans Directorate but later in charge of Air Force Security, had rushed up to Retford on the theory that Knickebein might be a system operated by fifth columnists, in the hope of catching them redhanded. The party had found nothing, as I would have expected.

I investigated the bombers available to Flieger Korps IV, and found that these were Heinkels 111's of Kampf Geschwadern 4 and 27. Therefore whatever equipment was used for receiving the Knickebein beam must be capable of being fitted to this type of aircraft. I immediately telephoned Denys Felkin because I knew that he now had prisoners from the bombers shot down during the preceding few nights, and briefed him about the information that I needed.

He duly interrogated the prisoners without at first getting anything of value. But when the prisoners were alone one of them said to another that no matter how hard we looked we would never find the equipment. This could not have been a better challenge because it implied that the equipment was in fact under our noses, but that we would not recognize it. I therefore obtained a copy of the full technical examination of the Heinkel 111 that had been shot down in the Firth of Forth raid, and looked especially at the various items of radio equipment. The only item that could possibly fill the bill was the receiver that was carried in the aircraft for the purpose of blind landing. It was labelled as E. Bl. 1 (which stood for Empfänger Blind 1—blind landing receiver type 1) and was ostensibly for the normal purpose of blind landing on the Lorenz beam system, which was by now standard at many aerodromes. I ascertained that the radio equipment had been evaluated by N. Cox Walker at Farnborough and so I telephoned him. 'Tell me, is there anything unusual about the blind landing receiver?' I asked. 'No', he replied— and then, 'But now you mention it, it is much more sensitive than they would ever need for blind landing.' So that was it. I now knew the receiver, and the frequencies to which it could be tuned, and therefore on which the Knickebein beam must operate.

I had argued myself through all these steps by the morning of the following day, 13th June. I went again to see Lindemann, taking with me this time a copy of Eckersley's computed map, which persuaded him to withdraw his objection of the previous day. Eckersley himself attended a meeting in Blandy's office and, unknown to me, he was given a copy of the vital Enigma message to consider. Lindemann now prepared a note for Churchill, which started, 'There seems some reason to suppose that the Germans have some type of radio device with which they hope to find their targets.' Churchill initialled the note and sent it to Archie Sinclair, who was now Minister of Air, adding, 'This seems most intriguing and I hope you will have it thoroughly examined.'[1]

The next day, Felkin told me that he had a fresh prisoner who said that Knickebein was indeed a bomb-dropping device; it involved two intersecting radio beams and it had been developed at Rechlin. As Felkin spoke, I mentally leapt at the prospect of putting in a false cross-beam to make the Germans drop their bombs before they reached the target.

The prisoner professed to be anti-war, and drew a sketch of what he thought was one of the transmitting towers which he had seen at Rechlin. This was square in cross-section and had sides which sloped somewhat together towards the top, rather like a magnified version of the bottom quarter of Cleopatra's Needle. I had through the winter been collecting information about any unusual towers that had been seen in Germany, and the prisoner's drawing agreed exactly, although on a larger scale, with a tower that had been photographed near an airfield at Hörnum on Sylt, where we knew that there was a Lorenz beacon.

On the same day, 14th June, Sinclair appointed Air Marshal Sir Philip Joubert, whose official post at that time was Adviser for Combined Operations, to take charge of the Air Ministry work on the beams.

On 15th June Joubert held a meeting in his office in the afternoon, at which both Lindemann and I were present, and where it was considered that the evidence was now sufficiently strong to show that immediate action was needed. Joubert therefore called a meeting of the Night Interception Committee for the afternoon of the following day, a Sunday. What a change from my inactivity of only a week ago! During the morning Scott-Farnie and I went out to see Felkin to pick up the most recent items of information from the prisoners, and we arrived back just in time for the meeting. I there encountered for the first time the Commander-in-Chief of Fighter Command, Air Chief Marshal Sir Hugh Dowding. After I had given my evidence Joubert turned to Dowding and said, 'Well, C-in-C, what should we do?' Dowding answered in one word: 'Jam!' But although he answered so positively, his note to Tizard, written after the meeting, was less positive: 'The meeting was called to discuss some rather nebulous evidence about

[1] Ronald Clark, *Tizard*, p. 228.

German long-distance navigation by Lorenz beam. Various plans were made to find out what the Germans were doing, and these may or may not be effective.'[1]

But, typical of any occasion on which Joubert was in the Chair, the meeting came to some crisp decisions. Air Commodore Nutting, the Director of Signals, should proceed with the formation of a flight of aircraft fitted with equipment to try to find the beams. Watson-Watt and I should investigate the possibility of putting listening receivers on our radar towers, where the high siting should give us a good chance of hearing the beams. Group Captain Blandy should evolve a jamming system and should co-ordinate all reports and recommendations. Group Captain Blackford should continue to search for concealed instruments that might be operated by fifth columnists, and Joubert himself should co-ordinate all investigations and should prepare a report every Friday for the Prime Minister. Professor Lindemann was to take up the question of designing new receivers, capable of detecting radio waves down to wavelengths of 40 centimetres.

So far, Tizard had not come into the picture at all, beyond noting earlier[2] from what I had told him about the X-Gerät in February and March that 'The Germans obviously have something in the way of R.D.F. (radar) and have ideas of using it for bombing at night'. It happened that he was out of London for most of the week, and only returned on the morning of Monday 17th June. To bring him up to date, it was arranged that I should meet him at 9.15 a.m. in the office of Air Commodore Nutting, the Director of Signals. I told him of what I had found in the preceding few days, and felt that he was not altogether enthusiastic. This was a little surprising in that I was in a sense his own protégé, and I think that he must for once have reacted much as Lindemann would almost certainly have done had it been Tizard to whom I had told the story first. Lindemann would almost inevitably have tried to think of reasons for doubting, and this is what Tizard himself now seemed to do. In a note written that day he said, 'I may be wrong, but there seemed to me to be unnecessary excitement about this latest alleged German method for dealing with the country. One cannot possibly get accurate bombing on a selected target in this way. It would, of course, be perfectly simple to use this system to bomb a place like London under completely blind conditions, but if we on our part had the task of bombing Berlin under blind conditions we could do it with-

[1] Ronald Clark, *Tizard*, p. 229.
[2] Ibid. p. 231.

out this system. I feel that the use of the system is far more dangerous if it is looked at from the point of view of being able to concentrate large numbers of aircraft round a particular district in bad weather conditions by day. That is what we must be prepared for and it is on that occasion and that only that I should jam.' In view of the subsequently discovered inaccuracy of our bombing, and of my previously expressed doubts arising from our pre-war navigational accidents, Tizard's faith in our blind bombing ability was, in retrospect, surprising.

At the meeting with Tizard an interesting sidelight emerged. Nutting had with him one of his Deputy Directors, Group Captain Lang, who told us that the latest Chiefs of Staff appreciation of the war situation was that invasion was possible within a week, likely within two weeks and almost certain within three. I did not myself believe it, but it gives some idea of the atmosphere in which we had to operate.

I could see that despite the priority we already had, progress might be held up because of insufficient scientific manpower. I therefore persuaded Lindemann to minute Churchill for authority to devote to the task anyone whose research was not likely to affect production in the next three months. Winston initialled the minute with the comment 'Let this be done without fail'. Curiously, Hitler had given a very similar order regarding German research at about the same time, for the opposite reason that he regarded the war as nearly won.

In the afternoon of the same day I attended a meeting in Watson-Watt's office, to decide the ways in which we could fulfil the decisions of Joubert's meeting. We selected five of the radar stations in the main coastal chain as sites at which we would try to detect the beams from the ground. Ottercops, Staxton Wold, West Beckham, Bawdsey, and Dover. We also selected the R.A.F. Unit that would try to detect the beams in the air. This was the Blind Approach Development Unit stationed at Boscombe Down, whose pilots had more experience than any others in flying along Lorenz-type beams. Their Commanding Officer was Wing Commander R. S. (Bobbie) Blucke, with whom I had flown several times when he commanded the Experimental Flight at Farnborough, and who had piloted the Heyford bomber used as target in the very first radar trial in February 1935.

It may help here if I explain what a Lorenz beam is, for this is what we expected to find. If one arranges a number of aerial units ('dipoles', which look like the simplest type of television aerial) side by side, as in a fence and about the same distance apart as they are long, and feeds the radio energy to them in a suitable manner they will generate the beam which

emerges broadside to the fence; and, paradoxically, perhaps, the longer
the 'fence' the sharper the beam. But without a fence of prohibitive
length, the beam would not be nearly sharp enough to define a target
one mile wide at two hundred miles range. The clever trick in the
Lorenz system was to transmit two fairly blunt beams, pointing in
slightly different directions but overlapping one another in a relatively
narrow region which now in effect becomes the 'beam' along which the
aircraft are intended to fly. (Figure 1)

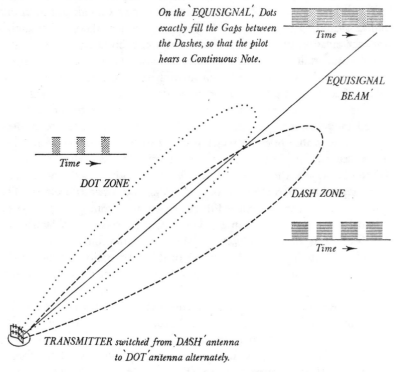

On the ʽEQUISIGNAL', Dots
exactly fill the Gaps between
the Dashes, so that the pilot
hears a Continuous Note.

Time →

EQUISIGNAL
BEAM

Time →

DOT ZONE

DASH ZONE

Time →

TRANSMITTER switched from ʽDASH' antenna
to ʽDOT' antenna alternately.

Fig. 1. Principle of the Lorenz beam

The two overlapping beams are most simply generated by two aerial
systems pointing in slightly different directions and mounted together
on a single turntable. The actual radio transmitter is switched from one
of these aerials to the other and back again in a repetitive sequence, so
that one aerial transmits for a short time followed by a longer interval,
giving a 'dot' to anyone who listens to it on a suitable radio receiver,
while the other transmits for a long time followed by a short interval,

giving a 'dash'. Anyone so placed as to receive the two aerials at the same strength would hear the one transmit a dot immediately followed by the other transmitting a dash, so that he would think that he was listening to a single aerial transmitting continuously. As he moved sideways into the zone in which one beam, say the 'dot' beam, was stronger than the other, he would begin to hear the dots coming up above the continuous note, and vice versa with the dashes. By listening for the predominance of dots or dashes he would know the direction in which he would have to steer to bring himself back into the narrow 'equi-signal' zone. This zone can be as narrow as one hundredth or even one thousandth of the width of the 'dot' or 'dash' beam alone. The aerials are therefore set on the turntable in such a direction that the equi-signal zone passes over the target. To warn the pilot that he is approaching the target, a similar beam system would be set up from one site well to the side of the director beam, and this second system would transmit a marker beam to cross the director a few kilometres before the target.

So this was what we had to look for. The radio frequency had to be within range of the 'hotted-up' Lorenz-type receiver in the Heinkel III which put it between 28 and 35 megacycles per second, and Rowley Scott-Farnie said that it would very likely be exactly 30 or 31·5 or 33·3 because these were pre-set frequencies in the German receivers. The observers who were to man the ground receiving stations were to be drawn from workers at Worth Matravers, near Swanage, to which the Telecommunications Research Establishment, which had started as the Air Ministry Research Establishment at Bawdsey, had been evacuated after a short stay in Dundee. The observers for the aircraft search were to come from the R.A.F. 'Y' Service.

On 18th June we briefed Bobbie Blucke and on the following day a search aircraft was in the air for the first time; but neither on that day nor 20th June was anything like a beam detected. This was slightly discouraging, but things done so hurriedly rarely work the first time.

There had to be two beams. One, I was reasonably sure, was at Cleves although our photographic reconnaissance was not yet adequate to find it. Felkin soon gave me the site of the other, for he found it on a paper salvaged from an aircraft shot down in France. This said:

1. Knickebein (Bredstedt no. ö Husum)
    54°39'
    8°57'

2. Knickebein
        51°47′5″
        6° 6′   (b. Cleve)

This fixed the second beam transmitter up in Schleswig Holstein: and another paper, this time from an aircraft shot down on 18th June gave 'Knickebein, Kleve 31·5'— which confirmed Scott-Farnie's guesses about the frequency. And on 21st June another paper gave us the frequency of the Schleswig Holstein beam as 30·0 megacycles per second.

One problem remained nagging in my mind: were Knickebein and the X-Gerät one and the same thing? On 20th June Felkin was told by a new prisoner that the X-Gerät was a bombing system which involved intersecting radio beams. This description exactly fitted what we now knew of Knickebein, but I determined to keep open the possibility that there were actually two different systems using the same principle. But long before that problem could be solved, much was to happen.

On the afternoon of 20th June, I heard rumours that there was to be a meeting the following morning at 10 Downing Street about the beam situation. But since no one had asked me to attend, and I could not very well push myself, I decided to go on with my work in a way that, although enormously more hectic than it had been ten days before, was now normal. In fact, the only surviving feature of my pre-beam routine was that I did not get into my office before 10 o'clock. There was little point in being earlier, because the night's incoming messages were hardly ready before then, and it was more sensible to start late-ish and work into the evening. So I caught the train from Richmond on 21st June at about 9.35 a.m. as usual, and arrived in my office at ten past ten. On my desk was a note from Daisy Mowat: 'Squadron Leader Scott-Farnie has telephoned and says will you go to the Cabinet Room in 10 Downing Street.' Well, in view of our lighthearted office relationships, it could just have been a joke, and so I checked with Daisy and Scott-Farnie before taking a taxi round to No. 10. I arrived at the Cabinet Room some twenty-five minutes after the meeting had started.

I hardly knew what to expect. As I was shown into the room through double doors (they can be seen in Plate 4(b)) I had an end-view of a long narrow cloth-covered table with a writing pad and blotter set before each place, and racks of black-embossed Downing Street notepaper distributed along the table. Churchill was sitting in the middle of the left side, his back to the fireplace; he was flanked by Lindemann on his right and Lord Beaverbrook on his left. Everyone else was sitting on the other side. Immediately opposite was Sir Archibald Sinclair, who had recently become Air Minister, and who was flanked by the most senior officers in the Air Force: Sir Cyril Newall, Chief of Air Staff, Sir Hugh Dowding, Commander-in-Chief of Fighter Command, Sir Charles Portal, Commander-in-Chief Bomber Command, and Sir Philip Joubert, nominally the Adviser on Combined Operations, but in fact in charge of all radar and signals matters in the Air Force. Sitting with them were Tizard, as Scientific Adviser to the Air Staff, and Watson-Watt as Scientific Adviser on Telecommunications. There were no secretaries, perhaps because the matter was so secret.

Immediately, I encountered a problem: the atmosphere was clearly tense and perhaps even that of a confrontation, and I stood for a moment waiting for an invitation to sit down. Lindemann waved for me to go to sit beside him, and at the same time the Air Staff beckoned me to sit with them. Lindemann was my old professor, and was probably responsible for my being there, but my post was with the Air Staff. I saw that I could conveniently resolve this conflict of loyalties by sitting in the chair nearest the door, which was in the 'no-man's-land' at the end of the table between the two sides; and so there I sat, somewhat isolated —the chair is visible to the left of Churchill's shoulder in the photograph at Plate 4(b).

Churchill's subsequent description of the meeting in *Their Finest Hour* was not quite correct, for he said there that 'according to plan' he invited me to open the discussion. Actually, it must have already been in progress for some 25 minutes when I arrived, and I listened for a time while some of those around the table made comments which suggested that they had not fully grasped the situation; only then did Churchill address a question to me on some point of detail. Instead of dealing with it, I said, 'Would it help, sir, if I told you the story right from the start?' Churchill seemed somewhat taken aback, but after a moment's hesitation said, 'Well, yes it would!' And so I told him the story. The fact that my call to the Cabinet Room had been so sudden had given me no time to rehearse, or even to become nervous. The few minutes of desultory discussion that had ensued after my entry showed me that nobody else there knew as much about the matter as I did myself and, although I was not conscious of my calmness at the time, the very gravity of the situation somehow seemed to generate the steady nerve for which it called. Although I was only 28, and everyone else around the table much my senior in every conventional way, the threat of the beams was too serious for our response to be spoilt by any nervousness on my part.

Churchill himself recorded that I spoke for some twenty minutes, which is quite a time to have the Prime Minister listening at the height of the greatest crisis that had ever confronted the country. He went on to say: 'When Dr. Jones had finished there was a general air of incredulity. One high authority asked why the Germans should use a beam, assuming that such a thing was possible, when they had at their disposal all the ordinary facilities of navigation. Above twenty thousand feet the stars were nearly always visible. All our own pilots were laboriously trained in navigation, and it was thought they found their way about and to their targets very well. Others round the table appeared concerned.'

Again, I sensed that Tizard had perhaps overdone his scepticism about the beams, but Churchill asked me what we could do. I told him that the first thing was to confirm their existence by discovering and flying along the beams for ourselves, and that we could develop a variety of countermeasures ranging from putting in a false cross-beam to making the Germans drop their bombs early, or using forms of jamming ranging from crude to subtle. Churchill added all his weight to these suggestions. In addition, he said that if the Germans were to fly along beams, this would be the ideal case for our sowing fields of aerial mines, which he had been pressing on the Air Ministry for some years, adding as he angrily banged the table, 'All I get from the Air Ministry is files, files, files!' And then the meeting ended. There were no minutes, because the matter seems to have been deemed so secret that no secretaries were present, and the only record was the one that I made for my report written during the following week. After the meeting, Archibald Sinclair came across to me and introduced himself, adding that he understood that I was working with his old friend, Stewart Menzies in M.I.6.

I returned to my office much elated at having convinced the Prime Minister. My elation, however, was to be dashed by the events of the afternoon. There was a conference in the office of the Director of Signals, Air Commodore Nutting, to discuss the possibility that the Germans might exploit pulse transmissions as navigational aids over this country, and on which Mr. T. L. Eckersley was to give evidence. The meeting, however, reverted to Knickebein, because Eckersley wanted to give instead his views on how wrong I was about it. It will be remembered that he had been given the Kleve message by Group Captain Blandy on 13th June, and he had interpreted it for himself. He said that it could not refer to a beam and that 'Kleve' might well be an error for 'Klebe', which meant 'to stick' and that the message might well be an instruction to paratroops to 'stick like glue' to position 53° 24' north 1° west. When I asked him why he rejected the idea of a beam, he said that a short-wave beam from Cleve could not possibly be heard at twenty thousand feet in England—it would just not bend sufficiently round the earth. If this were true, it would completely destroy my case and, ironically, it was on the basis of Eckersley's earlier calculations that I had demolished Lindemann's objections and thus succeeded in raising the alarm. I reminded Eckersley of his calculations, which contradicted what he was now saying: he replied that I ought not to have taken them seriously, what he was doing then was to calculate how far they might go under some circumstances, and that he did not believe them himself. And to support his argument there was the fact that our aircraft had failed to detect any beams on the two preceding nights.

At that point the principal Deputy Director of Signals, Group Captain O. G. W. G. Lywood said something like, 'Well we now have the greatest expert on radio propagation in the country and he says that the beam theory is all wrong. We have wasted a lot of effort and let's not waste any more. This evening's flight should be cancelled!' I weighed up my position, and pointed out that Eckersley's evidence had neutralized itself, because he had said one thing a few months before and now something quite different. In that case I proposed that his statements should be ignored, and that I already had so much other evidence that I was convinced that the beams existed. I told Lywood that if he cancelled the flight, which I myself had heard the Prime Minister authorize that very morning, I would see that the Prime Minister came to know who it was who had countermanded his orders. This was a strong line to take, but it was a case of risking all; Lywood backed down and the flight plans went ahead. I was asked where the aircraft should search, and I suggested that we should assume that the director beam was on Derby, because the most crucial target in England at that time was the Rolls Works where the Merlin engines for Spitfires and Hurricanes were made.

I also gave the expected frequencies on which the aircraft should search, and it was arranged that it should take off from Wyton in Huntingdonshire to fly northwards so as to cross the beams. From the chair, Nutting said, 'And what do we do if we find the beams?' Quietly I whispered to Scott-Farnie, 'Go out and get tight!' At the end of a long day I went home and spent a thoroughly uneasy night. Had I, after all, made a fool of myself and misbehaved so spectacularly in front of the Prime Minister? Had I jumped to false conclusions? Had I fallen for a great hoax by the Germans? Above all, had I arrogantly wasted an hour of the Prime Minister's time when Britain was about to be invaded or obliterated from the air?

Fortunately, this period of wretched introspection was dispelled the next day when the results of the search flight were reported. We held a meeting in Joubert's room in the afternoon, and the pilot, Flight Lieutenant H. E. Bufton, was there to tell us what he had found. Neither he nor the observer, Corporal Mackie, had been told the Knickebein story, but merely to search for transmissions with Lorenz characteristics and to locate the equi-signal line after taking off from Wyton and flying northwards. His flight report read:

(1) That there is a narrow beam (approximately 400–500 yards wide), passing through a position 1 mile S. of Spalding, having dots to the south and dashes to the north, on a bearing of 104°–284°T.

(2) That the carrier frequency of the transmissions on the night of 21/22 June was 31·5 Mc/sec. modulated at 1150 cycles and similar to Lorenz characteristics.

(3) That there is a second beam having similar characteristics but with dots to the north and dashes to the south synchronized with the southern beam, apparently passing through a point near Beeston on a bearing lying between 60°+ and less than 104°.

The guess about Derby proved a good one, at least in anticipation. The diaries of the German Chief of Air Staff, Ernst Milch, for 21st July show that Goering thought that air supremacy 'could be achieved only by destroying the R.A.F. and its supporting aero-engine industry—an industry the enemy would be forced to defend. . . . As to their tactics, Goering suggested they should make these factories the targets for nuisance raids by night at once.'

The impact of Bufton's brilliant report on the meeting was all that might be expected. Our conclusions had been confirmed: there were indeed two beams, whose bearings were consistent with transmitters at Cleves and Bredstedt. There was even jubilation: I can recall 'Daddy' Nutting—who, I felt, was always on my side, even in the bitter disagreements that I had with some of his staff—actually skipping round the room in delight. All doubts were now removed, and plans for countermeasures could go urgently ahead. As our meeting ended Rowley Scott-Farnie said to me, 'Remember what you said yesterday?' and so he and I went across to St. Stephen's Tavern, on the other side of Whitehall, to indulge in a celebration that was tempered only by the knowledge that

I had to drive down to Boscombe Down on the following day to take some equipment for chasing fifth columnists.

During the following week, I wrote an account of the whole episode under the title 'The Crooked Leg', for this or 'Dog Leg' is one of the meanings of 'Knickebein'; more recently I have found that it is also the name of a cocktail. My report concluded:

> It is a fitting stage at which to close the account as far as Secret Intelligence is concerned. In the course of ten days the matter has developed from a conjecture to a certainty, with a healthy organization for its investigation. Several technical points remain to be cleared up, but their elucidation is only a matter of time.
>
> There are many lessons in this story, most of which are too obvious to point out. It shows the German technique is well developed—almost beyond what we thought possible; if they can place an aircraft to within 400 yards over this country, they may well have an extremely accurate system of R.D.F., and one might guess that they are concentrating on the C.H.L. principle.
>
> The possibility that Knickebein is an elaborate hoax may be discounted. At least sixteen independent sources have been obtained, and while some of them could conceivably have been inspired, the physical evidence of the sharpness of the beam, which would never have been gratuitously revealed, and of the increased sensitivity of the Lorenz receiver, are too subtle even for German thoroughness to have executed.
>
> The writer trusts that an expression of his appreciation of having worked with the group of officers mentioned in this report, as well as with others whose contributions are nameless but necessary, will be accepted. If our good fortunes hold, we may yet pull the Crooked Leg.

CHAPTER TWELVE

Reflections

1940 WAS dominated by Churchill. Throughout the preceding decade his career had been commonly judged a brilliant failure, his eloquence denigrated as extravagance, his robust living rated for showmanship, and his changes of party branded as disloyal careerism. Even though he had consistently shown his great qualities, many of his countrymen preferred to see him as the perpetrator of folly in the Dardanelles, as the diehard breaker of strikes, and now as the exploiting war-monger between Britain and the Axis powers. Had there been no Nazi movement, his posthumous reputation might have been at best a matter of dispute. But, now that the hour had come he was uniquely matched to its demands. Tory Democrat, Liberal, Anti-Socialist, Constitutionalist and Conservative, he had been in politics for forty years. He had been head of each of the three Service Ministries, of the Home Office, the Colonial Office and the Board of Trade, and he had been Chancellor of the Exchequer. Yet he had been out of office for ten years; and even this was a qualification for leadership, for it provided the period of isolation which he deemed ingredient. He had served in eight regiments. Pre-eminent in courage—the quality that, he wrote, guarantees all the others—he had learnt from Antwerp in 1914 (or so it seemed) that when directing supreme affairs one must not 'descend into the valleys of direct physical and personal action'. He understood the essence of supreme decisions: yea or nay, right or left, advance or retreat. He knew the strengths and weaknesses of experts. He knew how easy it is for the man at the summit to receive too rosy a picture from his Intelligence advisers. His humour and fairness had made friends of those enemies who had proved true fighters. Alone among politicians he valued science and technology at something approaching their true worth, at least in military application, and he had for seven years been warning his countrymen of the very disaster that had now befallen them. He had even, forty years before, pictured London in the position that it might shortly face, and had confided that there would at least be some who rather than surrender would die like the Dervishes at Omdurman.

If he had at times overstrained the eloquence of his language and had seemed to live 'larger than life', 1940 was a time which eloquence could not exaggerate, and which demanded a man of more than life size. Throughout his life he had had a sense of history and a feeling of destiny. Now they were fulfilled together. 'I felt as if I were walking with destiny, and that all my past life had been but a preparation for this hour and for this trial': this was the truth, simple and deep.

He never overclaimed his part in 1940. Disaster had united rather than disrupted us, as he knew it would. Although as a nation we were alone, as individuals we were all in it together. He felt our temper exactly: 'There is no doubt that had I at this juncture faltered at all in the leading of the nation, I should have been hurled out of office. . . . It fell to me in these coming days and months to express their sentiments on suitable occasions. This I was able to do, because they were mine also.' All this was true, but there was much more. Churchill could turn even a minor occasion into a memorable one by a happy phrase or a humorous comment. Here he had one of the big occasions of history, and it called for the summit of language, for 'There was a white glow, overpowering, sublime, which ran through our island from end to end'. In speech after speech he helped the people of Britain to see where they stood in history, he convinced them that the direction at the centre was now both firm and good, and he called from them their supreme effort.

But it was not to his eloquence, or even to his humour, alone that they responded; disaster had struck the scales from their eyes, and suddenly they saw the towering courage that had been Churchill's all his life. Everyone knew, in that mysterious way that tells true from false, that here was a man who would stand to the last; and in this confidence they could stand with him.

From our encounter, I of course felt the elation of a young man at being noticed by any Prime Minister, but somehow it was much more. It was the same whenever we met in the war—I had the feeling of being recharged by contact with a source of living power. Here was strength, resolution, humour, readiness to listen, to ask the searching question and, when convinced, to act. He was rarely complimentary at the time, handsome though his compliments could be afterwards, for he had been brought up in sterner days. In 1940 it was compliment enough to be called in by him at the crisis; but to stand up to his questioning attack and then to convince him was the greatest exhilaration of all.

As I was speaking at the Knickebein meeting, I could sense the impression that I was making on him. One day after the war, when I was sitting at his bedside, he told me about it: having surveyed our position in the early weeks of June 1940, he thought that we ought just to be able to hold the Luftwaffe by day. And then, when this young man came in and told him that they could still bomb as accurately by night, when our nightfighters would still be almost powerless, it was for him one of the blackest moments of the war. But as the young man went on the load was once again lifted because he said that there could be ways of countering the beams and so preventing our most important targets being destroyed.

I did not in fact see Churchill again for some two years after the Knickebein meeting, although many of my reports went to him, and the impression throughout the senior staffs in the Service Ministries was that I had his ear the whole time. That was certainly very useful, in that men frequently did what I recommended, not so much because they believed in it, but because they were afraid of the Prime Ministerial wrath if they did something else.

The ten days, 11th to 21st June, had brought me from obscurity to the highest level of the war. But, if 21st June was a turning point in my own fortunes with Churchill, it was a disastrous—and quite unfair—episode for Tizard. During the previous few days I had been worried about his attitude, although I had seen none of his deprecating minutes; and in the Cabinet Room I sensed that he had put himself in a dangerous position, but I had no idea of the extent to which he had actually done so, because I thought he would be much too sensible. After all, when I had been entirely in Lindemann's laboratory, he had been almost incredibly fair in applauding my efforts although they had seemingly been done under the aegis of his rival. So when, a few days after the 21st June meeting, I wrote up the whole episode to Churchill and the Air Staff, I therefore did my best to repair any damage that he might have inflicted on himself by saying that at the beginning of the war I 'had been appointed to be responsible for Scientific Intelligence, and if, incidentally, this present account be considered to justify that appointment, it should be remembered that it was fostered by Sir Henry Tizard, Mr. Pye, Wing Commander Winterbotham and Mr. Woodward Nutt (and opposed by the Treasury!).'

Tizard himself felt so miserable about the affair that even before it was clear that I was right, he went across to the Athenaeum that afternoon and wrote out his resignation. Had I known I would have been desperately sorry. It was bitter irony, because but for Tizard I would probably not have been in Intelligence and therefore the whole episode would not have taken place; and that was far more important than whether or not on this occasion he himself allowed his judgement to be upset. And had he, instead of Lindemann, sent for me on 11th June, as could easily have happened, their roles would very probably have been reversed.

It was long before I began fully to realize the damage which had been done to Tizard. As Ronald Clark—his biographer—pointed out to me, I had missed more than twenty minutes of the vital meeting, and so could not know the extent to which his scepticism may have gone. It was only two years later that I began to get some idea, when Lindemann said to me, 'The Prime Minister was speaking very warmly about you the other night!' When I asked Lindemann why, he told me that Tizard had once again threatened to resign, this time from the Ministry of Aircraft Production (in 1940 it had been from the Air Staff). The new threat of resignation had been discussed at either the Cabinet or the Defence Committee, and someone had said what a tragedy it would be if Tizard were to go. Churchill had disagreed, and had said, 'If we had listened to Sir Henry Tizard in 1940, we should not have known about the beams. As it was, it was left to that young Dr. Jones, who spoke so well at our meeting!' And a good deal later, I was to receive the same picture from Lord Portal. Tizard himself was magnanimous enough never to hold any resentment against me. In fact, he continued to help me throughout the war, and afterwards right up to the time of his death.

Besides the sense of personal fulfilment that the episode gave me, for of all the tasks I could possibly have done this one, of standing in some ways alone in a vital gap in our national defences, was the one I would have chosen above all others—there was also the fact that I had put Scientific Intelligence 'on the map'. Moreover, it was a prime example demonstrating the fallacy in Buckingham's argument regarding the merit of information from the Intelligence Services being interpreted by our own experts. If we had been running on this system, the last word would have rested with Eckersley and we would therefore have taken no action until markedly later, and probably not in time for the Blitz. Thenceforward Scientific Intelligence was to become an essential component in defence, and not in our own country only.

5

Of the many laudatory verdicts that have been passed in the books, I think that the one that I value most—apart from Winston's own[1]—was that by Telford Taylor, Professor of Law in Columbia University, New York and incidentally the Chief Prosecutor at the Nuremberg Trials, in his book *The Breaking Wave*: 'The early detection and partial frustration of Knickebein—a feat then known only to a few—was an early and major British victory in the Battle of Britain.' If that was right, I was in the best of company, few though it may have been.

[1] See pages 181 and 248.

CHAPTER THIRTEEN

The Fortunes of Major Wintle

THE GRIM situation in 1940 was tempered by lighter episodes; and although to record them may appear to hold up the narrative, it may serve to correct the impression of a perpetually breath-taking pace that would be suggested by a compact account merely of the high peaks of my activity. Fortunately we could usually afford the time to laugh, and could then tackle our problems all the better. For me, one of the brightest of such episodes started on 17th June in the middle of the Knickebein flurry, and it was brought about by the impending collapse of France—now only five days away. I was walking back across Horseguards Parade to my office after lunch, perhaps one of the rare lunches that I had as Lindemann's guest in The Athenaeum, when there were military footsteps behind me, and I received a hearty slap on the back from the brisk figure of Freddie Wintle.

'Hello, old boy, how's your war going?' he asked. I told him that for me it had taken an interesting turn, and in reply he told me why he thought we were generally in such a mess. 'The trouble with this war,' he said, 'is that you can't criticize anybody. It's "Well done, Neville", or "Good old Tom" or something like that. Why man, you're not in a decent Cavalry Mess five minutes before you have been called a bloody fool—and you're the better for it!' With that we parted, he towards the Air Ministry in Charles Street, and I to Broadway.

Evidently Wintle proceeded to put his doctrine into immediate practice, but I did not at first correlate it with what I read a day or so later on a placard: 'ARMY OFFICER IN THE TOWER'. When I bought a paper I found that it referred to Freddie Wintle. The basic reason for his annoyance on Horseguards, which he had not told me, was that he had been ordered back to his Regiment when he believed that if only he could go to France he could so stiffen the morale of the French that they would not give in. He claimed to know the French better than most because he had been an instructor at the Ecole de Guerre, the French Staff College at St. Cyr. After leaving me, he had gone straight to the Director of Air Intelligence to protest at his posting whereupon, it seems, that he thought that the Director had accused him of cowardice in not wishing to rejoin his Regiment. This of course was fatal, for no one could question Wintle's gallantry. He thereupon drew his revolver in indignation and said, 'You and your kind ought to be shot,' or words to that effect. He was arrested and sent to the Tower.

Looking forward to his Court Martial was one of our light reliefs during the Battle of Britain. It duly came off, and he appeared in immaculate uniform, leather and brass shining brightly; drawing a silk handkerchief from his pocket he flicked some imaginary dust from his beautifully pipeclayed breeches, returned the handkerchief to the pocket, crossed his legs, screwed in his monocle, folded his arms and glared at the Court. He had to answer three main charges. The first was that he had faked defective vision in his right eye, the implication being that he thereby wished to avoid Active Service. This he was easily able to refute, because not only did he have one eye useless as a result of being wounded in World War I, but he had also bluffed the examining specialist into thinking that he had two good eyes, and he called the Chief of the Imperial General Staff, Sir Edmund Ironside, as a witness. This charge was therefore dropped.

The more serious charge was that he had produced a pistol in the presence of the Air Commodore whom he had threatened to shoot, along with himself, and had 'said words to the effect that certain of His Majesty's Ministers or Officers of the Royal Air Force above the rank of Group Captain and most senior Army Officers ought to be shot'. Instead of denying this as regards the Ministers, he proposed to substantiate it as a patriotic action and read out a list of the Ministers who he suggested should be shot. When he got to Kingsley Wood, at No. 7, the Prosecuting Advocate interrupted to say that he did not propose to proceed with this charge, which was accordingly dropped.

Finally Wintle was asked, 'When you produced the pistol in the presence of the Air Commodore, was it your intention to intimidate him?' With his monocle held more firmly than ever, he replied, 'Intimidate the Air Commodore? Oh dear me, no! Why, I have worked with the Air Commodore for over a year, and I well know that he is the type of Officer that if you rushed into his room and shouted at the top of your voice "The Air Ministry's on fire!" all he would do would be to take up his pen and write a minute to someone about it!' He was on a pretty good wicket, in that he was being tried by an Army Court Martial for being rude to an Air Force Officer, and he escaped with a severe reprimand.

I lost sight of him after that for some time; being the reverse of a coward, and finding service with his Regiment too inactive, he had volunteered to go into France as an agent with the Special Operations Executive, where he was captured by the Vichy French and we heard of him languishing in Toulon jail. He escaped into Spain at the second attempt, and I again lost trace of him.

At the end of the war he was to make a dramatic reappearance, this time in the house in which I had been born. The lady of the house was much alarmed to hear a great crash in her sitting-room and found that a motor car had come through its front window. The house was on a bend, which the driver had obviously taken too fast. When he stepped out, it was Freddie Wintle, who at the time was standing as Liberal candidate for Norwood against Duncan Sandys. 'My dear lady,' he said, 'I am most frightfully sorry. I must have upset your nerves. What you need is some sherry which I will now go and get.' And just as on the occasion of my first meeting him, he went to the local pub and returned with the sherry. I am sorry that he did not become our Member of Parliament.

Again I lost sight of him, until I read of a retired Army officer who had lured a solicitor to a secluded flat and removed his trousers because the officer—who once again turned out to be Wintle—thought that the solicitor was tricking one of his female relatives into making over her money. The solicitor summoned him for assault, and Wintle was sent to prison for six months. Nevertheless, when he came out he managed to prove his case against the solicitor and he fought the legal battle right up to the House of Lords, without any professional aid. He won, *The Times*' headline being 'CAVALRY OFFICER JUMPS LAST FENCE TO WIN'.

Wintle died in 1966. Fittingly, his friend ex-Trooper Cedric Mays of the Royals on the occasion of his funeral drank a bottle of Glenfiddich and then, through a mist of whisky and tears, sang the Cavalry Last Post and Cavalry Reveille to the astonished worshippers in Canterbury Cathedral, the Chapel of the Cavalrymen of Britain.

CHAPTER FOURTEEN

The Fifth Column

THE STORY of the engine-stopping rays on the Feldberg (pp. 50 and 84) was one example of how the human imagination can conjure up fear under conditions of stress; these conditions were much intensified with the direct threat to Britain in June 1940. With the example of Quisling in Norway and with stories of fifth columnists causing confusion during the retreat of our Army in France and Belgium, it was not surprising that a scare about fifth columnists swept through Britain. It was, indeed, quite conceivable that the Nazis had infiltrated some of their own agents among the stream of Jewish emigrés who had come to Britain before the war, and it was therefore not unnatural, although unfortunate, that the Government decided not to take any risks and rounded up many of them for internment. The Lander Committee (p. 83) lost two of its members in this way, and it took us months to get them out again. Some were taken to the Isle of Man and others to Canada: they bore this great inconvenience with much patience.

As far as I could see at the time, and still more in retrospect, the fifth column in Britain was completely imaginary. But great zeal was expended by security officers in chasing reports of fireworks being let off while German aircraft were overhead. Our countryside was scanned by aircraft of the R.A.F. looking for suspicious patterns laid out on the ground which might serve as landmarks to aid the navigation of German bombers. More than one farmer was surprised by a call from security officers to explain why he had mown his hay in such a manner as to leave a striking pattern which could be seen from the air. One chapel, whose gardener had unconsciously laid out paths in the pattern of an enormous arrow as seen from the air, and which did indeed point roughly in the direction of an ammunition dump ten miles away, was raided as a suspected Fifth Column Headquarters. In this instance, as in the Knickebein hunt, the raid was led by Group Captain Blackford.

Late in the evening of Sunday 30th June, I was telephoned at home by Blackford, who told me that he had just returned from investigating another case, this time in Norfolk, and there was so much to it that he was sure that it was 'up my street'. He was sufficiently convinced to have some R.A.F. policemen sent up to the area and to have persuaded the Chief Constable of Norfolk to issue search and arrest warrants. He wanted me to fly there the next morning to look over the evidence and sanction the search and arrest parties. It was an unusual job for a scientist, but it promised excitement.

I went into the Air Ministry first thing in the morning to look at the evidence. It was indeed much stronger than in any other fifth column case I had seen. The file started, as did so many others about that time, with a letter from an R.A.F. Station Commander along the lines: 'Sir, I have the honour to report the following suspicious incident in the vicinity of my station in the recent past. . . .' The station concerned was near The Wash, and the Commander claimed to be the oldest group captain in the Air Force. Certainly, he was one of the most energetic, and he had insisted on coming back from retirement, well over sixty, to 'do his bit' once again. He had organized his own dummy aerodrome, complete with fireworks, which he manipulated himself when German aircraft were overhead. From watching these aircraft he concluded that there was a fifth column radio transmitter near his station, because aircraft always approached from the same direction and then turned when almost immediately overhead to go on a new course to their targets inland. Also, he thought that he had some fifth column rivals in letting off fireworks. These factors, fireworks and aircraft changing course overhead, were common to innumerable stories all over England at that time, and the Air Staff had come to take little notice of them. Nothing therefore was done until another letter arrived from the Group Captain, again starting 'I have the honour. . . .' but it was quite clear that by then he considered it anything but an honour to deal with the seemingly lethargic Air Staff.

The Group Captain's second letter described events that were quite remarkable, and it was this letter that had led to the hurried visit from Blackford and thus to my own impending trip. Briefly, there was a radar station a few miles from the aerodrome; this station, one of our main chain, was being troubled by jamming, and the C.O. had formed the impression that the jamming was originating locally. There was a small town a few miles away, and he had made private enquiries with the police for any suspected character who might be capable of making a jammer. The police said that they only knew of one man in the town with the necessary competence, and he was the local electrical engineer. It was here that things became interesting, because on looking into his background the police found that he was a Blackshirt, and had actually appeared on the same platform as Oswald Mosley.

Up to this point, there was little concrete evidence to go on, but within the past few days someone had brought into the police station a six-inch local map which he had found under a seat beside a public footpath. This map had pencil lines on it which were as suspicious as one could hope for. They were line bearings from local points of vantage on to four crosses which represented the towers of the radar station. Now it was at that time an offence to make a sketch or map of any Service installation, let alone anything so secret as a radar station, and yet it was quite obvious that someone had deliberately triangulated on to the towers for the purpose of locating them accurately.

The police recognized the map as being one sold by the Ordnance Survey through the local stationer, and they therefore visited him to see whether he had sold any such maps recently. The stationer identified the map as one that he must have sold, but said that he had sold none recently. The police were disappointed at drawing blank; but they were visited that evening by the stationer's younger son, aged about 21 or 22, who was obviously agitated and who claimed the map as his own. He was the local scoutmaster, and said that he must have lost it while explaining map-reading to his scouts. He was not asked to account for the markings, but he was not given back his map, because the police immediately realized a remarkable fact: *the stationer's elder son was the Blackshirt electrical engineer.*

I left for Hendon after reading this, and flew to the aerodrome in time for lunch with the Group Captain. After lunch, I went with the station security officer to visit the radar C.O., and held a conference at which there were, in addition, the Chief Constable, the C.O. of the local coast defence troops, and the two R.A.F. policemen specially brought over from the depot at Uxbridge. We went over the evidence: it was good, but not conclusive. The weak point, I felt, was that the scoutmaster had unnecessarily put his head into the jaws of the police, but it might conceivably be a double bluff. Anyway, everyone else was convinced, and the decision whether to raid the electrical engineer's and the stationer's houses rested with me. I looked at their expectant faces. If I decided against the raid, and went back to the Air Ministry, rumours would still go on and the Air Ministry would be blamed for inaction. On the other hand, a raid would decide the thing one way or the other, and the policemen's eyes lit up when I therefore gave my verdict in favour.

We then got out large-scale maps of the town and planned our raid. The two houses, about half a mile apart, were to be surrounded simultaneously, to prevent one house being alerted by secret radio from the other. The electrical engineer had a wife, and we therefore took the 'Queen W.A.A.F.' of the station to look after her. Search warrants were produced, and after a cup of tea we set off; I was with the party going to the electrical engineer's—he was thought to be the more likely to have any apparatus, and the other party was merely to hold everything static until we had finished with the engineer, and were able to rejoin them. We took up positions around the house to give covering fire if necessary to the Chief Constable and the Army Commander as they rushed up the garden path to give a thunderous knock on the door.

The door was opened by a patently astonished young man who turned out to be the Blackshirt engineer, his alarmed wife clinging to his shoulders. She was gently taken into one room by the W.A.A.F., while we started our search. It stands out in my memory as one of the worst things that I have ever had to do. It is not a nice thing to ransack someone else's house, and rudely search through all the minutiae and debris of domestic life; it turns out to be so pathetically like one's own. It would have been still worse if there had been any children and we had had to go through their toys. None of these thoughts, however, seemed to affect the R.A.F. policemen, who went about their search as enthusiastically as dogs after a winged pheasant hiding under a gorse clump. We inspected the wireless set: nothing unusual. 'Look at this, doctor,' said one of the policemen, 'pages of secret calculations!' I looked; it was an old lecture notebook compiled by the engineer when he was a student, and nothing more. The policeman went away as disappointed as a dog would be when his master reproved him for retrieving a tame hen. Soon he brought back something else, but again it was nothing of importance. This was repeated many times. I could hear the policemen rummaging about upstairs. Then one of them came rushing down, saying 'Here it is!' He had found it hidden away at the bottom of a drawer of clothes, and it was a smallish polished wooden box which might house some scientific instrument—or might not. It was locked; we asked the engineer for the key. He astonished us by saying that he had never seen it in his life. This appeared to be an obvious lie. The policemen fiddled with the lock and ultimately got it open. They gave a yelp, and handed it to me in triumph. There, inside, was an induction coil, some

5*

wire, and some crocodile clips. Remember, we were looking for an electrical jamming apparatus, and so their yelp was certainly justified.

I looked at the engineer. His face showed surprise and embarrassment: he protested that the thing was not his. I looked at the box again; there were some instructions inside the lid. I read them, and realized that this was an electrical hair-remover. His wife, modest woman, had bought it for her personal use, and had been practising a mild deception on her husband. Our search had wrecked her secret—I hope that their domestic happiness survived.

After a pretence at a further search, we all left the house—at least some of us somewhat discomfited. We still had the stationer's house to explore, but it was an anticlimax after the stirring events of the last half-hour. One look at the scoutmaster showed us that he could never have the nerve to be a cold-blooded spy. His explanation was quite simple: he had bought an old prismatic compass the year before, and had fitted it with a new crosswire. He had wanted to check the accuracy of the new sight, and so had gone out onto local eminences, and had taken bearings on the most prominent local objects, the radar towers. Actually, the sight was not aligned quite correctly, and he had accordingly triangulated the towers into the wrong field—as could be seen from a more thorough inspection of the map. He had done all this during the previous year, when it had not been an offence. Technically, we could still have charged him with being in possession of a marked map, but it would have been unkind.

Our mission had therefore been fruitless. All we had done was to explode the main evidence. The jamming of the radar station was almost certainly accidental, and I doubt whether it originated from the hair-remover. The change of direction of German aircraft in the neighbourhood was most probably due to the fact that we were on the coast of the Wash, which served as a very convenient and recognizable landfall taking the aircraft further in towards any of their Midland targets than would any other landfall that they could have made.

It was too late to get back to London that night; and since the radar station was fortunately one of those where we had fitted one of our Knickebein listening receivers, I stayed through the night at the top of one of the towers listening to the beams that Eckersley had said would not be detectable even at twenty thousand feet. I had some fun with Bobby Blucke, who was in charge of the Knickebein watch at Fighter Command, because I was able to telephone him, as it were, from the wrong side. He naturally assumed that I was still in the Air Ministry, and was much surprised to find me taking one of the actual Knickebein watches out on the coast.

As dawn broke, I was myself to hear familiar sounds coming unforgettably from the wrong side. They were of larks invisibly far below us, gradually becoming louder as they rose from the darkness to greet the dawn.

CHAPTER FIFTEEN

The Edda Revived

WITHIN A few days of the final proof of the existence of Knickebein, there was on 27th June another mention of it in an Enigma message. This simply said 'IT IS PROPOSED TO SET UP KNICKEBEIN AND WOTAN INSTALLATIONS NEAR CHERBOURG AND BREST'. So what was Wotan? And why was it mentioned along with Knickebein? Was it complementary or alternative to Knickebein? Just as there might be a clue in the meaning of Knickebein as Crooked Leg, was there some clue in Wotan? I knew, of course, that he was the Zeus of the German Gods (and still honoured, incidentally, by Wednesday) but was there anything unusual about him? I telephoned Bimbo Norman, whose scholarship in German heroic poetry even I was coming to realize. His qualities are best portrayed by what his colleague Leonard Forster wrote of him in *The Times* after his death in December 1968: '. . . the man known characteristically throughout the academic profession as "Bimbo". Nomen est omen: the Italian word for a child in fact revealed something very deep in Norman. There is a sense in which he remained a small boy all his life. He preserved until the end the gusto, the quickness of wit, the intellectual curiosity of the formidably intelligent schoolboy that he must have been—and the immediacy and charm. These qualities gave life to his academic teaching and informed the influence he exerted on generations of students. His medium was the spoken, not the written word, in informal conversation rather than in the lecture room; his use of it was memorable. In this way he communicated in a uniquely personal manner his learning, enthusiasm, and the fruits of his wide-ranging, lightning-swift mind.' I was immediately to have a demonstration of this last quality, for as I asked him about Wotan, he replied, 'Yes, he was Head of the German Gods. . . . Wait a moment. . . . He had only one eye'. And then, shouting triumphantly into the telephone, 'ONE EYE—ONE BEAM! Can you think of a system that would use only one beam?'

I replied that I could, for in principle one could have the bomber fly along a beam pointing over the target, and have something like a radar station alongside the beam transmitter so that the distance of the bomber could be continuously measured from the starting point of the beam. A controller there could know both the distance of the bomber from its target and its speed, from which he could work out the correct instant at which the aircraft should release its bombs to hit the target.

As for the radar system employed, it could be something like our own, in which pulses were sent out to the bomber and reflected back to base; this system could be improved by having a receiver in the bomber which would amplify the signal before re-transmission to base, giving a positive identification of the bomber rather as in our own system of I.F.F. (Identification Friend or Foe). Alternatively the range-finding system might not use pulses but a continuous wave, such as had been mentioned in the Oslo Report, and which I had also found published in a Russian technical journal. In view of the Oslo evidence, I was inclined to look for something like a Knickebein beam with the continuous wave method range measurement. Norman enthusiastically applauded this suggestion, and together we chased every possible clue.

A few days later we encountered another Nordic deity, when on 5th July we learnt that German fighters had been able to intercept some of our aircraft owing to the excellent 'Freya-Meldung' ('Freya Reporting'); and on 14th July we learnt that there was something called a 'Freya Gerät' ('Freya Apparatus'). So Freya appeared to be associated with air defence and to involve specific items of equipment. I knew that Freya was the Nordic Venus: and since Wotan's one eye had seemed to give us a clue to a new bombing system, so I wondered whether there might be something about Freya that would provide a clue in air defence.

I went to Foyle's bookshop and bought a book on Norse mythology, and I described the result which I wrote on 17th July under the title 'The Edda Revived':

Actually the Decknammen Department of the Luftwaffe could hardly have chosen a more fruitful goddess, but few of her attributes have any possible relation with the present problem. She did, however, have as her most prized possession a necklace, Brisinga-men, to obtain which she not merely sacrificed, but massacred, her honour. The necklace is important because it was guarded by Heimdall, the watchman of the gods, who could see a hundred miles by day and night. There is a possible association of ideas with a coastal chain and a detecting system with a range of a hundred miles. Moreover, in Germany, the Brocken is pointed out as the special abode of Freya, and the mystery of the tower on the Brocken is well known. It is unwise to lay too much stress on this evidence, but these are the only facts concerning Freya which seem to have any relation to our previous knowledge. Actually Heimdall himself would have been the best choice for a code name for R.D.F., but perhaps he would have been too obvious.

It is difficult to escape the conclusion therefore, that the Freya-Gerät is a form of portable R.D.F. Freya may possibly be associated with Wotan, as she was at one time his mistress, although it would have been expected that the Führer would have in this case chosen Frigga, who was Wotan's lawful wife.

My report recorded that there were Freya stations near Cherbourg and Brest, and we learnt later that the former had detected our destroyer H.M.S. *Delight* at a range of about sixty miles, with the result that she was sunk by the Luftwaffe on 29th July. Since she had neither balloons nor air escort, the Freya apparatus must have been able to detect her directly. It appeared to be sited near the village of Auderville on the Hague peninsula north-west of Cherbourg, but it had to be very different from our own coastal chain stations, since it was completely undetectable on the best air photographs that we possessed of the area. This confirmed the idea that Freya was a fairly small apparatus, which had already been suggested by the fact that it had been set up so quickly after the Germans had occupied the Channel Coast.

By this time Norman and his colleagues in Hut 3 at Bletchley were so fascinated by the use that I was making of their information that they asked me if I would give them a lecture explaining what I had found. Bletchley had been organized into a series of Huts; and Hut 3, which had originally been Winterbotham's headquarters if we had to evacuate Broadway, became the centre for co-ordinating the signals of air interest that came out of Enigma. The head of Hut 3 was Malcolm Saunders, a naval officer with an excellent knowledge of German and a great sense of history, and he had on his staff a number of distinguished academics including, besides Norman, F. L. Lucas and Geoffrey Barraclough. 'A. J. Alan' chaired my lecture, which aroused such enthusiasm for divining intentions from code names that one cryptographer, learning that the Germans had in hand an operation called Freischütz, spent a whole night reading the score of *Der Freischütz* in the hope of finding a clue.

But if there was enthusiasm at Bletchley, there was reviving doubt in some quarters of the Air Staff. In particular, the Principal Deputy Director of Signals, O. G. W. G. Lywood, now dismissed Knickebein as a 'nine days' wonder', since after all the fuss at the end of June it had so far not materialized as a major threat: this was a singularly ungrateful reaction to a timely warning but Lywood may have felt understandably resentful of my youth. In fact, there were no air attacks on London or other major cities in July, and the only night alarm in London had been caused by an aircraft that had been sent up to investigate the beams and had accidentally strayed across London. We knew, indeed, from Enigma that Hitler had specifically forbidden the bombing of London for the time being; and fortunately Lywood's view did not prevail because I continued to receive pointers to the fact that the Luftwaffe intended to make use of the beams on a large scale.

On 27th July Felkin circulated a document recovered from a German bomber which said that to use Knickebein at long range, the aircraft receivers were to be tuned up by special tuning squads, whose services would be made available to bomber formations on request. And on 27th July an Enigma signal said that one of these squads was requested by Kampf Geschwader No. 54 (a Bomber Group, with a nominal strength of 3 Gruppen each of 27 aircraft) in the week beginning 5th August. Since this Geschwader was primarily to operate in the west of England up to Liverpool and Manchester, which would be beyond the range of the Cleves Knickebein, the information implied that the foreshadowed Knickebein beam near Cherbourg was coming into operation early in August. I was able to give this warning on 4th August: major night bombing appeared imminent.

During the same period we decided to institute bombing surveys to record the pattern of German bombing. I was asked to nominate two towns for particularly careful observation, and I suggested Liverpool and Birmingham, my argument being that Liverpool with the outline of its docks visible even on fairly dark nights would provide a useful contrast with a target well inland such as Birmingham, where we could expect the beams to be especially important. P. M. S. Blackett, who was then with Anti-Aircraft Command, was at the meeting and afterwards he told me that he could not see how the Germans could have made beams as sharp as I was claiming, on an argument that I had had to meet earlier; this was because he had not realized what could be done by over-lapping two broad beams in the way that I have already described.

(For the benefit of students of physics, the problem is how precisely one can define a direction by a beam generated by an aperture which is a given number of wavelengths wide. At first sight this may appear to be the resolving power as calculated by Lord Rayleigh—and indeed Rayleigh thought it was. But the Rayleigh criterion applies properly to the closeness to which two sources can approach before they appear to merge into one when viewed through the aperture, i.e. of establishing that two separate diffraction patterns are involved. By contrast, the precision with which the direction of a single source can be defined is the precision with which the central direction of a single diffraction pattern can be established when no other pattern is present, and this precision may be a million or more times greater than the resolving power.)

The day battle in the air had been going on since about 10th July, the target being almost entirely coastal shipping. On 12th August the German attack switched to our radar stations and aerodromes, and it seemed only a matter of time before the night attacks developed, too. Vera and I went up to Hoar Cross for a short holiday in the second half of August, and on the 23rd we watched a night attack on Birmingham some twenty miles away, reminding me of the scenes of searchlights, bomb flashes and fires that I had witnessed in the first war. As I watched, I wondered whether Knickebein was now coming into large-scale use.

I had the impression that Churchill was as sceptical as I was about the imminence of invasion in July 1940, despite military appreciations that it was likely to happen soon. For some weeks there was no suggestion of it in Enigma, and then we began to get strong indications of an intended operation to be mounted by the Germans under the code name 'Seeloewe' ('Sealion'). This information was passed up to Churchill by Winterbotham, but it seems that the former was still so doubtful that Winterbotham and Stewart Menzies had to have a special meeting with him to convince him of its authenticity. Winterbotham asked me if I could prepare a note establishing the reliability of our information; this I duly wrote, pointing out that the source was exactly the same as that which had given us the crucial message about the Cleves Knickebein which had been so dramatically verified.

Churchill was now convinced, and he said that he would like to see all future information but that it might compromise our source if we continued to use the German code name. So he told us that in future all teleprints on the subject should be headed 'Operation Smith'. His instructions were carried out, with the surprising result that the War

Office appeared to lose all interest in information coming from Bletchley regarding the invasion.

After some time, the reason was found. It turned out that the War Office had its own Operation Smith, which was indeed concerned with the invasion. It was the code name for the movement from one of its minor administrative branches from its current headquarters in somewhere like Stroud or Tetbury to some place further north if the Germans should have invaded and posed a threat to south Gloucestershire. The result was that when the Bletchley teleprints were received in the War Office, duly headed according to the Prime Minister's instruction, they were immediately sent to the Colonel in Gloucestershire, who no doubt impressed by the service that the War Office was providing but realizing that the material was too secret for general circulation, locked them in his safe and told nobody.

We returned to London before the end of the month, where I chased a miscellany of details besides, of course, my main targets of Knickebein, Wotan, and Freya. I found some satisfaction in learning that the Germans, too, could form their own wild theories when under stress. The pilots of one bomber formation, Kampf Gruppe 100, had been asked to investigate a theory that whenever one of our Observer Corps posts heard a German bomber overhead at night it switched on a red light, so that our patrolling fighters could thus get a rough clue to the whereabouts of the bomber. Actually, we had no such procedure, but after three weeks the pilots of this crack formation reported that from their own observations the theory was undoubtedly correct. Probably we had so many red lights showing accidentally that at least one was always within visual range of an aircraft flying anywhere over England, but this was a pleasant lesson in how a false theory could be built up.

As an example of the many minor distractions at this time, there was an Enigma message which seemed to say that a particular region in France would be suitable for the use of 'FLAK GAS'. Since there had been earlier stories of anti-aircraft shells filled with a gas to burst in front of an aircraft which would paralyse its engines as it flew through the cloud of gas, there was an immediate alarm, improbable though the story seemed. The scare arose from nothing more than a missing letter in the message, for there should have been a 'T' at the end, the letters GAST standing for 'Geräte Ausbau Stelle', which merely meant an anti-aircraft equipment depot. I was reminded of this alarm later in the war, when the Germans in turn had a scare when they found that the American Air Force in North Africa was stocking up with enormous quantities of GAS, and so they began to brace themselves for the onset of chemical warfare, which in turn alarmed us. Fortunately a German Intelligence officer realized in time that the Americans were merely referring to petrol.

CHAPTER SIXTEEN

Knickebein Jammed—And Photographed

TOWARDS THE end of August, the Germans began to supplement their day-time efforts with fairly heavy night attacks and on 24th August a few stray bombs fell on central London. This prompted Churchill to order a retaliation on Berlin on the following night. Hitler's expected response was not immediate, but instead there were successive heavy attacks on Liverpool on the last four nights of August. My recommendation of both Birmingham and Liverpool for our bombing surveys was thus already justified, and it was now time to bring countermeasures to Knickebein into play; the first of these was fortunately ready just in time.

As a result of our finding Knickebein in June, a special R.A.F. organization was set up to deal with the beams. This was No. 80 Wing under Wing Commander E. B. Addison, who had his headquarters at Radlett, just north of London; Addison, a signals specialist who had recently returned from the Middle East, had been present and had supported me at the meeting when Lywood proposed cancelling the vital Knickebein flight. The technical design of countermeasures had been entrusted to a Section under Dr. Robert Cockburn in the Telecommunications Research Establishment near Swanage. Both the organization and the technical development of countermeasures were accorded the highest priority: they made great demands on all concerned. The first jammers were simply diathermy sets which could be made to transmit a 'mush' of noise on the Knickebein frequencies, but these were quickly superseded by higher powered equipment called 'Aspirins' (to deal with the Knickebein beams which were code-named 'Head-aches'). These transmitted a dash sounding very like the genuine dash transmitted in the Knickebein beam so that if a German bomber was flying correctly along the equi-signal he would in fact hear this signal plus a dash superimposed on it, which would make him think that he was too much into the dash zone of the overlapping beams, and thus steer further into the dot zone to try to make the dots as strong as the boosted dashes. If our dashes had been synchronized with the genuine ones, the effect would have been to 'bend' the beam, which would seem to have been displaced to the dot side. In practice, there was not enough time to develop a synchronized system, so that all that we could hope for on most occasions was to confuse the German pilots and thus deprive them of the inherent accuracy of the beams; but as the battle went on the legend grew up on both sides that we were genuinely bending the beams.

Apart from its accidental night bombing on 24th August London was still immune from attack until the afternoon of Saturday 7th September. I was in my office when the sirens sounded, and soon both bombs and machine guns were audible. Since they did not seem to be very near I joined Winterbotham and others on the roof. Against the clear blue sky we could see, away to the east, bombs bursting and smoke billowing from fires in the London docks. High in the sky were formations of German aircraft with our fighters attacking individually. Still higher a dozen or more aircraft, presumably German fighters, were flying in a circular daisy-chain, each aircraft protecting the tail of the one in front of it. There was an occasional parachute.

I went back to Richmond wondering whether this was the beginning of the end. The fires in the docks were enormous: they could never be put out before nightfall. Even if we jammed the beams completely, the night bombers would have perfect markers, for the flames in the docks could be seen from the coast. All the Luftwaffe would then have to do was to keep the fires stoked up with successive raids, while its main force aimed a few miles to the west and so pulverized central London. As we watched from Richmond, it was clear that the fires were still raging, and the night attacks on London began. But they were put out within a few days, despite all the odds, by the gallantry of the Regular and Auxiliary Fire Services, who continued to work throughout the raids. There must be few tasks so frightening as trying to put out a fire knowing that you are at the target for bombers overhead, and have no power to hit back.

One offsetting advantage that might have been expected from the dock fires was that the sky was so well lit up we could hope the German bombers would be visible to our nightfighters; but despite this, and despite their previous successes during the short June nights, our fighters inflicted almost no losses on the night bombers. Clearly we badly needed a good airborne radar, and this was not yet available. Anti-aircraft guns, too, were relatively ineffective, and so our blunting of Knickebein was almost our only hope.

In parenthesis here, I may mention that at least one A-A gun crew started their war well, for about this time I read one of the most elated accounts that I was to see during the war. It came from a Territorial gun crew near Farningham in Kent, whose first prospect of action occurred when three Dornier 17 bombers flew over in formation during daylight on 8th September to renew the attack on the London docks: according to the gunners they had one shot at the formation as a 'sighter' and then carefully aimed their second shot at the leading aircraft. All three aircraft promptly vanished, the gunners claiming that they had hit the bombs in the leader which had exploded and blown up the other two. Certainly survivors of two aircraft were picked up from this remarkable shot (A. I. 1(k) Report 485/1940).

The climax of the daylight attacks came on Sunday 15th September with Fighter Command stretched to the limit; but so was the Luftwaffe, and it decided henceforward to concentrate on attack by night. For this it had a unique weapon in Knickebein—or would have had if we had not been able to jam it. From 7th September until 13th November London was bombed every night except one, the average number of bombers being 160. Even without any beams, it was, of course, not difficult to hit such a large target as London, with the Thames as marker, but a substantial proportion of bombs went astray, all the more so when raids were made on cities of smaller size. At least some of the credit for this must be given to our counter-measures, because in principle any German bomber flying on Knickebein ought to have been able to hit a target of about one mile square.

The knowledge that Knickebein was jammed spread through the Luftwaffe and there was a story current at the time that although the pilots were well aware of it, no one wanted to take the responsibility of telling Goering, with the result that Knickebein was persisted in for the next two months although it was substantially useless. Dr. Plendl, who was responsible for much of German beam development, told me after the war that ultimately special listening sorties were sent out to check the crews' reports, and that the German scientists came to the conclusion that the beams were not merely jammed but bent.

But although Knickebein was now effectively countered by the

'Aspirins', we had still not seen what a Knickebein beam station looked like. Aerial photography had been neglected between the wars by the R.A.F., and it was left to individual and unorthodox initiative to overcome the deficiency; and since photographic reconnaissance was to play a vital part in my later work, it is worth recounting how this work benefited from my association with Fred Winterbotham.[1] About the time of Munich he had approached a buccaneering Queenslander, Sidney Cotton, who had been a pilot in the Royal Naval Air Service. Cotton was already well known for the development of the 'Sidcot' flying suit and was currently involved in marketing the Dufay process of colour photography. Winterbotham obtained the money for Cotton to purchase an aircraft and to make unofficial flights over Germany to photograph various items of interest.

In the few days before the actual outbreak of war, Cotton succeeded in photographing Wilhelmshaven, and it soon became clear that he was better at operating both cameras and aircraft than the regular Air Force. The latter's cameras suffered, for example, from condensation on the lenses and other components in the low temperatures prevailing at altitude: Cotton's mechanical and physical insight enabled him to remedy these faults by ducting warm air to flow around the cameras, and thus to operate R.A.F. cameras when the R.A.F. itself could not. In addition, Cotton recognized the importance of speed, and he succeeded in getting an extra 20 or 30 m.p.h. out of aircraft such as the Blenheim by removing excrescences, and giving the surface a smooth gloss finish.

Before long the Air Force was brought to admit the effectiveness of Cotton's treatment, and he persuaded Dowding to let him have two Spitfires from Fighter Command. By 'Cottonizing' he improved their speed from 360 to 396 m.p.h., and his next problem was to get adequate cameras installed. The original R.A.F. cameras had been F24's with lenses of 8-inch focal length; but these gave much too little detail to see objects of less than about 30-feet diameter on photographs taken from the operational height of thirty thousand feet.

He therefore wanted to install larger cameras, and he told me how he had succeeded in getting Farnborough to install two 20-inch focal length cameras into a Spitfire. The authorities at Farnborough had said that this could not be done because the cameras had to be installed behind the pilot, and that the weight of two cameras, about 120 lbs., would pull

---

[1] I am also grateful to him for my introduction to Broadway and Bletchley and to Barnes Wallis, whose ideas about big bombs were forwarded to the Air Staff through Winterbotham.

back the centre of gravity of the aircraft making it 'tail heavy' and dangerous to fly. Since he was dependent on Farnborough for the actual installation, Cotton could do nothing but profess to accept their ruling. He therefore sent one of the Spitfires to Farnborough for fitting, and he was duly told that the aircraft was ready.

He went to Farnborough himself, and met the men who had done it. He anxiously asked them whether they had tested it in flight and whether the centre of gravity was all right. They told him that it was, but that of course it would not have been had they acceded to his original request to fit two cameras instead of one. 'You are absolutely satisfied that the aircraft is okay?' he asked, and when they assured him that it was he then said, 'Well, now take off that tail panel!' When they asked him why, he merely insisted that they should do as he said. The removal of the panel revealed a 20 lb. lead weight attached to the tail which he had placed there before he delivered the aircraft to Farnborough. He told them that since they had now agreed that the aircraft was safe with one camera and 20 lbs. of lead in the tail, this would have pulled the centre of gravity as far back as the 60 lbs. weight of a second camera situated alongside the first, and he therefore demanded that the second camera be installed.

There is a twist to the story. In 1952 Churchill asked me to spend a year or so back from my University in the Ministry of Defence, to see what could be done to bring Intelligence back to its wartime efficiency; as a result, I was able to give only a few lectures to my students in that year. These were therefore summary lectures on topics that I thought would be useful, and one was on simple physical principles which I had myself found to be of great use in practical applications. Among these were centres of gravity, my thesis being that although calculations of centres of gravity were a dull process of seemingly little importance, there were many occasions when the exact location of a C.G. was vital, and I told the story of Cotton and his cameras. To add to the colour of the story I mentioned that the last I had heard of Cotton, whom I did not mention by name, was gun-running in the Mediterranean.

After the lecture one of the students who, as many were, was an ex-Serviceman, came up and asked me, 'Was your friend's name Sidney Cotton, sir?' When I replied that it was, the student said, 'In that case, sir, I can cap your story! In 1948 Cotton was running guns into Hydera-bad, and I was Flying Control Officer on the airfield where his aircraft used to land. On one flight he was flying in a field gun, which must have broken from its fixings, and moved as the aircraft came in to land. The result was that the aircraft became tail heavy and crashed, killing the crew.' So Cotton's encounters with centres of gravity did not always have a fortunate ending.

I was once more to hear of him, and of his Hyderabad venture when I encountered yet another buccaneer who had joined forces with him in order to evacuate the Nyzam of Hyderabad at the time of the Indian take-over in 1948. The idea was that Cotton would provide the air lift, and the second buccaneer would make arrangements for accommodating the Nyzam in the manner to which he had been accustomed. The proposal was that they should rent one of King Farouk's palaces in Egypt, and the second buccaneer approached the King. I cannot recall all the details, but the buccaneer told me that the King's terms were that 'I want 25 percent of all he brings out' and the buccaneer had replied '25 percent of one hundred million pounds, Your Majesty, is a lot!' The transaction was duly made, but not taken up because the Nyzam insisted on staying to say a last prayer as the Indian Forces were approaching, and the buccaneers had to escape without him.

But returning to the war, what the Royal Air Force had failed to realize was that photographic reconnaissance was a specialized activity well worth thought and trouble, and not just a backwater for personnel who were not much good for anything else—and the same applied to a greater or lesser degree to the attitude of the Services to all forms of Intelligence activity. Cotton, who had a genius for getting things done—and frequently doing them himself—had seen where the effort needed to be made; fast high flying aircraft of long range, with good cameras and outstanding pilots, and with specialist interpreters for examining the photographs. Before long, his irregular methods were too much for the R.A.F. and he was 'organized out' of his leadership of photographic reconnaissance. He had a raw deal, for his contribution was great: and I for one am glad to have known him.

On 8th September Enigma gave us the pinpoint to the nearest mile of the Cherbourg Knickebein as 49° 40·5′ north 1° 51′ west, and it should surely be visible on the 20-inch focal length photographs that, thanks to Cotton, were then becoming available. Nothing was reported by the interpreters, but I was in a better position to examine the photographs because I had at least some idea of what I was looking for: either a 'squat tower' or, more probably, some form of turntable. During a daytime raid on about 17th September, when we had to take cover in the basement, I took a collection of photographs of the Hague

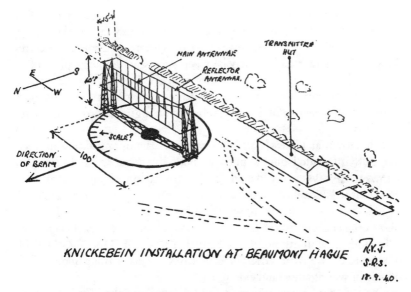

KNICKEBEIN INSTALLATION AT BEAUMONT HAGUE

R.V.J.
S.R.S.
18.9.40.

Fig. 2a Tentative sketch of a Knickebein beam transmitter made from the vertical air
reconnaissance photograph at Plate 5a

Fig. 2b. What this particular transmitter really looked like; but see Plate 5d for a Knickebein transmitter that more closely resembled the upper sketch

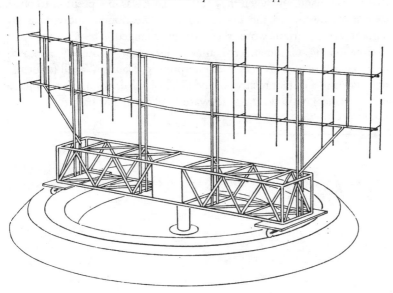

peninsula with me to make some use of my small space in the crowded cellar. Ultimately I spotted an object which looked rather like one of the circular filter beds of a sewage farm, with an arm some 30 metres long across it that had rotated between successive photographs just as the sprinkler arm of a sewage farm would do. But this was no sewage farm—it had not been there on photographs taken on 20th June—it must be the turntable of the Knickebein with a girder across it carrying the aerials.

It is shown at Plate 5(a); Figure 2a shows the optimistically detailed sketch that I made from the photograph, while Figure 2b and Plate 5(b) shows what it was really like. Plate 5(d) shows a low oblique photograph of the large Knickebein, 100 metres across, probably the one near Cleves, which bears a distinctly closer resemblance to my sketch. Plate 5(c) shows the entrance to the bunker of a second and later Knickebein near Cherbourg, with its pompous legend 'ERBAUT UNTER ADOLF HITLER IN KAMPF GEGEN ENGLAND 1941' ('Built under Adolf Hitler in war against England 1941').

On 18th September I wrote a report describing the identification of Knickebein, thanking the officers who had supplied the photographs. This caused a minor stir at the headquarters of the Photographic Interpretation Unit at Wembley. So far they had not taken my requests as more than a sideshow to the operational demands for photographs of invasion preparation: when they found that I was in a position to write reports going up to the Prime Minister mentioning individuals by name for meritorious work, their attitude changed. The Commanding Officer, Wing Commander Lemnos Hemming, promptly allocated to my work one of his very best interpreters, Claude Wavell (a former surveyor and a distant relative of the Field Marshal, whom he resembled in appearance), who was henceforward to play a major part in my story.

CHAPTER SEVENTEEN

The X-Apparatus

TWO OR three nights before the bombing of London started on 7th September, my sleep was interrupted by an event which made more impression on my memory than any bomb ever did. This was the telephone at my bedside ringing in the small hours of the morning and an excited voice saying, 'This is Norman at Bletchley. We've got something new here. God knows what it is, but I'm sure it's something for you!' By this time I had come to know that, although he was a technical tyro, Norman had a magnificent 'nose' for sensing that something was important even when he understood nothing of it, so I readily agreed to drive to Bletchley in the morning.

The cryptographers had broken a new line of Enigma traffic. There were mentions of beams, including one which said that the beam width was eight to ten seconds of arc, or an angle of one in twenty thousand, which would imply that the beam was no wider than twenty yards at two hundred miles. And there was the electrifying word 'X-GERÄT' which was being fitted to an aircraft with a call sign 6N+LK, which identified it as belonging to Kampf Gruppe 100. The unit had attempted to attack Birmingham on 13th/14th August; and, as we afterwards found, it was their raid on 23rd August that I had witnessed while at Hoar Cross. I quickly correlated the new beams with those which Scott-Farnie told me had just begun to be heard on frequencies around 70 Megacycles per second from the Cherbourg and Calais areas; and I asked Bletchley to put every possible effort into making further breaks into the new line of traffic. In this, I was in a much better position than if I had been simply in the Air Ministry because of the close and informal terms of my relationship with the Bletchley staff that had arisen through Winterbotham's agency.

So the X-Gerät was indeed something distinct from Knickebein, and by 11th September I had circulated my first report. By 24th September we had identified six beams to which the Germans had given the code names of rivers: Weser, Spree, Rhein, Elbe, Isar, and Oder, and we had the exact positions of the first two which were again on the Hague peninsula north-west of Cherbourg. The next three were near Calais, and the last near Brest. Kampf Gruppe 100 seemed to be working in somewhat irregular order through a book of numbered targets, and the chief scientist involved appeared to be a Dr. Kühnhold. We had the actual directions for the beams for 20th September: the Germans had specified them to the nearest five seconds, implying an aiming accuracy of about ten yards at two hundred miles—if they had heeded the same lesson as I had learnt in my school physics of not specifying a measurement to a greater accuracy than your practical achievement would justify.

Could such accuracy be attained with the radio waves of frequencies around 70 Megacycles per second that I had already associated with the X-Gerät (which would have wavelengths around four metres) or would it require still shorter wavelengths of, say, less than a metre? The Germans talked of coarse and fine beams, and the 70 Megacycle beams might be the coarse ones only. Further, there were mentions of centimetres in the Enigma messages. I had already been alarmed by the fact that we had no listening receivers for centimetric waves where, both according to the Oslo Report and to Bainbridge-Bell's examination of the *Graf Spee*, German radar might well be, so I used the centimetric beam possibility as a lever to get a special listening watch on these wavelengths across the Straits of Dover. This watch was undertaken by some young workers from the Telecommunications Research Establishment, including D. J. Garrard and E. G. Ackermann, and it was almost immediately fruitful for they detected radar-type transmissions on a wavelength of 80 centimetres, which appeared to be ranging on our convoys and directing the fire of the German guns.

There was fairly frequent mention of something called 'Anna' and this was usually associated with a number between 10 and 85 which was usually a multiple of 5. By 17th October I had collected the following numbers: 10, 15, 25, 30, 35, 44, 47, 55, 60, 75 and 85. Another set of numbers that I collected at the same time gave the frequencies (such as 8750 kilocycles per second) of crystals that were issued to the beam stations for stabilizing their transmissions. It is normal for the stabilized frequency to be eight times the crystal frequency and if you multiplied the crystal frequencies by 8, you obtained the following series: 66·5, 67·0, 67·5, 68·0, 69·0, 69·5, 70·0, 71·0, 71·1, 71·5, 72·0, 72·5, and 75·0 Megacycles per second (1 Megacycle = 1000 kilocycles, so 8 × 8750 kilocycles = 70·0 Megacycles). The crystals were very much in the range of frequencies of the new beams that we were hearing, and if, as I had come to suspect, 'Anna' represented at least the tuning dial of the aircraft receiver, if not the receiver itself, there ought to be a simple relation between the 'Anna' numbers and the actual frequencies. The chance that the one set should nearly always end in 0 or 5, and the other in 0 or ·5, was so small as to be hardly coincidental, and it was simple to deduce that the 'Anna' reading had to be divided by 10 and either added to or subtracted from some constant number.

One evening when the bombing in Richmond was fairly intense, and Vera and I had joined some neighbours with a flat on the ground floor, I left them and worked in the flat above because I thought that by now there ought to be sufficient numbers to resolve the problem unambiguously. Besides the numbers themselves, I knew that a Feldwebel Schumann had signed a return for three crystals for frequencies 69·5, 70·0, and 71·1; I traced him to the station at den Helder, which then had these three crystals only, and which was ordered to transmit on Anna numbers 30 and 35. I soon found that the constant had to be 66·5 if one tenth of the 'Anna' number had to be added to it or 73·0 if it had to be subtracted. And since I knew that crystals for 75 Megacycles per second existed, the second possibility could be dismissed. I obtained further confirmation from the two crystals whose frequencies were not exact or half integers, and the problem was solved. Looking over the figures in retrospect, it was only on 17th October that we had collected just sufficient figures, and my feeling that the problem could now be solved was purely instinctive—if I had tackled it even the night before I could not have found a unique solution.

A further fact that came out of the 'Anna' numbers was that the fine beams, as well as the coarse, were in the same range of frequencies between 66·5 and 75 Megacycles per second, so that wavelengths below one metre were not employed. It turned out that the occasional mention of centimetres referred to the precision with which a monitoring vehicle was to take up its position a kilometre or so in front of the beam station to align the beam in the desired direction.

A further value of the 'Anna' numbers was that if we could obtain the information in time, among the instructions sent out to the beam stations during the afternoon before a raid, we should be able to tell 80 Wing the frequencies on which they should jam. At first, however, my interpretation of the 'Anna' numbers was not accepted, because there appeared to be frequencies outside the range that I had determined. These, as it transpired, were due to bad measurements of the frequencies of the German beams on the part of our countermeasures organization, a feature that was to plague us through the whole battle. The fault in this case probably lay not with the observers but with the calibration of our receivers which were not up to the German standards of precision.

I had recommended on 11th September that similar countermeasures to those which we were employing against Knickebein should be developed against the X-beams, because even if we were only able to jam the coarse beams this might well stop KGr100 from locating the fine beams. We now knew that similar measures would work against both coarse and fine beams, and Robert Cockburn had the development in hand. Corresponding to the 'Aspirins' for Knickebein he produced the 'Bromides' for the X-system and these began to appear in October. However, they did not seem to have much effect on KGr100 which continued to bomb more or less as it pleased.

I began to think about other countermeasures, encouraged by the fact that a far miss by a bomb intended by Bomber Command for Cherbourg actually hit the second X-beam station on the Hague peninsula, some 20 kilometres away, destroying the station and, unfortunately perhaps, making the Germans think that we knew a great deal about their activities, and leading them to postulate several theories as to how this remarkable feat was accomplished. They proceeded to tighten their security regulations, examining the past history of all the personnel on the stations. I wondered if we could repeat the feat intentionally, by flying along the X-beam ourselves, which should at least lead us directly over the station, and we attempted to do this but without much luck.

During October KGr100 began to drop flares over its targets in England, and Lywood at once hailed this as either a success for our countermeasures, or at least as evidence that the X-beams did not work, because, he argued, the pilots were so unsure of the X-beams that they were dropping flares to find out where they were. I pointed out that we had no evidence that KGr100 had been so far disconcerted by our countermeasures, and that the real explanation might well be that they themselves could locate the targets with the X-beams, and were dropping flares in practice for operations where they would act as pathfinders for their de-Knickerbeined comrades in the rest of the Luftwaffe.

This interpretation did not please Lywood, and added to the unpopularity that I had already acquired in some quarters on the Air Staff shortly after 15th September. Robert Cockburn remembers that when it was claimed by the Air Staff that we had shot down 186 aircraft that day, I stated that we had only found the wreckage of 38 aircraft and that I did not believe that there were more than another 38 in the sea, which was the Air Staff explanation for the discrepancy between claimed certainties and the number that we actually picked up. After the war we found that even my estimate was rather too generous, in that the German losses for the day were no more than 62. The explanation was, of course, that the Air Staff was fooling itself because it was quite unreasonable to expect any pilot who thought that he had destroyed an enemy aircraft to follow it down to the ground and watch it crash, and overclaiming was inevitable. Despite any unpopularity, I survived because war is different from peace: in the latter fallacies can be covered up more or less indefinitely and criticism suppressed, but with the swift action of war the truth comes fairly quickly to light—as Churchill said, 'In war you don't have to be polite, you just have to be right!'

On my advice Lindemann minuted Churchill on 24th October: 'There is some reason to believe that the method adopted is to send a few KGr100 aircraft fitted with special devices to assist in blind bombing on these expeditions in order to start fires on the target which any subsequent machine without special apparatus can use.' And it turns out that on the other side Milch, the Head of the Luftwaffe, was advising Goering that the current policy of night attacks was useless without special radio-beam devices, like the new X-Gerät. He recommended that KGr100 should receive priority in personnel and aircraft, and that attacks should then be possible even on the darkest nights or through cloud.

If only we could decode the Enigma messages in time, we could find where and when KGr100 was going to attack, and so to counter them by having fighters waiting and by having our jamming ready on the right frequencies. This would make great demands on the codebreakers, for the orders did not go out to the beam stations until the afternoon, giving only two or three hours to make the break. But for such a prize they strained every resource of human intelligence and endurance; and it was a great day, late in October, when they achieved this fantastic feat for the first time. Thereafter, they were able to repeat it on about one night in three. I was then able (having first worked out the position of the cross-beam stations near Calais) to tell the Duty Air Commodore at Fighter Command the exact place of attack, the time of the first bomb to within ten minutes or so, the expected ground speed of the bombers, their line of approach to within 100 yards, and their height to within two or three hundred metres. Could any air defence system ask for more? Despite this detailed information—and much to our disappointment—

our nightfighters repeatedly failed to locate KGr100 aircraft, and I almost began to wonder whether the only use the Duty Air Commodore made of my telephone calls was to take a bet with the rest of the Command as to where the target would be for that night.

I could also on these occasions tell 80 Wing the frequencies of all the beams that would be used on the particular night. It may help at this stage if I explain a few details of the X-beam set-up.

In principle, the aircraft had to fly along a beam (Figure 3) that was laid directly over the target (the Director Beam) and release its bombs at a point rather short of the target. The information needed to compute the release point involved the height and speed of the aircraft, and where it was at any instant relative to the target and the type of bombs. The way this information was derived in the X-beam system was to lay two beams across the Director Beam, crossing it at pre-determined distances before the target. In general one, the 'Main Signal', crossed the Director Beam five kilometres before the target and the other, the 'Fore Signal' at twenty kilometres.

While the pilot flew along the Director Beam, either by listening to it or watching a direction indicator, the bomb aimer listened for the cross beams. The time interval between crossing the two beams would be the time taken to cover fifteen kilometres, which gave the aircraft's speed, and the main signal also told him that he was five kilometres away. The problem of determining the release point was simplified by a small mechanical computer involving a stop clock that was started by the bomb aimer as he crossed the Fore Signal and stopped as he crossed the Main Signal; and then, if he had fed in the correct height information from his altimeter, the mechanism would work out by itself when the bombs ought to be released.

Thus, strictly, only three beams were absolutely necessary for the operation of the system, but this was made easier by providing additional beams, one to give a rough indication of where the fine Director Beam lay and the other an additional cross beam to be laid 50 kilometres or so in front of the Fore Signal. A typical layout is shown in Figure 3, which indicates the layout for a raid on Coventry, with the Director Beam coming from near Cherbourg, and the cross beams from near Calais. To provide an insurance against the failure of the Director Beam, which was usually from the station known as Weser, a reserve Director Beam was provided by the nearby station, Spree. Thus on a typical night, with five beams operating (the Main Signal might also be duplicated in addition to the Director Beam) we needed to knock out at least three

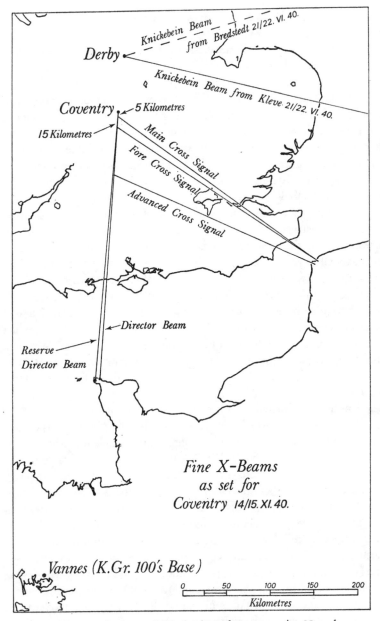

Fig. 3. The X-Beam dispositions for the bombing of Coventry 14/15 November 1940.
Also shown are the two Knickebein beams found by Flight Lieutenant H. E. Bufton and
Corporal Mackie for the night of 21/22 June 1940

beams, preferably the two Directors and one other, if we were to deprive the system of its accuracy.

Incidentally, the potential accuracy of the system was so great that in calculating the paths of the beams, it was necessary to take into account the fact that the earth is not a simple sphere, but is somewhat flattened towards the Poles. This made a difference of three hundred yards or so in where a beam starting from Cherbourg would actually cross London, compared with where one would calculate it to be on the assumption that the earth was a true sphere. It was necessary to be able to perform rapid calculations, working with a spheroid that more accurately approached the true figure of the earth, and I enlisted the help of Colonel C. J. Willis, who was then in charge of Maps in the Air Ministry. He put me in touch with Dr. L. J. Comrie of the Scientific Computing Service, who did most of the work that ultimately led us to establishing the exact positions of the beam stations in the Calais area, as well as enabling me to deduce the nightly targets accurately.

As for the accuracy which KGr100 realized in practice, I doubt whether they ever did as well as they might have hoped, although frequently a few bombs actually fell on the pin-point target. On one occasion, we were able to obtain a clear 'signature' of their efforts, when they attacked a factory in Birmingham on 26th/27th October. We were able to plot all the bombs, with the result shown in Figure 4. The bombs lay in three pencils running roughly south to north, with the central and heavier pencil 150–200 yards east of where we had calculated. The length of the pencils was presumably unintentional, and due to the difficulty of establishing the exact instants of flying through the cross beams. The two side pencils, lying roughly half a mile on either side of the main, have never been explained, either by me or the Germans, who were surprised when I told them after the war. I thought that they must have included a deliberate offsetting device in the X-Gerät so as to be able to mark an area, but this turns out not to have been the case.

If my narrative gives the impression that my work was done in a state of unruffled calm, this would be false. We were bombed, or at least alerted for more than seventy consecutive nights with the exception of 3rd November, and slept on the fifth floor. We did indeed sleep, despite all the noise and risks, because we knew that not to sleep would result in exhaustion; and this—as far as my unravelling of the German systems was concerned—would have been fatal. With the disruption to trains, I had often to use my car, and even then getting to the office was not easy. On one morning after I had crossed northwards over Putney Bridge I

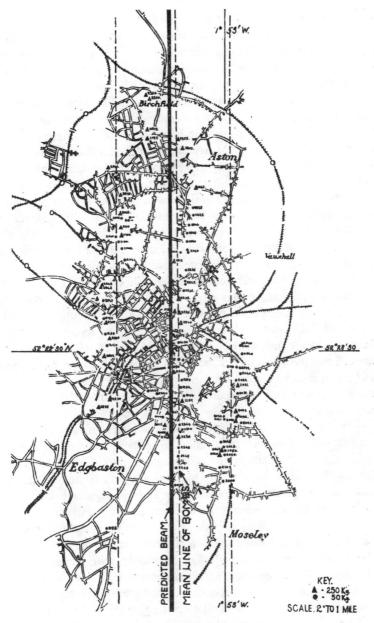

Fig. 4. Plot of bombs dropped on Birmingham on 26/27 October 1940 by Kampfgruppe
100 using X-Beams

found Kings Road blocked, where I would normally have turned east-wards towards Westminster, and indeed all alternative routes blocked right up to Notting Hill Gate, where I finally got through. One of the advantages of the Blitz was that if trains were running people went home so early you could get a seat in the normal rush hour.

Despite the fact that I was a rather vital cog in the defence machine, I had no special privileges. There was indeed talk of giving me a Class C.C. commission in the Royal Air Force at the height of the invasion alarm—but although I would have accepted it if it had materialized I would have felt it was a masquerade, because I had been brought up to regard anyone in uniform who was not in the Front Line as bogus. I had no official transport, either at this time or throughout the war. Indeed, I had no help, apart from what Daisy Mowat was able to give me as secretary when she was not occupied with Fred Winterbotham's work. His Second-in-Command, John Perkins, knowing that I was beginning to predict nightly targets, suggested that one of his officers, Harold Blyth, should be attached to me. Harold, an old Harrovian who thought his greatest achievement was to have clean-bowled Victor Rothschild, was a concrete specialist in private life, and a good draughtsman. He established the format of all my subsequent wartime reports, and intro-duced me to the only type of filing system that I have ever found to work. This consists simply of box files into which papers of any size relevant to a particular subject can be hurriedly deposited. I ended the war with more than four hundred files built up on his system, and I have continued to use it ever since.

Helpful though Harold was, there was obviously going to be a gap if I myself were killed during the Blitz, for nobody but another scientist could know the details of the work, and Fighter Command would therefore have been deprived of some basically very useful information. And so at last I persuaded the Director of Scientific Research, D. R. Pye, to let me have the assistant he had denied me earlier in the year. Naturally I wanted Charles Frank, who by this time had moved to the Chemical Defence Establishment at Porton; he managed to extricate himself and it was arranged that he should join me around 5th November. As recognition of the importance of my work I was promoted as from 11th November to the grade of Senior Scientific Officer, which meant a rise in salary from £575 to £680 per annum.

Before Charles Frank joined me, I accepted an invitation from A. P. Rowe to visit the Telecommunications Research Establishment at Swanage, partly to tell his people about what I had so far found, and

partly to be briefed regarding the newer developments, including what
was happening in generating and using waves of around 10 centimetres
wavelength. Several of us before the war, including Watson-Watt and
myself, had been pressing for new generators of centimetric waves
because this was obviously the way to improve the sharpness of the
information that radar provided, and several laboratories had been put
on to this work at the outbreak of war. A great breakthrough had been
made in Birmingham by Randall and Boot, and this was now being
applied to airborne radar at Swanage. It was to give us a great advantage
in the radio war.

CHAPTER EIGHTEEN

Coventry

BY EARLY November 1940 the X-Beam stations had become so adept at setting and resetting their beams that KGr100 could mount attacks on two targets in succession on the same night: on 4th November Birmingham and Coventry, on 5th November Coventry and Birmingham, on 8th November Liverpool and Birmingham, and on 12th November Liverpool and Coventry. On some of these raids the X-beam flyers may well have been acting as pathfinders for fairly small forces drawn from other bomber units. One homeward bound KGr100 aircraft, call sign 6N+AH, suffered a compass failure on the night of 5th/6th November, and was then misled by our 'masking' of German radio beacons (this was achieved by sending out signals on a British beacon identical to those being sent by the German beacon) into thinking it was over France when it was still over England. Running short of fuel, it landed on the beach near Bridport in Dorset in the early hours of 6th November. It was potentially a unique prize, for it carried a complete X-Gerät; but there then followed an episode as grimly humorous as the Porter's performance in *Macbeth*, and equally incongruous as a prelude to high tragedy.

There are various accounts of what happened but, as I first heard it, the aircraft was found by an Army unit stationed there for coastal defence. The Officer in command left two Other Ranks as guard; he did not, of course, recognize the unique importance of this particular aircraft, with its complete X-Gerät, but he was well aware that it ought to be properly guarded. He left the soldiers with the instruction that they were to let no one touch it until further orders and, unfortunately, added the phrase, 'I don't care if even an Admiral comes along. You are not to allow him near it!'

Now the aircraft had come to rest between high and low water and, as the soldiers watched, the tide inexorably came in. A local naval detachment offered to help the soldiers drag it above high water mark; but the latter, remembering their instructions, stopped the Navy from doing anything, with the result that the whole aircraft was awash. By the time Technical Intelligence officers were available to examine it, all the radio gear was full of sand, and all the light alloy components corroded. This failure to save the aircraft intact may have contributed to the disaster eight days later at Coventry.

Versions of the story of the Coventry raid have recently appeared, in which Churchill is said to have been presented with the dilemma of evacuating Coventry because of our prior knowledge of the raid, or of doing nothing and so preserving the security of our Enigma work. To the best of my knowledge, this is not true, and I will give my account of what happened.

By 6th November I was back in London after the visit to Swanage, and on the afternoon of, I think, Sunday 10th November I received a teleprint of a decoded Enigma signal to the X-beam stations. It had been sent the previous day, and it was most unusual in telling the stations to prepare for operations against three targets numbers 51, 52 and 53. It gave the beam settings for the three targets, and it was only a few minutes' work to find that 51 was Wolverhampton, 52 Birmingham, and 53 Coventry. Instructions for three targets had never been sent out at the same time before: it might be that KGr100 was getting even more ambitious, and intending to attack three targets in one night, but never before had any target instructions been sent out more than a few hours in advance of the attack. Moreover, whereas for the previous month or so all the beam settings had been specified to the nearest second of arc, for the three new targets the settings were merely specified to the nearest minute, implying a coarsening of the accuracy by a factor of 60. Were the seconds to be specified later, or was it that whoever had drawn up the instructions had been as well trained as I had myself in not specifying a higher degree of accuracy than the operation required? I inclined to the latter alternative: remembering that we had already found KGr100 dropping flares, it seemed likely that unless the beam orders were to be made more precise subsequently, the Gruppe was expecting to drop something less accurate than ordinary bombs, which could be either flares or incendiaries. I alerted the proper authorities, for it seemed that the foreshadowed change in German policy was now imminent, but I could not say when or in what order the three targets would be attacked.

There were other signs that a change was in the offing. On 3rd November we had some indication that preparations were being made for an abnormal amount of signals traffic between Luftflotte 2, commanded by Kesselring, and its subordinate formations. And on 11th

November a long Enigma decode of a signal sent on 9th November contained orders for what was evidently to be a very major operation under the code name 'Moonlight Sonata'. KGr100 was to be involved, and among its tasks was to check the positions of the Knickebein beams. Four target areas, A, B, C and D, were mentioned, and there was one inexplicable word which, had we been able to interpret it, could have given us a clue: 'KORN'. It meant 'Corn', and I wondered whether it might be a code name for the appearance of radar screens when jamming was present, which we ourselves often called 'Grass' or when spurious radar reflectors were to be dropped, which although we were subsequently to call them 'Window' received the American code name 'Chaff'. What we did not guess was that it was an alliterative code name for Coventry, which the Germans spelt with a 'K'.

Where were target areas A, B, C and D? Since a map from a crashed aircraft had shown some larger areas thus lettered in the south of England, Wing Commander 'Tubby' Grant of Air Intelligence made a dubious correlation, for the map areas were too large to be suitable as bombing targets; they would have made much more sense as dropping areas for a large airborne invasion. Grant's interpretation was circulated by teleprinter, but it was hard to believe. I would have much more likely believed something that Felkin reported, had I seen it. This was that a prisoner from KG1 had said that the heaviest possible attacks were to be made between 15th and 20th November on Birmingham and Coventry. Grant's interpretation, however, tended to hold the day as far as the Air Staff was concerned, and a series of countersteps was planned on the assumption that the main objectives of Moonlight Sonata were somewhere in the south of England. For some of our proposed counters, these misjudgements hardly mattered: these were the offensive measures against the German bomber bases, and against the beam stations, which were to be attacked by flying specialist bombing aircraft down their own beams, as I had previously suggested.

My own part in the operational story was the detailed forecasting of KGr100's targets on a night-to-night basis; and although I had pointed to the unusual threat to Birmingham, Coventry and Wolverhampton, and to KGr100's pathfinding role, I had no standing in the making of the general Intelligence assessment. If someone had correlated my warning with that of Felkin, and especially if the KG1 prisoner had mentioned Wolverhampton as well (which he did not) thus making the correlation complete, the Air Staff appreciation might have been less in error. Whether or not this would have made much difference to what happened to Coventry is nevertheless doubtful, because we did not yet know the exact order in which the towns were to be attacked, and we might reasonably have expected Wolverhampton to be first; and even if we did know the correct order, both previous and subsequent experience showed that neither our nightfighters nor our guns could seriously damage the Luftwaffe.

On 11th November, while we were speculating about Moonlight Sonata, KGr100 was to have attacked Liverpool (target No. 34) and Coventry (target No. 49, different from 53) but these operations were cancelled on account of weather. The Gruppe came out against these two targets on the following night, and then on 13th November it had no operations. So far there was nothing unusual—the target directions were specified with the old accuracy. By this time Charles Frank was with me, and I had introduced him to the Enigma situation, commenting that—thanks to Bletchley—if we could hold out through the winter we had a chance of winning in the end.

Together we braced ourselves for the following night, and for whatever 'Moonlight Sonata' might mean. It happened to be one of those afternoons when the Enigma signals to the X-beam stations were not broken in time, and we were therefore left guessing. There was, of course, the evidence that could be gathered by flying our own aircraft along the German beams and establishing where they were pointing. Moreover we could listen and obtain the beam frequencies, so that we could set our jammers appropriately. Somewhere between half-past-five and six o'clock Addison telephoned me from his headquarters at 80 Wing asking for my help in deciding the frequencies on to which to set his jammers. He was fairly sure that the target was somewhere in the Midlands, and his problem was to decide which beam was which, and therefore which to try to obliterate with the three or four jammers that he had available. He then read out to me the list of radio frequencies as determined by our listening aircraft. I could see at once that the measurements must be wrong, in that they did not match up with the figures that I knew from the 'Anna' code. I therefore made a mental correction of the measurements as far as I could—for example, 68·6 should probably have been 68·5, if our receivers had been properly calibrated, or 70·9 should have been 71·0. But deciding what, for example, 66·8 meant, was more of a lottery.

The one other clue that I had spotted was that there seemed to be a convention that the director beams would generally be on frequencies between 66·5 and 71·5 and the cross beams between 71·5 and 75·0

6*

Megacycles per second, the division being presumably due to operational convenience. Remembering that we needed to knock out the main and reserve director beams and at least one of the cross beams, I then made my mental gamble, and suggested a set of frequencies to Addison which he said he would adopt. All this took no more than five minutes on the telephone: but I was well aware that in these snap decisions I was probably gambling with hundreds of lives. Sobering though this thought was, the fact remained that someone had to do it, and I was easily in the best position.

Because of the abruptness in his move to London, Charles Frank was staying with Vera and me, and I can recall driving back with him to Richmond and wondering, as we passed in bright moonlight through Roehampton, where the target really was. I for one did not know, and I do not think that anyone else did, either. Certainly I have no recollection of Coventry being mentioned in an Enigma message in the way that some accounts have stated; the teleprinter room into which the messages came was immediately across the corridor from my own, and no message mentioning Coventry was brought to me, as it certainly should have been if it had existed. As for any argument as to whether or not Coventry might have been forewarned, I knew nothing of it.

The suggestion that Churchill was warned in the afternoon that the target was Coventry, and that he then had to decide whether the city should be warned or not, has been effectively disposed of in a review in *The Times Literary Supplement* for 28th May 1976 by Sir David Hunt, at one time his Secretary, drawing on evidence of Sir John Colville who was on duty at No. 10 Downing Street on the night in question. Churchill that afternoon had set out from London for Ditchley Park (the house a few miles north of Oxford which he used as a retreat in place of Chequers on moonlit nights) when he opened his box containing the latest Enigma decodes. A heavy raid was foreshadowed, and Churchill at once turned the car back to London. To those of us who knew him this could mean only one thing: he thought that the attack was to be on London and that his duty, in character with his lifelong inclination, was to be where the fight was hottest. This conclusion is borne out by Sir John Martin, who was with him as Secretary in the car, and by the fact that he sent Colville and Martin to take refuge in the deep air raid shelter at Down Street Underground Station, telling them that their young lives were valuable for Britain's future, while he went up onto the Air Ministry roof.

For myself, I spent a very uneasy night, wondering whether my gamble had been right, and switched on the wireless for the eight o'clock news, only to learn that a city in the Midlands had been heavily bombed. I forget whether the news mentioned Coventry at that stage, but it was evidence enough that the gamble had failed. There were 554 killed and 865 seriously injured. It would have been tremendous luck if I had in fact guessed the beam frequencies correctly, but I felt very miserable at having been instrumental in a negative way in contributing to the disaster.

My wretchedness turned to bewilderment when, later in the day, the Enigma signals to the beam stations for the Coventry raid, target No. 53, were decoded. It turned out that, by luck, I had guessed the frequencies correctly. But in that case, where had the failure been?

The answer came some days later when on 21st November Frank, Scott-Farnie, and I visited Addison in his headquarters at Radlett. By that time, the aircraft at Bridport had been salvaged, and the X-Gerät receiver had been taken to 80 Wing. There it was, full of sand and corrosion, with its dial covered up so that we could only see one number. I commented to Addison, 'It's a funny thing, but I have never known an "Anna" number to be above 85. Could your chaps get the cover off so that we can see whether it stops at 85 or goes up to 100?' We had lunch, and when we returned there was the exposed dial: 85 was indeed the top number. This, of course, hardly increased our knowledge; but what did so was an investigation of the filters which were fitted to the receiver to let through the audible notes of the beams as the pilot listened in his headphones but to exclude any note that sounded differently. Moreover there was a course indicating meter which would tell the pilot whether he was to the right or left of the beam, and this was insensitive to any sound that did not get through the filters.

In a commendably thorough examination which must have played its part in the later successes of our X-beam countermeasures, the Royal Aircraft Establishment at Farnborough found that the filter was tuned to two thousand cycles per second, a high-pitched note corresponding roughly to the top 'C' on a piano. Our jammers had been set not on this note but on one of fifteen hundred cycles per second, corresponding to the 'G' below top 'C'. So the filter could distinguish between the true beam and our jamming, even though we had got the radio frequencies correct.

It was one of those instances, of which I have since found many, where enormous trouble is taken to get the difficult parts right and then a slip-up occurs because of lack of attention to a seemingly trivial detail. Of all the measurements in connection with the German beams, easily the simplest was to determine the modulation note, because this could be done at any time in comfort; and yet whoever had done it had either been tone deaf or completely careless, and no one had ever thought of checking his measurements. I was so indignant that I said that whoever had made such an error ought to have been shot.

My anger was increased by the prevarication I then encountered. The argument was that the Germans originally had their modulation on fifteen hundred cycles per second, which had been correctly measured, and they had changed their filters in order to avoid our jamming. But, if so, then we should have noticed the change in modulation of the German beams; and I finally managed to prove that KGr100 had had the same set of filters ever since the beginning of their operations. So that defence was untenable.

What made things worse was that the countermeasures organization was already claiming successes in jamming the X-beams, when there was no evidence whatever of this either in the Enigma traffic or in failures of KGr100 to find its targets. This was the second time (the first being the 186 aircraft that we did not shoot down) I had to insist on facts because officers were kidding themselves. I have no doubt that had I been part of the countermeasures organization, instead of having an independent voice through Intelligence up to the Chief of Air Staff, my criticisms would have been suppressed.

An alternative defence was that even if the jamming had been perfect, Kampf Gruppe would still have found Coventry because it was a bright moonlit night. Some nightflyers maintain this point, while others say that from eighteen thousand feet towns are only visible when seen against the moon, and so could not be attacked from the south by flying along the beam. One relevant fact is that on a later raid, when KGr100 attempted to bomb Derby on a similarly moonlit night (8th/9th May 1941) but when radio countermeasures were effective, the bombs intended for Derby fell on Nottingham, and those intended for Nottingham fell on open country.[1]

After Coventry, the Germans mounted a similar large attack on Birmingham under the code-name 'Regeschirm'. Since this was the

[1] One problem still remaining in the Coventry postmortem was: where had areas A, B, C and D been? From what we obtained from a captured map of a later raid, they were probably each 3·5 kilometres long × 2 kilometres wide, situated quadrantally about the aiming point with their longer sides parallel to the director beam, making a total target area 7 kilometres long × 4 kilometres wide.

German for umbrella, which was associated with Neville Chamberlain, who in turn was associated with Birmingham, someone at Bletchley correctly guessed the target. As foreshadowed, the Kampf Gruppe 100 target was No. 52, and it was attacked on 19th and 20th November. On the latter night, at least, Bletchley broke the target instructions some hours before the raid, but again our defences could achieve little. As I thought about the target during the night, the obvious thought occurred: first target No. 53, now 52—it left only target 51, Wolverhampton. At least we could be ready for that one.

Officers at Anti-Aircraft Command who knew of my work had told me that if only I could give them twelve hours warning, as opposed to the two or three hours that at most were usually possible, they would move anti-aircraft guns to wherever I said. I therefore telephoned the Command and told them to move guns to Wolverhampton. This was the day on which I was to visit Addison at Radlett, and so before leaving the Air Ministry, I made a point of seeing Sir Philip Joubert, one of the liveliest of Air Marshals, and told him why I thought Wolverhampton was 'for it'. He reacted suitably, and the result was that our defences were braced as never before for a raid on a particular target. And then—nothing happened.

Those whom I was myself criticising for their previous mistakes immediately seized their opportunity to turn the tables: I had alarmed and upset the defences of the whole country on a false deduction, and even some of my friends were not anxious to discuss the matter for the next week or so. And then I had an enthusiastic telephone call from Felkin, who said, 'You know that you were saying that there was to be a big raid on Wolverhampton and that nothing happened. Well, we've overheard a conversation between two prisoners. One said he was in the Coventry raid and what a good show it was. The other said he was in the Birmingham raid. The first then said that there was to have been a similar raid on Wolverhampton under the code name "Einheitspreis".' Felkin explained that 'Einheitspreis' meant 'unit price', as at Woolworths, where most things cost sixpence, and this was the obvious link between the code word and the town.

I do not know at which stage the attack was cancelled, but in a further check on security of the X-beam stations, it was stated that German photographic reconnaissance had shown that anti-aircraft batteries were installed in apparent anticipation of a large and already scheduled raid. And, in contrast to all the other 40 or so targets for which we had intercepted the beam instructions, target No. 51 was never attacked.

CHAPTER NINETEEN

Target No. 54

TRAVIS AT Bletchley was very anxious that I should pay another visit to tell his staff about the use I was making of their information; and this, of course, I very readily agreed to do. Bletchley was divided into various 'Huts'; and Hut 3, to whom I had spoken previously, was primarily concerned with taking the rawly decoded messages from the Enigma codebreakers, and passing them on, after classification, to whomever was entitled to see them. Norman, for example, had thus become in effect my agent in Hut 3. But there was some degree of feeling between the huts; in particular Hut 6, whose staff did the actual codebreaking, may have felt that Hut 3 was getting the kudos while Hut 6 was doing the hard work. And so on the morning of 28th November I drove down to Bletchley with Charles Frank and gave Hut 6 an account of what I had been doing.

At lunch, I encountered Malcolm Saunders and some of my other friends in Hut 3 who were upset that I had been to Bletchley without Hut 6 letting them know. They therefore demanded that I should stay for the afternoon and lecture to them all over again. On the personal side, I could see trouble ahead, because I could certainly not get back to London before nightfall, and there was quite a chance that London would be raided that night, and Vera, already six months pregnant, would be left by herself. However, there was no doubt where duty lay: I was enormously indebted to Hut 3, as the whole country would have been had it known of the work that was being done, and I owed it to them to let them see how things were going. So we did not get away from Bletchley until about 4.30.

Realizing that I would be driving against traffic streaming out of London in anticipation of the nightly air raid, I checked that my headlamps, which were feeble enough anyway with their wartime screens, were pointing well down so that I should not blind anybody coming the other way. The result was that I was repeatedly dazzled by the ill-adjusted lamps of oncoming cars. Finally, just where the A5 road narrows on the northern outskirts of St. Albans there was a particularly dazzling chain of vehicles coming northwards, and I could hardly see ahead at all. Suddenly I saw the rear wheels of a lorry in front of me, and braked hard. It was much too late and we crashed.

The rear of the lorry, which should have been painted white, was so covered with mud that it was hardly visible, and the lorry had been left by its driver who, thinking that he might be running out of petrol although he still had some left, had gone off to find a supply. We were doing less than fifteen miles an hour, but there was so little time for braking that my own car was a complete wreck. Charles and I both went through the windscreen; he had a cut over his eye and I had one in the middle of my forehead, and all due to a driver who had panicked.

Granted this disaster, we were then distinctly fortunate. We had crashed precisely outside St. Albans' Hospital, and we walked into the casualty ward and were stitched up. We were then taken to the police station, where I telephoned Vera. The raid had in fact started before we crashed, but she was going to join neighbours downstairs. I remembered that my old pupil, Mark Meynell, was a curate in St. Albans' Cathedral: he had two spare beds for the night, and so we stayed with him. I also knew that Winterbotham's driver, Mrs. Yvonne Vereker, lived in St. Albans. She was able to pick us up in the morning and so we arrived in the office at the normal hour, bandaged and with pronounced headaches, but with no loss of working time.

During the morning, Scott-Farnie told me that there was to be a conference at Fighter Command on the following day on the best way of making use of the beam information that I was providing, and that the Commander-in-Chief would be glad if I would attend. Scott-Farnie himself would be going and would have a staff car. He would route the car through Richmond to pick me up and he asked how he would find my flat. I told him that he should drive up Richmond Hill until he came to a large U-shaped block of flats, with a tennis court between the arms of the U. 'You can't miss it,' I said, 'because at the entrance there is a large clock at one end of the tennis court.' And so we agreed to meet in the morning.

Earlier in the week, on 25th November, Sir Hugh Dowding had been replaced as Commander-in-Chief at Fighter Command. Personally, I was sorry to see 'Stuffy' go. I had been with Lindemann and Watson-Watt when the press announcement was made, and Watson-Watt was quite pleased. I defended 'Stuffy' for his forthrightness (incidentally I knew that when Watson-Watt had offered him some hundreds of airborne radar sets 'Stuffy' had said, 'Give me ten that work!'). But Watson-Watt said that he had been unreceptive to new ideas. Most of the argument had been over whether Dowding was right in his method of intercepting German day raids on the way in. Leigh Mallory and Douglas Bader had advocated mass formations of fighters, which inevitably took time to assemble, and which could therefore only attack bombers on the way out, and they may have had the ear of those higher up. One further factor might have been the failure of Fighter Command by night. Certainly the new Commander-in-Chief, Sir Sholto Douglas, who as Deputy of Air Staff had known of my work, was concerned about the little use that so far seemed to have been made of my information, and it was for this reason that he had ordered a conference.

It was going to be an interesting weekend. Besides the Fighter Command conference on the Saturday morning, we were to have Charles' wife Maita, join us in Richmond.

Maita had stayed in Salisbury because she was nervous about London, but she wanted to come for a sample weekend, and when would I recommend? No one was in a better position than I to give advice on this matter, and I suggested that she should come for the weekend beginning on 29th November, when there would be no moon, because the German Air Force was tending to concentrate its heavy attacks on moonlit nights; but that was before Coventry which, although it was of course a moonlit night, showed the Luftwaffe that they could now attack on dark nights, using KGr100 as pathfinders.

Maita arrived in Richmond some time on the Friday afternoon, and Charles and I left the office about six o'clock, having now, of course, to travel by train since we had left the car wrecked in St. Albans. About twenty past six, while we were in the train, the sirens went, and we arrived home about twenty minutes later. Vera had dinner ready, and we sat down to soup. Bombs began to fall, and were getting alarmingly close; but knowing that we had a nervous visitor, we pretended that this was absolutely normal, even though we were on the top floor and the building was at times swaying so much that the soup was slopping about in the bowls. And then we heard a noise that is unforgettable to anyone who has experienced it, sounding rather like ghosts in hollow chains rattling across the roof. Having once had an incendiary fall within three yards of me, I knew what it must be, and I went over to the back door of the flat, from which we used to admire the view across to Windsor Castle.

The sight was fantastic—a panorama stretching far away to Kew Gardens, with all the domes, spires, and trees silhouetted in the pale blueish light from the ignited incendiaries which had been strewn everywhere, with here and there the orange glow of a fire that had already started. I recognized the handiwork of KGr100, and therefore what we were in for. I called the others to the door, saying, 'Come quickly, this is a sight you may never see again!' And then after a few spellbound seconds I said, 'Now run downstairs like hell!' We rushed down the darkened stairs, but we were not completely down to the ground floor when there was a tremendous noise, the building swayed violently backwards and forwards, and all the lights went out. We had been straddled by a stick of four 500 lb. bombs, two of which had fallen on the tennis court and burst in the garage underneath, demolishing the clock tower that I had told Scott-Farnie he couldn't miss. The same evidently applied to the Luftwaffe.

The first bomb had killed several people in a dug-out in the Earl Haig poppy factory across the road and the last bomb had missed us on the other side of the flat by no more than seven yards. Fortunately it had burst in soft earth, sending most of the explosive upwards. One of the two bombs in the tennis court must have come off somewhat early, otherwise it would have hit us directly. A curious feature of the explosions was that all the handles of the casement windows on one side of the building were bent back outwards through the adjacent panes, and these were the only panes lost.

The raid still had a long time to go, but all of us in the flats rallied in the way that people do. The flicker of a candle appeared in the bottom flat and Mrs. Butler, the frail but imperturbable occupant, invited us all in. Our companions were a select lot—selected by the simple test of refusing to budge from London after nearly three months of bombing. With Mrs. Butler were her teenage daughter June, and a rather exotic child psychiatrist, Madam Foussé. From the flat opposite there was Miss Loman, who worked in a bank, and from the flat above Mrs. Butler were a couple in their sixties, the Bryants, whose son Denys, was out at the time with the Auxiliary Fire Service, and whose daughter-in-law, Lilian, a girl of magnificent courage and humour, was driving an ambulance. From the flat opposite the Bryants there were the Radcliffs; and neither of them said much but quietly stuck it out. Finally, there were the four of us intent on our quiet weekend.

Somehow Madam Foussé got enough heat to boil a kettle, even though all the grates were stacked high with dislodged soot, and made tea. Tradition in this situation clearly expected my mouthorgan, and so I began to play. When I ran out of breath, we took to story-telling; quite the best that night was one told us by Madam Foussé. She had at one time lived in a flat in San Francisco with a companion, and they had been shopping in a drug store. Among other things she had bought a loofah sponge which she left for her maid to unpack from her shopping bag. Madam Foussé noticed that the loofah did not duly appear in the bathroom, and she wondered what had happened to it. She was served it at dinner, steamed and with white sauce.

Thoughts of bathrooms made me wonder what had happened to our water supply. It was almost certain that our mains had been cut, and we might well be in difficulty, especially if a fire started. I therefore climbed the stairs by the light of the fires outside, and went back to our own flat to fill the bath with water. It seemed to take a very long time, as there was only a slow trickle of rusty water, but eventually the bath was full. The flat was still shaking with the thud of bombs; we had three further sticks within a hundred yards, and furniture was thrown about the rooms, fortunately with little damage. I then went downstairs again, and started a second round on the mouthorgan.

Suddenly someone fresh burst in through the door. It was Mrs. Anderson, the resident in the one other occupied flat in the block whom we had assumed to be away when she failed to appear with the rest of us. She was notorious for her stream of complaints to the management about almost everything from the behaviour of the porters to the sticking of the lifts, and the noise from other people's wireless sets, including mine. She was well known, not only in our own block of flats but in most of the others owned by the same syndicate.

We were not surprised now to find her hysterical. At least, that is what we thought she was when she burst in with 'Ealing cemetery's on fire!' Actually, it was quite true. She had been visiting another part of London and had tried to make her way home through the raid. She had come as far as she could by bus, and then had to walk through the brunt of the raid in Richmond. Incendiaries had fallen in Ealing cemetery and the grass, uncut for lack of labour, was long and dry, so that the cemetery really was in flames. Mrs. Anderson was one of those who complain unceasingly about the pin-pricks of life, but who have tremendous guts when there is a real disaster to face. She was actually quite calm and collected, and not at all unnerved by walking alone through the blazing streets of Richmond, with the bombs still falling.

Gradually the intensity of bombing died away; and by three o'clock we were able to get some sleep. Charles and I, of course, had to be up at the normal time the next morning, because Scott-Farnie was coming to take us to Fighter Command. He finally appeared climbing over the rubble that surrounded us, having searched in vain for the clock tower.

I could hardly have been in a more suitable mood for attending a conference at Fighter Command to discuss what use the Command was making of the information that I had been supplying. Charles and I both had bandaged heads and headaches from the car crash. The Senior Air Staff Officer, Air Marshal Douglas Evill, was in the Chair, and I said very little until the end of the meeting. I was not altogether satisfied with the way things had gone, and I finally said that I would like to know just what the Command had so far been doing with the information, since I could see very little result. The Air Marshal gave the usual stalling reply that I must realize that mine was not the only information which the Command had available, and that they had to take this other information into account when making their dispositions. My intervention had caused something of an uncomfortable stir among the Command representatives and I could feel their relief at the skilful reply of the Air Marshal, but I knew that it was untrue and I made a direct counter: 'In that case, sir, I have evidently overrated the importance of what I and my sources have been doing. We have a good many other things to do, and if you can get most of what you want in other ways, I will redirect my sources on to other problems.' This did the trick, for the Air Marshal then saw that the Command would be left without its main source of information for making its nightly dispositions, and he capitulated. The Command was very attentive to us after that.

After lunch we returned home, to find that the water had indeed been cut off, and I went proudly into our bathroom to contemplate my prize, gained at such a risk. The bath was empty. I asked what had happened to it. Vera said, 'Oh, it was full of dirty water, so I emptied it.' For days we had to traipse for water down six flights of stairs and hundreds of yards to a stand pipe in the road. Life between us has never been quite the same since.

When we went to the office the following day, the relevant Enigma signals had been decoded. The target number for our lively night had been No. 54. It would have been flattering, and disturbing, if I myself had been the main objective; but, as far as we could see, the intended aiming point was situated some hundreds of yards away in Richmond Park. The only explanation that I have ever been able to offer is that the

Germans did indeed suspect that there was an underground factory in the Park. I have sometimes wondered what I would have done had the Enigma messages been decoded, as so often happened, before we went home.

CHAPTER TWENTY

The Atrocious Crime

EVEN THOUGH we now had the radio and audio frequencies of the X-beam correct, and although Bromide jammers were now in operation, there was still little sign in early December that our countermeasures were troubling KGr100. Our remaining defect probably lay in the simple operation of picking up the German beams on a receiver, noting the dial reading and converting this to a frequency, and then setting a jammer on this same frequency. Put simply, British instruments were not as precise as they were supposed to be—and many people may have died as a result. I myself had been interested in many aspects of precision before the war, from straightening the ranks at Trooping the Colour to making accurate measurements in science: but even if I had had no previous inclination in that direction, the experience of Coventry and the other cities would have burnt precision into my mind.

The countermeasures organization was nevertheless claiming success. It even argued that the Coventry raid was evidence for the success of countermeasures because KGr100's accuracy had been destroyed so that they could do nothing more precise than fire-raising. In a way, Coventry was indeed evidence of success, not against KGr100 but against Knickebein, the countering of which had forced the Luftwaffe to use KGr100 in a different role from that originally intended. But if Round One in the Battle of the Beams had resulted in the defeat of Knickebein, Round Two against the X-Gerät had gone heavily in favour of the Germans. Once again, the importance of an independent voice was vital, as Churchill himself had commented in writing of Haig in the first war: 'The temptation to tell a Chief in a great position the things he most likes to hear is the commonest explanation of mistaken policy. Thus the outlook of the leader on whose decisions fateful events depend is usually far more sanguine than the brutal facts admit.'

Nothing but detailed chapter and verse would enable me to pin down those in the countermeasures organization who were painting too rosy a picture: the most effective way would be, I thought, to write a full report. This took all the December evenings at Richmond. The report ran to twenty thousand words and covered all aspects of the X system, both technical and operational, as we then knew them. Entirely written in longhand, it was typed by Daisy Mowat direct from my manuscript. I can still see her with duplicator ink smeared over her elegantly groomed and smiling face in the rush to get it finished. Harold Blyth drew the diagrams, Claude Wavell provided the photographs, and Charles Frank contributed an Appendix on the theory of bombing on the X system. Together we assembled and stapled some thirty copies and gave them as wide a circulation as I dared in view of the security. This obviously took time; the report was only finished on 12th January 1941, and action had to be taken well before then. Although hitherto I had always observed Benjamin Franklin's dictum that 'I shall never ask, never refuse, nor ever resign an office' I felt that the time had come to demand more power.

Although I had now been in Air Intelligence for more than a year I had never met the Director, Air Commodore Boyle; nor, for that matter, had I met Stewart Menzies. When the Air Ministry was split into two in the summer of 1940 the Directorate of Scientific Research to which, strictly speaking, I belonged, had been transferred to the Ministry of Aircraft Production, and so I was technically in a different Ministry from the Air Staff. I would have a better say if I had a recognized position on the Air Staff, and shortly before Christmas I asked to see Boyle and Pye. Both interviews were arranged for Boxing Day.

To my surprise, Boyle was full of enthusiasm, telling me that what I had done was the finest piece of Intelligence he had ever seen, and that he would very readily agree to my becoming one of his Assistant Directors. I also saw Pye; and so arrangements for my official transfer to the Air Staff could be put in train. In the meantime, I was working to complete my report on the X-beams, and this appeared on 12th January 1941, before any transactions between the two Directors had got very far.

Besides the details of the X-beam system the report outlined the principles of countermeasures policy:

14.2 There are three possible aims of countermeasures: (1) To mislead the enemy, so that he erroneously thinks that he has attacked the correct target; (2) To induce a mistrust in his pilots, so that they are not sure whether to believe their instruments and/or their senses, and thus jeopardize their efficiency; (3) To wreck the particular system of instrumental aids employed in such a crude and rapid way that the enemy knows that they are useless, so that his staff may be discouraged from developing similar aids. . . .

14.4 With the X–Gerät, we have fallen between two stools because we have probably not discouraged the Germans from beam bombing. They will hope to repeat their transient success, with an improved system. With Knickebein, our crude methods have probably led them to discard the idea of ever again putting such a system into the entire bombing force—at least during the present war. We must therefore expect from time to time to be faced with small formations using specialized methods, and we will be forced to counter them in turn, or we can use crude but rapid counters: if we succeed in killing three methods as soon as they are tried on us, we shall have established a moral superiority which may lead the German staff to abandon all hope of developing a successful method. This is going to make great demands on Intelligence, and on a countermeasure organization, and will require the best technical assistance that can be obtained. The war can be lost without a good, clear thinking, Countermeasure Policy.

The report had a little light relief in the misfortunes of Feldwebel Ostermeier, where after describing the X-beam transmitters in France it went on:

8.7 In addition to the above stations, there are other transmitters in Germany, which are used to establish a system of beams on which the crews of K.Gr.100 can practise. The source of the director beam is at Klein Helle, N.W. of Neubrandenburg. This station was under the charge of Feldwebel Ostermeier, whose misfortunes and plaintive garrulity rival those of Donald Duck. He seems to be well known throughout the whole company for his comic stupidity, and those in charge of the other stations delight in sending him dud equipment. The month of October was particularly unfortunate for Ostermeier, as he started it by receiving a complete transmitting set which was defective in so many ways that no one piece of the apparatus could be tested individually. He then waged an epic struggle in which he no sooner put one component right than another went wrong, while the replacements which he ordered from the stores at Koethen repeatedly arrived in unsound condition. At last the transmitter worked: within a day it had broken down again. Koethen then came to his assistance and on 14.10.40, one transmitter was working fairly satisfactorily, but by the end of the month, Ostermeier was in trouble again, describing his plight in somewhat euphonious letters to the stores. About this time he began to express fears about the effects the ravages of the winter might have on his monitoring vans, and was trying to get huts built for them. It is not known whether he was successful, for at the end of November he was removed and sent to HITLER[1] (the beam station, not the Führer) by an exasperated senior officer. The reason for his removal was that K.Gr.100 had been asked to give a demonstration to Reichsmarshall Goering, and required the practice stations to be operating at their best. The use of the French stations working over France had been contemplated, but as they had been sited for forward transmission over England only, the proposal fell through. The demonstration had therefore to be made at the practice stations, and the presence of Feldwebel Ostermeier was thought not to be conductive to maximum efficiency. It was with sincere regret that we heard of his passing to a subordinate position.

The trickiest part of the report was how to criticize our own countermeasures organization. I thought that this might best be done by following Hamlet—the play's the thing . . . so I wrote the minutes of an imaginary German Air Staff conference under the chairmanship of the Director of Signals on the future of the beams:

13.1 The chairman's introductory remarks would probably be to the effect that while the British had wrecked Knickebein, they had fortunately been surprisingly slow in countering the X–Gerät. They were now, however, seriously interfering with the present X-beam transmissions, and the meeting had been called to discuss future policy.

13.2 Dr. Kuehnhold would then be called upon to describe the type of interference experienced, and would begin by pointing out that he and his colleagues had originally been seriously perplexed by the appearance of numerous dash transmitters in the Anna band (66·5–75·0 mc/sec) at the beginning of November. These transmissions had been modulated at a frequency of 1500 cycles per second, but as the X-beam modulation frequency was 2000, it was hard to see why the English had chosen exactly three quarters of this figure. It must have been some extremely subtle form of jamming, but had evidently

---

[1] We ourselves had renamed Weser, as the main director station, after the Führer, to avoid using its correct name, which we knew only from Enigma. Spree, as the reserve director, was renamed Göring. The cross-beam stations Elbe, Oder and Rhein were renamed Himmler, Ribbentrop and Hess, and the entire system as 'the Ruffians' instead of 'The Rivers'.

proved unsuccessful, as the British had since changed to a frequency of 2000.

13.3 A German navigation officer, if one happened to be present, would probably say that as he had warned them before, they had been jammed, and that in his opinion all radio navigational aids were useless.

13.4 Dr. Kuehnhold would point out with some vigour that even though they might now be jammed, they had had a good run of luck, and the German Air Force had them to thank for getting to its targets in the autumn bombing season of 1940. Moreover, when he was able to erect some more stations, there was some hope that K.Gr.100 would still get through, particularly if the modulation were changed.

13.5 Hauptmann Aschenbrenner, as O/C., K.Gr.100, and being extremely jealous of his position as leader of the leaders of the German Air Force would endorse Dr. Kuehnhold's remarks, and would add that Wotan II was still unjammed and for the rest of the winter they might be able to use that.

13.6 Dr. Plendl would be glad that his particular system would now become of direct operational importance, and would add that while this was probably as easy to jam as the X-Gerät, newer systems could be developed which did not in fact involve beam flying but depended entirely on distance measurements from two ground stations, either by frequency modulation, phase measurement, or pulses.

13.7 Dr. Kuehnhold would probably interrupt with a defence of beam flying, pointing out its operational advantages, and saying that they had only to decrease their wavelength, preferably to the decimeter region, in order to foil the British jamming. With luck, even if the British did discover the change quickly, it would take them some months to develop a jamming system which would, in any case, be even more difficult to operate successfully than that against the X-beams.

13.8 A representative from Rechlin might point out that even if they could not go to decimeters, the use of frequency modulation with the present system might provide some degree of immunity from jamming.

13.9 The Director of Signals would end by recording a number of recommendations, and would point out that German radio research had entirely recouped any loss of prestige over the defeat of Knicke-bein by extemporizing use of the X-Gerät to lead the German Air Force to its target. They had learned from this lesson that it was better to have several alternative systems ready, with one Gruppe specializing in each, instead of equipping the whole Air Force for one method which might at any moment be rendered useless by countermeasures. Therefore, he intended to pursue the development of several systems, and in particular the Wotan method, Knickebein Dezi, and a decimeter X-Gerät. In the meantime, Dr. Kuehnhold's extra stations, which were already erected, would be equipped with the transmitters now in production. This might give the X-Gerät a new lease of life. The main body of the German Air Force would continue to be mass produced, but K.Gr.100 would be raised to the status of a full Geschwader and would be asked to be responsible for the service development of most of the above methods. Operating first on one system, they would continue to lead the G.A.F. to its targets. When that system was countered, they would change to another. They would thus, with comparatively little equipment, proceed through a succession of systems towards a centimetre ideal, each being more difficult to counter than its predecessor.

13.10 The success which they had achieved this winter would probably enable the conference's recommendations to be accepted by the German Air Staff.

Not all of my forecasts proved correct, but several did. The modulation change forecast in paragraph 13.4 did take place two years later when, despite our detailed warning, the countermeasures again missed it, and therefore failed to deflect the Baedeker raids. The method of using pulses to determine distances from two ground stations was taken up not by the Germans but by us, and developed as 'Oboe', the most accurate radio bombing system produced by either side. And Oboe became especially effective when it was used at centimetric wavelengths, as forecast in paragraph 13.9. And within a month or so of the report Kampf Gruppe 100 was raised to the status of a full Geschwader, thus becoming K.G.100.

I prefaced the report by Goering's New Year message to K.Gr.100:

At the close of 1940, I express to the C.O. and to this Gruppe my sincere thanks for an achievement unique in history. I know what enormous personal effort it has entailed on the part of each individual, and I am convinced, my comrades, that in 1941 as well, you will know only victory. So I wish each of you much luck and continuous success in the coming year. Heil Hitler.

In our own minds Charles Frank and I endorsed the message with an item of snark-hunting:

> 'And hast thou slain the Jabberwock?
> Come to my arms, my beamish boy!
> O Frabjous day! Callooh! Callay!'
> He chortled in his joy.'

As I expected, the report produced a most violent reaction, particularly on the part of Lywood, and the next thing I knew was that the report had been recalled by Sir Charles Portal, the Chief of Air Staff. This proved the most effective way possible of getting every copy read from cover to cover before it was returned; and I noted the fact for use later in the war because the natural reaction of anyone who is asked for the return of a document is to peruse it intently to find out what it is that ought not to have been revealed.

Lindemann sent for me, and told me that Portal had been discussing the report with him at Chequers, and had asked for his advice. Portal commented that he was as amazed by its brilliance as he was appalled by its indiscretion, and added that in his opinion I was worth twelve squadrons of Spitfires to the Air Force. Lindemann told him that he thought that my criticisms had been entirely justified, and together they decided that I should be transferred to the Air Staff with the rank of Deputy Director.

Portal then consulted Tizard, who agreed, and minuted the Secretary of State, Archibald Sinclair, accordingly. The latter wrote to Lord Beaverbrook on 12th February 1941 as follows:

Dear Max,

I write to consult you about the position of Dr. R. V. Jones. You know the importance which we attach to his work on the German radio methods of navigation and our own countermeasures. If, as I am inclined to believe, we are at the moment on top in the silent and secret battle of the beams, the lion's share of the credit should go to him. . . . If, on the other hand, you agree with me that his work would gain in value if he were to be put definitely under the Air Staff here, I would appoint him as Deputy Director of Intelligence (Scientific Intelligence).

I would be grateful if you could agree to this proposal and if you would let his assistant Mr. Frank come with him.

Yours ever,

ARCHIE.

Beaverbrook thereupon sent for me to know whether the proposed move accorded with my own wishes. 'It strikes me, Doctor, that they are trying to discipline you! Will you be happy at moving across?' I told him that I thought that I should be able to look after myself, and indeed that I had suggested the move in the first place. In that case, he said, he would agree, but he was prepared to defend me if he thought I needed it. He also made a comment about Lindemann which I never understood. He said that the Prof had been under a bad influence, but was now under a good influence, and could be a great help.

And so my move took place. At the same time, a difficulty cropped up which could have jeopardized our future. It all arose because our first baby was due early in February and I had to point out to Charles Frank that glad as Vera was to look after him she would be quite unable to do so in less than a fortnight. Charles was most apologetic, and asked me what he should do while he looked round for lodgings. I knew that there were a few beds in the basement of our Broadway offices, and suggested that he might stay there for a few nights, which was duly arranged. A few days later I was intercepted as I entered the building by Fred Winterbotham and the Chief of Staff. 'Who's this man Frank?' they asked. 'He is working with me,' I replied. 'Then, who let him in?' 'Technically,' I replied, 'you did, because I put all the papers through you to arrange for his security clearance.' 'In any case,' said Winterbotham, 'he's got to go!' I then asked what he had done and met with the reply, 'He's offended the Chief!'

As I could piece the episode together, it seemed that Charles had sat down at breakfast at the same table where a middle-aged man had been chatting to the duty secretaries and something that the man had said was known by Charles to be incorrect. Charles, who had a rigorous feeling for truth, intervened in the conversation and told the man where he was wrong. The man turned out to be Stewart Menzies, who was understandably put out at being contradicted in front of the secretaries of the organization in which he was Chief.

It was a desperate moment because I knew that Charles' help was going to be invaluable. And so, although I had not met Menzies before, I asked to see him as soon as possible. I told him that I understood that my chap Frank had upset him, but that I would very much like him to stay because he was one of the ablest men I knew. 'That's alright, then,' said Menzies. 'I'll stand anything if a man's efficient—he can stay!' This episode, which looked so disastrous, in fact put me into cordial contact with Menzies, to the benefit of my standing in the organization.

Despite such distractions, of course, we were in full cry against the beams. In my report I had suggested a way in which we might bomb the stations using the beams themselves, because a beam station hardly ever emits a single beam, but usually a fan of beams of which one points in the right direction and the others out to the side. So if an aircraft could fly down the main beam and drop a stick of bombs which would ignite as flares when they hit the ground, the result should be a line pointing to the station. If another aircraft flew down one of the side beams, the result should be a second line intersecting with the first at the exact location of the station. Other bombers could then bomb the intersection by normal visual aiming.

Sir Philip Joubert was keen that such measures should be employed, and he minuted the Deputy Chief of Air Staff, Air Marshal A. T. Harris, to this effect. 'Bert,' as Harris was generally known on the Air Staff, was notorious for writing pungent minutes—I was told that one of them read 'In order to get on in the Army, you have to look like a horse, think like a horse and smell like a horse!' And he gave a similarly pungent reply to Joubert. Among other things he said, 'Are we not tending to lose our sense of proportion over these German beams? . . . We use no beams ourselves but we bomb just as successfully as the Germans bomb, deep into Germany. . . . I do not agree that the beams are in fact a serious menace to this country, or that they have proved to be in the past. They are simply aids to navigation, and it is within our experience that such aids are not indispensable to the successful prosecution of bombing expeditions. I would go further and say that they are not even really useful. . . . Long may the Bosch beam upon us!' The date of that minute was 1st February 1941, and I took a copy wondering whether its writer would one day see the light. On 22nd February 1942 he went to Bomber Command as the man selected to introduce the new policy of bombing by the radio aids about which he had been so scathing.

The final twist to this chapter came from the recirculation of my X-beam report. When the original copies were being recalled, the duty fell to officers who were judged reliable enough to handle them and who were already in the Enigma picture. Winterbotham's staff were therefore involved, and in particular Harold Blyth who had been of so much help to me. By luck, he was detailed to collect Lywood's copy, and he recounted to me the exchange that then took place. On learning his mission, Lywood laughed and said that the doctors were now in trouble, and that he personally had caused the report to be recalled. 'That's very interesting, sir,' said Harold, 'but please may I have your copy?' 'No,' said Lywood, 'I was the one who had it recalled so I don't see why I should give mine up.' 'I'm sorry, sir, but I have the Chief of Air Staff's orders to collect your copy.' 'But it's very useful to me,' said Lywood. 'It's got a lot of information in it, and what's more, I have got all my own comments written in it, the ones I am going to shoot up Jones with. I can't possibly give it up.'

Although Lywood was four ranks above him, Harold persisted loyally, 'I'm sorry, sir, the Chief of Air Staff said nothing about comments, but I have his orders to collect your copy. If you don't believe it, please telephone the Director of Intelligence.' Lywood had little alternative, and the Director of Intelligence confirmed Harold's statement. After further protest Lywood made it a condition that he should put his copy in a sealed envelope to be taken by Harold to the Director of Intelligence and kept sealed by the latter until the time came for re-issue. This arrangement having been made, Lywood gave Harold the envelope and then, as Harold was leaving his room, said, 'By the way, which Section do you come from?' 'AI 1C, sir.' 'AI 1C,' said Lywood, 'isn't that where Jones works?' 'Yes, sir,' said Harold, saluting, 'I am his personal assistant. Good afternoon, sir.'

I do not know exactly what happened next but the Director of Intelligence's office sent all the collected reports back to me. There was none in a sealed envelope, and yet they were all there. Indeed there was Lywood's copy, out of its envelope, and I could only assume that the Director of Intelligence wanted me to see it.

Comments were passionately sprinkled all through it. In the section describing the imaginary German conference, Lywood had risen to the bait about the uselessness of radio aids to navigation, and had adorned my own remark with, 'The navigation officer might also have pointed to success with astro navigation methods and the increasing success in finding targets by dropping flares as practised by the British.' As we have seen, this was widely believed by the Air Staff at the time, and even by Tizard, as he had said at Churchill's Knickebein meeting. But, already, I was beginning to collect evidence that our bombing raids on Germany were rarely finding their targets.

As I read the next comment by Lywood on my conference, I was reminded of Thomas Henry Huxley's remark on Wilberforce's outburst in the famous British Association debate on evolution, 'The Lord hath delivered him.' For what Lywood had written was this: 'This sort of play-acting in a report of this nature, if advisable at all, would be more useful if the characters had some real experience of their jobs and were not merely puppets of one inexperienced young scientist's mind.' All I had to do was to write underneath, with due acknowledgement, Pitt's reply to Walpole: 'The atrocious crime of being a young man, which the Honourable Gentleman has with such spirit and decency charged upon me, I shall attempt neither to palliate nor deny; but content myself with wishing that I shall be one of those whose follies shall cease with their youth, and not of that number who are ignorant in spite of experience!'

When the time came for the report[1] to be re-issued on the more limited circulation approved by Portal I sent back the appropriate copies to the Director of Intelligence with a minute saying that I understood that the Principal Deputy Director of Signals was extremely anxious to have his original copy back, because it contained some valuable comments. If the Director would be good enough to look through it, he would see that I was at least as anxious that the Principal Deputy Director of Signals should have his wish.

Tempers ran very high for a time, especially because Lywood had circulated a 'refutation' of my report which was full of inaccuracies.

In the end Lindemann was brought in to try to make peace between me and Lywood. It was a strange role for him, but he did his best. 'Now admit it,' he said to me. 'You lost your temper with them and said things you didn't mean. I know, because I've done the same myself.' It was very rare for him to make such an admission, and I much appreciated the effort that it must have cost him. But I told him that I had not lost my temper and that I meant everything that I had said. But I added that I now felt that I had had my revenge, and related how I had dealt with the charge of youth and inexperience.

We happened to be going the same way from Cabinet Offices for lunch, and we walked together as far as the Haymarket, where he stopped to turn into the Carlton. He told me that he had a lady to take to lunch. 'What, *you*, Prof!' I said. 'Yes,' he replied and, with a jaunty wave of his umbrella, 'You know, the atrocious crime. . . .'

---

[1] It had, incidentally, concluded with a provocative tribute to our sources: 'They have enabled us to appreciate our enemy in a way that can rarely before have been given to a country in time of war. It is our duty to them and to the country to ensure that more worthy use is made of the results of their efforts.'

CHAPTER TWENTY-ONE

Wotan's Other Eye

M Y REPORT on the X-Gerät had emphasized that there was yet another system in the offing which, as related earlier, seemed to be called Wotan, and which involved a beam plus a ranging system, the latter very possibly being on the lines suggested by the Oslo Report. This suspicion had been strengthened when on 6th October an Enigma message to a new station 'Wotan II', somewhere on the Hague peninsula (north-west of Cherbourg), said 'TARGET NO. 1 FOR Y CO-ORDINATES 50 DEGREES 41 MINUTES 49·2 SECONDS N 2 DEGREES 14 MINUTES 21·2 SECONDS W'. The co-ordinates were those of the Armoured Corps Depot at Bovington Camp in Dorset, and they indicated a very significant difference from the X system. In the latter a series of *beam directions* were always sent out, each station being instructed to set its beam in the specified direction. In the new system, which may have been called Y as a successor to X, the *position of the target was given to a single station*, and so presumably this station had the entire means of directing the bomber to the target. The easiest way of doing this would be by determining the bearing and range of the target, and then getting the bomber to fly along a beam directed over the target until it was at the correct range for releasing its bombs, in the way that I had three months before conjectured for Wotan.

A few nights later Bovington was attacked by two aircraft. They were not very accurate in direction, but were good as regards range. We had little evidence of any further attacks but our listening service began to report beams on frequencies of between 40 and 50 Megacycles per second which had quite different characteristics from those associated with Knickebein and the X-beams. Instead of right and left signals being labelled by dashes and dots, the signals were of equal duration, but there was a short pause in transmission and one signal, say the right, came immediately after the pause and then the other signal followed, in the sequence: pause, right, left, pause, right, left, pause, and so on. We gradually unravelled these new beams, which had been designed specifically to work a beam-flying indicator in the aircraft without the pilot having to listen to them. All he needed to do was to watch the instrument indicate whether he was to the right or left or accurately on the beam itself. As it turned out, such a beam was even easier to jam than either of the other two systems, but we did not realize this until relatively late in the battle. What attracted our interest, of course, was to find out whether the ranging system was indeed like that fore-shadowed in the Oslo Report, and it was not long before we were able to confirm this suspicion.

The aircraft using the new system were not from KGr100 but from Third Gruppe of KG 26, commanded by an outstanding officer, Major Viktor von Lossberg. The scientist in charge was Dr. Plendl who to some extent was the German counterpart of T. L. Eckersley. When I discovered this I asked the latter what he thought of Plendl, and met with the reply, 'He's not much good—he bases his theory on experiment!' I talked to Dr. Plendl after the war, and he told me that he had been responsible for the development of the X system, which he handed over to Kuenhold while he himself went on to develop the Y system. He had tried out the measuring principle at Rechlin in 1938, and in 1939 had started to develop the ground stations. Flight tests had only started in the spring of 1940, and so the Oslo Report had warned us of the Y system before any of the equipment was in the air.

Plendl was proud of having taken the system into operational use within six months but thanks to the Oslo Report we were on the lookout for the Y transmissions, which we were quickly able to find and thus devise countermeasures. These were already being prepared when a KG26 aircraft was shot down near Eastleigh on 19th January 1941. The aircraft was so badly damaged that we could only see that it carrried equipment resembling but not identical to the X-Gerät. All members of the crew were killed, and almost the only useful relic was the radio operator's notebook, charred at the edges, which Felkin sent to me. This included two handwritten tables of figures, of which the first ran:

Loge	244	142	10
Schmalstigel	454	149	11
Bruder	372	120	11
Süden	272	117	11
Bild	405	137	11
Rückflug.			

Charles Frank and I were able to make sense of the table on the basis
that we knew that III/KG26's home airfield was at Poix, 20 miles south-
west of Amiens. We also knew that Loge was the German code name for
London, just as 'Korn' had been for Coventry, and our interpretation
was:

Objective	Distance to Poix	Rhumb bearing to Poix	Magnetic Variation
London	244 km	142°	10°
Sheffield	454 km	149°	11°
Bristol	372 km	120°	11°
Southampton	272 km	117°	11°
Birmingham	405 km	137°	11°

Homeward Flight.

The second table in the logbook ran:

Hinflug	
294	10
318	11
283	11
274	11
302	11

By assuming that the entries referred to the same towns as those in
the corresponding rows in the first table, and that the three-figure
entries were bearings, we found that these intersected at a point near
Cassel, in north France, and so could interpret the table as follows:

Objective	Approach bearing from Cassel	Magnetic Variation
London	294	10°
Sheffield	318	11°
Bristol	283	11°
Southampton	274	11°
Birmingham	302	11°

We could therefore deduce that:

(a) the aircraft approached its targets from the direction of Cassel.
(b) it was not concerned with distance calculations on the outward
flight, which would be consistent with the distance being determined
by a distant ground station, and,

(c) after it had reached its targets it intended to return direct to an aerodrome near Poix, and since it was now navigating on its own it needed to know the distance from the target back to Poix, as well as the direction.

All these deductions were consistent with what we so far knew of the Y system, and they additionally indicated that there was a ground station at Cassel similar to that on the Hague peninsula.

A third table in the log book gave us the frequencies both for the beam itself and for the ranging system employed by each of these ground stations.

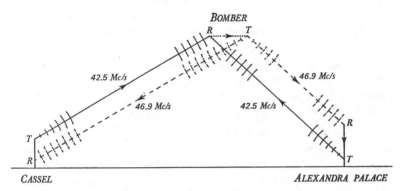

Fig. 5. *The method of interfering with the Y-Ranging system, January 1941. The signal re-radiated by the bomber on 46·9 Mc/s is picked up at Alexandra Palace and retransmitted back to the bomber via the television transmitter on 42·5 Mc/s*

Following what I had already said in my report on the X system about the desirability of using a more subtle type of countermeasure, it was easy to see a delicious method of upsetting the ranging system: and this time I had my way. To take a specific case, the ground station at Cassel radiated a (sinusoidally modulated) signal to the aircraft on 42·5 Megacycles per second, which was picked up by the aircraft and its modulation there transferred to a transmitter on board and then re-radiated back to the ground station on a frequency of 46·9 Megacycles per second (Figure 5). The ground station could then calculate the distance the aircraft was from it by the delay in the return signal. But we could pick up the signal from the aircraft on 46·9 Megacycles per second even better than its own ground station could, and we could in principle re-radiate this already re-radiated signal back to the aircraft on the same frequency, 42·5 Megacycles per second, as that being used by the ground station. This would therefore be fed in to the aircraft receiver, along with the fresh signal coming in from the ground station and in turn be fed back to the ground station again. The effect would be rather like that which occurs in public address systems where the noise from the loudspeakers impinges on the original microphone, and is therefore picked up and relayed back to the loudspeakers again. The effect on the ground station would be to make it think that the aircraft was at a false distance, because the returning waves would have travelled round an extra loop between the aircraft and our own station before getting back to their original base, and if we used a powerful transmitter ourselves the whole system would 'ring' just as a public address system squeals if the gain of the amplifier is made too high.

The powerful B.B.C. television transmitter at Alexandra Palace would be excellent for the task, because it worked in the right frequency band. Robert Cockburn therefore commandeered it for re-radiating the German aircraft's own signal. It turned out that this countermeasure, known as 'Domino', came into use the very first night that the Luft-waffe had decided to replace KGr100 by III/KG26 because we were at last jamming the X system effectively. There had been a few minor raids by the Y-bombers during January, and the Germans hoped that they would now have this alternative formation to act as their path-finders for the rest of the winter.

I had advised that for the first few nights we should use a minimum of power, so as to inject into the German system just enough of a signal to give them a false range, without arousing their suspicions too much. The effect was very satisfactory. One aircraft became involved in a puzzled exchange with the ground station, which informed him that he must have a wire loose in his receiver, and that he would have to abandon the use of the system for the night. Over the next few nights, we gradually turned up the power of Alexandra Palace, and the Germans realized that the system was unusable. My original objective was that, since I was not sure how long a period of success they had already had with the Y system, we should shake their confidence by making them think that we might have been interfering with it in a way that they had not detected for a period stretching some distance back into the past. This subtlety was probably unnecessary, as it happened, because we had effectively countered the system from the very first night on which it was to be used on large scale, and this by itself completely shook the German confidence.

Once the idea that we were interfering with the system became known to the German air crews, we obtained a further benefit. Since the aircraft had to be instructed by the ground station when to release its bombs, it had to be monitored all the time during its bombing run, and the ground station could handle only one aircraft at a time. The aircraft would therefore fly to a convenient area from which it could be ordered onto the beam by the ground station, and so commence its bombing run. In principle, all we needed to do was to transmit false orders to the aircraft. In fact we did not do this, but it seemed such an easy countermeasure that the German crews thought that we might, and they therefore began to be suspicious about the instructions that they received.

Coupled with the kind of misunderstanding that so often occurs in operations, it was not long before the crews found substance to their theory. On one occasion, for example, the ground station ordered an aircraft to steer a course of 270° (i.e. due west) presumably because it was east of the beam, and this was the vector required to bring it to the right point to start its bombing run. For some reason the aircraft failed to hear any further orders from the ground station and went a long way west, only to return to base and complain that the British had given him a false order. What with our real countermeasures and those imagined by the crews, Y operations became a fiasco and the system was withdrawn; we had restored our moral ascendancy for the rest of the winter.

This of course did not stop the bombing. London was such a large target that it could be attacked without any aids; and our ports, especially those in the south where the Germans could hear their beams strongly enough to give them at least the right direction of approach, were heavily attacked. But inland towns were now much more difficult; and the Germans had little further success against them.

Only later did I find that there was no foundation to our original reasoning that the Y system would involve a beam and a range measurement, correct though the conclusion was, and important as it had proved in the Battle of the Beams. The fact that it was known as Wotan had nothing to do with its method of working. Had I known enough, the Y system was code-named 'Wotan II'; and the X system was 'Wotan I'. And so while Wotan may have had one eye for Y, he could not have had crossed eyes for X.

We could see from vertical air photographs that the turntables for the beam transmitting aerials were made the same for the X and Y systems; and later in the war when a Y station was erected in Norway. One of our Norwegian friends photographed it (Plate 8(a)). Incidentally we called the system 'Benito' because we reckoned that Mussolini was the one-eyed end of the Axis.

CHAPTER TWENTY-TWO

Retrospect and Prospect

BY FEBRUARY 1941 the Battle of the Beams was as good as won. We had another three months of bombing to endure, but all three major German systems, Knickebein and X and Y, were defeated. Many bombs therefore went astray, often attracted by the decoy fires that were now part of the countermeasure programme. Moreover our fore-knowledge of the German targets was at last beginning to result in the destruction of their bombers, as our nightfighters were becoming equipped with good airborne radar and as our ground controlled interception technique improved to the extent where they could now effectively hunt along the beams. With the last major raids of April and May 1941, the Luftwaffe was therefore not only tending to miss its targets, but it was beginning to encounter losses on a potentially prohibitive scale.

As information flowed in, we could see more of the Luftwaffe policy. The X-Gerät had been developed at least as early as 1937, and X-beam stations had been set up for the bombing of Warsaw in 1939, and then transferred to the Eifel region for operations against France—it was probably a French report about them that Woodward-Nutt had mentioned to me at lunch. Nevertheless the German Air Staff had not appreciated the importance of the X-Gerät until they were driven to bombing by night after the Battle of Britain, and had found Knickebein jammed. The main bombing force had been intended primarily for day-time operation, and even the X-beam flyers had been squandered in ordinary operations in the Norwegian campaign. The unexpected command of all the coast from den Helder to Brest gave the Luftwaffe an enormous geographical advantage: it could attack Britain from any direction ranging from north-east to south-west, and the situation was ideal for the beams. Fortunately, we were just beginning to parry the X-beam threat at the time that the German Air Staff realized what an important weapon their radio men had given them. The X- and Y-beam stations were then described in a contemporary Luftwaffe appreciation as 'enormously important and hardly replaceable', and Dr. Plendl was created a Staatsrat by Goering in recognition of his work for the beams.

Luckily for us the Germans made the classic military mistake, which we were later to repeat, of trying out devices on a small operational scale before depending on them for major efforts. It was only for this reason that I was able to unravel the beam systems in the nick of time. Since we had no technically minded agents in Germany I had foreseen in my original design for a Scientific Intelligence Service that an attack on the operational trial stage was the only one that would offer much hope of success; and this was what I did, much aided in the case of the Y system by the insight given by the Oslo Report.

So what difference had my attachment to Intelligence made? Suppose that I had not been there, or that I had agreed to Pye's recall, or that I had accepted Eckersley's opinion about Knickebein?—What would have happened? We should certainly have been slower with radio countermeasures, and the bombing of our inland towns must have been worse, perhaps much worse. With our nightfighters and guns powerless, radio countermeasures were our only means of defence. Not only could there have been many more Coventrys, but Milch's aim of knocking out our aero-engine factories might have been achieved.

Scientific Intelligence was now established as a branch having its place alongside and interlocked with the more traditional divisions of Naval, Military and Air Intelligence, and we had the beginnings of a Scientific Intelligence organization. I had been able to share in the effort by the relatively small band of scientists and engineers which had affected the outcome of the Battle of Britain and the Blitz. Beyond its effect on the immediate outcome it had made a great difference to the position of science in national affairs, for it had shown the government, and indeed governments abroad, that science and engineering could be essential to national survival. The effect on Winston Churchill was profound: 'Thus', he wrote, 'the three main attempts to conquer Britain after the fall of France were successfully defeated or prevented. The first was the decisive defeat of the German Air Force during July, August, and September . . . our second victory followed from our first. The German failure to gain command of the air prevented the cross-Channel invasion. . . . The third ordeal was the indiscriminate night bombing of our cities in mass attacks. This was overcome and broken by the continued skill and devotion of our fighter pilots and by the fortitude and endurance of the mass of the people, and notably the Londoners, who, together with the civil organizations which upheld them, bore the brunt. But these noble efforts in the high air and in the flaming streets would have been in vain if British science and British brains had not played the ever-memorable and decisive part which this chapter records.' This extract comes from *Their Finest Hour*, of which he sent me one of his earliest copies; and in an accompanying letter he commented, 'You certainly did "pull the crooked leg". It makes me very proud of our country that there were minds like yours playing so keenly around the unknowable, and I am also glad that through my friendship with Lindemann I was able to bring these deadly beams into relation with the power of the British State.'

The Battle of the Beams had sorted out those of us who knew that we could rely on one another, and stand the test.

> If you can keep your head when all about you
> Are losing theirs and blaming it on you,
> If you can trust yourself when others doubt you
> But make allowance for their doubting too

Taking them in the order I met them, there was Bimbo Norman at Bletchley delving into the Enigma messages, and behind him the brilliant band of cryptographers in Hut 6, Denys Felkin with prisoner interrogation and captured documents, Rowley Scott-Farnie with the R.A.F. wireless listening service, Claude Wavell in photographic interpretation, and now Charles Frank was with me. These were among the men, to borrow my mother's phrase, 'who went first'.

But this was no time for mutual admiration, for the position of Britain in February 1941 was still grim. Ports were being heavily bombed. Rationing was biting hard; and any remaining amenities of peace-time life were disappearing fast. A German invasion in the summer still seemed likely, and a counter-invasion of the Continent by us extremely improbable for long into the future. Even if they did not invade, the Germans were in a commanding geographical position, with the Luftwaffe disposed in a great arc from Norway through Denmark, Holland, Belgium and France to the Spanish border. Their U-boats, operating from ports in the same great arc out into the Atlantic, were sinking more and more of our shipping; and with further ingenuity in mine design and with a more systematic mining campaign they might well strangle our ports and with them the whole island.

I used to look at my wall map every morning and wonder how we could possibly survive. Anyone in his right senses would do the best deal he could with Hitler—but we had no thought of it. Even though we

7*

were tired by the Blitz, there was that 'white glow overpowering, sublime that ran through our island from end to end'. It can hardly be described to those who did not experience it; it must lie very deep down among human emotions, giving the individual a strange, subdued elation at facing dangers in which he may easily perish as an individual but also a subconscious knowledge that any society which has a high enough proportion of similar individuals is all the more likely to survive because of their sacrifice.

And there were some hopeful signs in February 1941. In North Africa Wavell's Army was sweeping westwards and capturing Italians in thousands. Those of us who listened on short waves could hear generous American voices campaigning among their countrymen for help for Britain: and, relayed by the B.B.C., the strong voice of Franklin Roosevelt was saying, 'The British and their Allies need planes and ships and tanks. From America they will receive planes and ships and tanks.' Above all, there was the great advantage of being able to read much of the Enigma traffic. If only we could hold on, sooner or later this could turn the tide.

Much would depend on what happened in the air, and the Chief of Air Staff, Sir Charles Portal, was strengthening his organization. Intelligence was elevated to become the responsibility of a new post, the Assistant Chief of Air Staff (Intelligence) with the rank of Air Vice Marshal instead of the previous Directorate headed by an Air Commodore. My own position, though, did not entirely materialize as Portal and Archibald Sinclair had intended. They had secured my release from Lord Beaverbrook on the understanding that I was to be a Deputy Director of Intelligence, which would have meant a promotion of three grades over that of Senior Scientific Officer to which I had been promoted as recently as November 1940. Such dramatic elevation was too much for the Civil Service, which gave me a promotion of only one grade, to Principal Scientific Officer. This was, of course, far less rewarding, and I would have had a very good case had I pressed my claim, in view of the written commitment by the Secretary of State and the Chief of Air Staff, but it would take a long time to fight the Civil Service and in the meantime I might acquire a reputation as being a man with a grievance, which could well be fatal. So I decided not to fight, but to depend for my authority on the value of the work that I was doing, aided by the general impression that I had at any time only to go to Churchill to ask him to issue appropriate orders.

So instead of becoming a Deputy Director I became the 'Assistant

Director of Intelligence (Science)' or 'A.D.I. (Science)' for short. But Assistant to whom? In Air Staff nomenclature an Assistant Director indicated a grade rather than a function, and did not imply, strictly, that I assisted a higher officer who held the post of Director. In the reorganization of Air Intelligence, Archie Boyle moved out and the new Head was Air Vice Marshal C. E. H. Medhurst, who was styled Assistant Chief of Air Staff (Intelligence). He had two Directors under him, one for Operations and the other for Security. I was made directly responsible to him and so was effectively in parallel with these two Directors, which in a way made up for the grudging manner in which the Civil Service had treated me, and I became the only civilian in an executive position on the Air Staff.

Charles Medhurst quickly sent for me, and we at once established a rapport. His last post had been as Director of Policy, but before that he had been in Intelligence and also an Attaché; I believe that he had recently been concerned with the secret deal by which Britain was allowed to use facilities in the Azores. He understood Intelligence and he was excellent to work for: if I went to him with a problem he would take immediate supporting action, and there would usually be on my desk within twenty-four hours a copy of the minute describing the action he had taken. At our first talk together he told me how impressed he had been by my work on the beams, and that he would like me to take over responsibility for analysing how the German night defences worked because he was sure that it was a problem that demanded a scientific mind.

To set the problem in perspective, I need only quote Churchill's minute of 8th July 1940 to Beaverbrook:

But when I look round to see how we can win the war I see that there is only one sure path. We have no Continental army which can defeat the German military power. The blockade is broken and Hitler has Asia and probably Africa to draw from. Should he be repulsed here or not try invasion, he will recoil eastward, and we have nothing to stop him. But there is one thing that will bring him back and bring him down, and that is an absolutely devastating, exterminating attack by very heavy bombers from this country upon the Nazi homeland. We must be able to overwhelm them by this means, without which I do not see a way through.

A sustained air bombardment of Germany was therefore a major instrument of military policy, all the more appealing to the nation as a whole because of the Blitz. As Churchill himself said, the almost universal cry was, 'Give it to them back!'

The problem could be more closely defined by considering the choice of attacking by day or by night. The former would result in increased precision, so that it would be possible to attack selected objectives, such as oil plants, the destruction of which should paralyse the German military effort. But our early experiences in attacks on naval bases such as Kiel quickly showed that bombers could not defend themselves against fighters, even when flying in close formation where cross-protection between the bombers had been carefully rehearsed. Therefore if major attacks were to be made by day, these would require fighter escort, and it was easy to prove, or so it seemed, that this, too, would be bound to fail. The argument was simple: the Germans would be fighting over their own territory, and near their home bases: their fighters would therefore only need a short range, whereas ours would require a very long range: and since short range fighters have to carry far less fuel, they could therefore have a higher performance and so shoot down our long-range escort fighters. Moreover the German fighters could be under control from the ground and choose the time, place and manner of interception. All these factors were confirmed by the experience of our early raids, and so it seemed that a daylight bombing offensive against Germany would be quite impracticable. We should therefore have to attack by night, when the German fighters would be severely handi-capped in finding us; and, again, our experience during the Blitz had shown that bombers had a very good chance of getting through against free-lancing fighters. The question would therefore arise sooner or later of German progress with radio and radar aids to nightfighting and also, indeed, to anti-aircraft guns. Their successes in this direction would be a major factor in determining whether or not our bombing policy would itself succeed; and the understanding of German developments in the radar field was a problem as congenial to me as the beams had been, at least in technicality if not in morality.

I therefore drew up my plan of attack. There were other Sections in Air Intelligence who would be more expert than I was myself in such details as fighter performance and armament, and such details would better be left to them. As regards anti-aircraft guns and searchlights, the work had been transferred, with the disappearance of Freddie Wintle, back to the War Office, where it became a branch of Military Intelli-gence. Its new Head, I was delighted to find, was 'Gubby' Allen, the England Cricket Captain; he was a most friendly colleague right through the war. I myself would concentrate on German radar, because I was sure that the Germans would find, as we had found ourselves, that sooner or later they would have to depend on it for nightfighting, and if I could only understand the performance and limitations of their particular equipments, this might well prove the key to understanding their whole system of night defence.

PART TWO

CHAPTER TWENTY-THREE

Freya

IN CONCENTRATING our effort against German radar, the problem was how to get at the kind of radar that the Germans would use for defending their homeland. Here the strength of their position could also be a weakness, for they would almost certainly bring some of their radar equipment forward to the Channel coast. Indeed we already knew that they had done so, and that the name of their basic equipment was Freya. So the first phase of my attack must be to find out what Freya looked like, what its radio characteristics were, and how it performed: this should at least acquaint us with German radar technique, and the necessary information should be obtainable by photographic reconnaissance and by listening for the radar transmissions.

The second phase would probably be more difficult, since the night defences of Germany were likely to lie well back from the Channel coast, perhaps in Germany itself, where we had almost no agents operating, and which would be much less accessible to photographic or radio reconnaissance. Moreover, we had very few agents operating in Holland, Belgium or France in early 1941, because as a matter of principle we had never spied on allies and consequently had no underground networks ready to operate as soon as the Germans took over the territories. It would be some time before the Resistance movements began to operate coherently, so in early 1941 the immediate attack must be on the Channel coast in the hope that what we learnt there would enable us to brief our various agencies when these were able to operate further back.

The first scratch, if not the first blood, had been drawn when we had learnt of the existence of Freya in the summer of 1940. Would aerial photography ever improve to the extent that we could see it? The first glimmerings of an answer came one day in January 1941 when Claude Wavell, now definitely established as my main contact with photographic reconnaissance, telephoned to say that there were various curiosities that he would like to show me. These were mainly photographs of beam stations, principally on the Hague peninsula, north-west of Cherbourg, where there was a Knickebein, and two X-beam stations and one Y-beam station, all of which had circular turntables. At the end he threw in another pair of stereo photographs, also of the Hague peninsula, adding that they might well signify nothing but that there was a pair of much smaller circles about 20 feet across at the edge of a field, and these had not been there some months before. They might be nothing more sinister than cattle feeding troughs or 'cow-bins', as he called them, but I might be interested. They were near a village, and I asked him its name. 'Auderville,' he replied and a bell rang loudly in my mind—for Auderville was the name of the village near which a Freya five months before had been instrumental in the sinking of H.M.S. *Delight*. Could these 20 foot circles be the Freya for which we had been so fruitlessly searching?

Charles Frank and I examined them in turn. We could see the shadows of some fairly tall structure, which might merely have been like a maypole, at the centre of each circle: and then Charles spotted the vital clue that the shadows were of different widths in successive photographs. Recalling that I had found the first Knickebein by a similar observation, he suggested that the different widths might be due to whatever it was rotating between exposures, so that at one instant it had been more or less end-on to the direction of the sun, and at a subsequent incident more nearly broadside-on. In fact, the difference in breadth was only about a tenth of a millimetre on the print, and it was a very fine observation; but it was positive, and I decided to ask the Photographic Reconnaissance Unit to take a low-level oblique picture of it. Although my desire to see a photograph was urgent, I told the Unit that it should exercise complete operational freedom in picking the time and the weather for the sortie. As a result, this did not occur for some days.

When it did, the pilot returned saying that I had sent him out to take a photograph of an anti-aircraft gun. A more foolhardy request it would be hard to imagine, and it was difficult to argue with him because he had been there and risked his life, and I had not. But, although I felt rather silly, I was not entirely convinced, and I examined the photograph that he had brought back. It was indeed of a light anti-aircraft gun, but it was not quite where I had specified—it was some hundred yards or so away; and there, on the very border of the picture where it was almost lost in the distortion of the gelatine was the edge of the structure that

I had asked to be photographed, and it did look like the edge of some kind of aerial. I therefore told the Unit that I was sorry but that I would have to ask for another photograph. This time the new pilot, Flying Officer W. K. Manifould, had the two objects beautifully centred in his picture (Plate 9(c)); there was no doubt that they were radar sets. His sortie took place on 22nd February, and on the following day Claude Wavell telephoned me to say that he had the pictures and that they confirmed our suspicions. I went out to his headquarters on the morning of 24th February to collect them, returning in time for a meeting that Air Marshal Joubert had convened for that afternoon with one item only on the agenda: 'To discuss the existence of German radar.'

The photographs were not the only evidence that I was able to take to the meeting, for we had also at last heard Freya's radar transmissions. These should have been easier to observe than its physical appearance, for all we needed to do was to listen in the right frequency band. But despite my warning in December 1939 (p. 74) that no proper listening service existed, and despite the fact that in our search for the X-beams we had discovered the German naval radar transmissions on 80 centimetres, our Listening Service was still inadequate, and the gap had once again to be filled by individual enterprise. This came about because in early November 1940 Air Marshal Joubert, concerned that I was still single-handed, had instructed the Telecommunications Research Establishment that they must detach an officer to help me.

The first that I knew of this was when my telephone rang and a voice said, 'This is Mr. Garrard of T.R.E. Air Marshal Joubert says that I have to come to help you!' This was not without embarrassment for, glad as I was to have further help, Charles Frank was just joining me, and it would take some time to get any further newcomer 'cleared' with Security to come to work in Broadway. The best that we could do in the meantime would be to let him work in my Air Ministry office alongside Joubert's, and this was relatively dull.

But Derek Garrard was not a man to remain inactive. . . . Impatient at having so little to do in my Air Ministry office, Garrard acquired a suitable radio receiver and took it in his own car down to the south coast to see if he could find the missing Freya transmissions since the official listening service had failed. In the course of a few highly profitable days, which included his getting arrested as a Fifth Columnist for his unauthorised activity in a Defended Area, he succeeded in hearing the Freya transmissions on frequencies of about 120 Megacycles a second, or 2·5 metres wavelength, and even in getting rough bearings on where they came from. Some of his bearings in fact intersected near the very equipment that we had now photographed north-west of Cherboug. It was a most valuable individual effort, and Garrard returned with his results on the very morning of Joubert's meeting on 24th February.

So when the meeting started, I let it run on for a little to let the doubters say that they did not believe that the Germans had any radar, and then I produced both the photographs and Garrard's bearings. Joubert looked hard at me and said, 'How long have you had this evidence, Jones?' He obviously suspected that I had kept it up my sleeve just to make fools of the doubters, perhaps for weeks. I pointed to the date inscribed on the sortie showing that it had been taken only two days ago. That was the end of disbelief in German radar.

So at last we knew what one type of German radar looked like; moreover, we had heard its transmissions and had heard similar transmissions coming from other stations, whose exact locations it should now be possible to determine on aerial photographs—it is always much easier to search when you know what you are looking for. We could thus find the deployment of the coastal radar chain; and although this was only one step on the way to the main German night defences, whenever these might be built up, it also had its own significance, as I pointed out to A. P. Rowe when he visited my office and we may have been showing signs of elation at our new discoveries. He commented, 'This is all very pretty, but what good is it?' My reply was, 'Some day we're going back, and we shall need to deal with those stations if we are going to land successfully.' So we set to work to build up a complete dossier of all the German radar stations that we could find.

It was unlikely that Freya was the only type of radar equipment that the Germans had. Indeed, we knew that their naval radar was different, at least as regards the wavelength (80 centimetres) on which it operated. Moreover the Oslo Report had told us that there was another system working on about 50 centimetres with paraboloidal aerials: what had happened to it? The first glimmering of an answer came at much the same time as the Auderville photograph was taken, when we heard through Enigma that a Freya equipment was being sent to Rumania along with another equipment called 'Würzburg' for coastal protection, and that two Würzburgs were being sent to Bulgaria for a similar purpose. Since radar equipment was not very plentiful, I assumed that these were the minimum number of equipments that would just cover the Black Sea coastlines of the two countries, 260 kilometres for

Rumania and 150 kilometres for Bulgaria. Each Würzburg in Bulgaria would therefore have to cover 75 kilometres of front, which it could just do if it had an all-round range of 37·5 kilometres. If this were so, the Freya in Rumania would have to cover (260–75) kilometres, which meant that a Freya must have an all-round range of 92·5 kilometres.

We already knew from Garrard's observations that Freyas sent out 1000 pulses per second, so that their designer was expecting to get the reflected pulses back within a thousandth of a second; and since radio waves travel with the speed of light, roughly 300,000 kilometres per second, the double journey to the target and back could not be longer than 300 kilometres, giving a range of 150 kilometres as a maximum. So the 92·5 kilometres deduced from the slender Rumanian evidence as a minimum was of the right order. This led us to hope that the equally slender evidence for the Würzburg range as 37·5, or say 40, kilometres might be good, too. And hope it was, for we had another clue which encouraged us to think that Würzburg might be the key to our major problem. This was the institution of a nightfighting area which was defined as a circle of 40 kilometres radius centred on den Helder in north-west Holland.

From what we could see of Freya, it was unlikely to be able to measure the height of aircraft, but we ourselves were already finding that for effective night interception the ground controller needed to know the height of the bomber as well as its position on the map. The Germans must encounter the same difficulty, and would therefore be tempted to use a second type of radar equipment which could measure height, and they would have to restrict their nightfighting radius to whatever range this second equipment might have. Was this the explanation of the den Helder circle, and was it more than coincidence that its radius was 40 kilometres, when we had deduced at least 37·5 for Würzburg? The paraboloidal system foreshadowed by the Oslo Report should be capable of measuring height, for in contrast to the vertical flat mattress-like aerials of Freya, the paraboloid could be tipped up as well as rotated.

So, tentatively, the key to German nightfighting would be the Würzburg apparatus, which would have a paraboloidal aerial looking like a large electric 'bowl fire'. If Oslo were right again, its transmissions should be on a wavelength of about 50 centimetres: and, if 40 kilometres were its maximum range, its pulse repetition rate should not exceed 3750 per second. With these figures in mind, we searched and found the transmissions: their wavelengths were about 53 centimetres, and the pulse repetition rate was 3750. The first transmissions that we detected came from the Channel coast, and the obvious next step was to locate a site accurately enough for photographs to be taken. For the moment, though, this was impossible—it had been difficult enough to find the first Freya on a photograph, and Würzburg was almost certainly smaller. What I hoped was that the Germans, faced with problems of security in unfriendly territory, would try to minimize their difficulties by keeping their equipments as 'bunched' as possible, so that sooner or later they would decide to put Würzburgs alongside Freyas. We would therefore photograph as many Freya stations as often as we could, in the hope that one day we would spot a Würzburg.

On the basis of the first Freya photograph, my relations with the photographic reconnaissance pilots were now very good. I think that they must have realized the difficulty in which I had been placed by having to ask that another of them should go out after the first pilot had said that I had sent him out to photograph an anti-aircraft gun, and they were obviously ready to undertake any task that I asked of them. I was therefore rather worried when I was told by Claude Wavell that a re-organization of Photographic Reconnaissance was occurring, and that it was to come under a new Assistant Directorate of Intelligence, A.D.I. (Photos). He was Peter Stewart, who up to that time had been running the Air Ministry War Room which among other things produced the Daily Summary of Operations. I was told that he was a man who had his own way of doing things, and much would depend on whether or not we hit it off together. I therefore called on him, half expecting trouble but, as with Medhurst, we took an immediate liking to one another. Peter was a member of Lloyd's and belonged to a City insurance firm, and before the war he had joined the Auxiliary Air Force. In fact he had been Commanding Officer of No. 600, the City of London, Squadron; and he had an intense sense of duty and patriotism. There was a story that he had received an adverse report from an Inspecting Officer about his conduct of 600 Squadron; being adverse, this had to be shown to him for his comments. The point of criticism was that he was on too familiar terms with his junior officers, who actually called him by his Christian name; his comment was, 'I would rather be called Peter to my face than Stuffy, Sausage or Ginger behind my back!'—the nicknames applying to Air Marshals Dowding, Gossage, and Harris.

He assured me that he wished to interpose no hindrance between me and the pilots and interpreters; in fact he immediately took me to lecture to the pilots of the Photographic Reconnaissance Unit which had just moved to Benson near Oxford.

We soon had a chance to link photographic reconnaissance with the interception of wireless signals associated with the control of German day fighters in France. This came about because across the road from my office was the large block of Edwardian, if not Victorian, flats known as Queen Anne's Mansions. An Army Signals Interception Unit belonging to Home Forces was stationed there, under the command of Lieutenant Colonel B. E. Wallace. Somehow we came to know him, and to learn that his Unit was intercepting radio traffic of German origin. Because the codes involved appeared to be simple, we thought that we would try to break them ourselves. This turned out to be a foolish thing to do, since we were not members of the code-breakers' trades union, and it was a long time before they forgave us. But first Derek Garrard and then Charles Frank succeeded in deciphering the traffic, which turned out to be plots by the same coastal radar stations that we were photographing, and the information in the messages could therefore provide us with valuable clues about the performance of German radar.

Once we came to identify the traffic we could see that the vital information was contained in the form of ranges in kilometres and bearings in degrees from the particular radar station involved, and it was often so elementary that only the bearing alone was encoded, and this in such a way that the figures were substituted by letters which did not change for several days on end. It was therefore a matter almost of common sense to find the appropriate de-coding figure-for-letter substitution after the reception of a few messages. We were never clear why the Germans used such an elementary system. Possibly it was because there was little available time—radar plots had to be used almost immediately if fighters were to intercept—and so there may not have been enough time for a more elaborate coding procedure.

It was perhaps because the messages were so easy to decipher that our code-breakers had tended to think that they could not contain information of much importance, and had therefore put them aside. Alternatively, some code-breakers had misgivings, perhaps subconsciously, at making much use of their decodes: this would be tempting a bountiful Providence which had given the code-breaker the luck to make his break and which could at any time withdraw the luck by leading the enemy to change the code.

The German plots presented us with much opportunity. We could, for example, fly our own aircraft in sorties towards any particular radar station that we had identified, coming in at various heights and seeing when we were first detected. We could thus chart the extent of the German radar cover, and also investigate the accuracy of their plotting. In general, this was high, because they had built their radar equipment with their usual eye to precision of performance. Moreover, we could ascertain the German reactions to any one of our raids and we could build up a minute-by-minute picture of what the German fighter controller was seeing. We took this to the stage of organizing a plotting table at Fighter Command Headquarters alongside the famous table on which our own radar plots were displayed, and so the controller for our fighter sweeps over north France could see not only what our own radar stations were recording there but also the information available to his German counterpart. We set this up at Fighter Command, much to the approval of the Commander-in-Chief, Sir Sholto Douglas, and arranged for plots to be fed in from Colonel Wallace's Unit and various other R.A.F. and Army Interception Units.

Most of the plotting was done by two girls who had now joined us: Mary Francis, a mathematician from the radar establishment at Swanage and 'Ginger' Parry, who before she had married was 'Ginger' Girdlestone. She had started from school as cashier in a butcher's shop in Felixstowe, and had been taken on with two other girls at Bawdsey by Watson-Watt to see whether girls would make good radar-plotters. Not only did these girls succeed but they went on to train as their successors the famous band of W.A.A.F.s who staffed the plotting tables of the Battle of Britain.

A further benefit from the German plots was that they enabled us to locate stations that we had not previously found. We at first achieved this by chance when a photographic reconnaissance aircraft had flown a sortie over the cruiser *Hipper* in Brest, making an easily recognizable track which we could plot on to a map from the photographs. It happened that this sortie was also plotted by a German radar station north-west of Brest; we did not know exactly where the station was but we could plot the ranges and bearings from this unknown station on a piece of transparent paper on the same scale as we had used for the photographic track, and we found that these gave a track of similar shape to that which we had plotted from the aerial photographs. We then slid the transparent paper over the photographic map until there was the best fit between the photographic and radar tracks (Figure 6), and the plotting origin on the transparent paper had to lie, within a

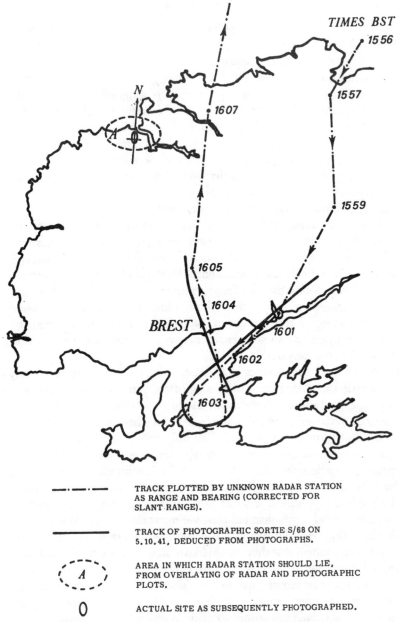

TIMES BST
15 56
15 57
15 59
16 07
16 05
16 04
16 01
16 02
16 03
N
A
BREST

─ ─ · ─ ─ · ─   TRACK PLOTTED BY UNKNOWN RADAR STATION
AS RANGE AND BEARING (CORRECTED FOR
SLANT RANGE).

───────   TRACK OF PHOTOGRAPHIC SORTIE S/68 ON
5.10.41, DEDUCED FROM PHOTOGRAPHS.

A   AREA IN WHICH RADAR STATION SHOULD LIE,
FROM OVERLAYING OF RADAR AND PHOTOGRAPHIC
PLOTS.

O   ACTUAL SITE AS SUBSEQUENTLY PHOTOGRAPHED.

Fig. 6. Example of locating an unknown German radar station through its broadcast plots on a British photographic aircraft. The radar track is plotted on transparent paper which is then slid over the track as mapped from the aircraft's photographs until the best 'fit' is obtained. the unknown station must lie at the origin of the radar plots

small limit of error, at the point where the radar station itself was. All we had then to do was to request that the next aircraft flying a sortie over Brest should photograph the small region in which we now knew the station must be located, and it promptly showed up. As a result of this success, Peter Stewart arranged that all photographic aircraft would run their cameras for a few minutes on crossing the French coast, which was the region in which they were most likely to be plotted by German radar anyway, and we would then examine the radar plots at the time shown on the photographs, and correlate the radar and photographic plots, thus locating any station that was plotting the aircraft at the time. This proved to be a very fruitful method of locating the remaining stations whose whereabouts were not exactly known to us.

Besides de-coding and using the German radar plots of our aircraft, we could of course examine the characteristics of the radar transmissions themselves. This told us such details as the width of the radar beam, and the way the individual stations scanned their field of view. And evidently the Germans found that the Freya equipment was capable of detecting aircraft at greater ranges than those allowed by the original pulse repetition rate of 1000 per second, for they subsequently lowered the pulse repetition rate to 500 per second, which would allow a detection range of 300 kilometres.

We also noticed changes in German radar philosophy during 1941. It appeared to us that at the beginning of the war the Germans had not thought nearly so much about the use of radar as we had ourselves, in contrast to the navigational beams, where they had obviously thought a great deal further than we had. The difference could be explained by our having thought almost entirely defensively whilst they were giving priority to offensive action. As a result in Britain, the serving officers and the scientists and engineers had been thrown much more together by the bombing threat, and had thus come to appreciate one another's problems much more than did their German counterparts. What would happen, for example, was that our serving officers would tell us the kind of equipment that they would like to have, and we might well have to tell them that they could not have what they wanted but that if they could relax their requirement in one direction or another we might be able to give them something that would be better than nothing. Similarly we could sometimes ask them whether, when we had thought of some new device, they would have a use for it.

As a result of this interchange at the working level, Britain had a radar system in 1939 which, although imperfect, was adapted to operational needs and moreover was handled by serving officers who from its beginning had been able to think out how it could best be used. And the essential point of our radar philosophy was that it enabled us to overcome the fundamental problem of intercepting the enemy not by flying continuous patrols, which would have been prohibitively expensive, but by sending up our fighters so as to be at the right place and the right time for interception. In other words, we regarded the main contribution of radar as a means of economizing in fighters, one of our most precious commodities.

The Germans, by contrast, did not have the same close relationship between their serving officers and their scientists. When radar became a technical possibility, and this was realized at least as early in Germany as in Britain, the German Services drew up specifications which the scientists and engineers then tried to satisfy. And very well they did so, within the limits imposed by the specifications. German radar was much better engineered than ours, it was much more like a scientific instrument in stability and precision of performance. The philosophy of using it, however, seemed to have been left to the German Services, and the Luftwaffe in particular made a philosophical mistake by focusing on the wrong objective.

German philosophy ran roughly along the lines that here was an equipment which was marvellous in the sense that it would enable a single station to cover a circle of radius 150 kilometres and detect every aircraft within that range. Thus it could replace a large number of Observer Corps posts on the ground, and so was a magnificent way of economizing in Observer Corps. Moreover, where we had realized that in order to make maximum use of the radar information the stations had to be backed by a communications network which could handle the information with the necessary speed, the Germans seemed simply to have grafted their radar stations on to their existing Observer Corps network which had neither the speed nor the handling capacity that the radar information merited. It was only after nearly two years of war that I saw the real value of radar recognized by a senior German officer. This was in North Africa, where Flieger Führer Afrika (probably Lieutenent General Hoffman von Waldau) said he needed more radar so as to economize in fighters. From that point onwards we could expect the German use of radar to improve.

As for the scale of German radar deployment in 1941, we could make a guess from the few serial numbers that were mentioned in the Enigma messages referring to Freyas: these numbers were 22, 59, 82 and 132. It was an interesting problem for a gambler faced with these numbers and assuming that they started from unity: how many Freyas were there altogether? My guess was that there was likely to be about 150; and by the end of 1941 we had actually located more than 50. Two of them were brought to our notice in a spectacular way which deserves to be recorded as an outstanding example of courage and individual initiative.

I was telephoned one morning in the summer of 1941 by an officer on Denys Felkin's staff of prisoner interrogators, who asked me to accompany him to the Royal Patriotic Schools in Wandsworth because M.I.5 had detained there a man who had just arrrived in this country and said he was a Dane. His story was so improbable that M.I.5 were very suspicious and they wished to have it checked by experts in every detail. So Charles Frank and I accompanied the officer, Flight Lieutenant Gregory, to the Schools, where we found the man under close guard. He said that his name was Thomas Sneum and that he owned an estate on Fanø, the island just offshore from Esbjerg. He had been a lieutenant in the Royal Danish Naval Air Service, but had returned to his estate when the Germans occupied Denmark. He and a friend had found that another of his friends had a Hornet Moth lying dismantled in an old barn on the island of Odense in central Denmark and so they had formed the idea of making their escape to England. They had therefore reassembled the aircraft, sometimes having to use odd bits of wire instead of proper fasteners, and somehow they had gathered enough fuel to take them to England, although this was well beyond the range of a Hornet Moth. Their plan was to carry the extra petrol in cans and to refuel the tanks by a hose from the cockpit while in flight.

The whole escapade was full of danger because the take-off had to be made within earshot of German guards, and the aircraft engine had not been run for some time, at least not since Denmark had been occupied more than a year before. They intended to swing the propeller, fling open the barn doors as soon as the engine started, taxi straight out and take off. They timed their exit to occur as a train was passing nearby, so as to mask the noise of their engine. There were electricity cables across their path and they did not know whether they would have to go over or under them. In the event, with the extra fuel load they had to go under, and they then set course for England. Over the North Sea Sneum had to climb out onto the wing, and insert the end of the hose into the fuel tank, while his companion poured petrol from the reserve cans into the hose at the cockpit end. They were duly intercepted, much to the astonishment of the Royal Air Force, since no one could believe that a Hornet Moth could have flown so far. The story was a tall one, and it was not unreasonable to suspect that the whole thing had been rigged by the Germans so as to infiltrate two agents who would gain our confidence.

Why I had been drawn into the episode was that Sneum had brought some undeveloped cine film with him which he said that he had taken of the radar station on Fanø, showing the aerials turning. Unfortunately M.I.5 had taken the film and had it processed by, I believe, the Post Office, and between them they had ruined nearly all of it; Sneum was justifiably indignant. There were just one or two frames left from which I could see that he very definitely had filmed two Freyas in operation. Figure (7) shows the sketches that I made by projecting the film on to a

Fig. 7. The only relic of Thomas Sneum's film of the German radar station on the Island of Fanø: sketches traced from a 'still' of the film

sheet of paper and tracing the outlines of the Freyas; these are the sole relics of a most gallant exploit. Gregory, Charles and I were all convinced that Sneum was genuine, and we could entirely sympathize with his indignation. Not only had he and his friend risked their lives several times over, but also they had brought with them very valuable information only to have it ruined by the hamhandedness of our Security Authorities; moreover they were treated as spies because their story was so improbable. At the same time, there was an almost inevitable irony about such episodes, because the more gallant and therefore improbable that they were, the harder it was to believe that they had really happened.

So we extracted Sneum from M.I.5 custody, and did our best to make up for his wretched treatment. He volunteered to go back to

Scandinavia. There was some difficulty in Stockholm because, I believe, he wanted to go into Denmark but S.O.E., which by agreement with M.I.6 was in sole charge of direct activity in Denmark, thought that it would be too dangerous for him, with the result that he fell out with them. He was even incarcerated in Brixton Prison, but was ultimately released. He joined the Royal Air Force, finishing the war in a Mosquito Squadron. I tried at the end of the war to make some slight amends for the way in which he had been treated, when I persuaded the Royal Air Force to let him lead his squadron into the airport at Copenhagen as the first of the Allied Forces to take it back from the Germans.

It might be thought that after all this Sneum would have become the national hero that he deserved to be. But he found himself cold-shouldered by those in control of Denmark at the end of the war, perhaps for this very reason. Some of them had been equivocal so long as Germany was in the ascendant, and their patriotic record would bear no comparison with that of Sneum, who had committed himself to resistance as soon as the Germans invaded Denmark. It would have endangered their positions if Sneum came back, and they were able to make play of his imprisonment in Brixton; he ultimately left Denmark to live in Switzerland. If they survive, the men who go first are rarely popular with those who wait for the wind to blow.

CHAPTER TWENTY-FOUR

Beams On The Wane

ONE REASON why we had been able to pursue Freya to the extent described in the previous chapter was that our counter-measures had gained us a respite from the beams. Even so, we dared not relax our watch for new stratagems and devices. It looked as though the Germans hoped to bludgeon their way through our jamming by building so many beam stations that we could not jam them all. They erected seven more Knickebeins, making a total of eleven: the position of each is indicated by a 'K' on the map in Figure 8, which also shows

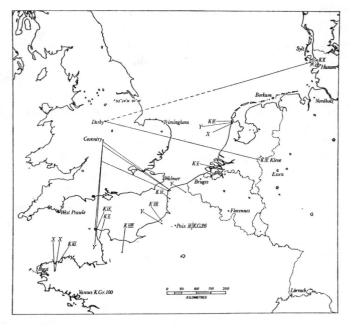

Fig. 8. Map showing the increased deployment in Summer 1941 of German beam stations (K, Knickebein; X, X-Beam; Y, Y-Beam), which the Luftwaffe hoped to use on its return from Russia

the positions of the X- and Y-beam transmitters. (The Cleves and Husum Knickebeins were much larger than those erected subsequently, their aerials being about 300 feet wide by 100 feet high; there was a third larger Knickebein at Lörrach near the Swiss border. These three huge constructions were clearly set up deliberately before the outbreak of World War II; they were so sited on the western border of Germany as to give the best possible crosses on targets in England and France.) To counter any one beam effectively we needed to deploy three jammers, because these were fixed whereas the beam could be swung from one target to another over the whole of southern Britain. Addison at 80 Wing therefore had a heavy task; although the Luftwaffe was never to return in force, his preparations had to be made.

At first we expected to see the Luftwaffe back in the autumn, but our hopes began to rise. There was always the promise offered by the Enigma decodes, although for one reason or another this promise was not always fulfilled. As Wavell's troops pushed right forward in Africa, Enigma messages showed that German rations and fuel supplies in some quantity were being sent to Tripoli; yet Wavell himself told me after the war that the presence of the Germans was a complete surprise to him when his forces encountered them, with the result that Rommel was able to roll us back easily. Wavell said that he would have changed his plans had the information been available to him.

Even when all possible information was available to our commanders, they often had insufficient resources to stop the Germans doing as they wished. In fact, Charles Frank and I were one day lamenting to an officer from Bletchley that reading the Enigma signals was just like reading to-morrow's paper today. He agreed with us but said that it was now going to be different—for example, we had just deciphered the complete German invasion plans for Crete at least three weeks in advance of their intended date of operations. Yet even all this notice did not stop the Germans from taking Crete, partly because our Commander, Lord Freyberg, could make only the most limited use of the foreknowledge for fear of giving the Enigma secret away. But the German parachute forces received such a mauling that they never took part in a major operation again.

Besides this, Crete is to be remembered for the decision of the Naval Commander-in-Chief, Admiral Cunningham, when it was clear that Crete was no longer tenable, and he was faced either with leaving the Army there and saving his ships, or playing the traditional part of getting the Army out. He declared, 'It takes the Navy three years to build a new ship. It will take three hundred years to build a new tradition. The evacuation will continue.'

Before Crete drew to a conclusion, there were already signs of major German moves which only made sense if Hitler intended to attack Russia. When I read the report from Bletchley that drew this conclusion I could not help exclaiming, 'Those whom the Gods wish to destroy...!' It seemed incredible that Hitler could be so mad as to attack Russia, where Napoleon had failed, before he had knocked us out—and yet what a relief it was. The Joint Intelligence Committee was much slower in arriving at this vital conclusion than Bletchley had been, or indeed Churchill himself. They appeared only on 12th June to have come to the conclusion that Hitler would attack Russia, earning the comment from Churchill, 'I had not been content with this form of collective wisdom and preferred to see the originals (messages) myself . . . thus forming my own opinion sometimes at much earlier dates.'

Among a miscellany of technical matters, we had been following up the Oslo story that the German Air Force was encouraging the development of radio-controlled rocket-driven gliders for use against ships at sea. We also had evidence that a television head was being developed for a ballistic bomb which would be steered from the launching aircraft on the receipt of the televised picture sent back by the bomb. The rocket-driven glider bomb appeared two years later as the HS293, which was used successfully against our warships in the Mediterranean. The ballistic bomb with a television homing head was too much in advance of the technology of the time, but it has since appeared in various forms.

In the background of our minds there was of course the possibility of the devastatingly powerful atomic bomb. As soon as I had joined Intelligence I had briefed agents and other sources to look for traces that might indicate German developments, including the production of heavy water at the Rjukan plant in Norway, where surplus hydroelectric power was used on a routine basis to electrolyse natural water and so leave a concentration of heavy water in the residue. I therefore jumped one afternoon of 1941 when I received a telegram from Norway saying that the Germans were stepping up the production of heavy water at Rjukan and that the sender of the signal would be ready to supply further information if we would say what we required. I contacted the Head of the Norwegian Section, Eric Welsh, who was a chemist and Manager of the International Paint Company's factory in Norway before the war, and whose wife was a niece of the composer Grieg.

When I told Welsh that I was interested in the telegram he said something like, 'Bloody silly telegram! Whoever heard of heavy water?' I told him that it meant something very serious, and that it must be followed up. He accordingly sent a signal on my instructions, and we awaited results. These were not quite what I expected for, instead of providing information as he had promised, the sender of the signal now demanded a reassurance. Yes, he would answer our questions if we could guarantee that our interest was genuine, and that it had not been inspired by Imperial Chemical Industries for, he went on—and I loved him for this—'remember, blood is thicker even than heavy water!'

I met him subsequently, and he turned out to be Leif Tronstad, Professor of Physics at Trondheim, who had worked at Cambridge before the war, and we knew of one another's work. He proved a most loyal colleague, and we looked forward to meeting in different circumstances after the war. Unfortunately, he was far too gallant a man to remain inactive in England, and he was killed in a Commando raid in Norway. But his signal played its part in the atomic bomb story, for one of the factors that led to the American decision to make the bomb, which was then in the balance, was the knowledge that the Germans seemed to be taking it seriously as evidenced by their demands for heavy water from Norway. Another, and more important factor, of course, was that the British Committee under Sir George Thomson, having been convinced particularly by Otto Frisch and Rudolf Peierls, had decided that a bomb was feasible.

Scientists were being increasingly drawn into operational problems, and there were now several of us scattered through the Air Ministry and the various Air Force Commands. Watson-Watt conceived the idea that we should all be formed into one organization with himself as head. Portal very wisely referred the proposal to Tizard, who was by now much in the background, but who might be expected to see whether the proposal amounted to more than self-interest on Watson-Watt's part. Tizard proposed to inspect all the scientific activities connected with the Air Force, and I was asked to let him see our work in detail so that he could assess whether or not we would be better as part of Watson-Watt's empire. I of course knew Tizard well, but I thought that we ought at least to give him evidence of our competence to run our show for ourselves by appearing to be as efficient as possible. We were therefore on our best behaviour for the afternoon of his visit, and I first showed him the maps on our wall. I thought that these would appeal to him, partly because he could see the way in which we had worked out the targets for the German beams and partly how our knowledge of the deployment of German radar was progressing. Moreover he himself had advised me at the beginning of the war to put a map up on my wall, when he told me that although I might having nothing to put on it for a start and might feel that it was a bit ostentatious, sooner or later I should have plenty.

I then took him over to my desk, to let him have a chair while drinking tea. There he happened to spot one of the volumes of Gibbon's *Decline and Fall.* 'Hello,' he said, 'who's reading this?' 'I am,' I explained, 'I read it in the train between here and Richmond.' He then remarked, 'You know, there is some very good stuff in this,' and went on, 'I wonder whether this is the right volume. Let me have a look.' A few moments later he said, 'Yes, here it is. Listen to this!' He then proceeded to read part of what Gibbon had said about the younger of the two Gordians: 'Twenty-two acknowledged concubines, and a library of sixty-two thousand volumes, attested the variety of his inclinations, and from the productions which he left behind him, it appears that the former as well as the latter were designed for use rather than ostentation.' After this promising start, we settled down to a serious exposition of what we did, and I showed him how we spotted radar stations on stereo-aerial photographs. For this I sat him at Charles Frank's desk and let him look through the stereoscope. He was very interested, and we thought that we were doing rather well and certainly giving the impression that we were so efficient that we required no co-ordinating direction from above.

Our impression of efficiency was shattered in a manner that we could never have foreseen. The door of our room was pushed open and a girl's head appeared. It belonged to Margaret Blyth, whose husband, Harold, had been my first assistant. A cryptographer herself, she had the run of our office on her visits to London from Bletchley, and she asked, 'Hello Doc, have you seen Harold?' Harold was evidently somewhere in the building, having come up from Kim Philby's Unit (to which he was now posted) but we had not seen him and I told her so. In that case she decided to come in, and was evidently feeling even more lighthearted than usual because she skipped up to Charles Frank's desk and said, 'Hello, Charles!' As she was covering the few yards between the door and the desk I realized the situation. She was a pretty girl but short-sighted, and refused to wear glasses which would have spoiled her looks. So she could not see that the figure seated at Charles Frank's desk, which had thinning hair and spectacles as Charles had, was not in fact Charles. She actually got within a yard of Tizard when she stopped and said, 'Good God, it's H.T.!'

I could only conclude that she was drunk, and I had visions of Tizard reporting that we were such an irresponsible Unit that no form of co-ordination could be too rigorous for us. Our façade of efficiency had been shattered and I was absolutely nonplussed: how could I possibly account for such wildly disrespectful behaviour? I was then equally astonished to hear Tizard say, 'Hello, Maggie, whatever are you doing here?' It turned out that Maggie's home in Wimbledon had been next door to the Tizards', and that their families were very close acquaintances over many years. Tizard evidently knew that she was a very bright girl, in more senses than one, and he was delighted to see her, especially in the present context. So we were 'home' in a manner entirely unexpected, and all threat of co-ordination vanished.

At the same time, there was a case for bringing those engaged in the various scientific activities together periodically, especially as regards what was now known as Operational Research. Watson-Watt himself had initiated the first Operational Research Section to study the use of radar by Fighter Command; the idea was now being extended to the other Commands and, indeed, to the other Services. The heads of the various Sections were therefore formed into the Operational Research Committee, with an Operational Research Centre as part of the Air Staff.

These developments are generally taken to signal the beginning of Operational Research, but its origins are really much older. Viscount Tiverton carried out a substantial amount of operational research for the Royal Naval Air Service and the Air Department in the 1914-18 War. And although Benjamin Franklin's attempt in 1775 was perhaps light-hearted, it anticipated his country's problems in quantifying American experience against the Viet Cong, when he wrote to Joseph Priestley: 'Britain, at the expense of three millions, has killed 150 Yankees this campaign which is £20,000 a head. And at Bunkers Hill she gained a mile of ground, half of which she lost by our taking post on Ploughed Hill. During the same time 60,000 children have been born in America. From these data any mathematical head will easily calculate the time and expense necessary to kill us all, and conquer our whole territory.'

I was asked to join the Operational Research Committee, so as to provide sidelights on what the Germans were doing, and how they were reacting to our various developments. After the first meeting of the Committee I met its Secretary, Wing Commander A. C. G.

('Sandy') Menzies. He was indeed a pilot, but that had been in World War I; then, as a physics lecturer at Leicester he had C. P. Snow as his first research student, and since 1932 had been Professor of Physics at Southampton. Not long before he died in 1974, he told me that he had been briefed by other members of the Air Staff to get to know me and find out how I worked. But he was far too straight to engage in anything that was not entirely above board and instead of spying on me became one of my strongest allies and warmest friends.

We formed a special Sub-Committee to determine the best tactical countermeasures for Bomber Command to use against the German night defences, both fighters and flak. The Chairman of the Sub-Committee was the Deputy Director of Air Tactics, Group Captain G. H. ('Tiny') Vasse. 'Tiny' was one of the largest of men both in body and in heart, and he and Sandy made a marvellous pair as Chairman and Secretary.

Tiny patiently let every member of the large Committee have his say, which literally took all day, starting at 10.30 a.m. Somewhere from 4 o'clock onwards he would decide that the meeting ought to pass a resolution, despite the conflict of views, for example, between Fighter and Bomber Commands. He would say something like, 'Well, gentlemen, I think that we need a resolution, and so I shall move from the Chair that we recommend . . .' And then would follow a long ramble about which nobody would be clear but with some part of which each member would have his own disagreement. There would be an awkward silence, and then Sandy would whisper something to Tiny which resulted in puzzled dismay coming over Tiny's face and he would say, 'Oh, can't you? In that case I withdraw that resolution, gentlemen!' After one such meeting I asked Sandy what it was that produced this magical effect and so relieved the meeting of the uncongenial task of disagreeing with our very good-natured Chairman. 'It's simple,' replied Sandy, 'Tiny knows that I am a professor, and he has a great respect for professors. So all I say to him is, "You can't say that, it isn't English!"'

Sandy collected a lively staff around him, and they had many tasks which demanded great tact. Not only were existing organizations suspicious of any enquiry into their modes of operation, as Operational Research was bound to demand, but also the scientists associated with Operational Research had themselves sometimes to be tactfully handled. This latter task Sandy could safely leave to his Deputy, a man well versed in civil life in dealing with prima donnas, the impresario Leslie Macdonnell.

I had already encountered the kind of difficulty that Operational

Research was up against when early in 1941 I had drawn Lindemann's attention to reports that indicated that we were not hitting our targets in the way that was being claimed. I remember particularly a raid on the Skoda Works at Pilsen, duly announced by the B.B.C. A friendly Czech indignantly told us that everyone in Pilsen knew that there had been no raid, and that the nearest bomb that had fallen was fifty miles away. Such incidents stimulated Lindemann to institute an investigation; this involved installing cameras in our bombers, so that photographs could be taken at the time of bomb release in the hope of subsequently establishing exactly where the bomber was. This aroused much resentment among the aircrew, who thought that the Air Staff must doubt whether they had actually gone in to attack their targets. Ultimately, they were convinced that no one doubted their courage, and enough photographs were collected by the summer of 1941 for Lindemann's secretary, D. M. B. Butt, to show that over the Ruhr, only one tenth of our bombers were within five miles of their target. It was this that finally convinced the Air Marshals that astronavigation, dead reckoning, and ordinary radio beacons were thoroughly inadequate; and the drive at last started for us to emulate the Germans in their radio navigational techniques.

Up to this time it had been difficult to persuade Bomber Command to take science seriously. The contrast with Fighter Command had been remarkable. If, as a scientist, you visited Bentley Priory, Fighter Command's Headquarters, you were likely to be bombarded with questions from officers at all levels up to the Commander-in-Chief. The Command realized that it was up against desperate odds and was therefore keen to try new ideas. Bomber Command was still nearly as complacent as it had been when Tizard had tried to help it with the Committee for the Scientific Survey of Air Offensive. To one technical problem, however, it thought that it had discovered a solution for itself. Bombers were frequently being caught in German searchlights, and the idea had grown up that the searchlight control could be upset if a bomber switched on its I.F.F. (Identification Friend or Foe) radar recognition set, and so the bomber could then escape. The proffered explanation was that the searchlights were directed by radar which was somehow jammed by British I.F.F.

I did not believe the story, especially since I had seen rather similar stories propagated inside the Luftwaffe about our own defences, which I knew to be untrue. Moreover, it was possible to show that switching on one's own identification device was the most dangerous thing that one could do. Either it had an effect on the German radar control, or it had not: if the latter, you were relying on a useless countermeasure and might therefore fail to develop another countermeasure which would be effective; if the former, a radiation was coming out of the bomber that positively identified it as British, and it would be a very simple step for the Germans to develop a special equipment to challenge the I.F.F. set properly, and obtain both its identification and its exact position. So this alleged countermeasure was either of no use or it was a very positive danger.

I argued that the practice should be most emphatically discouraged, ultimately to such effect that it was decided to hold a special meeting at Bomber Command. I thought this would do the trick because if first-line pilots were present at the conference, my argument must at least shake their confidence in the practice, and general distrust would gradually ensue. I well remember Lywood's comment on the problem of suggesting a Chairman. He himself ultimately suggested the name of a suitable officer on the basis, 'He should make a good Chairman—he doesn't know anything about it!' Since Lywood now effectively disappears from my story, in which he has inevitably figured in an unfavourable light, let me record that some of his contributions were substantial. He was, for example, one of the originators of the British 'Typex' encoding machine, which had points of similarity to, but was more advanced than, Enigma. It was widely used by our Services and as far as we know was never broken.

The conference was held on 26th September 1941 at Bomber Command, not only with members of the Bomber Command Staff but also with pilots such as Leonard Cheshire. To my amazement, Cheshire and his fellow pilots stated their belief in the efficacy of using I.F.F. to jam searchlights, and my rational argument failed to prevail. The only concession I could gain was that there would be an objective assessment over the next few months by the Bomber Command Operational Research Section to ascertain whether I.F.F. had any beneficial effect or not.

The result of the assessment, when it appeared some months later, seemed to show that it had no effect one way or the other. But Bomber Command argued that it was a good thing to let the pilots go on using I.F.F. because it would encourage them to press home attacks over defended areas when they might otherwise be inclined to turn tail if caught by searchlights. This was a thoroughly immoral argument which sooner or later must lead to trouble.

About a fortnight after the Bomber Command conference I was telephoned by a very respectful Flight Lieutenant Smith, who said that he would like to speak to me urgently on a matter of some personal importance, and suggested that I should join him for lunch at his Club, the Thatched House, just across the other side of St. James's Park. Over a very pleasant lunch (he was also a member of the Athenaeum, where he said he went for high thinking and plain living, but came to the Thatched House when he wanted the reverse) he told me what his problem was. He was Reader in Anglo-Saxon in University College, London, but had joined the Royal Air Force and was currently a Flight Lieutenant in one of the personnel branches. Partly because of a motorcycle accident and partly a duodenal ulcer, he was on the point of being invalided out of the Air Force and he wanted to stay in. He had therefore looked through the various branches of the Air Staff to see whom he might persuade to take him on, and he thought that I might have a use for him.

The use that he proposed was in examining charred documents from German aircraft, his qualification being that he was used to deciphering old and fragmentary documents. In particular, he had resolved a major puzzle presented by the Anglo-Saxon Chronicle. He himself had started as a clerk on the Lancashire and Yorkshire railway before going to Leeds University and reading English. By inclination he was an engineer and he had marvellous hands. He had managed to use them, even in English studies, where he solved some problems in early typography by constructing a replica of an early printing press, one by Moxon, which showed what the early printers were up against, and therefore why they developed some of their techniques.

He had also turned to photography, and had developed ways of detecting forgeries by the way different inks showed up in infra-red and ultra-violet photography. It was this capability that had led him to solve the problem of the Anglo-Saxon Chronicle, because a number of puzzling entries all turned out to be written in the same ink, which was different from that of the rest. What appeared to have happened was that some monk in Canterbury in the eleventh or twelfth century had 'got at' a copy of the Chronicle and inserted various items of false history, usually to the effect that someone had died, and had left his lands to the See of Canterbury; and part of the present wealth of Canterbury had been gained in this way.

So Hugh Smith, as his name was, thought that he might be useful to me. Frankly I could not see that we would have many problems in this particular direction, but he was such a good and entertaining chap that I

Fig. 9. *Drawing of a Freya radar by Hugh Smith, based mainly on air reconnaissance photographs*

thought that if possible I would try to make a place on my staff for him. I therefore accepted his invitation to take Vera and our daughter, Susan, then eight months old, to his country cottage, a farmhouse at Alstone in Gloucestershire for the weekend.

It was a thoroughly enjoyable break, and the first of many. There was usually an evening visit to 'The Hobnails' which was Hugh Smith's 'local' and which—characteristically—he had managed to prove ante-dated (1474) the first mention of hobnails in the Oxford English Dictionary (1594). Its landlord, Phil Fletcher, belonged to a family that had run the Inn continuously since Lady Day 1743, and its patrons were basically Gloucestershire farmers, starting with 'Sheddey', 'Matey' and 'Artey' Chandler, three of seven brothers who had all been in the Gloucesters in the First War, and if there were five Sundays in a month, the fifth was 'Pewter Sunday' when all beer was served in tankards.

On my return to London, I consulted Bimbo Norman who before going to Kings College had been at University College, and who knew Hugh Smith well. He was full of enthusiasm for the prospective appointment, and so I persuaded Charles Medhurst to allow me to recruit Hugh Smith, despite the fact that he had no scientific qualifications. It was a singularly happy appointment because Hugh had a tremendous personality, and was outstandingly good in smoothing our way over all kinds of administrative difficulties. He was also a first class draughtsman, and he took over the drawing of the diagrams for my various reports, using his own ingenious method of making perspective views of objects such as radar stations. An example of his craftsmanship in this direction is the drawing of a Freya shown in Figure 9. More of his attributes were to appear as the war proceeded.

CHAPTER TWENTY-FIVE

'Jay'

DECEPTION HAS been an important stratagem in war at least since Gideon scared the hosts of Midian into a disastrous stampede and Thomas Hobbes valued it so highly as to write in *Leviathian* 'Force and fraud in war are the two cardinal virtues'. The schoolboys of my generation had a hero in Richard Meinertzhagen who, by feigning being shot and dropping a briefcase, misled the Turks into thinking that Allenby's attack in Palestine in 1917 was coming on the wrong flank; and many will know from J. C. Masterman's book *The Double Cross System* the story of our using captured German spies in World War II to provide misleading information to their headquarters.

We of course had no monopoly of this art, and one of its greatest masters was a German officer, Colonel H. J. Giskes, who so brilliantly turned 'Operation North Pole' against us. This was an operation in which the Special Operations Executive parachuted sabotage agents into Holland, and Giskes succeeded in catching one of the first to be dropped. By getting this first agent to send suitable messages back to London, Giskes ensured that he knew where all subsequent agents were to be dropped, and so captured them all, at the same time getting enough signals back to London to make S.O.E. think that the agents were at large and operating a successful campaign.

Why I admired Giskes, as it were 'across the havoc of war', was that in the middle of this very serious deception he counterfeited a signal asking S.O.E. to drop a load of tennis balls instead of explosives, on the pretext that the agent was in touch with the King of the Belgians, who was known to be keen on tennis, and who was more likely to be friendly if we could replenish his diminishing stock of tennis balls. Actually, had Colonel Giskes known more of English history he might have realized that tennis balls were a dangerous international commodity: a previous consignment had led to Agincourt.

We ourselves had faced much the same problem as Giskes had, but of course in reverse. I can remember that during the early part of 1941 we knew from the Enigma traffic that a German agent was to be dropped by parachute somewhere in England, but we did not know where. We even knew the night of the operation, and we went home wondering what the chances were of catching him. When we enquired the following morning, we found that he was already in custody, in hospital in fact. He had been dropped with a radio set so that he could keep in contact with his base, and this had been suspended with him on the same parachute but, fortunately for us, between him and the parachute. As he landed, the radio set hit him on the head and knocked him out, and he was discovered unconscious by the police in, I believe, a ditch somewhere in Northamptonshire. I have sometimes used this incident as an illustration of the value of following the precept of Horace Darwin, son of Charles Darwin and founder of the Cambridge Instrument Company. He used to make the point in instrument design that whenever you think that you have made a good design, try reversing the arrangement of some of the parts—it might then work better. And had the Germans reversed the position of parachutist and radio set, the latter might have been demolished, but the agent would have been at large for much longer.

My own contact with our deception work started through my first assistant, Harold Blyth, going to work with Kim Philby, who was in that part of M.I.6 which liaised with M.I.5 on matters of internal security. Harold told me that he would like me to meet one of the M.I. officers concerned, whom I will call 'George'. Although I did not know this until after the war, George was the key man in 'The Man Who Never Was', the deception in which a body dressed up as a Major in the Royal Marines was put into the sea off southern Spain with a dispatch case containing documents which made it appear that we were going to land in Sardinia and Greece in July 1943 when in fact we were going to invade Sicily. The deception was so successful that the Germans diverted an armoured division to Greece, and did not realize until much too late that our landing in Sicily was a major operation.

Incidentally, I came to learn the truth about 'The Man Who Never Was' only in 1952, when Churchill asked me to come back to the Ministry of Defence for a year as Director of Scientific Intelligence. I was now a member of the Joint Intelligence Committee, and at my first meeting I heard a discussion about what should be done because Ian Colvin, later Deputy Editor of the *Daily Telegraph* and one of the men who kept Churchill informed on Germany in pre-war days, had worked out the facts of the operation, and had written a book which he had submitted for security clearance. Colvin told me that he had come to write his book because of Duff Cooper's *Operation Heartbreak*, ostensibly a work of fiction but in which a deception operation was described so vividly that Colvin thought that it must have a basis in fact. The key point was the planting of a body of an army officer in the sea off Spain, with false documents calculated to mislead the Germans. Colvin therefore worked his way round the cemeteries on the coast of Spain until he found the actual grave, and one way or another he established most of the truth. Duff Cooper, then Ambassador in Paris, was approached by the security authorities and, as I heard it from George, said that if they attempted to prosecute him for a breach of security he would state that he had the story from Churchill himself, without any warning that security was still involved. The Joint Intelligence Committee decided, very unsportingly, I thought, to hold back Colvin's account while they invited Ewen Montague, who had been in Naval Intelligence and was involved in the deception, to write an officially approved account which came out as *The Man Who Never Was* in 1953.

My opportunity for working on the grand scale with George came in August 1941 when I was urgently summoned by Tizard one morning to discuss an unexpected operational emergency that had arisen. The background for this emergency was that a new radio navigational aid had been developed, particularly by R. J. Dippy at the Telecommunications Research Establishment, which was very much along the lines that I had proposed to the Air Ministry in 1938, and which had been turned down, partly because it was believed that the range of radio devices would not be great enough to permit accurate navigation over Germany, and partly because Bomber Command and others were convinced that these radio aids were not needed, anyway. The inaccuracies in our bombing revealed by the Butt Report had now come to light, and the Command was prepared to consider radio devices despite the fact that various senior officers had hitherto termed them 'adventitious aids'.

The system developed by Dippy was known as 'Gee' and it involved sending synchronized pulses from three stations in Britain. From the differences in the times of arrival of the three pulses at the aircraft, the navigator could determine his position. Trials of the system had been made over Britain and out into the Atlantic, and it worked very well. Bomber Command, however, still had misgivings, and would only be convinced if it could be tried out over Germany. The Command therefore fitted trial receivers into three aircraft and proceeded, without telling the Air Staff, to fly them over Germany, and the crews concerned were enthusiastic about the accuracy with which they were now able to find their way. Someone at Bomber Command then decided to use these three aircraft as primitive pathfinders for the rest of the bomber force, again without telling the Air Staff. Of course, it was only a matter of time before one of the aircraft was lost, and this in fact happened on 13th August 1941, when an aircraft of No. 115 Squadron was missing after leading a raid on Hanover. Bomber Command had thus repeated the error of the Germans in 1940, and this was an even more serious example, for wreckage of the aircraft could provide the Germans with information about the new system that was coming into use, but which in fact would not be available (apart from the three prototype receivers) until March 1942, some seven months ahead. At Portal's request, Tizard had therefore called a meeting to discuss what should now be done.

After the facts had been presented to the meeting, and it was made clear that for most of 1942 Bomber Command was either going to be committed to Gee or to continue to use its existing methods which had proved so inaccurate, Tizard asked me to assess how much the Germans might have discovered. We guessed that there was roughly a one in three chance that they had captured the receiver, although this was probably damaged because it had been fitted with demolition charges. Knowing the weakness of our own radio interception efforts, I thought that it was unlikely that the Germans would have so far recognized the pulse transmissions from the ground stations in England as being associated with a navigational system, and also that it was unlikely that they would have received reports from spies, especially since I knew that most of these were already locked up.

Where the main danger lay was in the fact that 78 aircrew had been lost in the interval between the first Gee receiver being installed in a bomber at Marham (which was the base from which 115 Squadron operated) and the receiver being lost, and probably twenty or thirty of them would now be prisoners-of-war. From our experience over the beams and other matters, I reckoned that with as few as six prisoners from the Luftwaffe who knew about a particular development we should very probably have acquired some clue, either by interrogation or by eavesdropping on their conversations, of what was afoot. In general, air crew were more lively and interested in new devices than their counterparts in the other two Services, and as soon as some new device came into use at a particular station, everyone wanted to know what it did and how it worked. So if the Germans had twenty prisoners, it was quite likely that they might have overheard some reference to Gee, and this would have alerted them to investigating particularly the wreckage of any aircraft from the squadron involved.

Since it was a matter of either Gee or nothing for most of 1942, Tizard asked me whether I thought that I could possibly mislead the Germans and throw them off the track until Gee should come into large-scale use, in seven months' time. I replied that it was a long shot, but I would be glad to try. I immediately drew up a plan of campaign, which was endorsed by the meeting. It was, of course, a marvellous opportunity and the culmination of all my pre-war efforts in practical joking, with virtually as much of the national resources at my disposal as I wished. The issue at stake, the success of our bombing campaign, was so great that I could have anything I wanted within reason.

My plan involved two aspects: the masking of any clues that the Germans might have already gathered or would gather in the future regarding the true nature of Gee, and second the planting of other clues to make them think that we were adopting an entirely different technique, since we could not avoid providing clues that some kind of new equipment was going to be installed in our bombers. The first step was to get the word 'Gee' abolished. The next was to get the type number changed from one in the 'R3000' series, which indicated its true nature as a receiver of pulse-type transmissions, which the Germans could have known from the airborne radar equipment that they had already captured (I.F.F. and A.S.V.). The new type number should be one in the ordinary communications series, and 'TR1335' was chosen, since this would suggest a new transmitter/receiver system for radio telegraphy or telephony. This solved two problems: I was told that for some months before Gee was installed on a large scale all aircraft coming off the production line would have to be fitted with the necessary hooks and so forth to accept the Gee receiver, and it was necessary that these fittings should be labelled from the start. The Germans would therefore have a long warning that something new was coming along, and an R3000 number would have given them a fatal clue. As it was, by changing the type number to one that was thoroughly misleading, we turned an awkward situation to our advantage. Finally, the Gee transmitting stations in England were camouflaged to look like ordinary radar stations by providing them with extra masts and by removing the exact synchronization of their pulses which might otherwise have given a clue had the German interception service been alert enough to spot it.

The next step was to provide something on which the Germans could focus their attention. Since it was likely that they would get wind that we were introducing some new radio navigational system, what better than to flatter them into thinking that we were going to copy them and use beams? I found that we had in fact already made some beam transmitters to give our bombers a line when they were attacking the German naval units in Brest, and so these beams were commandeered and re-erected on the east coast of England; I gave them the title of 'Jay beams'. The new bombing system was to be called 'Jay' and I hoped that if the Germans had previously overheard British prisoners-of-war talking about Gee they would be misled into thinking that they had misheard the prisoners, who had really been speaking about Jay. And to give the Jay beams a further touch of authenticity, bomber crews were to be actually encouraged to use them as a directional aid when returning to bases in England, and possibly on the way out, too.

A further channel of communication was open to me, and this was the possibility of providing false information via George and the German agents in Britain who were under his control. I therefore suggested that one of these agents should purport to have overheard a conversation on the evening of New Year's day 1942 between two R.A.F. officers chatting in the Savoy. One who was rather 'browned off' said: 'Why did Sir Frank Smith get his G.C.B.? All he has done is to copy the German beams—and a year late at that! In any case, it wasn't him alone, but the chaps under him.' 'But,' said his companion, 'you must admit that at any rate we now have the Jay beams to get us to our targets; they worked okay on Brest, and we shall soon have them over Germany.' In the ensuing argument the second officer demonstrated the Jay system by having the salt cellar as one beam station and the pepper pot as the other and impressing the lines of the beams on the tablecloth with the end of a fork.

Another agent who was supposed to be in contact with R.A.F. personnel reported that he had been told that a 'Professor Ekkerley' (whom I hoped the Germans would identify as Eckersley) had been giving special lectures to R.A.F. units in which he described the new 'Jerry' radio navigational system using Lorenz-type beams. I left it to my German opposite number to work out whether 'Jerry' stood for 'Jay' or for 'German' or for any other object with which his knowledge of English may have acquainted him. The agents were enthusiastically thanked by their German masters for their very valuable information.

I could not know in advance whether or not the hoax would be successful, but the enthusiasm mentioned in the last paragraph was a good sign, and we might therefore hope for perhaps three months' life for Gee once operations were started on a large scale, before the Germans were able to revise their ideas of what we were doing and develop suitable jammers. In fact large-scale Gee operations started on 8th March 1942, and no jamming was experienced until nearly five months afterwards. We had therefore obtained considerably more than the three months for which we had hoped at our most optimistic, and prisoners were still being interrogated about the Jay beams as late as July. In his book *Instruments of Darkness*, Alfred Price has provided further evidence because he discovered an account of a meeting in Berlin on 26th May 1942 to discuss our new navigational system. The Intelligence Officer in charge of the Intelligence investigation was Engineer-Colonel Schwenke, who reported:

> We have also carried out a systematic interrogation of prisoners. The following facts have come to light. As a result of the extensive use by us of the Knickebein and X- and Y-Gerät systems these devices fell into British hands; this was because we did not fit demolition charges.
>
> In mid-1940 orders were given for the immediate construction of copies of the Knickebein and a year later, in August or September 1941, these were ready for service. The British found it comparatively simple to copy the German set, as the airborne Knickebein uses the installation for (Lorenz) blind beam (airfield approach) receivers, and the British had obtained the licence for the Lorenz set before the war. . . . From the interrogation of prisoners, we know that this system was used under the designation 'Julius'.

He went on to tell how captured Gee sets now indicated that we had also developed another system, and then gave an accurate account of the genuine Gee principle. He went on to say that the Director General of Air Signals, General Martini, was going to call a conference on the question of jamming Gee, and so it seems that jammers for Gee were not even designed more than two months after we were using it on a large scale. In the meantime the Air Signals Experimental Regiment (who had operated the beam stations against us in 1940) had themselves set up listening stations to investigate the Jay beams, and I was able to report at the beginning of 1943, 'It is pleasing to find among the personnel some of those who were previously operating the X-beams against us, so that some of our old scores against the Regiment are being wiped out.' A final twist to the story was that when the Germans realized that they had been hoaxed they ceased to pay any attention to the Jay beams, which continued to work throughout the war, and thus provided a useful homing service for our bombers when more sophisticated aids were jammed.

CHAPTER TWENTY-SIX

Würzburg

B Y THE middle of 1941 we had a fair knowledge of the Freya stations in the Channel coast and we were scanning photographs of their sites in the hope that we would ultimately find evidence of a Würzburg, the smaller paraboloidal equipment whose transmissions we could hear on wavelengths around 53 centimetres. If, as we suspected, the Würzburg could determine the height as well as the plan-position of an aircraft, it could be the key to whatever system of night-fighting the Germans might develop. It turned out that the same thought had occurred to General Ernst Udet, the World War I air ace, who succeeded in the summer of 1940 in making a practice interception of a target aircraft, on the basis of information from two Würzburgs, one following the target and the other Udet himself. On 16th October 1940 a British bomber was successfully intercepted for the first time using this technique; it was probably this experience that led to the setting up of the circular nightfighting zone of 40 kilometres radius at den Helder.

In September 1941 we heard of another nightfighter circle, this time of 60 kilometres radius, centred near Bad Kreuznach, the wine capital of the Nahe region. Had the range of the Würzburg been extended and, if so, how? I asked for photographic cover, and was advised by Claude Wavell that it would be well if I visited Benson and met Geoffrey Tuttle, the Commanding Officer of the Photographic Reconnaissance Unit because he liked to know the reasons why he was asked to risk his pilots. I felt much sympathy, for it was too easy to ask for photographs without thinking of the risks that had to be run to get them. I readily went to Benson, and the meeting with Tuttle resulted in a lifelong friendship. He had the embarrassing and difficult task of taking over from Sidney Cotton, who he thought was the greatest leader he had ever met; but he himself set a splendid example, and he was able to call on the most able pilots in the R.A.F. to join his unit. Somehow we never found the Kreuznach station, although the area was carefully photographed;

perhaps the station had not been set up, or we had insufficient idea of what we were looking for. But the disappointment had its compensation in the even warmer contact with the pilots that resulted from my visit.

Had I known it, a photograph was already in my hands. It had come into Air Intelligence through our American liaison and had been taken in May 1941 by the American Embassy in Berlin. It showed an object on the Flak Tower in the Tiergarten (Plate 13(a)). The photograph took some months to reach me, and it was indistinct; moreover there was no indication of its scale. At first I thought it was a searchlight with some sort of control box mounted on its back, and I could only keep it in mind as an unsolved problem. Enlightenment came in an unexpected and literally roundabout way from a Chinese physicist who had worked in Berlin and was on his way back with his wife to China via Ankara. There our enterprising Naval Attaché met him, and persuaded him to come back to England in case he might have useful information. When he and his wife arrived they were most discourteously treated by M.I.5, who failed to appreciate that they had made the long and risky detour simply to help us.

The two were locked up and stripped, and the physicist was very justifiably indignant. All his papers and suitcases had been gone through without his permission—he had been bright enough to place threads in tell-tale positions to show if anything had been disturbed. When I met him he was literally 'hopping mad'. He was so angry that he could not keep both his feet on the ground at the same time, saying, 'They have no right to do this to me! I am an individual man! Individual man!' It was indeed appalling treatment for a pair who had made the relatively dangerous journey from Ankara to England instead of going directly back to China, and it was not easy to change his frame of mind. However, in the course of a day or so I managed to make a few amends on the part of His Majesty's Government, and we discussed what the Chinese physicist had seen during his years in Berlin. I had with me the photograph of the object in the Tiergarten and asked him whether he had seen it. He had. I then asked him whether the 'bowl' was solid, and bright like a searchlight mirror viewed from the front, or whether the bowl consisted of a mesh more like a sieve or colander. He told me that he was not sure, but he thought that it was a mesh. If so, it could not be a searchlight, and might well be radar equipment and by that time I knew that P.R.U. was flying sorties over Berlin. I therefore asked Claude Wavell to send me some photographs, and I was able to relate the dimensions of the tower to those of the Tiergarten as a whole, which gave me the scale of the photograph and showed that the diameter of the reflector must be about twenty feet.

Such a diameter would make the apparatus at least as large as a Freya and it should therefore have been visible on photographs of the Channel radar stations, had it been there. So the mystery of Würzburg was not yet solved. But at about the same time in the autumn of 1941 Charles Frank made the vital observation that was ultimately to clear everything up. Claude Wavell had sent us photographs of the Freya station at Cap d'Antifer, the chalk headland about 20 kilometres north of le Havre. There were two Freyas situated at the top of the four hundred foot cliff, and a track appeared to run southwards from them for some hundreds of yards to a large villa further along the cliff and nearer the village of Bruneval.

The inference was that this was the headquarters of the radar station and the track had been worn by traffic between the house and the Freyas. At least, that is what most observers would have deduced; but Charles pointed out that the track did not run quite up to the house but ended in a loop rather further away from the house than it should have done had the vehicles been driven up to it. By the loop there was a small speck which was so indistinct that we had to look on several photographs to check that it was not simply a speck of dust on the negative. Photograph No. 10(a) shows, not the photograph on which Charles made the observation, but one which was a good deal better and taken from low altitude—and even then the speck is barely visible. I requested a photographic sortie at low level, as usual giving complete operational freedom for the sortie to take place only when conditions were favourable. In the meantime I told Claude Wavell what I had done, so that he could look out for the photographs when they were taken, along with my suspicion that the object might well turn out to look like a large electric bowl fire.

A few days later two pilots from the Photographic Reconnaissance Unit, Gordon Hughes and Tony Hill, happened to visit Wavell, who told them of my interest in the object. Tony Hill said that he would go and have a look: I had already heard of him, although not by name, as a photographic pilot who was practising most assiduously at taking low oblique photographs but was almost always missing his target. His enthusiasm never wavered, and he just went on trying.

Later, when I came to know him well, he told me that his trouble was that he was 'a bit slow' in his personal reaction time, with the result that by the time he had pressed the shutter the object was past the camera.

Actually, it was a very difficult thing to get right because no one had worked out properly how low oblique photographs should be taken. The only arrangement that had been made was for a camera to be pointed sideways and looking somewhat aft from the fuselage of a Spit-fire just behind the pilot's seat (Plate 14(c)). Therefore what a pilot had to do was dive and fly past the object to be photographed; the object would disappear under his wing, and he had to guess when it would reappear behind the wing and fire the shutter accordingly. Since all this had to take place while he was flying at fifty feet and three hundred miles an hour, with quite possibly a light anti-aircraft gun firing at him, it is not surprising that he found it difficult.

It turned out that Tony Hill's father, Colonel Hill, ran Fordham's Brewery in Hertfordshire which had brewed the beer for the 1937 Coronation, and Hugo Meynell had been one of the Brewery's pupils. Tony Hill himself was my idea of every schoolboy's hero—modest, lively, and ready to go on trying indefinitely until he got things right. Actually things did not go right on his first sortie against our object—his camera failed. But he returned and telephoned Claude Wavell, telling him to tell me that he had seen the object and it looked just like what I had expected, a large bowl fire. He would go out again tomorrow and get me a photograph.

All this was completely unofficial. Although I had formally requested a sortie, this had been allocated to another Squadron based at the same airfield, Benson, and they had decided to send three aircraft on the very same morning that Tony Hill was making his second unofficial attempt. As he climbed into his Spitfire he was told that the other aircraft were taking off for the same target, whereupon he taxied over to the other Squadron and told them that if he found any of them within twenty miles of the target he would shoot them down. As a result he had a free run; this time his camera worked—and in contrast to so many of his practice efforts he had the Würzburg almost exactly in the middle of his two photographs. They became classics; they are reproduced as Plate 11. They led to the Bruneval Raid, as the following chapter describes.

What was already clear was that whatever electronic apparatus would give a range of 40 kilometres in a paraboloid of 10 feet diameter should be able to give at least 60 kilometres range in the 20 or so feet diameter of the paraboloid of the Berlin Tiergarten provided that the pulse repetition rate was dropped from 3,750 to 2,500 per second or less, to give the pulses time to return from the longer range.

Our bombers had for some months been reporting the existence of a great belt of searchlights along the western frontiers of Germany, and our pilots believed that these were controlled by radar. As the next phase of our attack, now that underground movements were being organized in the Occupied countries, we could brief them to look for such installations as Freyas in the hope that their presence would be reported by friendly Resistance workers. Pre-eminent among these at this stage were the Belgians. My contact with them was through Major Jempson, our Belgian liaison and, I believe, a former policeman. He had a rather flamboyant manner—I can recall him saying, 'Tell me what you want,' and then, with a wave of his hand, 'I will get you anything!' For a time I thought that this was an idle boast, but events were to show that there was substance to it.

In February 1942 he produced for me a report of an object which, from its description, seemed to be a Freya about 5 kilometres north of the German nightfighter airfield at St. Trond and about 35 miles east of Brussels.

Now that we had a pinpoint I could ask for a photographic reconnaissance, and the result was sent up to me from Medmenham by Claude Wavell, saying that besides a Freya there was a tower-like object on the photograph which he had not seen before. When I looked myself, I realized that he had been misled by the low angle of the sun, and that when one allowed for this the object was almost certainly a large open-work paraboloid just like the one in the Berlin Tiergarten. It was in fact what the Germans called a 'Würzburg Riese' (Giant Würzburg) and I was so impressed with it that I represented it on our map by a gold-headed pin.

Moreover, there were three searchlight emplacements around it, and a later photograph showed that there was also another Giant Würzburg, this time with no searchlights, and a Freya on the site.

It was not long before we found another station, but with two Giant Würzburgs at Domburg on the Island of Walcheren in the Scheldt Estuary. This second station was well placed for a low-level photographic reconnaissance and I let Tony Hill know that I was initiating an official request for a sortie, so that he could make sure of getting it. Once again, as at Bruneval, he came back with just two photographs, giving full face and side views of the new equipment (Plate 13(b) and (c)). Plate 13(d) also shows a photograph of another Giant Würzburg taken by a Belgian Resistance worker.

The Domburg station had one Freya and two Giant Würzburgs, but no searchlights. At this point I became involved in an argument with our own radar experts as to how the German system worked. Our own philosophy had been to control night interceptions by means of a single radar equipment, which rotated continuously, with its information displayed on a circular cathode ray screen in which the position of the radar set itself was represented at the centre. Returning echoes were displayed along the radius that corresponded to the direction in which the radar set was 'looking'. The result was a map showing the returning echoes as luminous points which indicated the position of any aircraft within range. This device, which was so simple and obvious that we believed that anyone could have invented it, was known as the 'Plan Position Indicator' or 'P.P.I.'. Both the bomber and the intercepting fighter would show up as luminous points, and the task of the ground controller was to estimate the bomber's course and so direct the fighter on to its tail, assuming, of course, that information was also available about the heights of the two aircraft.

One great merit of the system was that the mapping did not need to be absolutely accurate—if, for example, the bomber were misrepresented (owing to errors in direction finding) as 5 degrees to the left of where it really was, so would be the fighter; when the controller steered the latter into the same position on the screen as the bomber, the interception might occur somewhere different from where he believed it to be, but it would still occur, which was the main object of the whole system. Thus our system automatically cancelled out any errors in locating the bomber, and we did not need to know exactly where it was. To make a radar set accurately enough to avoid these directional errors would have been much more trouble, for which no effective return could have been derived. Our system therefore depended on relative measurements of the position of the fighter with respect to the bomber, and not on absolutely accurate independent measurements on each aircraft.

Our experts therefore could not believe it when I said that I thought that the reason for their being two Giant Würzburgs at a single German station was that one was intended to follow the bomber and the other the fighter, and that somehow the plots from the two separate instruments were married together so that the controller could direct the fighter towards an interception. Our experts thought that the second Giant Würzburg was to act as reserve in case the first broke down. I pointed out that in that case it was hard to see the reason why one of the two Giant Würzburgs in the searchlight belt always had three searchlights around it and the other none, because if the second had been a reserve, duplicating exactly the functions of the first, it should have had searchlights as well. Moreover, it was hard to believe that the Germans were so well stocked with such elaborate equipments that every night-fighter control station should have had a spare Würzburg.

What, of course, my explanation assumed was that every Giant Würzburg was so accurately made and performed so well that its absolute accuracy was good enough for it to tell where the bomber was with sufficient precision for its plots to marry up with those of a second Würzburg, at least within the error which would still bring the fighter close enough to the bomber for either a visual or an airborne radar contact, i.e. not much more than a kilometre.

It turned out that my interpretation was the correct one, and it was not the only surprise that we received of the same kind. Later in 1942, for example, we discovered a new form of German radar installation on the Channel coast, which was much bigger than Freya, and which I believed to be used for long-range detection. Because of its appearance I called the new equipment a 'Hoarding', because it resembled the kind of erection on which large bill posters are displayed on major roads; the Germans, because of its size, called it 'Mammut' (Mammoth). When I directed T.R.E.'s attention to the new equipment, they listened for it and found that, as we had guessed, its radar characteristics were very similar to those of Freya, so that the extra performance was being obtained from the same transmitting and receiving equipment, through the extra directing power of the larger aerial array.

However, our experts concluded that it was not a simple radar system but one that was intended for precision long-range bombing, and they backed their argument by the fact that the radio frequency and the pulse repetition rate were far more stable than would be required for ordinary radar purposes, and would only be necessary where extremely accurate range determination was necessary, such as determining the absolute position of an aircraft relative to a ground target. By this time there was more than one Mammut on the Channel coast, and every one had this same stability. It was not easy to challenge the experts on matters of technical detail, when these were supported by rational argument, but I got them to agree that the ordinary Freyas were intended merely for radar and not for long-range bombing; I then asked them to go out and check how stable the Freyas were, because I suspected that the high stablility that we had observed was merely another example of German thoroughness and precision, even where it was not required. A fortnight later the experts came back and told me that I was right: the stability of every German radar station was better than that of the best instruments that we had available to check them. In fact, Martin Ryle, afterwards to win a Nobel Prize for Radioastronomy, was one of our observers, and he told me that ever afterwards if he wanted to know whether a radar transmission was British or German, all he had to do was to check its stability.

I had come to have a 'feel' for the way the Germans did things. They would take simple ideas, and put them straight into practice no matter what technical effort was involved, because they had a far greater command of precision engineering than we had (some notable exceptions such as Rolls Royce apart). When we contemplated a development we would take the simple idea, look for the technical snags in the way of its realization, and think of ways of getting round them without having to go to the trouble of great precision of design or workmanship. In the end, I suspect that we often took as much trouble in avoiding the difficulties as the Germans did in overcoming them by good workmanship; as it turned out in the War, the advantage in the end lay with us, because while the German equipment was technically very good, it was also less adaptable, and we could more easily change ours to meet a new situation.

If the German night interception procedure seemed unduly elaborate, the precision of the Giant Würzburg was not entirely wasted on the war: in 1945 specimens were brought to Britain and America and converted to radio telescopes for radioastronomy. Another specimen that remained on site in Holland was used by Dr. van de Hulst to discover the radiation coming in from the hydrogen atoms in the spiral arms of our galaxy on a wavelength of about 21 centimetres.

As soon as I saw Tony Hill's photographs of the Domburg Giants, with their lattice-like frames for the paraboloids, I was seized by a feeling that I had seen that kind of construction before: where was it? Then, in the spring of 1943 we heard a rumour that the paraboloids were made at Friedrichshafen on Lake Constanz. That was the clue: the old Zeppelin works! What I had been reminded of were photographs of the skeletons of shot-down Zeppelins in the 1914–18 war. A photographic sortie over the works showed them surrounded by scores of Giant paraboloids. I showed the evidence to Lindemann, now Lord Cherwell, and on 22nd June—on Churchill's personal intervention—the works were attacked by No. 5 Group of Bomber Command; many paraboloids were destroyed and no aircraft were lost because they flew straight through to North Africa, to the bewilderment of the German nightfighters who were waiting, as usual, to catch them on the way back from the target. As we shall see, we had unconsciously struck a blow at more than the Würzburgs.

As I write this book and look at Tony Hill's pictures of the Bruneval Würzburg and the Domburg Giants, I am once again amazed by the precision of his photography. Just two photographs on each occasion, one full view and one profile, almost in the centre on each exposure from an aircraft travelling at more than three hundred miles an hour and the photographs taken over the shoulder. I was to be acquainted with him for less than a year, and yet in that time I came to know him well, boyish ambitions and misdeeds and all, with his exceptional perseverence, skill and courage. Twice I had the pleasure of writing citations, first for the Bar to his D.F.C. after Bruneval and then for his D.S.O. after Domburg. And then on Trafalgar Day 1942 I had a dread telephone call from Wing Commander MacNeill, the Operations Officer at Coastal Command who supervised photographic activities. He simply said, 'Tony Hill has not come back from a sortie on le Creusot. Can you find out what has happened?'

On 17th October 94 Lancasters had made a daylight raid on the Schneider armament works at le Creusot, and Bomber Command was anxious to check the results. On the following day the weather was bad and only low level photography was possible, so Tony Hill flew a round trip of more than 1,700 miles and took low obliques. On his return it was found that his camera had been loaded with previously exposed film. His friend Gordon Hughes went out on 19th October, but his photographs showed mainly the undamaged side of the works. Bomber Command—which had been complaining that it did not have a big enough share of photographic reconnaissance—pressed for full cover, and on 21st October Tony Hill went out again, considering the sortie so dangerous that he would not ask any of his subordinates to do it. This time the German guns were ready for him, and he broke his back in the crash.

Bill Dunderdale, our liaison with the French, found that Tony was in hospital, badly injured, and we organized a Resistance party to get him out. It was an occasion when I would have gone myself if it would have helped, but I arranged for the Resistance men to carry a message from me so that he would know that it was safe to go with them. I do not know how far the attempt got, but Andrew Brookes in *Photo Reconnaissance* says, 'A special aircraft was laid on to fly him home, but as he was being carried out to it he died'.

I felt his loss more than any other in the whole war. Another young pilot, G. R. Crakenthorp, volunteered to take over the low oblique work, modelling himself—as he told me—on Tony Hill. He could not have done better.

CHAPTER TWENTY-SEVEN

The Bruneval Raid

THE PROBLEMS of dealing with the renewed radio beam threat on the one hand and of penetrating the German night defences on the other were so fascinating that we hardly noticed how depressing the general situation was as the winter of 1941/42 wore on. The fact that America had been drawn into the war on 7th December 1941 of course gave us great hope for an ultimate victory. But the success of the attack on Pearl Harbor and the loss of *Prince of Wales* and *Repulse* on 10th December showed that battleships could not survive against bombers, despite Navy doctrine. And, if this were not already enough, *Barham* was sunk by torpedoes; and *Queen Elizabeth* and *Valiant* were both settled on the bottom in Alexandria, having been put out of action by two-man torpedoes by the Italian Navy. We had been amazed by the capture of the first riders of these underwater chariots and could hardly believe the story, since it required courage of a type that we did not normally associate with the Italians. Once again we could not avoid respecting courage wherever we found it, even when it was being exerted so spectacularly to our disadvantage. To add to the gloom, there was the fall of Singapore on 15th February 1942. Some of us had long been worried about the Japanese threat, but had met with the argument that Singapore was three thousand miles from Japan—to which I always pointed out that it was six thousand miles from Britain.

A further exasperation had occurred three days before when on 11th/12th February *Scharnhorst* and *Gneisenau*, along with *Prinz Eugen*, steamed up the Channel. There are many accounts of this event, includ-the Official Enquiry which was published as Command Paper 6775 in 1946, on which Watson-Watt commented at some length in *Three Steps to Victory*, and Adolf Galland's account from the German side in *The First and the Last*. I was only on the sidelines for this episode, since no problem of Scientific Intelligence was involved; but it was impressed on my memory because of the morning of 11th February Colonel Wallace (who had been such a help with his Radio Interception Unit in Queen Anne's Mansions when we were taking the German radar plots) called to see me. I can remember his imploring tone as he said 'Will you chaps take me seriously? No one else will. For days our radar sets down on the coast have been jammed, and the jamming is getting worse every day. I am sure that the Germans are up to something!' Wallace was referring to the Army radar sets under the control of Home Forces, and he had reported the increase in jamming to the proper radar organization, but it seems that the increase from day to day was so gradual that most operators failed to realize how intense it had now become.

I was reminded of the particular technique of practical joking which which may be termed 'acclimatization by slow change'. A classic example was perpetuated by one of the most famous of American experimental physicists, R. W. Wood, for many years Professor of Physics at Johns Hopkins University, Baltimore. Some of his jokes were simple and effective, such as leaving a suitcase on a railway platform with a large gyroscope spinning inside it, so as to disconcert anyone who picked it up and who attempted to carry it round a corner. As for acclimatization by slow change, Wood at one stage in his early career worked in Paris and lived in a block of flats. He observed that the lady in the flat below kept a small tortoise in a window-box. He secured a supply of tortoises of various sizes and by means of a grappling device consisting of wire at the end of a broom pole he fished out the original tortoise and replaced it by one that was slightly larger. Over the course of a week or so, by successive small increases of size of tortoise, the lady was convinced that her pet was growing at an astonishing rate. Knowing that Wood was a scientist of some kind, she consulted him and Wood at first referred her to a French scientist in the same block, hoping to make a fool of him, too. When the scientist refused to take any interest, Wood then suggested that the lady might write to a newspaper about it. This she did, with the result that the tortoise became the object of attention by reporters; and when these were well and truly 'hooked' Wood reversed his nightly procedure, and to everyone's astonishment the tortoise gradually shrank to its original size.

This is just what the Germans did to us across the Channel, and what no one but Wallace spotted. I knew him well enough to accept his story completely, and I told him that I would get Derek Garrard to accompany him down to the coastal radar stations on the following day, 12th February—the very day that *Scharnhorst* and *Gneisenau* sailed through the Straits. The German radar officers, headed by General

Wolfgang Martini, had subtly increased the intensity of their jamming over a period so that we would get acclimatized to it, without realizing that it was now so intense that our radar was almost useless. Once again they had scored against us.

To make things worse, the German warships should have been spotted leaving Brest, where they had been for nearly a year, and on which we kept a continuous watch. But despite the fact that there was more than one appreciation that they might make a dash up the Channel in the period between 10th and 15th February, it proved to be yet another example of a point made by Francis Bacon in his essay *Of Delayes*: 'Nay, it were better, to meet some Dangers halfe way, though they come nothing neare, than to keepe too long a watch, upon their Approaches: For if a Man watch too long, it is odds he will fall asleepe'. In detail, the break-out was missed because of the failure of a radar set in a Coastal Command aircraft, which should otherwise have detected the ships, but had the watching system been on its toes and not perhaps lulled into dullness by months of waiting, some reserve arrangement might have been brought into operation.

One comic item was revealed in the post-mortem into why the watch on the battle cruisers had slipped. A report had indeed come in from France on the night of 11th February that they had moved out of dock, but it was not passed on by a duty officer. When asked why, he said he had already read it in a London evening paper and therefore assumed that the Admiralty knew of it.

The shock to our defences caused by the German ships getting so far up the Channel before they were spotted was such that all normal chains of command broke down. I was told that there were even air marshals sitting on one another's desks during the course of the day thinking of individual pilots whom they might telephone and ask to find the ships which, even after their first spotting, were lost several times. After the war, I met Captain Giessler, who had been Navigating Officer on *Scharnhorst* for the operation. He had been appointed as my temporary A.D.C. when the Germans invited me as Guest of Honour to their Radar Conference in 1955. He told me that their most miserable half-hour was when they were hove-to, not very far past Dover, after they had struck a mine and were stationary for half-an-hour. Fortunately, there was low cloud and in the entire half-hour not a single British aircraft found them.

Morale was to some extent restored a fortnight or so later by our successful raid on Bruneval. It was undertaken as a result of Charles

Frank's alertness and Tony Hill's superb skill in photographing the Bruneval Würzburg. Not long after we received the photographs I had happened to say 'Look, Charles, we could get in there!' pointing to the fact that although the Würzburg was on top of a 400 foot cliff, there was a continuous slope down to a small beach a few hundred yards away. I had sometimes noticed the legend 'Descent des Anglais' on French coastal maps, recording that at some time in the marauding past British forces had landed at the indicated spots, and it might be possible to add a similar legend at Bruneval. However, I doubt whether by myself I would have asked for a raid to be made, partly because I disliked risking lives unless it was absolutely necessary, and partly because I had developed something of a professional pride in solving all the characteristics of a German equipment before I actually had it in my hands.

What decided me was a chat with W. B. Lewis, the Deputy Super-intendent of the Telecommunications Research Establishment, who by that time had seen the photographs. He told me that if I were inclined to suggest a raid, T.R.E. would strongly support me. Added to that was the fact that it had been part of Churchill's policy ever since Dunkirk to occupy as much German attention as possible by isolated raids, and there was no doubt that useful information might well be obtained from this particular target. The idea was therefore passed from the Air Staff to Combined Operations Headquarters, whose Chief was now Lord Louis Mountbatten. He and his Headquarters accepted the suggestion enthusiastically, and plans were put in hand to mount the raid as soon as possible.

One of the prerequisites for the raid was a detailed knowledge of the dispositions of German forces to guard the Bruneval locality and the radar station. Signals were accordingly sent out from London to the French Resistance, and the responsibility for reconnaissance fell to Gilbert Renault, known to us as 'Rémy'. When France collapsed, and with his wife expecting their fifth child, he had come across with one of his brothers to England and joined General de Gaulle. Such was the spirit in his family that before the war ended his mother and five of his sisters had suffered imprisonment by the Germans, two of them in Ravensbrück; his brother Philippe, also deported, was killed in Lübeck Harbour a few hours before it was taken by British troops. After a short stay in England, Rémy returned to France to organize intelligence networks, having been given the whole of the French coast from Brest to the Spanish frontier to cover. Then, when the network covering

North France from Dunkirk to Brest was destroyed by the Germans, Rémy was asked to build it up afresh.

One of the men he recruited was Roger Dumont, known as 'Pol', who proceeded on Rémy's instructions to reconnoitre the Bruneval terrain. This he did, along with 'Charlemagne' (Charles Chauvenau, a le Havre garage proprietor). Together they established the positions of German strong points and the troop dispositions: they also made the important discovery that despite German notices to the contrary, the beach was not mined. All their information came back to Britain in time for the planning of the raid. Rémy survived the war but Pol was betrayed, cruelly, by the congratulatory message that he received after Bruneval; he died before a German firing squad in 1943.

As the plans for the raid developed, it was decided not to go in by sea in the first place but to attempt to capture the Würzburg by paratroops, who would also capture the beach so as to make a landfall for the Navy, through which the captured equipment could be evacuated. Obviously it was important that someone with technical knowledge should go on the raid and, much to his credit, Derek Garrard volunteered to go. Of course, as soon as he had volunteered, I had also to do so; but I was distinctly relieved when Portal forbade either me or any of my staff to go because we were in possession of so much information that we should be a bad security threat if captured. I tried to counter this by pointing out that we might also be all the more successful in misleading the Germans by giving them false clues about our own developments if we fell into their hands, but Portal wisely refused to entertain this argument. It was, however, agreed that a scientist who was less in the general security picture than we were should accompany the Naval force, so that he could land if the military situation were favourable, and for this D. H. Priest of T.R.E. was selected—I had known him as one of the original Bawdsey team with a penchant for high-powered cars. But the dismantling of the equipment might well have to be done by someone dropping with the paratroops and therefore at greater risk, and it was decided to call for a volunteer from the flight sergeant radar mechanics who manned our own radar stations.

Victor Tait, who was Director of Radar on the Air Staff, interviewed a possible volunteer on 1st February 1942. This was Flight Sergeant C. W. H. Cox, who before the war had been a cinema projectionist, and who had never been in a ship or an aeroplane. He was married with a few weeks' old baby, and all he knew was that he had volunteered for a dangerous operation that required the services of a radar mechanic.

9

Within a few days he found himself practising parachute jumps and committed to the Bruneval operation. One awkward aspect of the plan was that he should accompany 'C' Company of the Second Parachute Battalion, whose personnel, of course, would all be in Army uniform whilst—if nothing were done about it—Cox would be in Air Force uniform. Garrard drew my attention to this, whereupon I did my utmost to get Cox into Army uniform for the operation, and also given an Army number. Otherwise, if he were captured, he would clearly be 'odd man out' and thus the object of special attention from German interrogators.

It seems incredible, even at this distance of time, but the War Office adamantly refused to co-operate, with the result that Cox had to go in his Air Force uniform. The only thing that I could do was to see Cox personally, tell him what had happened, and warn him about the danger if he were captured. 'I've been thinking about that, sir' he said, and then went on to tell me that he proposed to say that he was really the Despatcher in the aircraft and in a moment of enthusiasm had dropped with the paratroops. I told him that I doubted whether the German interrogators would 'wear that one', and he regretfully agreed. So I went on to warn him about the dangers of special interrogation, saying 'Don't be worried too much about physical torture, because I don't think that they are using it. What you have to be tremendously careful about is being thrown into solitary confinement in a cold damp cell, with nothing but bread and water for a few days. Then a new German officer will come round on a tour of inspection, and will himself protest about the way that you are being treated. He will take you out of the cell, and explain that he will try to make amends for your bad treatment, giving you cigarettes, a decent meal, a warm fire and something to drink. After a while you will feel such a glow and so grateful to this very decent officer that when he starts asking you questions you will hardly be able to resist telling him anything he wants to know. So for God's sake, Cox, be on your guard against any German officer who is kind to you!' I can still remember Cox standing to attention and replying 'I can stand a lot of kindness, sir!'—that was the sort of man he was.

Cox's job, of course, was to examine the Würzburg and, if possible to dismantle the key units: but it first had to be captured. This was what 'C' Company of '2 Para' had to do: commanded by Major J. D. Frost, they were largely drawn from Scottish Regiments, including the King's Own Scottish Borderers (Lieutenant E. C. B. Charteris), the Black Watch (Captain John Ross, Second-in-Command, Company

Sergeant Major Strachan and Sergeant Jimmy Sharp) and the Seaforths (Sergeant Grieve) with an Engineer Detachment under Lieutenant D. Vernon. The total force to be dropped was about 120 strong, and was carried in twelve Whitley aircraft. Detailed accounts of the raid are to be found in *The Red Beret* by Hilary St. George Saunders and *The Bruneval Raid* by George Millar, himself the holder of the D.S.O. which he won for escaping and working with the French Resistance. Roughly, the plan was to drop the force in three components inland from the Würzburg (Plate 12). The first component (Captain Ross and Lieutenant Charteris) was to advance towards the beach and capture it, the second (Major Frost, Lieutenants Naumoff and Young) to head towards the cliff and capture the Würzburg, and the third (Lieutenant Timothy) to act as rear-guard and reserve for the other two. When the Würzburg was captured an Engineer party under Lieutenant Vernon with Flight Sergeant Cox was to advance and dismantle it.

The raiding party was ready for action by 20th February—it had rehearsed as much of the operation as possible, partly with the aid of a scale model made by the Photographic Interpretation Unit at Medmenham and partly at full-scale on the south coast of England. Rehearsals had not gone well, but the operation had to be made within a few days, since a full moon was necessary for visibility on landing, and the tide had to be right for getting the landing craft in to the beach. A further limitation was wind—the night needed to be relatively calm if casualties were to be avoided on landing.

Night after night the operation had to be 'stood down' because the weather was unsuitable. In fact, Thursday 26th February had been originally reckoned as the last night of the Moon, but when weather again destroyed any prospect of operations, it was decided to risk the raid on 27th February if the weather changed, rather than wait for a further month. The morning was bright and frosty: the wind had dropped: the raid was 'on'. The Naval relief force headed into the Channel during the afternoon; some hours later the paratroops were played into their aircraft by a piper and took off. I was already home, wondering how many would return in the morning.

It would have been remarkable if the raid had gone entirely to plan, for time had been too short to get everything right. What in fact went wrong was that two aircraft dropped their 'sticks' of paratroops about a mile-and-a-half south of the intended position, and these were the sticks that had been intended to capture the beach. They were under the command of Lieutenant Charteris who quickly realized that they were badly out of position, and succeeded in establishing the direction in which he would have to advance towards the beach. He and his twenty men set off at the double.

The entire terrain was covered with several inches of snow but the parties that were intended to capture the Würzburg (Young's) and the adjacent house (Frost's) had no difficulty in finding their way. When Frost's party arrived at the front door of the house there was a moment's hesitation when someone said 'What do we do now?' and another replied 'Ring the bell!'

Flight Sergeant Cox afterwards gave the following account of his experiences:

I met Mr. Vernon at forming-up point at approx. 12.35. We proceeded under Mr. Vernon's direction to pull trolleys up towards house over various barbed wire defences and through snow, which was rather rough going.

In about 200 yards Mr. Vernon went on to house and said we must make our way to left hand side of house and conceal ourselves until he whistled or shouted for us. This we did, and lay in a small ridge for what seemed to be quite a long while, but was really a very short time. Then one of the Sappers went over and said we must go through and meet up with the equipment immediately. Then we all went forward and through some more barbed wire to the equipment.

I saw Mr. Vernon and he said 'this is it!'.

The barbed wire was not more than 2 ft. high, a criss-cross network about 10ft. thick. Range of distance round equipment about 50 yards radius.

In view of the obstacles, it would have been better to have made arrangements for carrying the equipment and tools etc. in haversacks, rather than on trolleys.

I surveyed the apparatus and found it to my surprise just like the photograph. The first point of interest was the aerial, which I looked at, and one of the Sappers proceeded to cut it from its centre. I went round the back tracing the aerial lead to the top box of the paraboloid. A compartment behind the paraboloid contained a big box, at the top; two smaller boxes underneath; at the right hand side of the small boxes was a panel of push buttons, and in the base of the compartment was a thing which appeared to be a large metal rectifier, but this had round fins instead of square. I then proceeded to attack the equipment with the tools to try to get it out without damaging it. This proved unsuccessful except in one case, which came away easily, so we proceeded to rip the rest of the stuff out by sheer force.

By this time the soldiers were getting impatient, and we were told to withdraw. During the whole period of working at the equipment, bullets were flying much too close to be pleasant, but while we were working at the back of the paraboloid we were protected by the metal of the paraboloid itself.

I noticed on the paraboloid before the aerial was cut out, on the left hand side, slightly above centre, the letters W.D. and a row of lines, horizontal lines arranged in a vertical scale, and against each line was a number about an inch apart.

The whole equipment was very solidly made and turned on its base with the slightest pressure. All leads were sealed into it in concentric plugs and sockets. The aerial socket ended in a type of attachment known to us as a Niphan plug.

The mounting was not on wheels, but looked as if it had been mounted on wheels and the wheels removed. There was no barbed wire on the boxes surrounding the equipment. We retired when the Army made us, and found that the equipment could be carried much better on our shoulders than by the trolley, so the trolley was abandoned. On coming down the slope we were met by a hail of machine gunfire from the opposite side of the cliff and we tried to dig ourselves in. Mr. Vernon told me to take charge of the Sappers while he went back with the rear guard. We lay on the bank for about 15 mins. and then received a hail from the village that the beach defences had been taken. We made our way down the slope to the beach and found we had to wait, so we stowed the equipment in a safe position under the cliff and as there was nothing else we could do, we just sat down and waited.

After about half an hour the Navy came and we got the equipment aboard, with the wounded, and after the rearguard had time to make the beach and get into the boats, we pushed off. Slight enemy fire was directed against us from the cliff tops but was soon silenced by Bren guns on the boats.

The withdrawal of the Würzburg party was delayed because the beach was still in German hands owing to the misplacing of Charteris' men in the original drop. Only two of the four sections (of ten men each) intended for the attack on the beach were therefore at the assembly point. Sergeant Sharp was in charge of these two sections, and he decided to attack as best he could with one section while he sent the other section under Sergeant Tasker to take the German posts on the cliff half-way between the Würzburg and the beach. Sharp worked down towards the beach and reached the position on the German wire from which he was to have given supporting fire to Charteris' sections if they had been in position. In their absence he had decided to attack on his own, when he heard the shout 'CABAR FEIDH', the war-cry of the Seaforths, which told him that somehow Charteris' men had got into position. With much resource, Charteris had succeeded in finding where he had been misplaced on landing and had led his men northwards at the trot for a mile and a half along the road to Bruneval and round the village to their prescribed position. Their war-cry was the signal that they were attacking, and Sharp now knew that his section could revert to its original function of covering fire. The guardroom and strong point at the beach were captured, the Navy could come in, and the raiders with their booty and prisoners could be evacuated. Among those who had fallen in Charteris' assault was a Gordon Highlander and an inveterate gambler, Corporal Stewart, whose pockets had been full of his winnings as he took off for the raid. Finding that he had been hit in the head, and thinking that the wound was fatal, he called to his nearest friend 'I've had it, Jock, take my wallet!' Lance Corporal Freeman (later a senior magistrate of the City of Nottingham) took it and examined Stewart's head, telling him that the wound was only a gash. 'Then gie us back my bluidy wallet!' said Stewart and got to his feet.

By 0235 hours on 28th February the operation was nearly over, and most of the force embarked. They left behind two men killed (Privates MacIntyre and Scott) and six missing (all of whom survived the war); the German report on the raid recorded the German losses as five killed, two wounded, and five missing. Two prisoners were brought back, one of them being an operator of the Würzburg equipment, as we had hoped. In his efforts to conceal himself on a patch free from snow, he had slipped over the edge of the cliff and fell about fifteen feet before he could save himself by grasping a projecting rock. He managed to climb back to the top, but was seen against the snow and captured.

When I arrived in my office the following morning a signal had been received telling us of the successful execution of the raid, and that we could expect the captured equipment in the Air Ministry on the after-noon of Monday 2nd March. That morning I had agreed to go to the Headquarters of No. Eleven Group at Uxbridge, to advise them what they could do about the German radar, which was detecting the

'Rhubarb' fighter sweeps the Group was carrying out in the Pas de Calais. When I arrived I met a party headed by Air Commodore Harcourt Smith in the chair and including Wing Commander 'Sunshine' Wells, in peacetime a grammar school headmaster from Gravesend way, but now Chief Intelligence Officer of the Group. My hosts were adamant that the Germans must have developed a new form of radar that could detect bombs in aircraft. When I asked them for their evidence they said that they carried out two kinds of sweep. One included a few Blenheim bombers, which represented the 'teeth' while the other was exactly similar, except that it consisted purely of fighters. The main aim of these sweeps was to get the German fighters to come up and fight, in the hope of gradually wearing them down and establishing air superiority. This had at first been fairly successful but now the fighters would only come up if the bombers were present and the problem therefore was how the Germans could detect six or so bombers in the presence of fifty or a hundred fighters. The theory was that somehow the German radar could see the bombs in the aircraft.

When I assured my hosts that as far as I knew about German radar, or indeed any other radar for that matter, it did not have the ability to achieve such a feat of detection, I was then challenged to say how the Germans could possibly know the difference between the one kind of sweep and the other. There was a silence while I thought, and then such an obvious solution occurred to me that I hardly dared to make it. Finally I said 'Bombers have not got the speed of fighters. When the fighters are escorting the Blenheims, do they slow down?' There was a stunned silence broken by Sunshine Wells exclaiming 'Christ!' It turned out that when there were no bombers the fighter sweeps were executed at standard fighter speeds, whereas the others were at the slower speeds of bombers so the Germans had a perfectly obvious clue. Thereafter we flew all sweeps at the same speed.

I then went on to discuss with the Group what could be done about German radar, especially to provoke the German fighters to come up, and I told them of a scheme which I had outlined in my main report at the beginning of the year on German radar which would involve a receiver in an aircraft detecting the pulses from the German radar stations and then sending them back longer, beating echoes to make it look as though a whole formation of aircraft were present. This scheme had so far been dismissed as too elaborate, but I told Eleven Group that if they would press for it, it was technically quite feasible. They did, and the result was a device known as 'Moonshine' which was successfully used later in the year.

After lunch, I went back to Air Ministry as quickly as my old Wolseley car would allow. The Bruneval booty was already in the Air Ministry, and it was obviously much better engineered than our own radar equipment, a fact which was readily admitted by our own radar men in their final report. Cox and his escort had done an excellent job. Only one important component had been left behind, an achievement all the more impressive because they had had only ten minutes at the Würzburg instead of the thirty which had been planned.

Before the equipment went to T.R.E. at Swanage for detailed examination, we took some of it out to Felkin's headquarters, to discuss it with the operator who had been taken prisoner, and who was very co-operative. We were disappointed that despite his readiness to help, his technical competence was far lower than that of any of our own operators. In fact, up to that stage in the war, he had had more time in jail than out of it. We spent the afternoon sitting on the floor with him, fitting the various pieces together, and listening to his comments. On his last leave he had remarked to his wife that his station was so isolated that the English might easily make a raid and capture it, and he was now wondering whether she might have been a Fifth Columnist.

The low technical ability of the operator and the high engineering standard of the equipment were not altogether dissociated. When I met General Martini, the Head of German Air Signals and Radar, after the war, I told him that these two factors had surprised me, and he pointed out that he had a very low priority in demanding personnel and had to make do with those who were deemed unsuitable for other duties. He had no skilled reserve to draw upon among radio amateurs, as we had, because Hitler had banned amateur radio before the war since it might provide communication links for disaffected organizations. Martini had therefore to ensure that the equipment was so well made, and so easily replaceable if any part broke down, that the system could be operated by relatively unskilled personnel.

Despite the relative ignorance of the prisoner, which was certainly disappointing, we succeeded in extracting a large amount of information from the raid. For example, various items in the equipment had been replaced at various times, and each of them included a works number and the date of manufacture; and from these I was able to work out that the average rate of production of components was about 150 sets per month which, allowing for the production of spares, indicated that there was a total production of around 100 Würzburgs per month. We also knew by the time of the raid that the Bruneval Würzburg was of an early type, with a simple aerial, and that the later Würzburgs had a spinning aerial which would enable them to determine the direction of the target much more accurately. And we suspected that our main opposition as regards fighter control would come from the larger equipment such as the Americans had photographed in the Berlin Tiergarten; but it was clear that the same electronic components could be used throughout, and we therefore had the vital samples in our hands.

So what had we gained? A first-hand knowledge of the state of German radar technology, in the form in which it was almost certainly being applied in our principal objective, the German nightfighter control system. We now knew the extreme limits of wavelength to which the Würzburg could be tuned, and that it had no built-in counter either to jamming or to spurious reflectors; moreover it seemed that German radar operators were probably less able than our own. Besides giving us an estimate of the German rate of production and a knowledge of the German quality of design and engineering, it had provided us with the equivalent of a navigational 'fix' in confirming the 'dead reckoning' in our Intelligence voyage into the German defences.

It was, of course, a pleasure to write a report on the Intelligence aspects of the raid because it had gone so very well. In my report I included a map to show where Bruneval was, and added what I described as the track of a somewhat older and larger 'raid' in the hope of providing historical encouragement. It looked very like radar plots on an aircraft, and I actually had an officer ring me up and say 'I didn't know that we'd made that other raid—when did we do it?' I then happily pointed out that if he would look at the beginning of the raid track, which started at Bosham he would see that it was timed as AD 1346 (Figure 10) and was in fact Edward III's route to Crecy.

The raid had major repercussions both on the Germans and on ourselves. One minor objective during the raid was to demolish the villa adjacent to the Würzburg, because we imagined that it would be the local headquarters. In fact, it appeared to contain very little and it was left undamaged. We were therefore amazed to see, on aerial photographs taken a few days after the raid, that the Germans had demolished the villa themselves. They had concluded that it was the presence of the villa that had given the Würzburg away, and so they proceeded to remove it. Apart from shutting the stable door after the horse had gone, the action was ironic because it was the presence of the villa that

very nearly caused us to overlook the Würzburg, and only Charles
Frank's astute observation saved us from thinking that the path from
the Freyas had no other object than to go to the villa.

Another delicious consequence was that orders were issued that
henceforth all German radar equipments were to be protected by
barbed wire: since this soon shows up strongly on aerial photographs,
because the grass grows longer underneath it or it catches rubbish blown
by the wind, the enclosing circles of barbed wire enabled us to confirm
several objects that we had previously suspected of being Würzburgs
but where the photographs had been insufficiently clear (Plate 10(b)).

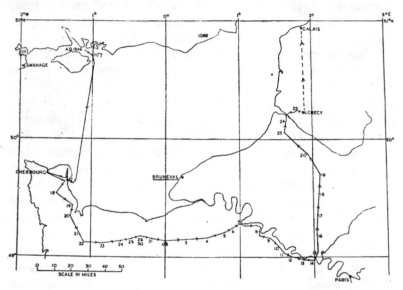

Fig. 10. *The position of Bruneval, and the route of an older and larger raid. From Air
Scientific Intelligence Report No. 15:* The Intelligence Aspect of the Bruneval Raid,
13 July 1942

At the end of the war we came across German appreciations of the
raid. They surmised that a new phase in the Hochfrequenzkrieg ('high
frequency war') had begun, and that henceforward aggression of all
forms could be expected against radar, including jamming and the
dropping of spurious reflectors such as I had suggested in 1937 and which
we were now developing. On the military side, the Germans expressed
admiration for the discipline of our paratroops: 'The Operation of the
British commandos was well planned and was executed with great discipline. During the operation the British displayed exemplary discipline

when under fire. Although attacked by German soldiers they concentrated entirely on their primary task'. And after the war Burckhardt, the German Paratroop Commander, expressed the opinion that Bruneval was the best of all British raids during the war.

On our side, an unexpected bonus was the nervousness engendered regarding the situation of the Telecommunications Research Establishment at Swanage, where all our new radar development was undertaken. I had been pressing for the Establishment to be moved from Swanage ever since the Germans had occupied the Channel coast. Even if they did not invade, they had a good chance of hearing transmissions from our new types of radar sets under development, but Swanage was such a pleasant environment that the Establishment was reluctant to move, and I had no success in attempting to dislodge it.

However, the Bruneval raid made people speculate about the possibility that the Germans might plan a retaliation, and where better than on Swanage? Apprehension increased when we discovered that a German parachute company had moved into position near Cherbourg, although there was no indication of what its intentions were. The news of this move leaked down to T.R.E., and I saw my opportunity. I was due to visit the Establishment, anyway, to see how the investigation of the Bruneval equipment was going, and so Hugh Smith and I drove down to Swanage. We said nothing about the possibility of a German retaliation, but merely carried our tin hats everywhere and had revolvers ostentatiously strapped to our belts. We also contrived to give the impression of nervousness and an anxiety to get back to London as soon as possible. The next we heard was that T.R.E. was moving in a hurry to Malvern where, as the Royal Radar Establishment, it still is.

A further repercussion of the Raid stemmed from its success and a general feeling that echoed Cox's comment when he first saw the Würzburg: 'I found it to my surprise just like the photograph'. Apparently few other proposals for raids had had such clear objectives, with such effective prior Intelligence, and as a result I received a stream of calls from budding planning officers in Combined Operations who wished to make their mark by planning a successful raid. I forget how many radar stations were earmarked for raids in this way, although there was relatively little point in that we had found most of what we wanted to know at Bruneval. One proposal, however, did have repercussions which could have ended my career in M.I.6, as I shall tell later.

Decorations were awarded to some of those who took part in the raid, but hardly on the scale that its success merited. Frost and Charteris received the Military Cross, while Flight Sergeant Cox, Sergeant Grieve and Sergeant MacKenzie were awarded the Military Medal. Young was mentioned in Despatches, Company Sergeant Major Strachan (who had been badly wounded during the evacuation of the Würzburg equipment to the beach) was awarded the Croix de Guerre. I tried hard to have Cox awarded either the Distinguished Conduct Medal or the Distinguished Flying Medal; the latter would have been the Air equivalent of the Military Medal, and would have been more unusual for a radar mechanic, but protocol did not allow it.

I had no idea that I, too, was considered for a decoration, but evidently Archibald Sinclair must have made the proposal to Churchill for, after the war, the latter gave me a copy of his reply dated 3rd April 1942, which ran 'Dr. Jones's claims, in my mind, are not based upon the Bruneval raid, but upon the magnificent prescience and comprehension by which in 1940 he did far more to save us from disaster than many who are glittering with trinkets. The Bruneval raid merely emphasised and confirmed his earlier services. I propose to recommend him for a C.B.'

Lord Cherwell told me that when the Prime Minister's proposal came before the Committee on Honours and Awards the head of the Civil Service, Sir Horace Wilson, 'threatened to resign' if I received a C.B., since I had been merely a Scientific Officer and I could not possibly have done work of such merit in my lowly position. The most that would have been justified would have been an M.B.E. or O.B.E. Finally a compromise was reached on a C.B.E.

Had I known this story I should probably have refused the decoration —in any event, Churchill's minute was worth far more to me, and so was a reunion that occurred in December 1976 when, as part of a programme for Yorkshire Television, I met some of the few survivors of Bruneval (many were killed in later operations). Along with General Frost and Flight Sergeant Cox were Major Vernon, Sergeant Sharp and Private Dobson and another whose expert knowledge and unusual bravery I had hardly till then appreciated, Peter Nagel. He had come with his father to Britain from Germany before the war to escape the Nazis. Enlisting in the Pioneer Corps, he had volunteered as an interpreter. Even more than Cox, perhaps, he was in a specially dangerous position if captured, because the Germans would have had no mercy if they had discovered his origin; but he went, as 'Private Newman', and without his coolheadness we might not have brought back the radar prisoner.

A month after Bruneval the great raid on the dock at St. Nazaire took place. Among those killed was my cousin Eric Beart, in command of Motor Launch No. 267 'A solicitor of about 30–35 or so, tall, fair and a most attractive personality. He had brought a rugger ball with him, hoping for a game on the quay while the commandos were about their business' (C. E. Lucas Phillips, *The Greatest Raid of All*). Peter Nagel went on that raid, too, and was captured; fortunately his story was so convincing that the Germans never detected that he was not English. I was moved when after the Yorkshire TV programme such a gallant man should come quietly up to me and say 'We would like you to know that if you had asked us we would have gone on another hundred raids'.

The success of the Bruneval raid clinched the future of paratroops in Britain, as Brigadier Alastair Pearson (who won four D.S.O.s in parachute operations) related at a dinner of the Scottish Territorial Battalion. The 1st Airborne Division and the 1st Parachute Brigade were immediately formed; and 'Bruneval' is the first battle honour inscribed on the drums of the Parachute Regiment.

CHAPTER TWENTY-EIGHT

The Baedeker Beams

ALTHOUGH WE were beginning to settle our scores with the German Air Signals Experimental Regiment, it was by no means defeated. By the summer of 1941 there were twenty beam stations on the Channel coast waiting to be directed against our cities, and it was therefore with considerable relief that we saw the Luftwaffe irretrievably committed in Russia. Moreover it gradually became clear that the Germans were going to be disappointed in their expectation that their Russian campaign would be over before the winter. I remember seeing a plaintive signal from a German commander saying that his transport was immobilized because the engine oil had frozen solid. Moreover, the Russians were showing technical ingenuity in defence. I noted that a German tank commander complained that his mine detectors would not work, because the Russians were using wooden mines. Hitherto, most anti-tank mines had been made of cast iron or steel, and the conventional way of detecting them was by the local changes that they produced in the Earth's magnetic field. Even if non-magnetic metal were used, there were ways of detecting this also: but none of the standard methods would work against non-conducting materials such as plastic or wood, and it was therefore a very sensible thing for the Russians to use wooden cases which were both cheap and undetectable.

At one stage, however, the Germans tried to hoax us into thinking that they were coming back to bomb us, by sending a considerable number of false radio signals in a relatively simple code in the hope of making us think that a new Kampf Geschwader, KG11, had been formed and was occupying aerodromes in France and the Low Countries. The radio intercept operator who was listening on our side took down the signals, and sent them on to his headquarters—but with a note saying that in his opinion all the signals had been sent by a single man. It turned out that to an experienced listener the way an individual operator makes his Morse characters is as personal as his handwriting, and our radio operator had been alert enough to spot the attempt at radio forgery in this way. He was entirely vindicated a night or two later when the German spoof continued, and the spoofers got so mixed up that one had to send a signal to another saying that he was supposed to be an aircraft but was sending signals that should have come from a ground station. Actually, there would be so many clues obtainable from the prior arrangements for a genuine move back of the bomber force that I offered to give six weeks' notice of any major new bombing threat to England.

As it turned out, six weeks was almost exactly the length of the warning that I was indeed able to give when the bombing threat reappeared in the shape of the 'Baedeker' raids on 23rd April 1942. This came from watching what our old opponents, KG100 and the German Air Signals Experimental Regiment, were doing. We found that on their practice grounds in Germany they were developing a new variant of the X-system, under the code name 'Taub' which means 'deaf'. What they were attempting was one of the stratagems against which I had warned in 1940—that when the X-beams were jammed, they might well change the modulation frequency. In the new system they left the old modulation frequency on the transmission, so that we could continue to hear and jam it, but they superimposed a supersonic frequency above the limit of human hearing. If we failed to spot that, they could filter out our jamming and use the supersonic modulation to work a directional indicator in the aircraft by which they could fly along the beam.

The basic information came, as so often, from Enigma—not explicitly, of course, but there were various incidental clues which enabled us to put the foregoing picture together. I briefed Denys Felkin, and by good luck a prisoner appeared who had actually taken part in the supersonic trials. He had at times sat in the bomb-proof bunker near Märkisch Friedland from which the accuracy of bombing on the experimental range could be observed, but he showed a sturdy resistance to telling us anything about the trials. I well remember Felkin ringing me up and telling me that the prisoner would not give anything away, but that he might just 'break' if Felkin could persuade him that we knew so much already that there was no point in holding the rest back. 'Can't you give me anything?' asked Felkin, and I said that I would look over what we knew and see whether we could pull something out of the bag. Charles Frank and I talked the problem over: one thing that we did know was the exact co-ordinates of the observation point. We therefore took the appropriate German map and imagined what the view might be from the observation point—hills, woods and roads—and we telephoned Felkin with the result. He then told the prisoner what he must have seen when he was watching the bombs fall, much to the astonishment of the prisoner who then said something like, 'Well—if you have got hold of a traitor like that, there is no point in my trying to hide anything', and promptly told Felkin what he knew.

We were therefore aware of every important detail of the new system many weeks before it came into effect, and No. 80 Wing was able to add supersonic modulation to its jammers in good time. The one condition that I laid down was that the supersonic jammers should not be switched on until after 80 Wing had heard the supersonic modulation of the German beams for themselves. Otherwise if we came up with the supersonic jamming before the Germans started to use supersonic beams, it would give them a very valuable clue regarding the source of our information. The Wing scrupulously obeyed my instructions, but we were puzzled to find that when the Baedeker raids started the 80 Wing observers could find no trace of supersonic modulation on the X-beams and yet KG100 seemed to operate unimpeded and successfully led the bomber force to its targets. Exeter, Bath, Norwich, York and Cowes were hit in succession between 23rd April and 4th May, with an average of about 50% of all bombs being on target. I could not believe that this was being achieved with the ordinary modulation of the X-beams, which was of course jammed, but 80 Wing insisted that no supersonic modulation was being used, and therefore they could not switch on the supersonic jamming. In the end we managed to prove that despite what the observers had said the Germans had been using supersonic modulation all the time, and an enquiry took place. Supersonic jamming was now employed, with dramatic results. The average percentage of bombs on target over the next month fell to 13%.

The enquiry revealed that despite all the detailed warning we had given, the designers of the listening receivers had overlooked the fact that supersonic reception involves a wider bandwidth than normal in the high frequency circuits of the receiver, and these circuits had not been suitably modified. As a result, the supersonic modulation was being cut out in the early stages of the receiver, and the operators had no chance of detecting it. Once again, an elementary mistake which should never have been made had cost many lives. This time I was so sickened that I did not even say that someone should be shot.

It is possible to estimate the number of casualties caused by the error, for the Official History shows that between 23rd April and 4th May a total of 447 tons of bombs fell on the target cities. Had the countermeasures been as effective throughout this period as they were after 4th May, the tonnage on target would have been reduced by about 80% or about 360 tons. On the experience of the Coventry raid, 503 tons on target had killed 554 people and seriously injured 865. The 360 tons that fell on the early Baedeker targets and which would presumably have fallen on open country had our countermeasures been effective, thus killed about 400 people and seriously injured another 600. Fortunately our early warning had at least ensured that suitable jammers were in position, and so there was no delay in countering the supersonic beams once their existence had been proved, and this in itself must have saved many lives.

None of this story is in the Official History, which merely records that after 4th May, 'almost everything went wrong for the attackers'.

CHAPTER TWENTY-NINE

El Hatto

ALTHOUGH THE Intelligence attack on the German night defences was our main work throughout 1942, we had a wide field of other activities to cover; and there was always the danger that by concentrating exclusively on the German nightfighters, important though they were, we should fail to detect some other and even more important development and so fail to avoid a national disaster. I had no golden rule for this general watch—it depended on having alert colleagues like Charles Frank, Bimbo Norman, Denys Felkin, and Claude Wavell, who had sharp instincts for anything that was odd; we were all so saturated at times that something could have been missed, but I still know of no automatic substitute for the human mind when some new situation has to be faced.

In the episode which I now recount, the alert mind did not belong to an immediate colleague but, most probably, to Kim Philby. My first assistant, Harold Blyth, had gone to work with him and was very impressed by his ability. Moreover, he was so critical of the way in which M.I.6 was run, and of the abilities of some of its officers, that it seemed a matter of touch and go whether he would be thrown out, at least after the war. So long as the war was on there was always the chance that he would survive on Churchill's principle that, 'In war you don't have to be polite, you just have to be right!' And Philby had a habit of being right. I think that these characteristics completely prevented any doubts about his ultimate loyalty to the country, if not to various officers in M.I.6.

Philby's main task was to watch and frustrate the activities of the Abwehr, the principal German Secret Service. Thanks to another type of cryptographic break, it was clear that that the Abwehr was mounting some kind of operation near Gibraltar, and Philby had the relevant signals sent to me. In his own words from *My Silent War*, 'The Abwehr code-name for the operation was Bodden. The Bodden is the name of the narrow strip of water separating the island of Rügen from the

German mainland, not far from the wartime scientific research station at Peenemünde. Taken together with additional evidence that the Bodden experts, with their instruments, seemed to be closing in on Algeciras, this seemed a clear enough indication that something affecting the Straits of Gibraltar was brewing. We therefore consulted the formidable Dr. Jones, head of the scientific section of S.I.S., who . . .' The adjective 'formidable', coming as it did from Philby, was quite a tribute.

When I looked at the evidence, it seemed peculiarly relevant to my pre-war interests, because it suggested that the Germans were trying to set up a great infra-red burglar alarm across the Straits of Gibraltar to count our ships in and out of the Mediterranean. There were to be three parallel barrages, with infra-red searchlights mounted on the southern coast of the Strait, just west of Perejil Island. The searchlights were directed northwards across the Strait and were to be detected from a point near Algeciras. The distance across the Strait was about ten miles, and I suspect that the Germans might well have found the barrage unreliable because of the 'twinkling' that occurs in the disturbed atmosphere near the surface of the ground or sea. Certainly, when the Admiralty had tried similar barrages over much shorter distances for harbour protection this had been found a difficulty. In any event, the Germans were going to supplement this barrage with an infra-red detector rather similar to that which I had made for the aircraft detection trials at Farnborough in 1936 and 1937, but much bigger and therefore with a longer range. This was to be sited near Algeciras, looking southwards over the Strait, to detect any ship with hot exposed parts such as funnels. I arranged for photo reconnaissance of the suspected sites, and these confirmed that they were active. We also had some agents on the ground who were able to supplement in a minor way the information we had obtained from cryptography.

The problem now was what to do. Obviously the Admiralty had to be brought in, because their activities were clearly the main target for the operation. If we could not stop it going on, our ships would either have to have their funnels lagged and screened, or we should have to provide so many false indications by interrupting the barrage and steaming backwards and forwards across the infra-red detector that the Germans would not be able to see our real activities. The results of Philby's work and my own were therefore sent to the Director of Naval Intelligence, who passed them up to the First Sea Lord, Sir Dudley Pound. The threat was a serious one, for this was the summer of 1942, and we were hoping to pass many ships into the Mediterranean for Operation Torch, the landing of American and British troops in North West Africa to drive eastwards as the Eighth Army chased the Afrika Korps westwards from Alamein, and we wished to avoid giving the Germans an indication of our build-up.

As for the fighting in North Africa, Rommel himself had swept eastwards at the end of May and this had resulted in our retreat to el Alamein. His main hold-up had been at Bir Hacheim, which was magnificently held by the Free French. I can still remember Rommel's signal saying that he was held up by a 'fanatical resistance at Bir Hacheim' and that until he had overcome this his right flank was pinioned. It conjured up a picture of the band of men, led by General König of the Cuirassiers, to whom the honour of France still meant something, with a determination to fight to the last. To me, it was the beginning of a French revival that has continued long into the subsequent peace. It is today an encouragement that we, too, could again revive after the age of abdication that has paralysed us since 1945.

Before proceeding with the Gibraltar narrative, we must also remember the defence of Malta, where three old Gladiators, Faith, Hope and Charity, for a time faced the Luftwaffe alone. I had a little to do with that episode, for the Germans had installed some powerful new jammers on Sicily so as to render our radar on Malta useless. This would, of course, deprive the Malta air defence of any early warning, and a signal arrived in Air Ministry from the Signals Organization in Malta telling us that they were now badly jammed and asking if we could provide any help. I knew that the Germans judged the success of their jamming by listening to our radar transmissions to see whether, for example, they ceased to scan, as they might well do if they could not be used. I therefore signalled Malta to go on scanning as though everything were normal and not to give any kind of clue that they were in difficulty. After a few days the Germans switched their jammers off.

At the end of the War, I spent several days talking to General Martini, the Director General of Signals of the Luftwaffe, when he was a prisoner-of-war. He had been in his post since 1933, and had a long and detailed memory of the many events in which he and I had been opponents. At one point he specifically asked me about the jamming of Malta, and he told me that he had installed the jammers fully expecting to paralyse the Malta radar, but they seemed to have had no effect. He wanted to know what kind of anti-jamming devices we had installed in our radars so as to render them immune. He laughed ruefully when I told him that he had in fact succeeded, but that I knew the clues on which he would judge his own success, and had therefore advised the Malta radars to pretend that they were still working.

As for the Gibraltar barrage and the Admiralty, I found myself facing an extraordinary problem. Because of the opposition of their Directorate of Scientific Research, there was still no scientist in the Admiralty in the corresponding position to mine on the Air Staff, and I was in effect doing their Scientific Intelligence for them, in collaboration with part of the Signals Section of the Directorate of Naval Intelligence, N.I.D.9. The Directorate of Scientific Research had, however, to be brought in if countermeasures such as the lagging of ships were to be developed, and so a member of that Directorate was shown the evidence on which my conclusions were based. Actually, there was no need for him to be told that the main source was cryptographic, and N.I.D. certainly did not intend to tell him because of the ultra high grade of security imposed.

Somehow, though, the First Sea Lord overlooked the security considerations and passed down to the officer concerned some of the raw cryptographic material. This officer was highly conscientious and thought that it was all wrong that such material should be available and that his superiors in the Directorate of Scientific Research could not be shown it, and he refused to keep the information to himself. An officer from the N.I.D. came to me and asked for my help in persuading the scientist involved that the First Sea Lord had committed an indiscretion, and that the matter was so secret that it must not be revealed. The N.I.D. officer and I saw the scientist concerned but we completely failed to dissuade him from what, according to his own lights, was his duty. We had reached an impasse and my N.I.D. colleague was near desperation, when I said, 'Well, we had better come clean'.

I gambled on the distrustful nature of the human mind, and went on, 'As a matter of fact, we have been telling the First Sea Lord a cock-and-bull story about the cryptography, because we haven't really broken the German codes at all. What we have actually done is to infiltrate an agent into the German Secret Service headquarters in Madrid, whose position is so delicate that we dare not tell even the First Sea Lord, and so we have made up the cryptographic story. What you have seen are messages alright, but our chap has pinched them from the Abwehr office! What I will do is to write a full account which you can see, and which you can show to your Director if you like—but it must be kept to a very small circle!'

I returned to my office and wrote a report on 'German Equipment for Ship Detection in the Straits of Gibraltar' which started:

> The information upon which this Report is based has been gathered by the S.I.S. through three separate channels: (A) our agent network operating in the Straits area, (B) the technical investigations of Mr. D. J. Garrard, (C) the reports of our 'el Hatto' source who has fairly frequent access to the German H.Q. in Madrid and whose duties with the German S.I.S. enable him to visit out-stations from time to time. Since much of the evidence depends upon the reports of this last source, it may be mentioned that although he is non-technical, he has reported faithfully on even more important subjects than the present, and there is a good deal of internal confirmation in his statements. The other agents, in the Straits area, have not the same penetration and can only be relied upon for grosser details such as positions of activity and the passage of large items of equipment.

This did the trick, for the scientist had found something to justify his suspicions for our reticence, which were now directed towards the duplicity of N.I.D. in kidding the First Sea Lord that we had broken the German code whereas we had really got an agent in the Abwehr. I received the grateful thanks of N.I.D. for extricating them and the First Sea Lord from an awkward situation. The humour of the story lay in the naming of the source as 'el Hatto' for Hatto was indeed the name of one of the men at Bletchley who was handling the Abwehr decodes— Mr., now Professor, A. T. Hatto, of the Department of German at Queen Mary College.

The problem now was to deal with the Abwehr, and it was decided first to make a diplomatic approach to the Spanish Government, in the hope of getting them to stop the German activity. Our Ambassador in Madrid was Sir Samuel Hoare, and we had to brief him by telegrams. This proved a severe challenge because he had no technical knowledge, and yet he had to make a convincing case to the Spanish Government, without providing any clues which, if they were passed on to the Germans, would indicate the true source of our information. It proved a most tedious and delicate process, but in the end it was successful in that we showed the Spaniards enough to give them cold feet about any further support for German operations. The German effort was therefore withdrawn, and our build-up for the autumn offensives in North Africa could proceed without undue risk of our intentions being detected.

The episode, though, had a further repercussion. The following year I found evidence that the Germans were setting up a station near Lugo in northwest Spain, of the type known as 'Elektra Sonne' which would transmit a fan of beams out into the Atlantic and over the Bay of Biscay. This, with a similar station near Brest, would provide a cross pattern of beams by which an aircraft or a U-boat could very easily determine its position. Remembering what difficulty I had had in briefing our Ambassador in the Gibraltar instance, I boggled at having to go through the whole process again for the new station. Happily, the thought occurred to me that we were operating more aircraft over the Bay of Biscay than the Germans were. I therefore telephoned the Chief Navigation Officer at Coastal Command and asked him whether, if I could provide him with a fan of beams from northwest Spain, he could honestly say that Coastal Command could make better use of it than the Germans themselves. He held an enquiry at the Command and two days later called back affirmatively, adding that the Command would very much appreciate the service.

All that we now had to do was to photograph the station; from the separation between its aerials, and their direction of alignment, the necessary instructions could be worked out. The code name 'Consol' was given to this system, and Coastal Command used it with much success. So much so, in fact, that its use was continued for civil purposes after the war. It was beautifully simple, requiring only the necessary charts, a simple receiver and a stop-watch in the aircraft, not special receivers as were necessary for our own systems such as Gee. In fact, it competed successfully with these systems after the war, to Watson-Watt's disappointment, and has spread throughout the world and is still in operation.

CHAPTER THIRTY

Pineapple

O F ALL the attempts to emulate the Bruneval raid, the one that had the most lasting effect started with a telephone call from a young officer, Captain Hesketh Pritchard of the Special Operations Executive. He asked if he could come and discuss an operation which he had in mind. At our meeting he told me that he thought that my Unit was doing more than any other to win the war, and that he would like to help us. What he wanted to do was to steal a German nightfighter.

When the difficulties of his original proposal became clear to him, he pleaded with me to give him a target, and I showed him a picture of a new radio navigational beam station that was probably intended to provide a navigational service for the German nightfighters, but about which we so far knew relatively little. It had been photographed by G. R. Crakenthorp, emulating Tony Hill; actually his aircraft was hit by gunfire while he was taking the photograph, but he then coolly proceeded to 'stooge around' over France for another ten minutes, reckoning that if the damage did not make him crash within that time it was probably not serious enough to stop him getting across the Channel with his photograph.

The photograph, which was aimed as accurately as Tony Hill's had been, was blurred by aircraft movement; but it was good enough for Hugh Smith to make an accurate sketch. Both photograph and sketch are shown in Plate 15, the former at the bottom left and the latter at bottom centre. The six sketches in the top and middle rows were made of the same object by different agents, and are of interest because they show the kind of material we usually had to deal with: a sketch tests an agent's ability and technical competence far more than does a verbal description. One sketch, that at middle right, is good: its author is the subject of the latter part of this chapter.

I told Hesketh Pritchard that if he could get inside the control hut, which was carried on the turntable along with the beam aerial it could be helpful. He reappeared triumphantly two or three days later saying 'It's on! From now on, I'm Pineapple!' It appeared that Pineapple was the name to be given to the operation of getting into the new beam station, with the aid of the local Resistance, and Hesketh Pritchard was himself to be parachuted in to take part in the raid. Ever afterwards we referred to him as Hesketh-Pineapple.

He explained that there would first have to be a ground reconnaissance to establish the details of guards and so forth, and we duly briefed him with instructions that he could transmit to the Resistance workers. Within a few days there arrived a report from one of these workers and, to my astonishment, it showed very high technical competence. It was clear that this was no ordinary member of the Resistance, but someone who knew a great deal about radio installations and physics generally. I asked further questions, and within a few weeks we knew so much about the station, thanks to the ability of whoever it was who was making the observations, that I did not feel justified in asking anyone to risk his life with a physical attack.

When I told Hesketh-Pineapple 'The chap you've got on the ground is so good that he's really made your raid unnecessary' he was obviously relieved but said that it would put him in difficulty because he had worked up so much enthusiasm among the Free French, they might now be disappointed and think we had been rousing them for nothing. He said that he must report to his superior in S.O.E., who came and told me he was delighted their ground work had been so good, but it would help future relations with the Free French if I could arrange for a letter to be sent to him from the Air Staff for transmission to the Free French, thanking them for this splendid piece of reconnaissance, and carrying as many official stamps as possible. This I could easily do because of my official position on the Air Staff, and I signed the letter myself. Pineapple's chief rang me up to say that this was exactly what he wanted: and that, I thought, was the end of the matter.

One Sunday morning two or three weeks later I happened to be in my office when the telephone rang. It was Sir Claude Dansey, the Vice Chief of the Secret Service, who asked if I would come and talk to him. As others have told, Dansey had an unusual outlook. He struck me as a man who might spend a lifetime building up an Intelligence organization, and then be delighted if you proved to him that his most trusted agents were in fact in the pay of the enemy. When I went to his room, I found him almost incoherent with indignation about 'Those buggers in S.O.E.' I could not see how I was involved but he went on to say that

S.O.E. had sent a memorandum to the Chiefs of Staff proposing that they should take over the Secret Intelligence Service, quoting in support of their claim a letter from the Air Staff saying that they had done the finest piece of Intelligence work since the war started. As the details came out, it became clear that this was my letter to Pineapple's chief which Dansey was completely unaware that I had written.

Actually, I had only spoken the truth: it certainly was the best piece of technical observation on the part of a ground agent I had seen, even taking into account the magnificent work of the Belgians—the difference was that the observer was obviously a highly qualified physicist or engineer who could both draw diagrams and write out mathematics accurately. Dansey had merely sent for me because he knew that I had connections with the Air Staff, and might therefore be able to find out where the letter had originated. I drew a deep breath and said 'I wrote that letter—but before you explode let me tell you why I wrote it!' I then told him the story, and when I had finished he walked round and round his room saying 'THE CHEATS, THE CHEATS, THE CHEATS!' And then 'As a matter of fact, he was our agent anyway!'

Again, I thought that the matter was at an end: but not so. Some months later Hesketh-Pineapple telephoned me to say that he had thought it would be nice if I could meet the man who had written such good reports, so S.O.E. had pulled him out of France and flown him to London. In fact, they could not have done a more embarrassing thing. In the first place, it was much more useful to us to have a good observer on the other side of the Channel than kicking his heels in London. We might well have to spend time looking after him, if only as a matter of courtesy, when we were already very short-handed.

S.O.E. explained that they intended to send him back within a few days, and I then had the pleasure of meeting him. He turned out to be Yves Rocard, Professor of Physics at the Sorbonne, a fine physicist and a very gallant man. S.O.E. in fact failed to get him back within the short time that they had hoped, with the result that it would then have been too dangerous for him to return, so he spent the rest of the war up to D-Day in England. Fortunately he was not the kind of man to remain inactive, and he joined the Free French Navy and became their Director of Scientific Research. The Gestapo were after him in Paris, but in letters to his wife he led them to think that he had fled to Corsica and they ultimately lost interest. He was imperturbable. When, in February 1944, the Luftwaffe staged some minor raids on London, he had a room on the fourth or fifth floor of a house in Queen's Gate. This was struck by a bomb and most of the house destroyed. He was in bed at the time and, fortunately, the bed remained perched, as it were, on a shelf formed by the surviving fragment of the floor. He felt all round his bed in the dark and found that most of the floor was missing but, deciding that he was at least safe where he was, went to sleep again, and awoke to find a crowd in Queen's Gate pointing to the spectacle he presented. What is more, although he was frequently in my office, one of the only two non-British nationals who so gained our confidence, he never mentioned to us that he had been bombed. We heard it after the war from his son Michel who, to his father's embarrassment, turned out to be ultra Left-Wing, and figured prominently in the French student riots of 1968. He even put himself up as a Presidential candidate against General de Gaulle.

Yves Rocard was as staunch a friend as Britain could ever find. After the war the German cryptographers had fled from their headquarters at Treunbritzen and had ended up in the relatively small sector of Germany that was allocated for French control. Our own cryptographers at Bletchley were very anxious to talk to their German counterparts, particularly to investigate how far the latter had been successful in breaking our codes. A formal diplomatic approach to the French had failed completely. I therefore offered to see what I could do, and told Rocard of our problem. Within twenty-four hours he was back with full permission from the French for our men to enter their zone and interrogate the Germans—and the only request the French made was that if we found anything that affected the security of France, would we please let them know. We were all delighted when Rocard received the C.B.E. for his services to us.

He told us that on his return to Paris he noticed that various of his friends treated him curiously, sometimes even to the extent of seeming to wish to stay on the other side of any convenient table. It turned out that Madame Rocard was faced with the problem of explaining his disappearance when S.O.E. failed to get him back, and she managed to convince everybody that she had not been unduly surprised because he had shown signs of going off his head, and that she could only assume he was now completely mad. She succeeded in convincing not only the Germans but his close friends.

CHAPTER THIRTY-ONE

The Kammhuber Line

G ENERAL JOSEF Kammhuber had been appointed by Goering on 17th July 1940 to take command of German nightfighters. His first concept was a great belt of searchlights deployed to the west of Germany proper, through which our bombers would have to fly to reach their targets. Warned by the Freyas on the coast, the German nightfighters would orbit suitably placed beacons in front of the searchlight belt ready to swoop on any bomber caught in the lights. The setting-up in 1941 of what came to be called the 'Main Belt' was of course soon reported by our bombers, and the question for us was: how did it work?

Our own experience strongly suggested that searchlights were unnecessary for nightfighting if a proper radar technique was available, and the apparent German dependence on lights was therefore something of a puzzle—all the more so because the 40 and 60 kilometre night-fighting circles we had already found suggested that searchlights need not be involved. Our bombers crews' reports repeatedly suggested that the accuracy of initial aiming of the lights was due to their being radar-controlled, along the lines of our own 'S.L.C.' (Search Light Control) radar, in which a special radar set was directly attached to an individual light, but we could find no true German equivalent. On the contrary, we had encountered various mentions of searchlights in Enigma, but none associating them with a radar control. Two direct lines of attack could be made on the puzzle, for if the lights were radar controlled the obvious equipment would be the Würzburg or something derived from it. We could therefore fly special aircraft carrying observers with suitable receivers for the 53 centimetre transmissions of the Würzburgs over the Main Belt; we could also attempt to photograph the searchlights and see whether any had a radar equipment associated with it.

The first line of attack was already available, in the R.A.F. unit which had made the original flight to discover the Knickebein beams in 1940, for later in the Battle of the Beams the same personnel had taken to flying down the beams in order to bomb the transmitters, and thus to making radio and radar observations over France. Specialist observers from the Telecommunications Research Establishment had volunteered for the flights, and had received R.A.F. Commissions in case they were lost on operations.

This indeed happened to one of the first observers, Howard Cundall. Cundall had been flying over France in the early hours of 4th November 1941, when a stray A-A shell fragment damaged an engine, and the crew had to bail out. The loss of a crew would have been a serious enough matter, anyway, but Cundall knew a good deal about our own radar, including the new centimetric devices which were coming along, and might thus be a valuable prisoner for the Germans to capture. The crew all landed without undue damage, and they remained at large for some days. After several adventures Cundall reached the coast near Mont St. Michel on 18th November, and seized a rowing boat in which he tried to hoist a make-shift sail and get back to England. He was seen by the Germans and captured. All the other members of the crew were caught except for the second pilot, who succeeded in escaping to Spain. This was fortunate because the Germans thought that they had captured a full crew, and therefore did not suspect the nature of Cundall's duties. While in Stalag Luft 3 he not only concealed his knowledge of our new radar devices, but built a radio transmitter with which he opened contact between the camp and London, maintaining it even during the long march eastwards as the Germans pulled back the prisoners in the late stages of the war. In this way he provided information from captured air crew regarding their experiences with the German night defences, and thus aided our offensive even from behind the barbed wire.

An even earlier observer on radar listening flights was Eric Ackermann, who in two years made more than 90 flights, including more than 40 on which bombs were dropped against the beam stations. Most of his later flights were over the Main Belt, listening for Würzburg transmissions. Not only did he hear these transmissions very frequently over the Main Belt, but he also concluded that some of the lights were radar-controlled.

Besides the radar transmissions themselves, we had the possibility of listening to the instructions transmitted by radio telephony to the German nightfighters from their ground controls. In these instructions there was frequent reference to something called 'Kleine Schraube' (Little Screw), which we ultimately realized was nothing more than a code-name for the radio beacon which the nightfighter was to orbit.

The other thrust of our attack, the location and photography of searchlights and radar stations, drew first blood in March 1942 when we photographed the Giant Würzburgs near St. Trond (p. 227) following a report from the Belgian Resistance. The photographs partly solved our puzzle, because the searchlights around one of the Giants were presumably controlled by it: these could be 'master lights' which showed other searchlights where the target was. We had already encouraged the Resistance workers to report as many searchlights positions as possible, with the intention of asking P.R.U. to photograph the positions reported.

The Belgians had become tremendously active, producing an enormous amount of information of all kinds which they took across France to Lisbon. One of the main routes was the express that ran from, I think, Lille to Lyons, where the fireman acted as courier. He hid the reports under the coal, so that all he had to do if the train was searched was to shovel the whole lot into the fire box. It seemed more difficult to get the information back to Britain: Jempson told me that at one stage there were 15 hundredweights of reports waiting in Lisbon for a plane back to England.

Many years afterwards I met some of our Belgian helpers at a Human Rights Conference in Brussels in 1970, and I was remarking to them that it seemed to me that half Belgium had been working for us, even to small children sitting by the wayside carefully noting the numbers of every German vehicle that passed. In fact espionage seemed so compulsive to the Belgians that I could not help wondering whether if we had occupied them instead of the Germans, they would have been just as professional in helping the Germans as they had been for us. One of their leaders said 'You are quite right. You must remember that Belgium has had a long history of being occupied and of finding ways of living with and getting the better of whoever was occupying us' and he went on to say that the tradition was so strong that it seemed almost automatic for them to get organized once the Germans had taken control.

But just as the information began to come back from Belgium the searchlights disappeared, and our reconnaissance photographs showed nothing but empty emplacements. What had happened was that Hitler had personally ordered all the searchlights back to Germany, where they could make a show of defending the towns. Bomber Command was now beginning to hit Germany despite Goering's assurance that no bomber would ever appear over Berlin, and Hitler wished to show the German people that something was being done to defend them. So on

5th May 1942 the searchlights were withdrawn back to Germany, reversing the move by which Kammhuber had originally brought them forward into the Main Belt. By 20th May, when P.R.U. went out to reconnoitre, they had all gone.

A few weeks after this disappointment I went into Jempson's room to see whether anything more of interest had come in. In his own way he was a professional who reckoned that his task had ceased once he had got the information, and that it was not his job to worry about whether any use was made of it. He waved towards his top shelf, and told me that there might be a map 'up there', indicating several dishevelled piles of documents. I asked whether he would mind if I looked through them, and after a few minutes I found the map: it was a breath-catching moment for, as I unfolded it, I saw that it must show the deployment of a whole searchlight regiment covering the entire southern half of Belgium. I like to think that one of our Belgian friends, daunted by the prospect of cycling round the countryside laboriously plotting the sites of individual searchlights, thought that it would be simpler to break into the headquarters of the Regimental Commander and remove his map, for this is what it was. I warmly thanked Jempson and took it back to show Charles Frank. We could now see all the searchlight positions on 90 kilometres of the Main Belt, together with the various levels of headquarters. Everything seemed to be organized on the basis of a military trinitarianism. There were three lights to a Zug (squad), three Zugs one behind the other to a Batterie, three Batteries side by side to an Abteilung (battalion) and three Abteilungen to the Regiment. Each Abteilung covered a front of 30 kilometres, each Batterie taking 10 kilometres with the three Zugs 5 kilometres one behind the other and about 3 kilometres laterally between individual searchlights. In front of each Abteilung was a more elaborate sign, and fortunately one of them coincided with the Giant Würzburg station that we knew of near St. Trond. It therefore followed that the other signs at 30 kilometres on either side of it, one each in front of the flanking Abteilungen were similar Giant Würzburg stations. One section of the map showing a complete Abteilung is reproduced at Plate 16.

The intended mode of operation was now clear. The Freya associated with the Würzburgs would first pick up an incoming bomber and direct one of the Würzburgs to it. The other Würzburg would be watching the German nightfighter which would have been 'scrambled' and instructed to orbit a radio and visual beacon (the 'Little Screw') some kilometres in front. As the bomber approached, the ground controller would begin to direct the fighter on to a course of interception, while the Würzburg following the bomber would direct his surrounding three searchlights towards the bomber. If these succeeded in picking the bomber up, it would now be visible to the battalion of searchlights behind, which would now light up, and try to hold the bomber in view as it crossed the belt so that the nightfighter could attack it. This explained why radar control of searchlights had seemed relatively scarce—for the three searchlights actually directed by radar, there were another 27 behind which depended on visual pick-up from the first three.

I took the map to the Photographic Reconnaissance Unit at Benson to show the pilots, so they would know what it was I now wanted when my official request for sorties came through. Over the next fortnight they photographed many of the positions indicated by the map. It did not matter that the searchlights had been withdrawn, because the radar stations had been left in place, and we knew, as did no doubt the Germans, that the radar stations themselves were sufficient for interception, at least if backed up by an airborne radar system for the night-

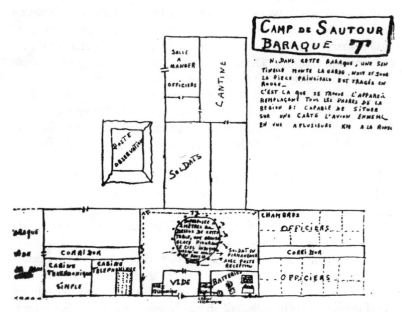

Fig. 11. Sketch of the German nightfighter control headquarters at Sautour, Belgium, made by a Belgium agent. The poor quality of the reproduction is due to the original having been transmitted to London on microfilm

fighters. The stealing of the map by agent 'Tégal' was therefore of very great value.

An interesting difference now emerged between the Giant Würzburg stations in the Main Belt and those such as Domburg on the coast. With the latter there was always a T-shaped hut, but when we photographed the Abteilung command posts in the Main Belt we found the T-huts some kilometres back from the Würzburgs among the searchlights. The T-hut was where the ground controller was situated, and it was evidently considered better for him to be among the lights when these were available. The next question was: what apparatus did he have at his disposal? More than one Belgian agent succeeded in getting into a T-hut and describing for us the 'Seeburg Table', on which the positions of the bomber and fighter were shown as spots of coloured light, red for the bomber and blue for the fighter, projected from underneath on to the ground glass screen forming the flat surface of the table. The projectors were moved by operators who received telephonic instructions from the two Giants. There was no cathode ray presentation such as we ourselves employed, and the plotting system was therefore ponderous and liable to human error.

Although I have said that the Belgians were almost automatically inclined to espionage, it would be entirely false to imply that they were without feeling. Later in the summer another report came through on microfilm from agent VNAR 2 of 'Service Marc'. It ended with the following:

(1) In view of the apparent current interest in similar installations, it seems to us odd that no attempts have yet been made to destroy them, especially since (a) except for No. 2, they are not powerfully protected, and (b) they were installed with difficulty in 4 *months* and it would not be at all easy to replace them. The Germans' interest in them is clearly shown by the extremely strict way in which they guard the approaches, which has several times resulted in our being fired at by sentries, fortunately with more zeal than accuracy. The Jauche installation is particularly easy to spot and to attack from the air.

(2) As far as our work is concerned, it would be helpful if we knew to what extent you and the British services are interested. We have been working so long in the dark that any reaction from London about our work would be welcome to such obscure workers as ourselves. We hope this will not be resented since, whatever may happen you can rely on our entire devotion and on the sacrifice of our lives.

10

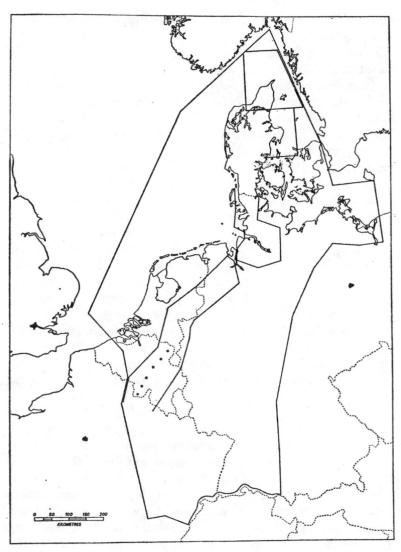

Fig. 12. The state of British knowledge of German nightfighter control stations in early September 1942. Six positions in the 'Kammhuber Line' were known in Belgium, and a seventh on Walcheren in the Scheldt Estuary. The parallel lines running south from Schleswig Holstein to Belgium were known to delineate the Kammhuber Line; the much larger area from Scandinavia to the Swiss border was designated as a general air defence region

As I read the message, and began to imagine the conditions under which it had been sent, it brought home to me what a pleasant safe job I had compared with those on whom I depended. The poignant humour of having been fired at 'fortunately with more zeal than accuracy' and the intention to work on despite the seeming lack of encouragement from our side made me more than ever determined not to let these men down. There was in fact no way of communicating with them directly at the time. I doubt whether anyone in Britain knew who they were, and I am not sure whether they were ever thanked, although I did my best. If any of them is still alive and reads this, I hope that he will now know that their message got through. As will transpire, I was able a few months later to arrange some direct action. The episode illustrates the enormous advantage of my personal position in Intelligence. Having such a vivid contact with those who were risking their lives to get the information on the one hand, and with those at the summit of power, like Churchill, Cherwell, Sinclair and Portal on the other, I was able to ensure that work in the field was appreciated at the top with as little hierarchic attenuation as possible.

Thanks to the Belgians and to Photographic Reconnaissance, we now knew how a typical sector of the Main Belt was organized, and the technical equipment on which it depended. The next advance occurred in September 1942, when Bletchley broke into a new line of Enigma traffic: I had encouraged them to look for anything that might be associated with nightfighter activities, and the hunt succeeded. When the cypher was broken it gave us some of the reports from nightfighter sectors back to their higher command.

Our first important break referred to reports from a Sector 7 on interceptions that had been made on our bombers by nightfighters during a raid on Frankfurt on the night of 8th/9th September. By finding where we expected our bombers to be at the times they had been intercepted, it seemed that Sector 7 must be in southern Belgium. There was mention of three controls, 7A, 7B and 7C, and it seemed that some aircraft had spilled over into Sector 8A, less into 8B, and none into 8C. This would be consistent with assuming that Sector 8 was south of Sector 7, and that the A, B and C sub-units were also in a north/south order. It was also tempting to assume that the three letters referred to a set of three control stations such as we had seen from the pattern on the stolen map. The one other piece of information that I had available was that the Luftwaffe generally had been informed of the existence of a closed area for nightfighting which roughly delineated what we believed to be a zone centred on the old Main Belt. Figure 12 shows this information, and Figure 13 shows the Bomber Command route map, with my pencilled speculation regarding the whereabouts of Sector 7.

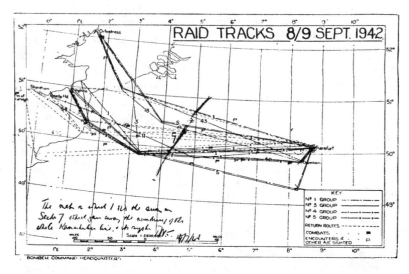

Fig. 13. *Bomber Command raid tracks for 8/9 September 1942, from which—in conjunction with an Enigma message—it was deduced that Sector 7 of the German nightfighter defences was in south Belgium*

As I was turning the information over in my mind I suddenly saw that if you assumed that a Sector covered a 90 kilometre front with radar stations at 30 kilometre intervals in a straight line, and try to fit a set of such 90 kilometre units into the declared nightfighter zone, and if you started at the top and assumed that Sector 1 was in Schleswig Holstein, the 7th Sector would fall exactly where I had deduced that it should be from the nightfighter interception reports. In a flash, the whole system of the night defences became clear. We could now guess at the position of every other radar station in the Main Belt, and could fill in much of the missing detail, so that the map shown at Figure 12 was now transformed into that at Figure 14. In front of the Main Belt there were the other nightfighter control stations of the Domburg type, extending all the way up the coast of Holland.

I first tried the idea on Charles Frank, who was sitting at the opposite desk at the moment on which it had occurred to me, and I then telephoned Charles Medhurst and arranged an immediate visit to show him

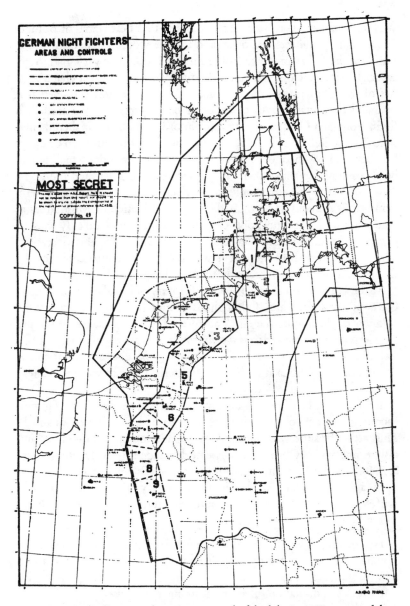

Fig. 14. The transformation of Figure 12 as a result of the deduction in Figure 13 and the stolen map at Plate 16. Taking a unit of three radar control stations in a row at 30 kilometre intervals, and assuming that this constituted a Sector and supposing that the Kammhuber Line was numbered consecutively from North to South, Sector 7 fell correctly into position, and the approximate positions of all the remaining 21 control stations could be deduced

what had happened. He said that he thought that Bert Harris of Bomber Command should see it at once, and that he would arrange for me to visit him the following day. I told him that I should be very glad to go, especially since the one gap in our knowledge was the exact characteristics of the German nightfighter radar. We were almost certain that it operated on a wavelength of about 61 centimetres, but we needed to fly in front of a German nightfighter in order to obtain final confirmation. Such a flight would be very dangerous if carried out in an ordinary bomber, and we therefore needed one or two Mosquitoes which would be fast enough to make their escape once they had detected the transmission from any German nightfighter that was about to intercept them. Bomber Command had almost the entire production of Mosquitoes at that stage and our one hope of getting Mosquitoes quickly was to persuade the Commander-in-Chief to release two for this operation. Charles Medhurst told me that it would be up to me to convince the Commander-in-Chief sufficiently to let us have them.

At the same time I showed the work to my old Professor, now Lord Cherwell, and told him I thought it would be helpful if the Prime Minister could minute the Air Staff to stress the importance of finding the German airborne radar wavelengths as the last essential step in our technical knowledge of the whole system, on which we were of course basing our countermeasures. Prime Ministerial pressure was accordingly applied.

In the meantime there was a happy outcome to the problem of giving encouragement to our Belgian agents who had contributed so much. This arose because we ourselves were developing a new bombing system known as 'Oboe'. This system, developed by A. H. Reeves and F. E. Jones at the Telecommunications Research Establishment, employed a principle which I had sketched in my imaginary minutes of the German conference in December 1940 about the future of radio bombing, where I ascribed it to Dr. Plendl:

'Dr. Plendl . . . would add that . . . newer systems could be developed which did not in fact involve beam flying but depended entirely on distance measurements from two ground stations, either by frequency modulation, phase measurement, or pulses'.

Reeves used to visit me from time to time in London, and told me he would like to develop a bombing system for our own use and tried out on me various of the alternative systems using range measurements from two stations. The attraction was that whereas our directional measurements were not very good, we knew that we could make range measurements very accurately. The idea was to fly an aircraft at a constant range from one station by sending out pulses from the ground which the aircraft would pick up and amplify and then return to the ground station. This ground station would then find the aircraft's range from the time it took the pulses to return. The path of the aircraft, if it flew at constant range, would thus be part of a circle centred on the ground station, and this circle would have to pass near the target, but slightly short of it, as the bombs went off tangentially after they had been released from the aircraft. All this could be calculated, if the aircraft's height and speed were known. Moreover, the pilot in the aircraft could be automatically informed by means of signals sent out from the ground station whether he was on track or to one side of it, just as in the German beam systems—but with the great advantage that since there was no beam the Germans could not pick it up as we had been able to do against their bombers.

A second ground station could also determine the range of the aircraft from it, and so instruct the aircraft to drop its bombs when it was at such a range that these should hit the target. The system was therefore a good deal more sophisticated than anything developed by the Germans. It had the same advantage as their Y-system in that the instant of bomb release was determined by a ground observer free from the harassment of a flight over enemy territory, but it also had two disadvantages of that system in that the traffic-handling capacity was very limited and the aircraft had to transmit a signal which might be homed upon by the enemy. The former disadvantage was not serious in the event, in that a few Oboe aircraft could be used to drop visual markers for the main force; the latter disadvantage was substantially avoided because Oboe was used by Mosquitoes which were too fast for the enemy nightfighters, and because it was later moved to centimetric wavelengths against which the Germans were almost powerless.

The potential disadvantages were given undue weight in some higher quarters—so much so that one scientist wrote:

I regret having to do this but I am sure it is true to say, quite bluntly, that these disquisitions from T.R.E. on OBOE are becoming ridiculous. If they came as inventions from the outside public and not from official sources, they would be rejected without hesitation . . . I repeat now, even more strongly, that it would be disastrous to permit the protagonists of this fantastic OBOE the chance of causing a sensible and

practical system like GEE to share the disrepute into which OBOE—
even if raised to Mark 20—will inevitably fall.

If I had the power I would discover the man responsible for this
latest OBOE effort and sack him, so that he could no longer waste,
not only his time and effort, but ours also by his vain imaginings.

As it turned out, Oboe was the most precise bombing system of the
whole war. It was so accurate that we had to look into the question of
the geodetic alignment of the Ordnance Survey with the Continent,
which effectively hinged on triangulation across the Straits of Dover.
F. E. Jones asked me if I could suggest a trial target from which we could
get precise information from ground observers on the fall of bombs, so
as to be able to see whether our triangulation required any correction. It
was then that I saw the chance of showing our Belgian friends that we

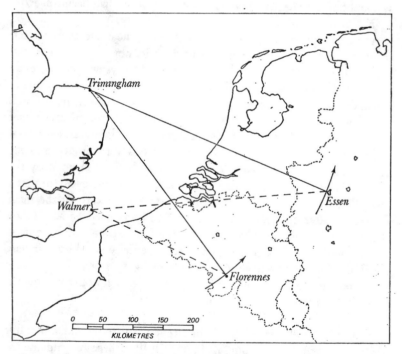

*Fig. 15. The 'Oboe' dispositions for bombing Florennes and Essen. The bombing aircraft
flies at a constant range from the ground station at Trimingham, taking it on an arc. When
it is at the correct range from the ground station at Walmer, the latter sends the order for
bomb release. The curved tracks are slightly (but exaggerated in the diagram) to the west
of the targets because the bombs continue on a tangent after release*

were making use of their information for by this time they had provided many more reports, one of which said that the headquarters of Sector 7 was in the Novitiate near the town of Florennes.

Entirely against the standard policy of not disclosing the target for a raid in advance, I obtained permission on this occasion for signals to be sent out to the Belgian network so that they could have observers in position for the night of the attack which was to be made by a small force of Mosquitoes in December 1942. Each aircraft flew on a constant radius from one Oboe station at Trimingham and the correct instant for bomb release was decided by a controller at a second station at Walmer (Figure 15). In the event, everything was so brilliantly successful that F. E. Jones afterwards said 'Within 48 hours we had reports of where the bombs had gone—even down to the fact that one had gone into a particular tree. Their distances from the aiming point were given in yards. And when I queried how this could have been done so accurately, R. V. pointed out that the Belgians, risking their lives in no uncertain manner, had actually paced out the distances for us before sending back the information to London.' And, to the delight of everyone concerned, including the Belgians, one of the bombs had actually hit the building in which the nightfighter headquarters were housed.

We had started tactical countermeasures against the Kammhuber Line in the winter of 1941/42, well before we knew its exact extent or location. The main tactic was to try to fly our bombers in a compact bunch, preferably all through the same nightfighter box in as short a time as possible. While the nightfighter controller was then concentrating on one bomber, many others should be able to get through unscathed. This tactic worked to some extent, but it was difficult to maintain concentration, especially on the homeward route where differences in speed and navigation between individual bombers caused them to be increasingly strung out and spread, and most of our lossses occurred in this phase. Kammhuber's reaction was to increase the number of nightfighter stations, so that instead of having to pass merely through his original Line our bombers had now to fly through a defence in depth. Figure 16 shows our knowledge of the increased deployment towards the end of 1943, when the original 27 stations of the original Line had now become an area defence involving more than 200 stations.

For locating the new stations as they appeared, we depended mainly on the Resistance movements in the Occupied Countries and on photographic reconnaissance. The stations, with their two Giant

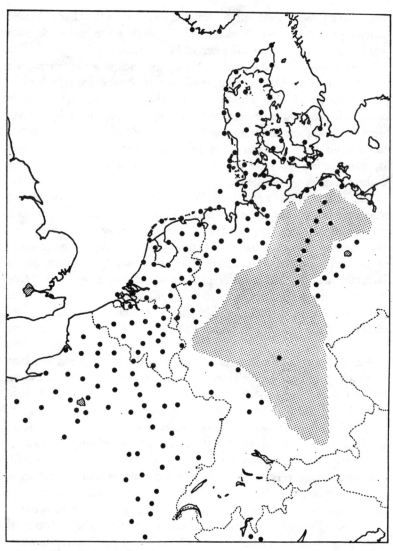

Fig. 16. General Kammhuber's reaction to Bomber Command's concentration tactics, spring 1943. His original Line is expanded to an area defence in depth, with many more radar control stations, each shown as a dot

Würzburgs, were difficult to conceal, and the Würzburgs were indeed objects of local wonder which strained the descriptive powers of many of our friends in the Low Countries. 'Inverted Umbrella' was a typical description, while 'Miroir Magique' conveyed an air of mystery. One Würzburg was so much talked about that it became 'Le Fameux Miroir d'Arsimont'. In areas where we had no direct contact with the Resistance movement, we used to get our bombers to drop homing pigeons in containers which would open after a few hours and release the birds if they had not been found by someone on the ground. Attached to the containers were questionnaires, asking a series of simple questions which, for example, a farm labourer might be able to answer, and which might be helpful to us. My own question was 'Are there any German radio stations in your neighbourhood with aerials which rotate?' This feature was an almost certain criterion of a radar station, and we dropped the pigeons wherever we saw a gap in our knowledge. Before the end of 1942 the pigeons had given us the locations of three stations hitherto unknown to us, and more followed during 1943.

Further clues regarding the locations of nightfighter stations could sometimes be derived from Enigma, where the stations were referred to by animal codenames, the first letter of the animal being the same as that of the nearest village or town to the site of the station. 'Hamster, Biber and Zander' were respectively Hamstede, Brielle and Zandvoort in the Scheldt Estuary, while 'Tiger' was Terschelling (incidentally responsible for the destruction of 150 of our bombers). 'Waal' was Wangerooge, 'Languste' was Langeoog, and so forth. As a result of this guessing game, and despite my ignorance of German, I came to know almost the entire German menagerie—to the bewilderment of a German forester who took me shooting at the end of the war.

Another tactic that we used against the Kammhuber Line in its original form was the obvious one of flying round its extremities. The outstanding examples were the attacks on Lübeck and Rostock in March and April, 1942. Great damage was done with relatively low losses. Kammhuber's reaction was to make an area deployment over the whole of Denmark, creating 29 new stations. Thanks to our friends in the Danish Services, and particularly Captain P. Winkel (later Major General and Chief of Defence Staff) and Captain V. Gyth (later Colonel and Chief of the Royal Guard), we knew the positions of all these stations before any was in operation. The Lübeck and Rostock raids had a further effect: Hitler resolved on a policy of retaliation, leading to the V-weapons.

CHAPTER THIRTY-TWO

Lichtenstein

IN BRITAIN WE had decided as early as 1935 that interception at night would very probably require a suitable detector for the nightfighter to enable it to close in on the bomber after the ground control had done its best to put the nightfighter into a favourable position. Such a detector had indeed been the main objective of my pre-war efforts in infra-red, but an airborne radar detector (A.I.—Airborne Interception) had proved more promising. In Germany, too, infra-red had been developed for nightfighter use and a brilliant equipment, the Kiel Gerät, had been produced using the infra-red detecting properties of lead sulphide. But it suffered from the usual infra-red defect of not being able to measure the range of the target, and so the Germans also ultimately preferred an airborne radar detector. This equipment, the Lichtenstein Gerät, first came to our notice through a prisoner in April 1941, and it appears to have achieved its first operational success on 9th August 1941 when a Messerschmidt 110 from Leeuwarden shot down one of our bombers with its aid. In the 'Little Screw' radio telephony traffic between German controls and their nightfighters there was increasing use during 1942 of the phrase 'Emil Emil' which seemed to indicate that a nightfighter had now been brought close enough to the bomber for the latter to be picked up in the nightfighter's own detector.

Since German radar technique was obviously strong at wavelengths of 50–60 centimetres, and since such short wavelengths would be particularly suitable for nightfighter equipment because of the small overall dimensions, we decided to search particularly in this waveband. And since nightfighters were operating in the Scheldt Estuary, not more than one hundred miles from the Suffolk coast, there was a good chance that we could pick up the nightfighter radar transmissions on listening equipment ground-based in Suffolk. Fairly soon we heard transmissions on a wavelength of about 61 centimetres with a pulse repetition frequency of 3,000 per second, which seemed to come from moving sources. Incidentally, the Giant Würzburg transmissions from Domburg were also heard, on wavelengths around 53 centimetres and with a pulse repetition frequency of 2,000 per second. On 16th May 1942 we even attempted to intercept a nightfighter controlled from Domburg with one of our own Beaufighters controlled from Foreness. Tracks of both nightfighters were plotted by Fighter Command; but, thanks to the skill of both British and German controllers, the attempted combat ended in mutual frustration. The German aircraft refused to be tempted more than about 60 kilometres away from Domburg, so as to remain within range of its Giant Würzburgs.

Although it was reasonably certain that one form of Lichtenstein operated on 61 centimetres, it was possible that this was only used by the coastal nightfighters, where the Germans must know we could intercept the transmissions, and that a substantially different wavelength would be used further back. This was why I had told Charles Medhurst that the next most important objective after the unravelling of the Kammhuber Line was to check whether the nightfighters associated with the Line also operated on 61 centimetres. Within an hour or so of my making the point Medhurst telephoned to say that he had arranged with the Commander-in-Chief, Bomber Command, for the latter to see me before lunch the following day, 20th September or thereabouts, at his Headquarters near High Wycombe.

On my previous visits to the Command I had always been courteously but disinterestedly received, rather after the manner of a gentlemen's country club. This time the atmosphere was different and I showed the Commander-in-Chief the outline of the German night defences as I now understood them, with the locations of a substantial number of nightfighter control stations. His immediate reaction was a grunt of satisfaction and the exclamation 'It shows I'm hurting them!', to which I replied that if we did not do enough about them it would be Bomber Command that would be hurt. I then told him of my requirement for a couple of Mosquitoes and he said that I had better explain the problem to his Deputy, Air Vice Marshal R. H. M. Saundby, whom I already slightly knew. It was nearly lunchtime and so Saundby took me into the Command Mess.

As we passed a portrait of George Washington, he told me that a few days before an American Air Force General with a Germanic name (it may have been General Spaatz) had been visiting the Command and had said something about the portrait as he and the C.-in-C. were passing it. Bert Harris' reply was 'I will bet you one thing, Spaatz: for every

one Spaatz that fought in Washington's army, there were ten Harrises!'
Saundby himself had a delightful sense of humour, and he proceeded to
divert me with the proof of a theorem that all cats have three tails. For
this it is necessary to make two premises, the first being that one cat has
one more tail than no cat, and the second that no cat has two tails.
What is more, he knew where the fallacy in the argument lay.

As soon as he had settled me with a drink he picked up a *Daily Mirror*
and asked me to excuse him while he read the strip cartoons. He
apologized saying that these cartoons were read by his bomber crews,
and that if he showed himself knowledgeable about the cartoons they
would be more likely to take notice of his instructions. I was not
entirely convinced of the sincerity of the argument, because he himself
was clearly interested and he became lost for a minute or so in one of the
strips, finally commenting 'Actually, this one is very funny. You see
this chap here—he has just entered for a vegetable marrow competition,
but his marrow has died and he is trying to make a dummy one by
stretching canvas over a wire frame. Here you can see him painting it!'
He then went on with a sigh 'It looks jolly good, but I am sure something's going wrong tomorrow!' After he had pulled himself away from
the cartoons, we went in to lunch, and it was not long before he was
cursing the idiots who had lowered the water-table of the whole
country by about four feet. I guessed that he was an angler, and he
needed little encouragement to go on. By the end of lunch he had
become so expansive that he told me 'As a matter of fact, the first time
I met my wife she had a rod in her hand!' and I began to see hope for
the Mosquitoes.

He was indeed a very fine angler. He was President of the Piscatorial
Society and after the war wrote a happy book, *A Fly-Rod on Many
Waters*. It contains some penetrating observations, for example on the
attraction of a red Mayfly, 'To the human mind a red Mayfly is incongruous—a ridiculous object. But there is no reason why the trout
should react to it in this way. The perception of incongruity—which
my ponderings have led me to believe is the basic requirement for a
sense of humour— is possible only to a creature possessing considerable
powers of reasoning.' I myself, by an entirely different argument—
based on seeing the object of a practical joke as the creation of an
incongruity—had come to the same conclusion.

What Saundby perhaps did not see was that he himself created
delicious incongruities by his ordinary behaviour. His colleague at
Bomber Command, Sir Arthur Saunders, told me that at a conference

which the C.-in-C. had called urgently one night Saundby was not to be found. He was not in his room, or in the Mess, but the sentries on the gate maintained that he had not left the compound. The conference had to start without him whilst a search was being made, and it was interrupted by the appearance of a corporal, who came in and said to the C.-in-C. 'Excuse me, Sir, but we've found the Deputy C.-in-C. He's up a tree, and we can't get him down!' Yet another of his interests were moths, and he had happened to spot an unusual moth high up a tree which he proceeded to climb, only to find that it was beginning to sway under his considerable weight, and he dared not climb any further. But neither could he see his way down again. It took quite an effort to retrieve him.

I had known none of this background before our lunch, and now that it was over I was in for another surprise. As we reached the door of the Mess to return to his office he gave me a sideways look and asked 'Do you like models?' I cautiously replied 'Yes, but what sort?' 'Model engines,' he replied, and then asked me if I would like to see some. There flitted across my mind the recollection that German Air Force prisoners had told us that Goering wiled away his time at Karinhall, dressed in a green silk dressing gown embroidered in gold and playing with toy trains. I asked Saundby what kind of trains he had, and he told me that they were Hornby. 'Not very good, are they?' I asked and he grudgingly replied, 'No, but I buy spare parts and modify 'em'. Fortunately this was a field in which I had schoolboy memories and so I asked 'Where do you buy your spare parts—Bonds?' His approving affirmative brought the Mosquitoes just a little nearer. Actually, Bond's shop in Euston Road was the mecca of every model railway enthusiast, and so it had been a fairly safe guess. But I at least felt that if he did not give me the Mosquitoes he would be more inclined, following his own principle with bomber crews, to believe what I told him about the German night defences.

He took me up to his bedroom, and showed me an ordinary Hornby No. o gauge track running on a shelf at waist level all round his bedroom except, of course, for the door. I would not have put it past him to contrive a kind of swing bridge which would come into operation as the door closed. But he told me that he had discussed his wartime policy with his son, who was then about twelve years old, and they had decided that they would concentrate on building rolling stock until the war was over. He showed me a goods train and invited me to test its lightness by pulling it along by hand. He then offered to let me into the secret of how he had achieved such lightness despite the fact that the trucks appeared to be full of coal. 'It's not coal, really,' he said. 'Actually, it's cork. What I do is to go round the Mess after a party on Saturday night and pick up all the old corks. Then I mix up linseed oil and bismarck black and put it in a tin with the broken cork. I usually pinch the C.-in-C.'s old cigarette tins for this, and put the cork and the black inside, push on the lid, and shake it up and down like a cocktail shaker. Then I tip the whole lot out onto a piece of blotting paper and let it dry.' And he went on, 'As a matter of fact, I get the trains even lighter, because these trucks are not really full of coal.' He grubbed the top layer on one truck aside with his finger and showed me that it hardly went below the top of the truck itself, because he had filled up the bottom with match-boxes which he had painted black.

Time was now getting on, and he looked regretfully at his watch and said 'I suppose we'd better be getting back to my office' and so we got as far as the door. In fact I was already in the corridor outside, but I can still see him, big man that he was, standing in his bedroom doorway with his hands on his hips surveying the room and saying 'Yes, No. o gauge is just about right! No. 1 gauge is too big, you can't get much of it into a room. Double o gauge is too small and fiddling, so you can't do any modifications yourself. No. o gauge is the gauge for me! And what's more, the engines weigh five or six pounds, and you can have a damned good smash with those!' As we made our way back to his office, I asked 'Now, what about those Mosquitoes?' 'Certainly' was his answer, and I went back to Air Ministry happy.

Next day I told Charles Medhurst what had happened and said 'You might have briefed me!' Medhurst apologized, saying that he thought Saundby's propensities were so well known throughout the Air Force that it did not occur to him that I didn't know. He told me that when Saundby was on the Directing Staff at the R.A.F. Staff College he sometimes had to take a session between noon and one o'clock, and somewhere towards half-past twelve he would begin to lose the theme of what he was saying and wander over to the window. This would happen with increasing frequency until finally the whistle or rumble of a train was heard in the distance on the line that ran past Staff College. At that point he would abandon all pretence at lecturing and stay at the window to watch the train out of sight, looking at his watch and making some such comment as 'Damn it, three minutes late again!'

It would be pleasant to record that the Mosquitoes were forthcoming within a week of my visit to Bomber Command; but this was not so. Since they would have to be allocated to the signals organization that was operating the listening flights, I handed the Bomber Command promise over to them, and awaited results. Unfortunately the Mosquitoes were still not available some two months later, and it was decided to risk flying one of the Wellington aircraft, which were much slower, in front of a nightfighter in the hope that the operator who was listening for the nightfighter transmissions would be able to give enough warning for the Wellington to escape.

Early in the morning of 3rd December a Wellington of No. 1473 (wireless-investigation) flight took off from an airfield near Huntingdon to accompany the raid that was directed against Frankfurt that night. Two hours or so later it was west of Mainz and was turning for home. The special radio operator was Pilot Officer Harold Jordan, who in peacetime had been a schoolteacher. Just after the turn for home he picked up weak signals on the expected wavelength and studied them for the next ten minutes as they increased in strength. He warned the rest of the crew what was happening and he drafted a coded signal saying that the signals had been picked up, confirming our suspicions as they were very probably coming from a nightfighter. The signal was dispatched by the wireless operator Flight Sergeant Bigoray. The nightfighter signals grew to a level which completely saturated Jordan's receiver, and he warned the crew that an attack was imminent. It was almost immediately hit by cannon shells, and the pilot, Pilot Officer Paulton, tried to throw off the attack. The nightfighter attacked repeatedly, and the rear gunner fired about a thousand rounds back, until his turret was put out of action and he was hit in the shoulder. Jordan was hit in the arm, but he drafted a second message, and then was again hit in the jaw and one eye. As each attack developed, he tried to warn the pilot of the direction from which it was coming by continuing to observe its radar transmission. Ultimately the nightfighter broke off, leaving the Wellington barely flyable. The port engine throttle had been shot away, and the starboard throttle was jammed. The starboard aileron and both the air speed indicators were out of action. Four of the crew of six were badly wounded.

Despite his wounds, Bigoray managed to send Jordan's second message, repeating it again and again in the hope that someone might hear. It was in fact picked up in Britain and an acknowledgement made, but this was not heard in the Wellington because its receiver had been damaged. Bigoray went on repeating the message until a quarter to seven in the morning. As the aircraft approached the coast of England Paulton decided that it was too badly damaged to risk a crash landing, and that he would bring it down in the sea near the shore. Since he still did not know whether Jordan's message had got through, and since Bigoray was so badly injured that he might not be able to get out of the aircraft before it sank, Paulton decided that he would fly inland and have Bigoray pushed out with his parachute with the vital information in case the aircraft and its remaining crew were lost in the sea. As Bigoray reached the rear escape hatch he remembered that he had not locked down his Morse key to provide the continuous note signal for ground direction finding stations to track the aircraft, so he painfully crawled back to fulfil his final duty. Paulton then flew back over the sea, and finally ditched in the sea some two hundred yards off Deal. The rubber dinghy could not be inflated since it had been holed many times and the crew stayed on the sinking bomber. Fortunately a few minutes later they were rescued.

It had been an epic of cool observation, great gallantry and resourceful doggedness. For some days we did not know whether Jordan was going to lose his eye, but the surgeons managed to save it. He received an immediate Distinguished Service Order, the next thing to a Victoria Cross. Paulton was awarded the Distinguished Flying Cross, and Bigoray the Distinguished Flying Medal. The last gap in our understanding of the German night defences had been closed.

The whole investigation, starting with the radar on the Channel coast, had drawn on our resources to the full. It had been a much more difficult Intelligence problem than the beams, where we had had prisoners and equipment presented to us, as it were, and where we could solve most of our problems without moving outside England. With the German night defences, by contrast, we had to go out to get the information by every conceivable means; and the risks run by the patriots in the Low Countries, by our photographic and listening air crew, and at Bruneval, will have been obvious from my account.

CHAPTER THIRTY-THREE

Window

O UR STUDIES of German radar were described in a series of reports of which the two most substantial were 'D.T.' (this was one of the original German names for radar, as ours was 'R.D.F.') dated 10th January 1942 and 'German Nightfighter Control' of 29th December 1942. As with the X-Gerät Report they summarized the knowledge we had gained during the preceding year, and ran to some twenty thousand words each. In making such comprehensive surveys we sometimes recognized weaknesses that might otherwise have gone unnoticed: for example, it was only when we put all the evidence together that we could come to the surprisingly negative conclusion that the Germans had no satisfactory method of identifying their own fighters, as we had in I.F.F. This, combined with their ponderous method of telling plots from the Giant Würzburgs to the Seeburg Table, in turn suggested that they might have difficulty in following a bomber that was not flying a straight and level course. This in fact sometimes happened: as the fighter approached the bomber, it was inevitably picked up by the 'red' Giant following the bomber; if the bomber suddenly turned away the 'red' Giant might continue to follow the fighter and plot it in mistake. This promptly suggested that when flying through the Kammhuber Line our bombers should take 'evasive action' as a matter of routine, and various manoeuvres such as the 'corkscrew' (a sudden twisting dive of a thousand feet or so, and subsequent recovery) were adopted. So besides the intelligence itself, our Reports inevitably considered possible counters to the German defences.

In particular, the 'D.T.' Report had a section discussing weak points in the German system, and pointing to the use of spurious reflectors, among other possibilities but first pressing for direct attack on the main radar stations:

The Report then went on to develop the theory of Spoof:

'10.3.0 *Spoof*

    10.3.1 R.D.F. [Radar] is a system which reports to the enemy the position of your forces by means of the radio echoes to which they give rise. To neutralize its value to him, it must be made to confound him. This may be done in two ways: by persuading him that you are either (a) where you are not, or (b) not where you are. Owing to the nature and good cover of German R.D.F. it may be taken, at least for this argument, that any aircraft within striking distance of the enemy coast will be observed as a positive signal on the cathode ray tube of an early warning station. It is therefore almost impossible to avoid giving to the enemy the necessary evidence from which he can deduce your true position. The art of Spoof lies in so colouring his appreciation of this evidence that he comes to a false conclusion. The only method philosophically possible, when you are bound to give him a positive indication of your position, is to provide him with a requisite number of imitation positive indications. No imitation can be perfect without being the real thing, but it is surprising what can be done by dexterous suggestion.

10.3.2 To any one R.D.F. equipment, an aircraft appears as a radio echo on a specific frequency. The fundamental elements of R.D.F. Spoof are echoes from spurious objects, and phenomena which simulate echoes or obliterate them. Obliteration, either by deliberate jamming or by sowing a dense field of spurious reflectors, corresponds to a smoke screen, and although in itself it is not a Spoof, it can be so handled that spoofing may result. For example, if a smoke screen generally preceded an attack, then the enemy will expect an attack whenever he sees a smoke screen. Thus, it is not of great use to obliterate his R.D.F. wherever and whenever a heavy attack is intended: the obliteration will itself provide the necessary early warning for the enemy to prime his defences. If obliteration be physically possible, then it must also be used at times other than those preceding attacks, so that the enemy can either establish no correlation or, better, can be induced to make false correlation.

10.3.4 Apart from obliteration, there remains the possibility of producing swarms of pulses which react as echoes off a large formation of aircraft, either from a ground station, or more easily from a single aircraft. This in itself is true spoof, which can be handled in mass so as to produce a greater spoof.

10.3.5 The enemy knows that an aircraft will show an echo which moves in the same characteristic way whatever radio frequency he projects, and therefore if he has a sufficient number of frequencies in reserve, he can discard those which give suspect indications. It is therefore necessary to be prepared to cover, say, 80% of his available frequencies, although in the heat of operations if even only one half his stations indicated a large raid, it would take a very cool controller to disregard them in favour of the others who truthfully reported only a small raid. It is easy to fall into the trap of thinking that the enemy is omniscient and panoptic and hence of believing that no spoof could fool him. German R.D.F. personnel are only human, and even relatively modest spoof might succeed.

The final paragraph discussed the timing of countermeasures.

10.3.7 It is unwise to be squeamish about taking countermeasures against any enemy development because of the danger of reciprocation. The enemy is not altogether lacking in ingenuity, and has probably thought of most of the counters. The true reason against undertaking countermeasures is that ultimately the enemy will learn to overcome them, and that it is only during the period of his education that we shall reap the advantage. This period must be made to occur only when we want it, no matter what action the enemy may take against our own system in the meantime. When the correct time arrives there should be no hesitation. Spoofing may require a very considerable degree of effort to be successful, but its cost must be weighed only against the relevant D.T. effort and against the additional damage which we could do with its aid.

The background to the foregoing paragraph had been a remarkable 'squeamishness' on our part regarding technical countermeasures against German radar, as far as the Air side was concerned. This contrasted with the readiness with which tactical countermeasures such as concentration and evasive action had been adopted. It also contrasted with what the Royal Navy had been doing in jamming the German coast-watching radar ever since we had discovered it in October 1940. I was amazed to sit through meetings of the Radio Counter Measures Board right up to the end of 1942 discussing whether it was advisable for us to start an 'R.C.M. War' and so invite German retaliation by the jamming of our own radar, when our Navy was already jamming German radar, and when the Germans had already jammed our radar very successfully in the *Scharnhorst–Gneisnau* episode. Although I repeatedly pointed to these facts, I encountered a nebulous but strong reluctance against taking technical measures against Luftwaffe radar.

The reluctance went right back to the early days of Bawdsey, and at

the heart of it was Watson-Watt. No trials of spurious reflectors had
been made after I had suggested their use in 1937; and A. P. Rowe, who
succeeded Watson-Watt as Superintendent at Bawdsey, told me after
the war that he did not hear of the suggestion until 1941. Writing to me
in 1962 Rowe said 'When I took over from W. W. at Bawdsey, I found
it was "not done" to suggest that the whole affair would not work'.[1]
In defence of Watson-Watt it could be argued that anything that might
have thrown doubts on the value of radar, such as the early development
of a successful jamming system, might have caused the Air Staff to lack
confidence, and thus not to support radar enthusiastically. We might
then not have had such an effective system ready in time for the Battle of
Britain. But it could equally well be argued that, had we been up
against a more thorough opponent who had developed a proper system
of jamming, our 1940 radar would have been rendered powerless, and
we should have been culpably unprepared to deal with such a situation.

Such arguments apart, the fact was that in 1941 and for almost the
whole of 1942 we shrank from technical countermeasures, and the most
generous interpretation of Watson-Watt's attitude was that he had
developed a 'bridge on the River Kwai' attitude towards radar, and it
hurt him emotionally to think of radar being neutralized, even German
radar. Perhaps, remembering our old enmity, I was in turn committed
to the idea of wrecking radar with clouds of spurious reflectors; but of
course I would never have wanted to see our own radar wrecked. With
some justice events were to lead to an ultimate confrontation between
Watson-Watt and me on this very issue, and I will now trace their
contorted evolution.

Among the various technical countermeasures to German radar, one
possibility was to fit a warning device to every bomber, telling the
crew whenever a Würzburg or a Lichtenstein transmission was directed
at them, so that they could take evasive action. This came into use as
'Boozer' in the spring of 1943. A much more elaborate device was that
of sending back amplified and extended echoes, to suggest a large
formation of aircraft; this was used on a small scale, following my
visit to No. 11 Group after the Bruneval raid (p. 243) from August 1942
onwards. On the first occasion when it was tried (6th August) eight
Defiant aircraft off Portland produced such a response that thirty

---

[1] In the same letter Rowe wrote 'Are you being modest in not claiming to be the
originator of Window?' It was such an obvious invention as to be hardly worth
claiming, and in any event I had the earliest and strongest incentive for thinking of it
because of the argument with Watson-Watt.

German fighters were sent up around Cherbourg to meet the imaginary threat. And on 17th August our 'Moonshine' Defiants with supporting aircraft managed to divert nearly 150 German fighters from an American Flying Fortress attack on Rouen. But the scheme was elaborate, and it would only work if a very limited number of Freyas had to be dealt with, so it was dropped after a few months, to be later revived for D-Day. We were able to use 'Moonshine' earlier than the simpler counter-measures, perhaps because it was too elaborate for the Germans to use on a large scale against us, and because our Moonshine aircraft could stay so far outside the German defences that there was little chance of their being captured. But the main reason probably was that the whole episode had occurred at the lower level initiated by my visit to No. 11 Group, and that formal approval was never sought at the highest level.

With the two major possibilities, jamming and spurious reflectors, the situation was different for their use would be on such a scale that formal approval would have to be obtained. Jamming appealed to me less, because it was cruder and moreover would jeopardize any aircraft carrying a jammer because it could be homed on by fighters carrying suitable receivers. Spurious reflectors would be simpler, and contained an element of hoaxing. The phenomenon on which they depended was that of resonance. If a reflector is made of a simple wire or strip of metal of length equal to half the wavelength used by the radar station, it resonates to the incoming radio waves and re-radiates them to such effect that it is roughly equivalent to a whole sheet of metal whose dimensions are a square which has sides equal in length to half a wave-length. Thus a few hundred such strips or wires would reflect as much energy as a whole Lancaster bomber. Originally I suggested that wires should be suspended from balloons, because the long wavelengths that were usual in 1937 would require lengths of at least 10 feet; but we found that the predominant wavelengths in the German radar that we had to counter were about 50 centimetres, so each wire or strip need only be 25 centimetres long, and could be made light enough to fall through the air at a slow rate, and thus remain active for many minutes.

As our knowledge of German radar built up during 1941 I pressed the idea again, especially with Lindemann, and it finally resulted in trials being done late in 1941 and early 1942. They were undertaken under Robert Cockburn's direction at Swanage by Mrs. Joan Curran, now Lady Curran. Her results were all that we expected, and she tried various forms of reflector ranging from wires to leaflets, each roughly the size of a page in a notebook, on which, as a refinement, propaganda could be printed. The form that we finally favoured was a strip about 25 centimetres long and between 1 and 2 centimetres wide. The material was produced and made up into packets each weighing about a pound, and the idea was that the leading aircraft in a bomber stream would throw them out at the rate of one every minute or so, to produce the radar equivalent of a smoke-screen through which succeeding aircraft could fly. So much progress was made, after the years of delay, that by April 1942 enough material had been produced for it to be used by Bomber Command. It was given the code name 'Window' by A. P. Rowe, the Superintendent of T.R.E., and the scheme went up to the Chiefs of Staff on 27th April 1942 for their sanction.

The Official History *The Strategic Air Offensive Against Germany 1939–45* suggests (Volume 1, pp. 400–401) that Window was thought of at this stage as primarily a weapon against radar-controlled A-A guns, but this was certainly not so in my mind. If the Chiefs of Staff took this view, it must have been because of the Bomber Command obsession with anti-aircraft guns rather than nightfighters. For the first three years of the war the Command seemed to be far more concerned about guns, and it needed much convincing that the fighters were the greater threat, my own conclusion being that 70% of our losses were due to fighters at a time when the Command would not agree to a higher figure than 50%. So wary were they of the guns that the Command Intelligence Officer told me they never routed a raid over the island of Overflakkee because of the possible effect on the morale of the crews.

With the Chiefs of Staff's approval, the Window packets were, I believe, actually loaded on to bombers for a raid in May 1942, and were then off-loaded again because there was a last-minute prohibition on their use. What had happened in the meantime was that my old Oxford colleague Derek Jackson had heard of them for the first time: he had given up research for Active Service at the beginning of the war and had become one of the most skilled nightfighter radar operators in Fighter Command, and he was now the Command's Airborne Radar Officer. Naturally, he was concerned about the reduction in our own nightfighting efficiency if the Germans were to use Window against us. He was always able to put his arguments with remarkable force, and on this occasion he called on Lindemann and swung the latter round from supporting Window to opposing its use. Lindemann went to Sinclair, convinced that Window should be withheld, and succeeded in getting its introduction deferred until the effect on our own night-fighters had been evaluated. Lindemann now had Jackson bombarding

him on one side and me on the other. For the time being Jackson pre-
vailed; and he was, of course, strongly supported by Watson-Watt.

All through the summer of 1942 the battle went on. I was quite sure
that the arguments against using Window were ill-founded, because
there was no prospect of the Germans attacking us on anything like the
scale that we were now mounting against them. What was left of the
German bomber force was mainly tied up in Russia. The only good
argument for withholding Window was the one that had been given in
my main report on German radar, which was that we should pick our
time when its introduction would have greatest effect; we could not
expect this effect to last indefinitely, as the Germans gradually found
ways of getting round the difficulties that it presented for them, and it
could be debated whether or not the optimum time had yet come. But
I was sure that we were delaying too long.

I thought that my chance had finally come when in October 1942 I
received a report which came from a Danish agent who had heard two
Luftwaffe women personnel talking in a railway train. The report ran:

A. A considerable number of women have lately been taken on for
work in aircraft control stations. Formerly this work was done by men,
but since this summer women are being used and their number is
constantly increasing.

B. Operations of night fighters are controlled entirely from such
stations, the pilot being almost a passenger. The direction of flight,
altitude and even the moment to open fire are given (in latter case by a
man) from the ground stations which are equipped with special
detectors (or predictors) for this purpose. The principle on which
such detectors (or predictors) work has something to do with the
metal in an aircraft.

C. Informant has heard of an instance when a British machine in
the Rhineland deceived a German control station by throwing out
aluminium dust and then changing its altitude. As the dust cloud
was nearer the control station than the plane, the detectors (or predictors)
guided the German night fighters in this direction and they are said
even to have opened fire on the dust cloud.

It was an extraordinary Intelligence situation, and unique in my
experience, because the value of the report was independent of whether
it was genuine or 'a plant'. The whole of the opposition to our use of
Window had been based on the argument that although the idea was
obvious, it had not occurred to the Germans. And yet, now we had the

report, either it was genuine, in which case Luftwaffe personnel were
discussing the effects of Window or it was 'a plant', in which case the
German Security Service had shown that they were well aware of the
possibility of Window. In either case, it proved that someone in
Germany knew of the Window principle, and therefore the argument
based on the premiss that the Germans did not know of it was now
substantially demolished.

I at once wrote a report about it, and circulated it to those concerned
on 24th October 1942. I telephoned Bomber Command and told
B. G. Dickins, the Head of the Bomber Command Operational
Research Section, that if the Command would now press for using
Window I had ample evidence to demolish the opposition. Portal
called a meeting for 4th November, and I made a point of seeing
Lindemann to try to talk him round before the meeting and to give
him the chance of changing his ground. This he refused to do, dismissing
my report as merely being something two W.A.A.F.'s had said to one
another in a train. When I told him that I would have to oppose him at
the meeting he said 'If you do that, you will find Tizard and me united
against you!' I could not help replying 'If I've achieved that, by God, I've
achieved something!' and we parted in laughter. Actually, he must have
been quite misinformed about Tizard's attitude, for the latter had
already minuted that my report had completed the argument for the
immediate introduction of Window.

The day of the meeting came, and I was looking forward to the fight.
I knew that I could expect opposition from Lindemann and also from
Sholto Douglas, the C.-in-C. of Fighter Command and, above all,
from Watson-Watt. But with Bomber Command and the evidence, I
thought that we must win. And had Tizard been there it would have
been a very interesting battle. But for some reason he was absent, and
Bomber Command, represented by Sir Robert Saundby, my train-
playing host of two months before, collapsed on me. Saundby said that
his C.-in-C. did not wish to press for Window at the present time since
he considered that other countermeasures, the jamming of the Freyas
with a device known as 'Mandrel' and the interference with the German
radio telephonic controls, would be enough for the time being.

The battle was therefore left to me alone, and I heard Lindemann
witheringly talk of the irresponsibility of basing major policy on what
someone had happened to overhear two W.A.A.F.'s saying in a train. I
therefore lost hands down, and in a last defiance I asked Portal whether he
would now advise our Security Services to call off the national effort

that was being expended in propaganda to prevent careless talk in our own country. For this was the one example in the whole of my experience where careless talk had really been important, and all that Lord Cherwell could do was to dismiss it as talk between two women in a train. Portal saw that I was indignant, and so he added a recommendation that we should now work out in detail just what the effect of Window both on the Germans and on our own defences might be. We should work out the amount of Window that we should need to drop on a typical raid, and estimate the effect that it would have in reducing our casualties. We should also work out how much Window would be needed by the Germans to produce something like the same effect on our defences. To get all sides of the case presented, he asked that Fighter Command, Bomber Command, and I should make independent estimates, after which we should have a further meeting.

In the meantime, jamming of the Freyas was started in December 1942, using the Mandrel jammers. Some of these were carried in Defiant aircraft in the form of an airborne 'screen' intended to blind the Freyas to our approach. This was at first partly successful, in that, with the Freyas blinded it was much more difficult for the Giant Würzburgs to be directed on to individual bombers; but the Germans overcame the problem in various ways, one of which was to change the wavelengths of the Freyas to others which the Mandrels could not jam. The other countermeasures brought into use at the same time was the jamming of the German ground to nightfighter communications by transmitters in our bombers, each using a microphone to broadcast the noise of its engines so as to superimpose these on the German conversations. I was rather worried when I heard that the code name given to this device was 'Tinsel' because it might suggest to any German Intelligence officer the metal foil strips that we were still withholding.

As for computing of the amount of Window required, we were to assume a raid of a particular magnitude on a typical target, and work out how much Window material would be needed to render the German radar system ineffective. Derek Jackson at Fighter Command was the first to come up with an answer: his figure was 84 tons. He also calculated that one ton of Window used by the Germans would wreck our own radar system. Charles Frank and I made our own calculation, pointing out that Jackson had calculated the worst case, and that if one adopted assumptions that were reasonable in the light of our special knowledge of the German radar system, the figure was much more probably 12 tons instead of Jackson's 84. Dickins at Bomber Command cautiously waited until Jackson and I had both made our bids, and then produced a calculation showing that 48 tons would be needed.

Our estimate had been completed by 4th January 1943, but Portal did not reconvene the Window meeting until 2nd April 1943. I knew from Lindemann's secretary that he was still adamant, and that he was going into the meeting to repeat his opposition to the use of Window. However, he was not called on to speak until all three calculations had been presented. On behalf of Fighter Command, now headed by Trafford Leigh Mallory, Derek Jackson explained how he came to a figure of 84 tons, whilst one ton would suffice for the Germans if they wanted to knock our radar out. Portal then called on me, and I showed where I thought the Fighter Command estimates were too stringent. He then called on Harris, who deflected the question to Dickins, who gave a longish account of how Bomber Command had arrived at its figure. When he had finished, Portal simply asked 'What has Bomber Command done beyond adding the Fighter Command and A.D.I. (Science) figures together and dividing by two?'

At this point, Watson-Watt intervened, saying that he would like to give a warning based on his experience, and that he considered Jackson's figure of 84 tons much too low, although he agreed that one ton would be sufficient to knock our own system out. His argument was that no radio or radar device in his experience had been more than 20-30% efficient in its initial stages of use and therefore Jackson's figure of 84 tons should be multiplied by at least three if we were to be sure that the German radar would be knocked out, because of the inevitable mistakes that we would make in using Window properly.

As he spoke, I could hardly believe the extent to which he had left himself open, for up to that time I had thought of him as a coldly calculating opponent who would keep himself completely covered. As soon as he had finished I intervened and said to Portal 'Are we to accept this, Sir? S.A.T. [i.e. Watson-Watt] has said that no electronic device in his experience is more then 20-30% efficient in the early stages of its use. If so, why does he apply this to our use of Window against the Germans, but not to the Germans' use of Window against us?' Portal hesitated for a moment as he grappled with my point, and turned to Lindemann for a clarification. Lindemann must have seen at the same moment that Watson-Watt's position was indefensible, and he explained to Portal the import of what I had said. Portal looked sharply round, pointed his finger at Watson-Watt and said 'S.A.T., you're clean-bowled!' To Watson-Watt's credit, he replied 'Not bowled, sir, but caught at the wicket, perhaps!' and that was the end, or almost the end, of the argument that had started between us nearly six years before, for Portal would have no further debate. He said that he would go straight to the Prime Minister to ask permission to use Window as soon as possible, which was understood to be 1st May.

But there was further delay, probably brought about by continued opposition by Fighter Command and Watson-Watt, for the Chiefs of Staff decided that Window should not be used until Sicily had been invaded. I have never been able to follow the logic of this argument. Portal now pressed for a further meeting of the Chiefs of Staff, with the Prime Minister in the chair, and this took place on 23rd June 1943. It was only the second time I had seen Churchill since the beams meeting of three years before. The intervening occasion had also been concerned, I think, with a discussion of the night defences. I remember that occasion because most of us had assembled in the ante-room to the Cabinet Room, waiting for Winston to appear, when I noticed out of the corner of my eye an individual in a boiler suit come padding into the room; I imagined him to be a Ministry of Works maintenance engineer who had inadvertently strayed into the room full of Generals while looking for some domestic installation such as a hot water radiator. It seemed kindest to pretend not to notice the poor chap, in the hope that he would realize his error and quietly disappear; but to my surprise, he turned out to be the Prime Minister in his famous siren suit and, picking me out from the group, he came straight up to me and said 'Mr. Jones, very glad to have you here!'

At this final Window meeting, Watson-Watt and I were once again in opposition, for Portal let me state most of the Air Staff case for using Window. Watson-Watt again emphasized the damage to our own night defences but Churchill then turned to Leigh Mallory, head of Fighter Command, pointing out that he was the man who would have to 'carry the can' if our defences failed, and what did he think? Leigh Mallory very decently gave the opinion that even though his defences might be neutralized he was now convinced that the advantage lay with saving the casualties in Bomber Command, and that he would take the responsibility. That concluded the argument, and Churchill said 'Very well, let us open the Window!' And just as Churchill could say that my appearance at his meeting in June 1940 reminded him of the passage in the *Ingoldsby Legend* that starts 'But now one Mr. Jones comes forth and depones', so could I now counter on Watson-Watt's behalf from Jane Austen's *Mr. Woodhouse*: 'Open the windows! But, surely Mr. Churchill, nobody would think of opening the windows at Randalls. Nobody could be so imprudent!'

We were still to wait until successful landings were made in Sicily, but this was now a matter of only a few weeks. At the end of the meeting Churchill called me over to him, and asked me, 'Has Mr. Sandys seen you yet?' I well knew the import of his question, which must wait till a later chapter, and I had to tell him, 'No, Sir!' He frowned deeply and said, 'Very well. I shall call a Staff Conference next week! Hold yourself in readiness!'

No doubt there would be many who would have some claim to credit if Window was the success we expected it to be, but it was equally clear that if it failed there was one above all others who would get the blame. This was I, for not only had I started the idea but, with fateful justice, I had fought the case right through to the catching out of Watson-Watt and now had scored again with Churchill. Night after night I thought about ways in which Window could go wrong. Might we, for example, be dropping so many metal strips that these would get into the air intake of subsequent bombers and clog their engines? Would the bomber crews drop the packets at the prescribed rates, or would they use too much at one time and too little at another?

I decided that the best hope for good Window discipline was to have the bomber crews fully understand what they had to do, and the best way of informing them was to have some of my own officers lecture on the German night defences to every bomber station. I had at least two very good lecturers in Hugh Smith and Edward Wright (an old friend, and Professor of Mathematics at Aberdeen, who had recently joined me), but the problem was to get them into the Command. In this, I was rather less than honest. I knew the Commander-in-Chief strongly resisted any direct contact between the Air Staff and his bomber crews although the crews were expected to send in reports of any encounters they had with German nightfighters, or any other experiences that might throw light on the German defences, and most of these reports ultimately came to me. I therefore telephoned not the Commander-in-Chief but the amiable Saundby and told him that I thought that I could get much more out of the crews' reports if two of my chaps could go round the Command and talk to them. At the same time, I said, it would be an opportunity for the crews to hear from us about the latest state of the night defences. 'That would be difficult,' Saundby said, 'because the C.-in-C. doesn't like anyone from the Air Staff going out to his stations!' To this I replied, 'These are good sensible chaps that I'd be sending. One of them is a magnificent model railway maker. In the office here I have a model that he has made of a Great Western County tank engine, in No. 1 gauge. It is coal-fired and super-heated, and you can come along any time yourself and we'll get it going for you. You can then see whether he'd be alright in going round the Command.' Saundby immediately said 'Oh, if he's a chap like that—that's different. When do you want them to go?' And so Smith and Wright spent a hectic fortnight each of them lecturing in at least two stations, and sometimes three, every day.

There was one further attempt to stop the introduction of Window. I do not know whether it was engineered by Watson-Watt, but somehow Herbert Morrison heard about it and was characteristically alarmed by the possibility that we should sustain civilian casualties if the Germans in turn used Window against us. Churchill had therefore to call yet another meeting, on 15th July, when Morrison threatened to raise the question of Window in the War Cabinet. Churchill replied that the matter was too technical for the Cabinet, and that he was personally prepared to accept the responsibility for the decision to introduce Window. It was to be used from 23rd July onwards.

So we were at last to employ Window. Although the only evidence that the Germans must be aware of the principle was that given in the report from Denmark, it was enough to make me wonder whether the Germans were keeping Window in abeyance because they feared that if they were to use it and we were to retaliate, their defences would suffer much more than ours. Following my example with the imaginary German beam conference in 1940, my colleague and ally (later Air Chief Marshal Sir) John Whitworth Jones wrote the minutes of an imaginary German Air Staff conference on the topic 'Operation Fenster' (window, in German) in which he portrayed the Luftwaffe's dilemma. After the war we found this to be very near the truth: from Bruneval onwards they had expected us to use Window, and were mystified by our not employing it or any other technical countermeasure against the Würzburgs, even after we had started to jam the Freyas. They themselves made trials first on the Düppel Estate near Berlin and later over the Baltic in 1942. The effects were so dramatically disastrous that Goering ordered all the relevant reports to be destroyed, and he forbade any further mention of the matter in case the British might acquire the idea. So for more than a year both we and the Germans had hesitated to use Window against one another in the fear of losing on the exchange.

CHAPTER THIRTY-FOUR

Hamburg

IN VIEW of my commitment to Window I wanted to watch for the first signs of anything going wrong. I therefore determined to follow the first few raids in detail by listening to the reactions of the German nightfighters and their control stations while the raids were in progress. This was possible because of the excellent 'Y Service' station at Kingsdown near Farningham in Kent, run by Wing Commander R. K. Budge; it intercepted many German radio transmissions including the nightfighter radio telephony. We arranged that Rowley Scott-Farnie, Charles Frank and I should all go there for the first night, 23/24th July 1943, on which Window was to be used. We were all set when, some time in the evening, the news came through that the raid had been postponed because of bad weather.

We went back to London in the morning and spent the day in our offices, returning to Kingsdown in the evening. This time the raid was on. The target was Hamburg. About 9 o'clock in the evening we went on watch, sitting alongside the operators who were listening to the Germans, and moving from one operator to another if the other had beckoned to indicate that he was listening to something of interest. We did not hear much that night, because of the distance from Hamburg to Kingsdown, but the few clues that we had suggested that, at least from the point of view of nightfighter interceptions, the raid had gone well. We went to bed at about 4 a.m., and awoke to hear the Bomber Command returns. Out of 791 aircraft only 12 had not come back, a loss rate of 1·5% compared with 6·1% for the six previous attacks on Hamburg. It could thus be argued that Window on that single night had saved between 70 and 80 aircraft.

The target for the following night was Essen, which was better placed for us to listen to the nightfighter radio telephony. It was a Sunday, and Charles Frank and I met at Victoria to catch the train back to Kingsdown. Charles had evidently estimated the number of Bomber Command personnel alive that night who might have been otherwise lost on Hamburg and said 'Well, there must be something like 300 men alive tonight who but for us would be dead!' This struck me as a rather odd way of putting it, and I could not help replying 'Yes, but how many more dead in Hamburg?' At the time, we had no idea of the casualties in Hamburg, still less of those that were to occur in the next few days.

The Essen raid started normally enough. One of our bombers was shot down a minute after midnight, presumably an early casualty unprotected by Window, since the first aircraft in a smokescreen must always be vulnerable. But soon we heard the ground controls in various states of perplexity, not only in trying to follow our bombers but also their own fighters. One control lost his fighter for eighteen minutes, repeatedly asking him to make the identifying right-left wing waggle ('Rolf-Lise') which should have caused his radar echo to wax and wane. I heard the controller getting more and more exasperated, presumably because his Giant Würzburg had fixed on a packet of Window instead of the fighter. Even his most stentorian 'Rolf-Lise machen!' produced no response from the Window, while another controller told his aircraft 'break off, the bombers are multiplying themselves'. A fighter complained that his control could not even tell him whether the bombers were coming from the north or the south. All these fragments indicated that the Kammhuber system was substantially disrupted; and this was reflected in our casualties, which, although substantially greater than those on Hamburg, were still only 23 out of 705 aircraft or 3·3%

On 27/28th July Bomber Command returned to Hamburg, where 17 aircraft out of 722, or 2.4% were lost. There were signs that the German defences were beginning to reorganize, with ground stations giving a running commentary regarding the course and height of our bombers. It happened that a unit of single-engined fighters had been formed in the preceding weeks by Major Hajo Herrmann, with the idea that these might be able to pick out our bombers with the naked eye in the glare created by fires at the target and, fortunately for the German defences, Herrmann's unit was ready just at the right time. His technique became known as 'Wilde Sau' (Wild Sow), and following early successes, his strength was increased to that of a whole Fighter Division.

On this second raid on Hamburg there was spectacular illumination from the fires on the ground, because we had unwittingly created what came to be known as a 'fire storm'. It was one of those instances where a change of scale produces a disproportionate effect. Once the density of fires exceeds a critical amount over a sufficiently large area the heat

of the flames causes the air to rise and cold air to be drawn in from the
sides at such a rate that a gale ensues, which thus fans the flames even
further. The result is complete devastation and the burning or asphyxia-
tion of every living being who is unfortunate enough to be caught. We
had no idea of what we had done until a few weeks afterwards, when I
can remember Tom Burgess and Richard Boord, who were responsible
for bomb damage Intelligence, putting all the evidence together and
concluding that something quite abnormal must have happened.

A third attack was made on the night of 29th/30th July, when the
fires were still burning from two days before. That night 27 bombers
were lost out of 777: the loss rate was still low—3·5%—but there were
signs that the German improvisation was achieving some success,
especially with Herrmann's single-engined fighters over the target. To
add to its agony Hamburg attacked in daylight on 25th and 26th
July, by the Eighth Bomber Command of the United States Army Air
Force. The final attack was made by Bomber Command on the night
of 2nd/3rd August 1943 when we lost 30 bombers out of 740.

In its four major actions Bomber Command had lost 86 bombers out
of 3095, a loss rate of 2·8%, compared with the 6·1% that had happened
in the six last attacks on Hamburg before the introduction of Window.
It is difficult to say how many aircraft had been saved, but the Air Staff
estimated that 78 were saved on the first night against Hamburg and
49 on the first raid against Essen. The casualties in Hamburg will never
be accurately known, but were at least forty thousand and possibly
more than fifty thousand.

Horrible though these figures were, they might have been justified in
terms of their effect in shortening the war, had the same terrible policy
been pressed home against other cities. The diary of Field Marshal
Milch, the head of the Luftwaffe, showed that he warned, 'These attacks
on Hamburg strike deep at our nation's morale. If we do not succeed in
smashing these terror attacks by day and by night very soon, then we
must expect a very difficult situation to arise for Germany.' At a meeting
convened by Hilter and addressed by Goebbels on 2nd August, Milch
repeatedly interrupted with the outcry, 'We have lost the war! Finally
lost the war!' And to his own officers a little later he said, 'It's much
blacker than Speer paints it. If we get just five or six more attacks like
these on Hamburg, the German people will just lay down their tools,
however great their willpower' (Irving, *The Rise and Fall of the Luftwaffe*, pp. 229–230). Speer must have accepted Milch's view, for in
interrogation after the war he said 'The first heavy attack on Hamburg

in August 1943 made an extraordinary impression. We were of the opinion that a rapid repetition of this type of attack upon another six German towns would inevitably cripple the will to sustain armaments manufacture and war production.'

So Hamburg in a sense was the nearest the area bombing policy came to success. We had started the war morally opposed to the bombing of civilian populations, and now we were pursuing it on a horrifying scale. How had this come about? It was convenient at one time to blame Lord Cherwell, but the fact is that in 1940 he was as keen as any of us to make precision raids on pin-point targets of strategic importance. Portal, too, was of the same mind; through 1941, so long as the myth of our bombing accuracy persisted, he pursued the policy of attacking oil installations, on the argument that if the German Armed Forces could be deprived of fuel their fighting ability would be destroyed. Then had followed the realization that we could not even guarantee to hit towns, let alone individual factories, and yet Bomber Command was the only weapon that we had which could reduce the German war potential. Given the fact that the Germans had bombed our towns more or less indiscriminately, the decision to bomb German towns was an emotional certainty. Moreover, with the failure of the campaign against oil, the doctrine grew up that attacks on what Bert Harris called 'panacea targets' were useless.

The question now was whether area attacks would ultimately destroy the German will and ability to fight. Apart from a few who clung to the immorality of area bombing, most of us answered this question in terms of how many bombers would be required, and lost, and whether we could afford to provide them without seriously weakening other aspects of our effort, such as the provision of aircraft, crews, and equipment for Coastal Command to limit the U-boat threat. Briefly, Lindemann thought that we could and Tizard was much more doubtful; but it was on the grounds of probable effectiveness and not of morality that the battle was fought.

It is easy to show that we probably lost more in airmen's lives and in expensive bombers and equipment than we did damage to Germany, but such an analysis may be too facile. German production went up spectacularly at a time when we had expected it to fall, a remarkable tribute to the increased determination of the Germans in response to our terrible attacks. But we saw many signs of German technical distress as a result of our bombing—for example, in delays in getting new electronic equipment developed as the radio war exploded—and this also has to be thrown into the balance, along with the large manpower that was tied down in German air defence. Had we realized the improvement in our bombing technique we might have abandoned area bombing earlier, or at least have put more effort into precision attacks at night. The precedent was already with us, for example in the raid that I myself had requested—that on the Zeppelin works at Friedrichshafen on 22nd June 1943. Here we used the Master Bomber technique, and when it was combined with Oboe pathfinding, precision attacks became distinctly feasible. Even without Oboe at Friedrichshafen, the random bombing error was no more than 400 yards. But we had become so indoctrinated with the area policy that few of us realized that Portal's original oil bombing policy could now have been revived with a hope of success.

As it was, we could not keep up the scale of attack that had caused such havoc at Hamburg, despite the fears of Speer and Milch; and instead of the Germans collapsing, they recovered magnificently. Their war production increased, and their night defences were reorganized to the extent that within three months they were—thanks to our mistakes—again a limiting factor of what we could achieve by bombing.

In the meantime, though, we were elated by our success, and on 3rd August I wrote a report summarizing our experiences of the first few nights, and pointing out that the Germans were already extemporizing by using day fighters over the burning targets. We should also need to improve our jamming against the Freyas, and to develop means of homing on the nightfighters, even though their Lichtenstein sets had been upset by Window. Finally, we must improve our concentration on the return journey if we were to keep up a sufficient density of Window to provide a smokescreen. As for the amount of Window we had dropped, and the original estimates that had been made by Bomber Command, Fighter Command and my own Unit, the amounts used in these early raids had been nearer to my own figure than to those of either Command, and they had worked as I expected; but as the Germans grew more expert we should certainly need more Window unless we took great pains to maintain concentration on the return journey.

It would obviously be an encouragement to the bomber crews if we could let them know something of the German reactions. One that we had not expected was an accusation of chemical warfare. A cow somewhere near Hamburg ate some of the Window strips and died; this caused the Germans to examine the strips in detail, and they found that the black paint with which we had coated them, so as not to show up in searchlights, did contain traces of arsenic, as we ourselves then confirmed.

But this was entirely accidental, and too small an amount to be serious, and so the accusation was dropped.

Other German reactions, such as those that we were gaining from Enigma, could not be broadcast to our crews; but fortunately a heavily-laden and very gallant pigeon arrived at its home base, having been dropped by Bomber Command somewhere in North France with my usual questionnaire. It had been picked up by a Frenchman who had been present in one of the German nightfighter control stations, perhaps as a cleaner, and when he saw that there was a question about radar he had clearly delighted in describing the events one night in the station at le Croix Caluyau as he had witnessed them. I have never seen a pigeon carrying such a profuse message. It ended with the exclamation by the German Station Commander, who had spent the night trying to intercept seven hundred separate bombers without being able to locate one: 'He would rather be attacked by a hundred bombers than submit to that torrent of paper again!' Since no source could be compromised by this message, we were able to circulate it to Bomber Command, where the Commander's comment was widely appreciated.

As for the Luftwaffe, its report written soon after Hamburg and entitled 'A study of the Present Window Situation' said:

'Since July 25, the enemy, first at night—in isolated cases in daylight too—combined with the raids into Reich territory, the dropping of "Hamburg bodies". The technical success of this action must be designated as complete. . . . By this means the enemy has delivered the long awaited blow against our decimetre radar sets both on land and in the air.'

While the Germans wrestled with the problem of dealing with Window, Bomber Command should gain some respite after its heavy losses earlier in the year, and I could now give rather more attention to other aspects of the war that threatened to overwhelm us.

CHAPTER THIRTY-FIVE

Heavy Water

L EIF TRONSTAD's 'Thicker than heavy water' telegram (p. 206) and his subsequent journey from Norway to Britain in early autumn 1941 had amply confirmed our suspicions that the Germans would be interested in heavy water as a 'moderator' if they intended to make an atomic pile; and it had thus indicated that they were taking atomic developments seriously. It turned out that Karl Wirtz, a pre-war friend of Charles Frank at the Kaiser Wilhelm Institut, had inspected the Norwegian plant at Vermork, the main European source of heavy water, to ascertain how far its output could be increased. A contract had been awarded to the plant to produce 1,500 kilograms of heavy water starting in the autumn of 1941, and it seemed that the Germans were on the way to making an atomic pile in which plutonium might be produced.

Later in the war, when Charles and I surveyed the evidence, we began to wonder whether someone in Germany had consciously steered his countrymen away from the plutonium route towards the construction of an atomic bomb, because—despite the demand for heavy water—it seemed that the Germans were not thinking along this line. It turned out that at least one German scientist, Fritz Houtermans, had indeed foreseen the possibility of making plutonium in an atomic pile and so making a bomb from the plutonium produced, and that he had written a memorandum about it. He submitted the paper to the German Post Office because, or so he told us, he thought it would be buried there and that no one would take any notice of it. At the same time, if there were ever a postmortem he could not be accused of not having told the German government about the possibility. Whether this was true or not, I had sympathy for Houtermans, when I heard about him after the war. He had had the almost unique experience of having been imprisoned both by the Gestapo and the Ogpu, both the Germans and the Russians having at different times suspected him of working for their enemies. In solitary confinement he had kept himself sane by trying to develop The Theory of Numbers, working out the various theorems by scratching on the whitewashed walls of his cell. I was reminded of Lord Cherwell who, in very different circumstances, adopted much the same policy; for during his wartime duties in Whitehall, he kept an interest in mathematics by working out a new proof of what is known as the prime number theorem, which concerns the probability that any given number may be a prime. When I met Houtermans after the war and told him how I had felt for him he replied, 'Well, it is the only experimental science that you can do without a laboratory.'

In March 1942 one of S.O.E.'s exploits was to capture a Norwegian coastal steamer and sail it to Aberdeen. Among the Norwegian volunteers in the exploit was Einar Skinnarland, who came from Rjukan, the site of the heavy water plant. When he landed at Aberdeen he was briefed by Tronstad, and parachuted back into Norway within such a short time that his absence went unnoticed. He made contact with the chief engineer of the plant, Jomar Brun, who provided full details of the plant, and in November 1942 Brun himself came to London, where Welsh, Frank and I talked with him and Tronstad.

In the meantime, the information about heavy water production at Rjukan was so positive that I was asked whether we ought to try to knock it out. When I agreed, the recommendation went up to the War Cabinet, which requested Combined Operations to prepare an attack. Direct bombing had been opposed by Tronstad, on the grounds that many civilian casualties would be caused if the liquid-ammonia storage tanks were to be hit, so the plan was formed to fly in two gliders carrying a force of 34 men of the First Airborne Division, who would attack the plant and attempt to escape into Sweden. The attempt was made on 19th November 1942, but met with utter disaster. One of the towing aircraft flew into a mountainside and all six of its crew were killed. Three of the men in the glider were killed and several others badly injured. They were caught by the Germans, and although they were wearing British Army uniform they were considered to come under Hitler's edict that all commandos should be killed. They were all shot or, possibly in the case of the three badly wounded, poisoned by a German doctor. The other glider, which the towing aircraft had thought to have come down in the sea, did in fact come down on land and again those who were not killed in the crash were executed by the Germans.

All we knew at the time was that every man had been lost. Eric Welsh broke the news to me, and told me that the decision whether or not the attack should be repeated would rest with me. I told him that since one day either way was not likely to matter, I would sleep on the decision and give it to him the following day. I spent much of the night arguing both sides of the case with myself, but finally decided that the argument for the destruction of the heavy water plant was just as strong now as it had been when we made the original decision; I therefore told him that I thought another attempt should be made.

I am unable to say whether my decision was the vital one that led to the next raid because I suspect in retrospect that Welsh was beginning to use me, as he ultimately used others in more eminent positions, as a puppet. Had his own opinion differed much from my own, I do not know what would have transpired. But he went to S.O.E., who agreed to mount a different type of operation involving a much smaller force— just six Norwegians under Lieutenant Joachim Rönneberg. They parachuted into Norway on 16th February 1943, and made their way to Rjukan which they attacked with brilliant success on the night of 27/28th February. It was an epic of daring, endurance, and sabotage. The German Commander in Norway, General von Falkenhorst, described it as 'the best coup I have ever seen'. The plant was put out of action for some months, and a stock of about 350 kilograms of heavy water was lost. At the same time, there had been no damage to the basic hydroelectric works, and no casualties on either side, for all six Norwegian saboteurs escaped. Lieutenants Rönneberg and Poulsson were awarded D.S.O.'s, and the others either M.C.'s or M.M.'s.

Matters were clearly warming up in the nuclear field. On 3rd December 1942 the world's first atomic pile had gone critical in Chicago, under the direction of Enrico Fermi, and the American effort was rapidly gaining momentum. Eric Welsh now began to grow in stature, and his next proposal seemed distinctly imaginative. It was that we should attempt to get Niels Bohr, the father of theoretical nuclear physics, to come to Britain from Denmark. For this he conceived the idea of using our own distinguished physicist, James Chadwick. He called on Chadwick in his Liverpool laboratory, stressing that he was in the Secret Service, and that it was Chadwick's duty to his country to try to persuade Bohr to come. Chadwick hesitated, thinking of the risk to Bohr, but Welsh then 'came the heavy father' and called on Chadwick in the name of England, as he told me, and Chadwick agreed to write a letter which was microfilmed and smuggled to Bohr in an ordinary household key. Bohr duly received the message but decided that his duty lay in staying at his post in Copenhagen—he used to quote Hans Andersen's poem: 'In Denmark I was born, and there my home is!'

For us, there was clearly enough in the Intelligence picture, coupled with what we knew of developments on our own side and in America, to justify the closest watch on German nuclear developments, long-term though these might be. I myself was very heavily committed to the work in support of Bomber Command and with anticipating the threat of the German V weapons, and since both these activities were more urgent, I thought the nuclear problem could be covered by getting Charles Frank and Eric Welsh together for meetings with Wallace Akers and Michael Perrin, both former I.C.I. employees, but now prominently in the British 'Tube Alloys' project, as our own nuclear bomb effort was called. I thought that Welsh, as the one Secret Service man with a science degree, and who had shown such an interest in nuclear matters after he had recovered from his first gaffe about heavy water, would work all the better for this direct liaison with those who were responsible for the British bomb developments, on the general principle that the more a man is involved, the better he works. In addition, Frank and Perrin were both Oxford chemists who could talk easily to one another.

After a month or two of their triumvirate meetings Welsh came to me with a confidential message from Perrin, asking if I would withdraw Frank from the meetings, and allow him, Welsh, to represent me alone, because Frank tended to rub people up the wrong way. Remembering the early brush with Stewart Menzies, I accepted that there could be just enough truth in this, but it was not a matter which I could very well discuss with Frank without hurting his feelings. I therefore suggested to him that we both had enough to do with the immediate issues of the war, and that we could safely leave the liaison with Akers and Perrin to Welsh. It was to have grave effects.

CHAPTER THIRTY-SIX

Revelations From The Secret Service

ONE FASCINATION of the war was the way in which it drew men and women of very different backgrounds together. This was especially true of the Intelligence Services, and I for one enjoyed the expanding range of human contacts. Beside the galaxy of talent at Bletchley, where I met mathematicians and Arts men in far warmer circumstances than in a university, there were men whose adventurous lives alternated between a desk and the 'sharp end' in the field, such as naval officers who spent weeks with us in the office, and then disappeared for spells when they took a four-master sailing ship from the Helford River right into the Breton coast under the noses of the Kriegsmarine.

One reason for such sorties was to bring back British personnel such as air crew who had evaded capture after being shot down in Europe. The principal figure in the escaping organization was a Coldstream officer, James Langley. He had joined the Coldstream Guards in 1936, his father having selected the regiment for him after recalling a 1915 discussion among the Greenjackets regarding the regiment out of the whole army that they would most prefer to have on their flanks in attack or retreat. The Coldstream won by one vote from the Grenadiers; but a regular Guards commission in peace-time was too much for the family pocket, and so Jimmy went on the reserve and into the City. Like most scientists, I had come to regard 'men in the City' as parasites who lived on the brains and labours of others; but meeting men like Jimmy changed my views. He was recalled in May 1939 and one year later found himself in the rearguard at Dunkirk.

Just as most of the Army had been evacuated, Jimmy was badly wounded while his Company was still holding its position. When their time came his Guardsmen carried him to the beach but the Navy would not take him because as a stretcher case he would occupy as much space on board ship as four men standing up. His wounds were so serious that in prisoner-of-war camp his left arm had to be amputated by a British surgeon; and injuries to his leg limited him to crawling. By October 1940 he had recovered sufficiently to escape from hospital in Lille, and he set out across France for the Spanish frontier. The long journey home took him until March 1941, when he landed in Liverpool: then, by the propriety that occurs more often in war than in peace, he was at once put in charge of the Section of M.I.9 that was attached to M.I.6 to organize the escape of British service personnel, especially air crew, from the Continent back to Britain.

From time to time he came to my office to seek advice about where a boat had best chances to reach the French coast undetected by German radar. In 1942 he was joined by Airey Neave, who had made a remarkable escape from Colditz, and they have described their experiences in Langley's *Fight Another Day* and Neave's *Saturday At M.I.9*. Although Langley's own modest comment was 'too little and too late' the achievements of his organization were remarkable: several hundred soldiers and some three thousand airmen were brought back, with invaluable effect on R.A.F. morale. The cost, though, was heavy: at least five hundred of those in Occupied Territories who aided the escapers are known to have been killed by the Germans, and the true total may be much higher. As Jimmy has said, quite possibly for every British serviceman brought back, a Dutch, Belgian or French patriot died.

I used to hear some of the stories from him as they were occurring, and there is one told by him and by Neave in their books to which I can add a detail that has escaped their memories. It concerns Harold Cole, or Paul Cole as he later called himself. The first I heard of him was when Jimmy told me how puzzled he was by the activities of an Englishman who was at large in France and who was running great risks to help our airmen escape. On one occasion he had shepherded a party of, I think, six R.A.F. evaders from the Occupied Zone across the demarcation line into Vichy France, and the senior officer had asked him for his name so that his gallantry could be recognized at some suitable time. 'Just tell them I'm Inspector Thompson of Scotland Yard,' was the Pimpernel's reply. But when Jimmy went to Scotland Yard, they had no trace of Inspector Thompson or, indeed, of any Inspector missing in France. Ultimately the 'Inspector' helped an Englishwoman who had been a governess to a French family in the south of France to escape. She was so certain of her story that Jimmy took her to Scotland Yard, where she was shown photographs of all their Inspectors who could possibly fit the bill, but she could recognize none of them. Finally one of the Yard men said; 'Wait a minute!' and went out of the room: he returned with a new album of photographs and before very long the governess picked 'Inspector Thompson' out.

The only difficulty was that this was no portrait of a Scotland Yard Inspector but one from the Rogue's Gallery of a confidence trickster who was wanted by the police on a charge of manslaughter or murder. He had disappeared before the war, and had turned up in 1940, posing as a sergeant in the British Army, in France where he was presumably continuing his career of crime. The German triumph seemed to have brought out all his patriotic instincts and, as for handling escapes, who better than a confidence trickster who was prepared not to stop at murder?

Not long after the war I happened to meet Jimmy by accident and asked him if he had any news of 'Inspector Thompson'. Jimmy had just heard that he had been shot dead by the Paris police. It was only later that the full truth emerged. His real name was Harold Cole, and he was born in 1903. He had stayed in France after Dunkirk, and had become involved with the famous escape line which was run by a Belgian officer, Albert Marie Guerisse, also known as Lieutenant Commander Patrick Albert O'Leary. Guerisse himself was finally trapped by the Germans in March 1943 after helping many of our men to escape, but he survived the concentration camp at Dachau and after the war became head of the Belgian Medical Corps. His many decorations included the George Cross and the Distinguished Service Order.

In the early days of Guerisse's organization, Cole had at first seemed genuine enough, but he must at some time have been caught by the Germans and offered his freedom if he would pretend to go on working for us. Against the numbers that he undoubtedly helped to escape, his treachery led to at least fifty French and Belgian helpers being murdered by the Gestapo. A few days before the liberation of Paris, he left it in the uniform of a German officer and some months after V-E Day he was arrested in the American Zone of Germany posing as a Captain in the British Intelligence Corps. Brought back to Paris under escort and put in an American prison, he stole an American sergeant's uniform and escaped. By sheer bad luck, for him, the landlady of the lodging house in which he took refuge reported him as a possible deserter, and he died in a shoot-out with the French police who tried to arrest him. Our romantic illusions about the villain who turned out to be a hero in the end had been finally shattered.

Besides Jimmy Langley there was another Coldstream officer with us, a Lieutenant Colonel who belonged to a famous Coldstream family.

Desk work did not appeal to him, and he thought that there were better ways of helping to win the war. To prove his contention, he used to come into the office in uniform, and change into civilian clothes, leaving almost immediately to do his day's work as second drayman on a dray from Watney's Westminister Brewery. He had simply walked into the brewery and offered his services; having been taken on, he found himself part of a team with another drayman and two draywomen, ferrying barrels around to the London pubs and sharing their lunch of beer and bread and cheese. At the end of the day he would return to the office, put on his uniform and go to his elegant house in South Kensington, satisfied that he had done more to help in the war than anything he could have done in 54 Broadway.

Amongst others with whom it was a pleasure to work were the Archibald brothers, Henry and Roy, Canadian lawyers practising before the war in Paris. Henry had been amateur golf champion of France, and one day he introduced me to a very gallant Frenchman whom I knew only by his code name 'Fitzroy'. He and his wife both worked for us, being frequently brought over by Lysander and parachuted back into France. I believe that Fitzroy himself made at least eleven trips. He and I cooked up a scheme for causing trouble to the Germans and benefiting ourselves, by tapping German telephone wires in open country and then putting the conversations back on the wire again after amplification in a radio transmitter. The messages would now be broadcast and we could pick them up in England while the Germans would have great difficulty in finding where they came from because they would have been radiated from a wire many miles long.

We never actually tried the scheme, but it led to Fitzroy telling us of one of his own escapades when, as a head agent, he had been parachuted back into France with six radio transmitter-receiver sets for distribution to his sub-agents. He got them safely to his first port of call, and was then faced with the problem of distributing the other five sets. Instead of trying to do this furtively he went into the local town and in the course of a few days made friends with the German garrison commander. As their acquaintance grew he let the German know that he was in the Black Market, and that there was a deal which he could bring off to their mutual benefit if the commander would co-operate. All that was needed was a German Army lorry and a driver, because the deal involved selling a load of carrots on the Black Market, transporting them from the original farm to another some twenty or so miles away. Fitzroy himself had no transport, but if the German could arrange the lorry,

Fitzroy would split the prospective profit with him. The deal was arranged and a German Army lorry driven by a German soldier appeared at the farm and the carrots were duly loaded. However, in addition to the carrots a large package went on board, and was about to be covered by the carrots when the soldier asked what it was, because there was no mention of a package in his orders. Fitzroy put his finger to his lips and said 'Zigaretten!' and tore open a corner of the package and pulled out a box of 100 cigarettes. He told the soldier that this was what the deal was really about, but that his commanding officer did not know, and that if the carrots and the package were safely delivered the soldier would receive a further 100 cigarettes. The driver was now happy, because he knew, or rather thought he did, how his commanding officer was being hoodwinked, and there were no further problems.

But this was not enough for Fitzroy. When he met the garrison commander to share the proceeds with him (the money of course being provided by us) they had a celebratory drink and then Fitzroy told the German that he had been thinking about the deal and that it had been Black Market. The German said that he realized that. 'But,' said Fitzroy, 'if you can pretend to find out that it was Black Market it is in your power as garrison commander to confiscate the carrots. If you will, we can sell them again—I know where I can find another customer!' And so the carrots were duly confiscated and sold again, and this time a rather smaller package went under them, one radio set having been left with the first 'buyer'. I do not know how many sets were distributed before the carrots went rotten.

Later in the war Fitzroy was caught by the Germans, tortured, and sent to a concentration camp. He survived and was, I believe, awarded a D.S.O. Tragically, as with others I knew, he found life in peace-time too dull, and sought excitement in high speed driving: he and his wife were killed when their car failed to take a bend.

Many of the aids associated with the dropping and picking up operations with agents were devised by 'Jane' Shaw, who delighted in making neat gadgets for such purposes; these included the magnetic trouser button which could be used as a compass, and which became a standard issue to air crew to help them in escaping. Another service was lessons in make-up, so that agents could disguise themselves. The officer in charge was Leon Thompson, who ran the photographic section and provided me personally with much help. We used to travel home together on the underground to Richmond, and on one of our journeys he told me that he had been surprised by a trainee who had corrected him on the appropriate make-up pencil to use; he had been an actor, and his name was Lindemann.

This Lindemann joined the French section, where he began to bring me agents' reports on German installations which were described as 'Radio Gonio'. With a chuckle, he told me that he had decided to bring these reports to me personally because they seemed to embarrass his secretaries who thought they dealt with some sort of venereal disease that would act at a distance. In further conversation, I remarked to him that he had the same name as my professor. 'Of course,' he said, 'I'm his brother. I'm the one he doesn't own!' It turned out that the Prof had two brothers: one was Charles, who had been partly a physicist and who had won the D.S.O. as a Colonel in the First War, and who was now a brigadier and an Attaché in our Embassy in Washington; the other was James, known as 'Seppi' who described himself to me as 'the black sheep of the family'. He had taken his share of his father's wealth and had proceeded to enjoy himself. At one stage on the Riviera, he owned two Rolls-Royces, one white and driven by a negro, and the other black, driven by an albino.

One evening in the Cabinet Offices, I told the Prof that I had met his brother. This was a shock to him because he never mentioned Seppi to anybody; but when I told him that Seppi was working near me he said that I had better get Seppi to telephone him so that they could meet for lunch. After the lunch Seppi appeared in my office, much amused: the Prof did not want his disreputable brother to know exactly where he worked, so he had offered to drop Seppi at Seppi's office. Seppi, on the other hand, thought that the location of M.I.6 headquarters was too secret even for the Prof to know, so he had insisted that the Prof should be dropped first. They drove round and round St. James's Park, neither prepared to give way to the other. In the end, Seppi persuaded the Prof to drop him at some quite irrelevant place, from which he made his way back on foot.

The Prof's secretiveness also amused his brother Charles, who told me that one of his tasks as Attaché in Washington was to arrange the transport of all nuclear physicists and others from Britain who were visiting or working at such stations as Los Alamos in connection with the atomic bomb project. Among these visitors was the Prof, who used to spin Charles the most fantastic yarns regarding the purpose of his visits, not knowing that his brother was already in the atomic picture and had in fact made all the travel arrangements for him.

I myself knew how the Prof felt about not disclosing where his headquarters were, since one of my pre-war colleagues in Oxford, Richard Hull, who was now a Fellow of Lincoln, posed me the same problem. We had had lunch together, and he was curious to know where I worked and so he proposed to walk back with me to my office. He had already asked me where it was, and I had told him that it was built underground on an island in the lake of St. James's Park. I explained that the entrance was also hidden from public view, and when he insisted on accompanying me there was nothing for it but to bluff it out. Fortunately I remembered that there was a gardener's hut hidden in the bushes by the side of the lake with an entrance marked 'Private' and when we came to it I shook hands with him and disappeared into the bushes while he went on his way. I had forgotten the matter when a week or so later the Chief of Air Staff called me over to his office to discuss something or other, and as I entered his anteroom his personal assistant, Cox, slowly smiled and said 'I was back in Lincoln last weekend' (he was also a Fellow) 'and I heard from Richard Hull where your office really is'. I was never quite sure whether Cox knew the truth or not.

We enjoyed another diversion when an Air Commodore was drafted into Broadway, along with a Colonel from the Royal Marines and a Lieutenant General, to improve the Service representation in the direction of M.I.6. As with other buildings in Westminster, our window-sills were infested with pigeons—and we persuaded the Air Commodore that our pigeons were our main means of communication with the French Resistance. For days, at our instigation, he solicitously provided them with saucers of water!

Thanks to Hugh Smith, the strain of the war was relieved by some hilarious weekends in Gloucestershire, where I became involved in a masquerade as the 'Bishop of Wigan'. This was nearly exploded when the victim of the masquerade discovered that the 'Bishop' was not listed in *Crockford's Directory*, but the situation was saved by telling him that it was a new diocese which had been created as a result of the increased population brought to Wigan by the 'shadow' aircraft factories, and that the Church had been forbidden to announce the increased ecclesiastical status because this could provide the Germans with a clue to the new centre of the aircraft industry. The 'Bishop' was therefore on the Secret List: he emerged, though, after the war, in Volume 39 of the English Place-Name Society, which deals with the North and West Cotswolds, under the entry for Little Washbourne, and alongside the description of The Hobnails as 'An ancient Inn', there appears among the field-names, '"Bishop's Piece" (named from an incident when Dr. R. V. Jones, Professor of Natural Philosophy in Aberdeen, appeared there as a Bishop of Wigan cf. *Early English and Norse Studies* presented to Hugh Smith, ed. A. Brown and P. Foote (London, 1963), 224)'. The name is attached to the piece of land not far from The Hobnails, and so I have taken my place with my old colleague Yves Rocard, who has had a submarine volcano near Tahiti named in his honour. Others may care to debate whether an acre in Gloucestershire is worth a volcano in the South Seas.

The title of this chapter was inspired by another weekend episode, this time in Broadway itself. Charles Frank was going away for the weekend, and in preparation had brought his suitcase to the office. It was a walking exhibition of Continental hotel labels, which Charles had accumulated in the course of his pre-war journeys. During the course of the afternoon I happened to spot that someone else in the office was reading a book with a lurid dustcover entitled *Revelations from the Secret Service*. I could not resist pasting the dustcover centrally among the hotel labels on one side of the suitcase while Charles was out of the room, and so it transpired that he left 54 Broadway, the headquarters of the Secret Service, carrying a Revelation suitcase with 'Revelations from the Secret Service' ostentatiously displayed on its side. But even that indiscretion did nothing to disillusion a girl in a nearby office across Broadway whose room looked out on the entrance of No. 54. From her observations she had decided that we were some sort of Government office where retired Serving Officers came to collect their pensions.

CHAPTER THIRTY-SEVEN

Full Stretch

B Y THE end of 1942 the resources of my small Section were stretched to the limit. Besides our main duties there were many facets of the war which called for our intervention. There was, for example, the imminent introduction of a new aid to our bombers which came into use under the code name H2S. This was a centimetric radar device which scanned the terrain for several miles around the aircraft and which presented the navigator with what was virtually a map of the ground, showing towns (which gave rise to large radar echoes), rivers, lakes, and coastlines. In fact it did exactly what I had at one time thought that the German X-Gerät might do. At that time, in 1940, our technical experts considered the idea impracticable, because they thought ordinary radio waves would be too coarse to give a sharp picture, while centimetric waves would be reflected strongly from many kinds of objects, even the furrows in a ploughed field. However, when—thanks to a brilliant invention by J. T. Randall and H. A. H. Boot—we were able to generate centimetric waves on a large scale and try the idea out, we found that it was easy to differentiate between towns and fields, and so the device appeared highly practicable. This would mean that any bomber equipped with the device would in effect be able to 'see' the ground below, in the dark and through cloud. The idea was taken up enthusiastically and developed by our Telecommunications Research Establishment, and notably by Philip Dee and Bernard Lovell, under the code name 'T.F.'.

Where I came back into this story was when I heard the initials 'T.F.' which I promptly guessed stood for 'Town Finding'. I thereupon warned Lindemann that once again our radar people had disclosed their intentions by the choice of a too-obvious code name, and he told me that he would see what could be done to change it. The following week, after visiting a 'Sunday Soviet', as A. P. Rowe's get-togethers were called, Lindemann told me that he had succeeded in getting the name changed, and that in future it was to be known as 'H2S'. He asked me if

I could see the connection between the new name and the device. When I failed, he said 'Ah, you see, it's very clever—H-S-H: Home Sweet Home!'

A few weeks later I was myself at T.R.E., and I told them that I was amused by the reasoning behind the new code name. They immediately volunteered that I did not know the true story. What had happened, they said, was that the Prof had told them that they must change the name, and had given them the lunch interval to think of a new one. When they were discussing it among themselves, someone suggested H2S because of the Prof's own part in the story. When they had originally shown him the possibility on an early visit to Swanage, he had not seemed very impressed, so they had not pushed ahead with the development. On a subsequent visit, after he had toured the Establishment, he told them that the last time he had been there they had shown him a very interesting device for mapping terrain from the air and wanted to know what they had done about it. They hardly liked to tell him that they had not done as much as they might because he had not given them any encouragement, and he became indignant at the various tactful excuses they offered. Finally he said of their tardiness 'It stinks! It stinks!' so when they were challenged for a new code name, H2S (the chemical formula for the gas associated with rotten eggs) happily suggested itself. But they had not foreseen his obvious question: 'Now why did you call it that?' There was an awkward silence until someone who deserved to go far came up with 'Please Sir, Home Sweet Home!'

The one factor in the story that I found hard to believe was that Lindemann could ever have failed to encourage the development of a device which would aid our bombers. Certainly, once he realized its potential, he was very keen to have it, being almost emotional about the theme of a scientific instrument in every bomber. It seemed to me that this was dangerously obsessive, because the same device had a quite different and possibly much more important use as a U-boat detector. Our original A.S.V. (Anti Surface Vessel) radar had worked on a wavelength of 1.5 metres and it was now becoming useless because the Germans had equipped their U-boats with receivers to detect it, and thus the approach of our aircraft long before they themselves could detect the U-boat. By the time the aircraft had reached the correct position the U-boat had dived and escaped. H2S offered much hope because it showed up the U-boats very clearly and worked on a wavelength of 10 centimetres for which, as yet, the U-boats had no detectors.

The question therefore arose whether Bomber Command or Coastal

Command should have priority in its equipment and use. When I heard that the priority was to be given to Bomber Command, I was so concerned that I wrote a note to Charles Medhurst, now Vice Chief of Air Staff, entitled 'Repercussions of H2S on Air-Sea Warfare' and dated 23rd January 1943. This concluded:

We may expect many months' life for 10 cms. A.S.V., providing that we do not give the Germans a clue to the wavelength. The capture of H2S will not only do this, but also show them a satisfactory receiver design. Moreover, having captured H2S, they may have some difficulty in producing transmitters to jam it (should they not resort to spoof reflecting devices), but this difficulty would not exist with A.S.V., for the only necessary counter is a receiver.

The fact is obvious that should we try H2S first, and should it prove relatively unsuccessful, 10 cms. A.S.V. will have a spoilt chance, and we shall have lost everything. Should we, however, reverse the order, we could test whether or not 10 cms. A.S.V. is an important factor in countering the mortal threat of the U-Boats, and still be in a position to use H2S later, should we choose. The latter finessing course therefore appears correct, unless there is some overwhelming operational factor in favour of a precipitate use of H2S, or of any other application of 10 cms. which is likely to fall into the hands of the enemy.

My intervention convinced Medhurst, who raised the matter on an inter-Service basis in a last effort to get the priorities changed; but he came back to tell me that the Services could do nothing to overcome Cherwell's enthusiasm for H2S going into Bomber Command first. Coastal Command now had to face the high probability that the Germans would recover the equipment from crashed bombers and realize that we were likely also to use it against U-boats, for which the only countermeasures needed would be to equip the boats with suitable receivers. The Naval Intelligence Division therefore requested that, as with Gee, I should attempt to mislead the Germans about how we were now finding the U-boats. There was an additional urgency to this request because we had another way of finding U-boats which was even more important that H2S, at least as regards their general location. This was the German Naval Enigma signals, which by a further feat Bletchley had managed to decipher. The Naval Enigma machine was more complex than that used by the Luftwaffe in that it included a fourth wheel, thus multiplying the number of combinations which had to be unravelled.

The basis of the deception was that we should give the impression that we were finding the U-boats not by radar, or by their Engima signals, but by infra-red. I therefore provided a series of clues, aided once again by 'George', and this appears to have been successful; for not only were the Germans very slow in realizing that we were using centimetric radar against them at sea, long after they had found it in our crashed bombers, but they also developed a most ingenious paint for their U-boats to camouflage them against infra-red as well as against visible light. If a normal grey-painted ship, which is thus camouflaged well against a typically grey sea, is viewed by infra-red it still looks grey but the sea looks blackish. They therefore had to make a paint which looked grey to the human eye, but blackish to an infra-red viewer. They achieved this by putting a black undercoat on the U-boats, and covering it by a varnish which contained a suspension of powdered glass in sufficient quantities to give a grey effect when viewed by the human eye. The glass and varnish were, however, so chosen that their refractive indices were identical in the infra-red, which went through the mixture and was absorbed in the black undercoat. It was a clever idea, and I much admired the German physicist who thought of it.

The new centimetric A.S.V. set was first used in the Bay of Biscay on 1st March 1943, and it was not until the following September that the U-boats began to dive on its approach, suggesting that they were at last equipped with centimetric receivers to give them advance warning. The six months uncountered use of centimetre A.S.V. was much longer than we had dared to hope, especially since the Germans must have found virtually the same equipment in our bombers. Writing of this episode in their book *Methods of Operational Research* published in 1951, Professor P. M. Morse of the Massachusetts Institute of Technology and Professor G. E. Kimball of Columbia University said, 'How this six months' delay occurred is one of the mysteries of the war (it can perhaps be explained only by a criminal lack of liaison between the German naval and air technical staffs).' An alternative explanation may lie in the infra-red hoax.

And another hoax may also have played a part. A British prisoner of war under interrogation ingeniously told the Germans that our aircraft were homing on to some kind of radiation that was coming out of the 'Metox' receivers which were used by the U-Boats to detect the approach of our original A.S.V.-equipped aircraft. It was a complete fabrication, but when the Germans investigated they found that there was indeed radiation coming out of the Metox receiver, and they went to some trouble to suppress it—without, of course, any success in reducing their U-Boat losses.

When the Germans finally realized that we were using radar after all, they fortunately blamed it for all their U-boat sinkings, Dönitz even going so far as to say that this one invention had changed the balance in the battle of the Atlantic, and our Enigma feat remained secure.

With all these side-efforts, in addition to our main activity, I was increasingly concerned that we should miss something vital. Altogether there were only five of us, and between us we closely read a daily input of about 150 sheets of foolscap paper, besides attending meetings, visiting R.A.F. stations, and so forth. I therefore submitted a paper to Frank Inglis, who had now succeeded Charles Medhurst as Assistant Chief of Air Staff (Intelligence), on 20th November 1942 pointing out that without a substantial increase in staff

> there is an extreme danger that something vital will be missed. In view of Hitler's recent statement that German inventive genius had not been idle in developing new weapons of offence against this country, we cannot afford to relax our watch as we have been forced to do . . . unless some relief is forthcoming, the present Assistant Directorate cannot accept responsibility for the surprises which are likely to be sprung upon us by the enemy without the timely warning which has been achieved in the past.

Four weeks after this warning, there arrived in my office a telegram from Stockholm dated 19th December 1942 saying that a new source 'overheard conversation between Professor Fauner of Berlin Technische Hochschule and engineers Stefan Szenassi on a new German weapon. Weapon is a rocket containing five tons explosive with a maximum range of 200 kilometres with a danger area of 10 kilometres square.' In answer to my enquiry, the reply came that the source was a Danish chemical engineer. His report was followed by another from Sweden dated 12th January 1943 saying that, 'The Germans have constructed a new factory at Peenemünde, near Börfhöft where new weapons are manufactured. . . . The new weapon is in the form of a rocket which has been seen fired from the testing ground'. Although the authenticity of this second report could be in doubt (for it went on 'It was previously tested somewhere in South America'), these two rocket reports, at that time no more than 'a little cloud out of the sea, like a man's hand' in fact foretold a deluge; but in the meantime there were further points in my memorandum to Inglis.

Before Medhurst had left Intelligence, he had advised me to expand my staff in my own interest, since status tended to depend on the number of men directly responsible to the holder of a particular post. I told him that I would prefer to define responsibility as the scope for 'dropping bricks', and that my basic difficulty was that the expansion of Scientific Intelligence had started much too late. Since I was not allowed to recruit anyone until after more than a year of war, all the ablest people had been fitted into posts, and it was now difficult to prise them out.

I now had to look for men whose qualities and background were not those of a normal scientist. Hugh Smith was such an example. At the same time, as my memorandum to Inglis had stressed, there was much to be said for using as few individuals as possible, and stretching them to their utmost.

It has been part of our policy to keep the staff to its smallest possible limits consistent with safety, because the larger the field any one man can cover, the more chance there is of those fortunate correlations which only occur when one brain and one memory can connect two or more remotely gathered facts. Moreover, a large staff generally requires so much administration that its head has little chance of real work himself, and he cannot therefore speak with that certainty which arises only from intimate contact with the facts.

It was an encouraging experience to find just how much a few individuals can do, and how even a single individual can sometimes be more effective than a large organization. During the Battle of the Beams in 1940 and 1941, I myself read every Enigma message. A full record of such messages came to me daily from Bletchley, and in the early days they were typed on different typewriters, or sometimes the same typewriter with different ribbons or different carbons. I could usually remember the date on which a message had been received, the colour of the carbon copy, and its degree of blurring, along with the part of the page on which the message had been typed. It was therefore usually a matter of seconds for me to flip through the file and pick out a particular message, even two months later. After I had done this a number of times over the telephone in discussions with Norman he had said enthusiastically, 'You must have a marvellous filing system! We have an enormous one here, and yet we can never find a message as fast as you can. Can we come up and see your system some time?' I told him that I should be delighted to show him and his colleagues, but it was hardly worth their making a special trip.

Norman's honest surprise when he found that the index was in my head was one thing; but the suspicions of others were less easy to deal with. The information must have been churning continuously around in my head, only returning to the conscious when some hitherto unseen correlation presented itself. The effect of producing these correlations out of the head, if not out of the hat, was to lead some of our associates to think that I had a great source of information that I never revealed to anybody outside.

There were at least three attempts made to infiltrate liaison officers into my Section to locate this great undisclosed source. In one, an officer from Bletchley was offered to me on a part-time basis to help but, as he told Norman and me afterwards, his main task was to uncover my mysterious source. After a month or so, he was called back and asked what he had found. He assured his seniors at Bletchley that there was no trace of anything other than what they already knew. When someone asked, 'Then how does Jones do it?' Bob Pryor, the officer concerned replied, 'Well, I suppose, Sir, he thinks!' Another officer who had been infiltrated became so enthusiastic as to have defended me to an Air Commodore who told him that I was a funny chap, and that he, the Air Commodore, had not been able to get on with me. 'Well Sir,' was the reply—and it came from a Flight Lieutenant—'You must remember, he doesn't suffer fools gladly!'

Be that as it may, we were all under strain. I had rowed at Oxford just under 175 lbs, which had increased to about 195 lbs by 1939. By the end of the war I was down to 170 lbs. I had no easements such as a staff car, and my civilian rations were substantially lower than those of the serving officers who worked under me. At the same time the strain was much greater on our wives, particularly one such as Vera, who was now bringing up a family in London, and who could not have the absorbing interest in the war that kept me going. Perhaps because she looked after herself last, she became so run-down that she suffered from a most painful series of abscesses.

Only once did my own interest divert from the immediate war. Irrelevant though it may seem, the issue deserves to be recounted at length, because it contains an element of eternal truth concerning the mentality of those who select themselves as planners. It was in January 1943, the period of this chapter, and of the optimism engendered by our recent successes in North Africa, when I read of the post-war plans for education in physics that had been put forward by a committee of the Institute of Physics. The plans, such as they were, prompted me to write to the Secretary of the Institute on 3rd February as follows:

Every time that the fortunes of war turn in our favour, up springs a crop of post-war planners. The recent sustained absence of bad news has swelled the latest crop to large proportions, and it is a matter of surprise that so many scientists—of whom we are so short—have so much time to spare at this period of the war. While at first sight it may appear wise to plan ahead, it is open to question whether we are beginning in the best way. . . . By 1935 at the latest, it was obvious to any man of foresight that there was a high chance that this country would shortly be involved in war. Those who realized the danger, and who had sufficient patriotism, abandoned their comfortable academic lives and accepted the more rigid discipline of Government service—not that they always approved of its machinery—in an effort to parry the military developments of science in Germany. Those with less foresight stood outside and often criticized destructively the efforts of Dr. Blimp. Those with less patriotism talked of the freedom of science and clung to their academic existences. The majority was merely apathetic and comforted itself with the delusion that Nazi Germany without Semitic inspiration was scientifically sterile. When war did break out, and foresight and public spirit were hardly required, most of the academic scientists of course flooded in, but they were mainly too late to have helped materially at the great crisis of 1940. Those scientists with foresight and public spirit therefore joined some form of Government service in the years before the war, and are likely to have been given responsible positions which require the devotion of all their energies to winning the war. Thus, those with the qualities necessary for planning are identically those most likely to be at present, and to have been for years past, completely absorbed in the war. Our best potential planners are therefore not available... the decision regarding the timely release of planners is surely beyond any body consisting purely of scientists. The best initial planning step that scientists could take would be to present this view to those concerned with the highest direction of the war, and in the meantime to ensure that no effort which could successfully shorten the war is wasted in premature planning.

My doubts were justified: the report of the Institute of Physics

Committee was not all that bad, but it was so phrased as to be misread, at least in Scotland, to the extent that the Committee on Secondary Education in Scotland (which met shortly afterwards), thought that the physicists had recommended that physics and chemistry should have an even lower priority in education than they previously had, and should be replaced by general science. It took me five years after the war to rectify the damage that had thereby been done. And many subsequent events have reinforced my doubts about the presumption of those who would be planners, not only in education but in the long list of grandiose government and civil projects that have led to disaster, ranging from the Ground Nuts Scheme to the Robbins Committee.

In contrast with the remoteness of post-war planning, my needs for more staff were immediate; and finally it was agreed that I should have an increase. John Jennings joined me towards the end of 1942: he was a physicist whom I had met in pre-war days when he had been taken on by the Philips Organization to liaise between the Admiralty and the Philips works at Eindhoven. Besides his physics, he had a knowledge of German, French, Spanish, Dutch, and Russian, and thus proved a valuable reinforcement. At about the same time Squadron Leader J. A. Birtwistle joined us. He had a science degree and had been an Intelligence Officer with Fighter Command, particularly at Kenley during the Battle of Britain. One of the first questions I asked him was about our overclaiming during the Battle, and why Intelligence Officers had let so many doubtful claims stand. As he put it to me, he was in the position of having to deal with pilots in an understandably excited state on coming out of an air battle, and it was quite impossible for an officer who had not been risking his neck as they had to say that he was not going to allow their claims.

One further reinforcement, who arrived on 1st April 1943, was E. M. Wright, who was then Professor of Mathematics at Aberdeen. I had first met him in 1932, when he was building an outstanding reputation as a pure mathematician in Oxford. He had been appointed to the Chair at Aberdeen in 1935, when he was still 29, despite having come up to Oxford late, and we used to meet on his periodical returns to Oxford. When I found, towards the end of 1942, that he was not directly involved in the war, I wrote asking whether he would care to join me. He readily agreed, and he had been with me little more than a month when Jack Easton, one of the Directors of Air Intelligence telephoned me on the morning of Monday 10th May to say that a Junkers 88 nightfighter had landed at Dyce, and suggested that I should go up there to take charge of it. Previously all that Dyce had meant to me was a monosyllabic aerodrome, like Drem and Wick, in Scotland. 'Isn't Dyce somewhere near you?' I asked Wright, and when he said that it was his local aerodrome, I offered him a trip to accompany me to Aberdeen. We travelled on the night sleeper, and went out on the Tuesday morning to look at the aircraft.

It was intact, and fitted with the Lichtenstein radar equipment (Plate 18) that only a few months before we had been at such pains to elucidate. Its crew of three told us that they had had little sympathy with the Nazis, and that when they had received orders to shoot down our civil courier flying between Scotland and Stockholm, it was time for them to get out of the war. So, during a normal sortie they signalled that they had an engine failure (or fire) and were losing height: in fact they dived down to sea level to get below the German radar cover, and then headed for Aberdeen. They were detected by our radar, and intercepted by two Spitfires from a Canadian squadron who recognized that their intentions were not offensive, and who took the risk of escorting them over Aberdeen and into Dyce. At the airfield, the ground defences opened fire, but fortunately missed, and the Junkers landed safely. I much admired the restraint of the Canadian pilots, because I knew of several instances where fighter pilots had shot down our own returning aircraft; and even though the German crew were waving white handkerchiefs, many fighter pilots would have opened fire. One of my more diverting efforts on returning to London was to try to get the two Canadians awarded the Distinguished Flying Cross for *not* shooting the Germans aircraft down. This was rather too much for the Air Staff, but they did finally agree that the pilots should be Mentioned in Despatches.

So we now had a German nightfighter, absolutely complete with its radar in working order. My first reaction was almost one of disappointment in that we should now have no technical problems left to be solved by normal Intelligence methods, but obviously the acquisition was a valuable one. One problem was to ensure that knowledge of its arrival did not get back to Germany. I had it hurriedly put into a hangar so that it could not be detected by German air reconnaissance, but already everyone on the station knew of its arrival, and it seemed almost impossible that the news should not get out. Fortunately, I found myself very much among friends, for it turned out that Dyce was the aerodrome from which the Operational Training Unit of the Photo Reconnaissance squadrons operated, and some of the instructors were actually officers who had flown sorties for me like 'Wattie' (Squadron Leader P. H.

Watts, D.S.O., D.F.C., who had taken the original high-level photographs of Bruneval). They took me up in their Mosquitoes, and I can still remember the thrill of reading 'This aircraft must not be dived at more than 360 m.p.h.', a speed far above anything I had flown before. I was taken up by John Merifield, whom the other pilots described to me as the 'best Mossie pilot in the Air Force', and who for many years held the Transatlantic crossing record of, I think, five hours and forty minutes. When I discussed with Wattie the problem of security I asked him whether he thought everyone could be so trusted that if I were to give the whole station a talk on German radar and what we hoped to do to counter it, and what the exact value of the German nightfighter was, they could be relied upon not to discuss it outside the station. Wattie was enthusiastic that this was a risk worth taking, so I asked the Station Commander to assemble as many of his personnel as possible, and I gave them an impromptu lecture; it was a risk, but it worked.

I had begun to make arrangements for the trials of the Ju 88, and returned south on Friday 14th May, not by train this time, but with one of the photographic Mosquitoes to Benson. I stayed overnight in the P.R.U. Mess, and took the opportunity to brief the pilots on the reasons why I wanted photographs of Peenemünde, and the angles from which the suspected rocket establishment should be photographed.

I went on to London the following morning; and in the afternoon Charles Frank and I went out to Latimer, where Felkin's headquarters now were, to talk to the crew of the Ju 88. They filled in various of the outstanding details about the German nightfighter system that we did not already know, and they offered their services at Farnborough to check over their aircraft before anyone flew it. This was helpful, because I could recall the first Ju 88 that Farnborough had intended to fly: it was built of parts recovered from crashed aircraft during the Battle of Britain and the Blitz, but there seemed to be something wrong with it although no one could say what it was. Finally a co-operative prisoner offered to look over it to see that all was well; and as soon as he saw the aircraft he burst out laughing. What Farnborough had not realized was that there were already two Marks of Ju 88, one with longer wings than the other; their aeroplane had a port wing from one Mark and the starboard wing from the other. The Dyce Ju 88, incidentally, was one of the few wartime aircraft to survive, and has recently been restored at the R.A.F. station at St. Athan.

I was convinced that the German pilot could be trusted to fly the nightfighter for us, but we needed its radar to be tested by one of our own expert observers, and I was delighted to find that he was to be my old colleague Derek Jackson, now a Squadron Leader Radar Observer, with a D.F.C. to add to his Oxford D.Sc. and other achievements. He telephoned to say that he was going to undertake the trials, and he wanted to discuss the pilot with me. I told him that the German pilot was willing to fly the aircraft for us, but he replied that he did not want to go flying with any bloody German, and that he wanted his own pilot. 'Is your pilot safe?' I asked, and let myself in for a typical Jacksonian broadside, 'Do you bloody well think that I would go up with him if I thought he wasn't?' And to that I had no answer.

So the trials were duly carried out, and we had two reports, one from Derek Jackson on the behaviour of the Lichtenstein radar and the other from the pilot, a Squadron Leader Hartley, on the handling of the aircraft as a nightfighter. One could take Derek's report as a matter of course—he had great skill with instruments, and all his observations would be highly cogent. The pilot's report, too, was very coherent and much to the point. My immediate reaction was, 'This chap can write—who is he?' I soon found out: he was Christopher Hartley, whose father was Sir Harold Hartley who had examined me for Scholarships at Oxford in 1928. We immediately became good friends. Incidentally, I had much the same reaction on reading a report by a young physicist who was primarily in the Operational Research Organization, but who at one time also looked after my interests in the Mediterranean. The clarity of his reports was admirable; he was J. C. Kendrew, now Sir John Kendrew, and a Nobel Prizewinner for his post-war work in molecular biology.

Another of our activities was advanced by my visit to Dyce. Ever since Tony Hill had told me how difficult it was to take low oblique photographs because of the sideways outlook of the camera fitted in the fuselage behind the pilot, I had been pressing for forward-facing cameras to be fitted on the wing-tips. This would have important advantages over the makeshift arrangement which had originally developed. In the first place, the pilot could simply dive at the target and fire his camera as he would his forward-facing guns. In the second, there would be no transverse blur superimposed on the photograph by the sideways motion of the aircraft; and in the third, with a camera on each wing-tip, a stereoscopic pair of photographs would be produced, which would add greatly to the information about the disposition of such items as the dipoles in a radar aerial.

The merits were so obvious that it is amazing that it took me more than two years to bring the change about, even though the pilots agreed with me and there was talk of making unofficial modifications. Technical matters such as this were not my responsibility: they had to be sanctioned by the Head of the Photographic Branch of the Air Staff, Group Captain D. D. ('Daddy') Laws, whose official position was D.D. (Deputy Director) Photos. For some reason or other he stubbornly refused to allow the modification to be made; but flying in Mosquitoes convinced me even further that with these aircraft wing-tip cameras would be a great advantage, and by this time I was beginning to get on personal terms with 'Daddy 'Laws. Finally, I found his weak point: of all the improbable hobbies for a Group Captain, his was the making of jam. If only I could convince him that I, too, was interested in jam-making, he might be more sympathetic to my ideas about cameras. My moment came when I asked him one day whether he had ever made quince jam. 'No!' he exclaimed—and then with a wistful look in his eye, 'But by God, I'd like to!' I offered to get him some quinces, and hence-forward photographic Mosquitoes for low-level work were fitted with forward-facing wing-tip cameras, with the much improved result we had expected.

Many more photographs were now coming in, and there was a rapidly increasing flow of all other kinds of Intelligence, including Enigma and reports from the Occupied Territories.

With our expanding activity, it was a relief when our secretarial arrangements were at last regularized. Well into 1942 we had been still depending on Daisy Mowat, who took on all our work in addition to her duties as Head Secretary of Winterbotham's Section. When she left for an overseas post we were helped out by 'Ginger' Parry whom we had recruited in 1941 to undertake the handling of the German radar plots; when it came to the emergency of having no-one to type our reports after Daisy Mowat left, it turned out that 'Ginger' could type, too.

When, much to our regret, she left us in 1943, Hugh Smith charmed M.I.6 into providing us with secretaries, the chief of whom was Joan Stenning. When she heard that she was to work for such a wild section as mine, and perhaps remembering some of my Oxford escapades, she burst into tears. But closer acquaintance must have shown her that we were not so bad, for when we broke up three years later, she was in tears again. In the meantime she had always been the staunchest of helpers.

We used sometimes to laugh together about what her father, the late Warden of Wadham, would think if he knew that his daughter and one of his undergraduates had been thrown together in this way. Actually, it gave me a chance to test out a theory that Tizard had once expounded to me when he had detected that I was uneasy in discussing secrets in front of his secretary. After she had gone out he told me that I need not be embarrassed, because in his experience women were more secure than men, his argument being that a men often felt obliged to brag about his work, and disclose that he was 'in the know', whereas women did not. Joan had told me that her father had no idea of what her work was, and so I mischievously decided to try this out next time I was dining with him at the High Table at Wadham. When I asked him what she was doing he said confidentially 'The same old thing—C.S., you know, C.S.!' My immediate reaction was that he must know more than we thought, for Joan had been in the Goverment Code and Cypher School when I met her, which was generally known as G.C. and C.S. It seemed that her father was saying just enough to let me know what she did, without disclosing it to anyone around us. When I returned to London I told Joan that it seemed, despite her care, her father had a fair inkling of what she was up to; but when I told her my evidence she burst out laughing. What he meant by 'C.S.' was Christian Science, of which she and her mother were devotees.

CHAPTER THIRTY-EIGHT

Peenemünde

THE MESSAGE about a rocket that we received from the Danish chemical engineer in December 1942 resensitized us to a possibility which, although I had reported it in 1939, had no more than stayed in the background of our thoughts over the intervening hectic years with the beams and German radar. The Oslo Report had mentioned Peenemünde, where, it had said, radio-controlled rocket gliders were being developed for use against ships under the code name FZ21 (Ferngesteuerte Zielflugzeug). The report also said, although it did not mention Peenemünde in this connection, that rocket shells 80 centimetres in diameter were being developed for use against the Maginot Line; these were gyro-stabilized, but were prone to fly in uncontrollable curves, and so radio control was being considered.

The Danish engineer's warning was timely: when he sent his message only three prototype V-2 rockets had in fact been fired at Peenemünde, the first successful firing having occurred on 3rd October 1942. This was as good a warning as we could hope to achieve in view of our lack of Scientific Intelligence before the war which had forced me to concentrate on detecting the development of new weapons at the trial stage i.e. later than the research stage but, hopefully, before the operational.

Over the next three months a few further reports appeared, but none substantially added to our knowledge. Indeed, they could have been no more than rumours, and the turning point, as far as I was concerned, occurred on 27th March 1943. It was a Saturday afternoon, and Hugh Smith was away for the weekend. Charles Frank was sitting at his desk opposite me when he looked up and said, 'It looks as though we'll have to take those rockets seriously!' He had been reading the transcripts of conversation between two German generals who had been captured after el Alamein, and who were now at our Interrogation Centre. One was Cruewell, who had been Rommel's Second-in-Command. The other was von Thoma whom I afterwards described as, 'The intelligent pessimist and most technically informed of our galaxy of German Generals'.

His comments on Hitler, for example, had already impressed me. He had told us how he had had to show Hitler some captured Russian tanks and the Führer had immediately said they could be no good. When von Thoma asked his reason, he said that the standard of finish was terrible, and that no one who was doing a decent job would leave his work in that state. So here we had the typical German view, with which I still have sympathy, that a good job should be well finished; but, as von Thoma pointed out, this judgement was very superficial because if you looked closer you could see that the Russian tanks were well machined where they had to be, but that the Russians had not wasted effort in smoothing and polishing surfaces where roughness and crudeness did not matter. In other words, their tanks were economically matched to their purpose.

The item which caused Frank to react was a remark of von Thoma to Cruewell on 22nd March 1943. Translated, this ran:

—but no progress whatsoever can have been made in this rocket business. I saw it once with Feldmarschall Brauchitsch, there is a special ground near Kunersdorf (?). . . . They've got these huge things which they've brought up here. . . . They've always said they would go 15 kms. into the stratosphere and then. . . . You only aim at an area. . . . If one was to . . . every few days . . . frightful. . . . The major there was full of hope—he said 'Wait until next year and the fun will start!'. . . . There's no limit (to the range).

Von Thoma also said that he knew their prison was somewhere near London and since they had heard no large explosions, there must have been a hold-up in the rocket programme.

His remarks transformed the situation. An Intelligence organization bears many resemblances to the human head, with its various senses. These will generally be on the alert, each searching its own domain and then as soon as the ears, for example, hear a noise and the signals are received in the brain, the latter will direct the eyes in the appropriate direction to supplement the information from the ears by what the eyes can see. So, if one kind of Intelligence source produces an indication, the Intelligence organization should then direct other kinds of source to focus on the same target. This was obviously what we had to do, and I started to take the appropriate steps.

It was a classic situation: we had now become aware of something without knowing enough to give the Operational Staffs something to act on and so take countermeasures. It was a point that I had discussed in my paper to Inglis of 20th November 1942, only a few months before.

We are sometimes criticized for withholding information, but while no instance has ever been proved, we reserve our right to do so because (1) to spread half-truth is often to precipitate erroneous action by the Air Staff, and (2) the steady and immediate broadcasting of each insignificant and uncollated fact automatically and insidiously acclimatizes the recipients to knowledge of enemy developments, so that they feel no stimulation to action. The presentation of the complete picture of an enemy development is the best way of stimulating the appropriate authority to action. The production of such pictures involves much effort, but it has been justified by results.
Although we think that the above policy is the best, it obviously has some defects, which we try to remedy by frequent oral communications to the appropriate bodies.

In summary, I regarded myself as a watchdog. If the dog barks too late it is fatal. But if he barks too early, he will bark so often at threats which do not subsequently materialize that his master will get tired of responding to false alarms. My duty over the rocket was clear: to pursue the Intelligence chase as energetically as possible, and to let men in key positions know that we were on to something. In this case, and at such an early stage, it would have sufficed to let Lindemann know, which I did.

The pursuit from then on would have been a perfectly normal, if exhilarating, one. But the whole situation was completely upset by the action of Military Intelligence in the War Office. All the information that had come to me had also gone to the War Office, and a very able Intelligence officer there had come to the same conclusion that Frank and I had, about the reality of rocket development. Where he differed was in his subsequent action. He warned the Director of Military Intelligence, who in turn warned the Vice Chief of the Imperial General Staff, who became so concerned that he took the matter to the Vice Chiefs of Staff Committee on 12th April. They decided that the Prime Minister and the Minister of Home Security, Mr. Herbert Morrison should be warned of a possible rocket attack and that scientific investigations should be put in hand. On 15th April, General Ismay, Chief of

Staff to the Minister of Defence, minuted the Prime Minister, 'The Chiefs of Staff feel that you should be made aware of reports of German experiments with long-range rockets. The fact that five reports have been received since the end of 1942 indicates a foundation of fact even if details are inaccurate.' The Chiefs recommended that a single investigator should be appointed to call on such Scientific and Intelligence Advisers as appropriate, and suggested the name of Mr. Duncan Sandys.

It did not seem to occur to the Chiefs of Staff that they already had a Scientific Intelligence component inside their organization, and the first I heard of Duncan Sandys' appointment was from Lindemann a week or two later. He sent for me and asked me whether I thought that there was anything in the rocket story. I reminded him that I had already told him that I thought that there was, and he in turn said that he thought that there was not. His view may have been coloured to some extent by the fact that he did not like Sandys, but perhaps even more by the fact that he did not want to accept any evidence that might throw us back on to the defensive.

After I left him I discussed with Charles Frank the news that Sandys had been appointed to do a job that we already had in hand, and for which our qualifications were much better. How had the Chiefs of Staff overlooked us, when we had already proved ourselves in the beams, the Bruneval Raid, the Gibraltar barrage, radar, Window, heavy water, and the German nightfighters? But, I added, this was no fault of Sandys, who had been called in out of the blue, and I supposed that I must regard myself as having been very lucky to have had the beams all to myself. It was no use being jealous of someone else having the luck this time. We would therefore stay in the background and see that he got all the information; but just in case he or his organization were not up to it we would continue to keep an eye on everything so as to be able to step in if there were signs of a breakdown.

In any event, I had the responsibility of warning the Air Staff if there was any threat to Britain which might require action on the part of the Royal Air Force, and in addition I was Head of the Scientific Section of M.I.6, advising on the direction of our agent effort, and of the direction of our code-breaking activities. So besides passing on to Sandys any information we might obtain, and making efforts to get it by means that might not occur to him and his advisers, I would continue to collate all the information as a reserve if he and his organization ran into difficulties.

It was a straight Intelligence problem, and I could therefore plan an attack with the resources at my disposal. Agents could be briefed; and in particular there was hope of information coming through the army of foreign labourers that had been recruited to work at Peenemünde. P.R.U. could be asked to photograph the Establishment there, and I was able to brief the pilots in detail. Felkin and his colleagues, who had of course provided the vital stimulus with the von Thoma conversation, could also be briefed.

In addition, there was one very long shot, in fact the longest that I made in the entire war. Contemplating the problem of monitoring the flight of a rocket from the ground, I recalled the story that Carl Bosch told me about the shells from the long-range gun[1] in World War I, which seemed to disappear 'into the blue' and were only found later, much further along the line of fire than expected, because a meteorologist who knew about the firing of the gun also happened to receive reports of three meteorites arriving at 20-minute intervals after three shots had been fired from the gun with this same interval between them.

Now, in World War II, the problem might be eased by following the rocket by radar. If, therefore, rockets with a range of 200 kilometres were being fired from Peenemünde then they would probably be fired east-north-eastwards up the Baltic, and quite possibly a set of radar stations would be strung out on the north coast of Germany, so as to follow the rocket over its trajectory. It would obviously be a very difficult job for the radar of those days, since the rocket would be moving ten times faster than an aircraft, and therefore the radar operators would have to be very expert. The German Army did not have much radar, and it would probably have to turn to one of the other two Services. Somehow, by that time I knew enough about German radar to say that the most expert operators were thought to be in the 14th and 15th Companies of the German Air Signals Experimental Regiment. I therefore told Norman at Bletchley of my line of thought, and asked him to see that Bletchley and the Y Service generally followed those two companies as closely as possible, and above all to let me know whether one or other of them moved up to the Baltic coast and showed signs of deploying itself from Peenemünde eastwards.

While we were putting this Intelligence attack into operation, there began to appear signs that I did not like. Sandys must have heard about me sooner or later, and indeed Lindemann made sure that he did so. For the one positive criticism that Lindemann could make of Sandys was that he would have been better advised to get in touch with me

[1] In trials that led to its later use against Paris in 1918.

than to set up a separate organization. Not only was there no contact between us but I began to sense signs of a move to 'corner' all the information. In particular instructions were issued that all photographs of Peenemünde were to go only to Sandys. This caused some discussion, and indeed disturbance, in the Photographic Reconnaissance set-up, all the more so since I had been briefing the pilots personally on how to take the photographs.

My contacts at all levels with P.R. were of course very good. So good, in fact, that on one occasion Peter Stewart asked me confidentially whether Wavell was my uncle. When I told him that we were not related, I asked the reason for his question. Apparently someone had complained that I got a far better service from the Photographic Reconnaissance organization than anyone else, and that this was because Claude Wavell was my uncle. I can only conclude that the complainer had heard someone say that it might be a case of nepotism and had looked up a dictionary. Anyway, from that moment onwards, Wavell became 'Uncle Claude' for the rest of the war, and no uncle could have done more for us.

Curiously, it was Peter himself who had a relative in his organization, for his father, 'Pop' Stewart, a former Brooklands racing motorist, served under him as a squadron leader. And it was 'Pop' Stewart and his colleague Roddie Nicholson, who played an essential part in my finding the first rocket. When they heard of a veto on the Peenemünde photographs going to anyone but Sandys, 'Pop' said to me, 'Our instructions from the Air Staff have always been to pass any photographs to you that might interest you, and so we propose to see that you get a copy of every photograph that goes to Sandys'.

In contrast with aerial photographs, reports from secret agents had of course to come through me, so that although I only saw aerial photographs some days after the Sandys' organization, I saw the agents' reports some hours earlier. There were two in particular in June 1943 that remain in my memory; they came from two Luxembourgers whom the Germans had conscripted into the army of foreign construction workers at Peenemünde. One was Leon Henri Roth, a student aged 20, who had been expelled from school for starting a Resistance cell. Along with other Luxembourgers he was sent to Peenemünde, and succeeded in getting letters through to his father, who was a member of a Belgian network, telling of the development of a large rocket which made a noise resembling that of a 'a squadron at low altitude'. The other Luxembourger whose report I remember was Dr. Schwagen, afterwards

Director of the Laboratoire Bactériologique de l'Etat in Luxembourg, who sent through an organization known as the 'Famille Martin' a report and sketch which reached me on 4th June. It is shown in Figure 17, and it clearly mentioned a rocket of about ten metres length, and showed where it was assembled. It also stated that for firing it was mounted on a cubical structure. Dr. Schwagen survived the war but tragically Roth, who was a student, was killed by fire from an American tank in 1945, while escaping with two Frenchmen in a German military

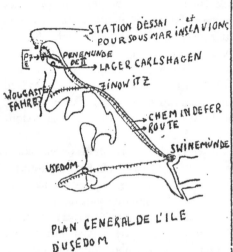

Fig. 17. A Luxembourger's message and sketch smuggled out of Peenemünde, June 1943. The poor quality is due to the original having been transmitted by microfilm. 'P7' was Prüfstand (test stand) 7, the oval enclosure visible in Plates 19 (a) and (b)

car; he was posthumously awarded the Croix de le Résistance and the Médaille d'honneur de l'Etoile, and was re-interred in Luxemborg in 1968.

Besides these reports from Peenemünde itself, there was an interesting one on 22nd June which came from a source in one of the Weapons Departments in the German High Command. This spoke of 'winged' rockets with remote control and launched by catapults, the intended target being London. Thirty catapults had been constructed of which fifteen were already serviceable. Although Hitler was pressing, the starting date of the bombardment had had to be postponed from the beginning to the end of July. We had no means of judging the reliability of this report, which was typical of many that now flooded in. Assessing them became extremely difficult, especially since the concern generated by the Sandys enquiry resulted in ill-considered questionnaires being sent out to all parts of our agent network. Briefing agents is a considerable art. With some you can tell them the whole story of what you already know, and you can trust them to use this information to guide their own enquiries. Others who are not so reliable will often take what you have already told them and feed it back to you with embellishments to cover up the fact that their own enquiries have been unsuccessful. This factor was to bedevil the rocket enquiry for the whole of the following twelve months.

The evidence from Photographic Reconnaissance was free from this difficulty, in that it was objective; but, even then, what one could see in a photograph was often a matter of subjective interpretation. The first sortie, on 22nd April, showed a large establishment with an enormous cloud of steam; although we did not recognize the cause of this until later, it was probably the condensed exhaust from the test of a rocket jet. And as the air photographs came in through May and June it was clear that there was great activity at Peenemünde both at the establishment and at the nearby airfield. A special section was set up at Medmenham, the Photographic Interpretation Unit, to undertake the interpretation for Duncan Sandys. In this he was unlucky because the principal interpreter assigned to the task supplemented his powers of observation by a remarkably fertile imagination. What were in fact catapults for flying bombs were, for example, interpreted as 'sludge pumps', a theory perhaps coloured by the interpreter's previous experience as an engineer with a river Catchment Board after his Cambridge Ph.D. thesis on classical hydraulic engineering—a thesis which was not accepted because, he claimed with rueful humour, Cambridge could not find as examiners either an engineer who knew Latin and Greek or a classical scholar who knew any engineering.

Since I only received the photographs from 'Pop' Stewart some days after they had been available at Medmenham there ought to have been nothing left for me to discover. The history of sortie N/853 is therefore revealing. Its photographs of Peenemünde were taken on 12th June. They were available at Medmenham the following day, and when the Prime Minister visited Medmenham on 14th June he was shown them by Sandys' interpreter, who issued his interpretation report on 16th June. I first saw the photographs on 18th June; after a quick lunch I was studying them with a stereoscope, convinced that sooner or later we must catch a rocket in the open, although we had little idea what its size and appearance would be, apart from the Luxembourgers' evidence that it was about ten metres long. The definition of the photographs was not good (Plate 19(a)), and I knew that by this time the Medmenham interpreters had had at least five days to study them: there ought to have been no pickings left. But suddenly I spotted on a railway truck something that could be a whiteish cylinder about 35 feet long and 5 or so feet in diameter, with a bluntish nose and fins at the other end. I experienced the kind of pulse of elation that you get when after hours of casting you realize that a salmon has taken your line—especially when someone else has had an exhaustive first chance at the pool.

To Frank I said in as level a voice as I could 'Charles, come and look at this!' He immediately agreed that I had found the rocket, which I then showed to Edward Wright. Now the only question was how we should play the advantage that the discovery had given us in demonstrating to the Intelligence world and the politicians that the 'old firm' had done it after all, despite all the effort and fuss that had been created by the Sandys approach, and despite a five days' handicap in seeing the photographs. If any justification were needed for our having continued to watch, this was it.

If Medhurst had still been in Intelligence, I would have gone to him. But Frank Inglis had taken over and, although he was a very decent officer, he was out of his depth when it came to technical matters. I could perhaps have bypassed him and gone to Portal, but the latter's position was already difficult in that he, as one of the Chiefs of Staff, had some responsibility for Sandys having been called in. So instead I went to Lindemann, if only to show him that his faith in us had been justified. I did not know it but on 11th June he had already minuted Churchill:

Jones, who you may remember is in charge of Scientific Intelligence'
has been following these questions closely, and I do not think there
is any risk of our being caught napping.

So I went across to the Cabinet Offices and saw Lindemann before he
left for the weekend at Oxford, to discuss how to proceed. We could
there and then have called for a showdown to decide whether there was
any further case for the abnormal Intelligence arrangements that had
been called into being by the rocket scare. Very generously, I thought,
Lindemann said that I should send a note to Sandys telling him that
there was a rocket visible on the photograph, to give him a chance to
react before I told anyone else. It was now late on Friday afternoon and
in the morning (19th June) I sent the following note to Sandys:

> Lord Cherwell has asked me to draw your attention to the fact—
> should you not have already noticed it—that a rocket seems to be
> visible on sortie N/853 of Peenemünde; it is about 35 ft. long.

This gave Sandys a chance to discuss the situation with me; and we
could perhaps have come to a reasonable arrangement where he would
be responsible for countermeasures and co-ordinating them with
Intelligence, whilst I provided him with the Intelligence. Instead, there
was no acknowledgement of my note: two or three days later there
appeared an addendum from Sandys' interpreter to his previous report,
saying that an object was visible on the photograph, without any
mention that anyone but himself had found it. This experience certainly
confirmed my impression that my help was being avoided, and that
Sandys wished to have others think that his arrangements were working
well.

Lindemann was no more pleased than I was, and he again spoke to
Churchill. He told me that he had told Churchill that he did not know
whether I was going to agree with him about the rocket or not, but that
my record was such that Churchill must hear me. To his credit, he
already knew that I did not agree with him, and the gesture must have
cost him much. It was this pressure from Lindemann, almost certainly,
that was the cause of Churchill calling me to his side after the Window
meeting of 23rd June (p. 298) and asking me whether Mr. Sandys had
been in touch with me. So with his instruction to hold myself in readiness
for the following week, I sat up that same night until 2.30 a.m. writing a
report to summarize what I could now see of the rocket picture.

12*

The report discussed and rejected the idea that the rocket story could be a hoax, and I appended my drawing of the rocket (Figure 18) as being about 35–38 feet long and 6 feet in diameter. It concluded that the scale of firing at Peenemünde was small, in that on no photograph had we seen more than one rocket whereas if there were, say, twenty available for test at any one time we should probably have caught more than one in the open at the same time.

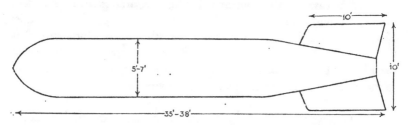

Fig. 18. Rough outline of rocket (not to scale) drawn from the aerial photograph of Peenemünde at Plate 19a, June 1943. The warhead was probably not fitted, decreasing the overall length by seven to nine feet. The drawing shows as much as could be extracted from the photograph and represents the limit of British knowledge at the time

As for the imminence of attack, this did not seem to me serious—in contrast with some other assessments—but there was always the chance that Hitler would press his technicians into firing a few against London if he was stung by our bombing attacks on German towns. For counter-measures almost the only thing we could do would be to bomb the development and production facilities, and in recommending an attack on Peenemünde I gave a written undertaking: 'Peenemünde would demand considerable priority over all other places, despite our curiosity to watch the development of the trials. Intelligence would be prepared to take the risk of the work being re-started elsewhere.'

I also noted that the long shot that I had planned in April showed some promise, for the 14th Company of the Air Signals Experimental Regiment had in fact moved a Würzburg to Peenemünde, and a radar detachment to the Island of Rügen, just north of Peenemünde. It might simply be a strengthening of the air defences, but dared we hope that we were 'on to something'?

In the report I made a mistake which I record as a salutary lesson for future Intelligence officers. When I measured the size of the rocket, I made a guess at its weight as 'perhaps 20 to 40 tons', and this is what I originally wrote in the report. On the afternoon of 26th June, however, Duncan Sandys at last asked me to see him, and the question of the

weight came up. I repeated my guess of 20 to 40 tons, but he told me
that our experts said that it must be at least 80 tons. When I expressed
surprise, he suggested that I should speak on the telephone to one of
them, Dr. W. R. (now Sir William) Cook, and so we put a call through.
Cook told me that to make a rocket you could not do better than a
50/50 fuel/carcase weight ratio, since the carcase has to be of steel thick
enough to stand the pressure of the cordite or other propellant burning
in the jet. This gives a mean density for the rocket of about four times
that of water, and so the total weight for a rocket of the size that we
had seen would be 80 tons. I tried to shake Cook without success, and
so I grudgingly altered the stencil of my report from 'perhaps 20 to 40
tons' to 'perhaps 40 to 80 tons'. As it turned out my original estimate
was much nearer the true weight than we were going to get for another
year; and it shows the dangers of letting one single item of information
that has come in at the last moment upset a judgement made on the
basis of all the previous evidence. Actually, of course, where our experts
were wrong was in assuming that the Germans were trying to make an
enormously enlarged version of a schoolboy rocket.

By the time I finished my report on 26th June, a further sortie had
been flown over Peenemünde on 23rd June with Flight Sergeant
E. P. H. Peek as pilot, and this showed a rocket (Plate 19(b)) so clearly
that nobody could argue about it—nobody, that is, except Lindemann.
The photographs were available for the meeting with Churchill who,
true to his word, had called it for 10 p.m. on 29th June; but instead of
this being a 'staff conference' it was a full meeting of the War Cabinet
Defence Committee (Operations).

Duncan Sandys gave an account of his conclusions, including the
estimate by the Ministry of Home Security that a single rocket would
cause 'up to four thousand casualties killed and injured'; but apart from
this, and a tendency to assess the threat as more imminent than I would
myself, there was not much that I would have questioned. He was
concerned that the rocket might be used before the Royal Air Force
could make a heavy attack on Peenemünde, the earliest date for which,
in view of the short nights, was mid-August.

Churchill then invited Lindemann to give his views. The Prof was
obviously not at ease, perhaps because he knew that I was going to
differ from him, but he proceeded in his best manner to fight a rearguard action. Trying to have it both ways, he said that he proposed to
act as *advocatus diaboli* against the case for the rocket as put by Mr. Sandys.
He made various technical points: he did not believe that a single rocket

would cause four thousand casualties, and he doubted whether the Germans had a sufficiently powerful propellant. As for the objects that we had photographed at Peenemünde they were either torpedoes or wooden dummies, deliberately painted white to show up easily on our photographs.[1] It was now that he touched his best form: the whole rocket story was a great hoax to distract our attention from some other weapon which would be much more vulnerable to countermeasures than the rocket if we were to detect its development in time, for example a pilotless aircraft. So if all our attention was focused on the rocket and on trying to think how we could counter it, we might miss the real weapon, the pilot-less aircraft. As was to transpire, this was a magnificent try, but it was not really valid—the chances were that if we were alarmed by the rocket story and were chasing it alone, we should in the course of the chase come across clues that would put us on to the trail of the other weapon, pilot-less aircraft or whatever it might be.

When Lindemann had finished, Churchill told the meeting that there was one man whose views he wanted particularly to hear. This was, 'Dr. Jones, who had been responsible for piecing together the evidence which had enabled us to detect and defeat the enemy's beams for controlling their night bombers'. He looked across at me and said, 'Now I want the truth!' The meeting was taking place not in the Cabinet Room in 10 Downing Street, but in the Cabinet's underground head-quarters (Plate 4(b)). Churchill was, of course, at the head of the table and flanked by Mr. Attlee and Mr. Anthony Eden. The other Ministers present were Oliver Lyttelton, Herbert Morrison, and Stafford Cripps. The three Chiefs of Staff and General Ismay were of course there; and Sir Findlater Stewart, Sir Robert Watson-Watt, W. R. J. Cook, and Kenneth Post (Sandys' assistant) were also present, in addition to Duncan Sandys and myself. Appropriately enough, Lindemann sat on one side of the table and Sandys on the other; and, as in 1940, I sat in No Man's Land which this time was at the foot, opposite Churchill.

I told him that although I did not think that there was a likelihood of a heavy attack for some months, I felt that the evidence for believing in the rocket's existence was stronger than that which I had presented to him about the beams in 1940. At this point Churchill called out 'Stop!' then turning to Lindemann he said, 'Hear that. That's a weighty point against you! Remember, it was you who introduced him to me!'

[1] Lindemann may have been almost uncannily right, to an extent: there were white wooden dummy rockets used for training purposes, and some may easily have appeared on our photographs.

He similarly interrupted my comments on two or three other occasions, for example when I discussed the theories that it might be a torpedo, which was one of Lindemann's alternatives, or a hoax. As for the torpedo idea, there was no aircraft in Germany that would carry a torpedo 38 feet long and 6 feet in diameter, or could lift 10 or 20 tons. As for a hoax, what would be the result, if it were successful? Almost certainly, we would attack Peenemünde, and there was enough evidence to show that Peenemünde was a major experimental establishment. It was as though we, in trying to mislead the Germans, had set out some dummy weapon at Farnborough for them to photograph. They would then attack Farnborough, and despite all the hard things we might have said in the past about Farnborough, we should think it a very silly hoax that resulted in its destruction. Moreover, in chasing a hoax-rocket, we should almost certainly come across traces of the weapon from which it was intended to distract us. As each of these points sank in, Churchill interrupted me, and asked Lindemann for a reply, repeating every time, 'Remember, it was you who introduced him to me!' All the Prof could muster was a rueful half-smile. At one stage Churchill actually said, 'I want no more of your *advocatus diaboli*!' stressing the Latin with his well-known dislike of that language.

In one sense it was as exhilarating as the beams meeting of 1940, but it was painful because I had effectively to refute my old Professor, but for whom I might well not have been called in. Had it been Tizard, as it was in 1940, it might have been the end of him, but fortunately Churchill's confidence in Lindemann was far too firm to be shaken. The personalities of various others of those around the table began to emerge. Herbert Morrison for some reason or other wanted to know whether the evidence from German personnel had come from officers or other ranks. Stafford Cripps seemed to be activated more than anyone else: he wanted Peenemünde attacked at once. Anthony Eden thought that the arguments were nicely balanced. Alan Brooke was in retrospect disappointing, in view of his high reputation. When I saw his notes of the meeting afterwards, they seemed distinctly superficial; and during the course of the meeting he described the German long-range gun used against Paris as 'Big Bertha' which any soldier should have known was not the long-range gun but a large calibre howitzer named after Bertha Krupp.

It was agreed that Peenemünde should be attacked by Bomber Command on the heaviest possible scale on the first occasion when conditions were suitable. Owing to Lindemann's having mentioned the possibility of pilotless aircraft, it was agreed that this should be investigated, too, and that I should be closely associated with Sandys in that enquiry.

There was another six or seven weeks before the raid could take place and, although we continued to watch the rocket evidence as keenly as ever, there was the whole of the Window operation to follow. The use of Window, in fact, made it possible to arrange a feint on Berlin, in the hope of distracting the nightfighters there while the main force attacked Peenemünde. At last, the nights were just long enough, and the attack took place on 17th/18th August 1943. I was not consulted about the aiming points in the raid, nor would I have expected this to be necessary; but, in retrospect, I wish that I had been. Bomber Command had originally intended to make its main attack on the development works and installation at Peenemünde, but Sandys convinced the Command that it was even more important to attack the housing estate which contained the homes of the scientists and engineers associated with the rocket project. I would probably not have agreed with this emphasis, because much of their essential work had probably been done, and the main object should be to smash up the research and manufacturing facilities. But with the emphasis on the housing estate, and with the unfortunate miscarriage of two important pathfinding 'markers' a substantial proportion of our bombs fell to the south of the establishment itself, and particularly on the camp which housed the foreign labourers, including those who had risked so much to get information through to us. We never had another report from them, and some six hundred of them were killed as compared with 130 or so German scientists, engineers and other staff. To add to the debit side of the raid, there was the fact that we lost 41 aircraft out of 600.

The effects of the raid in delaying the rocket programme have been variously estimated from four weeks to six months. We killed some key German personnel, such as Dr. Thiel, who was responsible for rocket jet design, and we burnt up many of the production drawings. We also did enough damage to the station itself to make the Germans decide that they ought to remove both development and production facilities to other places. Taken altogether, I think that the raid must have gained us at least two months, and these would have been very significant because the rocket could then have been used almost simultaneously with the flying bomb in 1944, and from a shorter range since the Germans still held northern France and Belgium and we should have had to face two threats at the same time.

Also on the credit side was the demonstration, despite our losses, that Window had given us a new factor in raid planning. For the eight Window-dropping Mosquitoes that had attacked Berlin had succeeded in attracting some two hundred nightfighters, and had got them up early. There were so many fighters over Berlin that some attacked others by mistake, and the German flak defences opened fire on their own fighters. With fuel running low, and in the absence of clear orders in the general confusion, many decided to land at the airfield at Brandenburg, where there was so much confusion that thirty aircraft were written off in collisions on the ground. By the time that the German defences realized that Peenemünde was the main target, relatively few nightfighters had the fuel left to get there; but these arrived in time to catch the last wave of bombers, and in the moonlight and at the low height of 7,000 feet from which the attack was made, they did great damage, shooting down 29 aircraft out of 200. This reinforced the lesson we had repeatedly preached about the need for short sharp raids with great care being paid to concentration on the way home.

Apart from Thiel, most of the leading German personalities survived the raid. Werner von Braun, the outstanding spirit in the whole rocket project, courageously rescued many of his documents from the flames. Dr. Steinhoff, Head of the Telemetry Department, and of whom we had already heard as visiting Bornholm as part of the rocket programme, escaped in his air-raid shelter, and so did the chief engineer, Walter Riedel, who moved with his family out of their cellar shortly before a bomb hit their house. The one completely unexpected casualty was the Chief of the German Air Staff, Jeschonnek. He had already had a bad day and had been harangued by Hitler because the American Eighth Air Force had succeeded in doing great damage to the ballbearing factories at Schweinfurt and the Messerschmitt works at Regensburg, even though Jeschonnek's fighters had shot down sixty bombers. Now Peenemünde had been attacked and shortly after midnight Jeschonnek had been called on the telephone by an infuriated Goering, because of the battle between the anti-aircraft guns and the nightfighters over Berlin. It was too much for Jeschonnek; by nine o'clock on the morning of the following day he had not emerged from his room. He was found by his secretary shot dead by his own revolver.

One of those who went to Peenemünde to inspect the damage was Colonel Leo Zanssen from the Army Weapons Office in Berlin. When I heard his name I wondered whether this was the engineer 'Szenassi' mentioned in the original rocket telegram from Stockholm. It reminded me of the episode in Erskine Childers *The Riddle of the Sands*, where the hero standing near a railway booking office just succeeded in hearing the sibilants in the station named by someone further up the queue, and correctly deduced the name of the station for which the latter had asked for a ticket as Essens.

To make one further Intelligence comment on the raid, I noted that in the information on which this major action had been conceived and carried out, there had been almost no contribution from Enigma. I always looked at such actions from this standpoint because, vital though Enigma was, it could at any time have been cut off, and if we had become too dependent on it, we should have been at an enormous disadvantage. The one point where it had entered in this instance was in providing me with a copy of an instruction originating from somewhere in the German Air Ministry, instructing personnel at research and experimental stations on new arrangements for drawing, I think, petrol coupons. The originating officer had addressed it to establishments in what seemed to be an order of precedence, starting with Rechlin, the nearest equivalent in Germany to our Royal Aircraft Establishment at Farnborough. Peenemünde was second on the list, ahead of several other establishments whose importance was already known to us. It was most unlikely that such a seemingly trivial clue, which the Germans had no idea would come into our hands, would have been part of a great hoax, and I was therefore able to cite this as independent evidence of the importance the Germans attached to Peenemünde.

One final item of Intelligence luck came chronologically at this stage, although we did not know it until after the war. Besides Peenemünde, one of the other assembly factories for the rockets was to have been the Zeppelin works at Friedrichshafen. The extremely light carcase of the rocket was, like the Giant Würzburg, based on Zeppelin-type construction, although our experts at the time were thinking of a substantial steel body. The raid of 22nd June 1943 that I had instigated to damage Giant Würzburg production also therefore damaged the assembly factory for V-2 rockets—so badly in fact, that the works at Friedrichshafen, which would have assembled 300 rockets a month, were abandoned. This was a valuable additional blow to the raid on Peenemünde itself.

CHAPTER THIRTY-NINE

FZG 76

AFTER THE flurry of Window and the Peenemünde Raid, we took the fortnight's holiday in Gloucestershire which Helen Smith, Hugh Smith's wife, had offered Vera and me. I discovered I could hit running hares with a pistol, and shot three in four days. I might have had more hares, but after only a week I was interrupted by a telephone call from Charles Frank saying that there was to be another Prime Ministerial meeting about the rocket threat on 31st August, and my presence had been requested. I therefore had to interrupt the holiday and go up to London by a morning train which arrived about lunchtime. This gave most of the afternoon for Charles to brief me on the events of the past week, before the Prime Minister's meeting started at, I think, 5 p.m. A number of interesting things had happened. First, on 22nd August an object had crashed in a turnip field on the Island of Bornholm in the Baltic, roughly half-way between Germany and Sweden. It was a small pilotless aircraft bearing the number 'V83', and it was promptly photographed by the Danish Naval Officer-in-Charge on Bornholm, Lieutenant Commander Hasager Christiansen. He also made a sketch, and noted that the warhead was a dummy made of concrete. He sent copies of his photographs and sketch to Commodore Paul Mørch, Chief of the Danish Naval Intelligence Service, who forwarded them to us. Several different routes must have been used, because I received three independent sets of copies, and it seemed that someone was determined that the information should reach us. Commodore Mørch thinks that besides the copies that he sent, others reached us by different routes from the photographic shop on Bornholm that processed Christiansen's film. Unfortunately one set of copies was intercepted by the Germans, who were able to identify the policeman standing in one of the photographs (Plate 20(a)) and hence discover who had taken them. Christiansen was arrested by the Germans on 5th September and tortured; but he held out and was transferred to hospital on 8th October. There he was rescued on 22nd October and smuggled to Sweden, where he underwent two major operations to alleviate the effects of torture. He reported for duty again in March 1944, and was awarded the Distinguished Service Cross.

At first, we were not sure what he had found. From his sketch it was about 4 metres long, and it might have been a rather larger version of the HS 293 glider bomb that KG100 was now using against our warships in the Mediterranean. Indeed, it turned out that this particular bomb had been released from a Heinkel 111, but it was in fact a research model (the 'V' probably stood for 'Versuchs' i.e. research) of the flying bomb about which we were going to hear so much in the next few months.

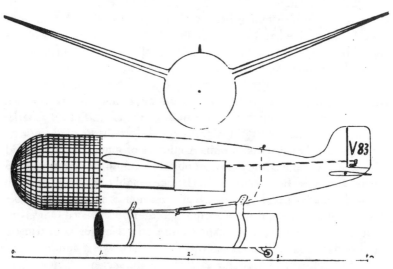

Fig. 19. Sketch made by Hasager Christiansen of an experimental V-1 that fell on Bornholm, 22 August 1943. See also Plate 20

The next report that had come in during my week's absence had originated on 12th August from the same disgruntled officer in the Army Weapons Office who had told us some weeks earlier of the plan for winged rockets. His new report was much more specific, and said that a pilotless aircraft officially known as Phi 7 was being tested at Peenemünde, but he knew nothing about it as it was not an Army project. In addition there was a rocket projectile known as A4. 20th October had been fixed as Zero Day for rocket attacks on London to begin.

The third report had come in from a French agent via the famous 'Alliance' network headed by Marie-Madeleine Fourcade, who had forwarded it to my colleague Kenneth Cohen in London. It was so remarkable that I reproduce it in full, as has also Marie-Madeleine in her book *Noah's Ark* (London, Allen & Unwin, 1973).

Information communicated by a captain on the active list attached to the Experimental Centre in question.

On the island of Usedon (north of Stettin) are concentrated laboratories and scientific research services to improve existing weapons and perfect new ones. The island is very closely guarded. To gain access, besides a military identity card, requires three special passes:

Sondergenehmigung	on watermarked paper
Zusatz	an orange card
Vorlaüfigergenehmigung	on white paper

The administrative services are at Peenemünde and at Zempin. Research is concentrated on:

(a) bombs and shells guided independently of the laws of ballistics.
(b) a stratospheric shell.
(c) the use of bacteria as a weapon.

Kampfgruppe KG 100 is now experimenting with bombs guided from the aircraft by the bomb aimer. These bombs could be guided from such a distance that the plane could remain out of range of AA fire. Accuracy is perfect if the plane does not have to defend itself against fighters (which is not the case in Sicily).

It appears that the final stage has been reached in developing a stratospheric bomb of an entirely new type. This bomb is reported to be 10 cubic metres in volume and filled with explosive. It would be launched almost vertically to reach the stratosphere as quickly as possible. The source speaks of 50 mph vertically, initial velocity being maintained by successive explosions. The bomb is provided with *Raketten* (vanes?) and guided to specific targets. The bomb is said to be fuelled with 800 litres of petrol, necessary even in the experimental stage, in which the shell is not filled with explosive, to enable it to carry. The horizontal range is slightly over 300 miles. Trials are said to have been made, without explosive charge, from Usedon towards the Baltic and to have reached as far as Königsberg. The noise is said to be as deafening as a Flying Fortress. The trials are understood to have given immediate excellent results as regards accuracy and it was to the success of these trials that Hitler was

referring when he spoke of 'new weapons that will change the face
of the war when the Germans use them'.

Difficulties have developed quite recently, only half the bombs
hitting the selected targets accurately. This recent fault is expected
to be remedied towards the end of the month. The trials have been
made by Lehr-und-Erprobungskommando Wachtel.

Colonel Wachtel and the officers that he has collected were to form
the cadres of an anti-aircraft regiment (16 batteries of 220 men, the
155 W, that is going to be stationed in France, at the end of October
or beginning of November, with HQ near Amiens, and batteries
between Amiens, Abbeville, Dunkirk).

The regiment will dispose 108 (one hundred and eight) catapults
able to fire a bomb every twenty minutes. The army artillery will
have more that 400 catapults sited from Brittany to Holland.

The artillery regiments will be supplied with these devices as and
when there is a sufficient production of ammunition.

Major Sommerfeld, Colonel Wachtel's technical adviser, estimates
that 50–100 of these bombs would suffice to destroy London. The
batteries will be so sited that they can methodically destroy most of
Britain's large cities during the winter.

Reinforced concrete platforms are reported to be already under
construction. They are expected to be fully operational in November.

The Germans experts are aware that British experts are working on the
same problem. They think they are sure of a three to four months' lead.

There is, incidentally, one important difference between Marie-
Madeleine's version and mine. Hers was unreadable as regards the third
word after 'Peenemünde' whereas ours read 'Zemfin', which we
amended to read 'Zempin', a village not far from Peenemünde.

The information about KG100 having used guided bombs which had
been developed at Peenemünde (reminiscent of the 'Oslo Report')
against our warships in the Mediterranean was correct: *Warspite*, the
most wayward of battleships, had been among those hit. Bacterial
warfare was an aspect which we were also on the watch for, but what
interested us most, of course, was the 'stratospheric shell.' This, and
much of the internal evidence, with its 80 kilometres into the stratosphere, pointed to the rocket; and somehow the source even knew the
colours of the various passes necessary to get into Peenemünde, and had
supplied a wealth of detail about the launching organization in France.
We learnt for the first time of the existence of Colonel Wachtel and his

Lehr-und-Erprobungskommando that was now to be formed into Flak Regiment 155W, and his technical adviser Sommerfeld. Some of the figures in the report were frightening: 108 catapults rising to more than 400, with 50 to 100 bombs sufficient to destroy London, and with a range up to 500 kilometres. What were we to make of it all?

All three reports I had to absorb in the three hours before Churchill's meeting, and although I could not have asked for a better briefing than that which Charles Frank gave me, I was not completely happy. Lindemann was again defiant. He argued that these new reports were typical of what might be expected once we had unwisely briefed our agents about what to look for, and he again threw doubt on the reality of the rocket. Despite this, the Ministry of Production was required to investigate the problem of providing another 100,000 Morrison shelters for London: Lindemann told me afterwards that the building of two battleships had to be postponed to provide the steel for these shelters. Because I was not sufficiently confident of the state of my information, I said almost nothing at the meeting, and afterwards walked across to his office with Lindemann. He obviously felt that he had done much better than the last time, and commented to me, 'You didn't have it all your way this time!'

The experience brought home to me what my real strength had been at the earlier meetings. It was that, in contrast to everyone else sitting round the Cabinet table, I had done all my own work for myself, and had forged out every link in the chain of evidence, so that I knew exactly what its strength was. Everyone else, in their more elevated positions, had had to depend on work done for them by their staffs, frequently only to be briefed at the last moment, as I myself had had to be on this occasion. And even with Charles Frank's understanding and skill, and even though I had been away from the work for only a week, I felt that there was too much sloppiness in my knowledge for me to pronounce positively on the various possibilities. On a previous occasion I had quoted Palmerston's statement of 1838 to Queen Victoria, and now I even more appreciated its force:

In England, the Ministers who are at the heads of the several departments of the State are liable any day and every day to defend themselves in Parliament; in order to do this they must be minutely acquainted with all the details of the business of their offices, and the only way of being constantly armed with such information is to conduct and direct those details themselves.

The following day I went back with Hugh Smith to Gloucestershire for a further few days; but I shot no more hares: while I was in London the vital strip of stubble had been ploughed up, and I could no longer predict the paths of the hares.

In the meantime I enquired about the source of the extraordinary Wachtel report, but all that I could learn at that time was that it came from 'Une jeune fille la plus remarquable de sa generation' who spoke five languages, and it has stayed in my memory throughout the intervening years. Some twenty years after I received the report I happened to meet Kenneth Cohen who told me that he was giving a reception that evening for Marie-Madeleine, and he invited me to meet her. I of course asked her if she could remember the report and its author; she at once replied positively and added that 'la jeune fille' was now la Vicomtesse de Clarens. When in 1973 Marie-Madeleine published her *Noah's Ark*, I searched it for details. Our source's maiden name was Jeannie Rousseau: strictly she was not one of the Alliance network where all the members were known by animal names (hence 'Noah's Ark') but of a smaller network known as the 'Druides', and her code name was Amniarix. At the time she sent in the Wachtel report she was 23 years old.

Shortly before D-Day it was planned to evacuate her and two other agents, Yves le Bitoux and Raymond Pezet, to England by sea, taking with them a large number of reports. They were to go to the small town of Treguier in Britanny but when, shortly after D-Day, they arrived there they found that the man who was to have guided them through the minefields had been arrested the day before. His house was full of troops, the town was encircled, and Amniarix and her companions were trapped. She was the first to be caught, and the Gestapo made her walk back with them to the car where two of the others were waiting, but even in her dire situation she succeeded in warning them by talking so loudly in German to her captors that the others had a chance to escape. Pezet got away: le Bitoux, since Treguier was his own town and might therefore be savaged by the Gestapo if he were to escape, allowed himself to be captured. He and Amniarix and two further companions were taken away to face imprisonment and perhaps worse in concentration camps, where le Bitoux and one of the others died.

Well, I now knew from Marie-Madeleine that Amniarix had survived the war but I hesitated to find her, because the revival of wartime experiences might have been distressing. But in 1976 the opportunity arose for us to meet for a Yorkshire Television programme, and so I

learned more of her story. In June 1940 she was in Dinard, the Headquarters of von Reichenau's Army Group for the invasion of England.
With her extraordinary gift for languages she was asked by the Mayor
of Dinard to act as interpreter in transactions with the Germans, and she
began to report what she saw and heard. This led to her being arrested
by the Gestapo in 1941, but there was insufficient proof for them to do
more than to prohibit her from staying in the coastal area. Back in
Paris she looked for a suitable 'cover' activity and joined an organization
entrusted by French industrialists with working out their problems with
the occupying forces. She was approached by Georges Lamarque, a
former university friend, who had set up an espionage unit known as
the 'Druides', he himself being the agent 'Petrel' in Marie-Madeleine's
'Noah's Ark'. He was a mathematician and statistician, and a man of the
Left who was in the end summarily shot by the Germans after he had
given himself up in order to save the village from which they had
detected his radio transmissions. 'No flourish of trumpets', writes
Amniarix '—the way he would have wanted it'. He had been a brilliant
intelligence organizer, and it was he who had forwarded her secret
weapon report.

Her work for the French industrialists had brought her in 1943 into
contact with a new German organization that was requiring work to be
done for a secret programme, and Amniarix recognized one of the
officers that she had encountered in 1940, now with a much higher
status. She succeeded in teasing him to boast about the new 'wonder
weapon' and in being engaged as an interpreter for the purchasing
commissions for contracts connected with the new organization, which
proved to be Wachtel's Regiment. Her report was the result.

As we shall see, Amniarix was to provide further information about
Wachtel, but we had first to clear our own minds concerning the nature
of the weapon he was to operate. Here our best clue came from an
Enigma message sent on 7th September, of which the most significant
part read:

(1) Luftflotte 3 again requests the immediate bringing up of Flak
forces to protect ground organization Flak Zielgerät 76. The urgency
of this is emphasized by the following facts:

(a) According to report of C. in C. West, Abwehr Station France
reports the capture of an enemy agent who had the task of establishing at all costs the position of new German rocket weapon. The
English, it is stated, have information that the weapon is to be

employed in the near future and they intend to attack the positions before this occurs.

I did not at first know quite how to interpret it, but its full significance struck me when Portal himself telephoned me personally and asked me what I made of it. Something he said made me realize that it was referring to the pilotless aircraft; and as I came off the telephone I said to Charles Frank 'C.A.S. is damned good—he was quicker than I was at seeing what that message was about!' Convinced now that we had unshakeable evidence about the pilotless aircraft, my first step was to see Cherwell because this would clearly 'let him off the hook' for any blunders he might have made about the rocket. His prediction that there would be a pilotless aircraft was completely fulfilled.

Much of my interpretation was based on the fact that 'Flak Zielgerät' would mean an anti-aircraft target apparatus, and we had in fact evolved our own 'Queen Bee' remote controlled aeroplane for use as an anti-aircraft target in the years before the war. To my astonishment Cherwell, instead of being grateful, at once disagreed with my interpretation, saying that he was well experienced in the use of German (which was undeniable) and that what was meant was an 'anti-aircraft *aiming* apparatus', in other words a predictor. He said that clearly the Germans were bringing in an important new predictor. I was in no position to argue with his German, and I could only point out that it was a very strange predictor that would require so many guns to protect it. I thought at the time, and I still believe it, that he was by now so concerned with the offensive that he subconsciously rejected any interpretation that might throw us back on the defensive, even at the expense of denying his own vindication by the appearance of the pilotless aircraft. On 14th September I issued a special note, concluding that

> The Germans are installing, under the cover name of FZG 76, a large and important ground organization in Belgium–N. France which is probably concerned with directing an attack on England by rocket-driven pilotless aircraft.

I also warned that in view of Lindemann's continued opposition to the rockets:

> There have been good reports from agents both of the development of the long range rocket, and of the rocket-driven pilotless aircraft; sometimes both have been mentioned in the same report. The messages under discussion appear to confirm the fairly imminent use

of the pilotless aircraft, but do not reflect on the question of the long range rocket except that they add credibility to it in those reports, manifestly competent, which state the existence of both weapons.

After my note, Portal congratulated me on the amount that I had been able to deduce from the message: when I told him that he himself had done it, he was surprised—it turned out that I had misunderstood him on the telephone and that he had not seen the interpretation of Flak Zielgerät as a pilotless aircraft.

We immediately increased the keenness of our search for the FZG 76 sites, and during the next few weeks reports began to come in from agents in North France about various emplacements that were being constructed ten to twenty miles inland, and which were said to be for long-range guns or rockets.

In London the situation was now somewhat eased by Duncan Sandys' proposal to the Chiefs of Staff that pilotless aircraft should be handled not by him but by normal Air Staff channels; but the arguments concerning the rocket still went on. Lindemann did so well with his scepticism that special meetings had to be held between him and the other scientists on whether it was possible to make a rocket with a range of 130 miles. When we heard of the argument, Charles Frank and I adopted the commonsense approach of asking how great a velocity was required in the rocket, to see whether any known fuels contained this amount of energy and sufficiently more to propel the carcase of the rocket to the required range. This was simply a matter of consulting the available physical and chemical tables, and it was clear that there were many combinations of fuel which would be suitable using liquid oxygen or nitric acid as one constituent and an organic fuel such as petrol or alcohol as the other. Therefore, in principle, the rocket could be made. We then stayed on the sidelines while Lindemann and the others argued. The episode is well described by David Irving in *The Mare's Nest*. The argument seemed to us so trivial that we thought ourselves well out of it. Actually, Lindemann almost won it so long as our experts could only think of cordite. But one British engineer, Mr. Isaac Lubbock, had just made successful experiments on a small scale with a rocket that would use petrol and oxygen derived from a liquid oxygen supply, and Goddard in America had been using liquid oxygen for some years. When Lubbock was at last brought in to the argument, our other experts realized that progress with liquid-fuel rockets might make the long-range rocket feasible. I can remember at one meeting Sir Robert

Robinson saying, 'Ah, Yes, liquid fuel!' and several others taking up the chorus as though the realization that the fuel could be liquid instead of solid completely exonerated them from their previous failure to refute Lindemann.

On 25th October, Churchill held another of his evening meetings. Again the arguments came up, Lindemann still expressing strong opposition, even to the extent of saying that the rocket was a mare's nest. Again Churchill asked me for my opinion in view of the latest evidence from our experts regarding liquid fuels. I could not help telling him that what really mattered was not the experts' opinions, but what the Germans were really doing. And that just because our experts had now thought of liquid fuels, there was no cause to assume that the rocket was either more or less imminent than it was before the argument had started: and the fact that they had 'learnt about two rare chemicals, to wit nitric acid and aniline, was no cause for panic.'

'Panic!' exploded Churchill, 'who's panicking?'

'It seems to me, Sir', I replied, 'that some of us around this table are getting pretty near it.'

Lindemann chuckled.

In any event, the Committee had before it a recent statement of my views, made on 25th September and circulated as a Chiefs of Staff paper, regarding the reality of both the rocket and the pilotless aircraft threats. After reviewing all the evidence, old and new, I had concluded:

Much information has been collected. Allowing for the inaccuracies which often occur in individual accounts, they form a coherent picture which, despite the bewildering effect of propaganda, has but one explanation: the Germans have been conducting an extensive research into long range rockets at Peenemünde. Their experiments have naturally encountered difficulties which may still be holding up production, although Hitler would press the rockets into service at the earliest possible moment; that moment is probably still some months ahead. It would be unfortunate if, because our sources had given us a longer warning than was at first appreciated, we should at this stage discredit their account.

There are obvious technical objections which, based on our own experience, can be raised against the prospect of successful rockets, but it is not without precedent for the Germans to have succeeded while we doubted: the beams are a sufficient example.

It is probable that the German Air Force has been developing a pilotless aircraft for long range bombardment in competition with the rocket, and it is very possible that the aircraft will arrive first.

Finally, Churchill turned to Field Marshal Smuts, who was attending as a member of the War Cabinet. 'Now, Field Marshal', said Churchill, 'you have heard the arguments. Tell us what you think!' Discussions round Churchill's table were usually conducted in a respectful tone, with everyone quiet except for the speaker at the time, but the silence seemed intensified in the second or two before Smuts spoke, as though the whole War Cabinet and the Chiefs of Staff were sitting at his feet. Smuts' comment was, 'Well, the evidence may not be conclusive, but I think a jury would convict!'

There were still further arguments after the meeting between Lindemann and the experts, and he even got them to go so far as to say that even if a rocket was possible the difficulties were so formidable that the Germans might not have attempted to overcome them. Finally Stafford Cripps was charged by Churchill to conduct an enquiry to establish the reality of the rocket threat. Cripps called me to his flat in Whitehall Court, and I was empowered to show him the full nature of my evidence, which now included a direct light on the progress of the pilotless aircraft itself.

I had set a watch six months before on two companies of the Air Signals Experimental Regiment, the 14th and 15th. If they were called in to plot the trajectory of a long-range missile by radar, we should hear of it irrespective of the nature of the missile—it would be equally valid against the rocket or the pilotless aircraft. During the autumn we found 14th Company on the Baltic coast, where it had strung out detachments, including one on the Greifswalder Oie, a small island just north of Peenemünde. To our delight, the detachments began to transmit ranges and bearings on a moving object, using exactly the same type of letter-for-figure code that we had encountered in 1941 with the German radar stations in north France. It did not take us long to sort everything out. Starting with the station on Greifswalder Oie, the ranges and bearings made sense of something that was taking off from Peenemünde, and was proceeding with a speed around 400 m.p.h. in an east-north-easterly direction. As it ran out of range of the Greifswalder Oie station it was picked up by one further along the coast and it was not difficult for us to locate this from the ranges and bearings it gave on the track that we had already established. We could locate the successive radar stations as each plotted a part of the track in turn. The stations were usually alerted before a firing took place, and there were security slips such as a reference to 'FZG 76' and so there was no doubt about what they were plotting. It was a great moment, for my very long shot had landed us in a ringside seat at all the trials of the flying bomb.

At the same time, many reports were coming in of new German constructions near the Channel coast. Were they the catapults of which Amniarix and others had told us? And were they for rockets or pilotless aircraft? On 28th October a fuller report came in which said that important work was proceeding at Bois Carré near Yvrench, and that a rough plan made by a workman showed 'a concrete platform with centre axis pointing directly to London'. It described the construction of various buildings on the site, including one which contained no metal parts; subsequent reports modified this to no magnetic parts. The information was confirmed by photographic sortie E/463 of 3rd November, which showed that the most prominent features were ski-shaped buildings 240–270 feet long, from which the sites were promptly named. If the non-magnetic hut story were true, this would indicate some kind of magnetic directional control in the missile. And I can remember Sandy Menzies pointing out to us that if he had to choose between the rocket and the pilotless aircraft, he would opt for the latter, since the entrance to the non-magnetic hut was a low, wide arch, which suggested that something with wings had to be wheeled through it. Medmenham was making a model of the Bois Carré site, but the interpreters there obviously thought that it was intended for a rocket, because they added a model rocket to their site, and we had to convince them that it was too long to be pushed round the curves at the end of the skis, where we assumed that the bodies of the missiles were stored, before they would give up the rocket hypothesis.

Personally I hoped to prove beyond any argument that the ski sites were for the FZG 76 by taking photographs of Zempin, about 15 kilometres south eastwards along the coast from Peenemünde, where Colonel Wachtel, so Jeannie Rousseau had told us, had one of his headquarters; and indeed we had now found radar tracks emanating from Zempin as well as Peenemünde. I therefore ordered a sortie, to cover both places; I even specified the optimum timing, since we were beginning to see the daily pattern of firing and, if lucky, we might catch an FZG 76 on its launching catapult. There was so much general activity at Peenemünde that it was not easy to be sure which elements were concerned with the pilotless aircraft, but at Zempin we hoped to have the aircraft and its servicing installations isolated, and we hoped

that these would be similar to those we were now beginning to recognize
on the ski sites. Unfortunately there was a delay of about three weeks in
getting the photographs because of persistent bad weather.

Obviously the ski sites had to be knocked out, if possible, whatever
their purpose, and so the question arose of how much bombing effort
was necessary. Sandy Menzies telephoned me with the result of his
operational research. A decision to bomb or not came down to one
simple question: the walls of the buildings on the ski sites were about
80 centimetres in thickness (actually 75 centimetres) and it was not clear
from the air photographs whether they were of reinforced concrete or
prefabricated concrete blocks. If the former, then little less than bombs
of two thousand pounds would do sufficient damage. If the latter, five
hundred pound bombs would suffice. There would thus be a factor of
four between the bomb loads required for the one possibility or the
other; with the smaller loads a bombing campaign would be feasible;
but if the heavier loads were required, the bombing effort would be
prohibitive. So could I find out how the walls were constructed? I put
the question to our Swiss station, which had provided some of the best
information from the French Resistance so far about the ski sites. The
information was back within a very few days that the walls were of
prefabricated concrete blocks, and so the bombing attack was 'on'. A
package of plans on tracing paper arrived on my desk, seemingly in
answer to my question, but they must have been already on their way.
As I heard the story at the time, two separate agents went out to answer
my question. One dressed up as a workman and surveyed the site,
while the other thought it simpler to steal the contractor's plans.

Quite possibly both stories refer to, if not the same man, at least a
single organization. Its head was Michel Hollard, whose story has
been told by George Martelli in *Agent Extraordinary*. Hollard had run
away from home to join the French Army as a boy of sixteen in the
First World War, and had won the Croix de Guerre. His father was a
distinguished scientist and he himself qualified as an engineer in the
years after the war. He was 41 years old when the Second War broke
out, and his feelings after the French capitulation were so strong that
he finally crossed into Switzerland to make contact with our Embassy
to offer his services in any capacity in which he could help. He was
subsequently to make another 48 unofficial crossings of the border. He
set up a small network which survived where others were caught,
because he used no radio. One of his contacts was a young, freshly
qualified, engineer called André Comps. Hollard himself had already

heard of the ski-site activity; and when he discovered one at Bonnetot le
Faubourg he made a personal reconnaissance, managing to penetrate
the site by collecting a wheelbarrow that he spotted in the ditch outside
it, and wheeling it in as though he were a workman. He noticed the
intended line of something that was probably a launching catapult, and
he was the kind of man who always carried a pocket compass. When he
worked out the alignment of the catapult later that evening, it pointed
in the direction of London. It had been his report that alerted us
specifically about the ski sites, and now he was to resolve our question
of the construction. He enlisted André Comps, and persuaded him to
volunteer for a job with the Germans as a draughtsman. Comps got
the job, and succeeded in copying the plans of every building at the
Bois Carré site, including the general outline of the base and rails of the
launching catapult. This last plan he had to copy from the original that
he had to remove temporarily from the coat of the German engineer
supervising the construction. The plan of the non-magnetic hut is
shown at Figure 21, while the general plan of the site is at Figure 20.
Comparison with the air photograph in Plate 21(b) will show how accu-

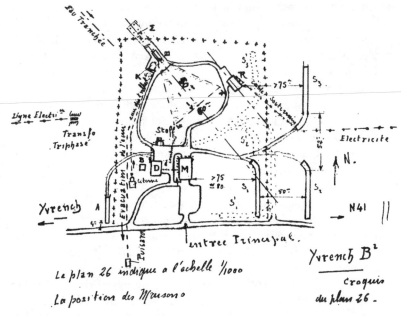

Fig. 20. Drawing of V-1 launching ('ski') site at Bois Carré near Yvrench (note the
'B²'). Comparison with Plate 21 will show the accurate draftsmanship

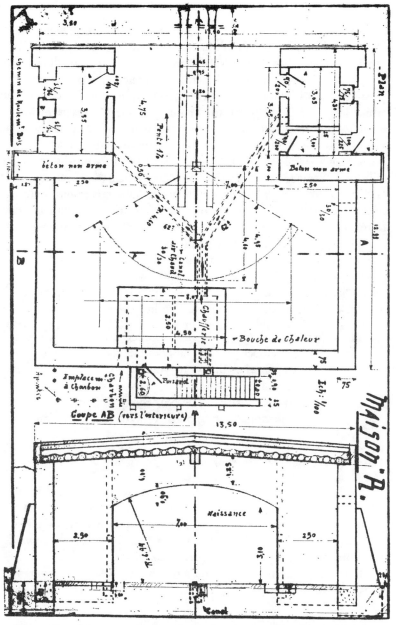

Fig. 21. One of the contractor's plans of a V-1 launching site obtained by André Comps and Michel Hollard, October 1943. This is of the 'square building' or 'R house' (Figure 20) which was reported to have no iron in its construction and in which the flying bomb was to have its compass set before going to the launching catapult. The broad arched entrance was a clue that the missile had wings, and the arc inscribed on the floor suggested that the missile was to be 'swung' to test its compass

rate it was. It was a brilliant piece of espionage, complementing what Hollard had already done for us. It also contained a neat element of humour, for it described the site as 'B²' as may be seen if 'B' is an abbreviation for 'Bois' and it is remembered that 'x²' in French is called 'x carré'.

As for Hollard himself, he went on working until he was finally arrested by the Gestapo on 5th February 1944. He was atrociously tortured by the Gestapo, including the bath treatment where the victim was submerged in a bath of cold water and violently beaten every time he put his head above the surface, so that he nearly drowned, only to be revived and have the treatment started all over again. The Gestapo failed to break him even after five or more repetitions, and they finally sent him to a concentration camp. He was one of those both fortunate and strong enough to survive, and I was to have the pleasure of providing the detail for the citation for his D.S.O.

It will have been obvious from this chapter that the French Resistance played a great part. Typical of their gallantry was that of one of Hollard's men, Olivier Giran, who was caught in 1943. Only 21, he was executed on 16th April. On 12th April he wrote to his parents:

I am condemned to death. . . . In all I write there are only two things I want you to remember: my eternal gratitude for a life of such great and constant happiness, as thanks to you two, I have had; and the strength of my love for you.

I won't say any more on that. There are things so great, so beautiful, so sacred, that one would only spoil them by trying to express them in words.

And as the executioners came for him four days later:

Among men I did what I thought was my duty—but I did it with joy in my heart. It was war, and I fell, as others did, and as many more must do. . . . I saw them on the Marne, buried in long rows. Now it is my turn—that is all. . . . Yes France will live. Men are cowards traitors, rotters. But France is pure, clean, vital.

I am happy. I am not dying for any faction or man, I am dying for my own idea of serving her, my country . . . and for you too whom I adore.

I am happy I love you. The door is opening.

Adieu.

He died giving the ageless call 'Vive la France!

There were many like Olivier Giran. Commandant Leon Faye, Marie-Madeleine's second-in-command, was another. Hidden in his cell after his death they found his last message to his colleagues in 'The Alliance',

> . . . I ask you to serve our unhappy country so that it may enjoy peace again and happiness, songs, flowers, and flower-covered inns. Close the prisons. Drive out the executioners. . . . Like many other countries France will have to tend, cleanse and heal cruel wounds and rebuild vast numbers of ruined places. But she is the only one whose moral unity was broken. Pulled and torn in all directions, she is a dyke bursting under the weight of water. That is the most serious and urgent task. Everything must be done to get out of this impasse. Later, historians will judge. For the moment the important thing is union and not reprisal, work and not chaos. Act to this end, my dear friends, that is my last wish. . . .

Faye had written this letter with his manacled hand on 14th July 1944.

While men like Giran and Faye, and women too, suffered torture and death for us alone among their perverted enemies, our squabbles in London went on. Some of these squabbles were both inevitable and fair, as when two of us found ourselves in posts with responsibilities which neither of us had framed but which had been drafted by others and which overlapped so that each of us thought certain tasks were his alone. But others were entirely avoidable; and I had hoped that now that the task of both rocket and flying bomb Intelligence had reverted to our normal organizations, the qualifications of my Unit to undertake it were clear. After all, it was I who had found the rocket and it was my 'long shot' that had given us the ringside seat at the flying bomb trials. But to my amazement the Air Staff stepped in, now that I had rescued them from an embarrassing position, and recalled from the Mediterranean Claude Pelly, an Air Commodore who was very pleasant to work with but who had no previous experience of Intelligence, to co-ordinate Intelligence and to direct countermeasures. And the Joint Intelligence Committee, whose record had been singularly undistinguished even to the extent of being far later than Churchill himself in recognizing the German intention to attack Russia, then stepped in to back Pelly up with an Inter-Service Committee. Their idea was that I should provide the Committee with the raw information, which it would then assess

13

and make into Intelligence appreciations. It was to meet every after-noon; and had I attended it, half of every working day would have been lost. I at once wrote to the Chairman of the J.I.C.:

It has been my duty since the beginning of the war to anticipate new applications of science to warfare by the enemy, and so to forestall new weapons and methods. Pilotless aircraft and Long Range Rockets are two such weapons which I have watched over the whole period. Unless I have failed in that duty, there can be little case for a Commit-tee covering much the same work and whose Chairman had had no experience of the type of problem. It is doubtful whether a Committee is needed at all, since problems such as scale of employment, deploy-ment, and places of production, are generally quickly solved once the technical nature of the weapon is fully understood, so that the main responsibility lies on those investigating the basic scientific and technical facts.

The establishment of a Committee to perform a function which I believe to be largely my own is therefore contrary to the way in which I have worked best in the past, and indicates a lack of confidence in my methods which—if I shared—would lead me to resign. More-over, since experience leads me to appreciate the Prime Minister's remarks about the possible otioseness of Committees, my section will continue its work regardless of any parallel Committees which may arise and will be mindful only of the safety of the country. I trust that we shall not be hindered.

If that sounded arrogant, it was simply because I knew that my Unit was far better able than any other group of individuals to deal with the problems that faced us, and I proposed to go on despite any arrangements made by those who knew far less about it. The situation was far too serious for any attempt at false modesty, and I would have gone at once to Churchill had anyone got in our way. More than anyone else, I knew what devotion was being offered by so many of our sources; and I was going to see that their sacrifices were turned to as good advantage as possible. This was the only way in which we could keep faith with them. Obviously I had no monopoly in my feelings towards them, but perhaps I felt more strongly because I had closer contacts with them than most others. For this privilege I shall be ever grateful.

A few days after my note to the Chairman of the J.I.C., who made no reply, I went down with tonsilitis and influenza. My temperature at breakfast, as I took it myself, was 108°F; by the time the doctor had arrived it was down to 105°. He prescribed opium and aspirin, and in the course of a day it fell off the bottom of the scale to, as far as I could estimate it, 92°F. The doctor forbade me to return to the office until my temperature was normal; but I had to disobey him after a fortnight, telling him that it only mattered whether I could last for six to eight months, after that I would not be so essential. I had in mind both D-Day and the onset of the German retaliation campaign.

While I was in bed, the weather at last became favourable for the sortie that I had requested over Zempin and Peenemünde. It was made on 28th November by John Merifield, who had flown me in his Mosquito at Dyce. Charles Frank brought the photographs out to me at Richmond. They showed the same buildings at Zempin as we had seen on the ski sites, giving the final proof that these were intended for the FZG 76. They also showed the catapult at Zempin: and once we had seen its shape (none so far had been installed on the ski sites) it was a simple matter to recognize the catapults among the many structures at Peenemünde—they were the erections that had been famously mis-interpreted as 'sludge pumps'! Moreover, on one of the catapults we had caught a flying bomb in position, just as I had hoped when I specified the optimum time of day for the sortie to be flown (Plate 21 (c)).

It is against this background that other accounts of the discovery of the V-1 should be read. All credit to a photographic interpreter who, not knowing the story leading up to the sortie, then found the V-1 and thought that the discovery was accidental; but in reality it was no accident. Where Medmenham may have been somewhat misled was that since the sortie was being flown at my request, and my interests were known previously to have been associated with radar stations such as Bruneval, the purpose of the sortie had been entered as a reconnaissance for radar stations. It was true that we were after the radar plotting stations as well, to locate them exactly, but our primary purpose had been to find the Zempin and Peenemünde V-1 installations.

I was now able to compile a fairly comprehensive report, which I circulated on 23rd December 1943. We could be positive, for example, that the whole V-1 programme had been hastily conceived, probably by the Luftwaffe in rivalry with the German Army which was developing the A4 rocket. In December the accuracy and reliability of the missiles were still so poor that if they had been launched from the ski sites, only one in six would have hit London. We could show this dramatically with our plots of the Germans' own radar tracks of their trial firings (Figure 22). Clearly the weapon was not yet ready, technical troubles were holding it up, despite the fact that Hitler wanted to open the retaliation campaign at the earliest possible moment, and I saw in the movement of the German bomber force to the West an indication that a substitute attack was being mounted:

> A pointer which may show that all is perhaps not well with the pilotless aircraft programme is the recent concentration of the German bomber force in the West, with the formation of a Pathfinder group. The Germans thus appear to be trying to increase their normal bombing, which indicates that they may not rely entirely on the pilotless aircraft.

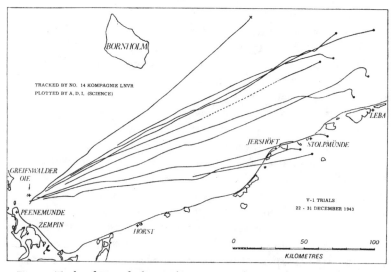

Fig. 22. Tracks of V-1s fired in trials at Peenemünde, December 1943. The crosses mark the positions of the radar plotting stations. By intercepting their plots, British Intelligence gained a 'ringside seat' at the trials, and so were able to assess the V-1 threat continuously. Note how scattered and inaccurate, at this stage, the missiles were

The attack thus foreshadowed started on 21st January 1944. Again there was the timely warning that I had promised in 1941 and 1942.

My report dealt in detail with every phase of the flying bomb problem from technical details to Wachtel's organization and deployment, to the manufacturing arrangements. Since we were getting from the Peenemünde trials not only the speeds and points of impact of the flying bombs, but also their heights and intended aiming points, the latter being frequently given to the plotting stations in advance, we could produce detailed figures for the expected performance of the bombs. I had let Cherwell have these figures beforehand, and he incorporated them in a note of 18th December to Churchill. We could get the approximate dimensions of the bomb from the Peenemünde photographs, and we could estimate the number of bombs to be stored in the skis. Making reasonable guesses about the time to service a bomb and its catapult, we could go on to estimate the intended rate of bombardment. The figures in my report may be compared with those that we established from German sources at the end of the war. On the technical side, the comparison is as follows:

	Estimate	*Fact*	*Remarks*
Type of Propulsion	Probably Rocket T & Z used somewhere.	Argus Tube	T- & Z-Stoffe used for starting.
Weight of Warhead	1000–3000 lb.	2000 lb. (1,800 lb. H.E.)	Estimate later finalized at 1 ton.
Speed	Varying between 200 & 400 m.p.h.	Varying up to 400 m.p.h.	German intention 370 m.p.h.
Height	Generally about 6,500 feet, but sometimes as low as 1,500 feet.	1,000–4,000 ft.	
Range	Generally 120–140 miles. Maximum 155 miles.	Generally 120–140 miles. Maximum 155 miles.	
Wing Span	Probably 19–22 feet.	17 ft. 4½ ins.	
Length	Probably 17½–20 feet.	25 ft. 4½ ins.	
Root Chord	Probably 4–5½ feet.	4 feet.	
Control	Magnetic.	Magnetic.	

As regards the operational intentions, the ski sites were of course knocked out by our subsequent bombing; but I have the statement by Colonel Eberhardt, Wachtel's Chief Technical Officer, regarding what was intended, and the comparison is as follows:

	A.D.I. (Science)	Eberhardt
Capacity of site	20	20
Maximum rate of fire	1 in 30 mins.	1 in 30 mins.
Time to fire all stored missiles	10 hours	10 hours
Replenishment period	2 days	1½ days
Total number of sites operating in one attack	50–100	64

The biggest mistake in my estimates concerned the nature of the propulsion. I had thought that this would be a rocket, and we had no idea concerning the ingenious nature of the engine until the campaign started. It involved simply a tube supported above the body of the bomb, with a combustion chamber at the front end. Air entered through the series of slats which acted as valves at the very front of the tube, and these slats closed automatically when the fuel was exploded in the chamber. The exploding gas drove a pressure wave down the tube and emerged at the rear end, which was open. The over-shoot then caused a partial vacuum at the rear end of the tube, and this started a pulse of rarefaction which travelled back along the tube to the combustion chamber. The consequent lowering of pressure there caused the valves at the front to open and a new charge of air was sucked in, and the cycle started all over again. It was like a large organ pipe with a valve at the front end, emitting an enormous sound for which the energy was provided by the combustion of the fuel, and the forward drive came from the reaction as the hot gases were pulsed backwards out of the end of the pipe. The engine was developed at the Argus Works, which were mentioned in my report as one of the seats of production, but none of us had any idea that a completely new engine was involved. The idea itself was not new: it had been partly developed as early as 1929 by Paul Schmidt and it had been at first financed jointly by the Army Weapons Office and the Luftwaffe. After 1934 it had been taken over completely by the Luftwaffe: and intensive development in 1942 enabled it to power the Luftwaffe's upstart rival to the Army's A4 rocket.

I had expected the engine to be a pure rocket, driven by decomposing hydrogen peroxide; and I had been more than usually pleased with the way in which I had been able to reach this conclusion. Since it involves an important point of principle it is worth recounting. When I saw the plans obtained for us by Michel Hollard, there was one building that was labelled 'Stofflager' which may be interpreted as 'fuel store'. It was of unusual construction, since it contained two compartments, but there was no communicating door between them. Each compartment had its separate door to the outside; and although these doors were adjacent, they were carefully separated by a blast wall. I therefore deduced that two fuels were involved, and that someone had taken great care in the design that the two should not come into premature contact. I already knew of two liquids used by the Germans in the rocket-propelled glider bombs they had been using against our ships. These were hydrogen peroxide and sodium permanganate, and these were known to the Germans as 'T-Stoff' and 'Z-Stoff'. I therefore conjectured that the Stofflager was intended to hold supplies of hydrogen peroxide and sodium permanganate. Following the same line, I found that some of the very squads that had been handling these materials for KG100 had been drafted to Wachtel's organization. The case for believing that hydrogen peroxide and sodium permanganate were involved therefore appeared complete, as indeed it was. I worked out the volumes of the two compartments, and found that they were big enough to store enough of the chemicals to provide fuel for twenty flying bombs and give them the necessary 200 kilometres' range for London. Moreover, I searched the site for any other building that might store some other kind of fuel, and there was none.

In view of all this reasoning, it was undoubtedly the simplest hypothesis to assume that the flying bomb would be driven by a larger version of the hydrogen peroxide rocket that we had previously seen in the HS293 glider bomb. Although this was the simplest hypothesis consistent with the facts, it turned out to be wrong. The bombs were driven by the Argus engine, which used a simple fuel like paraffin, and they came up to the ski sites already fuelled from the base depots. Hydrogen peroxide was undoubtedly used, but the purpose was different. It provided the steam power for launching the bombs from their catapults—a variant of the old 'atmospheric railway' which was after the war adopted by the British and American Navies for launching aircraft from carriers.

What I had done, after congratulating myself on spotting a clue that nobody else had seen, was to employ the principle known as Occam's Razor: *essentia non sunt multiplicanda praeter necessitatem* (hypotheses are not to be multiplied without necessity). For if you start allowing more complicated hypotheses than are essential to explain the facts, you can launch yourself into a realm of fantasy where your consequent actions will become misdirected. As one of my academic colleagues once put it to his pupil: 'If I tell you that the explanation of why I never see a tiger when I open the door is that there really is a tiger outside but that the tiger is frightened of me, so that every time it hears me opening the door it runs away and hides round a corner, you would say that I was mad—or, at least, a little peculiar!' Time after time when I used Occam's Razor in Intelligence it gave me the right answer when others were indulging in flights of fancy leading towards panic. But every now and again it will be wrong, as it was on this one occasion in my experience. By accident you may just have collected a set of facts that can be explained by a simpler hypothesis than what is really occurring; the answer is never to be satisfied but always to search for fresh facts and be prepared to modify your hypothesis in the light of those facts. But in general Occam's Razor gives much the greatest chance of establishing the truth.

As it turned out, the mistake was of no consequence, for the operational deduction was that we should try to knock out German hydrogen peroxide production, and had we been successful in this, the V-1 campaign would have been paralysed because there would have been no way of launching the flying bombs.

The vital performance figures were correct, of course, and they provided all the information that would be needed for countermeasures. To intercept the flying bombs, the performance of our fighters would need to be increased. To engage the bombs our anti-aircraft guns would need new predictors and proximity fuses that would have to be set sensitively enough to work on the relatively small targets that the bombs themselves presented. And all this information was available six months before a flying bomb was launched against London.

Finally, despite the overwhelming preoccupation of the radar stations with plotting the flying bomb trials, my report warned that the rocket should not be forgotten, for the stations were trying to plot the rocket trials, too, although these were far less frequent.

Long after the war, one of the members of the Committee that the J.I.C. had set up, Matthew Pryor, most generously wrote (in *The Times*, 19th April 1961): 'The debt the country owes to Dr. Jones' brilliant, if rather lone-handed, Intelligence work cannot be over-estimated'.

But in reality I was far from alone: What could I have done without the devotion of men like Bimbo Norman and Claude Wavell to their respective tasks, the pilots like John Merifield, and the men and women in the field who faced torture like Christiansen, Hollard, Comps,

Marie-Madeleine and Jeannie Rousseau? Or without the backing of men like Hugh Smith and Charles Frank, who also stood ready to take over if I became a casualty? We were part of a great team in which we all knew our parts; from past experience we had confidence in one another, as for example between Peter and 'Pop' Stewart and me, to know that the best hope of solving the problem lay in our continuing to work together, whatever other arrangements might be imposed. If 'brilliant' is a fitting adjective, it applies to the whole team and I was merely that part which took the fewest physical risks and yet—as Churchill said of himself—had the luck to give the roar.

Just as my report was completed, the first active countermeasures—the bombing of the ski sites—started on a large scale on 21st December 1943. Here the American Eighth Army Air Force came fully to our aid, and on Christmas Eve put out its greatest effort ever—thirteen hundred aircraft dropping 1,700 tons of bombs. Wachtel decided that we knew too much about his organization, and tried to throw us off the scent. As I first heard the story, he aimed to suppress the name 'Flak Regiment 155(W)' and replace it by 'FlakGruppeCreil', pulling back his headquarters 100 kilometres southwards from Doullens to a château near Creil, about 45 kilometres north of Paris. To change his personal identity he dyed his hair, grew a beard, and changed his name to 'Max Wolf'. The whole move was carried out in secret, even to the extent of his entire headquarters staff driving into the back streets of a town and re-emerging on the other side in different uniforms and with different transport. In this it was reported to have been so successful that its laundry never again caught up with it. But we were quickly informed, because we received the following report, dated the end of December 1943:

Following numerous air reconnaissance flights and bombing, the H.Q. of the A.A. "WACHTEL" regiment was transferred from DOULLENS to a chateau in CREIL region, exactly 55 Km. from PARIS, and in the immediate vicinity of a small town indicated in German by the initials: "M.b.B." that is to say: "Ms.B." or "M.e.B" (MARCQ-en-BAROEIL?). The transfer was made under conditions of the utmost secrecy; the H.Q. Staff believe that the emplacement is still unknown as there has not yet been any reconnaissance from the air.

However, the unit keeps at DOULLENS an important relay-station called "Dohle" in telephone conversations; the "WACHTEL" regiment is called "Flakgruppe Creil" in the Army telephone organization. The totem of the regiment is:

Fig. 23. The symbol for Wachtel's Regiment that was never used

which is made from the C.O.'s name.

The full Staff is expected at H.Q. for the beginning of January; it comprises 20 officers. Colonel WACHTEL himself will not be in continual residence at his H.Q., for he goes on inspection missions in BELGIUM and also makes frequent journeys to PARIS, BERLIN, ZEMPIN, to supervise the finishing touches to the stratospheric rocket. It is reported that the platforms are ready and the personnel standing-by, but the guns will only be set up on their emplacement in March.

The officers of this unit expect a Commando raid or even a landing having for mission to prevent the use of this weapon. The CREIL H.Q. is said to be very strongly defended (electric network, constant patrolling, A.A. Defences always at the ready).

It is reported that GOERING's and even HITLER's visit is expected in the near future.

It might be possible for an interpreter in charge of the purchasing for the account of the unit, and acting as liaison with the French authorities, to gain access into the H.Q.

Who had written this report? Again it was one that I remembered long after the war because of the pun in the 'totem', since the German for one-eighth is an 'Achtel'. At a reunion in 1955 I met one of Wachtel's officers, and congratulated him on the regimental sense of humour in choosing such a sign for its escutcheon. He was astounded, and asked, 'However did you know that? We *were* going to use it, but we decided in the end that it was so obvious that it could not be used, and we were ordered not to mention it again!'

I could not tell him how we knew because I did not know—then. But after I met Amniarix I looked up the report again: it bore all the stamps of her marvellous handiwork and virtually identified her in the last sentence. She has confirmed that the report was hers, and also that she sent others which neither of us could identify. The puzzle is why she spoke of the 'stratospheric rocket' with such circumstantial detail in place of the flying bomb, because she was punctilious in reporting things exactly as she heard them, even when they made no sense to her. Watchtel and his officers could not mislead her when it came to organizational matters, but is it possible that they had hit on Cherwell's very plan of using the rocket as cover for what they were really doing? Be that as it may, Amniarix's reports stand brilliantly in the history of Intelligence; and three concentration camps, Ravensbrück, Königsberg (a punishment camp), and Torgau, could not break her.

CHAPTER FORTY

The Americans Convinced

THE AMERICAN commitment in Britain had been steadily growing during 1942 and 1943. Its impact on Intelligence was perhaps most directly felt in photographic reconnaissance, where an American unit was attached to R.A.F. Benson, and where American pilots in P38s (Lightnings) were now flying regularly. For some reason that we never discovered their casualties were substantially higher than our own pilots flying Spitfires. I thought that this must be due to a difference in speeds but this turned out not to be so. I remember the episode particularly because it brought me into warm contact with the American Commanding Officer, Colonel Hall, a quiet friendly airman who won my respect by flying the first American photographic sortie himself, exemplifying Xenophon's dictum: 'there is small risk a general will be regarded with contempt by those he leads if, whatever he may have to preach, he shows himself best able to perform'.

In the radio war, American participation was less direct, for it concentrated on the countermeasures side and left the Intelligence to us. In fact one American Naval Intelligence Officer, Commander Kearley, not only told me that he intended to depend entirely on us, but asked me to put a legend at the head of all our reports stating, 'This Report is not to be reproduced except in entirety'. He was particularly concerned with radar Intelligence leading up to the landing in Normandy, and I was looking forward to a warm post-war friendship. But, in the same mould as Tony Hill, he felt that he ought to go on the D-Day landings and he was among the many who died on Omaha beach.

On the countermeasures side, an officer of the United States Navy, generally Captain (later Admiral) Solberg or his Deputy, Commander C. G. Mayer, regularly attended meetings of the Radio Countermeasures Board right through 1942 and 1943: and, following a visit to Britain by Dr. C. G. Suits, afterwards Director of the General Electric Company's Laboratories at Schenectady, a strong team of American scientists and electronic engineers was attached to the Telecommunications Research

Establishment at Malvern. The first Head of the team was Dr. V. H. Fraenkel, who then went on to General Spaatz's Staff and was succeeded by John N. Dyer. As the U.S. Eighth Army Air Force grew in strength it became of course acutely interested in what we knew about German radar, and we found that the rivalry between the U.S. Army and the U.S. Navy was even greater than that which we had sometimes experienced between our own Services. Fortunately, there was a freemasonry among scientists that usually enabled us to sort any problems out.

Besides our co-operation in scientific and technical matters, where the superiority of American production engineering was often a powerful—even vital—aid, we also shared our experiences in Operational Research. One salutary incident that I recall concerned a British mathematical physicist and an American theoretical physicist, Dr. Charles Kittel, who had been set together, side by side, to work on the problem of deducing the characteristics of German magnetic mines laid at sea, especially the sensitivity and polarity of the firing mechanism. The data from which the characteristics were to be deduced were the reports of our minesweepers as they exploded the mines, with the positions of the explosions being reported as ranges and bearings from the minesweepers. The first thing that Kittel wanted to do was to take a few trips on a minesweeper to sample the data for himself. The British theorist refused to do this, on the argument that he could only make a few trips, and therefore any experience so gained might be heavily biased, and therefore much too dangerous as a basis for generalization. So he stuck to his desk while Kittel went out minesweeping. What Kittel immediately found was that the reports from the minesweeping crews were wildly inaccurate as regards both range and bearing, and the only item of data on which one could rely was whether the mine had exploded to port or starboard. Simplifying all the later reports down to this extremely limited observation, he nevertheless succeeded in deducing the answer; but the British theorist went on accepting the data as accurate and never reached an answer.

The incident shows the importance of personal reconnaissance before taking a decision. Kittel had exemplified exactly what Isaac Newton had said in a letter to Nathaniel Hawes:

> If, instead of sending the observations of able seamen to able mathematicians on land, the land would send able mathematicians to sea, it would signify much more to the improvement of navigation and the safety of men's lives and estates on that element.

Although we were closely co-ordinated with the American forces as regards offensive steps against Germany, we had so far entirely looked after ourselves as regards German attacks on Britain, the famous 'Eagle Squadron' of American volunteers excepted. The threat of flying bombs, however, was clearly going to stretch us to the limit. Already the Eighth Air Force was attacking the ski sites but, assuming that the Germans would somehow get to the stage of launching large number of bombs, we had very few fighters that were fast enough to intercept them and they would be very awkward targets for our anti-aircraft guns. As regards fighters, it was mainly a question of 'hotting up' our existing aircraft and of speeding new aircraft, such as the Tempest, into service; this task fell to the Fighter Interception Unit, now commanded by Christopher Hartley.

Along with the guns, we should need new predictors and the new proximity fuses which, although originally a British project, had been developed and were being manufactured in America. Given this need, and the large-scale diversion of bombing effort that would be necessary against the ski sites and which therefore might detract from our joint bombing of invasion targets, the British Chiefs of Staff felt that we must ask for the aid and understanding of the Americans. On 20th December 1943, the problem was discussed at the Joint Chiefs of Staff in Washington, which had before them an appreciation from the U.S. Air Force that the United Kingdom might be devastated.

Opinions in Washington ranged from a wild over-assessment of the threat to the opposite belief that it was all a hoax by the Germans to divert our effort away from our intended landings in France. The first I knew of the difficulty was when Portal telephoned me to say he wanted me to show all my work to an American who would be sent over to assess it, and then advise the American Chiefs of Staff whether they should help us or not. I was annoyed, because I knew that our work was solid, and required no checking by any stranger especially since it involved revealing all our Intelligence methods. I told Portal that I would only do it if he would confirm that he was giving me a direct order, so that the responsibility would be his. This he immediately did, so we prepared ourselves for the coming of the American, whoever he might be.

The day of the American inspection duly came, some time in January 1944, and to our surprise a quiet, rather bulky man walked in and explained that he was H. P. Robertson, Professor of Applied Mathematics at Princeton. What he did not say was that, as we afterwards discovered, he was one of the world's leading theorists on Relativity, and one of the most senior staff members in the Office of Scientific Research and Development in Washington. It was clear, though, that here was someone to whom we could talk, and the morning went very well. We took him across to St. Ermin's Hotel and we were just settling back after lunch when 'Jane' Shaw came in, obviously fortified by a thunderstorm of his 'lightning snifters'. He did not know that we were the subject of an American inspection, and I was rather worried that his deportment might upset Robertson's impression of our efficiency.

It turned out that 'Jane' was determined to tell us a story of his career which had been sandwiched between his cavalry and his Air Force days. It was no use trying to stop him. He just went on: the incident concerned his earliest days in Salisbury[1], when he had been invited to a party and had got on with a girl there so successfully that he went home and spent the night with her. A week or so later he was in one of the Salisbury bars drinking with another man when he thought that he would improve his general knowledge and find out more about the girl. Gradually he worked the conversation round, and finally said what an attractive girl she was. 'Yes', said his companion, 'what a pity about her leg!' 'What's wrong with her leg?' asked 'Jane'. 'Didn't you know, old man, that she's got a wooden leg?' replied the other. 'Jane' was thunderstruck and said 'A wooden leg! She hasn't, damn it I ought to . . .' and pulled himself up, but it was too late. He said that for months afterwards whenever he went into a bar in Salisbury someone would come up to him, pluck at his thigh and say 'Excuse me, old man, a splinter!'

We must have had a Guardian Angel watching over us, but who delighted in teasing us. First he had sent Maggie Blyth as a *dea ex machina* when Tizard was inspecting us, and now he had sent 'Jane' Shaw in a similar capacity. For 'Jane's' story was exactly to Bob Robertson's taste. Signals went back to the American Chiefs of Staff saying that the British work on the flying bomb was entirely reliable, and that the Americans should give us all the aid within their power.

One point of special American concern was the timing of the flying bomb campaign and its likely targets. Would the bomb be ready before D-Day, and could it knock out our embarkation ports? Charles Frank prepared a report for S.H.A.E.F. (Supreme Headquarters, Allied Expeditionary Force) showing that the only worthwhile target, given the inaccuracy of the weapon, was London. As for timing, he and I reckoned that our bombing could probably postpone the opening of the

[1] Rhodesia, where he had gone as a tobacco planter.

campaign for some months, and that it would also take this time for the Germans to improve their accuracy in trials to an acceptable level. We might therefore be able to land in Normandy before the first bomb was launched, but we thought that the landing would provoke Hitler into ordering the pilotless bombardment forthwith, whatever the state of the trials. And since we reckoned that a military machine of the scale of Flak Regiment 155 (W) would have a reaction time of about a week, we suggested Day (D+7) as the best guess for the opening of the bombardment.

CHAPTER FORTY-ONE

'Flames': Problems Of Bomber Command

As soon as I returned from leave in September 1943 I went again to listen to the reactions of the German nightfighters and their ground controls. They had clearly reorganized, but on 29th/30th September we heard how they could now confuse themselves; the raid was on Bochum in the Ruhr and the German controller was broadcasting a running commentary on our route to his fighters. For some reason or other he convinced himself that the raid was instead to be on Bremen, and on 4th October I reported:

The present German system is unstable in that once the controller has formed a picture of the situation it becomes increasingly easy for him to convince himself that he is right. Having made his guess at the target from the early track of the bombers, he sends his fighters to a convenient beacon. These fighters are then reported by sound observations and, unless the observers are extremely skilled, they may easily be misidentified. The controller then interprets the observations as referring to British aircraft, and is thus confirmed in his initial misjudgement, and so may order up more fighters which may again be misidentified. At Bremen the self-deception went even further; the Flak opened fire, possibly delighted by the absence of Window, and at least one fighter dropped a flare presumably to illuminate our bombers which were in fact at Bochum, 150 miles away. The flare probably convinced the JD 2 controller that the Pathfinders had arrived for even when JD 1 announced that bombs were falling at Bochum, JD 2 countermanded the JD 1 order for the fighters to concentrate on Bochum.

So far the improvised system has worked fairly well on clear nights and against large raids, but the 250–350 aircraft raids of the last few days have shown that it has a very serious weakness. There is much to be said for raids of not more than 20 minutes duration, for such raids can take full advantage of any errors made by the German controllers. Longer raids will always be liable to attacks on their last waves whenever fighters can fly, whatever tricks are employed to mislead the controllers.

Surprisingly, the same weakness could also occur in daytime, to the benefit of the Eighth Army Air Force. Sometimes at night when the German controls became confused we would hear the lines cleared for take over by a higher command, and we wondered just how high this was—not that it usually succeeded in clarifying the situation. The answer may lie in an incident related by Adolf Galland, who now commanded the German fighter force, in *The First And The Last*. It concerned an American raid on Düren in the Rhineland by day above cloud, aided by 'Window'. Goering himself took over control and since the 'Window' cloud was drifting eastwards, he concluded that the Americans were heading for Schweinfurt, the ballbearing centre. He therefore ordered his fighters to Schweinfurt, and his reporting service now of course reported that there was the sound of many aircraft heading towards Schweinfurt. The fighters, unable to find any American bombers, overshot, and so aircraft were now reported east of Schweinfurt without any bombs falling there. Goering then concluded that the bombers were going to the Leuna Works at Leipzig, where the same process was repeated, causing Goering now to divine the Skoda Works near Pilsen in Czechoslovakia as the target. At last, over Pilsen, the sky was clear, and there were no aircraft but German fighters.

It was obvious to the whole fighter organization that Goering had literally taken them for a ride, which he had the sense of humour to acknowledge by sending out a signal congratulating himself and all participants on the 'successful defeat of the air-raid on the Fortress of Köpenick'—the reference being of course, to the classic German hoax of 'the captain of Köpenick', where a shoemaker in 1906 procured a secondhand uniform of a Prussian captain, and took command of a squad of soldiers, arrested the local Burgermeister, and confiscated the municipal treasury.

My report of 4th October concluded optimistically:

The German defences may of course rapidly change if we successfully exploit their present weakness, but in the meantime we shall have benefited by such exploitation. The Germans may have stampeded more than is justified by the present density of Window, but there can be little doubt that they have for the moment partly abandoned their former system. Window is fulfilling its function even better than could be hoped. So long as we can keep German detection equipment neutralized, the problem of getting our bombers through the present extemporized defence system lies with the tactician.

One night in October 1943 Charles Frank and I were again at Kingsdown listening to a raid, where the German Divisional Controllers called themselves 'Leander', 'Prima Donna', 'Kakadu' (Cockatoo) and 'Möbelwagen' (furniture van), and addressed their fighter units by code names, for example 'von Leander von Leander an alle Schmetterlinge' (From Leander to all Butterflies) and it was clear that their technique was to 'scramble' their fighters on a raid warning and instruct them to orbit one of a number of visual and radio beacons, selecting the beacon nearest to the predicted track of the raid. Then, as the raid approached, the fighters would be in a position to swoop. This system was known as 'Zahme Sau' (Tame Sow) in contrast to Herrmann's 'Wilde Sau', and was devised by Colonel Viktor von Lossberg, whom we had previously encountered as the skilled commander of the bomber formation III K.G.26, using the Y-beam and ranging system for bombing us in 1941. The Y-ranging system was now to be fitted to German nightfighters, since it would be immune to Window, and would thus enable the German controllers to know at least where their own fighters were.

In the morning train back to Victoria I said to Frank (who incidentally, subsequently named his hens after the Divisional Controllers, starting with Prima Donna) 'The next thing we must do, Charles, is to locate those beacons', but I had no idea of how we were going to do it.

That same morning there arrived on my desk a bundle of microfilm prints from the Belgians via our colleague, Jempson. The story behind them, as I now know it, was this: the strain on the German air defences created by the co-ordinated attacks by the Eighth Air Force and Bomber Command was telling so much by August 1943 that the Germans were beginning to send up their nightfighters by day, just as they were sending up their day fighters by night. During an American day raid on 17th or 18th August 1943 a German nightfighter from an airfield near Liège was shot down; one of the occupants escaped by parachute. While he was still in the air he dropped a leather bag containing the flight documents, and by good fortune one of our Belgian agents, Jean Closquet, was on hand. Closquet, who had worked for us since 1941, rushed to the bag, and fled with it into a near-by wood. He evaded the subsequent search, and it was the microfilm of his documents that now, some six weeks later, had arrived on my desk via the famous 'Service

Marc'. It was a marvellous piece of opportunist Intelligence, and it was clear from the Belgian legend 'Dérobé d'un chasseur 卐 descendu' that they were fighter documents. There were some fifteen altogether, containing call-signs, transmitting frequencies and navigational instructions. Would they have the one list that I wanted?

There, on the tenth sheet, it was: the code-names of the beacons, Ida, Kurfürst, Ludwig, Marie . . . , some twenty-one all told, with their ranges and bearings from various German airfields. Charles and I spent the rest of the morning plotting them on a map. We could then imagine ourselves as German controllers: if we could see a raid coming, and had a rough idea of its track, where would we place our fighters so as best to poise them to swoop? Immediately, I informed Bomber Command and Fighter Command, suggesting that if Bomber Command would let me know its route in advance, I might be able to guess the beacons that the German nightfighters would orbit: we could then send a few of our long-range nightfighters to mix in with their German counterparts, and thus create a classic state of alarm by opening fire and therefore, hopefully, starting a fight among the Germans themselves. Bomber Command agreed to let me try to direct our intruding nightfighters in this way, and I had an interesting time seeing how many of my 'bets' paid off. Number 141 Squadron, commanded by Wing Commander J. R. Braham, was principally involved. Chris Hartley, too, went out; and on his first night the guess was good enough to put him right into a swarm of nightfighters orbiting one of the beacons and indeed right through the slipstreams of two of them, only to find his own radar had failed. Once or twice we succeeded in so upsetting the German nightfighters that they opened fire on one another, but I would claim no more than that.

The Closquet documents were thus a bonus to Bomber Command from the Eighth Air Force, whose respective bombing campaigns were supposed to be co-ordinated under the 'Pointblank' plan promulgated at the Casablanca Conference in January 1943. But their philosophies differed. The Eighth Air Force believed in precise attacks on selected targets, such as ballbearings and oil, in contrast with Harris's disillusion over 'panacea targets'. And the co-ordination of the two campaigns went no further than Bomber Command area-bombing by night the towns in which ballbearing or other targets were being bombed by the Americans by day.

For several months it seemed that Harris was right. Despite the most gallant and precise attacks in October 1943 by the Eighth Air Force on

Schweinfurt for example, in one raid on 14th October, 60 out of 291 Flying Fortresses were lost and it was believed that 75 per cent of the ballbearing production had been knocked out—German production nevertheless somehow went on, and even increased. So it seemed that even at the expense of prohibitive losses the selective policy would not work. The basic, almost philosophical, difficulty was that precise attacks needed optical aiming in daylight so the bombers would always be visible to the fighters and intercepted. They must therefore fight their way in and out, and experience was exploding the idea that formations of bombers could achieve satisfactory mutual protection by cross-fire against attacking fighters. We had learnt this lesson in 1939 and the Americans were learning it now.

So precise raids, necessarily in daylight, would require fighter escorts, but it was entirely unreasonable to hope that a long-range fighter could ever be able to out-perform the short-range fighters operating over Germany, because it would have to carry a great deal more fuel. Thus the logic of the British position, which basically was one of evading the fighters under cover of darkness, rather than fighting them, seemed unassailable.

Whichever policy was pursued, my task was to help minimize our bomber losses. One could hardly dare contemplate what our bomber crews were up against. They frequently had to fly about 800 miles through the German defences, at a speed less than 200 miles an hour, and at any time they were liable to unexpected attack. The chances of surviving a tour of thirty operations in Bomber Command in 1943 were about one in six, but morale never faltered. I had the chance to meet the most able of the survivors when in October 1943 Charles Medhurst wrote suggesting that I should lecture to the R.A.F. Staff College at Bullstrode Park, Gerrard's Cross, of which he was now Commandant. On 28th October I spoke there about the German night defences. The audience consisted of operational officers, usually of Wing Commander rank, who were expected to cram a whole year's Staff Course into three months, as a relaxation from operations. Guy Gibson, who won the Victoria Cross with 617 Squadron (The Dambusters) and 'Sailor' Malan, for example, were on one or other of these courses. They were worked hard, and almost the only sport in this period of contrast with the stresses of operational life was to bait the visiting lecturers. The result was a marvellously lively audience, especially if one were, as I was, speaking about matters that had been life and death to them, and in all probability would be so again when they returned to operations. To talk to those audiences was one of the greatest privileges and most stimulating experiences that have fallen to me. I talked to every Staff Course in succession from 1943 to 1955, when I finally called it a day partly because I felt that I might be getting out of date but still more because of the mess that was being made of our peace-time organization, in which I felt that Scientific Intelligence was being so badly handled that I could no longer talk about it with confidence.

The interest in those wartime courses was terrific, one occasion starting at 9.30 a.m. and the questions only finishing when the Commandant called a halt at 1.30 p.m. Subconsciously I acquired the two secrets of lecturing from which everything else follows: first, to believe that you have something worth telling your audience, and then to imagine yourself as one of that audience. Nearly all the advice that I have seen given to would-be lecturers deals with the trimmings without mentioning the fundamentals: but if you get these right, they entail all the rest. You must, for example, talk in terms that appeal to the background experience of your audience. You must be audible at the back of the room, where the details of your lantern slides must be visible and your blackboard writing legible; and you should not distract your audience with antics and fidgeting. You must also detect by the change in tension when you are in danger of losing its interest. But all these follow from the simple consideration of trying to regard yourself from the point of view of a member of the audience in the back row. Even now I cannot claim to satisfy all these criteria: but if I have any merit as a lecturer it derives from those glorious days of lecturing to as gallant and alert a band of men as any speaker could ever address.

'Window' was still having its effect, so much so that on 8th October 1943 Goering had conceded us his admiration:

In the field of radar they must have the world's greatest genius.

They have the geniuses and we have the nincompoops. . . . The British would never have dared use the metal foil here if they had not worked out one hundred per cent what the antidote is. I hate the rogues like the plague, but in one respect I am obliged to doff my cap to them. After this war's over I'm going to buy myself a British radio set, as a token of my regard for their high frequency work. Then at last I'll have the luxury of owning something that has always worked.

(Irving, *The Rise and Fall of the Luftwaffe*, p. 247).

In the ensuing turmoil, Kammhuber was removed from the night-fighter command, and was replaced by General 'Beppo' Schmid, who had been a Nazi in the 1923 'Putsch'. This was a good sign for I had reckoned that if we could get Kammhuber the sack, it was a criterion that we were winning. On the personal side, I was sorry to see him go because I had much admired the objectivity of his claims.

Our losses remained reasonably low in October (3·9 per cent) and November (3·6 per cent), and we were, of course, supplementing 'Window' by other countermeasures, including some against the 'running commentary' which the German controllers were broadcasting to their nightfighters. One of the best of our efforts was on 17th November when, during an attack on Ludwigshafen, we succeeded in counterfeiting the controller's voice over a powerful transmitter of our own (known as 'Aspidistra' because it was the biggest in the world) and warning all German nightfighters to land because of the danger of fog. When the Germans found that we were intervening in this way, they substituted women for men to broadcast the commentary, but for this we were ready and had German-speaking WAAFs standing by. The next move by the Germans was to have a man repeat any orders that our WAAF gave, so that the nightfighters would know that these orders were spurious. All we then had to do was to have our man repeat any orders that their woman gave. As a further twist, they supplemented verbal orders with music, so that, for example, a waltz meant that the bombers were in the Munich area, jazz meant Berlin, and so forth, with the end of an attack being signalled by the March 'Alte Kamaraden'.

Since this chapter is primarily concerned with bomber losses, there is a point unconnected with Intelligence which nevertheless deserves to be told. The question to be decided was whether we should fit de-icing equipment to our bombers or not. At first sight it would seem that the fitting of de-icing equipment was bound to save aircraft but the matter was put to Professor George Temple. When he looked at the figures he came to the following conclusion: the weight of the de-icing equipment meant that each bomber fitted with it must carry a smaller bomb load. Therefore, to achieve the same weight of bombs within destructive range of the target, the total force would have to be increased. Knowing the rate of casualties inflicted by the German defences on our bombers, he could work out how many more bombers would be shot down than before. This number turned out to be significantly greater than the number of bombers that, on average, would be saved by de-icing equipment. Therefore the fitting of this equipment would have increased bomber casualties rather than saved them. This is an example of a phenomenon where an action can have the opposite effect than that intended, and a lesson always to be borne in mind by politicians and administrators.

With the onset of the Battle of Berlin in November 1943, our losses began to rise. This was hardly surprising in view of the great distance over which our bombers had to run the gauntlet of the German night-fighters, but at the end of December 1943 there was a very disturbing development. My personal attention was, of course, divided between supporting Bomber Command and elucidating the details of the flying bomb, but it was through this division of attention that the trouble came to light. The watch that I had set on the 14th and 15th Companies of the Air Signals Experimental Regiment had already told us that the 14th Company was plotting the flying bomb trials. Now it showed us that the 15th Company too, was engaged in something unusual.

I was telephoned by Scott-Farnie to ask what I made of the messages that the 15th Company was sending. Once again, they were ranges and bearings, and I told him that I would look at the evidence that night, 5th January 1944. The messages referred to 'Flammen' (flames), and they were unusual in that they gave ranges up to 350 kilometres, well beyond normal radar range. The 'flames' could be switched off, and were not under the control of the observing station, which seemed to find it easier to determine range rather than bearing. They could also sometimes be seen during the day, and from the positions of the few plotting stations we were able to locate, we realized they referred to the positions of our bombers. By a process of elimination, I was quickly able to argue that the Germans were 'challenging' and plotting the I.F.F. (Indentification Friend or Foe) sets that had been kept switched on in some of our bombers, and perhaps also in American aircraft, too.

This was the very danger about which I had warned so strongly in 1941, and which had been dismissed by Bomber Command. My note of 12th September 1941 had said, 'Therefore, either I.F.F. has no effect, or it contributes to our losses: we should refrain from the use of this treacherous device over enemy territory'. A year later, the Operational Research Section of Bomber Command had reported that the intervening experience over Germany had shown, 'There is no evidence that the use of the J-Switch (by which the I.F.F. was left switched permanently on) has had any appreciable effects on searchlights, flak defences, or the activities of enemy fighters, or the "missing" rate'. The O.R.S.B.C.

report had then gone on to make a fatal recommendation, all the more reprehensible for the clear warning of potential danger that I had given: 'It is known, however, that many crews think the device effective, and it should therefore be retained. . . . Since no evidence has come to light indicating the harmful effects of the J-Switch, the psychological effects on the crew alone is sufficient to justify its retention'.

What this meant was that in 1942 there was no sign that the Germans were utilizing our I.F.F. transmissions. This conclusion was doubtless correct, but its implication was that although it was of no use, it encouraged crews to press home attacks in defended areas where the flak was so intense that they might otherwise have stopped short. Now, in assessing the position fifteen months later, I had to be careful because my opposition to the I.F.F. legend was well known, and my interpretation of the evidence regarding 'Flames' might thereby be discounted unless the proof was complete. Two days later, I issued a formal report which concluded:

It appears inescapable that I.F.F. has betrayed some of our bombers. The legend about effect of I.F.F. on searchlights may now be reaping a tragic harvest, and future tragedies of similar type will only be avoided by the peremptory application of common sense to shatter quasi-scientific superstition.

While their Radar remains neutralized, the Germans will probably make every effort to utilize the radiations from our aircraft. In view of the encouragement which they must thereby have received, they will probably try other radiations should we now thwart them on I.F.F., and we shall therefore need to be even more circumspect than before in our use of all radio equipment which involved continual transmissions from our aircraft.

At first there was some disbelief in Bomber Command headquarters, which I had accused of the immoral practice of encouraging brave men to clutch at false straws in their hour of greatest danger (I actually used these words at a conference) and I was particularly critical of the Operational Research Section which, as scientists, should have been much more objective. I was able to point to actual raids during December where, according to the Germans' own (Enigma) reports 9 out of the 41 aircraft lost on 2nd/3rd December against Berlin had been shot down because of their use of I.F.F., 4 out of 24 lost on Leipzig on the following night and 6 out of 26 on Berlin on 16/17th December—and these may have been due to one plotting station alone. This crucial evidence was a marvellous bonus from our attempts to follow the flying bomb trials. I felt that we had achieved one of the best 'right and lefts' of all time by picking out the 14th and 15th Companies.

At last Bomber Command headquarters was sufficiently convinced to issue orders that I.F.F. should be switched off, and I was told that the Commander-in-Chief had sent a signal to all units flaying 'those idiots who believe in the joss-like protection of I.F.F.'. Nevertheless it proved difficult to enforce I.F.F. silence in all aircraft, and with our concentration tactics, it only needed one aircraft to leave its I.F.F. on for the whole bomber stream to be betrayed. Moreover, the 'flames' plotting was completely immune to 'Window', because of the different wavelength and because, as in the Y-system, the aircraft itself amplified the echo many times over that normally associated with radar and it positively identified itself as British.

Since I had to continue to report the I.F.F. activity for some weeks after the prohibition order had gone out, the Air Staff decided that the strongest representations should be made to the Command, and the Commander-in-Chief was called by the Secretary of State, Archibald Sinclair, to explain what he was doing. In the meantime, thanks partly to the treacherous 'flames' our losses had risen to more than 6 per cent in January 1944, and 7 per cent in February, and even nearly 10 per cent on bad nights.

Fortunately, at the same time as our losses to nightfighters were rising in the early months of 1944, the Eighth Air Force entered a new phase of effectiveness. The reason was the advent of the P51B, the 'Mustang' fighter. This aircraft resulted from a request from the Royal Air Force to North American Aviation, who built the prototype in 1940. More than six hundred had been supplied to the Royal Air Force by the end of 1941 but in their original form they were under-powered, with their Allison engines giving 1,150 h.p. Five aircraft were therefore fitted with Merlin 61 engines, and the production line was accordingly modified in America, with American-built Packard Merlins. These changed the performance of the aircraft from 366 m.p.h. at fifteen thousand feet to 425 m.p.h. at the same height, and 455 m.p.h. at thirty thousand feet. Moreover by adding extra fuel tanks that could be jettisoned, the operating range could be extended to more than 700 miles, and the Mustang could outperform all the standard German day fighters. Almost by accident the philosophically impossible had been achieved.

The result was that the American day raids could now have effective fighter escorts over a very large part of German territory. This completely changed the balance of air power, and in February 1944 the Army Air Force staged its Big Week, where immense damage was done to the German aircraft industry, including the destruction of 700 completed Messerschmidt 109s; moreover, the production of JU88s for nightfighting had been cut from 365 to less than 200 per month (Irving, *The Rise and Fall of the Luftwaffe*, p. 270). Despite this damage, however, overall aircraft production had risen to more than fifteen hundred per month compared with an average of about one hundred a month in 1943. But while aircraft could be produced and replaced, skilled pilots could not; and especially after the Mustangs were allowed to seek out the German fighters rather than merely escort their bombers, the end of the German fighter force was in sight.

In the meantime, though, the German nightfighters were by no means finished as regards Bomber Command. A new airborne radar set, Lichtenstein SN2 had been produced, and I reported its appearance in service during February 1944. I presumed that it was developed from the 'Lichtenstein S' which was an airborne set for detecting ships at sea, and that, if so, its radio frequency might be about 80 Megacycles per second, or a wavelength between 3 and 4 metres. This would be quite clear of our original 'Window' and we would need to produce strips of much greater length. The SN2 had a range of about 4 miles as compared with the 2 miles of the original Lichtenstein (type BC) of which we had been given a sample at Dyce in the previous May.

Even so, it would probably not have been of great use to the German nightfighters unless they could be guided into the bomber stream by some other system. Even as late as 15th February, more than six weeks after I had originally warned about the German exploitation of I.F.F., there were still ten I.F.F. sets switched on in our bomber stream. And, as I had warned, whetted by this experience the Germans were now plotting every other transmission emanating from our bombers. The Command was appallingly indiscreet in its use of radio transmissions, far beyond anything that I—with my education from the Navy in the virtues of radio silence—had ever thought possible. And, for that matter, had not the Commander-in-Chief himself written as D.C.A.S. of the German beams in 1941, 'They are frequently a means of giving us advance warning of the enemy's intention. On the whole, they have therefore been of more value to us than to the German bombing effort'?

After the war, one of the German scientists working in the raid tracking organization told me that he thought that we could have had no idea of the extent to which the Germans were making use of the

information that we were thus prodigally providing. I could tell him
that some of us certainly knew, but we had great difficulty in making
Bomber Command and even our own scientists at Malvern believe it.

As one example, there was H2S, the radar bombing aid working on
a wavelength of 10 centimetres. I obtained overwhelming evidence that
the Germans were plotting it (they had started as early as November
1943), and were in fact equipping their fighters with a receiver code-
named 'Naxos' to home on to the transmissions not only from H2S but
also on the kindred equipment that were being fitted to our bombers to
warn them of the approach of German nightfighters. Since H2S was
being switched on as soon as our bombers took off from their airfields in
England, the Germans could get very early warning of a raid, and get
their fighters airborne so as to be able to home on the transmissions
when they came within range.

Such was the disbelief in our evidence that Watson-Watt and A. P.
Rowe, the Chief Superintendent at Malvern, said that they would only
accept it if they could nominate one of their own officers to see every
detail of our evidence and the methods by which we had obtained it.
Fortunately they nominated Philip Dee, and although I suspected that
the opportunity was being taken to see whether I had some great undisclosed source, I was delighted to welcome Dee, who some weeks after
he joined us told me that he himself had found that the H2S aspect was
indeed partly a cover, saying, 'I have just realized that I have been sent
here as a spy!' Again, we became very firm friends, and I can remember
from those days his telling me that after the war he wanted to get back
to a university because he believed that the future of Britain lay in good
university education, and that we should have to rebuild after the war.
Having been at Cambridge previously with Rutherford, he went to
Glasgow as Professor of Natural Philosophy in 1945.

While the argument about I.F.F. and H2S had been going on, our
losses had risen to an almost unsupportable point, although on some
raids, thanks to good tactics by Bomber Command, they were gratify-
ingly low. For example on 1st March 1944 we lost only 4 aircraft out
of 557 against Stuttgart and on 26th March only 9 out of 705 against
Essen. But in the last attack on Berlin, on 24th March, the loss rate was
9·1 per cent, and on 30th March we sustained the greatest losses of the
war, 96 aircraft failing to return from the 795 sent against Nuremberg.
Martin Middlebrook has investigated this raid (*The Nuremberg Raid*,
Allen Lane, London 1973) and ascribes the losses to a number of factors,
including the clarity of the night and the persistence of condensation

trails in the half moonlight, along with the use of SN2 and upward firing cannon by the nightfighters. Anthony Cave Brown in *Bodyguard of Lies* (Allen, London, 1976) has suggested that the target was disclosed by us to the Germans in advance, so as to build up the credibility of an agent with which we intended to play a later hoax on the Germans, 'that was intended to save lives on D-Day' (p. 516). I have no knowledge of any such hoax, nor do I believe that anyone else has. The simple fact is that we were so prodigal with the information that we were giving to the Germans through our transmissions from the bombers themselves that the stream could easily be located; and in the failure of any effective diversion and in the general conditions obtaining that night, the losses were only to be expected.

Possibly we did not stress the importance of SN2 sufficiently. It showed up only rarely in the Enigma traffic in February 1944; this may be explained by the fact that at the beginning of that month only 90 out of 480 nightfighters were completely fitted with it. But as it was given first to the best nightfighter crews, its effect was greater than the simple numerical proportion. And although on 6th March I had set the establishment of the SN2 wavelength for countermeasures as one of our two most urgent problems, and even though some weeks before we had correctly guessed that its wavelength would be between 3 and 4 metres, our listening searches failed to detect it. Proof only came when American camera guns caught JU88s and ME110s fitted with SN2's ponderous aerials, and the photographs came to us in May (Plate 18); even then its transmissions were not heard until after an SN2-fitted JU88 landed in error and intact at Woodbridge in Suffolk on 13th July.

Even with this failure of Intelligence, however, the SN2 nightfighters would probably have been relatively unsuccessful had we been more careful in our use of radio and radar, as was indicated by our low losses on the nights on which the ground controllers failed to put the fighters into the bomber stream. In the event, Bomber Command was pulled back for the time being from raiding Germany during April and May 1944, because its effort was needed against targets connected with our impending landings in Normandy.

A further brilliant item of Belgian Intelligence that arrived early in 1944 may fittingly conclude this chapter. The Y-ranging system that von Lossberg had brought in for nightfighters was also applied to dayfighters, and complete stations for controlling dayfighters on the Y system were built. Since each equipment could handle only a few fighters at a time, as many as five complete ranging equipments and their

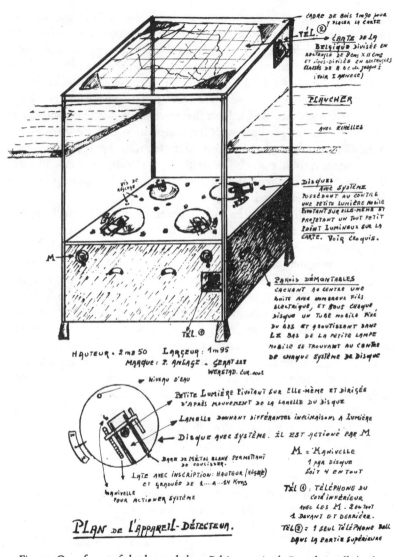

Fig. 24. *One of a set of sketches made by a Belgium patriot (a Brussels jeweller) who spent every night for a week in a German fighter control station which used the Y-system for locating its fighters. This sketch shows the details of the 'Seeburg' plotting table on which the positions of the bomber and the fighter were projected as spots of light, and from which the controller issued orders to the fighter*

plotting tables were incorporated into a single station. One of these was at Lantin, in Belgium, and a Brussels jeweller decided to investigate it for us. Surprisingly, it was not used by the Germans at night, and so the German personnel left it under a guard of Belgians who had been recruited into the S.S. Our jeweller friend bribed one of these men to let him into the station at night, and he spent every night for a week there, sketching everything that he could see. His sketches came to me, and one of them is reproduced in figure 24. The excellence of his draughtsmanship will be evident, especially when it is remembered that he was sitting alone in the German headquarters, with always the chance that one of the Germans might return. His sketch of the Seeburg (plotting) table gave us easily the best detail that we obtained until we at last captured specimens towards the end of the war.

CHAPTER FORTY-TWO

The Baby Blitz

OUR WARNING of 23rd December 1943 that there was a German bomber force concentrating in the West, and that this might have been assembled as a substitute should the flying bomb be delayed, was proved correct by the entries in Milch's diary. These show that the performance of the prototype bombs in trials had been disappointing; and an R.A.F. attack on Cassel on 23rd October had forced the evacuation of the Fieseler Works where the pilot series of flying bombs was being manufactured. In November it was estimated that another 150 bombs would have to be tested before the trials would prove satisfactory, and excuses had to be made to Hitler for the delay. On 27th November Goering promised him that the Luftwaffe would mount a heavy attack on London within two weeks in revenge for the raids on Berlin; but even then he had to delay, so the first attack did not take place until 21st January. It was the start of what came to be known as the 'Baby Blitz', which continued in a desultory manner until it fizzled out at the end of April 1944.

To me the Baby Blitz was memorable for two incidents. The first was the birth of our son, Robert Bruce, on 11th February, at home in Richmond, and with Vera and me and the two children having on various nights in the subsequent weeks to revert to sleeping on the floor with our heads protected by our dining table. The second incident started with the impression gained by our listening service that the fighter bombers sent over by the Germans were being controlled by a new method. Actually, it was much along the lines that the Telecommunications Research Establishment had suggested when in 1942 they would not believe me that the Mammuts (or 'Hoardings') were simply radar stations, because the precision of their transmissions was unnecessarily high. I had, of course, been able to show that they were not distinguished in this respect from any other kind of German radar station, but it helped to alert me to the possibility that at any time any German radar station, at least of the Freya type, was capable of directing bombers, especially if it were fitted with a device such as our own I.F.F.

The Germans now had such a device in the Funk Gerät 25A, and we soon heard transmissions from it on the fighter bombers that were hurtling across London. The method was to set a Freya station on the coast of France so that its split-beam pointed over the target in London (Figure 25). The aircraft then flew along the beam, being guided by verbal instructions by the radar operator, who having steered the aircraft along the beam to an appropriate range and having told him to fly at a given speed and height, then told the pilot when to release his bombs or flares.

At first the attacks were very scattered. In two raids on London (21st and 29th January) some 500 tons of bombs were dropped, with less than 40 tons hitting London, for the loss of 57 aircraft, or nearly eight percent of the sorties. But in one of these early attacks a few bombs fell fairly near Whitehall, which caused more interest at the top level than might otherwise have been the case, and once again I found myself summoned to the Cabinet Room. This time I was able to tell the Prime Minister not only of the German technique, as I suspected it, but also to give him the names of one or two of the German pilots.

We discussed possible countermeasures, especially in view of the fact that the Germans were at last dropping 'Window', and a few of them were even using captured Gee receivers of ours by which they could navigate on our own Gee stations. It occurred to me that we could play exactly the same trick on the Germans as they were playing on Bomber Command, for they had to have their I.F.F. sets on while they were being controlled from the radar stations in France. If we could make challenging transmitters and receivers, we could thus locate the bombers through any amount of 'Window', just as the Germans were doing against us. When Churchill grasped the point he said 'Let it be done!'

Once I had produced the idea, it was technically no longer my responsibility, but that of the research and countermeasures organizations. And so in the follow-up meeting in the Cabinet Room a week later, when my proposal came up as an item on the agenda for the review of progress in its exploitation, Churchill looked at Robert Renwick, whose care the development now was. Just as Renwick started—quite properly—to speak, however, I saw Attlee, who was sitting next to Churchill, nudge him and whisper something and point to me. Churchill thereupon stopped Renwick and invited me to speak.

14

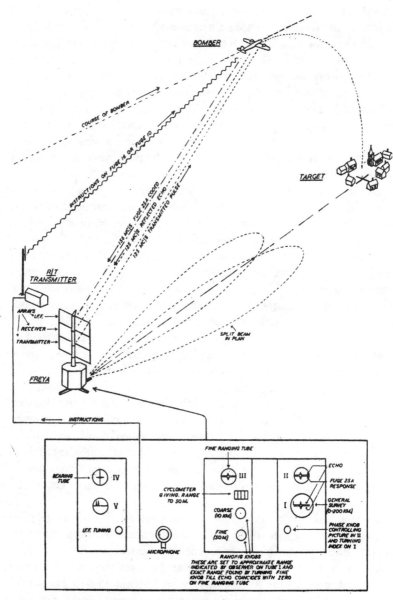

Fig. 25. *The bombing system used in the 'Baby Blitz', January/March 1944*

General Wolfgang Martini, Commanding German
Air Force Signals and Radar, 1939-45
(courtesy of General Kammhuber)

17b General Josef Kammhuber, Commanding German
nightfighters, 1940-43
(courtesy of General Kammhuber)

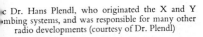

c Dr. Hans Plendl, who originated the X and Y
mbing systems, and was responsible for many other
radio developments (courtesy of Dr. Plendl)

17d Oberst Viktor von Lossberg, Commanding Officer
of III/KG26 in the Blitz, and who later developed the
'Zahme Sau' system for nightfighting
(courtesy of Colonel von Lossberg)

18a Lichtenstein receiver and presentation unit in the Junkers 88 nightfighter which landed at Dyce near Aberdeen, 9 May 1943

18b Lichtenstein BC antenna

18c Camera gun photograph taken by an America fighter of a Junkers 88 nightfighter fitted with the muc larger Lichtenstein SN2 antenna, 1944

18d Messerschmidt nightfighter fitted with Lichtenstein at Kastrup Airport, Copenhagen, photographed by a Danish agent, 1943

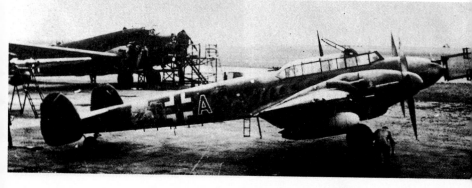

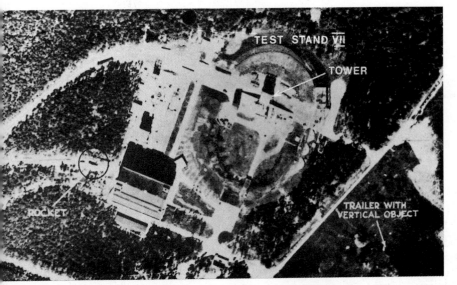

19a Air Reconnaissance photograph of Heeres Anstalt Peenemünde, 12 June 1943, on which a large rocket (left centre) was first recognized (Sortie No. N/853)

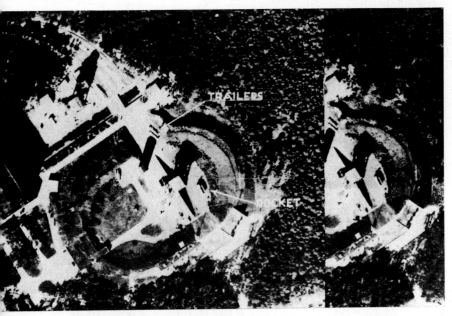

19b Stereo pair of Air Reconnaissance photographs of Peenemünde, 23 June 1943 (Sortie No. N/860) showing a rocket inside the elliptical earthwork

20 Photographs of the experimental V-1 flying bomb which crashed on Bornholm 22 August 1943, taken by Lieutenant Commander Hasager Christiansen and smuggled to London

20a Main bo

20b Automatic pilot

20c Compressed air
container

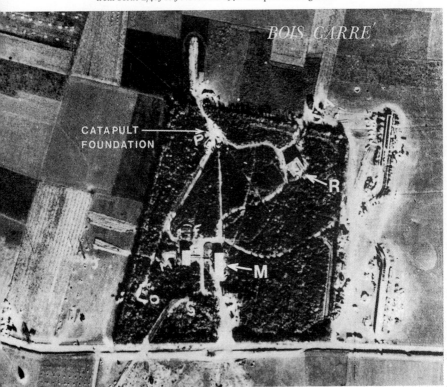

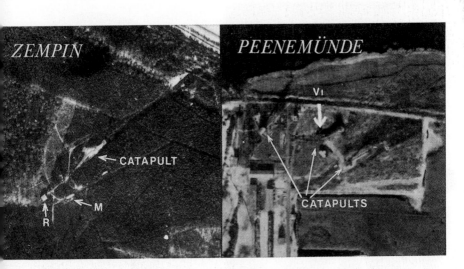

21b and c The R.A.F. Reconnaissance photographs of Zempin and Peenemünde from Sortie N/980 of 28 November 1943 which proved that the 'Ski Sites' were to launch V-1s. 21b: Trial launching site at Zempin, showing similar buildings (R and M) to those ski sites, and a launching catapult. 21c: Launching catapult at Peenemünde with a V-1 ready for firing (and spotted by Flight Officer Constance Babington Smith)

22a Dr. Howard P. Robertson, Chief American Liaison with British Scientific Intelligence (courtesy of California Institute of Technology)

22b Professor Yves Rocard, Chief French Liaison with British Scientific Intelligence (courtesy of Yves Roc...

22c Lieutenant Thomas Sneum, who flew to England from Denmark with a film of a Freya station (courtesy of Thomas Sneum)

22d Jerzy Chmielewski who collected parts from crashed V-2 rockets in Poland and brought them to Britain (courtesy of Dr. Jozef Garlinski)

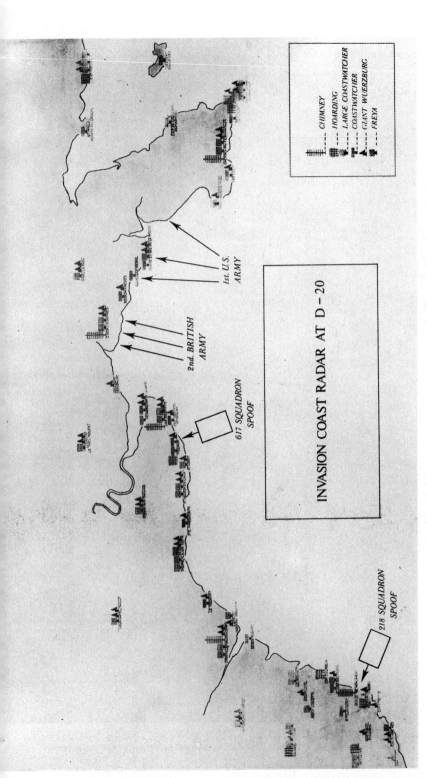

23 German radar on the Invasion coast before D-Day 1944, and 'spoofing' diversions

INVASION COAST RADAR AT D – 20

617 SQUADRON SPOOF

218 SQUADRON SPOOF

1st. U.S. ARMY

2nd. BRITISH ARMY

CHIMNEY
HOARDING
LARGE COASTWATCHER
COASTWATCHER
GIANT WUERZBURG
FREYA

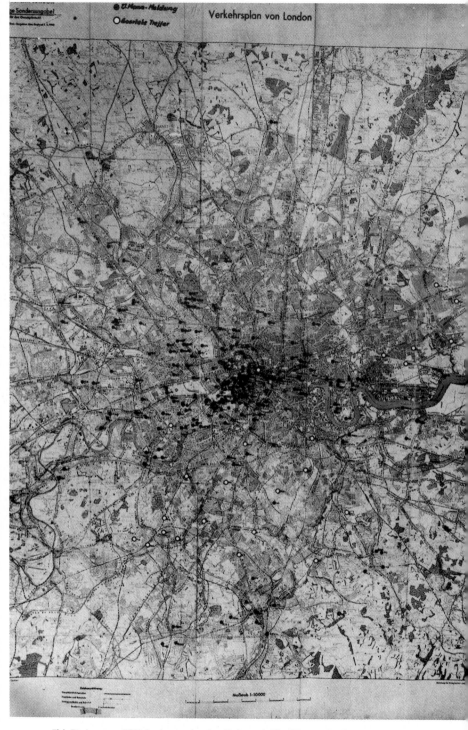

24 Flak Regiment 155(W)'s battle map showing (dark spots) fall of V-1s on London as reported by German 'agents' and (white spots) fall of V-1s as indicated by radio transmitters mounted in sample missiles

25a German photograph of a V-1 track across the Straits of Dover taken by a camera with its shutter left open at night. The continuous white track is traced out by the flame of the bomb as it travels towards Kent, and the white spots (whose pattern puzzled the Germans) are bursts of anti-aircraft shells fitted with proximity fuses

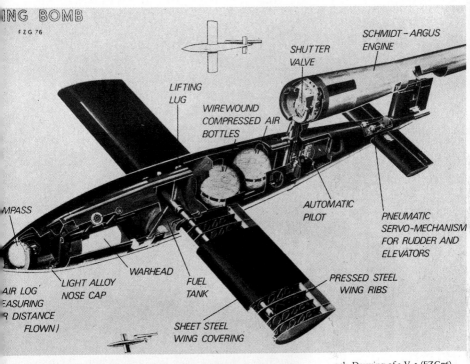

ING BOMB

FZG 76

SHUTTER VALVE

SCHMIDT–ARGUS ENGINE

LIFTING LUG

WIREWOUND COMPRESSED AIR BOTTLES

AUTOMATIC PILOT

PNEUMATIC SERVO-MECHANISM FOR RUDDER AND ELEVATORS

MPASS

WARHEAD

LIGHT ALLOY NOSE CAP

FUEL TANK

PRESSED STEEL WING RIBS

AIR LOG EASURING R DISTANCE FLOWN)

SHEET STEEL WING COVERING

25b Drawing of a V-1 (FZG76) after R. Castle

25c 'Kamikaze' V-1 fitted with a cockpit (courtesy of the Imperial War Museum)

HUTS
FUNCTION UNKNOWN

HUTS (50×16) SUITABLE FOR STORING ROCKETS

LIGHT RAILWAY

REVERSING LOOP

BARRACKS

TANK CARS

ASSEMBLY HALL (330×100)

VERTICAL
OBJECTS

T RAILWAY

CENTRES

UNEXPLAINED
ACTIVITY

SPECIAL VEHICLES

TRAIN POSSIBLY USED
FOR ACCOMMODATION

OCKET ON
EVERSING
LOOP

TRACK POSSIBLY LIGHT
RAILWAY LEADING FROM
ASSEMBLY HALL TO
FIRING POINT

LEMON SQUEEZER

SQUARE PLATFORM (26×26)

FLYING BOMB
INSTALLATIONS

26 Aerial photograph of V-2 test site at Blizna, Poland, on which (black circles) a rocket and its firing platform
were first identified (Sortie No. PRU385 of 5 May 1944). This photograph is reproduced at its original size,
and gives some idea of the difficulty of interpreting photographs even of the best wartime quality
(R.A.F. photograph)

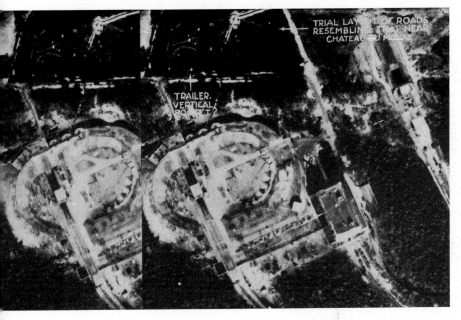

TRIAL LAYOUT OF ROADS
RESEMBLING THAT NEAR
CHATEAU MO...

←

TRAILER.
VERTICAL
ROCKET.

27a Aerial photographs showing (at top) the same road pattern traced on the foreshore at Peenemünde, February 1944, as was later recognized on the ground in Normandy (See Figure 29)

27b Photograph from the Peenemünde archives of a model made for Hitler in 1943, showing three rockets ready for firing from the same layout

28a A4 rockets set up for firing on the foreshore at Peenemünde
(courtesy of David Irving)

28b A4 rocket launched from inside th
elliptical earthwork at Peenemünde bes
the testing tower visible on Plate 19
(courtesy of Deutsches Museum, Muni

28c Wooden 'mock-up' of an A4 rocket on its transporter (Meillerwagen) for training purposes, inside the
elliptical earthwork, February 1942. Note the 'Lemon Squeezer' blast deflector at the rear of the rocket
(courtesy Deutsches Museum, Munich)

29a Jagdschloss plan–position–indicating radar near Ringsted in Denmark, photographed by Wing Commander D. W. Steventon, D.S.O., D.F.C., 24 September 1944. Note the improvement in definition due to the use of a forward-facing camera (R.A.F. photograph)

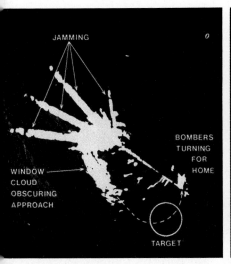

29b and c Photographs taken ten minutes apart of a Jagdschloss cathode-ray screen during a British Mosquito raid which was protected by jamming, and by clouds of Window sown during approach to the target and on the homeward journey. Distance between plotting centre and target about fifty miles

30a Dismantling the German experimental nuclear pile at Haigerloch, 50 km. S.W. of Stuttgart, April, 1945. Rupert Cecil nearest camera, 'Bimbo' Norman extreme right, Eric Welsh standing on outer rim, the second man behind Cecil

30b Examining captured nuclear files at Stadtilm, 20 km. S. of Erfurt. Cecil extreme right, Welsh nearest to Cecil, and Goudsmit extreme left (both photographs courtesy David Irving)

31 Buckingham Palace, 1946, with Vera, Susan and Robert

32 The Vicomtesse de Clarens at the Yorkshire Television Studios, December 1976
(Yorkshire Television)

I of course referred the matter back to Renwick, but I was much impressed by Attlee's memory and sense of fair play in that he had gone out of his way to see that I was to get the credit for the suggestion, even in a technical matter that must have been quite beyond him.

As it worked out, the method was an extremely powerful one, and even a single challenging station could plot the German aircraft, even though they were dropping 'Window', over the whole of southern England. It was not in fact much used because by the time it was ready the Baby Blitz, which fizzled out in April, was nearly over. But the lesson had been learned, for it was adapted for our intruding nightfighters to use against the German nightfighters if they had their I.F.F.'s on. Under the name of 'Perfectos' it was described by Alfred Price in *Instruments of Darkness*, p. 220, as one of the neatest electronic gadgets to come out of the Second World War. It achieved little tangible success, but it forced the German nightfighters to switch off their recognition sets, so complicating the tasks of their ground controllers.

Spring came as the Baby Blitz ended, and I was able to take a happy weekend with Hugh Smith in Gloucestershire. We awoke to see in the garden across the road someone who was familiar to us in Whitehall. He was Major Kingdon, one of our colleagues in M.I.8, the branch of Military Intelligence concerned with intercepting enemy radio communications. It turned out that by coincidence Hugh Smith's neighbour, Captain Rogers, had just joined the same branch and he had invited Kingdon, who was the Head of his Section, to the same village for the weekend. The weather was beautiful, the orchards of the Vale of Evesham were at their blooming best, and the two Military Intelligence officers had come to hear the first cuckoo. I myself have some competence in the art of cuckoo-ing—I used to try to persuade Susan to sleep with it, so much so in fact that one day in Richmond Park she heard a genuine cuckoo call and immediately said 'Mummy, Mummy, Daddy's up a tree!' Hugh and I enlisted the services of the lads of the village and, for a shilling a head, our military colleagues heard cuckoos in quantities that would have found Dame Juliana Berners speechless.

CHAPTER FORTY-THREE

D-Day

AT THE same time as we were watching the flying bomb trials, dealing with the Baby Blitz, and wrestling with the German night defences, another problem was approaching its climax: this was the coming operation to land in force in Normandy. Ever since 1940 I had known what my part must be, whether or not it was formally assigned to me: to see that everything possible was done to knock out, by jamming, deception, or direct action, the chain of coastal radar stations that the Germans would inevitably build up. This had been my answer in 1941 to A. P. Rowe when he asked me what good it was my collecting detailed Intelligence on all German radar stations: some time, I had replied, we were going back and those stations might stand between our success and failure.

In general by the end of 1943 we knew enough about the various forms of coastal radar to jam much of the system successfully, and to organize deceptions by using 'Window' to simulate large forces at sea as well as in the air. But if we could make direct attacks on German radar stations, some of them could be eliminated, and the operators in the others might be so disturbed as to observe less accurately in the presence of jamming and 'Window'. From the beginning, therefore, I had advocated direct attack.

Fighter Command at first said that it could not carry out attacks on such small targets as radar stations because fighters could not find them. I therefore suggested that each fighter squadron should be led by a photo reconnaissance pilot, and this suggestion may have shamed the Command into improving its low-level navigation. Anyway, by the beginning of 1944 there was serious consideration of using fighter squadrons against the radar stations in the Invasion area.

The work of building up the information about the positions and types of German radar equipment on the coast was shared between my unit and Claude Wavell's in the Central Interpretation Unit at Medmenham, and over the years we had jointly produced a series of dossiers for what were known as 'Rhubarb' operations, these being the general title of any offensive actions by Fighter Command over France and the Low Countries. To the general operational instructions there was a series of appendices, and ours was Appendix XII, of which we produced several editions as the intensity of German radar cover increased. The result was that, although we never had an operational requirement stated to us, there was a comprehensive dossier on every German coastal radar station, including maps, and high- and low-level photographs, in sufficient detail for accurate attacks to be planned.

Moreover, we produced recognition drawings of all known types of German radar equipment, and catalogues of all the radar stations between Skagen at the northern tip of Denmark, and Bayonne on the west of France near the Spanish frontier. Even though we knew that the attack was to be made in Normandy, we covered a very much wider coastline, so that if any leakage of information were to occur, the Germans would have no clue regarding the selected area. Our catalogue listed nearly two hundred separate stations which between them contained some six hundred individual radar installations.

We were now producing many copies of our reports—more than three hundred of each were circulated to headquarters and field units, both British and American, and we supplied the information for all three Services of both nations. In this, we had the enthusiastic support, particularly, of the United States Navy; but, even as late as March 1944, I still had no formal request for information on German radar, nor was I formally brought into the Invasion planning. At last, an officer who had been on the first Course to which I had lectured at the R.A.F. Staff College, came in to consult me, since he had officially been assigned to the problem of knocking out the German radar. But it was clear that his scale of operations would be much too small to be effective. I was therefore wondering how I could intervene, when I had to give a further lecture at the Staff College on 13th April 1944. When I arrived there, Charles Medhurst told me that Sir Arthur Tedder, the Deputy Supreme Allied Commander, would be giving the lecture after mine, and Medhurst wondered whether I would care to listen to him before we all went to lunch. I told Medhurst that Tedder was just the man I wanted to see, because of the inadequate planning of countermeasures against German radar, and that I would like a chance to talk with him. Medhurst, once again delighted to be able to 'fix' something, told me that he would see if he could arrange for a quiet half-hour between me and Tedder after lunch.

He left the two of us in his room, and I told the Deputy Supreme Commander why I thought that the plans were inadequate. He was quickly convinced and asked me what he should do—after all, the Invasion was less than two months away. I told him that he should send a request to the Air Staff for as high level a party as possible to be formed at the headquarters of the Allied Expeditionary Air Force, nominating Victor Tait, the Director General of Signals, to head the party. Then, almost certainly, Victor Tait would ask me to join him to provide the Intelligence, and I could then bring in those members of my staff who would best be able to help.

Medhurst wrote to me later that same afternoon saying, 'I hope that your talk with Tedder will bear fruit!' It evidently did, for a few days later Tait rang me up to tell me that he did not know how it had come about but there had been a request from Supreme Headquarters for him to organize a party at A.E.A.F. to run the countermeasures against the German radar stations, and that he would like me to join him and do all the Intelligence work. We quickly formed our party, and started on a much enlarged plan of attack.

One of my first steps was to visit Supreme Headquarters in Bushey Park to make contact with some of the Planning Staff. Among them was Major Manus, a Canadian, who greeted me with 'Dr. Jones? Good God! I thought that you were dead!' When I asked him why, he replied, 'I gave orders for you to be shot!' It turned out that he had previously been on the Planning Staff for the Dieppe Raid, and he had understood that I myself was going on the Raid. He had therefore detailed two men to guard me as far as possible but had also ordered them to shoot me if I were about to be captured by the Germans, because with my knowledge I was such a security risk. He told me that he had not been on the Raid himself, but that he had been waiting to meet the survivors as they landed and could find no trace of me, and he therefore thought it best not to make any further enquiries. This is the explanation underlying James Leasor's book Green Beach, and also a legal action fought by Quentin Reynolds about someone going on the Dieppe Raid who was to be shot if in danger of capture.

Green Beach is the story of Flight Sergeant Jack Nissenthal, who in fact did go on the Dieppe Raid as the expert ready to dismantle the German radar station at Pourville if it was captured during the Raid. This was in August 1942, some months after Bruneval, but it differed from the latter in being a very much larger Raid, and the radar was only a subsidiary target instead of being the main one. There was a suggestion that Flight Sergeant Cox should again go on the Dieppe Raid, but I advised him that I thought that he had already 'done his bit', and so another Flight Sergeant was selected from the volunteers. This was Nissenthal and somehow the order that would have applied to me had I gone on the Raid (and I have heard a story that there was a similar order regarding D. H. Priest, had he landed at Bruneval) was transferred to him. Actually there was no more reason for him to be shot than there would have been for Cox in the Bruneval Raid, since they knew comparable amounts about our own radar, and only as much about German radar as was necessary for dismantling captured equipment. It was the misapprehension of Major Manus regarding my own presence on the Raid that resulted in his dramatic order. Full credit, though, to Nissenthal who had a very rough time indeed and survived his guards. He called on me immediately after the Raid and told me of his experiences. It had been a day of utter contrast—at one time quiet enough to be drinking wine with the local Frenchmen who thought that the Invasion had started and were therefore celebrating, and later coming under such heavy fire that, as he said, the Canadians built a parapet out of the dead bodies of their comrades, and fired their machine-guns over it. Nissenthal, who described the Canadians to me as 'magnificent', finally escaped by swimming a quarter of a mile out to one of the departing boats.

For D-Day, it was important to know how much effort we should need to knock out a major radar installation, and so we decided to have a trial attack on one of the largest types of German equipment, known to us as a 'Chimney' because of the appearance of the large supporting column which held the array, and to the Germans as 'Wassermann 3'. It was rather like a Hoarding turned with its long side vertical and mounted on a swivelling column, and had the advantage that it could determine height as well as range. Figures 26a and b show drawings of various types of radar station, one set being made by the Germans and the other by my own Section—in the case of the 'Chimney' it is hard to believe that there was no collusion between the two artists, but we had certainly not seen the German drawings, and it is very unlikely that they saw ours.

I decided on a 'Chimney' near Ostend, because our Belgian espionage network was excellent, and we briefed our agents about the date and time of attack, so that they could observe its effects. The attack took place on 16th March with rocket-firing Typhoons of No. 198 Squadron, and was very successful. Two attacks were made, and the turning

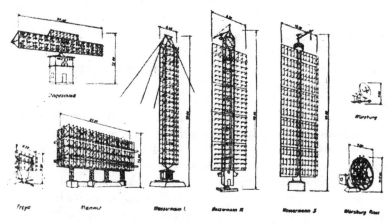

Fig. 26a. German drawings of their principal types of radar equipment

Fig. 26b. British sketches made without having seen the German drawings

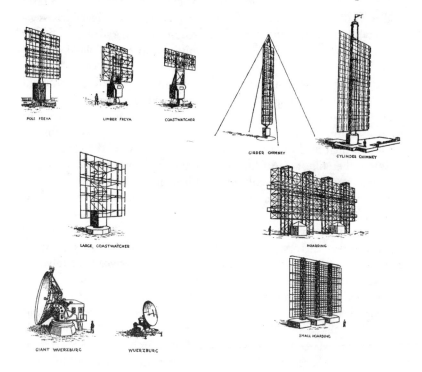

mechanism was so damaged that the station had to be dismantled for repair. Our Belgian friends reported the results enthusiastically, and added that there was an exactly similar installation 23 kilometres or so along the coast, with the implication that they should like to watch us attack that, too. But once the technique had been established, we then held off until the campaign for D-Day should start in earnest.

As regards the tactics of the campaign, it would clearly be dangerous to attack only the radar stations that could cover our intended landing area, and so we had a general rule that for every one attack that we made in the area there should be two outside it, so that the Germans should not be able to deduce from the intensity of our pre-invasion attacks exactly where the landings were to be made. Some idea of the distribution of the German radar stations may be gained from Plate 23.

It was also important that we should be able to assess the effectiveness of our attacks as the campaign proceeded, so that we could estimate how much of the German radar cover was left intact. We had, of course, the reports of the pilots carrying out the attacks, supplemented by evidence from their camera guns. We also had a strong photographic reconnaissance effort, carried out both by regular reconnaissance pilots and by specialist units devoted to tactical reconnaissance. In addition, we could listen from stations on our south coast to the transmissions from the German radar stations themselves, to see how many of them survived. As for ground agents, we did not use them for this operation, since there was much other work for them to do.

One vital concept of the whole campaign leading up to D-Day was that we should not only conceal our intention to land in Normandy but should also do everything possible to give the Germans the impression that we were going to land east of the Seine, so as to mislead them into keeping as much of their armoured forces there as possible and that we should then destroy all the bridges at the last moment so that they would be unable to come into action. On the night preceding D-Day, therefore, we aimed at giving the impression that a large sea-borne force was heading towards landings east of the Seine, and the development of 'Window' made this possible, with Robert Cockburn working out the technique with Leonard Cheshire, who was then Commanding 617 Squadron. The idea was that each of his Lancasters should fly in rectangular orbits eight miles long by two wide, moving the centre point of each orbit in a south-easterly direction at a rate of 8 knots, the speed of a sea-borne convoy. 'Window' would be dropped the whole time, with the Lancasters so deployed as to give the overall impression of an

14*

area sixteen miles long by fourteen wide full of ships advancing towards
Fécamp on the French coast. In addition to 'Window' dropped by the
Lancasters, 'Moonshine' simulators (p. 243) were to be carried on motor
launches to give augmented and extended radar echoes, so that a few
launches travelling under the 'Window' cloud would appear as a
massive convoy to any airborne radar reconnaissance that the Germans
might fly. A second spoof 'convoy' was to be created in the same way
by the Stirlings of 218 Squadron, heading towards Boulogne. The
scheme called for very precise flying, and it also required to be observed
by at least one German radar station. It was therefore decided to leave
one station intact, and the one at Fécamp was selected for this privilege.

About three weeks before D-Day the party under Victor Tait at
A.E.A.F. headquarters (housed in the famous Fighter Command
premises at Bentley Priory, Stanmore) came into regular operation. On
the technical side, Derek Garrard went from my Section, and on the
tactical Intelligence side I selected J. A. Birtwistle, who had been a
Fighter Command Intelligence Officer at R.A.F. Kenley during the
Battle of Britain. The third member of my team was Rupert Cecil, an
Oxford biochemistry graduate who was now a wing commander with
a D.F.C. and Bar, after two tours in Bomber Command. We had met
when I first lectured at the R.A.F. Staff College, and he joined me
shortly afterwards. We could now see bomber operations through a
pilot's eyes, and his presence assured Bomber Command that one of
their own men had the fullest access to our work. Moreover, he gave us
mobility; and although his airmanship was not always conventional,
I would have flown with him anywhere. In the weeks before D-Day he
regularly flew us to the stations from which the radar attacks were being
made. These began on 10th May, but for the first week or so I did not
take a direct part, because of the other activities that we had to maintain,
including setting up our own Overseas Party under Hugh Smith to go
in behind the initial attack on Day D+2, to seize any radar or other
technical equipment that should be sent back to England for examination.

The evidence from the first week indicated that the attacks were going
rather well, and Birtwistle—who had been briefing the pilots personally
and had clearly done it excellently—told me that he thought it was time
for me to come in. On his and Cecil's advice, my first step was to visit
the two main stations concerned, Thorney Island, where the radar
strikes were being flown by 20 Sector, under Group Captain Gillam,
and Hurn, where 22 Sector was operating under Group Captain Davoud.
So on Saturday 27th May Cecil, Birtwistle and I went out to Hendon,

having secured a Proctor communications aircraft with which Cecil was to fly us to Thorney Island and then on to Hurn and Odiham (from which 39 Reconnaissance Wing under Group Captain Moncrieff was flying the photographic sorties along with 35 Wing under Group Captain Donkin at Gatwick), and then back to Hendon at the end of the day.

I had not been in the air for some considerable time, and flying with such a spirited pilot as Rupert Cecil was a new experience. As we headed south-westwards from Hendon a Spitfire from Northholt thought that he would surprise us with a dummy attack from our starboard flank, heading straight for us. From his subsequent manoeuvre I imagined that he was as surprised as I was when Cecil, with all his old bomber pilot's reactions, banked us sharply into a turn heading directly at the fighter, at the same time shouting at the top of his voice, 'You should always turn into an attack!' Since I had almost forgotten the practice of going with the aircraft and was tending to use the horizon to maintain my orientation, I found myself still trying to sit vertically while we were in a vertical bank. The Spitfire duly missed us, and we went on our way, the flight itself being memorable for the sight of wild rhododendrons in bloom on the west Surrey hills—I have never been able to see them since without recalling D-Day.

Our final approach to Thorney Island was somewhat dramatic: one moment we seemed to be high in the air and then everything seemed to happen at once, but evidently not quite rapidly enough for Cecil, who was working several controls at the same time and shouting, 'Landing this aircraft is like delivering a bloody cow!'

The rest of the day was uneventful (apart from a characteristic Cecil landing at Odiham which earned as big a reproach as a Flight Lieutenant Flying Control Officer dared make to a Wing Commander with two D.F.C.s, 'I didn't see you make an orbit, sir!' only to be withered by Cecil's. 'Didn't you?') until our final landing at Hendon where a Dakota was immediately ahead of us and turning into his final approach. Cecil immediately recalled one of the few rules that he observed in flying, which was that the aircraft at the lower height has the right of way. Since he could out-turn a Dakota in a Proctor, he actually turned inside the other aircraft, commenting, 'Look at that idiot going off on a cross-country!' and succeeded in losing enough height so that when the Dakota pilot had straightened out for his final approach he was astonished to find us immediately in front of him, and we landed amid a shower of Verey lights fired from the ground, and only just skimming the railway

embankment that bordered the eastern side of the airfield. A train was
travelling southwards at the time, and we were only about fifty yards in
front of it—I can still recall the heads of the driver and fireman looking
out and wondering whether we would miss them.

Rupert Cecil had two other rules for flying. The first was to make
sure that your radio did not work because then you could not be
instructed from the ground, and in such a situation the captain of the
aircraft had complete discretion in all his actions. And since some of
Cecil's actions were not exactly conventional, he had one further rule
which ran, 'You can get away with anything—once!' And if my description of flying with him earns the disapproval of more orthodox airmen
I can only repeat that I would have flown with him anywhere.

It was a day well spent because both I and the pilots benefited from
the contact. At first they had been lukewarm about shooting up radar
stations, which did not explode spectacularly as, for example, railway
locomotives did; but as they came to realize the importance of the
operation, they began to take a direct interest, and were perusing our
'Rhubarb' Appendix for themselves. Most Freyas were surrounded by
blast walls (as in Figure 9, p. 213), but there had to be gaps in the walls
for the operators to enter the equipment. The pilots began to study our
photographs in detail and make their attacks so as to fire through the
gaps. Moreover, they began to suggest the stations they would like to
attack. These, of course, were decided on a central plan, and orders
went out to the Sectors from Victor Tait's party at headquarters. In
particular, the station at Fécamp had been left alone, but the Typhoons at
Thorney Island very much wanted to attack it. I told them that it was
part of the plan that Fécamp should be left intact, and that they must do
nothing unless an order came from headquarters.

A week later we were at Thorney Island again, and it was clear
from the camera gun and other photographic evidence that the attacks
were being very well carried out, and exceeding anything that we could
have hoped. Even before my first visit 29 sites had been attacked,
involving 619 sorties, and 20 radar equipments had been badly damaged,
as judged by the photographic evidence alone, and many others had
probably been damaged but not badly enough to show up photographi-
cally. During the subsequent week many more attacks were carried out
and I began to think that we could succeed in eliminating a substantial
proportion of the German radar effort by the time D-Day arrived.

On my visit of 3rd June I found the pilots clamouring to be allowed
to tackle Fécamp, and I weighed up the arguments. If I could persuade

the rest of the party at headquarters that an attack should be made, after all, and an order therefore be sent out to the Sectors, the pilots would have the satisfaction of knowing that they had had a direct influence on the conduct of the campaign. Although nothing was really necessary to boost their morale, the sense of participation would reward their enthusiasm. Also, I thought, the plan was quite possibly too rigid, in that it was all very well leaving a station alone, but it was in any event unlikely that we would eliminate all the stations that might observe our spoof convoys, and so even if Fécamp were knocked out the spoof would be duly observed by the Germans. I told the pilots that I would see what could be done, and we flew back to Hendon for the evening meeting at Stanmore. Finally I convinced the rest of the party that it was foolish not to make at least a minor effort against Fécamp: since it had not been so far attacked its radar operators were likely to be the least flustered of any in the whole coastal chain, and therefore the most likely to be able to detect that our spoof convoy was false. This argument won the day, and it was rather reluctantly agreed to send out an order to Thorney Island for a small attack to be made. The order went out on 4th June, and Birtwistle, Cecil, and I could guess at its effect.

On Monday 5th June we again travelled to Thorney Island, and found that the pilots had just returned from the Fécamp attack. They had interpreted their orders very liberally, and had given Fécamp everything they could carry. Before returning to Stanmore, we flew on to Hurn, and it was clear that the Invasion was 'on' because the large armada of ships which had been in Spithead two days before was no longer there. I was silently wishing them Good Luck when we had a head-on encounter with a whole wing of American Thunderbolts. It was like standing in a butt while a covey of enormous grouse is driven past you on all sides. What was more, the Thunderbolts with their big radial engines were climbing, and so none of their pilots could see us.

We duly landed at Hurn, my main memory there being of a Norwegian Wing Commander who had been taking part in the radar strikes. He had been shot down earlier that day, picked up out of the sea by one of our air/sea rescue launches, and had already flown another sortie. That evening at Stanmore, the meeting started with Birtwistle's report of operations for the day, finally coming to Fécamp. He reported in respectful terms that an attack had been made that morning, and that he would give the details. As he read out the dosage, it gradually dawned on the others how they had been 'conned'. Twenty-eight Typhoons had attacked, firing innumerable cannon shells and ninety-six 60-lb. rockets, and dropping seven tons of bombs, many of them with delayed action. Birtwistle read out the report, and I can remember his conclusion as he came to the delayed-action bombs, looking at his watch and saying, 'They should just be going off now, sir! Just a little raid, sir!' The others took it very well, and we went home hoping for the best.

Besides the German radar stations, there was another problem on my mind that night. This was whether or not the Germans would be able to jam our Gee navigational system that our Invasion craft were intending to use, and some of our vital communications links, especially those used for fighter control. My problem was that the radio listening stations operated by our own Signals Intelligence Service had taken many bearings on the German jammers, and had concluded that there were 23 independent sites, all of which would have to be eliminated. But we could only locate five sites, my own evidence being based on a dispute that we knew from Engima to have involved one of the German beam stations in 1940, when a jamming station had been sited on the same hill as it was, Mont Couple, near Boulogne. The beam station staff had been worried that the jamming station would upset their beam, but it evidently did not, for the jammer remained in position. We had thus been able to identify and locate it, and to watch its development over the next three-and-a-half years.

From its appearance, Claude Wavell had over the years found four other stations in the Invasion and Spoof areas which he thought must all have been designed by the same architect, and which were sufficiently similar to the Mont Couple station to be classed as probable jammers; but he could find no more. Where then were the other eighteen? It is the most difficult of Intelligence problems to prove a negative case; we had all the alleged sites (which had been specified by our direction-finding operators to the nearest mile) rephotographed but Wavell and his team scanned the pictures in vain. We were inclined to think that once again the radio evidence had let us down, and that the eighteen missing stations were merely the result of erroneous bearings. There was much misgivings at A.E.A.F. when I told them to eliminate the five jammers and see what happened. Since they had been budgeting for knocking out twenty-three stations, there was effort to spare; and we told them that it would be worth using some of this effort against two further stations, including one of the Hague Peninsula which, as luck would have it, proved to be one of the main German intercept stations for listening to our own radio communications.

As for the method of elimination, Rupert Cecil suggested that his old group, 5 Group, should undertake the job. I said I thought this was very unlikely to succeed because of the by now well established errors of night bombing. Cecil maintained that his Group could do it, and so we decided to try . On the first night, 31st May/1st June, they failed—but the photographs showed that all their bombs were concentrated in little more than a single field just to the side of the jamming site. Obviously there had been a minor marking error, and the concentration was so good that all the bombs had missed. Two nights later the Group went out again and this time the bombs completely destroyed the jammers. Incidentally, it was this that brought home to me the enormous improvement in our bombing accuracy which, if others had perhaps realized it, too, could have allowed us to revert to precision bombing earlier than we did. Anyway, the same technique was employed against the other four jamming sites, and we had no trouble whatsoever from the jammers over the whole period of D-Day and the following week. It had meant much anxious work for Claude Wavell and his staff in searching for the eighteen non-existent jammers, and we were all relieved at this vindication of their painstaking skill.

I drove out to Stanmore on the morning of D-Day to see how things were going. Almost the first officer I met was the Group Captain who had asked me to find the jammers, and who had been very sceptical about our disbelief in the missing eighteen stations. When I asked him how the invasion was going he replied, 'I haven't heard, but it must be going well—there is a marked increase in saluting, this morning!'

And so it turned out. Not only had we eliminated the jammers and the headquarters of the German Signals Intelligence Service in north-west France which might otherwise have detected our movements on Day D-1, but we had knocked out a large proportion of the German radar chain. Of the 47 radar stations that were in operation three weeks before D-Day, hardly more than half a dozen were able to transmit on the vital night, and these were so shaken that their operators fell easily for Cockburn's spoof, and German guns and searchlights were brought into action against the bogus Fécamp convoy. One operator in a station near Caen did, I believe, detect the approach of our genuine armada, but his reports were discounted higher up the chain of command because they were not confirmed by other radar stations. So we achieved a degree of surprise far greater than we could have hoped: four years' work had proved worthwhile, although I have sometimes wondered what would have happened without that after-lunch talk with Tedder.

Reviewing the results, Sir Trafford Leigh Mallory, the Allied Expeditionary Air Force Commander, said in his Official Despatch (*London Gazette*, 2 January 1947):

> The application of radio counter-measures immediately preceding the assault proved to be extraordinarily successful. . . . These results may be summarized as follows: the enemy did not obtain the early warning of our approach that his Radar coverage should have made possible; there is every reason to suppose that Radar controlled gunfire was interfered with; no fighter aircraft hindered our airborne operations; the enemy was confused and his troop movements were delayed.

And as for the attack that we had thrown in for good measure along with those on the five jammers, the Despatch said:

> The success of this last attack on the Headquarters of the German Air Force Signals Intelligence must have been a major catastrophe for the enemy, and it may well be that it was an important contributory factor to the lack of enemy air reaction to the assault.

But there was a cost. As the Official Despatch said, 'These Radar targets were very heavily defended by flak, and low level attacks upon them demanded great skill and daring . . . losses among senior and more experienced pilots were heavy'. In one case, that of an attack on a 'hoarding' on the Hague Peninsula, I received a German eye-witness account: three of our fighters had attacked in line astern, and one was hit by flak. The pilot had dived his aircraft into the hoarding, finishing it—and himself—for ever. The German said that it was the bravest thing that he had ever seen. It was agreed on the Air Staff that if I could find who the pilot was I should write a citation for a posthumous Victoria Cross; but two of the three aircraft in the attack had crashed with their pilots lost, and we could not establish which was the aircraft which had destroyed the hoarding.

The Official Despatch concluded: 'These attacks saved the lives of countless soldiers, sailors and airmen on D-Day'.

CHAPTER FORTY-FOUR

V-1

WHILE THE first five months of 1944 were heavily occupied with the misfortunes of Bomber Command and the coming landings in Normandy, we dared not relax our watch on the pilotless aircraft and the long range rocket. In principle, and not through pique, I could have disclaimed any further responsibility. What we had discovered by the end of 1943 had already given all the technical information necessary for countermeasures to the flying bomb: weight of warhead, size of aircraft, its speed and height, and so forth. And, indeed, now that the responsibility was firmly back with the Air Staff, which had appointed Claude Pelly as Director of Operations (Special Operations) and supported him with an inter-Service Staff, there might have seemed little more for my own Section to do. But, as I had expected, there were signs that Pelly's staff was less able than we were to form accurate assessments of the threat. Just as I was issuing my report of 24th December 1943 on the pilotless aircraft, the Chief of Air Staff on Pelly's advice warned that the Germans might be bombarding London with 300 tons of bombs in an eight-hour period by mid-January 1944. My own estimate was that 'a heavy bombardment could probably not occur until March 1944, assuming that the snags shown in the present trials are overcome, and that production and training are proceeding satisfactorily'.

In fact, production in Germany was far from proceeding satisfactorily, as we later discovered. Air attacks by Bomber Command and the Eighth Army Air Force, particularly on the Fieseler Works at Kassel, in October 1943, resulted in supplies of flying bombs to Peenemünde being halted from October 1943 to February 1944. The opening of the campaign against London had repeatedly to be postponed, and we could see from the radar plots of the Peenemünde and Zempin trials that the bomb was still not ready. Pelly had agreed that the evaluation of the radar plots should be left to me, as my Unit had developed the necessary expertise, and this work became the task of a young physicist from Ebbw Vale, David Arthen Jones, who had served as a civilian in 60

Group after graduating with First Class Honours at Bangor, and who held Welsh University 'Blues' for boxing, rugby, and cricket. He was in fact Glamorgan's fast bowler and would—according to Bill Hitch, the Glamorgan coach—have been England's fast bowler had the war not intervened, and had he decided to give up physics for full-time cricket. I had previously not believed such tales as the swinging of cricket balls by seam bowlers, particularly at Trent Bridge before lunch, until Arthen told me with modest confidence that he could do it, and I kept wicket for him while he told me what every ball would do. Watching his plots of the Baltic trials over the next few months, we could see that the reliability and accuracy of the flying bombs were rapidly improving.

The question arose of how much damage we might expect to be inflicted on London, and we found that even the size of London was variable, according to whether one wished to minimize or maximize the expected threat. In particular, Herbert Morrison was characteristically nervous and would assume as large an area as possible, whereas others such as Lindemann would go to the other extreme. Was 'London' to be taken as the London postal district or the Greater London area, or what? In the end, I presented the German trials results as objectively as possible by assuming that each bomb had been aimed at Charing Cross from the south-east, and superimposing the plot of the range and bearing

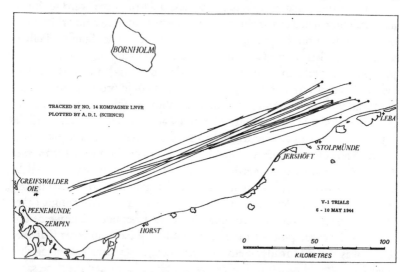

Fig. 27. Tracks of V–1s fired in trials at Peenemünde, May 1944, as plotted by Scientific Intelligence from the German radar plots. Comparison with Figure 22 will show the increase in accuracy since December 1943

errors for every bomb in the Baltic trials on a map where the built-up areas of London and its suburbs were shaded in, so as to indicate the proportion of bombs which would have fallen on built-up areas.

Figure 27 shows the plotted tracks in the Baltic trials for a few days in May 1944; comparison with Figure 22 will show how much the accuracy had improved since December 1943. Taking the end-points of all the Baltic plots for May 1944 and transferring them to a map of London on the assumption that they had been aimed instead at Charing Cross from the Abbeville area, we produced on 9th June 1944 the diagram shown in Figure 28b, which may be compared with Figure 28a which shows the actual fall of bombs in the first 24 hours of the main bombardment.

In the meantime, the bombing campaign against the 96 'ski' sites, from which the flying bombs were to be launched, was well under way, with Pelly directing the efforts of both British and American bombers. Besides the launching sites themselves, Medmenham had discovered earlier in February 1944 eight large sites that were obviously intended as supply depots, and which were heavily defended by A-A guns; these were not attacked for the time being. The effort against the ski sites was such that by the third week in April the Chiefs of Staff considered that all the ski sites would have been neutralized by the end of the month.

By that time, however, aerial photographs showed that the Germans were building what became known as 'modified sites', from which the familiar skis were missing, and which could be much more rapidly erected. Even so, there were some who thought that the main danger had been averted, and Pelly himself moved from his post, in which he had never been happy, to become Chief Intelligence Officer of the Allied Expeditionary Air Force, because he thought that in this new post he would see much more action. He was succeeded in the middle of May by Air Commodore Colin Grierson who, once again, was completely new to Intelligence. On the German side, too, there had been organizational changes. The most important of these had been in December 1943 when Wachtel, instead of having an independent command in control of Flak Regiment 155W, was subordinated to a new Army Corps, the LXVth, commanded by Lieutenant General Erich Heinemann, who was to co-ordinate Wachtel's operations with those of Major General Dornberger, who was in charge of long-range rocket development.

About the time that Pelly left I warned that, from what I could see of notices sent to the Baltic radar plotters, 'These announcements,

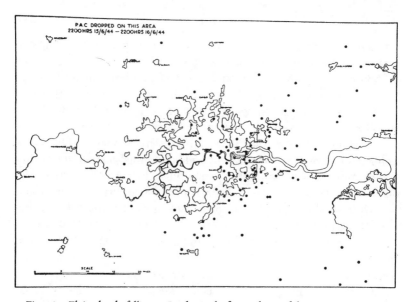

Fig. 28a. Flying bombs falling on London in the first 24 hours of the main V–1 campaign

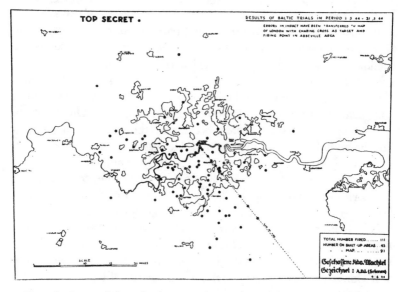

Fig. 28b. Scatter of flying bombs on London as predicted from the Baltic trials of Figure 27.
Note that both patterns tend to fall short of Central London

coupled with the generally high rate of activity during April and early May imply either an increased degree of urgency in the trials, or that they have now reached the stage where sustained rate of fire is being tested, the missile itself having been proved satisfactory' (13th May 1944). But Grierson's staff as late as 11th June reported that while eight ski sites might have survived and therefore be used, the sixty-six 'modified sites' would not be fit for use 'on any appreciable scale' for the next few weeks (D. Kelly: *The Defence of the United Kingdom*, p. 368). In fact, the routine watch on the launching sites had fallen into the classic error that had befallen the long watch on the battle cruisers in Brest: the watchers become so tired and jaded that they miss a vital development. On this occasion, honour was just saved because a Belgian agent reported on 10th June that a train of 33 waggons had passed through Ghent in the direction of France, with each waggon carrying three objects described as 'rockets'. Furthermore, the bad weather that had inhibited photographic reconnaissance since 4th June cleared on 11th June, and hectic activity was visible at several of the modified sites. The Air Staff was therefore able to give a last-minute warning that the flying bomb attack was imminent.

The first ten bombs were launched on the night of 12th/13th June. Five crashed shortly after launching, and a sixth one went missing; of the remaining four, one fell in Sussex, and the others near Gravesend, near Sevenoaks and at Bethnal Green. My first visitor the following morning was Jimmy Langley, who warmly shook my hand and congratulated me. It turned out that he had made bets regarding the day on which the first flying bomb would land in England, based on our passing prediction some months before that the day would be D+7. We had by accident hit exactly the right day, on a very general argument: assuming the Normandy landings would provoke Hitler into ordering an immediate bombardment we estimated that the reaction time of a large-ish military organization such as Wachtel's Regiment would be about a week, and so we had therefore suggested the starting date as 'D+7'. In fact, although Wachtel was not ready, the 65th Army Corps signalled on 6th June that he was urgently to prepare to bomb London, and the preparations took six days, enabling Jimmy Langley to win the bets which he had placed on the basis of our prediction, with a confidence that I would never have entertained myself.

I went over to the Cabinet Office to see Cherwell, who was tending to chuckle at the insignificance of the German effort and who said, 'The mountain hath groaned and given forth a mouse!' I told him that the night's effort had in my opinion been an organizational hiccup and that within a few days we should see a major bombardment. In any event, we knew that the Germans could launch twenty missiles a day at Peenemünde, so they could at least do that in France. I asked Cherwell to persuade Churchill to warn the country, but I assume that he did not do so. This was unfortunate, because I had heard Churchill say at an earlier meeting that the people of Britain would stand anything if you warned them in advance about what they were in for. And although he had in fact sounded warnings about the retaliation campaign both in 1943 and earlier in 1944, I am sure it would have helped the country, and perhaps his own position, if he had given the kind of warning on 13th June that I had suggested. As it was the Germans quickly overcame their deficiencies, and on 15th June the V-1 (as the FZG76 came to be called in Germany—'Vergeltungs 1'—'Retaliation 1') campaign opened in earnest, and the people of London tended to feel that the Government had been taken unawares.

In the 24 hours beginning at 22.30 on 15th June, Wachtel launched more than 200 flying bombs, of which 144 crossed our coasts and 73 reached Greater London. 33 bombs were brought down by the defences but eleven of these came down in the built-up area of Greater London. I was horrified to see our anti-aircraft gunners firing enthusiastically at the bombs as they crossed London, which was the worst possible thing to do. For if a bomb were hit, this made sure that it would fall on London rather than pass over and explode harmlessly beyond. Cherwell needed only the slightest persuasion to intervene, and the practice was dropped within a few days.

The guns were at some disadvantage through a misunderstanding regarding the operational heights at which the flying bombs were operated. In December 1943 I had reported that the height band mainly used in the Peenemünde trials was six thousand to seven thousand feet, although I also mentioned that some trials were made at heights as low as fifteen hundred feet. As the trials progressed at Peenemünde in 1944, the heights were gradually brought down, and we duly mentioned the fact. What I did not know was that Air Marshal Roderick Hill, who commanded our fighters and guns, had pointed out before the campaign opened that if the bombs were to fly at heights between two and three thousand feet, our guns 'would have a very awkward task, for between those heights the targets would be too high for the light anti-aircraft guns and too low for the mobile heavy guns which at that time could not be traversed smoothly enough to engage such speedy missiles.'

Although we reported the change in height of the Peenemünde trials as a matter of routine I would—had I known the Commander-in-Chief's anxiety—have made the point personally to him. His views, which were presumably sent to the Air Staff, did not reach me; and our information about the reduction in height did not reach him. Once again, this was an example of the hierarchical attenuation of information, and it underlined the need for the shortest links between Operational and Intelligence Staffs—whilst preserving the independence of Intelligence.

The fighters, on which our defences mainly depended during the first few weeks of the bombardment, quickly began to do rather well, even though they were not completely ready despite our six months' warning regarding the performance that they would need to have. The emergency resulted in Christopher Hartley having to take his experimental squadron into action, instead of continuing to develop techniques for other squadrons to use, and so he took his squadron to Tangmere, which they shared with two squadrons from the Second Tactical Air Force. After a week or so, the Station Commander told Hartley that he had been watching all three squadrons, and that somehow Hartley got about twice as much work out of his squadron as either of the other two commanders did, and asked Hartley how he achieved it. Hartley replied that, 'It is simple, Sir. I have the last *squadron* in the Air Force!' When the Station Commander asked him what he meant, he pointed out that the Fighter Development Unit was an experimental unit, and had therefore not yet been changed over to the 'planned servicing' arrangements now imposed on all the regular units in the Royal Air Force.

Since the point is of much administrative interest, it is worth further explanation. The Battle of Britain, for example, was fought on the older system of servicing in which each pilot had his own aircraft, and that aircraft was serviced by a devoted ground crew, so that they regarded themselves as part of a team with the pilot, and felt that they shared in any victories that he achieved. Obviously this could be extravagant in ground crew, and one of the early results of Operational Research was to show that substantial economies could be effected by changing over to a kind of central garage system into which aircraft were sent for servicing after each operation, and from which each pilot could draw a serviced aircraft, probably a different one from that which he last flew, for each new operation.

The scheme succeeded in Coastal Command, where the main criterion was the number of flying hours achieved per aircraft and per unit of ground crew, so well that it was extended to the other Commands as well. But it achieved flying hours at the expense of the espirit de corps that formerly existed between air crew and ground crew; and, moreover, as one pilot pointed out to me, if you were flying with one aircraft continuously and knew its various faults, you knew those which you could, literally, live with and could therefore afford to take out even if it were not in perfect condition, whereas with one that you were drawing from a central pool you had to make sure that it was fault-free before you could risk flying it.

The main point, though, was the esprit de corps, and this was what Hartley had meant with his 'last *squadron* in the Air Force'. The enthusiasm engendered by the direct interest of the ground crew in any particular aircraft and pilot somehow drew substantially more work out of them when an emergency arose. Since this is rarely quantifiable, it is not usually taken into account by any plan to improve administrative efficiency.

Within a few days of the opening of the V-1 bombardment a new problem arose. 'George', with whom I had been involved in supplying misleading information to the Germans through the agents whom they supposed to be freely operating in Britain, called on me one morning and asked my advice. The dilemma facing M.I.5 was that the Germans were now telling their supposed London agents to report the times and places of flying bomb incidents in London. If, to preserve the security of possible future deceptions, we were to supply truthful information to the Germans, this would be aiding the enemy. If, on the other hand, we supplied false information, then this could be checked by German photographic reconnaissance, in which case the agents would be 'blown' and future deception plans ruined. What should he do?

It immediately occurred to me that photographic reconnaissance could only reveal the points of impact, and not the times. Moreover, I knew from previous experience that while agents could usually define the place of an incident fairly well, they were likely to be wrong in other details, even the time.

I had noticed that in the Peenemünde trials the bombs tended to fall short of the target, and now knew from the plot of bombs for the first 24 hours (which is shown on Figure 28a) that the operational bombs were also tending to fall short, the centre of gravity being in south-east London, near Dulwich. In a flash I saw that we might be able to keep the bombs falling short, which would mean fewer casualties in London as a whole, and at the same time avoid arousing any suspicions regarding the genuineness of the agents.

We could give correct points of impact for bombs that tended to have a longer range than usual, but couple these with times of bombs which in fact had fallen short. Thus, if the Germans attempted any correlation, they might be led to think that even the bombs which they had reason to believe might have fallen short were instead tending to fall in north-west London. Therefore, if they made any correction at all, it would be to reduce the average range. This range was, incidentally, determined by an 'air-log' which was a small propeller which clocked up the air miles flown by the bomb, and everything depended on its having been correctly calibrated, and on due allowance for the wind. After the appropriate number of revolutions had been counted the fuel supply was cut and the missile put into a dive. It was those silent seconds between the noisy roar of the engine and the explosion on the ground that made the weapon such a nerve-racking one.

As I recommended this course of action to 'George', I realized well that what I was doing was trying to keep the mean point of impact in the Dulwich area, where my own parents lived and where, of course, my old school was. But I knew that neither my parents nor the school would have had it otherwise. 'George' said that he would adopt the plan, and we waited to see what would happen. Somehow, though, the dilemma got out, and it was discussed at the political level, with Duncan Sandys now back in the picture. Both he and Lindemann supported the policy we had already put into effect, but it was opposed by Herbert Morrison, whose constituency was a nearby one, Lambeth, and who seemed to think that the attempt to keep the aiming point short was an effort by Government officials and others in Westminister, Belgravia, and Mayfair, to keep the bombs off themselves at the expense of the proletariat in south London.

This was the second time that my own ideas about the bombardment of London differed from those of administrators and politicians. In the previous year, Herbert Morrison's adviser, Sir Findlater Stewart, had produced a paper on the evacuation of London in the event of a rocket bombardment, which seemed to me altogether to underrate the spirit of the Londoners, introducing proposed measures with such phrases as, 'If panic is to be avoided'. I could not help commenting that although I was at the meeting as a scientist, I lived in London, my parents were in London, my wife and family were in London, and never had I seen such an insult offered to the people of London. There was little further discussion.

I was not present at the meeting at which the deception policy was discussed, but Herbert Morrison was in the chair in Churchill's absence, and he finally ruled that it would be an interference with Providence if we were to supply the Germans with misleading information, because this might mean that some people would be killed through our action who might otherwise have survived—overlooking the fact that what we were hoping to do, while it undoubtedly might involve such cases, would also enable more to survive who might otherwise have been killed. 'George' came and told me of the ruling, asking what he should now do. Whether or not it is relevant that Nelson and I were both born on 29th September, I could not help recalling his comment at Copenhagen, and I did not even have to substitute my deaf ear for his blind eye, for I remarked that I had not been present at the meeting, and the decision was so incredible that I would only believe it if I received instructions in writing; and so until that time my instructions to 'George' were to continue as we had started, which he accordingly did.

When we overran Wachtel's headquarters two and a half months or so later, we were able to see the results of our work, for he had recorded the points of impact of the flying bombs, both as reported by the agents and as plotted by his own organization on sample bombs which had been fitted with radio transmitters. We had not known beforehand of these radio-transmitting samples, which, in correctly indicating that the bombs were falling short, contradicted the agent's reports which showed that they were tending to over-shoot. Plate 24 is a reproduction of Wachtel's own battle map showing both the radio plots and the spies' reports. A written comment by Wachtel's organization (which had been aiming at Tower Bridge rather than Charing Cross) on the discrepancy stated that the agents were particularly reliable, and therefore their information was to be accepted, and that there must be something wrong with the radio D/F method.

In this helpful conclusion, Wachtel was supported by the evidence of photographic reconnaissance, which incidentally revealed one of the biggest surprises of the whole war. It turned out that there seemed to have been no German photographic reconnaissance of London from 10th January 1941 to 10th September 1944. We had expected that the Germans would have flown regular reconnaissances of the whole of southern England, but Fighter Command had been so effective in interception that the Germans had not succeeded in making a reconnaissance of London for three years and nine months, no more than fifty miles inside our coastline, while our photo reconnaissance pilots were often flying over five hundred miles of German occupied territory. I knew of no more startling contrast in the entire war, a joint tribute to Fighter Command and to our Reconnaissance Units.

I had a slight inkling of the situation before we captured Wachtel's map, because I had read a glowing tribute to the new German twin-jet fighter, the Messerschmidt 262, which a secret Luftwaffe report said was so good it had succeeded in a photographic reconnaissance of London 'hitherto considered impossible'. By good fortune for us, there was cloud over much of south London, while north of the Thames it was clear, so the bomb damage plots compiled from the sortie were blank for an area south of the Thames, while there was plenty of damage north of the Thames—but much of it was not due to the flying bombs at all but to the late raids of Spring 1941. Wachtel's organization was, naturally, only too anxious to claim as much damage as possible, so they proudly showed all the 1941 damage, which was not of course there on the January 1941 photographs, as due to their weapon. By good luck, therefore, the photographic evidence appeared to support completely what the agents had been telling them.

It is possible to make a very rough estimate of the reduction of casualties in London caused by the flying bombs tending to fall short. The Official History, *The Defence of the United Kingdom*, states that, in all, 8,617 bombs were launched from the sites in France, of which 2,340 reached the London Civil Defence Region. These caused casualties of approximately 5,500 killed and 16,000 seriously injured. Figure 28a shows the distribution of points of impact during the first twenty-four hours of the main campaign when, of the 90 bombs plotted, only about 30 fell inside the built-up areas. If the same pattern had been shifted northwestwards by about four miles, roughly 45 out of the 90 bombs would have fallen in built-up areas, increasing the casualties and damage by fifty per cent. Assuming, therefore, that the Germans had quickly discovered their error and lengthened the range, up to fifty per cent more casualties might have been incurred in the campaign, or up to 2,750 more killed and up to 8,000 more seriously injured. Even if only a fifth of these figures is ascribed to the success of our deception, it was clearly worthwhile.

There was a happy postscript to this story at one of my Staff College lectures after the war. I had recounted the events that I have just described, and at the end of the lecture one of the Directing Staff stood up and said that he could complete my story. He was Group Captain (afterwards Air Chief Marshal Sir Alfred) Earle who explained that during the war he had been Air Secretary of the War Cabinet, and had been present at the discussion which had resulted in Herbert Morrison's incredible ruling. Earle had wondered what he could do, and then the bright idea struck him that he should persuade the Cabinet that the matter was so secret that the instruction to give the Germans correct information should not even be put into writing, 'And', he said, 'I knew that that would be enough for *you!*'

The actual flying bomb incident that remains most in my memory occurred on Sunday 18th June when Charles Frank and I were both in the office. Shortly after eleven o'clock I was on the telephone to Bimbo Norman at Bletchley when we heard the unforgettable noise of a flying bomb. Norman could hear it over the telephone, too, and then the engine cut out. I remarked to him that this was going to be pretty near, and that we were getting under our desks. There was a deafening explosion, and I can remember Norman's voice saying, 'Are you alright? Are you alright?', and I assured him that we were. I then went out of the office to see what had happened, and found that the bomb had fallen about 150 yards away on the Guards Chapel. It had struck during Sunday morning service, and had killed 121 of the congregation and the Coldstreamers' Band, including their Director of Music, Lieutenant Colonel Windram, one of the most human of military band conductors, who used to delight us in St. James's Park by telling us about every piece of music he was about to play. There was nothing for me to do, for the Guards had everything under control, and were already carrying out the dead. But that sight, coupled with the sea of fresh green leaves that had been torn from the plane trees in Birdcage Walk, brought home to me the difference between one ton of explosive in actuality and the one ton that we had predicted in the abstract six months before.

Despite the considerable successes of our fighters—and these were obtained at some risk to themselves, since an exploding flying bomb was not the safest of atmospheric companions—too many bombs were still getting through. Attacks on the launching sites were not very profitable since in their new form these were difficult to discover and easy to replace. Both Bomber Command and the Eighth Army Air Force had bombed them without substantial effect. The eight major supply sites were therefore an attractive alternative, and so Bomber Command was invited to attack them. Despite heavy attacks on 16th and 17th June, the rate of fire had not slackened off, and the Commander-in-Chief was therefore doubtful about the value of further attacks until the need could be justified. His doubts were well founded, for the eight sites turned out to be part of the original ski-site programme, and were not used in the 'modified' site campaign.

The resultant limited success of our various countermeasures, perhaps coupled with the tragedy of the Guards Chapel only a few hundred yards across St. James's Park from Whitehall, worried the War Cabinet. On 19th June the Prime Minister formed the 'Crossbow' Committee of the War Cabinet to report on the flying bomb and rocket and the progress of countermeasures, and on 20th June he decided that he would hand over the chairmanship to Mr. Sandys, who therefore came right back into the picture, and in a commanding position. Along with the Commanders-in-Chief of the appropriate Commands and various senior serving officers and scientists, I became a member of the Committee.

Shortly after this, there were changes in the Air Staff arrangements. the strain was beginning to tell on Colin Grierson, for whom I was profoundly sorry. He had been thrust into a very difficult post only a week or two before the flying bomb campaign opened, and he found himself having to work in a field in which he had had no previous experience. We had helped him as much as we could, but Frank Inglis, the Assistant Chief of Air Staff (Intelligence) sent for me at the beginning of July and told me that he had decided to relieve Grierson of his Intelligence responsibilities and hand all such responsibilities regarding the German retaliation campaign over to me from 6th July. This was very late in the day, but at last I had a chance of co-ordinating all our Intelligence efforts.

One of my first steps was to make sure that the Americans were completely in the Intelligence picture, since the Eighth Army Air Force was being asked to undertake much of the bombing of the flying bomb organization along with Bomber Command. I therefore asked Bob Robertson, who was now Eisenhower's Scientific Adviser with the rank of a four-star General, whether he would come right into our organization as my deputy for all flying bomb and rocket matters, and he very willingly agreed. A further step in the same direction was to try to bring Military Intelligence and Air Intelligence closer together, because relations were showing signs of strain. The War Office felt that the Air Ministry and the politicians were now completely obsessed by the flying bomb and were paying no attention to the rocket. Indeed Matthew Pryor, whose alarm about the rocket in April 1943 had aroused all the political interest, had just written a report which suggested that the Air Staff were now ignoring the rocket; I met him and told him that however much other branches of Air Intelligence might be pre-occupied with the V-1, my own Section had been watching for the rocket as keenly as ever, and I persuaded him to come across from the War Office and join us for the duration of the threat, with the particular responsibility for studying the military organization associated with the rocket while I took responsibility for the technical details.

As for the flying bomb, its violence did not seem to be affected much by Allied attacks on either the launching or the original supply sites. It seemed that the bombs must be distributed from some other sites, and reports began to come in from the French about three underground storage depots. The largest of these was at St. Leu d'Esserent, in some caves in the Oise Valley just north of Paris. The second site was at Nucourt, northwest of Paris, where there were also limestone caves, and the third at Rilly-la-Montagne, south of Rheims, in a railway tunnel. The caves at St. Leu had been used in peacetime for growing mush-rooms, and the French very helpfully supplied us with detailed plans. I therefore recommended that these underground storage sites should be attacked, and in the last week of June the Eighth Army Air Force made heavy attacks on both Nucourt and St. Leu. At the former, 241 flying bombs were irretrievably buried and another 57 seriously damaged.

St. Leu, however, was less vulnerable, owing to the greater thickness of the limestone roof, which required heavier bombs than were available in the American Air Force. It was an ideal case for 'Tallboy', the big streamlined bomb developed by Barnes Wallis, but even then it would require careful aiming and a precise knowledge of the tunnelling if the bombs were to be dropped in the right places. Fortunately we knew the exact positions of the tunnels from the French, and in urging the bomb-ing I had said at an Air Staff conference that I was prepared to go to 617 Squadron to brief them myself. This offer may have been taken some-what amiss by the Commander-in-Chief, who strongly discouraged any direct contact between the Air Staff and his squadrons, so Rupert Cecil drove me out to High Wycombe to see him. As soon as we met, he said that before I said anything, he would like to tell me what he thought. For ten minutes or so, he spoke sheer good sense, saying that he had ordered a raid for that same night, and then asked for my com-ments. I replied that what he had said to me was exactly what I had come to say to him, and he then showed us where he had placed the main aiming point. I showed him the French plans, and suggested that

the aiming point should be moved some 200 yards south-east, since his
aiming point was displaced by this amount from where I knew that the
main entrance tunnel ran. So far from resenting my interference, he
then picked up the telephone to speak to Air Marshal Cochrane, the Air
Officer Commanding No. 5 Group, which was to carry out the raid,
and said, 'I say, Cocky, about the raid tonight. I have Dr. Jones here and
he thinks that we ought to move the aiming point 200 yards to the south-
east to hit the main tunnel. Do you think that we can change it?' This
was agreed.

The raid took place on 4th/5th July and was extremely successful, to
judge by the subsequent aerial photographs. In contrast with Nucourt,
we did not get the detailed German returns for the number of flying
bombs wrecked, but we knew that it could have been holding 2,000,
and the site was rendered almost useless. The German Commandant
reported that many of the tunnels had collapsed, and that the approach
roads were impassable. Moreover, we saw the effects in the reduced
rate of fire against London which fell from an average of 100 a day
before 7th July to fewer than 70 a day for the next ten days.

The reduction in the rate of bombardment worked more in our
favour than the launching figures suggest by themselves, because our
defences were then less saturated and thus able to achieve a higher rate
of success. Before the attacks on the caves we were shooting down
around 40 per cent of the bombs entering our defences, and this rose to
well over 50 per cent after St. Leu had been bombed. The original
Wachtel plan had been to fire the bombs in salvoes, so that while one
bomb was being engaged several others would get through the defences.
Fortunately he never achieved the necessary synchronization.

In our successes so far, fighters had played much the larger part,
shooting down 924 bombs by the middle of July compared with 261 by
the guns and 55 by balloons. Several authorities, including Roderick Hill
and Robert Watson-Watt, thought that the guns would do better if,
instead of being sited near London and therefore behind the fighters,
they occupied a belt on the coast, where they could shoot over the sea.
Professor Edward Selant, who had been associated with the proximity
fuse development in America, told me towards the end of the war that
he himself had suggested this same deployment before the V-1 campaign
opened, but that Anti-Aircraft Command did not accept it at the time.
The Americans had provided us with the SCR584 gun-laying radar and
predictor, and also the new proximity-fused shells which, although
originally a British invention, had been developed and engineered in

America, and these were now to produce a profound effect. In his post-war despatch (supplement to the London Gazette of 19th October 1948) Roderick Hill said that the guns had originally been deployed on the North Downs because the plan 'had been drawn up at a time when jamming of our radar by the Germans was a threat which could not be neglected'. So here was the same concern about German jamming which had made A.E.A.F. so distrustful of our Intelligence before D-Day. The manifest success of Intelligence and the consequent bombing of German jammers now removed this fear, and so there was no further inhibition about moving the guns and their radar to the coast. The move was a courageous and tremendous feat of organization. 800 guns, 60,000 tons of stores and ammunition, and 23,000 men and women were moved to the coast in a few hours, and during the week the vehicles of Anti-Aircraft Command travelled a total of $2\frac{3}{4}$ million miles. Within 48 hours the new deployment was effected, and the guns were immediately more successful, their rate rising from 50 bombs a week before the move to 170 bombs a week after it. The fighters, now more restricted, dropped from 180 to 120 a week, but the overall gain was substantial.

The Germans were much puzzled. Plate 25a shows a long-exposure photograph that they took at night from the French coast of the track traced out by the exhaust flame of a flying bomb as it flew across the Straits of Dover. The track is recorded as a continuous line, and the anti-aircraft shell bursts as simple points of light. In contrast with the wide scatter of normal anti-aircraft fire with time fuses, all the bursts were very near the track of the bomb because of the action of the proximity fuse. Before long, one burst was near enough to explode the bomb; and in the first few weeks of proximity fuse operation, the average number of rounds to destroy a bomb was 77.

With these technical and tactical advances, the bombardment was brought down to a fraction of its original strength. On one of the last days, 28th August, for example, of the 97 bombs which approached England, 13 were destroyed by fighters out to sea, the guns then shot down 65, with another 10 brought down by fighters over land, leaving 9 to continue towards London. Two collided with balloons, three fell outside London, leaving only four to reach it. Understandably, with the advance of our armies in France, the impression began to grow that the flying bomb had been mastered. It was true that from July onwards to September some 400 bombs were launched not from ramps but from Heinkel IIIs, but their effect was comparatively insignificant. What was to worry us much more were developments in the long-range rocket, which the next chapter will describe.

But before we leave the flying bomb, we should remark its technical excellence as a weapon. Its simple construction (Plate 25b) made it cheap to produce, and it was designed to exploit the extraordinarily favourable situation in which the Germans found themselves, able to shoot at such a great target as London from an entire 90° arc running from east to south. The bomb was hard to shoot down, and if we had not had so much prior warning our defences would have fared poorly. As it was, an analysis of the economics of the campaign showed a large balance in the German favour: the cost of our countermeasures, especially in bombing the sites, exceeded the estimated cost of the campaign to the Germans. But the fact was that we started from a potentially disastrous position geographically, with London a great 'hostage unto fortune' at the focus and mercy of the great French coastal arc; and the balance on which judgement must be passed is not between British and German expenditure but between our expenditure on countermeasures and the damage that would have ensued in lives, material and morale if those countermeasures had not been undertaken.

CHAPTER FORTY-FIVE

V-2

E VER SINCE the attack of 17th/18th August 1943 on Peenemünde, the long-range rocket seemed to have been eclipsed by the flying bomb. Our ringside seat at the Baltic trials had shown us that, although there was an occasional attempt to plot the track of a rocket, they were almost entirely concerned with flying bombs. Now the bomb had arrived first, as we had forecast in September 1943, and the question was: What had happened to the rocket? In recommending the attack on Peenemünde I had offered: 'Intelligence would be prepared to take the risk of the work being re-started elsewhere'. Actually the raid did not drive all the experimental work from Peenemünde; but some of it moved eastwards along the Baltic coast to Brüster Ort, and what appeared to be an out-station of Peenemünde was set up at an S.S. camp known as 'Heidelager' at Blizna near Debice, some 170 miles south of Warsaw. We first got on to its track via some Ultra traffic, and it seemed to be primarily concerned with flying bomb trials over land.

Since we already knew so much about the flying bomb, studies of the activity in Poland could add little to our knowledge in this respect; but there were features about the messages that could not be explained by assuming that the flying bomb alone was involved. As for what the other activity or activities might be, these could have been anything from glider bombs to air-to-air missiles if the work were associated with the Luftwaffe alone, as the flying bomb itself was. But since the bomb was now co-ordinated with other retaliation weapons by the LXV Army Corps under General Heinemann, the rocket might be in course of trial in Poland, too. In March 1944 the Polish Intelligence Service reported that trials were being conducted at Blizna of a missile with a range of 10 kilometres which made a large crater, and that railway tank cars thought to contain liquid air were entering the establishment. Finally, there was one item from the Ultra traffic which could not be accounted for either by the flying bomb or a short-range missile, because one of the staff at Blizna was interested in a crater near Sidlice, some 160 miles away to the north-east, which was beyond the range of the flying bomb. This single fact made us think that we were once again on the trail of the rocket.

I therefore requested photographic reconnaissance of the Blizna area, and a sortie was flown on 5th May, 1944. The photographs went to Medmenham, where a flying bomb ramp was immediately recognized, but there was none of the other installations which we had previously seen at Peenemünde and which were thought to be associated with the rocket. Since the photographic cover of the area was far from complete, it seemed that there must be another compound in which the rocket activity was taking place, and I therefore requested further cover of the whole area. When Matthew Pryor voiced his concern that the Air Staff was taking no interest in the rocket, I was able to show him that all this work was indeed in hand—and, what was more, on the same day that the first flying bomb fell in England, a large rocket from Peenemünde fell in Sweden.

We subsequently learned the story of this stray rocket, and it turned out to be an experimental hybrid consisting of a genuine A4 rocket (of the type later to be known to us as 'V-2') fitted with an extremely elaborate radio guidance system primarily designed for a smaller rocket known as 'Wasserfall' which was being developed for anti-aircraft purposes. General Dornberger in his book *V-2* states that shortly after the rocket was launched the control officer had tried to change its direction by eye 'and lost contact with it when it unexpectedly moved sideways into low cloud'. It then flew on an unintended northerly course to Sweden. But as we heard the story, the control officer had been selected for this particular trial on the basis of his expertise as a controller of guided bombs, and had never seen a rocket take-off before. He was said to have been so awestruck by the sight that he unwittingly left his hand on the controls so that the rocket swerved to the left too and by the time he pulled himself together it was too late to gain control.

It took a few days before news of the incident reached London; the report from our Air Attaché in Stockholm was accompanied by some rather badly focused photographs of the remains of the crashed missile taken by the Swedish General Staff. Despite their lack of definition they showed components that were obviously not associated with the flying bomb, and we therefore wondered whether, just as with the bomb on Bornholm ten months before, a sample of the Germans' latest V-weapon had gone so far astray that we might hope to learn more about it. I therefore arranged for two Air Technical Intelligence Officers

(Squadron Leaders Burder and Wilkinson) to go to Sweden with a request to the Swedish General Staff that they might be allowed to inspect the debris. Their first report back to Air Ministry expressed surprise at the amount of electronic control equipment incorporated in the rocket, and gave their opinion that such expensive complexity would only be justified if the warhead were to weigh at least ten thousand pounds. So here seemed a piece of evidence for a warhead as large as our experts feared; and although I myself would have restricted the circulation of the message as a perfectly legitimate speculation from one Intelligence Officer to another, it unfortunately was widely circulated, and thus added to the general alarm.

Further confirmation of a large warhead seemed to come from the aerial photograph of Blizna, which showed a large crater a few kilometres from the S.S. camp; and Charles Ellis, the Scientific Adviser to the War Office, told us that his explosives experts had estimated that it would have needed about five tons of explosive to make such a crater. Much additional evidence was now being provided by the Poles: they had set up an organization for beating the Germans to the scenes of crashed missiles, and they had analysed the liquid recovered from one incident, and found it to be highly concentrated hydrogen peroxide. By 27th June they had reported that the missile was about 40 feet long and 6 feet in diameter, agreeing with the dimensions that we had measured on the Peenemünde photographs. They also found pieces of radio equipment, including a transmitter on a wavelength of about 7 metres and a receiver for about 14 metres; these were investigated by Professor Janusz Groszkowski, later the President of the Polish Academy of Science. Shortly afterwards the Poles reported on the construction of the main jet, and, from the dimensions they gave, this was identical with the rocket unit that had fallen in Sweden. During July the Poles also offered to send us what they had collected, if we could arrange for an aircraft to pick it up, and this operation was put in hand.

In the meantime, new evidence was coming to light as our Forces advanced in Normandy. Somewhat to my surprise (because it had seemed a less likely area) we began to find traces of an organization for storing and launching rockets from south of Caen and a prisoner told us that he had been on the Staff of an Oberstleutnant Beger, who had his headquarters at Isigny, and whose task was to select and construct sites for the storing and firing of rockets. One of the sites was found near the Château du Molay, west of Bayeux, and it was surveyed for me by David Nutting and Arthen Jones, whose sketch showed that it was simply a tree-flanked stretch of road into which concrete platforms had been set, and on either side of which parallel loop roads had been made among the trees. As soon as I saw the sketch I was reminded of a pattern that I had seen some months before outlined on the foreshore at Peenemünde, which had hitherto made no sense. I could now see an explanation: the pattern of the roads at the Château du Molay had been laid out on the sands at Peenemünde to see whether the proposed curves in the loop roads could be negotiated by whatever transporters were to carry the rockets. Moreover, a week or two later we captured many of Beger's papers, which gave us most of the firing sites and storage sites in Normandy.

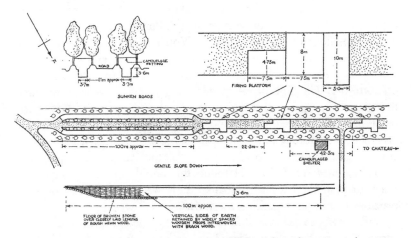

Fig. 29. Plan of a V-2 launching site near the Château du Molay, Normandy. Note the similarity of the road layout to the pattern previously observed on the foreshore at Peenemünde (Plate 27a)

Evidence was now accumulating so fast and so convincingly that it was clear that Cherwell would look very silly if he continued to deny the existence of the rocket. Apart from the fact that I did not want to destroy my old professor there was also the point that he might try to argue to the end, and that Churchill would be torn between the facts and a loyalty to his most trusted friend. I therefore went to see Cherwell and told him what a pile of evidence I had, and that if he continued to deny the existence of the rocket there was nothing I could do but shoot him down. If, however, he now realized his case was hopeless I would bring the new facts out as gently as I could over the next week or so to give him a chance to change his ground. Fortunately he agreed to this second course.

The build-up of information was fascinating; and had we been allowed to pursue it in our own way, it would have been exhilarating. Instead, for most of the time it was more nearly exasperating, because Duncan Sandys had brought back all the experts who had, with all their good intentions, so complicated the situation in the previous year. Almost every new item of undigested information was circulated widely, and all kinds of false trails were thereby opened up. Around 12th or 13th July, Frank Inglis insisted that I should write a report on the state of our knowledge for the Crossbow Committee, but I protested that the time was not yet ripe, for our information was still so incomplete and confused that there were likely to be serious errors in any conclusions that seemed to be suggested at that stage. I used the rather repulsive analogy of lancing an abscess. You have to wait until the abscess is well formed before you can successfully lance it—and so it is with Intelligence. However, Inglis continued to insist and so I wrote a report on 16th July. The bulk of the evidence regarding the warhead pointed to a weight between 3 and 7 tons, the expectations of our own experts being in agreement with the size of the crater seen near Blizna and the comment that Burder and Wilkinson had made on the Swedish rocket. Another seemingly firm conclusion was that the main fuel was hydrogen peroxide, since the Poles had found this liquid, and also there were traces of it in the Swedish remains. As it was to turn out, both this conclusion and that regarding the warhead were wrong.

Within two days I was able to correct the second error and also to express doubts about the warhead being so heavy. Burder and Wilkinson were now back in London, and Charles Frank had talked with them while I was at a meeting to discuss tactics against flying bombs. Charles had seized upon one item which Burder and Wilkinson had told him: this was the unusual nature of one of the pumps feeding liquid into the rocket jet. Instead of its bearings being lubricated in the ordinary way by oil or grease, this pump appeared to have no other lubrication than that provided by the liquid which it was pumping. This immediately reminded Charles and me of our school physics textbooks, where the Claude process of liquefying air was described. In this process the liquid air has to pass through a rotary pump, making it so cold that oil or grease would be frozen solid, and Claude had solved the problem by designing the pump so that the liquid air itself would lubricate the bearings. It therefore seemed highly probable that liquid air or, still more probably liquid oxygen would be one of the liquids being pumped into the rocket jet.

I now had the chance to think rather more easily about the rocket problem, for Vera had taken our two children away to Cornwall. I had usually depended on thinking over the day's new facts every evening at home, but this had recently become very difficult. A flying bomb in Richmond had blown out the windows of some friends, and they had taken refuge with us. This meant that besides Vera and the two children there was another husband and wife and two children all sleeping in the same room with us, all with our heads under tables, and it was not easy to get enough isolation to sort out the day's facts.

Before she left for Cornwall, Vera and I had had a disputation while we were doing the evening's washing-up. Life under the flying bomb was a strain, anyway, and she always held me responsible, as she has always done since, for any calamity that befell the country. In this instance, she was nearer the truth than on some other occasions, but it was hard to be charged with having been asleep while the Germans stole such a march on us as to get the flying bomb into operation. I could not tell her the whole story, but I was not a little annoyed to find that even my own wife was now distrustful. Her arguments were good enough in their way, but there would have been no point in replying to them one by one unless an external referee had been present. I would have fared no better than Alfred did with the cakes.

I could now stay in the office for the evenings and spend some quiet hours after dinner going over all the evidence. Something very odd had been taking place in Poland because Blizna was from time to time dispatching what were called 'Geräte' (apparatuses) back to Peenemünde. What could these be? I could understand things being sent from Peenemünde to Blizna for trial, but what would be worth sending back? I began to wonder whether these might be items such as rocket jets that had been tested, but there was no clue in the Ultra messages regarding their nature. Certainly there were plenty of them, to judge by the numbers by which they were identified. The first number that I had was 17,053, about which I had learnt on 17th June, and by early July the highest number I had heard of was 17,667. How could I prove that these were rocket components? If only we had complete photographic cover of the Blizna area we could have found the launching site or test rig, and perhaps found a rocket there; but even though I had requested further cover more than a month before, fresh photographs had not yet been obtained.

As I pondered, I tried to put myself in the position of the Germans working in unfriendly territory, and began to wonder whether—even with the rivalry between the German Army and the Luftwaffe—I would have used two sites, each of which would have to be defended, when there should be enough room in a single site to launch both flying bombs and rockets. I therefore took out again the 5th May photographs of the flying bomb compound, even though I knew that these had been exhaustively searched at Medmenham. Going over them millimetre by millimetre for many minutes, I suddenly realized that a familiar outline had 'clicked' into place with the memory of one that I had seen before— on the photograph of Peenemünde on which I had first found the rocket. Yes, there indeed it was: a rocket (Plate 26). Although there was almost no detail, it was no artefact for it appeared on two separate photographs, and it immediately transformed the Intelligence situation. In case I fell victim to a flying bomb during the night I telephoned Charles Frank at his home in Golders Green and told him that if such an event happened he was to secure a copy of photograph No. 3240 by 60 Squadron of 5th May, and to look at the object which he would find 90 millimetres down from the top and 26 millimetres in from the right-hand edge.

I also let Lindemann know that I had found a rocket at Blizna, and informed the Chiefs of Staff. But the account was not yet complete, because there was no sign of any launching apparatus. Our experts had assumed that the rocket would need to be fired from some sort of gun at a speed of about 100 metres per second to make it stable in its initial flight, and there was a large tower erection at Peenemünde which had been assumed to be for this purpose; but there was no such tower at Blizna. So on a subsequent evening I scanned the photographs again, looking for a concrete platform; ultimately in the centre of the compound, and showing only very faintly because that part of the photograph was so light, was a square of about 35 feet side. With this evidence and that from Molay, could it be that the rocket needed no launching equipment more elaborate than a flat pad, and simply stood vertical, nose uppermost? If so this would explain the 40 foot 'columns' that we had sometimes seen standing at Peenemünde. The rocket would take off by itself, stabilized by gyroscopes and the deflectable 'jet-rudders' that we had found among the components mentioned in the Enigma messages.

I tried to telephone Charles Frank, but the lines were out of action. So I wrote a note in case a flying bomb got me during the night, instructing the finder:

17th, July, 1944

In case I am killed during the night 17/18 July, whoever finds this paper must take it at once to Dr. F. C. Frank, Government Communications Bureau, 54 Broadway, S.W.1, and tell him that he will find a square concrete platform in the middle of the clearing at Blizna on Photo 3240 of PR385. It is fed by a carefully curved road leading direct from the rocket workshop, and is parallel to the P.A. launching ramp.

R. V. Jones.
A.D.I. (Science)
Air Ministry.

Finally, now that we were certain about the rocket, we could say from the Geräte numbers that it seemed likely that at least one thousand had already been made.

The day of Tuesday 18th July passed swiftly, most of my time being spent in committee meetings that, fanned by the general alarm, were occurring at a prodigious rate. I knew that at 10 o'clock that evening I was due to appear at the Crossbow Committee in the Prime Minister's War Room, and would be expected to give an account of the general Intelligence situation. In the two hours between dinner and the meeting I went over all the new evidence regarding numbers of rockets, and so forth, and then left for the meeting. The Prime Minister himself was in the Chair and he was clearly in a 'testy' mood, if by that adjective this meant a desire to test every piece of evidence submitted to him. It seemed to me that he had been briefed to 'gun' for the Air Staff, and he was in a mood to do so because the public had become increasingly critical of the Government.

This was the first meeting on which I had met him since the beginning of the bombardment and now that I was officially in charge of all V-1 and V-2 Intelligence, I had to answer for everything that had been done. I had the impression that Winston was himself surprised to find that I was going to be the target for his attack. Personally, I had some sympathy with his impatience, which was if anything due to the faults of my predecessors and the rather unwise arrangements that the Air Staff had made during the preceding months. However, I had now to speak for the Air Staff, and I saw that the main hope of defending it lay in getting the attack directed against things for which I myself had been directly responsible, since I could readily answer for any of them.

Winston's attack grew sharper as the night proceeded, but I began

to enjoy it. Claude Pelly was sitting on one side of me, now as the Chief
Intelligence Officer of A.E.A.F., and Colin Grierson on the other, since
he was still nominally directing countermeasures. They both remained
rather miserably silent as I took the whole attack. I was grateful that
Archie Sinclair was not there because with his gallantry he would have
tried to intervene to defend me, and he would not have had the facts at
his fingertips to do so effectively. Portal was of course there, but he
remained silent—I hope in the belief that I was well able to look after
myself.

The crisis came when I told Churchill that from the evidence I had
just evaluated I thought that the Germans must have at least a thousand
rockets. At this he exploded, and started to thump the table, saying that
we had been caught napping. He then produced, almost word for word,
the arguments with which Vera had belaboured me over the washing-
up a few nights before. This was too much. If I let him get away with
it, I should never morally be master in my own household again, and
so I respectfully thumped the table back.

I told him that if we had been caught napping, this was due to his own
directive issued before D-Day that in any conflict between requirements
for defence and offence priority should be given to the offence, and in
my field this meant concentrating on knocking out the German radar.
The fact that his army was now safely across the Channel testified to the
efficiency with which we had done that job. But, even so, we had not
been napping as regards the rocket. I had promised that we would find
the Germans again if we drove them out of Peenemünde, and we had
indeed found them in Poland. It seemed to me foolish to be surprised
that if the Germans thought a weapon worth making at all, they would
not have made at least a thousand; and as for the destruction it could do,
even if the warhead weighed five tons—which I did not believe—this
only meant a total of five thousand tons of explosive on London, which
was little more than Bomber Command was delivering on Berlin in a
single night. (Albert Speer in *Inside the Third Reich* retrospectively made
the same point: 'Even 5,000 long-range rockets, that is more than five
months' production, would have delivered only 3,750 tons of explosives;
a single attack by the combined British and American air forces delivered
a good 8,000 tons').

Winston then asked questions as to when the evidence had become
available. I pointed out that, as for the identification of the rocket on
the photographs in Poland this had been done by me personally a few
days before, and as for the numbers of what we could consequently say

were rockets, these too had only become available in the last few days. Then I added a further detail: the experts had advised us to look for the wrong things, and had we not been so misled regarding the nature of the launching apparatus, which again had only become clear by our own efforts in the last 24 hours, we might have got at the truth earlier. He then asked whether I had told the 'Prof' about the launching system and I replied, 'Not yet, Sir'. 'Why not?' he snapped. And I replied, 'I found it last night, and I have had seven committee meetings to attend since then, Sir'. There was a silence in which none of the Chiefs of Staff or the Ministers present saw fit to intervene until Colin Gubbins, the Head of S.O.E., introduced some unintentional comic relief by saying that S.O.E. had had a report that the rocket was to be steered to its target by a man inside it, who was to parachute out of it during its final descent. The tenseness having been broken, Portal came strongly to my support, testifying to the value of our work throughout the whole of the period, and Winston subsided. Evidently reports of the meeting got out, for Rowley Scott-Farnie, now a Group Captain and Chief Signals Intelligence Officer of A.E.A.F., came to see me a day or two afterwards, and told me that he had heard that I had shut Winston up. If so, I hope that I did it respectfully, because never in my life have I enjoyed a fight so much. Each of us had too much respect for the truth to resort to any subterfuge or sophistry, and we both knew that the truth was what we wanted to get at.

My own memory could perhaps have exaggerated the drama of the encounter, but after the war I received a letter from one of those present, Sir Oswald Allen of the Home Office, who was one of Herbert Morrison's chief civil servants:

Do I not remember you at the Rocket meetings? Far the youngest present, calm, cool, collected, the only one, or almost the only one prepared to take on the great man in his testiest midnight mood and argue patiently and respectfully with him!

A further comment came at the next meeting of the Crossbow Committee, on 25th July 1944, when an admiral whom I had not previously met, but who had been at the meeting, came and sat beside me and remarked, 'I thought that you did damned well last week!', a comment which increased my already warm regard for the Royal Navy.

Immediately afterwards Churchill himself came in, and after we were all seated, but before he formally opened the meeting said to me, 'Mr.

Jones, how many meetings have you had to attend today?', 'Six, Sir', I replied. 'What are they?' he asked, and I proceeded to catalogue the first five, some of which had been chaired by men now sitting round the 'Crossbow' table. Before I could go on he said, 'And now this is the sixth!' 'Yes, Sir', I replied, 'this is the sixth!' And I thought of reminding him of an adage that I had learnt from my grandmother: 'Every time a sheep bleats it loses a nibble.' He then said, 'I can well see that you can never get any work done if all your time has to be spent in committees. You have my authority to absent yourself from any committee that you do not think worthwhile!' It was a valuable concession, since almost none of the committees was genuinely useful, and most of them owed their origin to a general panic resulting from too much theorizing on too few facts. My job was to get the facts.

Later in the meeting there was the usual discussion of the ideas of our own experts regarding the weights, and one of them remarked that the Intelligence that was coming in was now agreeing nicely with their ideas. This was completely untrue, and Winston, who had been watching me immediately said to me, 'Is that true?' He always seemed to know when I was doubtful, because the same thing happened on several occasions, and I must have somehow unintentionally given away my disbelief in my face. I had of course to reply, 'No, Sir', to meet with his 'Why isn't it?', and I catalogued the errors in the statement that had just been made. 'What do you have to say to that?' he then asked the expert, and the latter began to flounder.

What I was objecting to particularly was the assertion that the Intelligence evidence was starting to agree with the experts' evidence that the rocket would weigh 32 plus or minus 7 tons when from what I could see of the Intelligence it certainly suggested less than 20 tons. I also noted that the experts were beginning to shift their ground, because only a week before they had said that the weight would be 40 tons. I was pretty sure that they had very little idea of how the rocket was designed and constructed, and that the only way in which we could arrive at the truth was to get more Intelligence.

One of the steps in this direction would be to explore the German site at Blizna if, as seemed very likely, it was about to be overrun by the Russians. I had therefore a week or so before minuted Portal:

It is most desirable that some Air Intelligence officers with a full knowledge of our background should immediately inspect the camp in the event of its capture. You may consider, as I do, that this matter is of sufficient importance to justify a personal approach to Stalin by the Prime Minister.

The approach was duly made and at the meeting of 25th July Winston told us that he had had 'a very civil reply from Mr. Stalin'. So the party was formed but, unfortunately, instead of the nominations of personnel being left to me, it was taken over by Duncan Sandys so that our 'experts' were well represented. Instead of our forming the team, Air Intelligence officers were included in a balancing rather than a primary capacity. One was Wilkinson, who had examined the Swedish rocket, and was obviously a good choice; and I nominated as my personal representative Eric Ackermann, who would be best qualified of the whole party to look at any aspects of radio control which I suspected might be used to fly a rocket along a beam.

In briefing Ackermann, I warned him that I thought the party had already been rendered ineffectual by its composition, but that he should continue with it as long as there seemed any hope. It would be well at this point to dispose of the fortunes of the party as they progressed eastwards. Their first signal, on 31st July, from Headquarters of British Forces in the Middle East included the ominous sentence, 'Party amalgamating well and very hopeful of good results'. This naïveté did not augur well for matching the wiles of the Russians. On 3rd August a signal from Tehran announced that the Russians were holding them up, because the party had left London without obtaining visas, and part of the signal ran, 'Position regarding visas unchanged . . . still confident that Mission will obtain extremely valuable technical information if allowed to visit sites'. Four days later the party was still in Tehran most of them down with dysentery, with two actually in hospital. By this time Ackermann managed to get an independent signal to me saying that the Mission was quite hopeless because of its incompetence, and requesting my permission to return. Since there was plenty of work for him to do on the Western Front, I readily agreed.

Ultimately the Mission reached Moscow, and on 1st September, five weeks after it had set out, there came a signal: 'We leave Moscow 0520 tomorrow morning. . . . We are all thrilled to be off at last and intend to do our best'. On 18th September, the Mission was at Blizna, and sent a signal describing its brilliant success: 'Russian Headquarters were undoubtedly a little sceptical about the existence of such large rockets until they saw us recovering and recognizing parts. This has made deep impression on the Russian officers with us. We may cause a minor sensation in Russian technical circles when we return to Moscow with the parts. Probably this is all to the good as regards future relations between the three countries.' By 27th September the Mission was on its way back via Tehran, from which there now arrived another signal saying: 'The Russians have temporarily lost main part of our R specimens in transit between Blizna and Moscow but they have promised to do all in their power to see that they follow us without undue delay'.

What of course the Russians had done was to put every obstacle in the way of the Mission reaching Blizna, while they themselves inspected the site. Then, as Wilkinson told me on his return, the Russians accompanied our Mission throughout the visit to Blizna, and Poles who might not have talked to the Russians gladly came forward to talk to the British, only to have their names taken by the Russians to be listed for their pro-British sympathies. So the Mission probably did positive harm and achieved no good whatsoever. When the crates which the Russians had forwarded to Tehran were brought back to England under top security and opened by members of the Mission, they were found to be not the items which had been packed at Blizna but parts of old aeroplane engines which the Russians had substituted instead. So much for the contributions of 'experts'!

This diverting débâcle, however, lay weeks into the future and well after the Germans had started to send us rockets direct; in the meantime I had to contend with the continuous sniping that was coming, understandably perhaps, from Duncan Sandys and his array of experts. There were so many complaints made to the Air Staff behind my back that on 26th July I minuted Portal:

I honestly believe that we shall only get the right answer by it being made clear that we are responsible for Intelligence regarding the Rocket, and that this responsibility includes calling in other scientists when we feel out of our depth. We cannot continue if the policy is pursued of calling in more and more experts regardless of their necessity, to discuss the evidence which we ourselves have obtained, and which we think ourselves competent to assess.

Three evenings later I drafted a further note, this time to Inglis, offering my resignation in protest:

I can make no stronger protest. Our sources will be mis-handled: collation will be wild and incomplete: presentation will be political ...

unless officers can be found who will defend the traditions of Intelligence to the last, so that the Intelligence system as a whole can work out its results in unmolested good faith.

The following morning the note was in my pocket when I saw Inglis, in a last effort to strengthen his resolve to stand by us. Instead he told me that he had decided to remove the responsibility for flying bomb and rocket Intelligence from me and transfer it to Jack Easton, one of his Directors of Intelligence. This drove any further thought of resignation from my mind, because it brought home to me the mess that might result if I ceased to watch the rocket. I told Inglis that whatever else he might do he could not remove from me the function of discovering the scientific and technical nature of the rocket. Since this fell squarely inside the Terms of Reference given to me at the beginning of the war, I proposed to take my investigation as far as that and write up the account to that stage, come what may. I then went to the desk in my temporary office in the Air Intelligence building in Monck Street and placed a notice on the empty desk saying 'sic transit gloria raketae' and returned to Broadway.

Another of my minutes to Portal—this time direct—had better luck. I was anxious that the items that had been recovered from the crashed rocket in Sweden should be examined in the greatest possible detail by our Royal Aircraft Establishment at Farnborough, and I had therefore suggested to Portal that an approach be made to the Swedish General Staff, and that we should be prepared to pay any reasonable price. I concluded, 'Probably if we offer the Swedes the results of our examination, together with any radio jamming equipment which we may subsequently design, the additional price in, say, Spitfires may not be unduly high. Perhaps you would consider action along these lines.' A deal was consequently arranged and the relics of the crashed rocket arrived at Farnborough towards the end of July.

Almost at the same time, some items arrived from Poland. The story behind them is truly a saga of which I can only give the merest outline here. The Polish organization for beating the Germans to the sites of rocket impacts had collected various items during the months of the German trials, including one that had fallen without exploding on 20th May 1944 near Sarnaki (about 80 miles east of Warsaw, near the Russian border), in a marsh on the banks of the River Bug. The Poles pushed it deeper into the water until after the Germans had ceased to search for it, and then they recovered some of the parts. These, with parts from other crashes, were placed in a sack, and carried on a bicycle 200 miles south-eastwards—almost back along the rocket's trajectory—to an area near Tarnow, which offered a suitable landing place for a Dakota flown from Brindisi. The bicycle journey was a precarious one, for it had to be made through the German forces that were now retreating in the face of the Russian advance. On 25th or 26th July S.O.E. Headquarters at Brindisi signalled to the Poles that the Dakota was on its way. It was piloted by a New Zealander, Flight Lieutenant Guy Culliford of No. 267 Squadron (afterwards Dr. S. G. Culliford D.S.O. of the English Department in the Victoria University of Wellington, New Zealand), with Flight Lieutenant Szrajer of the Polish Air Force as navigator.

The fate of the mission was in the balance, for unexpectedly two German aircraft had occupied the landing ground, and a small Luftwaffe unit had set up camp. Fortunately, at sunset the Germans evacuated the field, and the Dakota was able to land. The rocket pieces were put on board, along with the Polish Resistance worker, Jerzy Chmielewski, who had been responsible for the watch on Blizna, and who had cycled the 200 miles with the sack on his shoulder. It was then found that the aircraft could not take off, because its wheels were stuck in the mud. His feelings after running the gauntlet of the Germans so courageously, can be imagined. The field was brightly lit by the plane's lights; and the roar of the motors as the pilot tried to get the aircraft unstuck could very well have attracted any Germans in the area. Thinking that the sticking may have been due not so much to mud as to his brakes failing to release, Culliford in desperation severed the hydraulic pipes with a knife, but the aircraft would still not budge. A crowd of helpers scraped the mud away with spades and bare hands, while local farmers brought up cartloads of planks, ripped from the fences around their houses. These they forced under the wheels, and then laid a track. Culliford had been preparing to burn his machine and its papers when it was at last freed, and he finally succeeded in a brakeless take-off, while the Poles on the ground dispatched a German patrol which, attracted by the activity, was now approaching.

The rocket parts with the courageous Pole arrived at Hendon on 28th July, but he could speak no English, and he refused to let anyone see the parts until he had authority from one of the only two Polish officers in Britain whom he knew. One was General Bor, and the other was a Polish colonel. He sat on his sack, and drew a knife whenever one of our Intelligence Officers made any move towards it. This scene continued for some hours, reaching peaks of embarrassment whenever he wished to fulfil one of his natural functions, while we searched for the General and the Colonel. One of them, I think that it was the Colonel, was either ill or out of London, and finally we had to get the General himself to come along and tell our gallant Pole that it was alright for him to talk to us and show us his treasures.

He endeared himself to us by telling us that had the Russians not advanced, he had organized enough of the Polish Underground Forces to try to capture Heidelager, and so gain all the information that we wanted. This was now going to be impossible, but he still wanted to get back. He told us that he reckoned he could stay in London about three weeks, but that was about as long as he thought that he could leave his organization. He explained that he had left quite a good man, a colonel, in temporary charge. He had previously told us that he himself was only a corporal.

One item of information that he gave us was that the rockets often exploded high in the air, and that the Germans were very annoyed when they did so. It turned out that this fault had only been recognized after the firing range had been moved to Poland; the rockets fired from Peenemünde had carried bags of dye which coloured the sea on impact, and until the move to Blizna this was the only evidence that the Germans had of how and where the rockets had fallen. As we had predicted, after the Peenemünde raid Hitler himself had ordered the rocket trials to be transferred from Peenemünde (about the beginning of September 1943, according to General Dornberger in his book *V-2*) and as soon as firings from Blizna were started at the end of 1943, it became clear that something was wrong at the far end of the trajectory. It took the Germans a long time to discover the cause; one of the fuel tanks appeared to be exploding. This was partially prevented by lagging the tanks with glass wool but, as Dornberger said, 'it was not until the closing months of the war that we found the final solution by reinforcing the front of the hull with riveted sheet steel casing'.

The arguments in Whitehall concerning the weight of the rocket lasted throughout July and well into August. Herbert Morrison was near panic: on 27th July he was wanting the War Cabinet to plan immediately for the evacuation of a million people from London—he had already tried on 11th July to have our Invasion forces diverted to land in the V-1 launching area. But I was beginning to get near the truth as regards the weight of the warhead for, based on what I had told him, Lindemann wrote to Brendan Bracken on 1st August, 'The intelligence evidence such as it is indicates one ton or a bit more. The more pessimistic scientists say this is impossible, they themselves, they claim, could make a rocket of the desired characteristics carrying five to seven tons. . . . The answer seems to me that none of them so far as I know has ever made a rocket that flew at all.'

More information was coming in from Normandy, where we had captured many of Oberstleutnant Beger's papers, and where we found one of his storage sites at a quarry at Hautmesnil, between Caen and Falaise. In the tunnels there, we actually found a great white wooden dummy rocket, which had clearly been used to give the troops experience in handling the missile around the bends in the tunnels, and I have sometimes wondered what would have happened had we found this dummy earlier, since Lord Cherwell had for a long time contended that what we had been photographing at Peenemünde in 1943 were simply dummies left out in the open to hoax us. But before we found the dummy, we also found the trolleys on which the genuine rockets were to be supported, and one of these was sent back to Farnborough. There again, some of our experts saw it, and immediately complained that I had misled them because the curvature of the supporting cradle was much less (4 feet 8 inches) than I had stated the diameter of the rocket to be. The experts took this opportunity to reduce their weight estimates accordingly, but I telephoned Farnborough and asked them to take a second look at the cradle because I was sure that the diameter of the main body of the rocket was about 5 feet 7 inches, as we had said. The discrepancy could be explained if, by bad luck, what had been sent back was one of the cradles supporting the rocket not somewhere along its main diameter but on a reduced diameter nearer the nose-cone, in which case I would expect the inner surface of the cradle to be chamfered to match the slope of the nose-cone. Someone at Farnborough went off and looked, and came back to report that the chamfer was indeed there, and they had previously failed to notice it. Even so, the experts did not put their weight back to their earlier estimates, but brought it down to 24 tons.

To Charles Frank, Bob Robertson and me, the naïveté of our 'experts' was incredible. They were all eminent, some very eminent, in particular fields of science or technology, and yet they were completely out of their depth when dealing with the rocket. I can remember a Fellow of the Royal Society, for example, saying at one of the meetings that he was amazed at the accuracy with which the Germans would have to set the rocket before launching it. He had calculated the angle to which the rocket would have to be tilted in order to give it maximum range, and found that this was only half a degree off true vertical. If it were fired vertically upwards, it would of course fall back on the heads of those who had fired it, and so the whole of the range was determined by this small angle off vertical, which would have to be very accurately determined. What he had in fact calculated, quite possibly correctly, was the trajectory of a rocket fired, as on 5th November, with a stick attached, and launched in the familiar way from a bottle, where the rocket gradually curves over in its trajectory under the influence of gravity. Almost in chorus, Bob, Charles and I shouted out, 'gyroscopes!', because we knew that the Germans were using gyroscopic control, with information about the attitude of the rocket being transmitted via servo mechanisms to graphite rudders that were placed in the main jet so as to deflect the stream of incandescent gases and thus turn the rocket on to a pre-set trajectory both in bearing and in elevation. We had known this and reported it ever since the Ultra traffic on Blizna became available, because it contained reference to 'Strahlrüder' which, as far as we could translate it, meant 'jet-rudder': it was a basic invention that made advanced rocket technology possible. As we explained the system, our scientist looked Heaven-wards and said, 'Ah, yes, gyroscopes! I hadn't thought of them!' And that was about the level of the better contributions from the experts.

By 6th August, a week after they had given the weight as 24 tons, they said that this figure would now be the upper limit. I myself thought this would still be an overestimate, and I decided to look at all the available evidence over again. We had had many reports about prospective weights come through our Intelligence system, but many of these had been coloured by the mishandling of the system from the time the panic had started in April 1943, and it was almost impossible to assess the reliability of individual reports, and to allow for the fact that many of them may have been feeding back to us information which had unwittingly been provided in previous briefings. I therefore decided to accept only those reports which had mentioned liquid air or liquid oxygen as one of the fuels. This provided a touchstone, since it showed that any report which mentioned it had at least one element of truth, and might therefore reflect the knowledge of someone who had had a fairly direct contact with genuine information.

The effect of applying the touchstone was remarkable. Out of the many reports on our files it selected only five, as follows:

Date	Origin	Length	Diameter	Total Weight	Fuel Weight	Warhead
15.2.44	Agent	14 m	—	7	—	1 ton
22.2.44	Agent	12 m	$1/1\frac{1}{2}$ m	11/12 tons	8 tons	2 tons
3.4.44	Agent	12 m	$1\frac{1}{2}$ m	11 tons	8 tons	1 ton
21.5.44	P/W[1]	more than 9 m	$1\frac{1}{2}$ m	—	—	1, $1\frac{1}{2}$ tons
2.8.44	P/W[1]	16 m	$1\frac{1}{2}$ m	8	—	1 ton

[1] Prisoners of War, both from Peenemünde

They all pointed to much lower weights both for the rocket as a whole and the warhead in particular than those favoured by the experts. The last report had come from the interrogation of a prisoner-of-war, and Charles Frank and I went out to Latimer, the Interrogation Centre, to see him. Talking things over with Charles on the way back, I said—as we went round Shepherd's Bush—that I was now prepared to call everyone else's bluff, and declare for a rocket of 12 tons all-up weight with a 1 ton warhead. I was the more ready to do so because there were references in the Ultra traffic between Peenemünde and Blizna to items called 'elephants' which normally weighed one ton, and which, as far as I could tell, seemed to be something in the nose of the rocket. If these were warheads shaped to fit into the slender nose-cone, they might conceivably suggest an elephant's head or trunk. There was also mention of a material called 'A-Stoff' for which the normal requirement for a rocket was 4·3 tons. On the assumption that this was liquid oxygen, and that another main fuel, 'B-Stoff', which might be a liquid such as alcohol, was involved, the total fuel weight would probably be around 8 tons.

I informed Sinclair, Portal and Cherwell as soon as I had come positively to the conclusion regarding the weight of the warhead, on 6th August. The question now was: how should I make my statement more widely to secure maximum effect and to show up the follies of calling in men who were certainly experts in their own fields, but as regards Intelligence were utter novices compared with Charles and me? The opportunity presented itself almost immediately for, despite having been deposed by Inglis, I was still a member of the Prime Minister's Crossbow Committee, and its next meeting was at 6 p.m. on 10th August. Inglis was not a member of the Committee, but Easton was now there, to speak instead of me, and the meeting was rather more crowded than usual, so that it was possible for me to sit so that I was not easily visible from the chair. This I wanted to do, because there was a delay in Churchill's appearing; Herbert Morrison explained that the Prime

Minister had been held up, and that he was to take the chair in the meantime. I particularly wanted to make my statement about weights in Churchill's presence, and so I sat as obscurely as possible through the first half-hour or more of the meeting, in the hope that he would ultimately appear. But, as luck would have it, he had had an urgent call to go out to Italy, and as time went on it became clear that he would not be taking over the meeting. At last, someone remembered that I should be there, and asked for my comments on the statements of Easton and Charles Ellis, the Scientific Adviser to the War Office. The former's statement was limited and factual, the latter's conjectural, and trying to excuse some further lowering of the expert estimate of the weight of the rocket in the last week because the diameter was now known to be 5 feet 7 inches instead of 6 feet. Even so, the weight was still around 20 tons. So I then gave my own figures of about 12 tons total weight with a one ton warhead, which met with a generally incredulous reception, and the Committee's minute 'took note with interest of the above statements, but recorded their view that it was too early to draw a firm conclusion regarding the smaller size of the warhead of the rocket'.

The following morning Cherwell telephoned me and told me that he was very worried on my account, because I had made such definite statements about the weights, when he himself could not see how such a large rocket could possibly be so light. He added, 'They are all waiting for you to make just one mistake, and I am afraid that you have made it now!' He advised me to provide myself with a correcting statement which would allow me some loophole of escape, but I told him that I had done as honest a job as I could in assessing the evidence, and that all I could say was that the weights that I had stated were what the evidence pointed to. He then told me that he was going later in the day to look at the pieces of the Swedish rocket which were now at Farnborough, and which the Establishment were trying to reassemble. On the visit he was accompanied by Edward Wright, who had formed a friendship with him when Wright was a Student of Christchurch. After Farnborough, they went on to Oxford for the weekend.

On his return, Wright told me that the Farnborough reconstruction had vindicated what I had said. The only trouble was that they could not make the weight of the warhead more than about 1,300 to 1,500 lbs., compared with the one ton with which I had surprised the Crossbow Committee. By this time I was so sure of the weight that Frank and I went to Farnborough the next day to look at the warhead for ourselves;

it was an odd experience now to have to convince the Farnborough experts that their estimate was too low, having had only a few days before to argue with the Whitehall experts that their estimates were much too high. The Farnborough estimate depended on the piecing together of the rim of the warhead at its wider end, i.e. the end further away from the nose. This was in several segments, and I managed to show the Farnborough engineers that there was a segment missing which, if they had included it, would have increased the size of the cone significantly; when they made the appropriate correction, the warhead weight came out at 2,000 lbs.

A sidelight on the vehemence with which the battle of the warheads had been waged has been provided by Professor W. W. Rostow, the American economic historian who in the 60's became Special Assistant to the President of the United States. As an American Army Air Force officer he had been assigned in 1943 to British Air Intelligence, and was asked by Sir George Thomson, the Scientific Adviser to the Air Ministry, to examine the arguments on both sides regarding the weight of the warhead. Having talked to me in, as he says, my 'marvellously dishevelled office'. he then listened to those who believed in the ten-ton warhead and finally called a meeting of both sides. 'Although,' he wrote, 'I was at that time relatively young (27), I had acquired some experience with both academic and government bureaucratic structure and their capacity for bloodless tribal warfare. But I had never been present at, let alone presided over, a meeting with more emotional tension than that centred on the size of the V-2 warhead. . . . What emerged was a reasonably solid Intelligence case for a one-ton warhead.

'I concluded that the evidence Jones had mustered was essentially correct; called on Sir George Thomson and informed him of my conclusion: the warhead would be about one ton. He looked up at me with a twinkle in his eye and said: "You are a lucky young man. A few days ago a V-2 mis-fired from Peenemünde and landed in Sweden. We flew it back in the bomb bay of a Mosquito. We have now measured the venturi. Obviously it could not develop more thrust than that required for a one-ton warhead." After some exchange on the curious way that essentially rational problems of intelligence and science could generate emotional attachments of great strength, I departed.'

As for the heights to which emotions could rise, I had received a warning shortly after the meeting of 18th July, when I had alarmed Churchill by telling him that I thought that at least a thousand rockets had been made, based partly on my recognition of the rocket on the

Blizna photograph. A few days later Inglis showed me a letter that had been sent to him by Douglas Kendall, one of the Chief Photographic Interpreters at Medmenham, protesting that I had told the Prime Minister that I had found the Blizna rocket, and that I ought not to have done so before I had asked Medmenham to confirm my observation. This was clearly a sore point for, having missed the rocket on the Peenemünde photographs, the Medmenham interpreters had now missed it at Blizna. It would never have occurred to me to criticize them for this, for I regarded myself as a fourth phase interpreter to supplement what had been done in the first three phases of interpretation at Medmenham, and I had the advantage of being in closer touch with other forms of Intelligence, of necessity, than the normal interpreters were. It was hard enough to be criticized by Duncan Sandys and his Crossbow colleagues on the one hand for withholding information, and on the other hand by the interpreters for giving it out prematurely, but when the criticism, as in the latter case, came from friends, who in their letter to Inglis described me as an amateur interpreter (and added that what I had seen on the Blizna photograph was more probably a locomotive), this was a warning that feelings were getting out of hand. I told Inglis that the best thing would be simply to acknowledge the letter but that in the interest of good relations, I would not reply and reprove them, as I could have done, for once again missing the rocket.

A fortnight or so later they provided me with an opportunity for a riposte. Evidently stung by the fact that they had not detected the rocket, they scanned the Blizna photograph again for signs of the launching equipment for the rocket. Actually, this involved no more than a platform of wooden railway sleepers, and even concrete was unnecessary—General Dornberger indeed deplored the waste of effort that had been involved in making concrete platforms in France. A prisoner had told us that to protect the wooden platforms from the flame of the rocket jet during the first few seconds a conical deflector was placed below the rocket to deflect the hot gases sideways. Our experts elaborated this slightly by suggesting that the device would have four pads arranged at the corners of a square, on which the tail fins of the rocket would rest. The resultant structure would look something like a large lemon squeezer, and so it was called (it can be seen in Plate 28(c) mounted at the tail of the rocket on its trailer). The dimensions stated by the prisoner were somewhat increased by the experts, and somehow between them and Medmenham 'feet' got transposed into 'metres', so that the squeezers instead of being 3 to 4 feet high became 3 to 4 metres high. Medmenham therefore looked at the Blizna photographs for such objects, and quickly found them. They then produced an urgent interpretation report, No. BS780 announcing their discovery.

I could hardly believe my luck, because I had spotted these same objects even before I found the rocket at Blizna, and had quickly dismissed them for what they were: bell tents. There was enough evidence on the photographs to show that they were not substantial metallic structures because they had been surrounded by protective walls of sandbags, with a gap left so that the occupants could enter and leave the tent and some of the tents had been struck, leaving the sandbag wall intact. So, whatever the structure was, it could be folded up enough to get through or over the sandbag wall.

Happily, Hugh Smith had recruited one of his friends, Ronald Lampitt, who in peacetime was a commercial artist, to take over the drawing of our diagrams, and I asked Lampitt to draw me a cartoon of a rocket stuck on the pole of a bell tent with an astonished German soldier looking out from the flap with another holding a copy of the Medmendham report. I provided the cartoon with a covering page simulating one of our normal covers, but instead of having been headed, 'Air Scientific Intelligence Interim report', this one was headed, 'Air Scientific Intelligence Tentative Report'. I then sent a copy to Douglas Kendall, with a note saying that a fortnight or so ago he had sent a rather unkind letter to the Assistant Chief of Air Staff (Intelligence) about the dangers of amateur interpretation. If he cared to peruse my enclosed report, he would see that I thoroughly agreed with him but that, in the interests of an old friendship, I proposed to give it no further circulation. Douglas Kendall stuck the cartoon on his wall, and our relations resumed their former warmth.

Now that the weights were settled, most of my Intelligence task was over, and I settled down to writing up all the evidence. My report was completed on 26th August 1944; it ran to some 30,000 words, and gave detailed arguments for all my conclusions. A few points remained obscure, notably the nature of the radio beam control for those rockets (about 20 per cent of those subsequently fired against England) which were guided along a beam rather than by their internal gyroscopes and accelerometers —the first substantial use, in fact, of inertial navigation. The rocket that had fallen in Sweden, and which had so impressed us by the complexity of its radio control, was not in fact typical of those to be used for bombardment: its controls were much more complicated because it was intended to test out a guidance system for ground-controlled missiles.

As for the figures given in my report, these may be compared with those by German sources as follows:

	A.D.I. (Sc.) Estimate	German Statement[1]
Total weight	11½–14 tons probably 12–13	12·65 tons (experimentally down to 11·2 tons)
Warhead Weight	1 ton nominal	1 ton (down to ·97 tons sometimes)
Liquid Oxygen Weight	4·5 tons	4·9 tons
Alcohol Weight	3·5 tons	3·8 tons
Carcass Weight	2·6–3 tons	2·87 tons
Maximum Range	200–210 miles	207 miles
Total Stocks	Perhaps 2,000 (on 26.8.44)	1,800
Monthly Production	About 500 (on 26.8.44)	300 in May 1944. Average 618 (Sept. 1944 to March 1945)
Total Forward Storage	About 400	320
Intended Monthly Rate of Fire	About 800	900 as 'target figure'

[1] The German statements in the first six rows came from firing tables produced by Wa Prüf 10 in August 1944. The statements of stocks and production came from the Director of the rocket factory at Niedersachswerfen (the 'M Works') and his factory records, while the final two came from one of supply advisers to the German rocket organization.

One of the ways in which I estimated the intended rate of fire provides an example of the irony of security. When we captured a map in Normandy it showed the storage sites for rockets west of the Seine, and these had a capacity for holding 100–120 rockets. Also shown on the Normandy map were some other sites numbered 15 to 20 inclusive, the numbers running from east to west. These were sites that we had already photographed from the air, and which we had diagnosed as dummies erected to throw us off the scent of some unknown genuine sites. The map gave evidence that these were somehow connected with the rocket, and we could therefore conclude that there were 14 sites to the east of the Seine, some of which we had already photographed and identified as being of the same pattern. Assuming that all these sites were part of a deception programme, and that there was—with German consistency—a fairly rigid relation between the number of dummy sites and the number of genuine ones (none of which we had discovered), I assumed that since there were 14 dummies east of the Seine for six west then the rocket storage capacity east of the Seine would be in the same ratio. So to the 100–120 rockets stored west of the Seine there should be another 100–120 multiplied by 7/3 east of the Seine, giving some 400 rockets stored altogether. Further, assuming that the policy was to hold two weeks' supplies in the stores, as we had found to be the practice with the flying bomb, this would suggest that the Germans intended a rate of firing of about 800 rockets a month. The result of this admittedly tenuous argument, which was supported by others of a similar nature, was thus surprisingly close to the German intention of 900 a month.

An obvious countermeasure to the rocket was to bomb the factories that were making it. We had found the three main factories, Peenemünde, the Zeppelin Works at Friedrichshafen, and the Rax Works at Wiener Neustadt, each of which was to produce 300 rockets per month, and we had heavily bombed all three. This caused the Germans to concentrate the production of V-2s (and V-1s) in a great underground factory at Nordhausen which from August 1944 onwards produced 600 rockets a month. At the time of my report, all that we knew was that there was an underground factory the 'M(ittel) Works' somewhere in central Germany (actually it was in the Harz mountains north of Nordhausen) operating in conjunction with a concentration camp 'Dora'. Dr. Jozef Garlinski has since told me that these reports came from Polish workers in the camp.

Figure 30 shows a drawing from my Report that Ronald Lampitt made of the rocket, based on the Farnborough reconstruction and what we ourselves could add from our other knowledge. Almost the only modification which had to be made once we captured some intacr

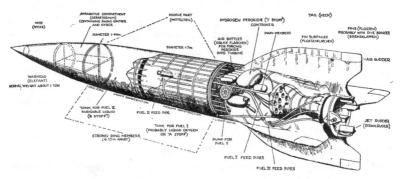

Fig. 30. Drawing by R. Lampitt of a V-2 before any fell in Britain. The outline was based on air photographs and on papers captured in Normandy. The nomenclature came from Enigma information, and the technical details overwhelmingly from the Farnborough examination of the remains of the V-2 that fell in Sweden on 13 June 1944. Later examination showed that the hydrogen peroxide container should have been below rather than above the pump

rockets was that the hydrogen peroxide container (which provided fuel to drive the pumps which fed the alcohol and liquid air into the rocket jets) should have been about 3 feet lower than where it was shown on our diagram. I was also able to provide a diagram (see Figure 31*a* overleaf) giving the trajectory that I expected for the rocket. Figure 31*b* shows for comparison a diagram of the trajectory of the first successful rocket at Peenemünde, which was found after the war in an album in the Peenemünde archives; while the general philosophy is the same, showing that we had divined the German intentions correctly, our diagram is more accurate in portraying a parabolic rather than a circular trajectory after the rocket has ceased to burn, and the German draughtsman has also erroneously placed the maximum velocity at the top of the trajectory instead of near the point of impact.

To complete my account, I included as appendices the reports on the rocket that I had written during the previous year, so that anyone could see the extent to which we had at any time been in error, and I concluded with a section on German policy in which I tried to answer the bewilderment still existing in Whitehall about why the Germans had developed such a weapon at all. I suspected that Hiter had been carried away by the romance of the rocket, just as our own politicians had been carried away by its threat: for some psychological reason they seemed far more frightened by one ton of explosive delivered by rocket than by five tons delivered by aircraft:

A rational approach brought us nearest the truth regarding the technique of the Rocket. When, however, we try to understand the policy behind it, we are forced to abandon rationality, and instead to enter a fantasy where romance has replaced economy.

The Germans have produced a weapon which, at the cost of years of intense research, throws perhaps a one or two ton warhead into the London area for the expenditure of an elaborate radio controlled carcase consuming eight or so tons of fuel. Their own Flying Bomb achieves the same order of result far more cheaply. Why, then have they made the Rocket?

The answer is simple: no weapon yet produced has a comparable romantic appeal. Here is a 13 ton missile which traces out a flaming ascent to heights hitherto beyond the reach of man, and hurls itself 200 miles across the stratosphere at unparalleled speed to descend— with luck—on a defenceless target. One of the greatest realizations of human power is the ability to destroy at a distance, and the Nazeus

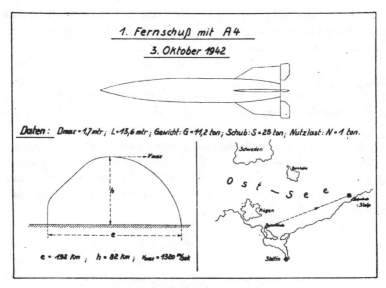

Fig. 31a. Diagram from a Peenemünde album showing the trajectory of the first successful
V-2 firing, 3 October 1942

Fig. 31b. Diagram from the Scientific Intelligence report of 26 August 1944, showing the
guessed trajectory. The German diagram erroneously has the maximum velocity at the top
of the trajectory

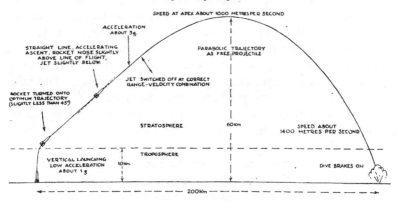

POSSIBLE TRAJECTORY

would call down his thunderbolts on all who displease him. Perhaps we may be permitted to express a slight envy of his ability, if not to destroy his victims, at least to raise one of the biggest scares in history by virtue of the inverted romance with which those victims regard the Rocket.

Finally, I added an epilogue, to state the case to which future Intelligence officers could point if they were ever threatened by such a muddle as I myself had had to face over the past sixteen months:

When Intelligence first detects a new enemy development, there are generally insufficient facts to eliminate all explanations but the true one. If therefore these insufficient facts are submitted to a body of experts, each can hold his own theory without the others being able to prove him wrong; this situation can only be resolved by getting more information, and generally when this information is obtained, an approach through Intelligence rather than through technical experience is the more reliable one for reaching the correct solution. Expert advice can be dangerous in Intelligence problems, for rather a simple reason. Our experts are engaged in developing weapons for British use; the enemy experts for German use. The requirements and stimuli are different, and in any case a few bad experiments may discourage either side. Four situations can therefore arise in any one technical development,

(a) Neither side makes it work. This presents no Intelligence problem.

(b) Both sides succeed. This is a normal Intelligence problem, for it soon becomes a matter of general knowledge, and Intelligence is reasonably well briefed as to what to seek.

(c) Our experts succeed, the Germans fail. This is an Intelligence worry, for proving the negative case is one of the most difficult of Intelligence exercises.

(d) Our experts either fail or do not try, the Germans succeed. This is the most interesting Intelligence case, but it is difficult to overcome the prejudice that as we have not done something, it is impossible or foolish. Alternatively, our experts in examining the German development are no longer experts but novices, and may therefore make wilder guesses than Intelligence, which at least has the advantage of closer contact with the enemy.

The positive contribution of technical experts to Intelligence problems can be great, and there are many cases where Intelligence would be remiss in not asking their advice; but from an Intelligence point of view, it must always be borne in mind that the advice comes from a British, and not from a German, expert. If this difference in background is not continually appreciated, serious misjudgements can be made. In the tactical field, Napoleon knew this danger well: he called it, 'making pictures of the enemy'. In the technical field the same danger exists: the present investigation is sufficient example.

I distributed 40 copies of the report, only to be telephoned two days later by Frank Inglis, who said that Portal was withdrawing them as a result of objections by Duncan Sandys. His objections were, I gather, to my epilogue, which he considered unjustified and unfair to the many experts whom he had called in. This was at least a way of ensuring that the report was read from cover to cover before the recipients returned it, but it was never recirculated. Indeed, when I requested its recirculation some months later, after the dust had died down, permission was still withheld on the grounds that the Chiefs of Staff had approved its withdrawal, and it would be difficult to get them to consider recirculation at that stage. It was, however, to be available for historical purposes, and I had some delayed gratification when I found that Winston Churchill had included a comparison between my figures and those of the Germans in the final volume of his war memoirs. And I am content to leave it to historians to decide whether or not its original withdrawal could possibly have been justified.

In some ways, fate seemed to be on my side. I had said in the summary of the report that a heavy attack 'could hardly be mounted before mid-September. Our threat to their launching area and to their lines of supplies may, however, cause the Germans to make an earlier, but smaller effort—if they can.' And, indeed, this was clearly going to be a 'near run thing', as our armies were now racing north-eastwards. Progress was so good that although I had given the range of the rocket as 200–210 miles, it seemed that we might make a clean sweep of all the possible launching areas. Certainly the Vice-Chiefs of Staff thought so (although Roderick Hill did not) for on 6th September they advised that the threat was over. Either on this advice or on his own, Duncan Sandys therefore decided to hold a press conference on 7th September to announce that the battle of London was over. Happily, I was not invited to the conference, although he was big enough to invite me to a cocktail party in his flat in the evening.

The papers for Friday 8th September therefore came out with headlines and pictures showing Mr. Sandys proclaiming the end of the battle. At twenty minutes to seven that evening Charles Frank and I were in our office when there was a double bang; he and I looked at one another and said almost simultaneously, 'That's the first one!' To mock the day's headlines, the V-2 had arrived. The one which we had heard had fallen near Chiswick and another had fallen near Epping. What most of those concerned with the celebration had overlooked was that our armies were held up by the rivers, and although they were now through Belgium, they had not been able to cross the Scheldt and the Rhine, and so there was an area around the Hook of Holland which was still in German hands, and within 200 miles range of London. Herbert Morrison was in the Slough of Despond.

The next morning, Charles and I went to Chiswick to inspect the crater, and after the weekend Rupert Cecil flew me down to Cornwall to take a few days off with my family. While I was away our Airborne Forces fought the action at Arnhem, with Colonel Frost—who had led the Bruneval Raid—holding the Bridge to the last. Unfortunately, despite tremendous gallantry, it proved a 'bridge too far', and the vital V-2 launching area remained in German occupation throughout the winter. The German records showed that by 7th April 1945 they had successfully launched 1,190 rockets against London with a further 169 failures; of these we detected the fall of 1,115, of which 501 fell in the London Civil Defence Region. We detected the rise of many of these rockets by radar, so that it was possible to give a few minutes' warning while a rocket was on its way. We should also not forget that Antwerp suffered more than London, in that it was the target for 1,610 rockets and 8,696 flying bombs, with Liège a target for 3,141 bombs.

In September 1944, one of the United States Army Air Force officers attached to Air Intelligence, Lieutenant Colonel Stuart McClintock, asked me whether I would write an article for the Eighth Air Force magazine on the future of the long range rockets, because he thought that the United States Air Force ought to be alerted to their possibilities. Charles Frank provided the basic calculations, and I wrote the article. It might be fitting to conclude this chapter with the closing paragraphs of our 1944 article:

There can be no doubt that with the A4 the rocket has come to stay for a long time, if only for its non-military applications; in no other way can we get free of the earth's atmosphere, with all that this freedom may mean to astrophysical studies. The attainment of the upper atmosphere will in itself be a major factor in experimental meteorology, and sooner or later someone will seriously try to reach the moon—and succeed. Military applications are bound to be made, whatever the limits imposed by treaties, and we should do well to keep an eye on the possibilities. If we were to allow ourselves more liberty of conjecture, we might consider using atomic fuels to drive an exhaust of hydrogen molecules, or perhaps lighter particles, giving an entirely different order of performance.

It is an often stated requirement that a weapon of war should have a probable error comparable with its radius of destruction, so that a few shots would ensure the obliteration of the target. Practical weapons seldom approach this ideal, although in the future it may be attainable through homing devices. With a very long range rocket we may have to accept errors, and it may be easier to increase the radius of destruction by the use of new types of explosive based on the fission of the uranium atomic nucleus. If such an explosive becomes practicable, it will probably have a radius of destruction of the order of miles, and on this account alone it might best be carried in some unmanned projectile, of which the rocket would be a particularly suitable type by virtue of its relative immunity from interception and of its potentially better accuracy at long ranges compared with pilotless aircraft. Speculation of this kind is fascinating, but can well wait for a paper at a later time when it is nearer realization.

Reviewing therefore what we have seen to be reasonable extrapolation from present practice, a two-stage rocket of about 150 tons starting weight could deliver a 1 ton warhead to nearly 3,000 miles range, with a probable error of 10 miles in range and 3 miles in line. This might be a feasible weapon for delivering a uranium bomb, should such a bomb become practicable. It would be almost hopeless to counter by attacks on the ground organization, because the increased range would allow an almost unlimited choice of firing site, while the trajectory could be so varied that the firing point could not be deduced without sufficient accuracy for countermeasures. Production would probably take place underground. At the moment such a rocket could not be intercepted, but by the time it becomes a serious possibility it may itself be a target for smaller defence rockets fitted with predictors and homing devices: but these would depend upon adequate warning, and the defences might also be saturated by a salvo of long range rockets.

The protagonists for the development of very long range rockets would probably have, in Britain at any rate, to meet the criticism that it would not be worth the effort expended. The A4 has already shown us that our enemies are not restrained by such considerations, and have thereby made themselves leaders in a technique which sooner or later will be regarded as one of the masterpieces of human endeavour when it comes to be applied to the exploration of Space. As it is mainly with our enemies that Intelligence is concerned, rather than with our own views on military economics, it suffices that the long range rocket can be developed much further. In the light of this fact, we must watch.

CHAPTER FORTY-SIX

V-3

BEFORE ANY of the ski sites had been discovered in 1943, we had found some very large concrete constructions which from their deployment seemed likely to be used for launching missiles against London. Three of them, Lottinghem (behind Boulogne), Siracourt (near Saint Pol) and Equeurdreville (near Cherbourg), proved to be artificial caves for the assembly and launching of flying bombs. Another two, Wizernes (also behind Boulogne) and Sottevast (behind Cherbourg), were to serve a similar function for the rockets, and one at Watten (behind Calais) was to be both a rocket launching point and a sheltered liquid oxygen plant. Despite the huge amounts of concrete used, and although we were for a long time unsure about the exact functions of the individual sites, we felt that we could keep these structures from being completed, thanks partly to Barnes Wallis' 'Tallboy' bombs.

We felt the same way about yet another great concrete structure, that at Mimoyecques, near Calais. It was heavily bombed, and could probably never have come into action, but we did not divine its exact purpose until our forces overran it. Under the name of 'HochDruck-Pumpe' (High Pressure Pump) it was to contain 50 smooth-bore barrels approximately 6 inches (15 centimetres) in diameter and 416 feet (127 metres) long, firing finned projectiles, each weighing about 300 lbs. at a combined rate of up to ten per minute at London. A final muzzle velocity of about five thousand feet per second was to be achieved by igniting further propellant charges in side ports up the main barrel, as the projectile passed them on its way out. The development of the scheme was pursued enthusiastically in Germany but, fortunately, it hit a basic snag: above about 3,300 feet per second the projectile became unstable and 'toppled', and thus fell badly short. This fact was only discovered after twenty thousand shells had been partly manufactured.

When the purpose of Mimoyecques was appreciated in London there was, inevitably, a feeling that Intelligence had failed. Actually some of our sources had reported that it was a long-range gun, but since the ski sites were also sometimes described in the same way this evidence was inconclusive. The Intelligence techniques that had been successful against the flying bomb and the rocket appeared to have failed against HDP, and there had to be a reason. Basically it was that with our limited effort we had to concentrate on the most urgent problems, and thus on catching weapons not so much at the research stage (although we sometimes achieved this) as in the development phase—which usually meant when trials were showing promise.

In the case of HDP the trials did not reach this phase: we discovered a letter from Professor Osenberg, who late in the war had been appointed to co-ordinate German scientific effort, to Martin Bormann, Hitler's Deputy. The letter had been written on 8th May 1944 and clearly had embarrassed Osenberg, who had been deputed by two large conferences at the testing establishment at Misdroy on 22nd March and 26th April and by another in Berlin on 4th May, to inform Hitler that the trials had been a failure, and to deplore the waste of material and effort. It was later said that Hitler nevertheless ordered the construction at Mimo-yecques to continue because it attracted bombs that might otherwise have been aimed at more vital targets. Actually, some improvements were made to HDP and in a much less ambitious form it was said to have been used against our land forces on the Continent in the winter of 1944/5. Had it approached a degree of success in trials comparable with that of V-1 and V-2, we should probably have heard something of it, and Mimoyecques would have been even more heavily bombed than it was. My contemporary conclusion on V-3 (26th April, 1945) was, 'There was little warning: there was little danger'.

A possible V weapon on which we received detailed information was a long-range glider bomb, the BV246. This had a range of about 200 kilometres when dropped from a height of seven thousand metres (23,000 feet) attaining speeds of about 350 m.p.h. at height falling to 250 m.p.h. at ground level, and carrying 430 kilogrammes of Amatol explosive. It was thus an early example of a 'stand-off' missile, along with the air-launched V-1; but although we were able to follow its development through the radar watch on the Peenemünde trials, it made no impact on the war.

Other developments that the Germans had in hand at Peenemünde were the A9, a winged version of the A4 rocket, designed to 'bounce' on the atmosphere at re-entry so as to glide to an increased range covering most of England, and the A10, a two stage rocket to reach

America. They also adapted their rocket technology to defensive missiles like 'Wasserfall', a ground-to-air missile, and the X-4 air-to-air wire guided missile. We had already seen two of their missiles in operation, the HS293 rocket-propelled glider bomb and the Fritz X guided ballistic bomb. With these developments, coupled with their advances in infra-red technique, the Germans could not substantially affect the outcome of World War II, but they initiated a new phase of warfare. Their most desperate proposal was a Kamikaze-type project to build manned V-1s to steer against vital targets; several hundred were manufactured, and about 100 pilots trained, but they were not used. The feasibility of such a project had been demonstrated by the courageous woman test pilot Hanna Reitsch, who actually flew a V-1 to establish the cause of its control troubles.

Both in the air, with the ME262 jet fighter, and at sea with the 'Schnorkel' U-boats and the fast Walther U-boats propelled by hydrogen peroxide, and with new homing torpedoes, the Germans would have had an impressive armoury if they had been able to sustain the war for another year or two. Moreover, in the nerve gases, they had a weapon to which we would have had no counter; fortunately Hitler believed that we must have equally lethal gases available, and in any event the war situation changed so rapidly that he was not tempted to start gas warfare. On 22nd December 1944 I had to write an appreciation of the new German weapons for Churchill, on the basis of which he gave a warning to Parliament. My report concluded.

The Germans have been consistently fertile in producing new weapons, and in several directions temporarily outshine us. The most notable examples are the new submarines and fuels, rockets, and jet propulsion generally. Few weapons starkly novel to Intelligence have been discovered during the past two or three months, but several of those previously discovered are only just coming into operation; if available in sufficient quantity, they would have a pronounced influence on operations. It is therefore production rather than invention, particularly of synthetic fuels, that is going to be Germany's main difficulty.

Fortunately for us, the production difficulties proved too great.

CHAPTER FORTY-SEVEN

Bomber Triumph

A S THE war entered its last year, the Germans were feverishly on the defensive. They were bringing out so many variants of their basic radar systems—and copying some of ours—that I had written in March 1944 'In 1940 the Germans regarded radar as a means of economizing in Observer Corps. In 1942 they used it to economize in fighters. In 1944 all signs of economy have disappeared, and radar is becoming an end in itself.' Even so, we were far from laughing at our opponents, for they were inflicting so many losses on Bomber Command that we were grateful for the respite offered when the Command was pulled back to bomb the Invasion targets.

Possibly adapting the idea from the panoramic cathode ray tube presentation in our H2S bombing equipment, the Germans at last built some ground radar stations with large aerials continuously scanning all around them, under the code-name 'Jagdschloss' (Hunting Castle). Finding one of these in Denmark, I asked for a low oblique photograph; the sortie was flown by Wing Commander Donald Steventon, a close friend of Tony Hill who used to visit my office with him. The resulting photograph is shown at Plate 29a; it was one of the first taken with the forward-facing cameras that we had had so much difficulty in getting adopted, and it gives some idea of the improvement in definition. Also shown in Plates 29b and 29c are two German photographs of the presentation screen of a Jagdschloss when it was tracking one of our raids, which we were protecting with jamming (the radial streaks) and Window, which blocked out whole areas of the tube.

During the spring of 1944 we continued to gather retrospective evidence regarding the losses caused by I.F.F. having been left on. In a single JagdDivision (JD2) the Germans credited it with 60 bombers by night and 150 by day during the first two months of 1944. Now that at last it was entirely switched off the Germans were puzzled, and there was one occasion, perhaps the 'Köpenick Raid' (p. 382) where an American raid was not intercepted because the Germans had been unable to locate it in its I.F.F. silence. But they were now prepared to listen for any radio or radar transmission that originated from British or American bombers, and they rapidly expanded their newly formed Raid Tracking Organization to exploit any weakness.

Not only could German fighters be directed on to the track of air raids by information gathered by the new organization, but the fighters themselves were now equipped with special receivers to home from a considerable distance on to any transmissions that might come from radar equipment carried by the bombers. One of these latter equipments was 'Monica' which was installed in every bomber and which was designed to detect echoes from nightfighters approaching from the rear. But it proved, as it was bound to be, much more effective in giving away the position of the bomber to the fighter, than vice versa. Trials with the JU88 nightfighter that had landed at Woodbridge on 15th July 1944 (p. 393) showed that its 'Flensburg' detector enabled the nightfighter to home from a range of fifty miles to within a thousand feet of a bomber fitted with Monica. As a result the Commander-in-Chief ordered the complete removal of Monica. A corresponding detector 'Naxos' for our H2S transmissions could home from 40 miles, and so orders were issued for a minimal use of H2S in checking navigation and in finding the target. These orders could have been issued months before, simply on the basis of commonsense, but they had waited for a cast-iron Intelligence case in each instance.

The return of Bomber Command to targets in Germany in the second half of July 1944 showed an immediate reward for our efforts. On 18th/19th July, the Command achieved complete surprise through radio silence in a raid on Scholven in the Ruhr; and on 23rd/24th July it lost only four out of 629 aircraft on Kiel, where the Germans—no longer able to spot our main force by its radio clamour—tried to intercept the spoof force instead.

General 'Beppo' Schmid, who had succeeded General Kammhuber in command of German nightfighters in the previous autumn, now found himself in as great difficulties—though of a different sort—as his predecessor had. He recognized that he needed 200 kilometres of warning before our bombers entered Germany if his nightfighters were to intercept us effectively, and he had come to rely on listening to our superfluous radar transmissions for this warning, rather than on his own battered radar. Now, at last, our transmissions were being denied him despite the security measures that he took to ensure that no clue should be given us that the Germans were exploiting our transmissions so successfully. On 16th November 1944 I happily reported

The difficulties of the Raid Tracking Organization apparently induced its commander to seek inspiration from his subordinates by a widespread appeal in the form of a competition essay. The subject matter of the essay, which was open to all officers, men, and women, of the German Y-Service, may give some indication of their recent lines of thought. The points to be considered were mainly the suggestion of new radiations from our bombers which might be utilized for early warning and recognition, and of methods whereby we might be induced to switch on existing radio equipment earlier in a raid. The above competition came to our notice through the misfortunes of a Y-Service company which since early September had been retreating through Greece to an ever-receding final destination. As it received by the same post a request for a return of the numbers of men taken prisoner, wounded, killed, and missing, the essay notice was probably treated a little flippantly. Only with difficulty could we restrain ourselves from entering in place of the unfortunate company; with luck, we should have won.

Besides achieving radio silence, of course, we now had the advantage of occupying France and Belgium up to the German frontier, so our jamming aircraft could now operate much further forward, and blind the German long-range radars. The Germans had therefore to react very rapidly once they detected a raid approaching, and in the resultant hurry, they inevitably made mistakes, especially when we were encouraging them to do so by means of 'Spoof' raids in which a few Mosquitoes would drop so much 'Window' that they looked like a large force. On 6th November, for example, we made two main attacks against Gravenhorst and Koblenz, putting in a 'Spoof' force against Gelsenkirchen. Seven Gruppen were airborne against these raids, with two more at cockpit readiness; of the total of nine, five Gruppen were drawn against the 'Spoof' force.

Besides providing diversions, 'Spoof' raids could be used to get the German nightfighters up, and so tire them, on nights when we were making no major raids. On 9th/10th November 1944, for example, although the Germans had originally thought that bad weather would prevent us operating, they were deceived into treating a 'Spoof' raid on Mannheim as a major one; and when they had unravelled the deception, they further deceived themselves by concluding that it must be the prelude to a major raid. As a result, aircraft of six Gruppen were airborne for $2\frac{1}{2}$ hours.

One of the examples that we enjoyed most occurred on 6th October 1944, when we obtained General Schmid's personal reaction to the fact that our losses were only 13 out of 949 aircraft. The night's major operations were twin attacks on Dortmund and Bremen. In the latter, our bombers made a low approach under radio silence, while the German early warning radar was jammed by a screen of 100 Group[1] aircraft operating their 'Mandrel' jammers; as a result the nightfighters were only able to attack after our bombers had been over the target for ten minutes. Similarly, the Dortmund force flew low over France and turned north and climbed towards the Ruhr again screened by 'Mandrel' aircraft, while a 'Spoof' force of Mosquitoes went on to threaten Mannheim.

The result was confusion to the defences, and General Schmid reacted with a castigatory diatribe to the whole German nightfighter organization: 'I am astonished that in spite of pains, admonitions, and orders throughout the whole year, I have not succeeded in bringing the Jagd Divisionen at least to the point of being able to distinguish in what strength and in what direction the enemy is approaching. In my view, there is no excuse whatever for this failure.'

We happily noted that his astonishment must have continued unabated, for he had no better luck throughout October, as the following table shows:

Date	Main Targets	First Plots	Sorties	Losses
5.10.44	Saarbrucken	Luxemburg	699	3
6.10.44	1. Dortmund	Bonn	949	13
	2. Bremen	Terschelling		
9.10.44	Bochum	Aachen	585	6
14.10.44	1. Duisburg	2 mins. after Target	1573	9
	2. Duisburg	Target		
	3. Brunswick	45 m. S. of Lippstadt		
15.10.44	Wilhelmshaven	60 m. N. of Groningen	674	11
19.10.44	1. Stuttgart	Metz	1038	9
	2. Stuttgart	Metz		
	3. Nürnberg	Trier		
23.10.44	Essen	20 m. S. of Aachen	1197	8
30.10.44	Cologne		1073	2
31.10.44	Cologne	Lille	658	3

[1] 100 Group had been formed in November 1943 to operate radiocountermeasures. Its Commander was Air Commodore E. B. Addison.

Our low losses could be attributed to the simultaneous operation of several factors. At last we had achieved radio silence, and at last we had effectively jammed all forms of German radar. We had pushed back the German night defences to the frontiers of Germany itself, which cut down their warning time, and the German nightfighters were now beginning to feel the shortage of petrol. All this gave scope which the Bomber Command tacticians exploited to the full. In addition, the operation of our long-range nightfighters now became a serious factor, and the German nightfighters began to sustain casualties so severe that they added an extra man to their existing crews of three, purely to divide up the radio and radar duties and to keep a backwards watch for the approach of our nightfighters. So we had the amazing situation of four men in a German nightfighter operating over Germany being harassed by two men in a British nightfighter operating from Britain.

At the same time, complacency on our part could have been dangerous. I commented: 'Looking now at the principles underlying our success, the classical method of conserving our bombers has been essentially one of evasion: by various countermeasures we have deceived or blinded the enemy as to the real position of our forces. It is the application of this method which has been mainly responsible for our recent low losses. If, however, we attack the remoter targets, the German problem will become easier both in identification and interception. Moreover, a relatively small change in the technical balance of the struggle, such as occurred following the German development of new A.I. could swing the loss rate on to the high side again, so long as we depend on evasion. The 100 Group nightfighters, however, represent an additional principle which reduces our bomber losses by direct attack on the enemy nightfighters, and is therefore still able to reduce bomber losses should the evasion policy temporarily fail.'

After some of my earlier reports, which had shown deficiencies in Bomber Command's tactics or countermeasures, the Chief of Air Staff— so his Staff Officer told me—would telephone the Commander-in-Chief to ask whether he had read my report and what he was doing about it. This time the Commander-in-Chief telephoned first.

One final triumph for Bomber Command was the sinking of the *Tirpitz* in Alten Fiord by the Lancasters of 9 and 617 Squadrons dropping 'Tallboys' on 12th November 1944. With their ship capsized, the doomed men inside were heard singing 'Deutschland über Alles' as the waters rose. What a tragedy it was that men like that had to serve the Nazi cause.

16*

The German defences were in great difficulty: the geographical situation was now as much against them as it had been against us in 1940. As for the possible technical factor that might have swung the situation in their favour, this did not materialize; and between 1st October and 31st December we lost only 136 bombers out of 14,254 sorties. Among our losses there were inevitably some 100 Group aircraft, whose activities were saving so many of their comrades. My second cousin, Robert Jones, was among the 100 Group crews who did not come back.

There was a tactical possibility that had worried us all the time, which was that the German nightfighters might operate a large-scale intrusion over England and attack our bombers as they were landing. In December 1944, I was able to warn that such an operation had been planned; and Bomber Command and Fighter Command were ready should it occur. But, fortunately for us, the Germans had not enough strength left to do it, and they spent themselves instead in their last great attack of 1st January 1945 on the allied airfields in France and Belgium; although they destroyed about 400 allied aircraft, mainly on the ground they themselves lost nearly 300 fighter pilots.

The German defences were now so weak, particularly as a result of the American day fighter attacks, that Bomber Command itself was able also to attack by day. Had the war gone on much longer, the Messerschmidt 262 (as Adolf Galland and his select band of pilots in Jagd-Verband 44 showed in the closing stages of the war) might well have swung the balance against the Americans and ourselves; and guided missiles, both from the air and from the ground, would have come into service, for in this respect—pressed by the need for new forms of defence—the Germans were well ahead of us all.

Fortunately, the war ended before these threats could materialize. It had been a 'long haul' in which we had identified 48 different types of ground radar, leaving only three rare types unidentified before capture. We had located 740 radar stations in Western Europe; and not more than six were unknown to us when our ground forces overran them. Our work in support of Bomber Command had been more difficult and less spectacular than any other that we did; it had extended over a wider field, and it had lasted longer than any other. When officers from Bomber Command and Fighter Command examined the German nightfighter system in Schleswig Holstein at the end of hostilities, they stated in their Report of 14th June 1945 on the German Air Force Nightfighter System, 'We heard of no equipment in operational use of whose existence indications had not been given by our Intelligence. Our Intelligence had clearly fulfilled its role admirably.' Bomber Command's main report, 'The War in the Ether' of October 1945, commented generously:

> It is, indeed, of the greatest interest to study the mass of information provided by the examination of documents and key personnel on the German side. The outstanding impression which such a study leaves is of the extraordinary range and accuracy of the technical Intelligence with which Bomber Command was provided for the conduct of the R.C.M. offensive. No praise can be too high for those responsible for producing this Intelligence, without which no worthwhile R.C.M. effort could have been possible. Nor is there any need to ask indulgence for labouring this point, since the critical reader cannot have failed to have been impressed by the importance which attached to the possession of accurate information regarding the enemy's methods and equipment.

We had certainly done our utmost; but, thinking of those hundreds of dreadful hours flown through the German defences by 200,000 airmen of whom 50,000 British and a comparable number of American did not come back, how could we have done less? And was it enough?

CHAPTER FORTY-EIGHT

Nuclear Energy

ALTHOUGH V-1, V-2, the Invasion and our Bomber Offensive had been our main preoccupations during 1943 and 1944, we had always to regard the possibility that the Germans were working towards an atomic bomb. Indeed, their interest in the Norwegian heavy water pointed in this direction, and we had therefore to go on watching. With my very small staff and our urgent commitments I had been glad to find in M.I.6 an officer with enough interest to help us: Eric Welsh, the Head of the Norwegian Section. And, as explained in Chapter 35 I arranged for him to meet Michael Perrin of the British Tube Alloys project periodically, originally along with Charles Frank but—as a result of a message from Perrin—later by himself.

Welsh's dragooning of James Chadwick into writing a letter to Niels Bohr seemed to have had little result for some months, since Bohr decided to stay in Copenhagen. Some of the other lines that Welsh stimulated, though, showed more positive results: we heard that the German nuclear physicists, headed by Werner Heisenberg, had left their laboratories in the large cities such as Berlin and Hamburg, where the bombing was intensifying, and were now working in or around Hechingen, a small town near Stuttgart. It seemed that their level of activity was not as high as we should have expected had they been as near to making a bomb as were the Americans and ourselves. We had the impression that they had originally been thinking of a bomb, but had decided that it would not be practicable inside the time span of the war, since in 1942 they allowed a number of relevant papers to be published on nuclear work done in the previous two years, which seemed to have been kept secret while they decided whether to go for the bomb or not.

In October 1941, as Niels Bohr was later to tell us, Heisenberg visited him in Copenhagen. There are still conflicting accounts of Heisenberg's purpose, one explanation being that he wished to discuss the moral issue of working on an atomic explosive; but Bohr was positive, as he told me, that Heisenberg at least implied that the Germans were already working on the atomic bomb.[1] After the war Heisenberg said that an investigation of the critical size was not undertaken (*Nature,* 160, pp. 211–215, 1947) but Irving says that in answer to a question from Milch at a meeting in June 1942, Heisenberg indicated that an amount of uranium as small as a pineapple would be enough to destroy a large city (Irving, *The Virus House,* p. 109).

All this was unknown to us. With all our other problems of Scientific Intelligence, we had had to rely on catching a weapon in the development and production stages, rather than in the research laboratory; and it was in the production stage, with heavy water, that we had caught the German nuclear work. We knew, of course, from pre-war scientific exchanges, who were the German scientists most likely to be involved, but in general we could only speculate on the state and direction of their work. One slightly false trail led to Peenemünde, when we found from a scientific publication that the theoretical physicist Pascal Jordan was now at 'Heeres Anstalt Peenemünde'—the first explanation, incidentally, for us of the letters 'H.A.P.' which Peenemünde personnel were known to wear on their uniforms.

A further result of Welsh's enterprise was that we were able to keep ourselves informed of the progress of Anglo-American relations, since he had persuaded our own authorities to send their signals to America

[1] If so, then it was one based on the fission of the rare uranium isotope, for Heisenberg told a conference of the Reich Research Council on 26th and 27th February 1942: 'If one could assemble a lump of uranium-235 large enough for the escape of neutrons from its surface to be small compared with the internal neutron multiplication, then the number of neutrons would multiply enormously in a very short space of time, and the whole uranium fission energy, of 15 million-million calories per ton, would be liberated in a fraction of a second. Pure uranium-235 is thus seen to be an explosive of quite unimaginable force.' (David Irving, *The Virus House,* Kimber, London 1966, p. 99.)

There is, incidentally, a loose detail of thinking here: the vital physical condition is not necessarily that 'the escape of neutrons from its surface to be small compared with the internal neutron multiplication'. What is necessary is that of the number of free neutrons released in each nuclear fission (say, between 2 and 3) slightly more than one neutron on average should be captured by another uranium-235 nucleus and cause it in turn to split. Suppose, for example, that the internal neutron multiplication were 3; then for 100 neutrons causing a first phase of fission, 300 neutrons will be released. If 160 of these escape, 140 will be left to start the next phase, and so there will be 40% more fissions in this phase than the first, and 40% yet again in the third phase, and so on. Since each phase occupies a minutely small time, the inflation will be catastrophic and lead to an explosion, even though for every 140 neutrons remaining in the lump, 160 will have escaped, in contradiction to Heisenberg's 1942 statement. This means that a much smaller amount of uranium would be needed to make a bomb than his statement suggested.

over our office link, which was especially secure. In one of the messages we read the terms of the agreement drawn up between Churchill and Roosevelt on 19th August 1943 in Quebec regarding the future concentration of atomic bomb work in America. I for one was shocked to read, 'The British Government recognize that any post-war advantages of an industrial or commercial character shall be dealt with as between the United States and Great Britain on terms to be specified by the President of the United States to the Prime Minister of Great Britain. The Prime Minister expressly disclaims any interest in these industrial and commercial aspects beyond what may be considered by the President of the United States to be fair and just and in harmony with the economic welfare of the world.'

It seemed to me that we had signed away our birthright in the post-war development of nuclear energy, and I immediately called on Cherwell to upbraid him for giving the Prime Minister such bad advice that the latter had signed our rights away because he did not realize how important nuclear energy was going to be. Difficulties had been increasing rapidly in the way of Anglo-American co-operation, due in part to American suspicions of our interest being more commercial than military, and I imagine that Churchill swept all these away with a magnificent gesture that could put us in a very awkward position after the war. I could to some extent sympathize with American suspicions, for in the Tube Alloys outer office the first thing that greeted a visitor was a large wall map of Britain divided up into the I.C.I. sales divisions, its presence in fact signifying nothing more sinister than that Akers and Perrin were I.C.I. employees seconded to the Government.

Shortly after this, on 6th October 1943, Niels Bohr came to England, after escaping to Sweden from Copenhagen when he had received a warning that he was about to be arrested. We flew him from Stockholm in the bomb bay of a Mosquito, and we very nearly lost him en route. He told me that his head was so large that he could not wear the headphone set which should have kept him in contact with the pilot, and he therefore failed to switch on his oxygen when instructed to do so, with the result that he lost consciousness. There was nothing that the pilot could do, except to travel as fast and as low as possible; but even when Bohr regained consciousness he still could not inform the pilot, who on landing rushed to the bomb bay and found to his relief that his important passenger was still alive. On his arrival in London, which was kept secret, Bohr was entertained to dinner in the Savoy by Stewart Menzies, the other guests including Cherwell, Akers, Perrin, Welsh,

Frank and myself. Aage, his son, who had escaped with his father and mother to Sweden, followed him to Britain a week or so later, and after a relatively short stay in London they went to see the work in America.

They returned in April 1944. Bohr, who in his original message to Chadwick had said that the prospect for the release of nuclear energy was remote, was at first astonished by the state of development that he had now seen, and it was interesting to see how far his attitude had changed. He was very worried about the prospect of nuclear explosives, especially on the stability of the post-war world. He and Aage were accommodated in a flat in St. James's Court in Buckingham Gate, and were allowed contact with no one outside a very small circle and it was suggested that Charles Frank and I should spend what time we could with Niels Bohr to give him the chance to talk about physics.

It was the most tantalizing situation that I have ever been in. Here was the chance to talk to one of the world's greatest physicists for as long as we liked, and he was only too glad to have someone to talk to. At the same time, it was less than a month away to the Invasion, and I was having to direct the attacks on the German radar stations, and also watch for the imminent flying bombs. So the time for discussing physics was very limited, but Charles and I did manage to receive a number of marvellous tutorials, in which Bohr showed us how, with his delightfully simple picture of the atomic nucleus as a charged liquid drop, it was possible to predict which nuclei could be split. Apart from finding the time to escape from our more pressing duties, our main problem was to keep him supplied in matches, because he would no sooner light his pipe than he would think of some new point to explain to us, and extinguish the tobacco with his finger. Every tutorial therefore ended with a pyramid of burnt matches and the pipe still unsmoked.

Bohr also told us of his concern about the post-war prospects, and of his wish that he could speak to Churchill. He had had an indirect contact with Roosevelt and he believed himself to be the bearer of a message from the President. He asked me whether I could arrange an interview with Churchill, and I was very ready to try, because I could see in it a chance to make Churchill realize just how vital the issue was. I thought that he had been inadequately briefed by Cherwell, because the latter did not really believe that nuclear energy would ever be released. In fact, he had said as much to me, as also had Tizard. It seeemd that each of them had become so alarmed at the destruction that atomic bombs could cause that they clung to the hope that God had not so constructed the Universe that he had put such power in the hands of men.

I therefore hoped that, even if Cherwell himself was doubtful about the prospect of the release of nuclear energy, the fact that so great an authority as Bohr was extremely worried about it would convince Churchill that he should take it more seriously. The one difficulty might be to persuade Cherwell, but in fact he fairly readily agreed. Apparently, as Margaret Gowing has related in *Britain and Atomic Energy 1939–45*, approaches to the same end were made to Cherwell by Field Marshal Smuts, Sir John Anderson, and Sir Henry Dale, the President of the Royal Society. But I believe that it was my persuasion that was decisive: at any rate, the message that Churchill would see Bohr came through Cherwell to me, with the request that I should tell Bohr. Immediately that I did so, Bohr himself asked for my help. He told me that he knew what he wanted to say, but that his English was not very good, and that he would therefore write out his statement and get me to put it into better English, which he would then learn by heart.

In parenthesis at this point, he told me that he used to think that he spoke very good English, and that he was a master of English idiom. He became so confident that at a dinner in London he thought that he would tell a funny story just to show off. It concerned a Frenchman whose pronunciation of English was faulty and who said that the speaking of English 'was not so much a matter of the voccabewlery as of the assent'. Bohr said that he told the story, but nobody laughed. 'Then', he said, 'I knew how badly I spoke English!'

I was far from happy about his suggested procedure, but I did my best, and after two or three re-drafts Bohr said that he was satisfied. The theme of his remarks was that sooner or later the Russians were bound to be able to make nuclear bombs for themselves, and that a very dangerous situation would result. He therefore believed that the world's best hope lay in making a gesture towards the Russians at the present stage, when the Americans and ourselves were almost certainly well ahead, by telling them the secrets of releasing nuclear energy. This, he argued, would show the Russians that they had nothing to fear from the West, and that their subsequent attitude would be both grateful and friendly. I was not sure how Churchill would receive this advice, but I hoped that he would at least see that if such a great physicist as Bohr was so concerned, then every step in nuclear energy development should be most seriously considered, including any further signing away of British rights.

The meeting with Churchill was to take place after lunch on 16th May 1944. I took Bohr along to Cherwell's office, and they went on to Downing Street while I went back to invasion preparations. About five o'clock the same afternoon I was returning from the Air Ministry building in King Charles Street to my office in 54 Broadway, by way of Old Queen Street where the Tube Alloys office was housed. To my surprise I saw Niels Bohr coming along the street in the opposite direction, with his eyes cast Heavenwards. He seemed to be in a daze, and he walked right past me. Fearing that something was wrong I went back and stopped him, to ask him how he got on. All he could say was, 'It was terrible! He scolded us like two schoolboys!'

Afterwards he told me the story, as far as he could reconstruct it. Expecting that Churchill would invite him to speak, he had been ready with his set speech. Instead, Churchill—who seemed in a bad mood—immediately started to upbraid Cherwell telling him that he knew why Cherwell had fixed the interview, which was to reproach him for having signed the Quebec Agreement. It therefore seemed that either I had misjudged Cherwell who had certainly defended the signing of the Agreement to me, or it is possible that, influenced by my earlier criticism, Cherwell had later expressed doubts about the wisdom of the Agreement. Anyway, Churchill went for Cherwell, and Bohr's set speech was completely lost.

When he did have a chance to speak, he no doubt suffered from his usual anxiety to be precise, for he used to say that accuracy and clarity of statement are mutually exclusive. If you want to be accurate you must put in so many provisos and qualifications that clarity will necessarily suffer; Churchill gained the impression that he was a muddled thinker, whose one anxiety was that we should give away our secrets to the Russians. Indeed, Churchill did wonder whether he was a Russian agent. As for the situation in the post-war world, Churchill told them that no difference in principle was involved, since the atomic bomb was simply a bigger one, and that there were no problems that could not be settled directly between him and his friend, President Roosevelt. So the only result of my good intentions was that Niels Bohr himself became suspect. Fortunately, the idea was so ridiculous that it had no lasting effect; what did last was the friendship that Bohr extended to me right up to his death.

When the question of nuclear intelligence had been discussed in 1943 it was agreed that the effort should be a joint one between the Americans and the British; and late in 1943 the first American officer, Major

Furman, appeared in London. His experience in such matters was so much smaller than ours that after he had left, Welsh and one of the Tube Alloys' officers shook hands with each other, in anticipation that we were so obviously going to be the senior partners in the exchange. But the picture gradually changed, especially when in the spring of 1944 Dr. Samuel Goudsmit appeared, and told us that he was Scientific Head of a mission code-named 'ALSOS', which had carte blanche from the President to investigate any captured equipment, papers, personnel or institutions that might throw light on nuclear developments in Germany. He did not seem aware of what we had done in Scientific Intelligence generally, and gave us the impression that he thought that we were even less experienced than he himself was. We considered whether we should form our own field team, such as the one that I was already operating for radar and similar German activities; but it was argued that it would be best for Anglo-American relations if, despite our greater experience, we should seek American permission to join the ALSOS mission under American leadership, and thus become very much the junior partner.

The main target for ALSOS would, of course, be the Hechingen area where we knew Heisenberg and his colleagues to be. We had recently had an alarm, because as a routine precaution I had arranged for periodic photographic reconnaissance of the area to watch for any unusual activity, such as might indicate a nuclear installation. I had briefed Douglas Kendall at Medmenham, to look for such an installation, and for unusual supplies of electric power and water. In the third week of November 1944 reconnaissance showed that several sites of feverish activity had suddenly appeared near Hechingen. We could not at first make sense of them, but such activity in any event needed to be taken seriously, and the proximity to Hechingen made us wonder whether we had at last found evidence of a frantic effort by the Germans to make a last minute attempt at a nuclear bomb. I showed the photographs to Cherwell on 23rd November, who immediately warned Churchill; and plans were made both for further reconnaissance and for bombing. I began to feel that nuclear intelligence had really 'taken off'.

Within a few days, though, the scare was dispelled. Kendall had spotted that all the sites were in the same string of valleys, and were on much the same level. After a visit to the Geological Museum in South Kensington, he found that a German geologist had reported low-grade oil shales in the area, and it turned out that all that the Germans were doing, now that their oil installations were being heavily attacked, was to try to exploit this unpromising source of supply. This salutary observation by Kendall much more than made up for the episode of the 'lemon squeezers'.

Having put our head in the American jaws, we were anxious to have as strong a moral claim as possible when it came to sharing the prospective nuclear information from Germany. This point was stressed to me by Eric Welsh in the early months of 1945, and he suggested that since the general idea was to air-lift the ALSOS mission into Hechingen at the earliest possible moment, we could press our claim for an appropriate share if we supplied the actual air-lift. This we could easily do, because Rupert Cecil was on my staff and an operational wing commander; and I persuaded Norman Bottomley, the Deputy Chief of Air Staff, to let us have the necessary aircraft and crews. Cecil had originally wanted Ansons, because they could land in confined areas, but accepted Dakotas because they turned out to be at least as good in this respect and carried a larger load. It was therefore agreed that Cecil should go as air-lift commander and as my representative, along with 'Bimbo' Norman, who was temporarily, to our delight, commissioned as a wing commander, to act as our main German linguist.

American forces approached Hechingen towards the end of April 1945, and the ALSOS mission moved in. Besides the German physicists and their experimental equipment, including a partly built nuclear pile, there were many documents. Anticipating that documents would be one of the most important finds I had asked Cecil and Norman to arrange that the documents should come back to London either for assessment by us, or at least for us to copy before they went on to America. Cecil signalled me saying that the Americans were being difficult, but that they had ultimately agreed to fly the documents back to America via London, where I could have them for 24 hours. This was clearly a token, and nearly empty, gesture because there were a great many papers, and it was perhaps thought that it would be so useless to us that we would decline the offer. Cecil asked me to signal to say whether I wished the documents to come. In the course of two or three hours, I arranged with the help of Leon Thompson, who had always been a very good friend to us, for every major copying service in the Ministries in London to take a share of the documents, and to work all night. I signalled Cecil, saying that we were accepting the offer; and the copying services stayed on duty.

Instead of the documents I received another signal from Cecil and Norman saying that while they had been absent arranging the details of the return air-lift, the Americans had reversed their agreement to the documents coming to London—on the advice of Perrin and Welsh who had told them that my officers and I were not secure enough: this from the men who had asked me to arrange the air-lift, and whom I had originally brought together in the nuclear intelligence picture!

So the documents were flown direct to America without copies being made in case of an accident to the aircraft, when neither we nor the Americans would have been able to examine them. In point of fact, they were not of very great interest, but this was not known at the time the decision was made. In *The Virus House*, David Irving has been led to postulate that there was an agreement between Sir John Anderson, who at the time headed the nuclear energy work in Britain, and General Groves that the documents should go direct to America. This theory is untenable: if there was such an agreement, why did the Americans in ALSOS agree to the documents coming to London even for 24 hours? And why did I not know about it? I was a member of the special Anglo-American Intelligence Committee which had been formed by Anderson and Groves themselves as recently as November 1944, the other members being Perrin and Welsh and Majors Furman and Calvert of the United States Army; would an agreement be made by Anderson without informing his own Committee? Would any responsible statesman, British or American, have agreed to a procedure in which the documents could have been lost over the Atlantic, without copies first being made? My belief is that there never was such an agreement, and that it has only been suggested to cover an entirely different explanation.

The fact is that the documents went to America, and when copies ultimately came back to Britain they went to Perrin and Welsh, who thenceforward held the whip hand in all nuclear intelligence matters. The fact that they, rather than I, then became the authorities for nuclear intelligence is unimportant as regards the quality of the work for, so far as I know, they did it well. But it was disastrous to Scientific Intelligence generally, for reasons that will later appear.

It was argued that we should do everything possible to keep in with the Americans, but I do not think that what happened was good for Anglo-American relations. Instead of relations being on an absolutely straight-dealing basis where individuals on either side stood up for the rights of their nation, those negotiating were tempted to seek temporary popularity by acquiescence, or otherwise, with negotiators on the other side, and so build up their positions in Britain by achieving reputations for 'getting on with' and 'being trusted by' the Americans. I would never do it: the Americans had rights and so did we, and I would expect an American officer to stand up for his country when he thought it was being outsmarted as I would do in my turn. I must have fought the Americans harder than most through this difficult period;[1] and I was astonished subsequently to be awarded two of their medals, including their highest civilian award and, as far as I know, to be the only British scientist whom they decorated twice.

The implication that my officers and I were insecure would have been laughable had not the general motive been so serious. For the same argument was used to keep Henry Tizard out of the nuclear energy picture when he went back to the Ministry of Defence in 1948 as Chief Scientific Adviser, presumably because some of those who were in positions of power wished to lose nothing to him—and this at a time when Klaus Fuchs was passing secrets to the Russians, and when pandering to the Americans had been shattered by the passing of the McMahon Act, which had broken the partnership the panderers professed to be fostering.

After Hechingen, we had the problem of what to do with the German nuclear physicists who had been rounded up, and who were temporarily held in an American internment camp in France known as 'Dustbin'. After they had been there a short while, Welsh suggested to me that we should get them moved to Britain because he had heard that an American General had said the best way of dealing with the nuclear physics problem in post-war Germany was to shoot all their nuclear physicists. Could I therefore please intervene, and somehow have the physicists held in England? Welsh's statements were sometimes made with a hidden motive, but the danger did seem possible, and we should at least have some residual advantage if the physicists came to Britain instead of going to America. I therefore suggested to Stewart Menzies that they might be accommodated in Farm Hall, the country house in Huntingdon which M.I.6 and S.O.E. had used as a staging-post for agents who were about to be flown into Occupied Territory from the R.A.F. Station at Tempsford, and which was now vacant. Menzies agreed, and I advised that before the physicists arrived we should have the house fitted out with microphones, so that we could hear their reactions when they realized how far the Americans and ourselves had

[1] Co-operation was not always good. James McGovern, later of C.I.A., has described (in *Crossbow and Overcast*, Hutchinson, London 1965, p. 161) how the 100 V-2 rockets that were to have been shared equally between Britain and America were all sent to the United States by an American officer despite British protests. No doubt there were examples the other way.

progressed. If this was an ungentlemanly thing to do, it was a relatively small advantage to be taken of the possible fact that we had saved them from being shot. The move bewildered Sam Goudsmit who afterwards wrote in *Alsos*, 'Just why these top German physicists were interned in England I never understood . . .'

By far the most interesting items that came out of the Farm Hall conversations were the reactions of the German physicists when the news of the bomb on Hiroshima reached them on 7th August 1945. Incidentally, we ourselves were almost awestruck, not so much at the power of the bomb, for this we had expected, but because the Americans had used it with so little notice. It had been clear to us that at least some Japanese authorities knew that they were losing the war, and that they were putting out peace feelers. So much so, in fact, that in March 1945 Geoffrey Tandy, of the naval section at Bletchley, had remarked to me that it was even money whether Germany or Japan would collapse first. For myself, I would have given the Japanese the chance of witnessing a demonstration before actually dropping a bomb on them, not entirely out of feeling for the Japanese who, although I have since come to like them, had conducted the war in a way (for example at Pearl Harbor and in torturing prisoners) that put them beyond the pale of normal humanity. But it was clear that with the dropping of the bomb another threshold would have been crossed, although it can still be argued that many more lives were saved on both sides by the sudden end of the war that would otherwise have been lost in its prolongation.

The transcripts of the reactions of the German physicists have never been published in full, because the official British attitude has been that they never existed. Transcripts were sent to America, of course, and they have been partly quoted both by Groves and Goudsmit. There is no dignity in denying their existence, which I myself have never tried to hide. Their historical importance lies in the light that they might throw on the question of the extent to which the German physicists had thought of making a bomb. Afterwards, Heisenberg gave the impression that he merely kept in with the Nazis because, as he explained to Robert Jungk in *Brighter Than a Thousand Suns*, 'Under a dictatorship active resistance can only be practised by those who pretend to collaborate with the regime'. And if he strove to keep control of nuclear energy in Germany, Jungk says that this was because he and his friends feared that 'other less scrupulous physicists might in different circumstances make the attempt to construct atom bombs for Hitler'.

I would accept that there was something to the comment of von

Weizsäcker, one of the physicists at Farm Hall, who said, 'I believe that the reason why we did not do it was that all the physicists did not want to do it, on principle. . . . If we had wanted Germany to win the war we could have succeeded'. But against this must be set the comment of his colleague Bagge: 'I think it is absurd for von Weizsäcker to say that he did not want the thing to succeed: that may be so in his case but not for all of us'. So the reactions at Farm Hall ranged from those of one or two who regarded themselves as defeated Generals, to others such as Otto Hahn, who was so upset that his original discovery of nuclear fission had led to so much destruction of humanity that he had to be restrained from commiting suicide. All this is clear from what has been published about Farm Hall.[1]

[1] What is still obscure is Heisenberg's own position. Bohr, it will be recalled, certainly thought that he had been interested in making a bomb. I can remember the relevant portion of the transcripts in which Heisenberg expressed astonishment at the news, because he could not see how the Americans could possibly have separated out the amount of uranium-235 that on his calculations would be necessary to make a bomb. His argument, according to my memory, ran thus: it would be necessary to produce fission in an amount of uranium that would contain of the order of 10^{24} atoms (i.e. 1 followed by 24 noughts). This is a number which is about the same as 2 raised to the power of 80. Assuming that two neutrons were produced by the fission of any one nucleus, this meant that chains of 80 fissions each starting from one original nucleus would explode of the order of 2^{80} (or 10^{24}) further nuclei. Each of the last nuclei to explode would be on the average a distance away equal to a 'drunkard's walk' of 80 steps each equal to the mean distance that a neutron would travel in the uranium before striking another nucleus. Since this vital distance was thought to be a few centimetres, say 8 to 9, the final nuclei would be 8 or 9 times the square root of 80, or about 80 centimetres away. This should be the radius of the bomb, giving a mass of about 40 tons.

The error in the argument is obvious, as pointed out earlier in this chapter, and it is hard to imagine Heisenberg making it. But he seemed to imply it also in his 1942 statement, and my own memory is firm. Moreover, Charles Frank wrote some years ago to me to say that his memory was exactly the same as mine, except that he thought that Heisenberg may have taken a shorter distance between fission events, say 4 or 5 centimetres instead of my 8 or 9. If our memories are correct, then one explanation of why the Germans did not go for a bomb is that they thought that far too much uranium would be required. But it is conceivable that we both misunderstood what Heisenberg said; and in fairness to a great physicist it is regrettable that the transcript has never been published. (Frank, who read the transcripts in more detail that I did, says that at a colloquium that Heisenberg gave at Farm Hall somewhat later he revised his original calculation of the size of bomb required by applying correct diffusion theory, and brought his estimate down from tons to kilograms).

As regards the feelings and motives of the German physicists they clearly ranged from those of Hahn to others who would have gone unashamedly for the bomb even under the Nazis. And, as for what the Nazis would have done with it Albert Speer has said in

CHAPTER FORTY-NINE

A.D.I. (Science) Overseas

THROUGHOUT THE war my primary job had been to remain in London directing the various collecting agencies, collating the information that they provided, and seeing that their achievements were used to best advantage. But it was vital from time to time for us to go into the field, partly to give advice on the spot to commanders, and still more to pick up information that might be missed by others without our specialist background. Thus Derek Garrard had gone out to Gibraltar in 1942 to investigate the German infra-red barrage, and subsequently to North Africa to examine German radar equipment.

Our main overseas effort lay in Western Europe after D-Day. Hugh Smith was keen to get into the field again, and so I made him head of my overseas party, and the Air Force gave him the honorary rank of wing commander. Besides Arthen Jones, we had officers from Technical Intelligence attached to us, notably David Nutting, who was a physics graduate and a squadron leader. Another physicist, Maurice Stephenson joined us; he was a captain in R.E.M.E.; and we had two other R.E.M.E. officers, Majors K. G. Dobson and R. A. Fell. They were seconded to us by the Army particularly to look at Würzburgs and other items of German anti-aircraft radar, because this kind of equipment was an Army responsibility in Britain.

Our first officers went over on D+2, and they were soon sending back a steady stream of information, documents, and equipment. On 18th July 1944, a whole 3-ton load of equipment came up to London, but

---

Inside the Third Reich that he has no doubt that Hitler would have used it against Britain. Perhaps the wisest comment is one made more generally on the subject of Germany by Churchill: 'Everyone is not a Pastor Niemoller or a martyr . . . I thank God that in this island home of ours, we have never been put to the test which many of the peoples of Europe have had to undergo.' We scientists in Britain may be thankful that we were not put to the fearful test that faced our German counterparts. Even the prospect of the personal power to be gained from association with the nuclear project was too much for some of us.

arrived just too late for anyone to examine it, and so it was parked outside the Air Intelligence building in Monck Street. Besides radar equipment it included 'something for the Boss' which was the reason why it had been brought straight to Air Ministry rather than going to Farnborough. This was an infra-red detector of the type that the Germans were using for ship detection. When I reached my office in the morning, I found that during the night a flying bomb had scored an absolutely direct hit on our lorry, and all our booty had been destroyed. But it had its compensation in the bewilderment that pervaded the Technical Intelligence branch for the rest of the day. For when they examined the wreck they of course found many items of electronic gear, which they assumed to have been on the flying bomb, and so led themselves to think that the Germans had a new and very accurately controlled missile which could be directed so precisely as to score the closest of near misses on the Air Intelligence building.

We had envisaged expeditions to some of the sites that we had studied from afar for so long, one proposal being that we should hold a celebration on the Hague Peninsula near Cherbourg, where several beam stations as well as our original Freya station at Auderville were located; but I myself went to France only once. This was to advise on countermeasures against the V-1s and V2-s, which were now being directed primarily against Antwerp, but my Air Force friends who had arranged it had also intended that there should be some fairly hectic entertainment. Unfortunately, they happened to pick 31st October for Paris, and 1st November for Brussels, overlooking the fact that these were All Souls Day and All Saints Day, and that everywhere was closed. They had even laid on an aircraft of the King's Flight, complete with pilot with white gloves, but to no avail. And still worse was our reception when we returned home. We had just one hour available for shopping on the morning of 2nd November, when the shops were open again, and we wandered round a large departmental store, looking for inspiration. None of us knew what our wives' measurements were, nor did we know their colours of lipstick or their favourite perfumes. At last, I was inspired. I saw a great tray of the kind of hairclips known as 'kirbigrips', about a shortage of which Vera had been complaining for the past two years. I said, 'This is it, chaps! I know they're short of kirbigrips, and this is the most welcome present that we can take back!' And was I wrong! If our relations have never recovered from the bathwater in 1940, they have never been quite the same after that visit to Paris and Brussels.

As more territory fell into Allied hands, the work of the overseas party widened. The enthusiasm of its members was such that they were sometimes ahead of our spearhead forces, and we accepted the surrender of at least one large German town. And Bimbo Norman, still looking the most unmilitary of men, even in his wing commander's uniform, was horrified when he was asked by some German villagers to round up a party of 'Werwolfs', the diehard Nazi Resistance.

There were, of course, other overseas parties besides ours. In fact, when the war ended there were a great many teams sent out from our Research Establishments under the aegis of the British Intelligence Objectives Sub-Committee, of which I was a member. Robert Watson-Watt headed a party to Eindhoven, dressed as a group captain. He did not feel that this rank reflected his true military equivalence, only to be told that the Prime Minister himself was content to be an air commodore, just one grade up, when he travelled in R.A.F. uniform. Watson-Watt arrived back in London very indignant, because the Philips scientists and engineers repeatedly told him when he asked them questions that they had already given the information to Appleton. He was furious that his rival should have received the information, but we could never tell him the true explanation. This was that one or two men from Philips had been coming across during the winter, making clandestine passages through the German lines. They were interviewed by officers in M.I.6, who asked me to suggest someone who could conduct technical conversations with them. I suggested Charles Frank, and they said that it would be better if the Dutchmen thought that he was someone already well known, and so they introduced him as 'Appleton'. If the Dutchmen wanted an explanation, for example if one of them already knew Sir Edward Appleton by sight, the M.I.6 officers proposed to explain that Charles was Edward Appleton's nephew. So the Dutchmen kept us informed of developments at Eindhoven, and we fed the information out through our normal channels. Somehow, we could only regard the unforeseen effect on Watson-Watt as an unexpected bonus.

The demands on our services grew; we purchased at a very favourable exchange rate chemical balances for the Agricultural Research Council: we supplied German radar components, which were generally much better engineered than our own, to both Bernard Lovell and Martin Ryle, to help them in their start on radioastronomy: and we distributed to British universities electrical and other instruments recovered from the German Research Establishments. This kind of activity became so substantial that I decided to convert our Overseas Party into a new Unit, the Air Scientific Equipment Recovery Unit, with the specific object of bringing back equipment for distribution in Britain. I put Eric Ackermann in command, especially since he was anxious to stay on whilst others such as Hugh Smith, Ken Dobson, and Andrew Fell, were intending to get back to civil life reasonably shortly.

Ackermann's enthusiasm could sometimes present problems. At one stage he had collected so much equipment that he signalled me demanding three Dakotas to transport it back to Farnborough. I thought that it was somewhat out of order for my junior to expect me to arrange transport for him, and so I sent a signal back saying, 'Arrange transport yourself', omitting the 'bloody well' before 'arrange' that would have more correctly reflected my mind. To my surprise, three Dakotas shortly flew into Farnborough with the equipment. I had not reckoned with Ackermann's resource: as soon as he received my signal he went to the Chief Transport Officer, showed him the signal, saying, 'Look Sir, Dr. Jones authorizes me to arrange the transport', and promptly got all that he wanted.

He was, incidentally, backed with a marvellous document that Hugh Smith had drawn up, with all his professional skill in English, which was headed, 'Subject: Orders'. Hugh had found that wherever one wanted to go in the American Zone such a piece of paper was essential because no American officer would act without written authority. It may have stemmed from having a written Constitution. At any rate, it did not matter very much who had written the orders, so long as they said something, and Hugh's masterpiece requested local British and American Forces to furnish the bearer with 'accommodation, permits, and such assistance as he may require'. It also authorized 'travel by service or civilian aircraft, road or rail transport, as necessary' and also 'the carriage of classified documents and photographic and scientific equipment.'

The arrival of the three Dakotas provoked an incident which had all Farnborough laughing. We were so fully stretched that the only officer that I could spare Ackermann at this stage was a recent recruit who had been a classical scholar at Oxford, and who before the war had gone into a Ministry of Labour office at, I think, Nottingham. He was ultimately in charge of sending out Calling-up notices for the Forces, until the day came when he had to sign his own notice. When Ackermann sent back the three Dakotas, he detailed our classical scholar as escort, saying, 'Remember, I want this equipment kept on ice at Farnborough till I get there!' What Ackermann was worried about was that some of my other officers might get at the booty before he himself had a chance, but Farnborough was astonished by our pilot officer classical scholar going round the establishment demanding a large consignment of ice so that he could place the equipment on it, since he imagined that Ackermann's instructions referred to the damage to the equipment that would result if its temperature became too high.

The most remarkable of all Ackermann's efforts started one afternoon in the autumn of 1945, when he appeared in my office with Roy Piggott, Edward Appleton's scientific assistant. They said that Appleton was interested in getting ionospheric research going again between Britain and Germany now that the war had stopped, and that there was an important German ionospheric research station, headed by Dr. Dieminger, that had fled to a location somewhere in Austria, and in the American Zone. Could our unit locate Dieminger's whereabouts, and arrange to transport him and his staff and equipment back to Lindau, near Gottingen, assuming that Dieminger were willing? Piggott confirmed that Appleton would like this done, and since Appleton had been a good friend to us, and was head of the Department of Scientific and Industrial Research, I tentatively agreed, asking Ackermann if he thought that he could 'work it in' with the rest of his programme. Ackermann said that he could, and the two left my office. Had I known more about Piggott, I might not have been so misled by his quiet air, for this proved to hide unexpected resource. Shortly after the war, for example, he and his wife had problems with cutting their baby's nails, because whenever they tried to do so, the baby screamed its head off. One night they heard a bump, and rushed into the baby's room to find that it had climbed out of its cot and fallen on the floor, knocking itself unconscious. Before Piggott went for the doctor he said, 'Here's our chance,' and cut the baby's nails.

Anyway, I had no idea of what I was in for. I heard almost nothing of either Ackermann or Piggott for about two months and then I began to hear rumours. A member of the Radio Security Service had called on Dr. R. L. Smith Rose, the Head of Radio Division at the National Physical Laboratory, and asked him whether he could throw any light on the activities of what was suspected to be a large black market gang operating in Germany and which used radio links. Most of the messages were in an unbreakable code, using frequencies allocated to the Royal Air Force but definitely not an R.A.F. code; there were a few words 'in clear', the three most interesting being 'Smith Rose', 'cheese machine' and 'fifty thousand Reichmarks'. Smith Rose was, of course, completely bewildered; the explanation was that the messages had indeed emanated from Ackermann, and that Smith Rose's name had come up in connection with the ionospheric project. The 'cheese machine' was a diffraction grating ruling engine in Hamburg which Ackermann knew interested me, and he was trying to bring its builder to England for me to talk to. The 'fifty thousand Reichmarks' was part of the money that he needed for the general support of his unit.

For the moment, I was merely amused by Smith Rose's bewilderment; but I myself was bewildered a few days later when Margaret Masterman, my W.A.A.F. Flight Officer, marched in with a file, saying rather pertly, 'I think that you should see this, Sir!' It was a standard War Office file with a great St. Andrew's Cross on it with the legend 'Hand of officer only'. Then I saw its astonishing heading: 'Obscene W/T Traffic'. I said to Margaret, 'What the Hell is this to do with me?' She replied, 'I think you'd better read it, Sir!' and fled. As I read, I realized that it was all part of the same story. There was this large gang, somewhere in southern Germany, and the radio bearings showed that it had been moving around, and the radio traffic was passed between the mobile part of the gang and its headquarters, which seemed to remain fixed. Most of the traffic had defied the cryptographers; unknown to them, this was because Ackermann had obtained Foreign Office 'one time pads' for encyphering his messages. The partial denouement had come when parties to celebrate the success of the expedition had occurred simultaneously both at the fixed headquarters and at the mobile unit, with a foreseeable result on their operators who, after a minor misunderstanding engaged in hurling 'opprobrious epithets' over the ether, scandalizing the Radio Security Service who thereupon redoubled their efforts to find who was responsible. When it was clear that R.A.F. frequencies were involved, these were traced to Ackermann, who had been missing for nearly two months.

The file ended with a certificate saying, 'I can personally certify that the traffic was obscene, because I listened to it myself,' signed by a major on the General Staff. When I called Margaret Masterman in to ask if she had read it she said, 'Yes Sir, but I don't think it was too bad!' And she had hardly left when of all people Ackermann himself appeared. He asked me whether I had been hearing things about him, and I pointed to the file. He said that that was only part of the story, and I had better hear the rest of it. The 'little job' that he was to do for Appleton turned out to be a prodigious undertaking. In the first place, it involved a journey of some hundreds of miles from north Germany down into the American Zone of Austria; and he had decided that they ought to have enough fuel to cover the whole of the expedition to Austria and back to base. The total requirement came to eighty 3-ton lorries with, of course, their drivers and 20 thousand gallons of petrol. Somehow he had charmed all this out of the Chief Transport Officer of the British Air Force of occupation (B.A.F.O.) along with five armoured cars and a full posse of motorcycle outriders. They had set out for Austria in deep winter and, apart from the indecipherable signals, little more was heard of them.

They found Dr. Dieminger very willing to return; and so, nearly two months after they set out, they were back in the British Zone and ready to set him up with his equipment at Lindau. But events now caught up with Ackermann, because at the Commander-in-Chief's weekly conference, the C-in-C himself—Sholto Douglas—had wanted something done, when the Chief Transport Officer told him that he did not have the necessary reserve of transport because he had lent it all to Flight Lieutenant Ackermann, who had said that he had a job to do for Dr. Jones. The C-in-C being frustrated, he then proceeded to the next item on the agenda, which was the Chief Signals Officer's report for the week. This included the matter of the obscene traffic, of which he had now been notified, and he had to report, once again, that the offending frequencies had been allocated to Flight Lieutenant Ackermann. So the latter was summoned to appear before the C-in-C.

Ackermann very sensibly decided that it would be better if I heard the whole story from him first, and so he had flown over from Germany for the afternoon to tell me. He was due to appear before the C-in-C the following afternoon, but he hoped that his path was going to be eased by the Chief Intelligence Officer, for the C.I.O. had invited Ackermann to lunch in the Senior Staff Mess, where it was hoped he might meet the C-in-C socially over a drink before the formal carpeting started after lunch. The C.I.O. himself told me that he duly took Ackermann into the C-in-C's office after lunch, and left him there, returning twenty minutes later, as he put it, 'to pick up the bits'. To his astonishment he saw Ackermann smoking one of the C-in-C's cigars, with the C-in-C listening attentively to Ackermann's story of his exploits and why he had done them. The C-in-C seemed quite disappointed at the C.I.O. breaking in, and remarked that he ought to be getting on with other work but he added that, 'This has been very interesting, Ackermann. I can quite see the importance of the work that you are doing, and if you don't get enough help in future, you just come to me direct!'

So Ackermann survived. He persuaded me to build him laboratories at Obernkirchen, not far from B.A.F.O. Headquarters at Buckeburg, where he spent several years. When I visited him in 1946, some of his captured German radio transmitters were the mainstay of the British Forces Network in Germany, which our Unit continued to transmit until a regular service could be set up. And the quality of Ackermann's radio work in Germany was so well regarded by the Americans that it did more than anything else after the war to ensure the continued exchange of electronic intelligence between us.

Another aspect of overseas operations that might ultimately have predominated was the war with Japan. So long as Germany was our main opponent my own duty was clear, for it was evident that the Germans were technically well ahead of the Japanese, and therefore that my kind of Intelligence would have much greater impact in the European Theatre. But we might be able to help the Allied Forces in the Pacific Theatre by letting them know what the Germans had made available to the Japanese in new military technology; and we could do something to estimate what developments the Japanese had made for themselves by what they told the Germans. The Japanese Attachés even sometimes had with them men who were specifically termed 'Scientific Intelligence Officers' to assist them in gathering information about their ally. We watched their activities with interest, and could say, for example, that the Germans had supplied early forms of Würzburg and Lichtenstein radars, listening receivers for submarines, and guided anti-shipping bombs, although we noted a reluctance to let the Japanese have the latest models. We also learnt details of Japanese developments in airborne radar as they revealed them to the Germans.

We were thus able to throw a useful sidelight on Japan, and one of my officers was posted for a time to Lord Mountbatten's Command in South East Asia. Had the Japanese war continued, we would have switched our main attention to it; but bearing in mind the crumbling state of Japan in early 1945 and the chance that the atomic bomb would be produced, I made no elaborate preparations.

CHAPTER FIFTY

The Year Of Madness

THE WAR with Germany officially ended on 8th May 1945. Amid the generally convivial atmosphere in Richmond, I personally felt miserable. It was partly because such an absorbing phase of my life was coming to an end, but still more because I thought that I could see the mess that lay ahead of all of us, now that our main national objective had disappeared.

In 1944, Ben Lockspeiser, now Director General of Scientific Research in the Ministry of Aircraft Production, had warned me there would be what he called, 'A year of madness' when the war ended, in which many ridiculous arrangements and plans would be made.

The first intimation that my own work might be affected came from one of our best friends, Clifford Evans, the Cambridge botanist who was in the Radar Section of the Naval Intelligence Division. He told me that N.I.D. had been discussing among themselves about what ought to be done regarding the post-war organization of Scientific Intelligence. The Admiralty, it will be remembered, had hitherto played a Puckish part: when Scientific Intelligence could have been rationally organized on an inter-Service basis in 1939, the other two Services had agreed but the Director of Scientific Research of the Admiralty had refused. Then, as German radar and infra-red had developed, I had had to keep watch on behalf of the Navy, with the cordial agreement of N.I.D. Actually, the Admiralty, having seen what a difference Scientific Intelligence could make, had a year or so before appointed a scientist, Edward Gollin, to N.I.D. to cover aspects other than radar, but had never told us. The War Office had still no scientist in Military Intelligence, and as regards radar matters its Anti-Aircraft Section, headed by Gubby Allen, relied entirely on us.

Well, it was fair enough that there should now be a joint discussion of the future. But what alarmed me was that N.I.D. had already gone to the Joint Intelligence Committee, and had suggested that this should form a special Committee to plan the future under an impartial and eminent Chairman, and had already named Professor P. M. S. Blackett.

Blackett had been a hero of my undergraduate days. Fourteen years older than I was, he had gone into the Navy via Osborne, and had fought at Jutland as a Midshipman. He had then gone on to Cambridge, where he read physics, and worked with Rutherford; his mastery of experimental technique led him to discover the positive electron in 1932, for which he was subsequently awarded the Nobel Prize. I had met him when he was one of the original members of the Tizard Committee, and I had seen him sometimes during the war, when he moved through a succession of posts in Anti-Aircraft Command, Farnborough, and Coastal Command, returning to the Admiralty as Director of Naval Operational Research. His contributions had been great, but I had seen him make mistakes. He tended to jump into a new field, thinking that his fresh ideas were better than those who had worked in the field for some time. Sometimes they were, but not always. He was given to 'rational' solutions of problems which sometimes completely overlooked the human aspects involved, and he would then press these solutions with a fervour that belied their apparent rationalism. He was a Fabian, and his approach was different from my own, if only because he would move from one post to another with relative ease, whereas I felt committed to whatever post I was in, to make as long-term a success of it as possible. I always hoped that if the world were collapsing, Blackett and I would find ourselves fighting side by side in the last ditch, but the routes by which we got there would have been very differrent.

It was worrying enough to have Blackett as Chairman, but the composition of the Committee gave no comfort, either. Apart from Gollin, who at least had a year's experience in Scientific Intelligence, and myself, no other member of the Committee had. Charles Ellis, the Scientific Adviser to the War Office, whose experts had made such a mess of the rocket Intelligence, was there; and since he and Blackett were both professors and Fellows of the Royal Society, my own opinions were completely outweighed—none of my wartime experience was considered relevant.

I did my best with Blackett, letting him see my organization and its results, and I wrote a paper for the Committee putting forward my own ideas about the future. The organization of an Intelligence system presents difficult problems because, as my report stated:

A fundamental difficulty of Intelligence work is that input is by source, and output is by subject. A changeover has thus to occur

17

inside the Intelligence machine, which therefore has to act as far as possible as a single perfect human mind, observing, remembering, criticizing and correlating different types of information, and then giving expression to the result. No card index can do it. although indexes are useful adjuncts. The larger the organization, the less can it resemble a single mind. An Intelligence organization has therefore to consist of as small a number as possible of individuals with abilities as great as possible. For the same reason, Intelligence is better done by a staff than by a committee.

Another fundamental difficulty in Intelligence organization is that the collators have the more responsible task in that they must direct the collecting services, if only because the collators alone see the whole picture; if there are any criticisms from the external world, it is the collation section which has to face them. At the same time, the collectors often have the more difficult task, and their work is the more fundamental. This inequality between responsibility and fundamental importance can only be solved by making collection and collation responsible to a common Head.

I then gave my own experience, indicating that our work was best done by working inside M.I.6, even in war. In peacetime this would be even more so, since the two main sources of Intelligence, our espionage system and our listening to radio transmissions, were both controlled by the Head of M.I.6, and the most important aspect of our work would be to influence these particular collecting services. All my own experience had shown the desirability of keeping the collecting and collating sides of the work as intimately together as possible, and it was this aspect that had given me such an advantage over all other branches of Intelligence, where they had been separate. My position had therefore been anomalous, through the historical accidents of 1939, but the anomaly had certainly been a profitable one.

The potential weak point in my arrangement, which I fully recognized, was that the bringing of collection and collation together could result in a great 'empire' where Intelligence might become an end in itself, without sufficient regard for those whom it should serve—for example, the Operational Staffs. For myself, I avoided this danger by maintaining as close contacts with these Staffs as possible; and it was a problem which could always be solved provided that its importance was continually recognized. Faced, though, with the problem of having to choose to sit alongside these Staffs or alongside the collecting agencies, I would opt for the latter because the links on that side would be the more difficult to maintain with the necessary intimacy and informality from a distance.

Blackett, though, would not listen. He told me that he realized the problem had been difficult, and that it had taken him two meetings of three hours to appreciate the problems fully and reach a solution; I told him that I had been in Intelligence for six years, rather than six hours, and that I could still not see a complete solution; I was sure that he did not appreciate the real difficulties, especially when human motives and interests were involved. His solution was to have each of the three Service Ministries with its own separate Scientific Intelligence and Technical Intelligence Section, and also to have separate Scientific and Technical Intelligence Sections inside M.I.6, and any other organizations that might become involved. This scheme bore some resemblance to the one that I had originally advanced in 1939, but the existence of so many separate sections without a single co-ordinating head (in my 1939 scheme, by contrast, it was clear that the three sections with the Services were to be subordinate to the central section) was obviously going to cause difficulties, especially when, as regards Scientific Intelligence, the Air Force one was so much larger and so much more experienced than those which the other Services would have to put up. And if I myself continued to head Air Scientific Intelligence, new personnel would have to be found for the Sections in M.I.6. But Blackett said that he would have no further discussion, and overruled my objections. I told the Committee that they had wrecked the future of Scientific Intelligence, but this produced no effect. I wish that I had been able to quote a passage in Macaulay which I have since encountered, as advice to would-be rationalizers. He described the objects of Whig legislation as, 'To think much of convenience and little of symmetry' and, 'Never to remove an anomaly simply because it is an anomaly'. If Blackett had heeded these, Scientific Intelligence in post-war Britain would have been much stronger.

Inevitably, the Joint Intelligence Committee, which itself consisted of senior officers with little experience in Intelligence, accepted Blackett's recommendations. Not only were all three Services to have their separate Sections but, accepting my point about the indivisibility of Scientific Intelligence (for example a new weapon developed by the enemy for use by its Air Force might be intended for use against our Navy, and therefore two Services were directly involved), Blackett recommended that all the new Sections should be housed together in one building; and, for symmetry, this could not be one of the existing

Service Ministries, so they were all to be housed together in derelict premises in Bryanston Square, far away from all three Services, and also from M.I.6. This resulted in the worst of all worlds in that the new organization would not have close connections with either the collecting agencies or with the operational staffs. Contact with M.I.6 was to be through the Joint Scientific and Technical Intelligence Committee, of which the total membership was to be thirteen, and to ensure perfect fairness and symmetry, the heads of the individual Scientific and Technical Intelligence Sections were to be Chairman in rotation, the chairmanship changing every three months among eight individuals or more. To add to the craziness of the scheme, Blackett overlooked the fact that Atomic Intelligence was not part of it. This was going to be done by Welsh and Perrin entirely independently of the main Scientific Intelligence organization, and it would have the foothold in M.I.6 that was denied to the rest of Scientific Intelligence.

So having been in charge of Scientific Intelligence throughout the war, I now found myself consigned to be a single member of a committee of thirteen, only one of whom, Gollin, had any experience of Scientific Intelligence at all, and I was to take my turn as Chairman for three months every few years.

When the new arrangements were promulgated, I called my staff together and told them what had happened. I had always said that, having had all the fun during the war, I had been prepared to go on through the dull days of peace to act as anchor-man to keep the nucleus of an organization available, which could be expanded again when trouble threatened. But that it was now going to be very difficult for me to go on, and I could certainly see no future for them in staying. Some, such as Edward Wright and Hugh Smith, were already going back to their pre-war university posts, and I offered the others all possible help in finding positions.

The most indignant of all was our very loyal friend Yves Rocard. He was now back in France, having moved from the Sorbonne to the École Normale Superieure, but he still visited us from time to time, and he felt so strongly about what had happened to us that he wrote a pamphlet on 'Co-ordination'; part of its preface ran:

'... De fait, le petit service anglais qui a, on peut dire, gagné la guerre en contrant la technique allemande, se trouve bouleversé; l'homme qui était seul, formé par une dure expérience de six ans, est maintenant noyé parmi treize, tous neufs et déraisonnables. Loin d'être le chef et de pouvoir les former, il n'est qu'un des treize et peut à peine parler. Excédé, il part, les treize tombent à douze, le rendement de 1/1 tombe à 0/12. Pourquoi? Parce que les succès même de la Recherche, la bombe atomique, les armes nouvelles, ont fait venir une nouvelle couche de personnes, qui sentent le pouvoir politique que comportent tous ces éléments, et qui les veulent. Pour les avoir, il faut les pénétrer. Comment les pénétrer? Par la Coordination. . . .'

'Indeed, the little British service which has, one can say, won the war by countering German techniques, has found itself in trouble; the man who was alone, matured by six years of harsh experiences, is now "drowning" among thirteen others, all new and naive. Far from being the chief and able to lead them, he is only one among thirteen, and can scarcely speak. Worn out, he leaves, the thirteen fall to twelve, the ratio of 1/1 falls to 0/12. Why? Because the very successes of Research, the atom bomb, the new weapons, have raised a new breed of people who sense the political power which all these elements allow to exist, and they want these elements. In order to have them, one must penetrate them. How can they be penetrated? By Co-ordination.'

How had this disaster happened? Unfortunately Blackett's enquiry had been conducted inside a frame of reference in which I had to fight entirely on my own; there was now nobody like Medhurst inside Intelligence who would have appreciated what we had done, except perhaps for Stewart Menzies, who had disliked what Blackett had forced through. Menzies, discussing the disruption with me, said that we had worked together through the war, and he would be glad to continue. He knew that he could work with me, but he was damned if he was going to try working with three different scientists. Since my wartime job was to be split right in half—the M.I.6 side and the Air Staff side, he hoped that I would stay with him; but the split would be an unhappy one, and probably unworkable, since whoever took over the other side would have had no experience, and I would for a long time know his job better than he did.

As for seeking support outside Intelligence, I had of course Cherwell and Portal: but the tide was running fast against individualism and in favour of egalitarianism: it was running against the Government, and everything was so much upset by the 1945 Election that nobody in high office could be expected to spend much time thinking about my problems. And unless they could have spent the time, they might merely conclude that I was trying to preserve my position for purely personal reasons. The explosion of the atomic bomb and the dropping of the Iron Curtain meant that our military stance had to be thought out afresh; and although a fundamental look at Intelligence should have been part of this thinking, many in senior posts were exhausted by the strains of the war.

The strain had told on Churchill, too, and it showed in his Election speeches, in which he conjured up a frightening picture of what Britain would be like under Socialism. Actually, his speeches do not sound so shrill now as they did at the time; but he was addressing a nation out of temper: for although the Allies had won the war with Germany, Britain—while bearing the brunt—had had to submit to America; and the submission was patent to the common man by such measures as the replacement of British markings by American on British tanks before D-Day. One general even said to me, 'What else could you expect from a man with an American mother?' I was alarmed by the tone of Churchill's first speech, and immediately went to Cherwell and asked him to advise Churchill to take a different line because he was misjudging the temper of the nation. I added, 'If he goes on in this way, the P.M. will lose the Election'. Cherwell said that he agreed with me, but that he was unable to do anything because Churchill had taken advice about his line of attack from Brendan Bracken and Duncan Sandys; but I note that Lord Moran has said that it was Bracken and Beaverbrook who were the men who had advised Churchill in this instance.

Anyway, the Conservatives lost the Election, and Churchill resigned on 27th July 1945. He felt the shock deeply—it was a sharper change of fortune than any man might expect to face. But no political misfortune could detract from the universal admiration for what he had done in the war. And so, after a moment of uncertainty in which he contemplated graceful retirement 'in an odour of civic freedom' his confidence returned. 'Many people,' he said to me eighteen months later, 'say that I ought to have retired after the war, and have become some sort of elder statesman. But how could I? I have fought all my life and I cannot give up fighting now!'

CHAPTER FIFTY-ONE

German Generals And Staff Colleges

IN THE chaos of 1945, I did what I could to round off my wartime work, and to salvage whatever remnants of organization might be valuable in the future. One of my more congenial tasks was to interrogate some of the German generals who had been my main opponents. They were now interned in a prisoner-of-war camp near Beaconsfield, and I went there to meet them. The headquarters was a large Georgian country house, Wilton Park, and as we approached it I saw an extraordinary sight. Fifty or more German generals were taking their exercise inside a barbed wire compound in the plan of an equilateral triangle of perhaps 80 yards side. Several were already famous names with us, including Field Marshals von Rundstedt and Milch, and I felt rather as one does in a restaurant on going up to a tank of swimming trout and pointing a finger saying, 'I'll have that one!'

Of the generals, Wolfgang Martini, General der Luftnachrichten-truppe, was the man I wanted to talk to most, because he had been in charge of all Luftwaffe signals and radar right through the war and indeed, as he told me, continuously from 1933. I wondered how I was going to interrogate a general, but I found it very easy because he also wanted to interrogate me. He had a very long memory, and could remember various incidents which had puzzled him. He immediately wanted to know, for example, why his jamming of Malta had failed in 1942, and he was ruefully amused by my explanation.

Another incident which he said had troubled him had occurred in the autumn of 1944, when he had brought into use a very powerful new jammer for our 'Gee' system and had sited it in the television tower on the Feldberg near Frankfurt. Within a few days we had sent out some fighter bombers and knocked the tower down—how had we done it? I could not tell him the complete explanation at the time, although I was able to do so later. It was due to the resource of a young R.A.F. Signals Officer who had been at one of our stand-by 'Gee' stations that was not actually transmitting. He locked his receiver on to the German pulses, and telephoned a colleague at another stand-by station to do the same. When the German pulses were coming in at the same instant as the genuine 'Gee' pulses at the other receiver, they were coming in somewhat earlier or later than the genuine pulses at his receiver. By measuring the time interval between the pulses at his receiver, he could then locate the jammer somewhere on one of the family of hyperbolae with the two stand-by 'Gee' stations as foci. The information was passed back to Charles Frank and me, and tracing the course of the particular hyperbola we saw that it passed near the Feldberg, which we knew was the site of the sister tower to the one on the Brocken (p. 50) that Charles had investigated in 1938. So we advised the Air Force to go out and destroy it. The jamming ceased immediately—and Martini told me that he had been so puzzled by our prompt action that he ordered a Court of Inquiry regarding the possible breach of security. We admired the resource of the young Signals Officer, but we did not know who he was. After the war, Charles Frank went to work in the Physics Laboratory at Bristol, where a new research student was just starting, having come out of the Air Force. He turned out to be the officer involved—Peter Fowler, son of Sir Ralph Fowler and grandson of Rutherford, and later to be Professor of Physics at Bristol.

I spent two or three days with Martini, talking over the war, and he was allowed the privilege of walking unescorted with me and our interpreter in the grounds. He tried to warn me about the threat from Russia, but I had to tell him that the Russians were our allies, and that it would be improper to pursue such a discussion. He himself was particularly worried about the welfare of his sister, who lived in Poznan. Towards the end of our conversations, he enquired whether he might ask my name. I told him, of course, but both the interpreter and I could see that he was not convinced. He was clearly acquainted with English surnames enough to know that Jones was one of the commonest, and he obviously concluded that it was a nom-de-guerre; but he could not very well express his disbelief. I was therefore delighted, after Volume II of Churchill's memoirs came out in 1950, to receive a letter which Martini had sent to Churchill, with the request that it should be forwarded to me. Part of this latter ran:

I have just read the description of the Battle of Britain in the summer and autumn of 1940 in the recently published translation of the Second Volume of Churchill's Memoirs. In this way I also read the appreciation of Dr. R. V. Jones's great services, in the form of suggestions and directions for the fight against German radio navigation techniques, for the British air defence and therefore for Britain. I remember a British civilian gentleman, from my time at a prisoner-of-war in a camp near Beaconsfield from the end of May until the beginning of August 1945, who visited me repeatedly, and with whom I had several discussions about the English–German radio war, which were conducted in a chivalrous manner. This gentleman was introduced to me under the name of 'Jones' by the English interpreter, and was referred to as a scientific adviser of the British headquarters for radio matters. I think it is therefore probable that Dr. R. V. Jones of the Memoirs is the same as my visitor.

I of course replied, and in his second letter he added:

I would not like to omit to mention, while acknowledging the receipt of your letter, that your visits, dear Professor, and the intellectual conversations that we had, were each time a ray of light in what for an old soldier were extremely hard and troubled times. It is unlikely that I shall visit England in the foreseeable future. It would therefore give me all the more pleasure to receive a visit from you when you are next in Germany.

I talked also with General Josef Kammhuber, who had commanded the German nightfighters up to the time when we used Window. He had hardly expected to meet a civilian in my capacity, or to find the readiness with which I could from memory sketch the deployment of his main belt of nightfighter control stations; I told him that we had called it 'The Kammhuber Line'. He smiled gratefully, for nobody in Germany had thought of the title; I hope that it compensated a little for the inconvenience of imprisonment. I told him how much I had admired the accuracy of his claims, and he modestly said that it was much easier for him than for us to get claims accurate, because his Line was so far back from the coast that the chances were that any bomber they shot down would crash somewhere on land, and he would allow no claim unless a piece of the aircraft was recovered. Eleven years later, when I was in Paris visiting the Supreme Headquarters of the Allied Powers in Europe (SHAPE), the most senior officer present came up, shook my hand, and greeted me as an old friend. It was Kammhuber, who was just about to be German Chief of Air Staff.

The German generals had been surprised by the completeness and accuracy of our information, and Martini naturally wanted to know

17*

how it had been achieved. It turned out that whenever they were faced with a new development, such as our using H2S, they set up a new committee to investigate it and to decide on courses of action, just as had happened with us with the rocket scare of 1943. Committees were slower and less responsible than individuals, especially when the latter were allowed to work and build up experience over several years, as had been the case with me. Martini told me that if ever he were fighting a war again he would use our system and, in fact, he hoped that he and I would be fighting together.

My third General was 'Beppo' Schmid, who had succeeded Kammhuber. He was different: I believe that he was one of the original Nazis in the 1923 Putsch. He had a less engaging character than the other two, and his views were very direct. He thought that we should have used Window six months before we did. He also said that our greatest mistake was to use H2S, because it had been so treacherous in giving away the position of our bomber stream, enabling him to inflict heavy casualties after Kammhuber's radar system had been neutralized. Objectively, this opinion would have to be weighed against the damage to German industry that could not have been done without the aid of H2S.

One name I looked for above all others was that of Carl Bosch. Sometimes during the war I had wondered what he was doing: was he my 'opposite number'? If so, he would know all my weak points; and he was such an expert hoaxer that he might easily have misled us. So I was relieved to find that, strictly speaking, there was nobody in the corresponding position to mine in Germany, and that all we could learn about Bosch was that he had worked on infra-red viewing systems. But that was not the whole story, as I found in December 1976 when he and I met in Miami (he works for N.A.S.A.) more than forty years after we had last seen one another. He had indeed also been concerned with Intelligence, and he knew Martini, Kammhuber, Speer, and many of the others mentioned in this book, but he was called in from time to time when emergencies arose, rather than on a full-time basis. When H2S was found in a crashed bomber, for example, he was one of those asked to examine it; and he told me that even in Berlin he could hear the H2S transmissions from our bombers over England. He had also been concerned with the U-boat listening receivers, and he had worked on the radio beam guidance system for the V-2 rocket. He had married but had lost his two children in an air raid. This personal tragedy of a friend with whom I had so much in common symbolizes for me the terrible tragedy that the nations of Europe should have wounded each other so much in the two World Wars and have squandered their great common heritage.

At the same time that I was talking to our German opponents, I was also meeting more of the men who had fought so successfully on our side. I had particularly looked forward to talking to the first post-war course at the R.A.F. Staff College because I knew that some of the ablest and most far-sighted officers had postponed going to Staff College until this particular course because it would be the course in which all the experience of the war would be available for the first time, and at which post-war doctrine would therefore be formed.

I was not sure that I was going to be invited, because of what had happened at the previous course. I had been smarting under the attacks of the various Rocket Committees, and had had a field-day at their expense in my Staff College lecture. I had, for example, remarked that one of the factors that had probably saved us from an earlier attack by V-2s was that the Germans had set up thirteen different committees to organize V-2 production. The Germans themselves may have had a Freudian abhorrence of Committees because the standard word in German for 'committee' is 'Ausschuss' which, perhaps by more than coincidence, also means 'rubbish'. Rather to my concern, the new Commandant, who had succeeded Charles Medhurst, took all my remarks seriously, and he seemed to be so shocked that I was afraid I was not going to be invited back.

However, the invitation duly came, and he asked me if I would address the Staff College on the morning of 17th October. In fact, he wanted me to give two lectures, because the College was now split into two. Part of it had remained at Bullstrode Park near Gerrard's Cross, where officers from Allied Air Forces were now attached, and the main British component was now at Bracknell, having taken over the former headquarters of the 2nd Tactical Air Force. So I lectured at Bullstrode on the afternoon of 16th October, one of the men on the course being 'Sailor' Malan, the famous South African pilot, and I then drove over to Bracknell, arriving there just before midnight. I was shown up into the Commandant's flat at the top of the house, and I found him sitting with his head buried in his hands. When I asked him what was wrong he replied, 'I have just had a mutiny!' I asked him if he would like to tell me about it, and he said that he had just been presented by a Round Robin signed by all the officers on the course, starting with forty group captains, protesting at various aspects of life at Bracknell. He read me the catalogue, which criticized the lack of married quarters, the absence of garage accommodation, the poor quality of the Directing Staff, and the poor quality of the visiting lecturers—of which I was the next one. He told me that the Round Robin had been presented by the two senior group captains on the course (one of whom subsequently became Chief of Air Staff) and I asked him how he had reacted. He told me that he had said to the assembled course, 'Very well, I see, chaps, you want me to raise the standard! So I will rise it all round, and not many of you will get through at the end of the course!' This was fatal. He had been a very gallant officer but, as I had sensed from my previous visit, he was inclined to be too serious. He told me that he did not know how I was going to manage in the morning, and we went to bed.

I wondered what to do: something was clearly wrong, because I was sure that those on the course were as fine a group of men as one could meet anywhere, and the idea of them being engaged in a mutiny was crazy. However, there was trouble, and I might well be at the receiving end. Somehow, I must strike a welcome chord in the first sentence, for if I could survive that, I knew that what I had to talk about would be of absorbing interest to them. Inspiration came to me, and I went to sleep.

That first sentence came back thirty years later, in December 1975, when we were visiting Belize where the Vice Chief of Defence Staff, Air Chief Marshal Sir Peter le Cheminant, had been a week or two ahead of us. He had met my daughter, Susan, and had told her how well he remembered the occasion, for he had been one of the group captains concerned. He said that I had walked straight on to the platform and had said, 'I sometimes think that strategy is nothing but tactics talked through a brass hat!' From that moment, the whole course was with me.

I learnt much from the experience, for the unlucky Commandant was almost immediately superseded by another, Air Marshal Sir Arthur Sanders, who had been Air Officer Administration in Bomber Command. On the next visit, I knew from the way the sentry had saluted at the gate that there had been a change of command; and the improvement in morale was a revelation of what a difference the personality of a Commander can make, even in a large organization.

It was not an entirely unproductive period for me, wrecked though my post-war hopes had been. I was so impressed by the value of Staff Courses that I proposed to Portal on 8th November 1945 that there should be a Staff College for scientists. Its introduction ran:

The life of a young scientist consists in the main of passing one examination in order to qualify as a candidate for the next. Then, when his final examination is over, he becomes a research student, frequently dependent for further financial aid on the results of his first researches. The number of permanent academic positions open to him is relatively small, and his merit is judged in competition with his contemporaries. Such a competitive system, while it has some merits, inevitably puts a premium on the short term worker, who concentrates all his energy on the immediate object, be it the next examination or the achievement of quick results in the first few researches. The young scientist who would commendably devote some of his time to external activities, to humane studies, or even to other branches of science, is likely not to reach such an immediately high standard in his own branch. He is thus at some disadvantage in the bitter competition for the early attainment of a permanent position in the academic world. The 'successful' scientist therefore tends to be he who shuts himself off from the external world, and even from other branches of science. The same is true, though perhaps to a lesser extent, in the fields of industry or Government service, where in peacetime scientists are largely recruited from those who have fallen out from the academic competition.

The premium thus placed in a modern scientific career upon undue concentration at an early stage encourages the production of men with a less-than-average appreciation (for their standard of intelligence) of the world at large. This ignorance may even become a habit in after life, when the energy of the hothouse-forced scientist declines, or when, finding himself outmanoeuvred in his first few clashes with professional and classically bred administrators, he retires embittered into his laboratory and decides that his ignorance is really a virtue, since the worldly-wise are such rogues.

Portal showed my memorandum to Tizard, and they were both enthusiastic. It finally failed, because nobody could see how to finance it. Lord Hankey revived the proposal a few years later, but with equal lack of success. There was one positive result, though, for Portal wrote to me on 21st December, 'I am therefore asking the Air Staff to examine the practical implications of sending a few scientists on Staff College and I.D.C. Courses'. This resulted in scientists in Government Service being allowed to attend the courses, which has continued to the present day: I am only sorry that such courses are not available for academics generally for, of all people, they need them.

A few days later I received a call to Portal's office, along with all the senior members of the Air Staff. It was 31st December, and he was about to leave. Never one to wear his heart on his sleeve, he made a halting speech, and then came to shake us individually by the hand. To me he said, 'Goodbye, A.D.I. (Science). You know what I think of you!'

For five years of utterly demanding war Portal as Chief of Air Staff had led the Royal Air Force with tremendous authority; it had been a privilege to work with him, and his support was one of the main sources of my own strength.

CHAPTER FIFTY-TWO

Swords Into Ploughshares, Bombs Into Saucers

ONE REFUGE from the politics of jostling for positions in post-war Whitehall was to think afresh about problems in pure science. The war had, for example, forced upon physicists and astronomers alike the fact that the sun emitted radio waves so strongly that it jammed our anti-aircraft radar on many occasions. The fact that cosmic radio waves were falling upon the earth had been established and reported by Karl Jansky, a radio engineer at the Bell Telephone Laboratories in America, as early as 1931, but his work was almost entirely overlooked until the radar jamming experiences of World War II. Several groups in Britain started to investigate the phenomenon when the war ended, and our part was to provide German radar equipment for these groups, including Martin Ryle in Cambridge and Bernard Lovell in Manchester.

Another wartime experience that made me wonder was the ability of pigeons which had spent their entire lives in England to home back to their bases after we had dropped them on the Continent. I spent some time with the Air Ministry Pigeon Service in the months after the war, learning from the experts what pigeons could do. There was evidence that the last twenty or thirty miles of their journeys were made by visual means, and that they used landmarks such as coastlines: the Norwich fanciers, for example, complained that in pre-war races from France their birds were always about twenty minutes later than those of the Lowestoft fanciers, the theory being that all the pigeons flew up the coast of Suffolk and Norfolk, when the Lowestoft birds could simply drop into their lofts, while the Norwich birds had another twenty minutes flying overland once they left the coast. Geographical landmarks, though, could not explain a good deal of the wartime flying, and I began to wonder whether the birds had developed a form of inertial navigation, based on the semicircular canals in their heads, which were known to be accelerometers. We tried to keep the Air Ministry Pigeon Service in being after the war, with a view to organizing a prolonged series of experiments, but the scheme fell through when both the pigeons and I left the Air Ministry.

Another line of thought had more permanent results. The fascination about discovering the methods by which pigeons navigate is much the same as that which I had experienced in working out how it was that German bombers could find their targets. Other animals besides pigeons have methods of locating targets, and these have an equal appeal. Among them are the moths: males home on to females from distances of miles, and the evidence here indicated that they must be super-sensitive to traces of scents emitted by the females. We found that a German chemist (probably Butenandt) had isolated the particular compound emitted by the female silkworm moth, and that a single drop of a solution of this compound at a strength of one part in a thousand million was enough to agitate all the male moths in the same room. Francis Griffin (the Secretary of the Royal Entomological Society, who had been attached to my staff in 1944 when the British Museum wanted us to secure an option on a collection of lepidoptera in Rennes as soon as it was captured) produced evidence for me that male moths home up-wind, and that they could do the coarse homing with one antenna removed, but that they needed both antennae for the final few yards. I was aware of these facts when I began once again to think about the problems of detecting U-boats, now that the Germans had developed the 'schnorkel' which enabled a boat to continue submerged and to 'breathe' by letting up a tubular trunk to the surface which only needed a fairly small capping valve at the top, and which would therefore give a relatively small radar echo, thus much increasing our difficulty of detection. All the exhaust products of the boat's diesel engines would be emitted into the atmosphere, and so why should we not try to 'smell' these products as they drifted down-wind? Moreover, the idea could be extended, in that it was very likely that plutonium factories would be emitting some radioactive products into the air, and so we could perhaps 'smell' these too. On 23rd November 1945 I therefore proposed to Ben Lockspeiser (Director General of Scientific Research in the Ministry of Aircraft Production) that these systems should be developed. Part of my proposal ran:

You are probably aware that various insects are able to home from distances of the order of a mile or more. . . . The foregoing facts indicate serious possibilities in homing by smell, and I am suggesting that now we are able to consider long term research again, it might be worth devoting some effort to applying smell techniques to airborne homing. By developing homers on to the exhaust products of internal combustion engines, such as carbon monoxide and dioxide (or preferably more peculiar products) or ions, we might be able to home along aircraft exhaust trails, or on to towns, or on to 'Schnorkels'. Radioactive smellers (probably using counters) would be a valuable aid in locating plutonium producing piles from the air; I put this possibility to the T.A. people two or three years ago, and they were not very optimistic, but it ought now to be reconsidered. Acid smellers might detect chemical factories, including plutonium separation plants.

The scheme was taken up and a smell homing device for schnorkels, known as 'Autolycus' was developed and put into service with Coastal Command. Its main drawback was that it would detect any oil-burning engine, whether this was in a U-boat or on a merchant ship, and so it never became more than an ancillary aid; and it was, of course, no use against nuclear submarines.

A further line of thought, which conceivably may have been seminal, came from our experience in transmitting a large amount of information as concisely as possible, for example in the 'microdots' used in letters from spies. (Incidentally, the first use of microphotography in war was in Paris in 1870, when microphotographed messages were sent by carrier pigeon.) How could the information necessary to create a complete human being be contained in a volume no larger than a sperm-head? I made a very rough estimate of the number of items of information that would be required, and came to the conclusion that it could only be possible if the data were somehow encoded on an atomic scale where the identities and positions of atoms were significant. I learned to observe bacteria and stain them with the standard agents. My interest had been stimulated, as so often, by Charles Frank, who thought that there must be some long-range forces (on the atomic scale, that is) involved in the separation of chromosomes; he told me that Max Delbrück had come to the same conclusion as I had about genetic information being on the atomic scale. Neither Charles nor I did any-thing further, because we became committed to more pressing ob-jectives, but perhaps the only good result of the reorganization of Scientific Intelligence was that we were joined by a young physicist who had been assistant to Teddy Gollin in the Admiralty, who still remembers the days when we relieved the dullness of our post-war situation by discussing these problems. He was Francis Crick, who went on to win the Nobel Prize for his part in solving the basic problem of the Genetic Code.

We had one diversion of an Intelligence nature, which no doubt arose from the general atmosphere of apprehension that existed in 1945 regarding the motives of the Russians, and which anticipated the flying saucer. We had already seen scares arise during the war by the imaginations of men under strain interpreting fearfully observations which had a natural explanation. KGr100 pilots had seen red lights over England. We had had to deal with reports of Fifth Columnists letting off rockets; and our bomber crews had reported single-engine nightfighters with yellow lights in their noses over Germany at times when we knew that no single-engine nightfighters were flying. So we were not unduly surprised when incidents began to be reported in Sweden, which regarded itself as in the front-line should the Russians attempt to move westwards. Stories began to be reported of strange objects seen in the sky, so much so that the Swedish General Staff put out a public request that all such objects should be reported. The result was, of course, a spate of 'incidents'. Some of these were probably imaginary, but one or two were genuine enough, in that they were seen by many people in Sweden. They were probably meteors, and by bad luck two of them were bright enough to have been visible by day.

The general interpretation, however, was that these were long-range flying bombs being flown by the Russians over Sweden as an act of intimidation. This interpretation was accepted by officers in our own Air Technical Intelligence, who worked out the performance of the bombs from the reported sightings in one of the incidents, where the object appeared to have dashed about at random over the whole of southern Sweden at speeds up to 2000 m.p.h. What the officers concerned failed to notice was that every observer, wherever he was, reported the object as well to the east. By far the most likely explanation was that it was a meteor, perhaps as far east as Finland, and the fantastic speeds that were reported were merely due to the fact that all observers had seen it more or less simultaneously, but that they had varying errors in their watches, so that any attempt to draw a track by linking up observations in a time sequence was unsound.

By this time I had been promoted to being Director of Intelligence, and the Technical Intelligence officers were now, at least nominally, part of my staff. They believed in the reality of the Russian flying bombs, as did Field Marshal Smuts, who became sufficiently convinced to warn the British public in a broadcast talk. For myself, I simply asked two questions. First, what conceivable purpose could it serve the Russians, if they indeed had a controllable flying bomb, to fly it in great numbers over Sweden, without doing any more harm than to alert the West to the fact that they had such an impressive weapon? My second question followed from the first: how had the Russians succeeded in making a flying bomb of such fantastic reliability? The Germans had achieved no better than 90 per cent reliability in their flying bomb trials of 1944, at very much shorter range. Even if the Russians had achieved a reliability as high as 99 per cent over their much longer ranges, this still meant that 1 per cent of all sorties should have resulted in a bomb crashing on Swedish territory. Since there had been allegedly hundreds of sorties, there ought to be at least several crashed bombs already in Sweden, and yet nobody had ever picked up a fragment. I therefore said that I would not accept the theory that the apparitions were flying bombs from Russia until someone brought a piece into my office.

My challenge had a diverting result. The other Director of Intelligence, Air Commodore Vintras, telephoned me to say that the Swedes now had several pieces of a bomb. When I asked whether it had actually crashed, the answer was that it had not, but that various pieces had fallen off it, and these were being given to one of his officers to bring across to show me. They duly arrived in my office, and turned out to be an odd assortment of four or five irregularly shaped solid lumps, none of which looked as if it had ever been associated with a mechanical device. To satisfy the curiosity of the believers, I sent the pieces to the Chemical Analysis Section at Farnborough for their verdict. Among the specimens was a lump two to three inches across that was hard, shiny, grey, and porous. Charles Frank and I immediately realized what it was but we sent it with the rest to Farnborough for analysis.

Instead of the Farnborough report coming straight back to me, it happened to go to Vintras who telephoned me excitedly as soon as he had read it and said, 'There, what did I tell you! Farnborough has analysed the stuff that you sent, and one of the lumps consists of more than 98 per cent of an unknown element!' I was amazed. But he turned out to be right, in that the Farnborough report gave the analysis of this particular lump as consisting of fractional percentages of several elements like iron, nickel and copper, but all these traces added up to less than 2 per cent. The chemists had been unable to identify the remaining 98 per cent. Excitement on the Air Staff was mounting—not only had the Russians a flying bomb of fantastic performance, but they were driving it with a fuel made from an element that was new to the world of chemistry.

I telephoned the head of chemistry at Farnborough, and asked him whether he really believed his own analysis, or whether he was playing a joke on the Air Staff, on the principle that silly questions deserve silly answers. He replied that his report had been perfectly serious, and that his Section was indeed baffled by the other 98 per cent. I then asked him whether he had taken a good look at the lump, and whether it had not struck him as being remarkably like an ordinary piece of coke. There was a gasp from the other end of the telephone as the penny dropped. No one had stopped to look at the material, in an effort to get the analysis made quickly, and they had failed to test for carbon. The other lumps had similarly innocent explanations.

Our flying bomb enthusiasts were somewhat dampened by this experience, but it was not long before they were excited again. The new excitement was brought to my notice by a signal to the Air Staff from the Senior British Air Officer on General MacArthur's Staff in Tokyo. The signal asked for the latest Intelligence concerning Russian flying bombs, and for confirmation of a story that a Russian flying bomb had fallen in England within the last few days. Vintras telephoned me to ask how we should frame the reply to Tokyo. I told him that we should simply say that there was nothing in the story that a bomb had fallen in England, and that we much doubted whether there was anything to the story of Russian flying bombs over Sweden. He replied that this was all very well, but did I not think that it might tie up with the 'Westerham Incident'. I asked him what the devil he was talking about. He then replied, 'Oh, I forgot that I was told not to tell you about that!' and added that since he had let the cat out of the bag he had better tell me the whole story.

It appeared that on the previous Saturday the Technical Intelligence Staff had been telephoned by an irate caller who said that his name was Gunyon and that he wanted the Air Ministry to come immediately to remove one of these 'darned contraptions' which had fallen from the sky on to his farm. The Intelligence Officers had asked where they should go, and he gave them instructions to drive out from Croydon towards Westerham, and that when they reached a public house called the 'White Dog' they should turn up the lane, and they would find his farm at the end. Knowing my disbelief, the Technical Intelligence Officers had jumped at the opportunity of surprising me. So, in great haste and equally great security, they drove in two staff cars to the area indicated by farmer Gunyon. Their doubts began to arise when they could find no public-house called the 'White Dog'. However, being good Intelligence Officers, they realized that they might have misunderstood Gunyon's message, and so they made enquiries about other public-houses to see whether there was one which had a name which they might have mis-heard over the telephone. Indeed there was one—the 'White Hart', and to this they duly went. They asked the publican whether he knew of anyone named Gunyon in the neighbourhood, but he did not. Then, repeating their technique, they asked him whether he knew of anyone who might have sounded like Gunyon. He did: there was a farmer named Bunyan two or three miles away over the hill, and so they set off again. They descended on an astonished Mr. Bunyan who finally convinced them that he had never telephoned the Air Ministry.

As they drove sadly back to London, having wasted their Saturday afternoon leisure, they began to theorize about the incident. They concluded that farmer Gunyon was none other than their own Director, myself. They knew that I had played various practical jokes before the war, and had sometimes hoaxed the Germans, and they concluded that I had determined to make fools of them because they believed in flying bombs, while I did not. It is always flattering when you are credited with an excellent joke that you have not yourself played; but this particular joke would have broken one of my own rules, which was that one ought never to take advantage of one's juniors in this way—or at least, only under the most extreme provocation.

CHAPTER FIFTY-THREE

Exeunt

FOLLOWING THE acceptance of Blackett's recommendations for the future of Scientific Intelligence, I was uncertain about what I should now do. I warned Inglis, who was still Assistant Chief of Air Staff (Intelligence), that it would probably result in my leaving, but he asked me to stay for a year to see the organization through its transition. He offered me a full Directorship, with responsibility for both Scientific and Technical Intelligence—although this offer at once reintroduced an asymmetry between the three Services, since the other two would not have corresponding Directorates.

Then, on 12th November 1945, Edward Wright wrote to me from Aberdeen, to which he had returned as Professor of Mathematics in the preceding April. An incidental sentence in his letter ran:

> I gather from Norman that things are being very troublesome for you. If they are too bad, why not apply for our vacant Chair of Natural Philosophy?

The suggestion astonished me. I had had my own idea of professorial standards before the war, and had never thought of myself as measuring up to them. True, my ideas had sometimes been jolted during the war by the incompetence of various professorial experts, but I had thought that my academic boats had been thoroughly burnt when I forsook pure research for infra-red detection of aircraft in 1935, for little of my work in the subsequent years could be published. In a way, though, the very trouble that I had had from professors was a challenge to meet them on their home ground. I therefore wrote to Wright to ask him whether his question had been a serious one. When he replied positively, I thought about the prospect and decided to apply. Two testimonials were necessary, and three referees. Portal and Cherwell wrote warm testimonials, and I asked Tizard, Appleton, and Medhurst to act as referees. On hearing of my application, Archie Sinclair characteristically offered to be a referee.

Edward Wright remarked that there was one referee who might well be decisive. This was Sir George Thomson who, as G. P. Thomson, had held the same Chair from 1922 to 1930 and who won the Nobel Prize for his work at Aberdeen in demonstrating the wavelike properties of the electron. The fact that such work could be done at Aberdeen, coupled with the fact that I already had a friend there in Wright, were two of the attractions about this particular Chair. However, I viewed the suggestion of Thomson with some misgiving, because he and I had been in conflict from the time to time when he was Scientific Adviser to the Air Ministry, and our terms of reference therefore tended to overlap whenever it came to a consideration of what the Germans were doing in the application of science to air warfare. I therefore wrote him a very tentative letter, saying that I should be grateful if he would agree to act as referee, but in view of the differences we had during the war he might well prefer either not to support me or to support another candidate. To my surprise, I received an enthusiastic telephone call, saying that he had at once written to 'Butchart'—a name which meant nothing to me, but in fact belonged to Colonel H. J. Butchart, the Secretary to the University, and one of G.P.'s best friends. I was deeply grateful for G.P.'s support—he evidently recognized, as I did, that in our wartime differences there had been substance to each of our points of view and that we were both trying to do our jobs according to our terms of reference.

Overlapping terms of reference are to some extent inevitable, especially in a changing organization; but they are to be avoided wherever possible. It is not merely that they can lead to personal friction, especially if one of the parties is ambitious: nor is it only that unnecessary duplication can occur and effort be wasted. The worst danger is that in a time of crisis each party may think that he can leave the problem to the other, with the result that neither tackles it—just as in doubles tennis a ball between the partners may be missed because each leaves it to the other.

I was asked to Aberdeen for an interview on 30th April 1946. I arrived the previous day, which I spent alone. I wondered if I would ever like Aberdeen. The houses were grey, the streets were grey, the sky was grey and, when I walked to the beach, the sea was grey, too. Halfway along the beach between the Rivers Dee and Don there was a notice which stated that bathing to the south of that point was permitted only from Corporation bathing huts, which could be hired for a suitable fee. Ominously the notice concluded, 'Bathing to the north of this point is dangerous'.

As a professorial candidate I had some worthy opposition, including two applicants who were already professors in other universities; but after the interviews, I was offered the Chair. The Principal, Sir William Hamilton Fyfe, then said to me—I thought a little ruefully—'A friend of yours was here last week'. When I asked who it was he replied, 'Winston Churchill!' On returning south, I visited Oxford for the week-end, and told T. C. Keeley that I had accepted the Chair, and that Churchill had been there a few days before. Keeley told me that Cherwell had asked him to put in a word for me, and had enquired on his return (Churchill had himself been receiving an Honorary Degree at Aberdeen) whether he had remembered to mention me. Churchill's reply was, 'I spoke of nothing else!'

When I visited Aberdeen with Vera some weeks later, the Fyfes invited us to lunch, and the story of Winston's visit came up. When I told Hamilton Fyfe what Winston had said he replied that it was absolutely true; and many years later, in 1971, Lady Hamilton Fyfe wrote to me giving her personal account:

> I have lately been re-reading the very long letter I wrote to our family overseas the day after Mr. Churchill was in Aberdeen to receive his Laureation from Tom Taylor, the Promoter in Law, and my husband, the Vice-Chancellor (27th April 1946).
>
> As we walked home, W.H.F. said to me that every time he encountered Mr. Churchill during the day, Churchill began *again* that the University MUST appoint R. V. Jones to the advertised Chair of Physics—the man who 'Broke the Bloody Beam'. And I see in my letter that at the final hurried tea party in the Lord Provost's parlour 'Mr. Churchill *again* pressed his candidate, and you will all be glad to hear the University Court today appointed him'.

Churchill always remembered his visit to Aberdeen. He afterwards told me that Tom Taylor's speech was the finest in his honour that he had ever heard, 'You know, he said the things about me that ought only to have been said after I am dead!'

Another sidelight I heard many years later came from Chief Superintendent Halcrow of the Aberdeen City Police who, as a sergeant, was in charge of security at the railway station as the train awaited Winston after a celebratory dinner. Nobody was supposed to be on the platform but Halcrow noticed a figure lurking in the shadows, whom he recognized as Patsy Gallagher, a newsvendor who was something of an

Aberdonian Figaro. Patsy delighted in giving an imitation of Winston, who was his hero, and shortly before closing time in one or other of the Aberdeen bars Patsy's grinning head would appear around the door, giving Winston's 'V' for Victory sign. Halcrow decided that Patsy meant no ill, and left him in the shadows on the platform until Winston himself came padding down the platform alone. Just as he was getting into the coach he spotted the figure standing some ten yeards away in silent worship, and advanced from the coach towards him. At the same time, Patsy moved forward and the two men met halfway, shook hands silently, and Winston returned to the coach.

On returning from the interview at Aberdeen, my immediate step, of course, was to inform the Air Staff of my resignation. I wrote a formal minute to the Chief of the Air Staff, Lord Tedder, who had succeeded Portal:

> . . . The implementation of the J.I.C. proposals is now taking place, and is one of the main reasons for my resignation. . . . A single Head in Intelligence is far better than a Committee, however excellent the individual members of the Committee may be. A Committee wastes too much time in arguing, and every action it undertakes merely goes as far as common agreement and compromise will allow. Common agreement and compromise, as every Commander knows, generally do not go far enough. The Head of an Intelligence organization is really in the position of a commander planning a perpetual attack on the security of foreign powers, and he must be allowed all the privileges of a commander. . . . The J.S.I.C. regime is the main reason for my resignation; but there are others. The first is to some extent another consequence of the J.I.C. control of Intelligence, and concerns the arrangement made for Atomic Energy Intelligence. Here the J.I.C. acquiesced in an irregular arrangement made with the Americans by Sir John Anderson, whereby another authority, 'The Anglo-American Combined T.A. Intelligence Organization' has been set up in parallel with the J.S.I.C. Moreover, to this organization in the shape of its British Head has been accorded the privilege of simultaneous membership of the S.I.S., the very privilege that is being removed from my own section. . . . In resigning, I criticise the arrangements made in this country for Intelligence. . . . The reason probably lies in the facts that Intelligence is rather despised in the Services, that the individual members of the J. I. C. change rapidly and are therefore on the average inexperienced in the basic principles of

Intelligence, and that they feel bound to put the interests of their particular Services, on which their promotion depends, before the interests of Intelligence as a Cause. . . . I regret leaving Intelligence more than anything else I have ever done, because I believe it to be most important for this country that it should have a strong Intelligence service, and I was prepared to spend my life in building it up, had I been allowed to do so in my own way. I have already enunciated many of the principles and I am reasonably confident that whatever arrangements the J.I.C. or any other body may make, the crises of a future war will show that something on the lines of my own ideas will have to be set up again; I hope that the demonstration will not come too late.

Regarding my own future, my course is fairly clear. We are very short of scientists, and I may yet be of service in training new ones, incorporating the many lessons which I have learnt in my seven years as an Intelligence Officer. Moreover, my election to the Chair of Natural Philosophy at Aberdeen provides me with an opportunity for removing one disadvantage, admittedly irrelevant, that I constantly encountered in my Intelligence duties. It was clear that one had to be a 'Professor' to command the respect of the J.I.C. I fear that had I gone on in Intelligence, the next crisis would have seen the calling in of yet another Professor, no matter how good my qualifications to tackle the task might have been. . . . Lest it be thought that I resign entirely embittered by the events of the last year, I would say that even knowing this sorry conclusion to the present phase of my association with Scientific Intelligence, I should have undertaken it in 1939 almost as readily as I in fact did. The results obtained during the war would have alone justified that. In addition, we have been able to extract many of the vital principles of Intelligence; and though the J.I.C. and others may choose to ignore them now, I have no doubt that these principles will outlive the J.I.C. My work has brought me into close contact with the Royal Air Force on the one hand, and with the Intelligence sources on the other; and I only resign my connection with them with very great regret. I hope that whatever form the Air Force of the future may take, its Intelligence service will prove worthy of it.

My final word must refer to my staff. Continuously overworked, they nevertheless gave me their fullest support throughout; most of them have now left, and I shall do my best to see the others settled before I leave. I am confident that, should another war threaten, most of us would be prepared to come back again; but we should hope that our experience would not then be ignored.

Of my wartime staff, Edward Wright was now, of course, back at Aberdeen, where he later became Principal and was knighted. Hugh Smith had returned to University College London, where he became Quain Professor of English, and headed a very happy and effective department. He became President of the Place-Name Society, and personally compiled several of its county volumes. His work for Scandinavian Studies was recognized by the Swedish Order of the Royal North Star, the Icelandic Order of the Falcon, and the Danish Order of Dannebrog. Bimbo Norman returned to King's College London as Professor of German, and was awarded the Gold Medal of the Goethe Institut, Munich. Rupert Cecil returned to Oxford, where he became Vice-Principal of Linacre College. John Jennings became a Senior Lecturer at Birkbeck College, and J. A. Birtwistle became Education Officer for Hampshire. Of the members of my overseas party, Eric Ackermann remained in Government Service for many years, one of his achievements being the organization of the 'Skynet' Satellite Communications Network. David Nutting became President of the Institute of Measurement and Control. Ken Dobson, after a spell as a financier, returned to technical work and pioneered the first 'Black Box' flight data recorder; it proved its value when it successfully analysed the cause of the crash of the prototype BAC III Aircraft. Andrew Fell became Principal of the National College of Horology, and Maurice Stephenson Chief Engineer of the Shell oilfields in Venezuela.

I had much hoped that Charles Frank would accompany me to Aberdeen, because we had found ourselves so complementary to one another. Unfortunately for me, this did not prove possible, and so I suggested to Neville Mott that he should invite Charles to Bristol. Charles rapidly established himself there, and latterly succeeded to the Headship of the H. H. Wills Laboratory; he became a Fellow of the Royal Society in 1954 and a Knight in 1977. Derek Garrard stayed in Government Service, and Arthen Jones accompanied me to Aberdeen.

My last few months were much occupied in setting the affairs of Scientific Intelligence in order, as far as this was possible, and arranging for our files to be transferred to the miserable premises in Bryanston Square, at the same time preparing myself for the work at Aberdeen. Although it was a period of running down, it had some enlivening episodes. One morning just before a weekend, the Security Officer rushed round the M.I.6 offices telling everyone to take down all maps off their walls. It turned out that the M.I.6 offices were only rented and the landlord had heard that we were thinking of moving. Anxious to re-let the premises in such an event he had somehow made contact with the Russian Trade Delegation, and he wished to take them round on the Saturday afternoon. Could it happen anywhere but Britain that representatives of its major prospective opponent should be allowed a tour of the offices of its Secret Service? The Russians must have wondered whether Philby had been telling them the truth.

Another incident from the same period was also illuminating. Stewart Menzies, the Chief, was one evening about to depart for a cocktail party in Mayfair or Belgravia when a very secret message came in after his safes had been locked. He stuffed the message into his pocket and thought no more about it until he found that at the party his hostess had hired an entertainer whose forte was removing such items as watches and braces without his victim being aware of it—and whom should he select for the victim but Stewart Menzies who, as he told us, stood apprehensively there while the entertainer removed various of his possessions but somehow missed the message. But if all this seeming ineptitude made us easy to exploit by men like Philby, there was another side: Niels Bohr told me after the war that he had no hesitation in working with the British Secret Service because he had found that it was run by a gentleman.

I officially left the Air Staff on 30th September 1946, having completed exactly ten years as a civil servant. Two or three days later I was in Aberdeen, preparing for the beginning of term, where I found that I would have to deal with between 300 and 400 students with a staff of nine (including myself), three of whom were new graduates aged under 21. It was clear, though, from my first lecture that despite the drawbacks of limited and inexperienced staff, and the almost complete absence of textbooks, my relations with the students would be warm. They and the two or three succeeding years were vintage, as far as I am concerned. There was a tremendous esprit de corps, and a great deal of experience. After a lecture on hydrostatics, in which I had talked about the physics of diving, and the new method of escaping from submarines, a slightly-built student came up to me afterwards and said, 'Excuse me, sir, but I found this lecture most interesting—I have done a bit of diving!' It turned out that he had a D.S.O. for the midget submarine raid on the Tirpitz.

In retrospect, although the students were older than average, and 'rusty' because of the gap in their education, there was one tremendous advantage: almost every man had been out and seen matters of life and death for himself, and had decided of his own free will that he wanted to come back to a university and get a degree. There had been no pressure by parents or teachers, or conformity to a fashion. Some of the men actually said to me that they realized how lucky they were—but for the war, they would never have had the chance of getting to a university. Although this was really the beginning of another story, it is too relevant to omit completely. If the war underlined our need for more scientists, and therefore inclined me towards bringing on the next generation, it also strengthened my interest in research into methods of precise measurement. I might well have gone into radioastronomy but Bernard Lovell and Martin Ryle already had a start, and so I concentraed instead on small-scale research in the hope of improving instruments of measurement, with the twofold objectives of using them to discover new physical phenomena and to increase our national ability in measurement—which episodes such as Coventry and the fictitious D-Day jammers had found so sadly wanting.

Because there was no house available in Aberdeen I had to leave Vera and the children in Richmond, so I returned there for Christmas. On Christmas morning the telephone bell rang and Vera handed the telephone to me. A voice said, 'This is Winston Churchill speaking from Westerham. Mr. Jones, how long are you going to be in the southern regions of our Island?' When I told him about ten days he asked me if I would be good enough to come across and have lunch with him, to which I of course very readily agreed. He went on, 'Do you know that there is a poem about you in the *Ingoldsby Legends*?', and he then recited to me the verses that he subsequently quoted in Volume II of his Memoirs.[1]

Two days later I went across to Westerham, only to find him in a four-poster bed, with a cold. He wanted to talk over the war, and especially those parts in which I had been concerned. Two or three days later, I spent another day with him, and these two days were among the most interesting of my life. For most of the time we were alone, and I was able to ask him about things which had puzzled me in his actions. At one point I asked him what he really thought of Macaulay. I told

[1] 'But now one Mr. Jones comes forth and deposes how fifteen years since, he had heard certain groans on his way to Stonehenge (to examine stones described in a work of the late Sir John Soane's) that he followed the moans, and led by their tones, found a raven a-picking a drummer-boy's bones.'

him that I knew that he had called Macaulay a liar because he had said that John Churchill had gained his original preferment by selling his sister Arabella to James II, but what did he really think of Macaulay as a writer because I myself thought that his own style resembled Macaulay's? He at once said, 'You've hit the nail on the head! If I had to make my literary Will, and my literary Acknowledgements, I would have to own that I owe more to Macaulay than to any other English writer. When I was a boy at Harrow there was a prize that you could win if you could recite 800 lines of any poet or 1,200 of Macaulay. I took the 1,200, and won!'

I told him that I did not like the way the country was going, with strikes and the clamour for a 40-hour week, and he replied, 'I could have given them a 40-hour week—if they would work for 40 hours!' And he wept as he told me that he never thought that he would see the British Empire sink so low. I found no anxiety on his part to argue that he had been right in everything he did—in fact at various points he quite tentatively asked me whether I thought that he had been right, for example in advocating the development of aerial mines.

I had a final impression of him as I left, and he had accompanied me in his dressing-gown to the top of the stairs. He had asked me how my family were, and I had told him that I was rather concerned because I could see that in my absence during the term the two children were getting rather much for Vera, as children tend to do when they have only a mother to deal with. I remarked that I had myself as a child seen this happen in World War I, for my own mother had pointed it out to me at the time, as regards some of my cousins. I still have the vision of him at the top of the stairs calling out, 'Remember, discipline those children!' If the country had taken more heed of this advice, its subsequent problems would have been less. And I sometimes recall his advice to me as a scientist, 'Praise the humanities, my boy. That'll make them think you're broadminded!'

Epilogue

A LECTURE TO the Royal United Services Institution on 19th February 1947 gave me the chance to survey what had happened in World War II, and to summarize my philosophy for the benefit of anyone in charge of Scientific Intelligence in a future war:

It is, first of all, to remember that the truest criterion of a good Intelligence organization is its ability to plan, to carry out and to exploit Intelligence attacks. You must frame the organization to do these things with the utmost efficiency; do not be hidebound by any pre-conceived fetishes of organization in securing the objective. You must remember that Intelligence depends more than anything else on individual minds and on individual courage, and your organization should only provide a smooth background on which these can operate. You must employ as few links as possible between the source and the operational staff who make use of the information. You must never forget to stand by your sources: they will repay you. Do as much of the actual Intelligence work yourself as you can; you will find that you can then speak with increased confidence at the highest conferences, which you will certainly be required to do. The fact that you have done much of the work yourself will give you a great advantage. Remember, as the cardinal principle of Intelligence, Occam's Razor, 'hypotheses must not be multiplied unnecessarily.' Lastly, to anyone on whom my mantle may fall, I would say: remember Kipling's

> 'If you can keep your head when all about you
> Are losing theirs and blaming it on you. . . .'

In a time of crisis you will find that a tendency to lose one's head is apt to appear at any level in administration. You will find yourself confronted with many frightening bogies conjured up by the agile imaginations of men often at higher levels than yourself. You will be unable to lay all these bogies at once, because to prove a negative case is one of the most difficult of Intelligence exercises. But you must find the simplest, commonsense hypothesis and stick to it until a fresh fact proves you wrong, however eminent an authority is attached to another view. You will find yourself blamed on the one hand for not telling everybody every conclusion you come to, even before you have thought of it, and on the other for indiscretion by the Security authorities. You will be accused of hoarding information, even though this is often a legitimate thing to do. And you will learn that in the Intelligence work there is an enormous premium placed upon going off at half-cock. The World seems to prefer a busy show of promptness to quiet, mature action, however timely. But you must never succumb. In a crisis, you will find that these distractions may easily take up to 80 per cent of your time. Your nights, or what is left of them after the work which you would have done during the day but for the distractions, will often be spent sleeplessly wondering whether this time you have not been too phlegmatic in decrying other people's flights of fancy or too rash in extrapolating from too few facts in forming your own hypothesis. But if in all this you can use the remaining 20 per cent of your time in encouraging your sources, directing your staff, correlating the Intelligence pictures for yourself and presenting it in logical and clear reports, you will generally find yourself vindicated by events. And if you can persuade someone to take countermeasures in time, you may have the satisfaction of seeing danger averted for thousands of your unsuspecting countrymen.

The future of Intelligence is hard. In the past war, the nature of the weapons, the brilliance of our sources and the mistakes of our enemies all weighed the balance in our favour. It may well not remain so in the future. But though the fortunes may vary, and its methods change, the principles will remain the same. And if in that war our work helped to clarify those principles, this may well be its most lasting contribution.

If any one man would have carried my hopes that ability in Intelligence would ultimately win the day over the organizational disasters brought upon us by Blackett, he would have been Francis Crick, who was one of the Admiralty contributions to the post-war Scientific Intelligence effort. He wrote to me on 18th February 1947, the day before I gave the R.U.S.I. Lecture, saying, 'I am opening the campaign for a central organization, and have been to see Lee and Admiral Langley'. By this organization he meant a proper Scientific Intelligence staff, in contrast to the three disjointed sections that had been thrown together by the Service Ministries. He went on, 'It would really help if they got another angle on all this, especially one founded on some experience. I wondered if you could find time to have a chat with Lee (he lives at the Cabinet Offices) while you were in town. Better still, to see Tizard himself. One point needs bringing out strongly. It's no use reorganizing with just the same old gang. We *must* have someone rather more lively to head the thing'.

I duly talked to Tizard, who had taken the chair at my R.U.S.I. Lecture, and an enquiry followed which resulted in Professor David Brunt being appointed in 1948 as permanent Chairman of the Joint Scientific and Technical Intelligence Committee, in place of the chairmanship which had rotated at three-monthly intervals between the several heads of the Scientific and Technical Intelligence sections belonging to the Services. There was little noticeable improvement, though, for Brunt had no staff of his own, and Crick left Intelligence to go to Cambridge where in 1962 he won the Nobel Prize for the elucidation of the Genetic Code.

Brunt found his experience so exasperating that within a year he resigned to become Physical Secretary of the Royal Society in 1949, placing this comment on the Ministry of Defence files: 'I am sure that if there is any one man in this country who will take on the job, knowing the true conditions, he must be unique, and either a saint or a fool'.

Tizard, who himself had been called back as Chief Scientific Adviser to the Ministry of Defence, sent for me and told me that he had been asked by the Joint Intelligence Committee to invite me to take the job on again. He warned that things were still in a very unsatisfactory state, and I ultimately wrote to him declining the invitation, saying

> The reasons which weigh most with me against returning are all connected with my work here. The Chair which I now hold suffered much through the War, and the Department needs a great deal of work to put it into a healthy condition; a change of Professor now would delay its progress very seriously. . . . In a few years' time none of these arguments might be valid: the Department may be flourishing, and we may well have available younger physicists in the country who could do the job better than I can. In the meantime I see a major national need to produce such physicists, and I am prepared to do my bit towards it.
>
> All these arguments would of course go by the board if, say, war was going to break out within a year. As you know, I believe deeply in the need of this country for a good Intelligence Service, and I often

18

said during the War that, having had the fun then, I was prepared to
keep the flag flying in the duller times of peace. It was not of my own
will that I did not do so, and if war were imminent I would return
now. . . . Please convey my thanks to the Joint Intelligence Committee
for the honour which they have done me in offering me the job. In
view of what has been said on both sides in the past, I appreciate it
probably more than they might expect.

In the event, Dr. B. K. Blount was appointed. He had been Head of
the Scientific Department of the Control Commission in Germany and
besides being a distinguished chemist had parachuted into Greece with
S.O.E. during the war. Following my earlier recommendation, he was
given the title of Director of Scientific Intelligence with a seat on the
Joint Intelligence Committee in parallel with the Directors of Naval,
Military, and Air Intelligence; and the Service scientific sections were
now made up into his Directorate in the Ministry of Defence and
rescued from Bryanston Square to offices, again decrepit, but much
closer to Whitehall. One old stumbling block remained in the way, as
he related in the final summary of his experiences when in 1952, speaking
of the future, he said: 'First it is necessary to remove the anomalous
arrangements for atomic energy intelligence, which are actively harmful to good Scientific Intelligence'. So in this respect the situation in 1952
was no better than in 1946, when the arrangements for atomic energy
intelligence had been one of the main causes of my resignation. Blount
himself resigned after three years in 1952, to become Deputy Secretary
of the Department of Scientific and Industrial Research.

By this time Churchill was again Prime Minister, and he asked me
to come back for a time to try to get things straight. Such a request I
could not refuse, and the University agreed. It meant leaving my family
behind in Aberdeen and once again abandoning research, but I returned
to Whitehall in September 1952: and I gratefully found on my desk the
legend 'Sic *Resurrexit* Gloria Raketae' which had been placed there by
John Mapplebeck who, as a wing commander, had worked with me
in the V-1–V-2 Summer of 1944 and who had recalled the departing
notice I had then placed on my desk.

I was promised that atomic energy intelligence would return to be
part of the general Scientific Intelligence organization, and would be
under my control. But I found that the Ministry of Defence was not
what I had expected. Instead of the streamlined Chiefs of Staff organization that I had known during the war, there was now an administrative

jungle of such inefficiency that, for example, papers sometimes came out over the signatures of the Chiefs of Staff, when in fact none of the three Chiefs of Staff had ever seen them. Part of the trouble was due to the fact that each of the three Services tended to send to the Ministry of Defence only their second-best officers, so as to keep their own ministries as strong as possible.

The promise to bring back atomic intelligence into the normal Scientific Intelligence organization was not implemented even though the one argument that had been used to justify its independence, that of playing along with the Americans, had been completely abused. For what the Americans had in fact done was to follow my own wartime example regarding the organization of Scientific Intelligence and so had created a special Office of Scientific Intelligence inside the Central Intelligence Agency, and their atomic intelligence organization was part of this office. So if we were genuinely to march with the American arrangements, atomic energy intelligence should have been part of the Directorate of Scientific Intelligence in the Ministry of Defence.

American relations were in fact quite the happiest aspect of my experience. Thanks to Blount, they were already cordial before I took office, and if possible they became even more cordial. I spent June 1953 in America, crossing to California to see Bob Robertson, now the theoretical physicist in Pasadena associated with the Mount Wilson and Mount Palomar Observatories. Like myself, he found that he could not refuse a call back to Defence work and had obtained leave to become head of the Weapon Systems Evaluation Group in the Pentagon.

Although I did some useful things inside the Ministry of Defence, I could not justify prolonging my absence from the University, and so I left the Ministry again at the end of 1953, having recorded the strongest possible protest about the way in which things were still drifting. I pointed out that to keep atomic energy separate from Scientific Intelligence generally was the equivalent of keeping submarines out of Naval Intelligence or jet engines out of Air Intelligence; and I was also unhappy about the arrangements made regarding what has come to be known as Electronics Intelligence. Following Civil Service procedure, I demanded that the papers be laid before the Minister, who must then see me. He happened to be Field Marshal Lord Alexander, and I intended to tell him what I thought was wrong with the Ministry. But before I could start, he insisted on telling me how unhappy he was in his post, which he had never wanted. He had been much happier as

Governor General of Canada but, as with me, he had been recalled by Winston and could not refuse. I felt so sorry for him that I spent most of the interview giving him advice on how to argue with Lord Cherwell at Cabinet meetings, because he said the Prof could always produce his slide rule and outwit him; but it was clear that I could make no headway with my own problem. As for what has happened since, I am not in a position to comment. Substantial improvements have obviously occurred, but it may be worth retailing the remark of a senior officer in Intelligence who a year or two ago had come across my protest of twenty years before, and said that the troubles to which I had then pointed had by no means entirely been put right.

It may be wondered why, with Churchillian backing, I could do so little. The fact was that I tried to play the game according to the rules inside the Ministry, without invoking Prime Ministerial intervention; and by the time that I did tell Churchill of the situation he was too exhausted to act. He had already had a stroke. After I left, the Ministry failed to find anyone to take my place; and the Directorate of Scientific Intelligence was down-graded and placed under the Director of the Joint Intelligence Bureau, so that Scientific Intelligence once again had no independent voice at the top level.

Even when the organization is faultless, the reluctance of reputable scientists to give up active work in science for a spell in Intelligence is understandable. Some may well feel that it is a degrading activity for their talents, and that it is at best a dirty business, prying into other countries' secrets. I do not share this view, for we must accept that struggles, military or otherwise, between individuals and nations are a fact of existence. And any individual or organization who thinks that he or it has developed something worthwhile is entitled, within limits, to safeguard its survival and further development. Since the consequent struggle will be better conducted the more an organization knows about its opponent—and since a struggle may not only be avoided but turned into co-operation if it becomes clear that the opponent does not represent a threat or if he has something better to offer—then a sensible nation will seek to be as well informed as possible about its opponents, potential or otherwise, and, for that matter, about its friends. It will therefore set up an Intelligence organization, and provided that this organization observes some moral limits in the methods that it employs, its task is an honourable one.

I have more sympathy with the reluctance of a scientist to go into Intelligence when he fears that he may find less creative satisfaction than he would in pure science. I was always aware that, exciting though Intelligence was, and important though its results manifestly were, it was on a lower plane of difficulty than research in pure science. Intelligence is a parasitic activity, in that you are always trying to discover what some other man has already done, in contrast to entering an uncharted field yourself. One of the greatest difficulties in scientific research is to build up your observational experience in this new field, and to develop concepts that have never entered any human mind before. They may even appear to contradict long-established ideas, as when Einstein proposed the equivalence of mass and energy, or when de Broglie postulated that material particles could also behave as waves. Sometimes in Intelligence we experienced this kind of difficulty, when for example it was necessary for us to postulate that radio waves bent further round the Earth than our own experts thought, or that rockets could be made with a range greater than 100 miles; but all the time I knew that we were trying to discover something that had already been discovered and formulated in the minds of our German opponents, and that it therefore should be within our mental grasp.

To the extent I felt that we were parasitic, and tackling a basically easier job than that of research in pure science, although we sometimes had difficulties comparable with those of scientific innovators when we had to persuade our experts to abandon some of their hitherto accepted concepts. Moreover, the methods we used in gathering and collating information were much the same in principle as those employed in pure science. Where we could claim to be genuinely creative was in developing new methods of Intelligence, such as listening to radar transmissions, and in welding them into a great system for observing the enemy by as many means as possible, and in directing this system and correlating the information that it obtained by these means into a comprehensively reliable estimate of enemy intentions.

We were remarkably fortunate in our opportunity. Just as the impact of radio in the '20's gave a unique chance for everyman to dabble in the 'marvels of science' by making his own receiver—a task complex enough to be fascinating without being so complex, as television later was, that it was beyond the competence of the average man—so it was with Scientific Intelligence in World War II, and for much the same reason. The very development in science and technology that led to everyday radio in the '20's also led to the radar and radio navigational systems of World War II, and these were relatively simple to understand and, if necessary, frustrate.

Moreover, these developments in radio were of such universal application in military technology that they gave me the entry to fields which at first sight might have seemed quite remote. Radar provided the key to the German night defences, and thus enabled me to attack those defences more fruitfully than through any other channel; and it also enabled me to attack the flying bomb in a positive manner by going for the German radar plots. I was therefore able to reduce some of our major Intelligence problems to the field that by good fortune I knew best.

Possibly the opportunity of Enigma might be viewed in the same light, for it involved radio communication at a stage of sophistication that was just within the limits of human ingenuity to 'break'. Its importance in my own field will have been obvious at various points in my narrative. Sometimes, as with Knickebein, a single short decode provided the clinching evidence. And because there was every likelihood that the Germans felt that they were secure in Enigma, even a single message was likely to provide an anchor of truth on which any explanation of German activity could be confidently based, or a touchstone against which previously formed theories of German intentions could be tested. Care was of course necessary—although any one decode was likely to be one hundred per cent reliable, it might well contain much less than the whole truth—a fact that must always be borne in mind regarding information from any source, however reliable. But the confidence with which Enigma decodes could be used in constructing or testing theories of enemy intentions was outstanding among all the sources available to us.

As will have been evident from my story, it was worth squeezing every drop of information out of the decodes. But it would have been dangerous to have come to rely on them too much, and thus to have neglected the other sources, for in a sense cryptography was the most vulnerable source of all in that it could have been extinguished at any time by a few simple changes in the Enigma machine. At the end of every investigation I therefore looked back to see how far we could have done without Enigma. As the outstanding example, it was reassuring to find that we would very probably have raided Peenemünde without any help from Enigma. This observation is not intended in the slightest to belittle the enormous contribution made by those who broke the Engima traffic—quite the reverse. And it is a pleasure to know that in a war in which science, and especially physical science, gained great esteem, the contributions of our colleagues in mathematics and in some of the Arts subjects can at last be publicly recognized.

As for a counterpart to myself in Germany, this is a matter in which I was again fortunate. For much of the war, I was concerned that I might have an opposite number in Germany, quite possibly my pre-war friend Carl Bosch, who might have provided me with false clues, as Bosch himself certainly could have done. This would at minimum have made my task more difficult, and could easily have misled me on to several false trails. As it turned out, though, there was no such co-operation between science and the Services in Germany, and so we were spared this problem—and many others. It was the great contribution of the generation of scientists before mine, headed by Tizard and Lindemann, and accentuated by the emergency in which Britain found itself after 1933, that Serving officers and scientists worked together to an extent far exceeding that of our opponents.

Further, there was leadership. In Churchill we had a Prime Minister with a genuine and strong interest in the possibilities opened up by science, such as none of his successors has had. Even his controversial dependence on Lindemann was evidence of this interest which, for example, made him anxious to be flown—even at some discomfort—in experimental aircraft to see for himself the state of airborne radar. After our first meeting I felt that there was now so strong an appreciation at the top that in emergency I could have appealed to him with confidence, although I also felt that so long as Portal was Chief of Air Staff no appeal would ever be necessary. 'Your name', Churchill once said to me, 'will open all doors!'

To conclude this catalogue of good fortunes, I must remark the scale on which we operated. Right through to the end of the war I was able to keep my immediate organization small, and to use the initiative of individuals to the full. Had we been a little bigger, we should have had to institute an internal communication system, instead of depending on personal contacts to the extent that we did, and this would have slowed our daily working. But there are many tasks in Intelligence that require large numbers of people, and these tasks have multiplied since 1945; there are, for example, many more radar and guidance systems compared with those with which we had to deal, and they require armies of recording operators and interpreters if they are to be unravelled. Scientific and Technical Intelligence organizations therefore now have to be larger, and the consequent change of scale from that on which we operated may well involve a different balance of qualities in those heading the organization.

Napoleon and Wellington both made the point that when handfuls of men are involved in combat, the outcome depends on individual fighting ability, but that when armies are involved individual ability may be less important than ability for an army to fight as a whole, Napoleon's example being that two Mamelukes would beat three French cavalrymen, but that any army of one thousand French cavalrymen would beat fifteen hundred Mamelukes. It would therefore be dangerous to suppose that what we did on the small scale in World War II would provide a satisfactory precedent for what could be done in the future, for we had the advantage both in timing and in scale.

But this is not to say that Scientific and Technical Intelligence will be less important in the future. Just as the cryptographers of World War I thought that machine codes could never be broken and therefore that the day of the cryptographer was over, so it would be foolish to conclude that what we did was a mere flash never to be surpassed if not repeated. Perhaps our lessons have been taken to heart more effectively in America than in Britain for in *The Craft of Intelligence* Allen Dulles wrote, 'Eloquent testimony to the value of scientific intelligence collection, which has proved its worth a hundred times over, has been given by Winston Churchill in his history of World War II. . . . Science as a vital arm of Intelligence is here to stay. We are in a critically competitive race with the scientific development of the Communist Block, particularly that of the Soviet Union, and we must see to it that we *remain* in a position of leadership. Some day this may be as vital to us as radar was to Britain in 1940'.

It will have been obvious from my account that our work was exhilarating. Tragedy, such as the loss of Tony Hill or the men of the first Rjukan raid, was always near; and tension, as in the Blitz or the 'V' campaigns, was often acute; but there were moments of tremendous excitement, as in the finding of the Knickebein beams. And these moments continued throughout the war: the first time we knew an X-beam target in advance of the raid; the photographs of the first Freyas and Würzburgs; the Bruneval Raid; the searchlight map; the unravelling of the Kammhuber Line in a flash; Window; the finding of the rockets at Peenemünde and Blizna; the first V-1 tracks in the Baltic; D-Day; the true weight of the V-2. I felt matched to the task, with an operational reward awaiting almost everything that I did; and I worked with as brave a company of men and women as any one man might hope to meet.

Finally, let me set our contribution in perspective. There were several occasions on which I could conscientiously say, with Wellington after Waterloo, 'I don't think it would have done if I had not been there' (Creevey Papers, Ch. X, p. 236) but this is far from saying that I or anyone else can claim the major credit. Even such a simple operation as countering the beams involved a multitude of men and women, every one of whom played an essential part; patiently cataloguing the call signs of German aircraft, poring over innumerable air photographs only a fraction of which had anything interesting on them, working away at breaking the seemingly unbreakable Enigma machine, interrogating prisoners, examining captured equipment, listening to the beams and scouring the country to find suitable jamming transmitters, and setting these on to the right frequencies, all played their part—and the whole system would fail when any one part broke down. When to all this are added the contributions by those who risked and sacrificed their lives, our own efforts may perhaps be seen in a more realistic perspective. We all depended on the efforts of a great body of men and women whose existence in Lord Slim's words, 'is only remembered when something for which they are responsible goes wrong'.

If any one of these many components had failed, our entire effort would have come to nothing. Just as any one link in a chain is essential to supporting the weight at its end, or as a breakdown in any one compenent can ruin a machine, so could any one of many agencies have lost us the war. What none of them would have claimed is that it won the war by itself. This lesson, so clear in war, has to be re-learnt in peace, where the successful functioning of a civilized state depends on the efforts of many professions and agencies, each one of which can truly argue that its contribution is vital. But if by threatening to withhold this contribution any one section holds up the rest to ransom in order to gain for itself a larger slice of the national cake it will start a movement that—if followed by others—will lead to the nation overpaying itself beyond its true income, and thus to ruin. Until we learn that lesson we shall have lost the battle that we in the war fought so hard to win.

Notes

Chapter 2

For the beginnings of radar in Britain, I have drawn on an unpublished memorandum by A. F. Wilkins.

Another account is in R. A. Watson-Watt's *Three Steps to Victory* (Odhams, London, 1957) which is a useful source book on early British radar developments.

Vol. 93 of the Journal of the Institution of Electrical Engineers for 1946 is another useful source.

For more details of early British infra-red developments see R. V. Jones, *Infra-Red in British Air Defence 1935-8* (Infra-Red Physics, Vol. 1, pp. 153-162, 1961).

Chapter 4

Watson-Watt's opinion of Lindemann comes from his article in *The Sunday Times* for 7 July 1957.

Chapter 8

F. W. Winterbotham has described his work in *Secret and Personal* (Kimber 1969) and *The Ultra Secret* (Weidenfeld and Nicolson, 1974).

Chapter 11

Sources of quotations in this Chapter are:
R. W. Clark, *Tizard* (Methuen, London, 1965).
D. Irving, *The Rise and Fall of the Luftwaffe* (Weidenfeld and Nicolson, London, 1973).

Chapter 12

Sources of quotations in this Chapter are:
W. S. Churchill, *Thoughts and Adventures* (Thornton Butterworth, London, 1932).
R. W. Clark, *Tizard*.
Telford Taylor, *The Breaking Wave* (Weidenfeld and Nicolson, London, 1967).
For a fuller account of Churchill's appreciation of science and technology see R. V. Jones, *Winston Leonard Spencer Churchill* (Biographical Memoirs of Fellows of the Royal Society, Vol. 12, pp. 35-105, 1966).

Chapter 13

Wintle's life, largely written by himself, can be found in *The Last Englishman* (Joseph, London, 1968).

Chapter 16

Cotton's life can be found in R. Barker, *Aviator Extraordinary* (Chatto and Windus, London, 1969).
The subsequent history of photographic reconnaissance is given in Andrew J. Brookes *Photo Reconnaissance* (Ian Allan, 1975).

Chapter 17

The X-Beam antenna appears to have been a simple two-dipole interferometer with a phase switch for shifting the pattern from dash lobes to dot lobes. The dipole separation was 14·75 metres in one version and 20·5 metres in another, and the waveband 3·9 to 4·5 metres.
Reflector dipoles were normally added, but these are not present on Plate 7a.

Chapter 18

A general account of the Coventry Raid is given by N. Longmate in *Air Raid* (Hutchinson, London, 1976).

Chapter 20

Sir Arthur Harris's minute of 1 February 1941 was on Air Ministry file S.7347 entitled 'Offensive action against German W/T stations'.

Chapter 23

The photographs on which the Freyas were discovered (p.190 and Pl. 9a and b) were taken on a brilliant November day when the low sun cast long shadows — the most favourable photographic conditions.

Chapter 24

The quotation of Admiral Cunningham at Crete comes from W. S. Churchill, *The Second World War*, Vol. III, p. 265 (Cassell, London, 1950).
The contribution of Enigma to the Bismarck and other naval actions is discussed in P. Beesly's *Very Special Intelligence* (Hamish Hamilton, London, 1977).

Chapter 25

Meinertzhagen's life has been written by John Lord in *Duty, Honour, Empire* (Hutchinson 1971).
H. J. Giskes has told his story in *London calling North Pole* (Kimber 1953).
Much credit is due to 'George' (p.216) but at the request of the Security authorities his real name was withheld from the text. However, it has now been revealed by his former colleague, Ewen Montagu, in *Beyond Top Secret U* as that of Squadron Leader Charles Cholmondeley.

Chapter 26

There was a bullet hole through part of the antenna unit that Cox brought back (p.241).

Chapter 27

An account of the Italian two-man torpedo effort is given in J. Piekalkiewicz's *Secret Agents, Spies, & Saboteurs* (Morrow, 1973).

Rémy (Colonel Gilbert Renault) has described his part in the Bruneval story in *Bruneval: Opération Coup de Croc* (Editions France Empire, 1968).

Flight Sergeant C. W. H. Cox's report was written immediately after the Bruneval raid and was included as an appendix to my Air Scientific Intelligence Report No. 15, *The Intelligence Aspect of the Bruneval Raid,* dated 13th July 1942.

Chapter 28

Philby described his work in *My Silent War* (MacGibbon and Kee, London, 1968). His judgement of personalities was penetrating until it began to break under the strain of his double-agency.

Chapter 30

For an excellent account of Underground activities in Occupied Europe, see M. R. D. Foot's *Resistance* (Eyre Methuen, London, 1976).

Chapter 31

F. E. Jones's account of the Oboe attack on Florennes comes from R. W. Clark's *The Rise of the Boffins.*

Chapter 32

An account of the German nuclear effort, and of the British/Norwegian sabotage effort, is given in David Irving's *The Virus House* (Kimber, London, 1964).

Chapter 38

The development of the long-range (A4) rocket has been described in General Walter Dornberger's *V-2* (Hurst and Blackett, London, 1954).

See also E. Klee and O. Merk *The Birth of the Missile* (Harrap, 1965).

Chapter 39

Constance Babington Smith's part in discovering the V-1 is described in her book *Evidence in Camera* (Chatto and Windus, London, 1958).

Glossary of Abbreviations and Code Names

British Officials and Department

A.C.A.S. (I)	Assistant Chief of Air Staff (Intelligence).
A.D.I.K.	Assistant Director of Intelligence (Prisoner Interrogation).
A.D.I. (Photos)	Assistant Director of Intelligence (Photographic Reconnaissance).
A.D.I. (Sc.)	Assistant Director of Intelligence (Science), (later D. of I. (R)).
A.I. 1(c)	Air Intelligence Liaison with M.I.6.
A.I. 1(e)	Air Signals Intelligence (later A.I.4).
A.I. 1(g)	Air Intelligence, Technical (later A.I. 2(g)).
A.I. 1(k)	Air Intelligence, Prisoner Interrogation (later A.D.I.K.).
A.R.L.	Admiralty Research Laboratory.
C.A.S.	Chief of Air Staff.
C.I.U.	Central Interpretation Unit.
C.S.S.A.D.	Committee for the Scientific Survey of Air Defence.
C.S.S.A.O.	Committee for the Scientific Survey of Air Offence.
C.S.S.A.W.	Committee for the Scientific Survey of Air Warfare.
D.C.A.S.	Deputy Chief of Air Staff.
D.D.I.4	Deputy Director of Intelligence (Signals).
D.D.S.(Y)	Deputy Director of Signals (Intelligence), later D.D.I.4.
D. of I. (R)	Director of Intelligence (Research).
D. of S.	Director of Signals (later Director General of Signals).
D.M.I.	Director of Military Intelligence.
D.N.I.	Director of Naval Intelligence.
D.S.R.	Director of Scientific Research.
M.I.5.	Security Intelligence.
M.I.6.	The Secret Intelligence Service.
M.I.8.	Military Intelligence (Signals).
M.I.9.	Military Intelligence (the escaping organization).
N.I.D.	Naval Intelligence Division.
O.R.C.	Operational Research Centre.
O.R.S.	Operational Research Section.
P.I.U.	Photographic Interpretation Unit (the forerunner of C.I.U.).
P.R.U.	Photographic Reconnaissance Unit.
R.A.E.	Royal Aircraft Establishment.
R.C.M.	Radio Counter Measures.
S.A.A.M.	Scientific Adviser to the Air Ministry.
S.A.T.	Scientific Adviser on Telecommunications.
S.I.S.	Secret Intelligence Service.
S.O.E.	Special Operations Executive.
S. of S.	Secretary of State.

S.R.3.	The forerunner of A.D.I. (Sc.).
T.A.	Tube Alloys, the British Atomic Energy project.
T.R.E.	Telecommunications Research Establishment.
V.C.A.S.	Vice Chief of Air Staff.
Y-Service	The organization for listening to hostile radio communications.

British Equipment

A.I.	Air Interception Radar.
Aspirin	Jammer for Knickebein.
A.S.V.	Anti-Surface-Vessel Radar. (Marks I and II wavelength 1·5 metres; Mark III 10 centimetres, identical with H2S).
Benjamin	Jammer for Y-Beams (which were nicknamed 'Benito' in Britain).
Bromide	Jammer for X-Beams.
C.H.	Chain Home Radar.
C.H.L.	Chain Home Low-level Radar.
Domino	Countermeasure to the ranging system of the Y-Gerät.
G or GEE	Pulse radio navigational aid. (German code-name: 'Hyperbal Gerät').
G.C.I.	Ground Control Interception Radar.
G-H.	Pulse radio navigational aid.
G.L.	Gun-laying Radar.
Headaches	General term for the German beams, alleviated by 'Aspirins' and 'Bromides'.
H2S.	Airborne radar for detecting towns, etc. (German code-name: 'Rotterdam Gerät')
I.F.F.	Identification Friend or Foe Radar.
J or JAY.	Bogus radio beams intended for deception.
Mandrel	Jammer for Freya radars.
Meacon	A 'masking' radio beacon.
Monica.	Radar device fitted to bombers to warn of approaching fighters.
Moonshine	Device used to amplify radio echoes to make one aircraft appear as a swarm.
Oboe	Precise radio bombing system using range measurements from two ground stations.
Perfectos	Nightfighter device for challenging and homing on I.F.F. (FuGe 25A) carried by German nightfighters.
P.O.I.	Plan Position Indicator.
Radar	'Radio Direction and Range'. Term first used by the U.S. Navy and since adopted generally.
R.D.F.	The original British term for radar (Radio Direction Finding).
R/T	Radio Telephony.
S.L.C.	Searchlight Control Radar.
Serrate	Device for homing on German nightfighter radar.
Tinsel	Jammer for German nightfighter R/T.
T.R. 1335	Airborne Receiver for GEE.
T.F.	Town-finding Radar, the original abbreviation replaced by 'H2S'.

| Window | (American 'Chaff') Aluminium foil strips dropped in packets to give radar echoes simulating a bomber. |
| W/T | Wireless Telegraphy. |

German

A4	The long-range rocket. (Aggregat 4) later called 'V2'.
D.T.	Radar.
Düppel.	'Window' or 'Chaff'.
E. Bl.	Blind landing receiver (Empfänger Blind).
Elektra	Radionavigational system transmitting a 'fan' of beams for long-range navigation. In its later form 'Electra Sonne' it was used and adopted by the Allies under the code-name 'Consol'.
Fi103	The flying bomb, so designated because it was made by Fieseler.
Flak	Anti-aircraft Artillery (Fliegerabwehrkanonen).
Flammen	British I.F.F. responses to German challenging (Flames).
F.M.G.	Gun-laying radar (Flakmessgerät).
Funkortung	Radar (Radio Location).
Freya	The original German defence radar, wavelength about 2·5 metres.
Fu. Ge.	Radio apparatus (Funk Gerät).
FZG76	Cover-name for the flying bomb (FlakZiel Gerät).
H.A.P.	Army Institute Peenemünde (Heeres Anstalt).
H.D.P.	The long-range smooth-bore gun (HochDruckPumpe).
Himmelbett	Close-controlled nightfighting.
HS293	The radio-controlled rocket-propelled glider bomb used against shipping.
Jagdschloss	Scanning radar with P.P.I.
J.D.	Fighter Division (Jagd Division).
J.G.	Fighter unit of 3 Gruppen (Jagd Geschwader).
K.G.	Bomber unit of 3 Gruppen (Kampf Geschwader).
K.Gr.	Unit of 27 aircraft in 3 Staffeln plus staff flight of 3 (Kampf Gruppe).
Kiel Gerät	Airborne infra-red detector.
Kleine-Schraube	Radio beacon for nightfighting ('Little Screw').
Knickebein	The original beam-bombing system.
Lichtenstein	Airborne radar. Version BC worked on 61 centimetres and SN2 on about 3·7 metres. These were used for nightfighting, the latter having been developed from the S version which had been used for A.S.V.
L.N.V.R.	Air Signals Experimental Regiment (Luft Nachrichtung Versuchs Regiment).
Mammut	Long-range early warning radar on about 2·5 metres (Mammoth, British code-name 'Hoarding').
Metox	Receiver for U-Boats to give warning of British aircraft carrying A.S.V. on 1·5 metres.
Naxos	Receiver for U-Boats to give warning of British aircraft carrying A.S.V. on 10 centimetres, also used on land to detect British bombers carrying H2S.

N.J.G.	Nightfighter Geschwader (Nacht Jagd Geschwader).
Seeburg	Plotting table used for fighter control.
T-Stoff	Highly concentrated hydrogen peroxide (Trieb Stoff=Propellant) used for the V-1 catapult and the HS293 bomb).
V-1	The flying bomb (Vergeltungs=Retaliation).
V-2	The long-range rocket.
Wassermann	Long-range early warning radar, with height-finding facility (British code-name: 'Chimney').
Wilde Sau	Freelance nightfighting.
Wotan	General term for the precise X- and Y-beam bombing systems.
W.P.G.	Thermal infra-red detector for coast watching (WärmePeilGerät).
Würzburg	Standard paraboloid radar working on wavelengths of about 53 centimetres (British code-name 'Bowl Fire').
Würzburg Riese	Giant Würzburg, with 7·5 metre paraboloid (British code-name 'Basket').
X-Gerät	Receiver for the X-Beam system of precise bombing, also known as Wotan I.
Y-Gerät	Receiver for Y-System of precise bombing, also known as Wotan II (Code-named 'Benito' in Britain).
Zahme Sau	Nightfighter system introduced in 1943 in which formations of nightfighters were directed into the bomber stream.
Z-Stoff	Permanganate solution used for decomposing hydrogen peroxide into steam and oxygen in the V-1 catapult.

Index